RENAISSANCE DRAMA

New Series 36/37   2010

Renaissance Drama

NEW SERIES 36/37

Italy in the Drama of Europe

Edited by Albert Russell Ascoli
and William N. West

Northwestern University Press

EVANSTON 2010

Title page image from *The Illustrated Bartsch*.
By permission of Abaris Books.

Contents

Submissions

RENAISSANCE DRAMA IS a peer-edited annual publication that investigates the traditional canons of drama as well as exploring the significance of performance, broadly conceived, in early modern cultures. We invite manuscripts for consideration, particularly those essays that question, or apply newer forms of interpretation to, the study of early modern plays, theater, and performance; that concern works written in languages and traditions other than English (although we publish only essays written in English); that examine the cultural discourses that shaped and were shaped by the varied institutions of drama across Europe and beyond its borders; or that address manifestations of performance and performativity during this historical period both on and off the stage. Occasionally, special issues of the journal are devoted to specific topics of general interest.

The editors of *Renaissance Drama* prefer to receive manuscript submissions electronically, either as Rich Text Format (.rtf) files or as Microsoft Word files (.doc or .docx). The journal does not accept submissions by facsimile. Scholars preparing manuscripts for *Renaissance Drama* should refer to the stylistic guidelines of *The Chicago Manual of Style,* 15th edition, including endnote reference citations. For initial review of manuscripts, photocopies of illustrations are acceptable, but should the essay be accepted, its author will be responsible for obtaining publishable-quality images and any necessary permissions.

Queries and submissions should be addressed to Nathan Mead at n-mead2@northwestern.edu. This information on submissions, as well as updates and information on any upcoming special issues, may be found at the Web site of the Northwestern University Department of English: http://www.english.northwestern.edu/resources/renaissance_drama_ journal.html.

Introduction:
Italy in the Drama of Europe

WILLIAM N. WEST

A N ACADEMIC GENERATION ago, in the pages of this journal, an important
article on cinquecento drama began unpromisingly by granting
that its subject was "aesthetically unrewarding." This was not an unprecedented judgment even among Renaissance Italian drama's most
interested scholars. In criticism and literary history, the drama of early
modern Italy tended to function as a literary subaltern, more of interest for its refractions into other genres or languages than for its own
achievements or characteristics. Even its recognized high points, like the
plays of Ariosto, Machiavelli, and Tasso, were overshadowed by those
writers' other works, more famous and more central to the canons of
Italian and European literatures; at the same time, those plays received
more than their share of attention precisely because they were by the
authors more important for the *Orlando furioso, Il principe,* or *Geru-*
salemme liberata. Italian drama suffered from comparison on the one
hand with other Italian genres that loomed more prominently over the
landscape of Renaissance European literature, like lyric poetry, romance,
or epic, and on the other with the dramas of other European languages
that seemed to play a more enlivening role in their literary histories, like
the drama of Shakespeare, Lope de Vega, Calderón, Gryphius, Corneille,
or Molière. The shaping influences of the scripts, practices, and theories
of Italian theater on the other dramas of Europe, both Latin and vernacular, were of course acknowledged, but this seemed simply to throw the

Italian theater further into the background as a mere source for these other works. At the same time, narratives of theater history for those languages tended to emphasize their debt to other precursors, whether native or classical, at the expense of a specifically Italian heritage.

Much of that changed, and has continued to change, with the publication twenty years ago of Louise George Clubb's *Italian Drama in Shakespeare's Time*, a collection of articles and chapters originally composed separately, but within which Clubb found an overarching counterargument to the prevailing account of Renaissance Italian theater as an elegiac of missed opportunities, frigid academicism, and untraceable threads. Clubb's innovative treatment began with her realization that early modern Italian plays exercised their influences on each other and on later institutions of theater across Europe not as a static archive, but as a generative matrix of what she called "theatergrams," those elements of dramatic composition such as character, situation, genre, and scene out of which narrative arcs and climaxes, catastrophes and dénouements of plays are assembled. Clubb's insight showed a new generation of scholars how they might make sense of the astonishing capacity of the Italian drama of the Renaissance to appear in, and to shape, even distantly related forms.

According to Clubb, Italian comedy, tragedy, and pastoral drama developed, refined, varied, and promulgated a lexicon of theatergrams to which later European drama returned again and again, rarely revealing strict lines of filiation but everywhere tasting of their Italian origins. Clubb's concept of the theatergram showed scholars how theatrical borrowing was almost never simple quotation and almost always transformation; further, she showed how those transformations were enabled by the multiple sources in classical drama, pastoral poetry, contemporary dramatic theory, residual medieval forms, and the like, which the innovators of Italian humanist drama had gathered in their own works. Since the recomposition of theatergrams in a play was always at the same time their reconfiguration into new shapes and to new purposes, Clubb's work on the relation and dissemination of Renaissance Italian drama thus also serves as a reminder of the originality of the Italian theater and of the theaters that followed it. Starting from the recognition that Italian drama served as far more than a passive conduit for classical drama or a sterile working-out of theoretical positions, Clubb's work showed that Italian drama was made in such a way as to facilitate its absorption and transformation into other traditions, even when it was not explicitly cited or referred to. Finally, Clubb's body of critical work signaled the interest of Italian plays in their own right, not just as sources for scholars of later dramas or as movements for theater historians, but as works that won a logic and coherence of their own from their repertoire of dramatic elements and as plays capable of addressing questions of the most serious theoretical and historical interest.

This special issue of *Renaissance Drama,* "Italy in the Drama of Europe," seeks to confirm, continue, and extend the claims of intertextuality and intertheatricality in Clubb's multiple projects of reappraisal and analysis, beginning with an overview of the state of the field by Clubb herself. Shakespeare of course retains his position as an important interlocutor and mirror for Italian theater, although the Italian materials that have long been recognized among his sources here strongly reflect their own vitality and autonomy. Kasey Evans's "Misreading and Misogyny: Ariosto, Spenser, and Shakespeare" begins with what looks like a traditional literary history, tracing a motif of male sexual servitude in *Much Ado About Nothing* to Ariosto's *Orlando furioso* by way of Spenser's *Faerie Queene.* But Evans powerfully shows how the form of such a literary history demonstrates not only the possibility of reading one text through another, but the possibilities of misreading it as well, and she thematizes such misreading as inherently gendered and misogynistic. When Shakespeare moves these episodes across modes, from diegetic to dramatic, to exploit the problems of embodied expression, interpretation, and action that are uniquely part of performance, he is directed not only by his romance pretexts, Evans shows, but by the traditions of Italian performance. Jane Tylus's "Imitating Othello: The Handkerchief, alla Italiana" and Albert Ascoli's "Wrestling with Orlando: Chivalric Pastoral in Shakespeare's Arden" similarly work chronologically backward from Shakespearean beginnings toward their Italian resources, only to find there unexpectedly determining structures in the figures of the web or the wrestling match that the English plays draw from them. Laura Giannetti refigures the Italian canon in " 'Ma che potrà succedermi se io donna amo una Donna': Female–Female Desire in Italian Renaissance Comedy" by examining more closely the recurring representation of same-sex eroticism among women in Renaissance Italian plays. The invisibility of such desire within early modern ideologies has sometimes been assumed by modern scholars, but Giannetti finds multiple examples within later Italian comedies to show that this very belief—that there was no meaningful same-sex female desire—is not only self-consciously displayed, but interrogated within the plays by its staging.

Other intertexts and interperformances surface in these essays as well. In their essays Ascoli, Tylus, and Evans necessarily address the problems of generic definition and *contaminatio,* that seemingly careless mingling of sources that simultaneously blurred and negotiated their boundaries, which Clubb so convincingly demonstrated were often put forth through the careful juxtapositon of theatergrams. In "Coincidence of Opposites: Bruno, Calderón, and a Drama of Ideas," Christopher Johnson traces these concerns with genre and tactics for exploring its resources through Giordano Bruno's *Candelaio* and Calderón's *El mágico prodigioso,* and finally to the work of Walter Benjamin on the German *Trauerspiel,* each of which he sees taking up the project of generic exploration through the paradoxical forms of the extreme case and the coincidence of opposites. Johnson traces these impossible performances of limits to the philosophical potential for the drama imagined by Bruno as well as by his humanist predecessors in both the theater and the library. Lorna Hutson's " 'Che indizio, che prova . . . ?' Ariosto's Legal Conjectures and the English Renaissance Stage" looks at the relations between legal and theatrical procedures by showing how theatrical problems of inference, persuasion, and conjecture work through differences between the Italian and English legal systems in addressing related problems of proof and evidence. Looking in particular at how Jonson's *Volpone* and Shakespeare's *Taming of the Shrew* negotiate Ariosto's *La cassaria* and *I suppositi* in relation to their shared Plautine heritage, Hutson outlines how such comedies assume different grounds for interpreting action and circumstance—and reflect their own mutual exchange.

Hutson criticizes the tendency of the criticism on early Italian drama to assume an inherent relation of perspectival setting to illusionistic mimesis. Fabio Finotti's "Perspective and Stage Design, Fiction and Reality in the Italian Renaissance Theater of the Fifteenth Century" also calls into question the well-rehearsed history of perspectival sets as self-conscious derivations from classical texts, especially Vitruvius, by adducing the practices of painters as sources rather than records. Inverting the received story of perspectival drama as classicizing and stressing the role of extratextual practices, Finotti suggests that the primary innovations in Italian Renaissance drama may have come from the visual arts, rather than the arts merely documenting stage practices. In "Performing

Anachronism: A New Aetiology of Italian Renaissance Tragedy," Kristin Phillips-Court likewise extends Clubb's broader and more oblique analyses of the practice of imitations and borrowings within Italian drama, as well as between it and other forms, by referring the performing arts to the visual ones. Comparing the strategic functions of antiquarianism and anachronism in contemporary Italian painting to the performances of Italian drama, especially Trissino's tragedy *Sofonisba,* and so extending the reach of the concept of theatergram beyond the theater, Phillips-Court shows how selective imitation in either field did not signal derivativeness, but produced a sense of the new creation of a work genuinely, and paradoxically, ancient.

Other articles in this issue extend the analyses of Italian drama and its influences beyond what is represented onstage and into the political and social spheres. In "Publish (f)or Paris? G. B. Andreini in France," Jon R. Snyder looks at the politics of publishing, as well as performing, Italian drama in France; in " 'Bawdy Doubles': Pietro Aretino's *Comedie* (1588) and the Appearance of English Drama," Bianca Calabresi shows how the idea of printed Italian drama influenced English conventions of print, and how one English printer, John Wolfe, returned the favor in his Italian-language books, published in London but striving to be more Italian than the Italian. Snyder and Calabresi both suggest how Italianness itself could become a tradable commodity, standing with equal conviction for traits like authenticity, perversity, or professionalism in the working circles of presses and theaters and in the audiences they developed.

Katherine Ibbett follows the expansion of such debates into a more overtly political sphere in "Italy Versus France; or, How Pierre Corneille Became an Anti-Machiavel," demonstrating how the drama of Corneille was represented as an ethical French corrective to the corrosive effects of Italian immoralism, both onstage and at court. Yair Lipshitz argues for a much less oppositional relation between two languages and cultures in "Performance as Profanation: Holy Tongue and Comic Stage in *Tsahut bedihuta deqiddushin.*" In Lipshitz's article, the Jewish humanist playwright Leone de' Sommi draws on the traditions of Italian erudite comedy and Hebrew biblical and midrashic textuality in his Hebrew *Comedy of Betrothal,* a play that Lipshitz argues ultimately raises the possibility of resituating the borders between two traditions to sketch a new "profane" one. Still more concretely social is Robert Henke's "Sincerity, Fraud, and Audience Reception in the Performance of Early Modern Poverty," which looks at performances that, broadly speaking, we might consider as real: displays of poverty and suffering that took place onstage, where they were evaluated for their art, and off, where they were judged on their sincerity. More explicitly political, Ronald L. Martinez's "Etruria Triumphant in Rome: Fables of Medici Rule and Bibbiena's *Calandra*" closely reads the multiple semiotic orders of one play to draw out the specific ideologies it was designed to propagate—including the claim that theater and spectacle itself could be associated with Etruscans, with Tuscans, and ultimately with the family that claimed to be their inheritors, the Medici.

In all, "Italy in the Drama of Europe" takes up the reverberations of early modern Italian drama in the theaters of Spain, England, and France and in writings in Italian, English, Spanish, French, Hebrew, Latin, and German. Its scope is an example of the continuing force and interest of one of the most rewarding, wide-ranging, and productive of early modern aesthetic modes, and a tribute to the scholarship of Louise George Clubb that, among work by others, recalled our attention to it.

RENAISSANCE DRAMA

New Series 36/37   2010

Looking Back on Shakespeare
and Italian Theater

LOUISE GEORGE CLUBB

THE NEW WORK in this volume so well illustrates the blooming state of today's scholarship on early modern Italian theater and its future that no prognostications from me are called for. The general bibliography attesting the invigorating Anglo-American wave of study shows the paths recently taken and where they lead: to performance theory, intertextuality, contextual revelations, new archival digs, and critical editions and translations that supplement or challenge the equally abundant current Italian approaches.

Instead, I can offer to measure the distance traversed to reach the present prosperity by contributing a view of the past, remembering what was available—and not available—to a neophyte venturing into a field that could almost be said not to exist half a century ago, when the scholarly climate was still postwar and precomputer. The challenging lacunae then faced by an aspiring Shakespearean with some knowledge of Italian literature dictated the shape of much of what I wrote thereafter and eventually determined a life's work.

Two mysteries appeared to me at the outset. First, Shakespeare's Italianate flavor was much stronger and more consistent than could be accounted for by the standard explanation that he had read many novellas in some form or other and put pieces of them into his plays. Second, however much his moods and themes changed from the beginning to the end of his career, his plays from the first were expertly theatrical.

3

Not for him a gradual progress from clumsy apprentice to master builder. The earliest comedies are fully stageworthy, as if he had already learned playmaking from professionals. Which is, more or less, what I think he did.

Years of reading Italian scripted plays and *canovacci* preceding or contemporary with Shakespeare have gradually shown me an international movement of playmaking recognizable as Renaissance Drama, a technology consciously developed by writers and actors in various ways from common principles of construction based on a Latin footprint and employing material from both classical and medieval narrative and drama, shaped into movable theatrical units, or theatergrams, which grew over time into a repertory of combinable parts that became the common property of the European stage.

The collection of reshuffleable pieces included types of characters, of relationships between and among characters, of actions and speeches, and of thematic design.[1] The existence of such a repertory is today widely, though not universally, acknowledged, but it was invisible in the way Renaissance drama and the relation of Shakespeare to Italy was presented fifty years ago.

Before recognizing the theatergram system, I had concurred in the general critical opinion that the innumerable similarities between Italian theater and other European theater were to be attributed to specific printed sources, narrative or theatrical, an assumption both justifiable and useful when a clear relationship could be established between an Italian play and its imitation or adaptation abroad, but bordering on the absurd when a situation, character, turn of phrase, or even a single word occurring in an Italian play could lead to deducing direct knowledge of it on the part of a later playwright who used it, as in the case, for example, of the scholar who claimed in 1916 that Molière knew Della Porta's *Astrologo* because in it a character says "sei un tartufo."[2]

The task I undertook originally turned out to be a comparatist's quest, in not one field, but three. Shakespeare was the starting point for me, the first field of research; the Shakespeare scholarship I encountered was concentrated on his plays, his context, his literary resources. Italian drama was the second field; Italian scholarship on this subject was deep but rarely broad, the angle more likely to be municipal, regional or, at the most, national. But the third field was my goal, the envisaged ground for a comparison between the other two that might illuminate their kinship and open a new view of Renaissance theater. Presenting Italian drama as Shakespeare could have known it required an approach that could be broad while not shallow. In those days the available works on Elizabethan drama and Italy were mostly source studies concentrated on English production; the few Italian plays known to most English scholars were written in the first half of the sixteenth century, to the exclusion of the mass of plays printed in Italy during the second half, and whoever gave thought to a comparison with Italian theater in Shakespeare's lifetime was likely to limit it to three or four *commedie* or to conclude that it was an "incontro mancato," a missed encounter.[3]

Among the great exceptions, Kathleen M. Lea's landmark work on the *commedia dell'arte* with reference to England should have revolutionized Shakespeare studies in the 1930s, but neither it nor the article of Ferdinando Neri seminal to it, had yet been taken to heart, and the paucity of documentation of the visits that troupes and individual actors undoubtedly made to England weakened their impact.[4] Allardyce Nicoll's and Winifred Smith's important works on the *commedia dell'arte* were at hand, and Marvin T. Herrick's descriptions of selected scripted erudite plays were soon to be printed, but the connection between *commedia dell'arte* (or *a soggetto* and *all'improvviso*) and *commedia erudita* (also called *osservata, regolare,* and *letteraria*) was dimly understood, and the same lack of documentation stood in the way of making convincing connections with the English theater. Yet the features of Shakespeare's plays insistently proclaimed a kinship, so it was apparent that, lacking sufficient archival records of visits and payments, a new methodology was needed to investigate it. More evidence for the link with Italian acting troupes would have to come from within, from comparing his plays with Italian ones, both the "writ" and the "liberty," the literary drama and the scenarios for improvisation. There was hardly anyone to talk to on this subject, but I was encouraged by the valuable resources offered by Lea, Nicoll, Herrick, and Daniel C. Boughner, and I began gratefully in their footsteps.[5]

Giambattista Della Porta offered a way into the Italian drama of Shakespeare's time. In the 1950s he was less studied than he is today by historians of science and of linguistics and was sometimes dismissed as a prescientific polymath, a curiosity who vied with his younger acquaintance Galileo for title to the invention of the telescope. My first knowledge of him came from Mary Augusta Scott's *Elizabethan Translations from the Italian,* where he was listed as the Italian playwright most often translated or adapted in England. His seventeen extant plays, published between 1589 and 1614, the year before his death, were counted important by Italian historians and even by some modern theatrical companies, but no critical edition then existed. Today major scholars are publishing the Edizione Nazionale of his complete works one by one, and Raffaele Sirri's four volumes of Della Porta's *Teatro* provide the excellent critical texts of all the plays, which in 1958 could be read only in the original editions or in incomplete versions.[6]

Della Porta's works displayed the peak of Italian fashion in regular drama in the late sixteenth and early seventeenth centuries, primarily the fourteen *commedie,* well-known and reprinted in Italy, sometimes adapted in France and England and often by the improvising players for their scenarios. A great variety appeared in these comedies, from farce to satire to tear-jerking love conflicts, representing high-tech dramatic theory, all constructed by masterly *contaminatio* of Plautus and Terence with dismembered and reconstituted plot elements from medieval narrative, especially Boccaccio's *Decameron,* and with a savvy stagecraft and comic liveliness that attest Della Porta's reciprocal appreciation of the professional *commedia dell'arte* that borrowed from him.[7]

By the time I came to edit and translate *Gli duoi fratelli rivali,* Della Porta's *commedia grave,* I had read enough to recognize the existence of a repertory of what the irreplaceable Mario Baratto first suggested I call *teatrogrammi,* the constantly recombinable units of playmaking, not simply plots, but raw micromaterials of plots and the techniques of putting them together that had been accumulated over years into a pool of exchangeable parts and practices, the unpublished common property of playwrights and actors. Recognition of these theatergrams in Shakespeare's works finally clarified for me the means and nature of his Italian connection and allowed me to compare Della Porta's and Shakespeare's treatment of them in dramatizing the same Bandello novella plot, arriving at different results highly illustrative of the way the system functioned in England and in Italy about 1600, in the hands of two playwrights presumably unknown to each other.[8]

Within the standard view of each Italian play as an individual text constructed by a single author, the principle of intertextuality had been considered relevant only to evidence of plagiarism or to the search for sources, each element in each play to be traced to an analogue in Plautus, Terence, Seneca, or medieval narrative. Judging from the handful of plays known to non-Italians, a reader might conclude that each has a unique relationship with its ultimate sources, the way he himself might resemble this or that portrait of his ancestors, but immersion reading in the thousands of Italian plays printed in the cinquecento and the seicento reveals a plurality of generations and combinations of features that suggests more complicated genetic connections and illuminates a method of composition different from imitation of discrete sources, one based instead on the existence of a repertory of theatergrams and of a default structure for each genre in which to combine them.

Most theatergrams show up first in regular drama (called *regolare* or *erudita* because written according to rules derived from classical sources), which laid the foundation on a combination of Latin drama structure with novella narremes and began amassing the repertory, which includes physical and verbal *lazzi* and *burle* of many kinds and thematic plot designs involving various character types and relationships that in turn generate patterns of dialogue, actions, stage loci, and props: an abundance of deceits and disguises (of sex, race, rank, nationality, profession); standard exposition dialogues; colloquies and confidences between lovers and with their servants or nurses; eavesdropping; utilization of doors, windows, balconies and *camere terrene;* patterned clashes between illiterate and learned speech; mad scenes; pastoral class distinctions; womanizing braggarts; friars managing love affairs; seamen; shipwrecks; twins; *contrasti* or monologues on such subjects as jealousy, cosmetics, honor and marriage; contests of friendship; duels; sorcerers and transformations; paired lovers contrasted and/or loving in the wrong direction; coffins, chests and laundry baskets; providential plot patterns; questions of succession; usurpers; clowns at court and in Arcadia, substitutions in dark rooms; wives condemned to death for supposed infidelity. . . .

If these seem too numerous and inclusive to constitute a well-defined collection useful for tracking resemblances, we need only consider how much of representable life and imagination was excluded from the repertory and to note the literally innumerable incidences of shuffled repetitions of the above prefabricated elements that had, by Shakespeare's time, become accessible in Europe through printed drama and performances by *commedia dell'arte* players. These elements were fitted together in different combinations and were fleshed out by the skills of actors, whether in memorized scripted five-act plays or in those improvised in three acts *a soggetto.* When Polonius describes the players to

Hamlet, he pairs these modes of performance as "the law of writ and the liberty."[9] In the latter case the dialogues, monologues, and gestures, including dancing, singing, and playing instruments, were part of the individual repertory created by each actor's reading, practice, and experience of interaction with his fellows.[10]

At the end of the 1950s Italian scholarship on Italian drama was plenteous, nationalistic, and richly detailed, faithful to the great nineteenth-century positivists, those exacting historians whose invaluable contributions were marked by a lingering Risorgimento combination of anticlassical romanticism and general Italian anticlericalism. They had unearthed texts and subjected masses of plays to critical investigation. While the eighteenth century had produced the updated version (1755) of Leone Allacci's 1666 *Drammaturgia,* the indispensable bibliographical tool for primary excavations, as well as some new editions (using questionable settecento standards) of major playwrights like Guarini and Della Porta, it was nineteenth-century scholars who delved into the mass of play texts listed by Allacci to construct the solid histories and narratives that, however tendentious, organized the field, as it were.

After the turn of the century Benedetto Croce's idealism had added interpretative latitude to the study of theater, and Mario Apollonio's inclusive panorama gave off original sparks, but the major thrust of the Italian scholarship I encountered in the 1950s was still toward classification of genres and teleological histories tracing the development of the vernacular and of the popular spirit. In addition to valuable local histories in the *storia patria* vein, there were some noncritical editions of scripted plays with standardized spelling and scattered printings of small clusters of scenarios, a few anthologies, and occasional source studies of individual plays. The *commedia dell'arte* had been taken up in France by Pierre Duchartre and Constantin Mic (Miklachevski) and earlier in the impressionistic studies of Maurice Sand, while Ruzante had been romantically celebrated by Henri Mortier; but Ludovico Zorzi's later monumental projects, as well as those of Cesare Molinari and the harvest of dialect studies fostered by Gianfranco Folena, were yet to appear.

Gradually it became apparent that the available Italian scholarship itself was as much an obstacle to the comparative goal I shared with the preceding generation of Lea and Herrick as it was a necessary source of information: not only did the huge mass of Shakespeare studies in English give very short shrift to Italian theater, as opposed to narrative sources, and not only was it almost totally out of touch with Italian theater history, but Italian scholarship on the native drama was equally out of touch with Shakespeareans, and its views of Shakespeare himself followed a Germanic notion of an untaught genius, or a Baroque natural psychologist, at the antipodes from its rather apologetic evaluation of Italy's own Renaissance theater. Romantic reaction against neoclassicism and a preference for whatever seemed vernacular, spontaneous, and popular still colored attitudes toward a drama derived from elite Latin models and constructed according to emerging rules about the unities, verisimilitude, and decorum. The handful of twentieth-century pioneers who began adding to or questioning this legacy had not yet made a dent in the positivistic evaluation of Italian drama, and as for the gap between Italy and the English-speaking scholarly worlds on the subject of Shakespeare, construction of bridges had barely begun.

The second half of the twentieth century would begin filling in the gaps with bibliographies and editions, heralding the present abundance: the editions and collections of both scripted plays and *canovacci,* the new panorama constructed by younger Italianists. The English scholars, even those who read cinquecento and seicento plays, usually had difficulty finding the texts or the time to read enough of them to gauge the enormous output and grasp the family characteristics of the dramatic genres and the innumerable variations they invite. But today's leading Shakespeareans, Stephen Orgel a stellar example, command a more cosmopolitan view, and new work in comparative drama and in theatrical music has further enlarged the horizon.[11]

Teaching Italian drama in the United States in the old days was pretty much out of the question, except as an arbitrary sampling, for lack of texts and translations. The UTET anthologies were only beginning to appear in the late fifties, Aulo Greco published eighteen comedies in 1959, but only in the sixties were they followed by Nino Borsellino's edition of eleven and by the Einaudi series of individual plays (precursor of the later admirable Italian drama collection edited by Guido Davico Bonino). Even Allacci's *Drammaturgia* was not available in facsimile until 1961.

Research in any depth was largely a solo struggle and could be done only in rare book libraries, beginning with the collections of Italian printed drama in the Folger Library, the Library of Congress, the University of Chicago's Regenstein Library, and later Yale's Beinecke Library, then proceeding to the British Museum, the St. John's College and Trinity

College Libraries at Cambridge, and naturally to Italy, where the great national and apostolic libraries (Florence, Venice, Naples, the Vatican) and the more specialized ones (the Sienese Intronati, the Paduan Biblioteca Civica, the Fondazione Cini, the Correr, the Ambrosiana, the Casanatense) all yielded treasures.

Most of the texts had to be read in the original editions. The available *canovacci* were limited to the fifty printed by Flaminio Scala in 1611 and to the selected handfuls published by Neri, Lea, Francesco Bartoli, Vito Pandolfi, and a few others. At the time, the Folger Library was acquiring what would become its rich collection of Italian drama. There were a few catalogues of other collections—Allacci and, eventually, Corrigan and Herrick were invaluable, but the easier access that later printed catalogues and the computer have provided was then impossible, so that much travel, domestic and European, was necessary, furnishing me with memorable scholarly experiences totally unavailable online.[12]

A misleading spin was put on decades of scholarship by nineteenth-century polarizations: scripted regular drama versus improvised *commedia dell'arte,* Church versus theater, native versus foreign origins, "ancient" versus "modern." Obviously such comparisons and oppositions are valid methods of analysis of some aspects of the field, but they are, after all, only organizing devices, unable to provide the widest perspective and, if treated as more than such, they obfuscate the internal tensions within the terms. Supplementary organizing devices are needed to reveal the nonoppositional relations of these binary pairs of concepts and their interactions and collaborations in a larger theatrical enterprise. The approach that focuses exclusively on conflicting forces obscures the international character of Renaissance theater; consequently, the very idea of a theatrical common market formerly seemed untenable and impossible to substantiate.

The Renaissance movement to define dramatic genres was a structural imperative acknowledged by the positivistic generations of the nineteenth and early twentieth centuries, but it was interpreted rather as aping of the ancients than as innovation in playmaking. The "scientific" approach to drama taken by humanistic playwrights bent on finding the principles of its construction in "literary nature" and applying them to the representation of modern life and its surrounding culture in the early *commedie* and *tragedie erudite* was noted but little admired as a breakthrough in technology. Even recent work that recognizes the innovative character of the *tragicommedia pastorale* and the *favola boschereccia* tends to treat cinquecento neoclassical tragedy and comedy simply as conservative forms associated with reactionary politics, ideologies, and poetics, again misleadingly pitting the "modern" Guarini against the "ancient" Denores, for example. Like the opposition of *commedia erudita* to *commedia dell'arte*, this controversy really belongs to infighting among moderns—the regular comedy and tragedy rooted in fifteenth-century humanism was still as experimental and innovative as humanism itself had been when its exponents first made a revolutionary turn toward ancient texts to search for principles on which to base their new constructions.

Compared with the newly investigated classical drama, the rambling stanzaic *feste, sacre rappresentazioni, farse,* and *favole mitologiche* of the quattrocento were perceived as formless, antiquated, unverisimilar, and irregular and were challenged by Ariosto's comedies and the plays of his contemporary experimenters. The search for rules in which they engaged was in itself an innovation, and in the latter cinquecento was still in progress. Finding the true form of modern tragedy continued as a critical quest into the seicento. The great drama of early modern France and England was nourished by it, and the fact that Aristotle was invoked and challenged should not automatically make the results appear "ancient"— the very fact of introducing Aristotelian criteria into the art of playmaking and the science of literary criticism was, if we view it from the right distance in cultural history, as completely new an undertaking in relation to medieval drama as twentieth-century aviation was to ground travel.

The polarization "ancient/modern" has long remained a useful means of sorting out the issues of genre and was actually necessary to the polemics of those who embraced it at that time, as in the quarrel over epic and romance, referring to the "ancients'" choice of Aristotelian classical structure imitating Homer and Virgil and the "moderns'" continuation of chivalric romance imitating Boiardo and the others writing in a form with a more recent origin in medieval narrative. But this polarization can mislead today's readers to the conclusion that the "ancients" were conservatives and the "moderns" innovative, with the further built-in conclusion that to be conservative is necessarily less desirable than to be innovative. Whatever relative values may be or have been attached to the "conservative/innovative" polarization, however, the humanistic turn toward classical examples constituted an innovation in literary theory and practice, while the continuing taste for vernacular theatrical forms such as the various *rappresentazioni, feste,* and *egloghe* dear to the grandparents of the "moderns" was a conservative stance. What David Quint has so well argued about the controversy over the chivalric romance and the epic, perceiving the multiplicity of Ariosto's *Orlando furioso* and his predecessors as "modern" and the controlled unity of Tasso's adherence to classical models in *Gerusalemme liberata* as "ancient," is not really applicable to Italian theater.[13]

Vestigially romantic nineteenth-century scholarship underestimated the innovative rediscovery and vernacular application of dramatic structure founded on Aristotle, Horace, Plautus, Terence, and Seneca that distinguishes sixteenth-century Italian drama from its medieval predecessors. As a playwright, Ariosto and the other early *commediografi eruditi* were performing, in fact, an avant-garde act of comparative literature, or comparative playwriting, the Plautine/Terentian model being one pole of the comparison and their modern *commedia erudita* the other, offered to a knowledgeable audience as a new bloom cultivated from an old stock and to be compared with it. Even when, at the dawn of the seicento, pastoral plays were more in vogue than comedy and tragedy, the latter were still a matter of theoretical controversy, their forms not yet fixed, as attested, for example, by Flaminio Scala's prologue on the form of comedy or Della Porta's attempting pure Sophoclean tragedy in *Ulisse,* as Carlo de' Dottori would still try to do at midcentury in *Aristodemo.* Nor do plays of the late sixteenth century support the assumption that making comedies continued to be a matter of choosing narrative sources and directly dramatizing them. This is not a false perception but one that, regarding plays from midcentury on, leaves out the essential middle term: the technology based on the resources accumulated by literary writers and expanded by commercial actors, who, even when beginning with a novella plot, reached into the repertory of theatergrams in order to put it onstage.

In the long course of reading, I learned why these and some other common assumptions were inadequate, for example, that the most Shakespeare may have learned from Italian theater was a technique of plotting intrigue comedy, and that the neoclassical *commedia erudita* was a mechanical construction, without sentiment or psychological depth, waiting for Shakespeare to invent romantic comedy and to give inner life or individuality to young female characters for the first time. As early as the predecessors of the Sienese Intronati, in fact, romantic comedy was in demand in Italy, and many examples were published from 1520 on, in growing number as professional women players took the stage after midcentury, influencing the style and content of both commercial and literary drama.[14]

The erstwhile notion that Shakespeare was the first to introduce "real," that is, lower-class, shepherds into Arcadian scenes and to mix hard with soft pastoral was another sign of the shallowness of knowledge about cinquecento drama. Pastoral drama was usually treated as a lyrical light-weight confection facilitating elite escapism, graceful bootlicking, veiled criticism—artificial and sensual at best. The principle of genre, on which the *commediografi eruditi* focused, while recognized by the positivistic source-oriented scholars, was conceived primarily in terms of its classical origins, and therefore the search for the "natural rules" of literary genres was not grasped as the revolutionary foundation of modern drama. The pastoral play, in particular, which in the absence of an ancient theatri-cal model declared itself a new-fashioned Renaissance form, a third genre observing the rediscovered rules, was treated mainly as an aesthetic and encomiastic court exercise and therefore did not receive the scrutiny that would have revealed the variety of theoretical, social, intellectual, and cultural forces that produced this enormously influential theatrical invention. Its religious potential, like the clearly fideistic bent of many late cinquecento or early seicento *commedie gravi* and *tragicommedie pasto-rali,* was likewise neglected as a subject distasteful to Italian anticlerical scholarship.[15] Only gradually did I perceive these fallacies as such, while pursuing my original goal to account for the theatrical Italianate quality in Shakespeare by learning more about Italian drama and seeing it as it might have come to him, not as Italian scholars had been presenting it for more than a century in self-perpetuating histories, nor as Shakespearan scholars had been seeing (or not seeing) it for the same length of time.

Formerly the evolving symbiosis between improvised and scripted plays was played down or acknowledged only cursorily by theater his-torians because of a preference for the idea of a conflict between the supposedly spontaneously improvised "liberty" and the observance of classical rules in the "writ." This romantic notion was supported by oc-casional documented evidence of some writers' scorn for the commer-cial *zannate* and of self-aggrandizing challenges from the actors, but the overinterpretation of such internecine clashes long retarded the needed investigation into the inclusive theatrical network that produced all kinds of theater in Italy in the cinquecento and seicento. The *commedianti dell'arte* plundered scripted plays as they did everything turned up by their constant reading. They memorized and performed regular drama, sometimes participating in court productions, as Isabella Andreini did in playing the title role of *Aminta*. From the regular drama they took structure, usable in all three genres, contracted the five acts to three in improvisation, expanded them again to five when, occasionally, they published them. In turn, *commediografi* like Della Porta and Pasqualigo borrowed characters and styles from the professionals.

When Shakespeare put together his only comedy in which there are no foreign names or characters, *The Merry Wives of Windsor,* he produced a perfect example of Italian comic construction by recombination of theatergrams native to both the "writ" and the "liberty": the jealous husband; the *inganno* to test his wife; the would-be seducer, impecunious and boastful as any *capitano;* the *innamorati* disguised to outwit a blocking father; the flattering go-between; the pedant; the word-games with his pupil; the *burla* that hides the seducer in a laundry basket and tosses him into the river; the *travestimenti* as fairies and ghosts—all directed to a reconciling finale of marriage and feasting. Translated into Italian terms for the page or the stage, minus the English names and references and assimilating the *commedia dell'arte*'s occasional latitude concerning scene shifting, it could have passed muster as an indigenous Italian *commedia.*

The specific contacts that generated Shakespeare's unmistakable familiarity with Italian drama are still in doubt. The probabilities are various. There were the court musicians, the Alfonso Ferrabosco who was once commanded to procure a "commedia all'italiana" for Queen Elizabeth, or the musical family of Emilia Bassano Lanier, a sometime candidate for the title of "Dark Lady." There was the likely acquaintance with John Florio, not to mention the extensive sojourn among actors in Italy of Shakespeare's colleagues Will Kemp and his fellow dramatist Anthony Munday. There was the presence in England of Italian diplomats, such as the Pasqualigo family, whose members served the Venetian Republic in London and included Luigi Pasqualigo, author in the 1570s of a comedy adapted by Munday and of the *Intricati, pastorale* that shares a blueprint with *A Midsummer Night's Dream.* Furthermore, in addition to the kind of knowledge of Italian theater disseminated by well-travelled Englishmen, such as is displayed in Sidney's *Apology,* by the performances at Cambridge in the 1590s and thereafter of adaptations of *commedie regolari* and *favole pastorali,* and by the plays in Italian issuing from John Wolfe's London press, there were visits to England of acting troupes, still sparsely documented, to be sure, but frequent enough to have been regarded as a plausible cover for Catholic spies from the Continent.

Early in my absorption with *commedia erudita,* I was asked by a colleague, an Italian scientist well-read in the humanities whose belief in the possibility of exactly measuring excellence had been bolstered by receiving a Nobel prize, whether the plays I was studying were any good, by which he seemed to be asking if they could attract modern audiences as Shakespeare's and Molière's do. While always diffident of absolute Platonic ideals of excellence, I nevertheless regard Shakespeare as peerless and so admitted that I hadn't found a single Italian play that could compete with his. Still, this opinion was neither universal nor timeless; although my distinguished colleague and I and everyone we knew revered Shakespeare, Voltaire did not.

Inevitably, having studied hundreds of Italian Renaissance printed theatrical texts in more than one genre for so long, I have developed a taste for them, have established my own hierarchy of values, and enjoy rereading not only from the top of the list—the *Mandragola*s, the *Aminta*s, and the *Pastor fido*s—but also comedies of Ariosto, Cardinal Bibbiena, the Intronati, the Divine Aretino, Giordano Bruno, and Della Porta; the tragedies of Tasso, G. B. Giraldi-Cinzio, Luigi Groto, Ludovico Dolce, and Pomponio Torelli; and the pastoral plays of Guidubaldo Bonarelli, Isabella Andreini, Giovanni Paolo Trapolini, or Pietro Cresci. These, of course, are only the best known members of the family. If we think of the unwavering esteem Lope de Vega's contemporaries enjoy in Spain, and the spirit that keeps Rotrou alive in France along with Corneille, or of the continuing viability of Middleton and Ford in England, there is no doubt that an equal claim could be made for any number of cinquecento and seicento Italian playwrights: Sforza Oddi, Girolamo Bargagli, Annibale Caro, Bernardino Pino, Giovanni Battista Andreini, Antonfrancesco Grazzini, Giovanni Maria Cecchi, Cristoforo Castelletti, and others, some still performed by Italian repertory companies.

The international theater movement that Shakespeare joined became visible to me during years of ingesting medieval *favole mitologiche, feste* and *rappresentazioni, commedie regolari, favole boscareccie, tragicommedie,* and *canovacci,* revealing a theatrical genealogy that can be followed from quattrocento Italy to Elizabethan/Jacobean England and beyond, and a stage technology that can properly be called the single most generative force in Renaissance dramaturgy. Without denying importance to the continued influence of national medieval traditions, we can recognize the global potential of the Italian repertory of combinable units and witness its use by Shakespeare and countless others.

Some initial reactions to my first demonstrations of Shakespeare's use of the theatergram system were negative, as if his achievement were thereby rendered less original, even mechanical, but on the whole scholars now agree that employing repertorial materials, even prefabricated ones, in recognizably individual combinations is more akin to intertextuality than to automatic assembly-line construction or to plagiarism. Though not universally acknowledged, the functioning of the repertory system is generally accepted now, partially by those who think of it as a collection of plots transmitted by *canovacci,* more fully by others who recognize the repertory as including the units of character, actions, relationships, language, gesture, topoi, and structural themes by means of which plots and variations can be staged. If disagreement and some lacunae persist, it is nonetheless satisfying to see how Shakespeare's kinship with Italy's theater is understood today and how much more we know about Italian drama itself.

Current analyses of communication and art in the digital age are peculiarly relevant to Renaissance drama and to the process of construction by *contaminatio* of theatergrams that had not been apparent fifty years ago. At the first plenary session of the fifth Media in Transition international conference in 2007 Thomas Pettit announced the

closing, in our time, and in the first instance in the mass media, of what might be termed the "Gutenberg Parenthesis," a period in the history of expressive culture dominated by the notion of the original and autonomous cultural product: (1) readily distinguishable from other products within the same cultural system; (2) acknowledged as the creation (and by implication the property) of a specific individual; (3) its stability and integrity sustained over time.[16]

According to the mission statement of this conference at MIT:

An emerging generation of media producers is sampling and remixing existing materials as core ingredients in their own work. . . . Readers are actively reshaping media content as they personalize it for their own use or customize it for the needs of grassroots and online communities. Bloggers are appropriating and recontextualizing news stories; fans are rewriting stories from popular culture; and rappers and techno artists are sampling and remixing sounds.[17]

In the context of this occasion and the cultural climate it breathes, the playmaking system of the Renaissance assumes a modernity—more precisely, a postmodernity—through the similarity of the modes of creative production before and after the parenthesis. Recognizing a "Gutenberg Parenthesis" makes it easier to recognize a theater technology that overlapped with the print culture of the era Marshall McLuhan called the "Gutenberg Galaxy," which fifty years ago was not yet established in the critical vocabulary as a perception of a major paradigm shift, much less of a passing phase. Shakespeare straddled the threshold, entering the parenthesis simultaneously with the actors of the *commedia dell'arte*, whose literary progenitors were already in it, at least insofar as their plays were written in the hope of printing, although those which were actually performed probably included elements—digressive, gestural, musical, balletic—characteristic of unstable cobbled preparenthetical theater that were excised when the texts were editorially stabilized for the press.

Cultural positions in the Romantic and Modernist eras founded on premises of the solitary author and the natural genius, of absolute originality and the paramount importance of text, encouraged a scholarship that obscured some important aspects of the Renaissance theater. Perhaps our own moment in a new millennium is more conducive to understanding the workings and the qualities of the fertile early modern Italian playmaking system, which produced an international drama that prospered precisely by displaying its shared origins, associations, and common materials.

Notes

1. On theatergrams and other issues touched on in this retrospective essay, see L. G. Clubb, *Italian Drama in Shakespeare's Time* (New Haven and London: Yale University Press, 1989), 6–8, and throughout; and Clubb, "Italian Stories on the Stage," *The Cambridge Companion to Shakespearean Comedy*, ed. Alexander Leggatt, 32–46 (Cambridge, England: Cambridge University Press, 2002).

2. Max J. Wolff, "Molière und Della Porta," *Archiv für das Studium der neueren Sprachen und Literaturen* 134 (1916); 148.

3. Antonio D'Andrea, "Giraldi Cinthio and the Birth of the Machiavellian Hero on the Elizabethan Stage," in *Il teatro italiano del Rinascimento*, ed. Maristella de Panizza Lorch (Milano: Edizioni di Comunità, 1980), 617. This follows in the line of R.W. Bond's *Early Plays from the Italian* (Oxford: Clarendon Press, 1911) and M.A. Scott's *Elizabethan Translations from the Italian* (Boston: Houghton Mifflin, 1916). Geoffrey Bullough's essential *Narrative and Dramatic Sources of Shakespeare*, 4 vols. (London: Routledge and Paul, 1957–66) did not challenge this general view.

4. Lea, *Italian Popular Comedy: A Study in the Commedia dell'Arte 1560-1620, with Special Reference to the English Stage,* 2 vols. (Oxford: Clarendon Press,1934); Neri, *Scenari delle maschere in Arcadia* (Città di Castello: S. Lapi, 1913). Neri published six *canovacci* (scenarios) from seventeenth-century manuscripts in Rome and Naples as examples of the *commedia dell'arte*'s pastoral plots, relating them to various Italian plays and to Shakespeare's, especially to *A Midsummer Night's Dream* and *The Tempest.* The first volume of Lea's voluminous history surveyed the known collections of scenarios between 1611 and 1734, one in print and eight in manuscript, described and classified plots and character types, identified the major troupes, reprinted some scenarios, and accounted for the background and practices of the professional theater. The second volume probed a substantial number of English analogues and references in drama and literature, with special attention to Shakespeare.

5. Nicoll, *Masks, Mimes and Miracles: Studies in the Popular Theatre* (London: G.C. Harrap, 1931), and later *The World of Harlequin: A Critical Study of the Commedia dell'Arte* (Cambridge: Cambridge University Press, 1963); Winifred Smith, *The Commedia dell'Arte: A Study in Italian Popular Comedy* (New York: Columbia University Press, 1912); Herrick, *Italian Comedy in the Renaissance* (Urbana: University of Illinois Press, 1960), and *Italian Tragedy in the Renaissance* (Urbana: University of Illinois Press, 1965); Boughner, *The Braggart in Renaissance Comedy: A Study in Comparative Drama from Aristophanes to Shakespeare* (Minneapolis: University of Minnesota Press, 1954).

6. Della Porta, *Teatro,* 4 vols., in *Edizione Nazionale delle Opere di Giovan Battista Della Porta,* 15 vols., ed. Raffaele Sirri (Napoli: Edizioni Scientifiche Italiane, 2000-2003). Gennaro Muzio had published the fourteen comedies in four volumes with standardized spelling (Napoli: Muzio, 1726), and Vincenzo Spampanato edited eight of them in two volumes (Bari: Laterza, 1910-11).

7. See Clubb, *Giambattista Della Porta Dramatist* (Princeton, N.J.: Princeton University Press, 1965).

8. Della Porta, *Gli duoi fratelli rivali / The Two Rival Brothers,* ed. and trans. L.G. Clubb (Berkeley: University of California Press, 1980). Baratto's beautifully succinct study *La commedia del Cinquecento* (Vicenza: Neri Pozza, 1975) focussed on other aspects of theater but appreciated the importance to the development of the genre of the repeatable "formula teatrale" or "modello topico," as he termed it (95 and following). The more detailed recognition of the concept and the system by recent scholars, Zorzi's heirs, is expressed by Anna Maria Testaverde's introduction to an admirable edition of texts, *I canovacci della commedia dell'arte,* ed. Testaverde and Anna Evangelista (Torino: Einaudi, 2007): "si era creato una sorta di immenso repertorio drammaturgico dal quale era facile attingere senza alcuna remora" (xxvii) and extension of the conclusion to Shakespeare's plays where the *commedia dell'arte* is present, "non limitandosi esclusivamente al 'riecheggiamento' di tematiche e al recupero di tipologie di ruoli, quanto piuttosto alla ricezione di topologie teatrali e alla condivisione di un metodo della pratica scenica" (lx-lxi).

9. *Hamlet,* II.2.387-92. See Clubb, *Italian Drama in Shakespeare's Time,* last chapter, "The Law of Writ and the Liberty: Italian Professional Theater," 249-80.

10. Daniele Vianello's study of the *buffoni* from the fifteenth century reveals that these were not merely predecessors of the *commedia dell'arte* actors but continued to ply their largely solo trade through the sixteenth century, sharing many techniques with the acting companies and building their own repertories by means of the same "continuo *bricolage*" that appropriated whatever materials were to be found in books, plays, popular entertainment and personal experience of all sorts. Both freelance *buffoni* and *comici* in troupes

improvised by drawing on a store of remembered variety. *L'arte del buffone: Maschere e spettacolo tra Italia e Baviera nel XVI secolo* (Roma: Bulzoni, 2005), 35.

11. Such scholars as Ferdinando Taviani and Mirella Schino, Franco Ruffini, Ferruccio Marotti, Giulio Ferroni, Maria Luisa Doglio, Riccardo Bruscagli, Siro Ferrone, Marco Ariani, Roberto Tessari, Elissa Weaver, and others too numerous to list have transformed the view of Italian theater. Anglo-Italian comparative studies also have bloomed, as attested by the contributors to this volume and by the distinguished work of Richard Andrews, Michele Marrapodi, Murray Levith, Leo Salingar, Christopher Cairns, Kenneth and Laura Richards, Nerida Newbigin, Keir Elam, Julie D. Campbell, Frances Barasch, Natalie Cohn-Schmitt, Donald Beecher, Pamela Allen Brown and Peter Parolin, and M. A. Katritsky, to name only a few. In addition, musicologists of the generation following Nino Pirrotta's, such as Anne MacNeil, Jessie Ann Owen, Ellen Rosand, Gary Tomlinson, and Giuseppe Gerbino. have illuminated another dimension of the theater.

12. Beatrice Corrigan catalogued the University of Toronto's Italian drama collection (1961-66), as Marvin Herrick did for the University of Illinois, Urbana (1966). These and Italian instruments such as Achille Mango's *Le commedie in lingua del Cinquecento* (1966) and Raffaele De Bello's, Franca Ritzu's, and Giovanni Favilli's catalogues of *pastorali* (1964-65), *drammi* (1962), and *commedie* (1963-64), respectively, at the Biblioteca Nazionale di Firenze were not available at the outset, although they were there to assist me in compiling *Italian Plays in the Folger Library (1500-1700): A Bibliography with Introduction* (Firenze: Olschki, 1968).

13. Quint, "The Multiple and the Modern: Towards an Account of Renaissance Aesthetics" (Chair of Italian Culture Lecture, University of California, Berkeley, November 8, 2007).

14. See Clubb and Robert Black, *Romance and Aretine Humanism in Sienese Comedy, 1516: Pollastra's "Parthenio" at the Studio di Siena* (Firenze: La Nuova Italia, 1993).

15. See Clubb, "Pastoral Elasticity on the Italian Stage and Page," in *The Pastoral Landscape*, ed. J. D. Hunt, Studies in the History of Art 36, 110-27 (Washington D.C.: National Gallery of Art, 1992); and "Pastoral Jazz from the Writ to the Liberty," in *Italian Culture in Early Modern English Drama: Rewriting, Remaking, Refashioning*, ed. Michele Marrapodi, 15-26 (Aldershot, UK, and Burlington, Vt.: Ashgate, 2007). New interest in the pastoral is now producing welcome editions such as Nicolas Perella's translation of Bonarelli's *Filli di Sciro* (New York: Italica Press, 2007) and studies such as Lisa Sampson's *Pastoral Drama in Early Modern Italy: The Making of a New Genre* (London: Legenda, 2006) and Maria Galli Stampino's *Staging the Pastoral: Tasso's Aminta and the Emergence of Modern Western Theater* (Tempe, Ariz.: ACMRS, 2005).

16. Borrowing the concept and term from Lars Ole Sauerberg, and referring back to Marshall McLuhan, Pettit compares pre- and postparenthetical cultures in "Opening the Gutenberg Parenthesis: Media in Transition in Shakespeare's England" (lecture, MiT5 International Conference: Creativity, Ownership and Collaboration in the Digital Age, Massachusetts Institute of Technology, Cambridge, Mass., April 27-29, 2007), 1.

17. MiT5: Creativity, Ownership and Collaboration in the Digital Age. Massachusetts Institute of Technology, April 27-29, 2007, http://web.mit.edu/commforum/mit5/subs/MiT5_mission.html.

Perspective and Stage Design, Fiction and Reality in the Italian Renaissance Theater of the Fifteenth Century

FABIO FINOTTI

THE EPISTEMOLOGICAL REVOLUTION that perspective generated in terms of European imagery is well known. The introduction of perspective during the Italian Renaissance appeared as the turning point from the vertical space of medieval universalistic culture to the horizontal space of the individual exploration of the world, beginning with Panofsky's essays up to their post-Lacanian revisions undertaken by Damisch, Holm, and Elkins.[1] But the emphasis on the triumph of perspective, as a characteristic feature of the transition from the medieval to a new age, sometimes forced the historical data. I intend to prove in my essay that the introduction of perspective to the theater of the cinquecento has often been described and interpreted according to a nineteenth century gaze that imposes *its own* perspective on the historical data, forcing them to conform to an abstract and crystallized conception of the Renaissance. At the root of this contemporary gaze lies the conception that the Renaissance artistic culture was wholly classicizing in its outlook, as if the historical category of Renaissance and the stylistic one of classicism were overlapping. The celebrated essay devoted to the "anti-Renaissance" by Eugenio Battisti, and recently republished in Italy, rests on this very premise.[2] Contesting Burkhardt's celebration of the Renaissance culture, Battisti's book focuses on the anticlassical, irrational, fantastic, and magic data celebrating the existence of a "marginal" culture during the Renaissance. By cataloguing this data under the rubric

21

"anti-Renaissance," Battisti reinforces the assumption of a wholly classicizing Renaissance culture.

This conviction further underpins Battisti's analysis of the relationship between perspective and the theatrical stage in his often quoted essay of 1957 titled "La visualizzazione della scena classica nella commedia umanistica."[3] This title is truly revealing. According to Battisti, both the humanistic and eventually the Renaissance settings correspond to visualizations of the classical setting (*scena classica*). By this account, perspective—in its application to stage design (*scenografia*)—is nothing but one of the phenomena of Renaissance classicism, which developed in the quattrocento in conjunction with the rediscovery and revival of antiquity.

This assumption produces the following consequences in Battisti's essay: One, perspective in the Renaissance theater is a natural and necessary application, born out of the study of Vitruvius. Two, perspective in stage design is a cultural phenomenon resulting from the rereading of ancient texts and finds in pictorial visualizations the domain of *its visual translation* rather than *the original locus of its discovery and exploration*. From the implications of the first two conclusions, the third naturally follows: that the Renaissance theater must have introduced perspective as early as the mid-1400s, a date that corresponds with the rereading of Vitruvius. The prejudice in favor of the Vitruvian influence seems to overlook the central importance of other traditions that inform humanist and Renaissance dramaturgy. These traditions are based in medieval performance practices. To arrive at a fuller understanding of the issue, therefore, it behooves us to look back at the late-medieval theatrical tradition. The criterion for representation in late-medieval theater was both juxtapositional and paratactic: different settings and times shared the same stage, one placed beside the other along the horizontal line of the backdrop. The habit of drawing these elements together, as well as the preeminence of the horizontal dimension, also played out in the interpretation of ancient theater during the humanistic period. The woodcuts accompanying the 1493 edition of Terence, issued in Lyon by Joannes Trechsel, are well known.[4] In these illustrations, the stage appears as a series of arcades or a portico, representing the various characters' houses as small cells united together and closed off by curtains. On the one hand, the architectural structure of the arcade combined with the unity of the scene on one platform is reminiscent of classical forms; on the other hand, the paratactic solution based on stringing together multiple places in horizontal fashion perfectly accommodated medieval customs, while deriving from the Romance tradition of staging known as the mansions or bathing huts.[5]

In "La visualizzazione della scena classica," however, Battisti suggests that this humanistic model has been superseded by Alberti as early as the first half of the 1400s in the stage plans proposed for his *Philodoxeos fabula* (ca. 1424–37), where the action classically covers not multiple physical spaces, but a single place.[6] According to Battisti, Alberti's classicism entails the application of Vitruvius and, inevitably, the application of Vitruvius corresponds in its turn to the implementation of perspective in theater. To support his hypothesis that perspectival treatment in stage design was already required under classicist influence in the *Philodoxeos,* Battisti engages in a radically strained interpretation of several passages in both Vitruvius's treatise and Alberti's *De Re Aedificatoria*. In particular, Battisti focuses on a passage by Alberti modelled after a related passage from Vitruvius to demonstrate that the theatrical use of perspective has been theorized and applied by fifteenth-century humanism under classical influences. But this correlation between perspective and stage scenery appears rather a projection of Battisti's assumptions onto the past, as neither Vitruvius's nor Alberti's passage hints at perspective in stage scenery.

The Vitruvian passage under discussion from his *De Architectura* (5.6–8) reads

Ipsae autem scenae suas habent rationes explicitas ita uti mediae valvae ornatus habeant aulae regiae, dextra ac sinistra hospitalia, secundum autem spatia ad ornatus comparata, quae loca Graeci περιακτους dicunt ab eo quod machinae sunt in his locis versatiles trigonos habentes in singula tres species ornationis, quae cum aut fabularum mutationes sunt futurae seu deorum adventus cum tonitribus repentinis ea versentur mutentque speciem ornationis in frontes. Secundum ea loca versurae sunt procurrentes, quae efficiunt una a foro, altera a peregre aditus in scaenam.[7]

The *scaena* itself displays the following scheme. The central doors have the ornaments of a royal hall. The doors to the guestquarters to the right and left are placed next to the area prepared for scenery. The Greeks call these areas *periaktoi,* because there are triangular pieces of machinery (Δ, Δ) which rotate, each having three decorated faces. When the play is to be changed, or when gods enter to the accompaniment of sudden claps of thunder, these may be rotated and present a face differently decorated. Alongside these places, are the projecting wings which afford entrances to the stage, one from the forum, the other from abroad.

Alberti's words on the subject read as follows:

Cumque in theatro triplex poetarum genus verseretur . . . non deerat ubi versatili machina, evestigio frons porrigeretur expictus et appareret seu atrium seu casa seu etiam silva, plout iis condiceret fabulisque ageretur.[8]

Three types of drama are performed in a theater . . . there would be rotating machinery, therefore, capable of presenting at an instant a painted backdrop, or of revealing an atrium, house, or even a wood, according to the type of drama and the action of the play.

Vitruvius's and Alberti's reference to theatrical machinery (*periacti*) enabling the presentation of comic, tragic, and satiric scenes, make no mention of displacement in the horizontal axis of the backdrop with respect to the vertical axis of perspective, creating the illusion of a landscape *behind the backstage*. As a matter of fact, in the classical scene, the *periacti* were rotating structures, placed *on the sides* of the scene, dominated by a fixed backdrop. The rotation of the machinery changed the sides of the stage settings, but it didn't open its backdrop to a vanishing point. Driven by the research for perspective Battisti considers the "frons" of Alberti's text as referring to the backdrop, instead of relating it to each different façade of the *periacti* themselves, on the side of the scene. Actually, Battisti's mistake is perfectly in line not with the fifteenth-century Vitruvianism, but with the perspectival Vitruvianism of the sixteenth century, when Daniele Barbaro places the *periacti* behind the doors of the backdrop,[9] opening them to an urban landscape with foreshortened buildings, a prelude to Scamozzi's scene at the Teatro Olimpico di Vicenza.

Battisti's inclination to force the historical data, inserting them within an interpretative framework of a classicist "perspective," reaches its maximum expression in the quotation of a passage of Vitruvius, chosen as decisive documentary evidence for the introduction of perspective in stage design as modelled after antiquity. The excerpt is exceptionally evocative: "scaenographia est frontis et laterum abscendentium adumbration, ad circinique centrum omnium linearum responses" (as for scenography, it is the drafted rendering of the front and the receding sides, and the convergence of all the lines on a point).[10] However, these lines by no means belong to the portion of text devoted to theater in Vitruvius's treatise. Rather, they appear at the beginning of the second chapter in the first book dealing with those elements that comprise architecture:

Architectura autem constat ex ordinatione . . . et ex dispositione . . . et euryth-
mia et symmetria et decore et distributione . . . Dispositio autem est rerum apta
conlocatio elegansque e compositionibus effectus operis cum qualitate. Species
dispositionis, quae graece dicuntur ιδεαι, sunt hae, ichnographia ortographia
scaenographia.[11]

Architecture consists of ordering . . . and of design . . . and shapeliness and symmetry and correctness and allocation . . . design is the apt placement of things,
and the elegant effect obtained by their arrangements according to the nature
of the work. The species of design, which are called *ideai* in Greek, are these:
ichnography [plan], orthography [elevation], and scenography.

As confirmed by Di Teodoro in his recent reconstruction of the history
of Renaissance translations and interpretations, it is impossible to interpret *scenografia* in the modern sense of the word, as specifically referring to theatrical perspective. Instead, the term is correctly understood
as referring to one of the planning stages or phases in architecture and
the description of the buildings in the architectural design.[12] Nonetheless, Battisti's distortion in terminology remains intriguing, for it demonstrates within the construction of Renaissance classicism the power
of what Gadamer calls "precomprehension" of texts. On the basis of his
radically forced interpretation of Alberti's theatrical Vitruvianism, Battisti proposes another hypothesis that leads to a thoroughly perspectival
reconstruction of the stage plans in *Philodoxeus fabula*.[13] In this manner, the "angiportus" or street where Alberti assigns the action magically
transforms into an arcade or even possibly a "loggia," according to Battisti's translation, which opens up to the city on the opposite side. The
cityscape undergoes its own transformation into a perspectival scene,
one that Battisti corroborates by late-quattrocento tablets[14] whose connection to Renaissance theater as models for scene designs now appears
untenable in that they constituted the backs of chairs that were painted
for private chambers or small study rooms.

It is precisely because of these debatable points that Battisti's essay
is of particular interest in terms of critical history. While striking in its
indefatigable will to trace the innovations of the Renaissance back to a
classicist foundation, his essay also reveals a penchant for assigning to
painting a documentary role of representing intellectual studies that are
primarily pursued elsewhere in literary and other fields such as architecture, mathematics, and theater—rather than treating painting foremost as

a forum in which to experience, theorize, and test spatial ideas that *subsequently*—thanks to a long, slow, articulated process—would intersect, shape, and transform other forms of discourse.[15]

In order to clarify the evolution of visual and theatrical space in the fifteenth and sixteenth centuries, it is crucial to acknowledge that Italian Renaissance theater, in comparison to medieval theater, contributed at least three innovations to stage setting. The first innovation consists in the possibility of implementing elements drawn from the ancient architectural repertory. The second innovation lies in the "realistic" unity of scene that replaces the juxtaposition of several places and times with the so-called simultaneous scene of Renaissance theater. The third and most significant innovation (almost always confused with the second) comprises *the radical inversion* of the relationship between the proscenium and the backdrop. As the first two are well known and documented, I will focus on the third.

In Roman theater, the backdrop (*scenea frons*) was the place from which the actors exited onto the stage representing the true center of the action to be played out. The real theatrical space was in front of the public and wasn't visibly opened behind the backdrop that worked as a sort of boundary of the area consecrated to the play. In medieval and humanistic theater the setting perpetuated this pattern: the stage setting was composed of a series of units or closed off spaces—at times exhibiting curtains—out of which the actors could emerge to play their parts or, alternately, into which they could retire. Even if these spaces did remain open to the view of the audience, they would nevertheless have rested against the back of a symbolic wall that separated the rest of the world from the realm of the theater, fulfilling much the same function as the canopies that were erected for the Mystery plays and tournaments.

The doors that served as entrances for the actors to walk out onstage were ordinarily placed in the foreground with respect to the backdrop and were closed off by curtains, thereby reinforcing the symbolic boundary beyond which the viewer's gaze could not venture.[16] Pietrini has pursued the medieval and early modern developments of this conception. It will suffice to recall an anonymous commentary on the life of Terence preserved in various manuscripts of the fourteenth and fifteenth centuries in which the scene is defined as "scena vere dicatur umbraculum habens cortinam protensam a quo *emittuntur* personae."[17] The classical foundation for this conception of space is very clear in Vitruvius:

Genera autem sunt scaenarum tria, unum quod dicitur tragicum, alterum comi-cum, tertium satyricum. Horum autem ornatus sunt inter se dissimili disparique ratione, quod tragicae deformantur columnis et fastigiis et signis reliquisque re-galibus rebus, comicae autem aedificorum privatorum et maenianorum habent speciem profectusque fenestris dispositos imitatione communium aedificiorum rationibus, satyricae vero ornantur arboribus speluncis montibus reliquisque agrestibus rebus in topoedi speciem deformati.[18]

There are three kinds of scenes, one called the tragic, second, the comic, third, the satyric. Their decorations are different and unlike each other in scheme. Tragic scenes are represented with columns, gables, statues, and other trappings of royalty; whereas comic scenes exhibit private dwellings, loggias with win-dows after the manner of ordinary buildings; satyric scenes, on the other hand, are decorated with trees, caverns, mountains, and other rustic features delin-eated in landscape style.

The scene is conceived rhetorically, as ornamentation to adorn the back-drop, and it rests against that impassable boundary delimiting the the-ater's space and the real world. Instead of opening backward from the imaginary line on which it rests, the scene opens forward, projecting it-self toward the viewers, with its decorations from which the actors enter the stage and in which they interact, all the while leaning on the back wall, as if against a solid division separating the theater from life.

In Italian Renaissance theater, however, the introduction of perspec-tive provokes a major breakthrough in the backdrop, undergoing an ini-tial pictorial change followed by an architectonic one. In the process, the theatrical space loses the imaginary boundary that once defined and sepa-rated it from reality. The players no longer enter the stage solely *from* the backdrop, but also from other directions *toward* and through the back-drop. In addition, a substantial part of the action is displaced outside of the spectators' gaze, toward an area that tends to coincide more and more with that of their daily experience, as might be confirmed by a reading of the spatialization in Machiavelli's *Mandragola* and in Ariosto's plays, filled with real names of streets and locations.[19] In sixteenth-century Ital-ian theater, the world that the perspective opens in front of the specta-tors is connected to the same one that they have left behind them, and the texts, as well as the stage setting, move toward the exploration and description of a well-specified reality.[20] The scene becomes the center for interplay between reality and fiction that fuses the space occupied by the spectators with that of the actors. The horizontal structure of theatrical stage, cloistered by the scenery, intersects the vertical articulation of the perspective lines, leading the spectators beyond the backdrop toward a part of their real world. In this way, it becomes possible to cross the threshold between the place designated for the scene and the depths of a civic space that threatens to swallow up the characters, like a vanishing point that remains perennially and menacingly open in their story.

The first comedy whose stage design used perspective is Ariosto's *Cassaria,* performed Monday, March 5, 1508, at the Court of Ferrara. The opening of act 4 illuminates the consequences of the new spatial treatment of stage setting. While the master appears to lose his way in the city streets, the servant feels threatened by their "breaking open." There is no better illustration for the dramatic, labyrinthine, and anamorphic appearance associated with perspective in the Italian Renaissance than Volpino's monologue in *Cassaria,* act 4, scene 1:

. . . lui, solo intento a spiare de la fiamma tolta, *va di là, di qua, tutta la città scorrendo* [. . .] da questo infortunio [. . .] mi saprei forse difendere, s'io avessi tanto spazio che vi pensassi un poco [. . .] Ma sì *da un canto* mi occupa il dubio che con la cassa il ruffiano non si fugga questa notte, *da l'altro* uno improviso timore che 'l vecchio patrone non ci sopragiunga e mi coglia e mi opprima in guisa che io non abbia tempo a comperarmi uno capestro con che mi impichi per la gola. Ma che lume è questo *che di là viene?*[21]

. . . he [Erofilo], intent on watching out for the missing girl, *goes here and there, all about the city.* . . . I could probably defend myself from this accident, if only I had the space in which to reflect a little. . . . *On the one hand,* I suspect that the procurer may run off with the safe tonight, and *on the other hand,* I fear that the old master might suddenly appear and discover me, overwhelming me before I even have time to purchase a noose. But what lamp is this *that goes there?*

The action played out on the stage is accompanied by simultaneous actions performed by characters who move beyond the domain of the scene, such that a real and uncontrollable space opens up, looming behind them like an imminent threat, ready to assault and devour them. A glimmer of light accentuates the depths implicit in the text: the fearsome father approaches in the dark, with a lamp that announces his arrival before he is close enough to be identified: "But what lamp is this that goes there?"

The visual breakthrough in stage design is not an automatic result of Vitruvian classicism. It is impossible to attribute it to Alberti's theater with absolute certainty. Nor is there evidence of it in Prisciani, who relies on

Alberti, for he makes no mention of perspective in his writings (*lettera-trattato*) on theater.[22] It is also absent in the classicist scheme designed by Giovan Maria Falconetto for the Odeo Cornaro in Padua, which witnessed the return of the loggia model, evoked by the woodcuts mentioned earlier in relation to Terence. Instead, the breakthrough in the backdrop of the theater was proposed *by a painter*, Pellegrino da Udine, in his staging of Ariosto's *Cassaria*, who opened the street up to the pictorial and there-fore architectonic articulation of the perspectival stage design destined to become popular in Italy and Europe during the sixteenth and seventeenth centuries. Michel Rousse affirms that the theater did not begin with the erection of a platform, but rather with the construction of a backdrop that cut off everyday life from the space occupied by the scene.[23] We could say that modern theater, or Renaissance theater, began once *this backdrop was broken down* and opened up, instituting a more intense interplay be-tween *theater and life, actors and their spectators, virtual settings and actual places, illusion and truth.*

Evidence for this complete overhaul of the stage space is documented in a number of accounts recording the reactions of the spectators. It will suffice to recall quite well-known letters, the most prominent of which is the one Isabella d'Este Gonzaga wrote to her husband on the occasion of the grand festivities in honor of the union between Alfonso and Lucre-zia Borgia celebrated in Ferrara in 1502. Performances at the festivities in-cluded five comedies by Plautus. Isabella recalls one kind of scene in which perspective and the opening up of the backdrop do not yet appear, even though the stage setting acknowledged a "realistic" need for a modern set-ting. On one side of the hall there were steps, while on the other side, Isabella writes,

. . . è facta una murata de legname, merlata a fogia de muro de cità, alta quanto è un uomo; sopra gli sono le case de le Comedie, che sono sei, non avantagiate del consueto.[24]

. . . there stood—as tall as a man—a wooden wall that was embattled so as to resemble a city wall; above this wall appeared the houses belonging to comedy, six in all, in their usual manner.

What we have, therefore, is a practicable stage with six houses *aligned along* the background that provide the spaces for a series of small con-tiguous rooms. Using our former classification, we could say that Isabella's letter acknowledges a unitarian but not perspectival scene. It is interesting, however, to compare this letter written by Isabella immediately after her visit to the theater, with Battista Guarini's description published in 1496 and likely altered by its author to adjust it to the taste evolving toward the triumph of theatrical perspective. This description suggests the use of perspective: "Vidimus efictam celsis cum moenibus urbem/structaque per latas tecta superba vias."[25] Though not yet in the scene setting, perspective was, therefore, in the mind's eye and in the expectations of those spectators who were abreast of the times at the end of the quattrocento.

Also fundamental to the understanding of this perspectival development is the letter written in 1508 by Bernardino Prosperi to Isabella d'Este relating the performance of *Cassaria,* once again in Ferrara, that adopts Pellegrino da Udine's stage setting:

Ma quello che è stato il meglio in tutte queste feste et rapresentationi, è stato tute le sene, dove si sono representate, quale ha facto uno Maestro Peregrino [Pellegrino da Udine] depintore, che sta con el Signore, ch'è una contracta et prospettiva di una terra cum case, chiesie, campanili et zardini, che la persona non si può satiare a guardarla per le diverse cose che ge sono, tute de inzegno et bene intese, quale non credo se guasti, ma che la salvaràno per usarla de le altre fiate.[26]

But the best part of all these festivities and performances were the scenes involved in the plays, such as the one realized by a certain Master Peregrino, the painter of the lord of Ferrara; the scene consisted of a street and a perspectival view of land with houses, churches, bell towers, and gardens, rendered with such diversity as to leave the viewer unsatiated; all this contrived with such ingenuity and skill that I doubt it will be discarded, but rather preserved for later use.

It is impossible to understand these letters' enthusiastic reaction to the new treatment of space without recalling that, precisely in the second half of the quattrocento, northern painting and miniatures emphatically thematize and dramatize the new conception of space.[27] The pictorial proscenium becomes the point of emergence of an ever deeper space, in which the school of Bellini, Mantegna, and the Ferrarese painters (figures 1–4) learned how to "transform the scenery into a sort of scenographic veil, which through its openings reveals a landscape behind it. Buildings, rock, or vegetable architecture, and even furniture are pierced, so as to dramatize the break-through of the backdrop,"[28] and to superimpose contemporary events vertically and mitigate the geometric axis of the single vanishing point with the multiplicity of the lines and images that

N.° 13464.ᴬ Verona - Chiesa di S. Zeno Maggiore. Ancona con la Vergine in Trono col Figlio e Santi, parte centrale. F.lli Alinari, Firenze 1937

FIGURE 1.   Andrea Mantegna, *San Zeno Altarpiece* (Verona, Italy), 1457–1459. Copyright © Archivi Alinari (Florence, Italy)

lead one's gaze into the depths of the scene (figures 5–7). Thus *before theater,* Renaissance *painting* took on a scenic spatialization that balanced and interwove order and multiplicity, unity and diffraction. The classic referents for this new conception of the pictorial and theatrical space probably aren't the backdrops of the ancient theater but some classical remains of urban scenery that looked like diaphragms and enhanced the possibilities of perspective: arcs of triumph and city doors (figure 8).

Thanks to the "visual thinking" of this new pictorial tradition, the classicism of ancient theater is not mechanically applied in the sixteenth century, but rather undergoes a kind of anamorphic deformation, anticipating the situation of Baroque spatial relationships, when the surfaces of

(Ed.™ Alinari) N.° 23158. PARIS — Musée National du Louvre. Le Parnasse (Andrea Mantegna.)

FIGURE 2.   Andrea Mantegna, *Parnassus*, Louvre Museum (Paris, France), circa 1497.
Copyright © Archivi Alinari (Florence, Italy)

buildings themselves begin to bulge and contract here and there, at the
risk of being sucked in by the vortexes radiating from the depths of the
scenographic space. Emblematic of this pictorial solution is the scene of
the Teatro Olimpico di Vicenza (1580), where the Vitruvian front drawn
by Palladio spreads open fanwise into a perspective toward various vanishing points in Scamozzi's interpretation (figure 9).[29]

Renaissance Italian and European letters dating between the fifteenth
and sixteenth centuries should be reexamined not only as historical
and social sources that provide insights into private matters but also as
documents that permit us to observe with the eyes of those who actually witnessed a new experience of the visible, one that anticipates a
post-Cartesian conception of space. Space isn't a material substance, or
res[30] but rather a fluid network of interrelationships between relief and

FIGURE 3.   Andrea Mantegna, *Minerva Chases the Vices from the Garden of Virtue*, Louvre Museum (Paris, France), circa 1502. Copyright © Archivi Alinari (Florence, Italy)

profundity, architectonic mass and pictorial vertigo, order and motion, centrality and centrifugal explosion, reality and scenic fiction.

Baldassar Castiglione writes to Ludovico di Canossa, regarding the performance of Bibbiena's *Calandria* (Urbino, February 6, 1513) for which Girolamo Genga designs the scene:

La scena era finta una contrada ultima tra il muro della terra e l'ultime case; dal palco in terra era finto naturalissimo il muro della città con due torrioni . . . la sala veniva a restare come il fosso della terra.[31]

The scene depicted a street in the distance between the city wall and the most remote houses; from the stage to the village there was a natural-looking representation of a city wall with two embattled towers . . . the parterre thereby became the ditch before the village.

FIGURE 4.   Giovanni Bellini, *Coronation of the Virgin*, Civic Museum (Pesaro, Italy),
circa 1471-1474. Copyright © Archivi Alinari (Florence, Italy)

I would like to underscore here the complete reversal in the customary
point of view with respect to late medieval conventions. Frequently in
the medieval or late medieval tradition of theaters, the structure rested
against a wall, such as in the famous case of the Passion of Velletri, in
which the backdrop coincided with the city wall itself that closed off the
theatrical space.[32] However, in the case of the *Calandria*'s perspectival
scene, the city wall is foregrounded, facing the spectator. It no longer

FIGURE 5.   Andrea Mantegna, *The Transportation of Saint Christopher's Body*, Ovetari Chapel (Padua, Italy), 1455–1459. Copyright © Archivi Alinari (Florence, Italy)

FIGURE 6.   Andrea Mantegna, *St. James Led to Martyrdom*, Ovetari Chapel (Padua, Italy), 1455-1459. Copyright © Archivi Alinari (Florence, Italy)

FIGURE 7.   Francesco del Cossa, *Allegory of April*, Palazzo Schifanoia (Ferrara, Italy), circa 1470. Copyright © Archivi Alinari (Florence, Italy)

represents the final threshold of the backdrop, but rather the initial threshold leading to the proscenium.

On the other side of this first threshold, the view of the entire city opens up:

> La scena poi era *finta* una città bellissima con le strade, palazzi, chiese, torri, strade *vere,* e ogni cosa di rilevo ma ajutata ancora da bonissima pintura e prospettiva bene intesa. Fra le altre cose ci era un tempio a otto facce di mezzo rilievo . . . *finte* le finestre d'alabastro . . . e in certi lochi *vetri finti di gioje che parevano verissime:* figure intorno tonde *finte* di marmo.[33]

Moreover, the scene gave the illusion of a beautiful city with streets, palaces, churches, towers, and real streets, each of which appeared in relief, being enhanced further by fine painting and well-rendered perspective. Among other things there was an octagonal temple in half-relief . . . with illusive windows of alabaster. . . . Certain areas were adorned with illusive glass of precious stones that looked absolutely genuine, freestanding illusive marble figures.

FIGURE 8.   *Porta dei Borsari* (Verona, Italy), first century A.D. Copyright © Archivi Alinari (Florence, Italy)

FIGURE 9.   Andrea Palladio and Vincenzo Scamozzi, *Perspective Scene*, Olympic Theater (Vicenza, Italy), 1584–1585. Copyright © Archivi Alinari (Florence, Italy)

"Real streets": the perspectival scene is thus no longer merely painted, but also practicable, at least in part. In this way, the stage becomes the imitation of an experience that appears authentic and no longer only theatrical. But, at the same time, the avid search for illusion colors the reception of the *Calandria*'s performance: "the scene gave the illusion of a beautiful city . . . illusive windows of alabaster . . . illusive glass of precious stones that looked absolutely genuine . . . illusive marble figures."

Letters such as Baldassar Castiglione's are key documents because they introduce to the scenographic game the necessary gaze of the spectator, who is the true accomplice in the deception that ambiguously intertwines reality with theater, truth and artifice, thanks to the new perspectival "realism." It is in these letters that we find the first fundamental testimonies of the enthusiasm for the *imitation of reality* that does not confine itself to the external space, but becomes the internal space, that profound and oxymoronic spirit of the Italian and European *illusion comique*.

Notes

Images for this article are reprinted with permission of the Archivi Alinari (Florence, Italy).

1. Erwin Panofsky, *Perspective as Symbolic Form,* trans. Christopher S. Wood (New York: Zone Books, 1991); Hubert Damisch, *The Origin of Perspective,* trans. John Goodman (Cambridge: MIT Press, 1994); James Elkins, *The Poetics of Perspective* (Ithaca, N.Y.: Cornell University Press, 1994); Lorens Holm, "Reading Through the Mirror: Brunelleschi, Lacan, Le Courbusier: The Invention of Perspective and the Post-Freudian Eye," *Assemblage* 18 (1992): 20–39. See also Allister Neher, "How Perspective Could Be a Symbolic Form," *The Journal of Aesthetics and Art Criticism* 63, no.4 (Fall 2005): 359–73.

2. Eugenio Battisti, *L'antirinascimento* (Torino: Aragno, 2005).

3. Eugenio Battisti, "La visualizzazione della scena classica nella commedia umanistica," *Commentari* 8 (1957): 248–56; republished, without illustrations, in *Rinascimento e Barocco* (Torino: Einaudi, 1960), 96–111.

4. See figures 18 and 19 in Nino Pirrotta, *Li due Orfei (da Poliziano a Monteverdi)* (Torino: Einaudi, 1975), and figure 25 in S. Pietrini, *Spettacoli e immaginario teatrale nel medioevo* (Roma: Bulzoni, 2001). See also Elena Povoledo, "Origini e aspetti della scenografia in Italia: Dalla fine del Quattrocento agli intermezzi fiorentini del 1589," in Pirrotta, *Li due Orfei,* 335–460: "Anche se alterate, le incisioni dovevano rispettare alcuni elementi di fondo, derivati dalle scene autentiche, quali il modulo ricorrente delle arcate chiuse da cortine di stoffa e la loro disposizione su un'unica linea frontale, a portico . . . le scritte abbreviate, lungo l'architrave, c'informano che ogni arcata corrisponde a una 'casa' della commedia."

5. A. Nicoll, *Lo spazio scenico: Storia dell'arte teatrale* (Roma: Bulzoni, 1971); F. Marotti, *Lo spazio scenico: Teorie e tecniche della scenografia in Italia dell'età barocca al Settecento* (Roma: Bulzoni, 1974).

6. Battisti, "La visualizzazione." A critical edition of Alberti's play is now available: L. B. Alberti, *"Philodoxeos fabula,"* ed. L. Cesarini Martinelli, *Rinascimento* n.s. 17 (1997): 111–234.

7. Vitruvio, *De Architectura,* ed. P. Gros, A. Corso, and E. Romano (Torino: Einaudi, 1997), 572.

8. L. B. Alberti, *De Re Aedificatoria,* in *L'architettura,* ed. G. Orlandi and P. Portoghesi (Milano: Il Polifilo, 1966), 7:7.

9. See F. Camerota, *La prospettiva del Rinascimento: Arte, architettura, scienza* (Milano: Mondadori Electa, 2006), 152.

10. Vitruvio, *De Architectura* 1.2.2;26.

11. Ibid.

12. F. P. Di Teodoro, "Vitruvio, Piero della Francesca, Raffaello: Note sulla teoria del disegno di architettura nel Rinascimento," *Annali di Architettura: Rivista del Ventro Internazionale di Studi di Architettura Andrea Palladio di Vicenza* 14 (2002): 35–54. See also *The Treatise on Perspective: Published and Unpublished,* ed. L. Massey (New Haven and London: Yale University Press, 2003), 269–74. It should be remembered that perspective itself is a Renaissance innovation in comparison to the classical sources. See F. Camerota, *La prospettiva del Rinascimento,* 46–47: "Perchè si possa parlare di prospettiva è necessario peró saper determinare geometricamente la digradazione delle misure in profondità, cosa che secondo le regole della prospettiva lineare avviene intersecando i raggi visivi con un piano corrispondente al quadro del pittore. Nessuna fonte antica fa riferimento a questo concetto fondamentale."

13. Only the first edition of the essay "La visualizzazione . . ." features the draft of Battisti's reconstruction.

14. The tablets in question are those housed today in Urbino (Galleria Nazionale delle Marche), Baltimore (Walters Art Gallery), and Berlin (Staatliche Museen). They have been attributed to Luciano Laurana, Francesco di Giorgio Martini, Cosimo Rosselli, and Piero della Francesca. See R. Krautheimer, "The Tragic and Comic Scene of the Renaissance: The Baltimore and Urbino Panels," *Gazette des Beaux Arts* 4, no. 33 (1948): 327–46. Magagnato and Battisti thought the tablets to be models for stage scenes by virtue of their affinity to the tragic and comic scenes featured in Serlio's *Second Book on Perspective* (1545). For the attribution history, see A. Conti, "Le prospettive urbinati: tentativi di un bilancio e abbozzo di una bibliografia," *Annali della Scuola Normale Superiore di Pisa* 6 (1976): 1,193–1,234, and R. Krautheimer, "Le tavole di Urbino, Berlino e Baltimora riesaminate," in *Rinascimento da Brunelleschi a Michelangelo: La rappresentazione dell'architettura,* ed. H. Millon and V. Magnago Lampugnani, 233–57 (Milano: Bompiani, 1994). For their use as decorated backs in private, domestic spaces, without any connection whatsoever to the Renaissance theater, see Conti; Damisch, *The Origin of Perspective;* and A. Chastel, "*Vedute urbane dipinte* e teatro," in *Teatro e culture della rappresentazione: Lo spettacolo in Italia nel Quattrocento,* ed. R. Guarino, 289–99 (Bologna: Il Mulino, 1988).

15. I completely agree with G. Mazzotta, "Politics and Art: The Question of Perspective in *Della pittura* and *Il Principe*," *Rinascimento* 43 (2003): 15–29 (21): "In 1435 Alberti wrote *Della pittura* (*On Painting*), a small treatise, which completely transforms the traditional understanding of representation and, by placing the perceiving subject at the center of the space of vision, he effectively ushers in the modern age. . . . Alberti's esthetics *elaborates for the first time what the artists' practice had adopted:* the one-point perspective system in the field of the visible."

16. See Pietrini, *Spettacoli e immaginario teatrale nel medioevo,* 152–63; 185–87.

17. Ibid., 162n93: "The scene is a shady place *in front of which* a curtain stretches and out from behind this curtain the characters *exit.*"

18. Vitruvio, *De Architectura* 5.6.9:572.

19. See A. Casella, *presentazione* to L. Ariosto, *Commedie,* ed. C. Segre (Milano: Mondadori, 1974), xliii–xlv.

20. Vasari gives an account of a performance of Machiavelli's *Mandragola* in 1518 "in casa di Bernardino di Giordano," stretching the use of the perspective: "Fecero la prospettiva, che fu bellissima, Andrea del Sarto e Aristotele [da Sangallo]." Quoted in Povoledo, "Origini e aspetti della scenografia in Italia," 382.

21. Ariosto, *Le Commedie,* ed. A. Gareffi (Torino: UTET, 2007).

22. See P. Prisciani, *Spectacula* [circa 1501], ed. D. Aguzzi Barbagli (Modena: Panini, 1992), 45: "Et adornavase [el pulpito] de colone, solari, et de quali se potesse andare da l'uno a l'altro ad imitation de case, cum ussi, porte, e cum una in mezo sì como regale per ornamento de templi, et in la quale potessero descendere et ascendere li personati et actori de lor senno sì como richercassero le fabule."

23. See M. Rousse, "La pratique théâtrale dans l'élaboration d'une farce," in *Artistes, artisans et productions artistiques au Moyen Age* (Paris: Picard, 1986), 533.

24. Alessandro D'Ancona, *Le origini del teatro italiano* (Torino: Loescher, 1891), 2:134.

25. B. Guarini, "Elegia," in *Carmina* (Modena, 1496), book 4.

26. D'Ancona, *Le origini,* 2:394.

27. About the pictorial search for perspective in the trecento, particularly in Giotto, see F. Camerota, *La prospettiva del Rinascimento,* 35–39.

28. See also book illuminations in Padua and Venice. An eloquent document is provided by Benedetto Bordon (Benedetto Padovano), *Digestum novum,* Venetiis, N. Jenson 1477 (Gotha, Landesbibliothek, Mon. typ. 1477), f. 12b, reproduced in G. Mariani Canova, *La*

miniatura veneta del Rinascimento (Venezia: Alfieri, 1969), fig. 108: the arches of the backdrop open out to an urban landscape.

29. See S. Mazzoni, *L'Olimpico di Vicenza: Un teatro e la sua "perpetua memoria"* (Firenze: Le Lettere, 1998); L. Zorzi, *Il teatro e la città: Saggi sulla scena italiana* (Torino: Einaudi, 1977).

30. See *The Treatise on Perspective*, 68: "it is important, also, to note that although *pictorial space* is a convenient, hence almost unavoidable, modern term, it is not one used by Piero [della Francesca, in his *De prospective pingendi*]. He considers only the construction of images of particular bodies. Each of these is then a measure of extension—the length of a body, the distance between two bodies, or some other expanse defined in regard to bodies. Space as an independent entity is a seventeenth-century invention."

31. D'Ancona, *Le origini*, 2: 102.

32. See Pirrotta, *Li due Orfei*, fig. 14.

33. D'Ancona, *Le origini*, 2: 102-3.

Performing Anachronism: A New Aetiology of Italian Renaissance Tragedy

KRISTIN PHILLIPS-COURT

B Y NOW IT is axiomatic that Italian experiments in tragic poetry at the end of the fifteenth century and in the first part of the sixteenth century resulted in texts that pale in comparison to those of the Elizabethan era. In our modern estimation, and particularly in the nonspecialist's view, early tragedians formidably attempted to resuscitate and to redress ancient Greco-Roman tragedy in contemporary garb, to present an erudite alternative to degraded comedy, and to reformulate the aesthetic and political divisions between comedy and tragedy. Already by the 1560s early cinquecento tragedy would lose on two fronts: it would fail to reach the cathartic heights of ancient tragedy, and it would fail to enact the proper catharsis prescribed by slightly later theorists such as Castelvetro and Giraldi-Cinzio and achieved by Shakespeare and Corneille.

This ossified narrative, parts of which are demonstrably false, emerges from a teleological portrayal of the rise of Renaissance tragedy and comedy as a progression toward an ideal of "modernity," which, for drama, could be alternately expressed as psychological depth, political relevance, or aesthetic autonomy. One aspect of modernity that concerns both Renaissance readers and post-Romantic readers like ourselves is the question of originality.[1] Beginning with the judgmental posture of the romantic movement, early Italian tragedy has not received high marks for originality in studies that look forward to Tasso or Shakespeare. Only works of the later sixteenth century—Tasso's *Aminta,* for example—seem to have

been judged for their intrinsic qualities, instead of for the way they absorb what came before.

Traditional accounts of drama's revival-by-imitation belie the cultural
subtleties and poetic play that characterize Renaissance anachronism. It
is difficult to determine whether this is the result of a misconstrued variation of the anxiety of influence that has infiltrated secondary criticism
and that trickles down to the historical object itself, or whether genre acts
as an insulating device within later accounts of drama's revival. Despite
the considerable contribution of genre studies to revealing drama's literary and historical meaning,[2] early tragedians' productive use of anachronism—by which I mean intertextual citation that results in a new literary
model—appears to be rote when that text becomes anthologized by genre
and placed within a developing narrative about a marginal literature.

Italy's "first regular tragedy," Giangiorgio Trissino's *Sofonisba* (1514),
for example, drew as much from Petrarch as it did from Euripides. *Sofonisba* has earned negative judgments for the author's inability to naturalize his sources, beginning with the negative assessments of his near
contemporaries, Benedetto Varchi and Torquato Tasso.[3] That Trissino
rejected the quattrocento Latin tragic tradition—by writing in Italian,
by writing in the Greek style without imposing acts and scenes, and by
writing a history instead of a fictive tragedy—signifies a genuinely innovative stance that has been buried under layers of criticism. Such criticism grapples primarily with the play's perceived theoretical failures and
with its supposed inability to resuscitate the profound meaning of Attic
drama.[4] Trissino's belatedness seems particularly pronounced when his
tragedy is compared to sixteenth-century comedy that boasts not only a
contemporary setting but also an updated ethics, like we find in Ariosto's
vernacular comedies and especially in Machiavelli's *Mandragola*.

Forty years ago, Lienhard Bergel argued in this journal that cinquecento
tragedy, a "literature that is aesthetically unrewarding," necessitated a
shift from the aesthetic field—understood as the formal realm of the
single text and related derivatives—to cultural history, for that might at
least provide some insight into intellectual currents of the time.[5] But to
abandon aesthetics altogether is to risk unintended results, which David
Quint has described with clarity:

For if the individual author was to be defined historically, his creation fell into the
realm of historical contingency, at a remove from any timeless or fixed standard

of truth. Historically delimited, the meaning and authority of the text might be just as relative as its literary style.[6]

In 1990 *Renaissance Drama* responded by presenting a collection of essays focusing on drama and cultural change.[7] Scholars like Marco Ariani, Carlo Dionisotti, Giulio Ferroni, and more recently Ronald L. Martinez have drawn out the ways in which early Italian tragedians responded intellectually to the politically unstable "crisis years" following the invasions of 1494.[8] But they have also demonstrated that aesthetics need not impoverish interpretive analysis by arguing that historical context can produce certain philosophical sensibilities, as Ariani has done in his discussion of Trissino's "utopian" poetics,[9] and can determine artistic models and choices, as Martinez has shown in two different explications of Machiavelli's iconographic use of the Roman figure of liberty, Lucretia.[10]

In this essay I would like to consider how we can illuminate another aspect of originality (and modernity) in early tragedy by reinjecting aesthetics into a historicist interpretation of Trissino's *Sofonisba*. Trissino's *Sofonisba* is a formal pastiche, and its political relevance may be argued in both pro- and anti-imperialist directions; but its cultural, artistic, and intellectual relevance emerges out of the pastiche itself. First, I look at the way in which tragedy's rocky start as an object of literary criticism has contributed to the difficulty of perceiving both Trissino's citation of visual art and his lyric modernity. Then I turn to the text to examine a concept of "figural anachronism" in *Sofonisba,* whereby the objectified characteristics of the beautiful queen combine with the subjective voicing of Petrarch himself to form a double historicity that is both ancient and modern. Taking some cues from Martinez's discussion of how Machiavelli and Trissino deployed the "tragic iconicity" of the ancient Lucretia and Sofonisba in their comedy and tragedy, respectively, I also follow in part a new, visual model of Renaissance anachronism put forth by art historians Christopher S. Wood and Alexander Nagel that helps to elucidate Trissino's artistic and poetic methodology. I argue that the citation and "retroactive power" of Sofonisba's familiar image in Trissino's tragedy comes forth as a kind of "performative" intertextuality that resembles the deliberate anachronism practiced by humanist writers but imports an image-artifact from the past, like words or phrases.[11] In Trissino's tragedy, this ancient visual citation folds together with modern, Petrarchan lyric imitation.

Finally, by way of conclusion, I maintain that for Trissino, just as for the more politically "relevant" Machiavelli, formal choices were ideological choices.

Tragedy's Firstcomer

Written in blank verse and without divisions between acts and scenes, Trissino's tragedy unfolds in Cirta, in North Africa, in 203 B.C. Trissino takes the tale of Sofonisba from book 30 of Livy's *History of Rome* but follows even more closely Petrarch's version of the story in book 5 of his epic, *Africa*.[12] Sofonisba was the daughter of a Carthaginian general at the time of the second Punic war. She married a prince of neighboring Numidia, allied to Rome, and, prior to the action of the play, she had succeeded in alienating her princely husband from his Roman masters. In Trissino's version, the queen confides that her husband, Siface, has been captured by the Numidian leader of Roman forces, Massinissa. Massinissa, who was once engaged to Sofonisba, would fall in love again upon seeing her and would likewise marry her. To prevent the loss of a second ally from the same cause ("la causa fu la bella Sofonisba," "it was the beautiful Sofonisba," says Siface, resigned to his doom), the Roman general Scipio demands that Massinissa surrender her to Rome. Her new husband, not daring to defy Scipio, opts for a lesser form of defiance: he sends Sofonisba a cup of poison, which she drinks. The setting of the play is the palace, where the action is narrated by the queen herself and by the chorus of women of Cirta. Competing with the lovers' plot are scenes from the Roman camp under Scipio's command, where Scipio, together with his second-in-command, Lelio (the Latin Laelius), airs the fittingly rational side of the debate over Massinissa's irrational decision to marry the conquered queen.

Trissino intended the tale of the beautiful Numidian queen who met her doom to be read by his friends, his critics, his patron Pope Leo X (Giulio de' Medici), and eventually, after he published it twelve years later, by anyone interested in reading a fine embodiment of Aristotelian principles. Tragic firstcomers like Giangiorgio Trissino and Giovanni Rucellai, who wrote Greek- and Roman-style tragedies in the Italian vernacular, and comic diversifiers like Ludovico Ariosto and Niccolò Machiavelli, who were revising Roman comedians Plautus and Terence for local audiences, did not yet have access to Aristotle's *Poetics*. Trissino had gleaned only generic prescriptions for his 1514 tragedy, *Sofonisba*, from parts of

Aristotle's *Rhetoric,* and he later noted that he had observed Aristotelian unities.[13] Trissino diverges from earlier neo-Latin tragedies of Castellano and Romano by following Greek structure. Importantly, he abandons a traditional tragedic schema of fortune and reversal found in Attic drama in favor of adopting Livy as a historical model.[14]

The revivalist attribution given to Trissino tends to align the "first modern tragedy" with a formalist approach. This textual-critical match is bolstered by Trissino's own controlling literary intelligence, already highly theoretical at the time he wrote *Sofonisba.* In the retelling of drama's revival in Italy we can perceive a fluctuation away from, perhaps even back toward, a politicized history. Some accounts attempt to place Italy's "first modern tragedy" into a context of either antiquarian interest or modern political practice. A formalist account of tragedy's revival in the early sixteenth century is neat and clean; it represents the most commonly recounted beginning of modern tragedy. Trissino's experimentation would eventually yield a fortuitous consequence—namely, after a few years of Senecan imitation, an Aristotelian model would replace medieval theater, culminating in seventeenth-century French classicism. Renato Barilli locates Trissino's *modernità* precisely in his adherence to classical models: that is, despite his ultimate "failure," Trissino should be admired for committing himself to the hard work of *integration* (my emphasis) of Aristotelian principles of verisimilitude and a modern vernacular language that sought to build emotion through its immediacy.[15] Barilli thus tries to improve Trissino's lot as a dry poet, but Barilli ultimately concludes that Trissino's achievement is that of providing one small step toward modern drama.[16]

A political-ideological approach that focuses on political allegories retrofitted uncomfortably to ancient tragedy provides an interpretive point of entry through which one could speculate about the author's prescriptive politics—did Trissino take an ambivalent view of Sofonisba's imperial conquerors, as Beatrice Corrigan suggested?[17] Does *Sofonisba* divulge "Machiavellian" themes within its lines? One might justifiably draw out the political implications of Trissino's association with Machiavelli. Such themes in early tragedy are probably better read in light of Seneca (and the pseudo-Senecan *Octavia*) while such themes in Giraldi-Cinzio's *Orbecche,* for example,[18] resulted from a longer chain of reactions to *The Prince* and later debates about tyranny. By concerning ourselves exclusively with how common political themes in tragedy (such as tyranny, liberty, and aristocratic privilege) correspond to historical events, we risk overlooking suggestive links between the text's formal properties and those same historical events. For example, why tragedy? Why did Trissino choose dramatic literature, and tragedy, its most rigid form? How did he seek to deploy his ancient sources within the rigid confines of the solemn genre? When Trissino co-opted Sofonisba, he created a poetic configuration, not a political symbol transmigrated clumsily from the Punic war to the pope's wars of acquisition and related allegories.

The purpose of encapsulating these narratives in a restrictive manner is to show how each, in its own way, elides the question of how aesthetics might relate to politics. What insight do we gain from the consensus built on rebirth narratives within the broader topic of Italian Renaissance drama, narratives that are most often already defined and compartmentalized by genre? And why should we insist on a purely literary chain of influence? The intertextuality and anachronistic display in Trissino's tragedy of Queen Sofonisba instantiate a much more evocative and culturally rich work than one might gather from judgments portraying Trissino as a pedant and purist.

A historicist approach to dramatic literature that takes into consideration Trissino's intellectual community, which included scholars and historians, including Machiavelli, who participated in discussions at the Rucellai family gardens between 1511 and 1514, provides the richest context for Trissino's decision to take up tragedy. Scholars in a number of disciplines have examined the meetings known as the "Orti Oricellari" as a trope of confluence and change.[19] Historians and political scientists take a keen interest in these Florentine conversations as a significant, fluid source of modern political thought, while historians of ideas see evidence of Ficino's influence across a broader intellectual community that would drive developments in sixteenth-century philosophy and aesthetics. Literary critics cite the meetings to identify when vernacular language overtook Latin in scholarly literature. And historians of drama know that at least two members of the Orti group—Trissino and Giovanni Rucellai—wrote vernacular tragedies in a bold new style, drawing from Greek and Roman drama as well as from ancient history and contemporary events.

What emerges from accounts of the Orti meetings is a microhistorical view of a common intellectual enterprise and shared intellectual property.[20] Most of the men who attended the meetings were in the process of composing larger literary works. Their choice to use the vernacular language in many of these works reveals more than an aesthetic debate over naturalistic expression versus ideal forms; their choice reveals a great concern for the contemporary world. Writing in the vernacular, as "younger generation" Oricellarians Machiavelli, Trissino, Giovanni Rucellai, Brucioli, and Gelli did, suggests that even behind the protective walls of the orchard these authors, like comic authors, were actively trying to identify with common culture rather than retreat from it.

Intertextuality; or, "Performing Anachronism"

As a way of contextualizing Renaissance authors' citation and imitation of the ancients, L. G. Clubb (1989) used the rhetorical term *contaminatio,* which had its roots in the proper historical period (often illustrated by Lucretius's lovely metaphor of bees gathering honey from diverse flowers).[21] The concept of contamination loosens the stricter philological approach to Renaissance revisers of Greek and Roman poets and underlines both the greater sophistication in the writer and the dynamic exchange of ideas in Renaissance Italy. Clubb's approach implicitly alleviated some of the difficult incongruities of Renaissance anachronism by shifting the focus to *contaminatio* in the confines of her study, which ultimately pursues Italian drama's placement in the build-up to Elizabethan drama. By engaging in further discussion of the nature of contamination we might shift the focus away from considering primarily whether the Renaissance author succeeded or failed in his "poetica imitazione," as Ariosto called it in 1508.[22]

One result of the trecento and quattrocento turn to the vernacular was that the distinctions between philosophers and men of letters were elided by a certain cultural permeability. The dramatic literature that attached to theatrical praxis brought social protocols and discursive formations together to reorder human experience, incorporating what Gombrich called the "beholder's share," not only onstage, but also in the mind of the reader.[23] Trissino's originality lies in his expansion of *Sofonisba's* referential field to visual images and traditions as well as to literary traditions. And his modernity, I suggest, can be located in the figure of the queen, who emerges as a conglomeration of literary voices and beloved icons to form the tragedy's cultural epicenter. The centrality of the queen's voice in the play, combined with an abiding emphasis on her corporeal image, provides Trissino with the vehicle for a moving story with a moral outcome.

In the remaining pages I will argue that Sofonisba's dual drive to *narrate* the scene and to *occupy* the scene reveals an indwelling reciprocity between the antagonistic categories of subject and object, which stems from Petrarch's creation of a radically divided self and from habits of beholding across the centuries. Trissino takes productive advantage of a devotional gaze that meets the seductive image of the queen. At the same time, however, this play counters a reductive erotic presentation of its protagonist by privileging her rational speech, her piety, and her own Petrarchan overtures, all establishing the queen as the play's ideological *logos* and structural *locus*. As the site of the author's own negotiation of history and politics on one hand and art and ideas on the other, the queen works as the tragedy's *ideologeme* as she represents the tragedy's ideological horizon by pulling its referential fields into herself. The "modernity" of Italy's "first vernacular tragedy in the Greek style" lies in the way it captures the originality and specificity of the Renaissance humanist's oscillation between objective rational ideas and a unified theory. Trissino sustains, in productive tension, two opposing positions that are the *Sofonisba*'s key intellectual ingredients: the need for a poetics of contingency and a heuristic defense of the classics.

Beholding Sofonisba

The culturally alert reader of Trissino's tragedy would have known of Sofonisba's beauty and suicide from Livy, from Boccaccio, and from Petrarch. Trissino then infused his icon with other anachronistic substitutions—not just of literary figures like Alcestis and Hecuba, but of recognizable iconic figures like Lucretia and Sofonisba, Virgil's Dido, Venus, and even the Virgin Mary. The link between Sofonisba and her more famous counterpart, the Roman Lucretia, a figure of liberty whose rape and suicide precipitated revolution, could hardly have escaped either Trissino or Machiavelli, as Machiavelli's *Mandragola* would make clear just a few years later. As Ronald Martinez has written, "for early *cinquecento* Florentines, the death of Lucretia was an established tragic icon, inviting to revolution and tyrannicide, complete with a stage set rendered in the purest classicism available."[24]

Indeed, Sofonisba's image in the Renaissance had become indelible in two media, first in the writing of Livy, Petrarch, and Boccaccio, and second in painterly traditions from antiquity onward. Tracking Sofonisba from the Roman period to the Renaissance cinquecento, we find that the Numidian queen secures her place not only in historical painting, in which she typically appears as part of an episode in the life of Scipio Africanus, but also in what I would describe as a combination of portraiture and cultic painting, in which she is pictured alone, without background or other narrative elements, resembling other female icons, both religious and historical or "secular."

Sofonisba's earliest appearance in painting was as the subject of a fresco at Pompeii, in which she poisons herself in Scipio's presence in order to avoid being carried off to Rome as a war trophy. In the medieval period Sofonisba appeared again in concert with literary texts in which she is a subject, notably in a decorated manuscript of Petrarch's epic *Africa* and of Boccaccio's verbal portraits of famous women, *De claris mulieribus*.[25] This last text came with a wave of interest in "illustrious men" in the Plutarchan vein and, more significantly, seems to have contributed directly to the inclusion of female heroines in iconographical cycles.

The most important fifteenth-century painter to take Sofonisba as his subject was Andrea Mantegna. Mantegna served as court painter at Mantua under Ludovico Gonzaga, where Trissino would take up residence between 1515 and 1516. Mantegna not only painted a grisaille of Sofonisba for Isabella d'Este's rooms at Mantua, he also included Sofonisba in one of the largest and most important imitation bas-reliefs painted on canvas for the Cornaro family.

Mantegna completed three panels before his death in 1506—*The Introduction of the Cult of Cybele, The Vestal Virgin Classical with a Sieve,* and *Sofonisba Drinking Poison.* Sofonisba and Tuccia are featured as part of a grander commission to celebrate the triumphs of the Roman Cornelii family, of which Publius Cornelius Scipio Africanus, hero of the Second Punic War, was the most famous representative. (The Cornaro family claimed to be the direct descendants of the Cornelii.) Mantegna conceived Sofonisba as both a historical subject and a cultic icon, whom viewers recognized by the iconography of her chalice just as they recognized Tuccia by her sieve. Together they also signify Summer (the sieve of the separation of grain) and Fall (the chalice of the *vendemmia,* the wine harvest).

Like Trissino's deliberate anachronism in the tragedy, Mantegna's colorless painting signals more than antiquarianism. Mantegna's canvas is a new and independent creation, like Trissino's poetic text. Mantegna was an intellectually accomplished artist who understood the highly

Andrea Mantegna, *A Woman Drinking*, 1495–1506.
Copyright © The National Gallery, London

mediated ontological status of artistic invention (*inventio*) and who demonstrated a deeply layered sense of the past. Jack M. Greenstein credits Mantegna with making the "diachronicity of invention a subject in its own right."[26] That is, Greenstein explains that Mantegna was interested in exploring scholarly abstraction, the abstraction that resulted when the past object or story was extracted from the flux of time. Mantegna refocuses the traditional ekphrastic rendering as a material and figural imitation: he makes a drawing that seems to copy an actual bas-relief. It is difficult to know if Trissino knew the painted bas-reliefs or if he emulated Mantegna's method; the associative link I aim to establish between Mantegna's intellectual painting and Trissino's poetic operation hinges on the mechanism of imitation, which sets word and image on equal footing in a historical narrative.

Voicing Petrarch

Sofonisba's aesthetic figuration owes much to Petrarch. In *Africa,* the effect of Sofonisba's sensuality is immediate: "Massinissa felt/a flame consume his marrows, even as ice/melts in the heat of summer or as wax/dissolves in the proximity of fire,/so as he looked he melted."[27] Trissino adopts the stilnovistic convention of praising the queen's physical attributes through the chorus of women and the would-be lover Massinissa, but Petrarchan words and phrases do not only reiterate Sofonisba's erotic allure as similar to that of Laura. Above, we can draw an analogy between Sofonisba and the *Canzoniere*'s Laura in terms of the objectification of the woman and her effect on the poet. Trissino relies on this communicative paradigm in the tragedy, but he folds these two perceiving bodies together into the queen, who appropriates the voice of the poet:

> [SOFONISBA:]
> E però quinci prendo tale ardire
> che, lasciando da parte ogni paura,
> io parlerò con voi sicuramente;
> benché *meco medesma mi vergogno* (467-70)
> . . .
> E solo io vi dirò, che tanta grazia
> non è mai per uscirmi de la mente,
> mentre *che di me stessa mi ricordi.* (565-67)

So I shall set fear aside and make bold to speak to you with confidence, although *I am ashamed of myself.* . . . I shall say only that I shall never forget such a great favor *so long as my memory lasts.*

Petrarchan rhetorical phrases reveal more than dutiful citation or a mechanical attempt to naturalize courtly love into tragedy. In this bold scene, in which the queen had the audacity to speak to Massinissa before he has spoken to her, Sofonisba echoes Petrarch not just in words but in state of mind. The queen's familiar and beautiful words, "meco medesma mi vergogno," which align Petrarch's words "di me medesmo meco mi vergogno" in the opening poem of his songbook, *Voi che ascoltate in rime sparse il suono,* endow Sofonisba with self-reflexive consciousness that is ancient, modern, and unmistakably Petrarchan. Trissino thus invites Petrarch's fluid subjectivity to permeate the tragedy and, to a large degree, determine its ethos.[28]

Petrarchan intertextuality in the *Sofonisba* serves Trissino's poetic enterprise by introducing to his tragic *dianoia* a striking integration of visual and psychological experience. Petrarch does not invest his Sofonisba with the transcendental quest that defines his *Canzoniere.* But Trissino inaugurates a new formula: when he gives his tragic muse a voice, he takes her amplitude, her fleshly presence, like that of Laura or Dido, and invests in her the voice of a poet-subject. By combining the objectified characteristics of Laura (and Dido) and the subjective voicing of Petrarch himself, Trissino brings together the Latin and the Italian Petrarchs, respectively. In this fundamental "historical anachronism," ancient Roman epic comes face to face with lyric modernity.

Sofonisba launches a Petrarchan existential appeal in the first verses of the tragedy as she laments with foreboding the news she has not yet received—that she will be taken prisoner by Roman soldiers who have conquered her city:

> Lassa, dove poss'io voltar la lingua,
> se non là 've la spinge il mio pensiero?
> Che giorno e notte sempre mi molesta.
> E come posso disfogare alquanto
> questo grave dolor, che 'l cuor m'ingombra,
> se non manifestando i miei martiri?
> I quali ad un ad un voglio narrarti. (1-7)

Alas, what else can I talk about, if not about what is on my mind? I am tormented, day and night, all the time. How else can I relieve my feelings unless I talk about what is worrying me? That is why I should like to explain the causes of my anxiety, one by one.

Sofonisba's monologue draws attention to the unity of language and thought in a presentation of the self that sets the tone for the entire piece. Stemming from her disorientation—an existential confusion that foreshadows the unsettling events to come—this embattled self contains within it a soul that is both resigned to the vicissitudes of fortune and resolved toward death. Trissino orders thought, speech, and action with sufficient deliberation. "Là 've [dove] mi spinge il pensiero": first thought, then speech, through which thoughts are made manifest. Sofonisba's monologue closes by insisting on a sequential ordering of thoughts "one by one" as personal circumstance and historical event unite in the queen's subjective world. The propitiary key of these lines, in which she foretells her telling, points to the dramatization of language throughout the *Sofonisba* tragedy. The point is driven home by her gloss on Dante's painful recounting of Ugolino's death in *Inferno* 33: "E come posso disfogare alquanto/questo grave dolor, che 'l cuor m'ingombra." (425).[29] (And Massinissa will echo this lamentation at the end of the tragedy with the words "per non rinovellar vechio dolore" that are even closer to Dante's "Tu vuo'ch'io rinovelli/disperato dolor.")

Conflating in Sofonisba the bodily-pictorial image of Dido-Laura and the poetic voice of Petrarch, Trissino cultivates within that visual citation what we might call an erotics of cognition. Concerned with tragedy's effect, this erotics of cognition builds upon two key factors: a certain permeability of other characters within the tragedy and an imagined public who was willing to be seduced by the image.[30] By selecting an erotically charged image like Sofonisba, the author created a stratification of meaning in the play in which language, thought, and ideology were intimately tied to image. Instead of propitiating the gods, Sofonisba's speech appeases the genre that requires it, so that the "where" of "là 've mi spinge il pensiero?" ultimately indicates the theater itself.

Despite Sofonisba's open appeal, these first two stanzas are closed off from the world, folded into the queen's myopic purview. The first stanza of Sofonisba's monologue above recalls Petrarch's "Lasso me, ch'io non so in qual parte pieghi," of which I transcribe only the first part:

Lasso me, ch'io non so in qual parte pieghi
la speme, ch'è tradita ormai più volte.
Che se non sparger al ciel sì spessi preghi?
Ma s'egli aven ch'ancor non mi si nieghi
finir anzi 'l mio fine
queste voci meschine,
non gravi al mio signor perch'io il ripreghi
di dir libero un dì tra l'erba e i fiori:
"Drez et rayson es qu'ieu ciant em demori." (*Canz.* 70)

Alas, I do not know where to turn the hope that has been by now betrayed many times. For if there is no one who will listen to me with pity, why scatter prayer to the heavens so thickly? But, if it happens that I am not denied the ending of these pitiful sounds before my death, let it not displease my lord that I beg him again to let me say freely one day among the grass and flowers: "It is right and just that I sing and be joyful."[31]

The poet has nowhere to turn his voice and thus turns into himself, drawing in an intersubjective universe around him, a dramatic *templum* that includes other characters who act as filters to the centralized self. But in terms of characterizing the centrality of Sofonisba's voice in the tragedy, we might make a broader comparison with the *Canzoniere*'s "establishing" poem. Sofonisba's overture, which reaches outward even as it focalizes meaning inward, evokes that of the great lyricist:

Voi ch'ascoltate in rime sparse il suono
di quei sospiri ond'io nudriva 'l core
in sul mio primo giovenile errore
quand'era in parte altr'uom da quel ch'i' sono,

del vario stile in ch'io piango et ragiono
fra le vane speranze e 'l van dolore,
ove sia chi per prova intenda amore,
spero trovar pietà, nonché perdono. (*Canz.* 1)

You who hear in scattered rhymes the sound of sighs on which I used to feed my heart in youthful error when I was in part another man, and not what I am now, for the vain hopes, vain sorrows I avow, the tears and discourse of my varied art, in any who have played a lover's part pity I hope to find, and pardon too.

Petrarch's opening poem encompasses myriad concerns, but if we may pay Trissino the compliment of possessing a Petrarchan sensibility, we might draw out two principal elements found in both overtures: the fusion of past, present, and future in the protagonist's voice, and the alignment of thought and words (*discorso*) with the literary project itself. The poet reiterates in 366 ways this initial act of containment in which the person in language and the text in space become one.

Similarly, Sofonisba's self-seeking words from the first strophe to her final breath establish her as the play's *locus* and *logos. Sofonisba's* fluid architecture produces a curious effect, which is the need to search for spatial unity. The stable, embodied image of the queen provides a *locus* that supplants Trissino's tenous unity of place; but she also generates the play's discourse as *logos,* as thought and speech come together in her voice and dominate the verses of the play. That she is the locus and logos of action is therefore due not to the tragic gesture of her suicide; rather it is Sofonisba's rhetorical skill, which constantly resurfaces, that determines her logocentrism. Actions and reactions in the play filter through the queen's logocentric character, so that dramatic action converges on a single point. Sofonisba enacts a kind of découpage, to use a cinematic term that is applicable to the likewise privileged sphere of the theater. Découpage refers to the arrangement of shots in a film that implies inclusivity and objective experience by reference to what is beyond the frame but that necessarily excludes peripheral information in favor of a subjective view. Sofonisba similarly brings the peripheral to center stage; she pulls all the fields of reference into herself in a play that exhibits no solid architecture. Worldly events—Roman conquest itself—are a backdrop filtered through the self. Thus, like Petrarch's project, this tragedy's dramatic structure and ethical thrust are established in a rhetorical sequence that calls the universal into the personal and repeatedly forces closure on what begins as an outward appeal.

Sofonisba's aporetic oscillation between pathetic resignation and heroic resolve signals an ongoing dialectic that takes hold of the tragedy from the first lines:

> Lassa, dove poss'io voltar la lingua
> *se non* là 've la spinge il mio pensiero?
> . . .
> E come posso disfogare alquanto
> questo grave dolor, che 'l cor m'ingombra,
> *se non* manifestando i miei martiri? (1-7)

> Alas, what else can I talk about,
> *if not* about what is on my mind? . . .
> How else can I relieve my feelings,
> *if not* by talking about what is worrying me?

While two hypotheticals in the same stanza underline an open-ended oscillation between existential options, the two ifs rationalize Sofonisba's speech and reveal a palpable element of censorship in her self-presentation.[32] The *Sofonisba* invites debates that cover the ethical-thematic concerns of tragedy, such as love versus duty, life versus death, and liberty versus tyranny, but these concerns do not spring spontaneously from the characters' words and actions. Instead, Trissino's tragedy focuses on the rhetorical formulation of ethical categories by inscribing conflict into the tragedy verse by verse. In any number of passages, Sofonisba tacks between submission and rebellion, between constancy and inconstancy.

Marco Ariani and others have questioned both the purpose and the effects of such deliberative rhetoric, or speech that is punctuated by what we might call "propitiary" words like *chiarire* and *ragionare* and demonstratives like *questo* and *quel.*[33] This tendency to lengthy deliberation led Martin Herrick to describe the *Sofonisba* as "a talky play" in which Trissino privileges *dianoia* or thought over action.[34] Giulio Ferroni has amplified this sensibility by arguing that Trissino's micromanagement of conflict reduces any notion of grand, tragic conflict to the level of mere verbal rhetoric.[35] Despite Ariani's careful study of the way Trissino stages within the queen's dialectic political debates and a longing for utopia, Herrick's and Ferroni's interpretations of the *Sofonisba* have dominated the contemporary critical landscape. Later studies, like Salvatore di Maria's, which surveys the development and themes of cinquecento tragedy, with the hope of "vindicat[ing] its theatrical relevance," tend to perpetuate nonetheless a dismissive attitude toward Trissino's poetic enterprise.[36]

But the tragedy's deliberative rhetoric has another function. It mediates both Sofonisba's emotionalism and the ardor of *Amor,*[37] which served Trissino's specific purpose of reconfiguring the exotic, adulterous Sofonisba into a model of grace and piety. Trissino foreshadows the compromise that Sofonisba and Massinissa will make by writing not only conflict but also moderation into her character:

> Ma questa dolce mia regale altezza
> Tosto mi fu cagion d'amara vita. . . . (72–73)

> But my lofty station brings me nothing but a life of sorrow. . . .[38]

> Ben conosch'io che quelo
> si deverebbe far che tu ragioni,
> ma 'l soverchio dolor troppo mi sforza,

e 'l senso ch'è rubella
de le più salde ed ottime ragioni,
subitamente il lor volere ammorza;
così mi truovo senza alcuna forza
da contrappormi al duol che mi distrugge;
se 'l ciel pietoso questa mia sciagura
non fa, che sia men dura,
ben son al fin, per cui la vita fugge. (166–76)

I know that you are right in what you say, but this overwhelming grief is stronger than I am. The emotions rebel against the dictates of reason and immediately override the will; I find myself without the strength to bear the sorrow that consumes me, and if merciful heaven does not alleviate this disaster, it will be the end of me.

Sofonisba's "bipolarismo"[39] in these lines surfaces on both linguistic-rhetorical and thematic levels. First we notice Petrarchan binary oppositions that ring out with the clarity of dyadic pairs in a structuralist reading: *dolce-amara, senso-ragioni, pietoso-men dura.* Image oppositions function as a performative mapping of ethical categories of life, death, power, and tyranny. Sofonisba's speech also prefigures her fall from glory to humility, from queen of *regale altezza* to lowly *serva de' Romani.* If we realign our perception that this pathetic fall constitutes the purgative moment, and not her protracted, drawn-out suicide, as Ferroni would have it, then the tragedy does succeed in permeating in a meaningful way the viewer's moral and ethical consciousness. If Sofonisba's pathetic fall, which will ultimately encompass the tragic fall from life to death, constitutes the moment of *recognitio,* then we might delineate further *which* emotion we are to experience. By folding the pluralities of literature, art, and political events into the figure of the queen, Trissino counts on the reader or viewer's ability to determine *Sofonisba's* edifying message.

Conclusion

Only a few years later, with a few chosen words, Machiavelli would direct his audience in another way. In the *Mandragola*'s mocking prologue, the author makes explicit the association between literary form—aesthetics—and politics:

E, se questa material non è degna,
per esser pur leggieri,

d'un uom, che voglia parer saggio e grave,
scusatelo con questo, che si'ingegna
con questi van' pensieri
fare el suo triso tempo più suave,
perché altrove non have
dove voltare el viso.
      . . .

And if this material is not worthy—on account of its being so light—of a man
who wishes to seem wise and grave, excuse him with this: that he is trying with
these vain thoughts to make his wretched time more pleasant, because he has
nowhere else to turn his face. . . .[40]

Machiavelli's juxtaposition of comedy and tragedy and his simultaneous
blending of comic and tragic registers questions, as Trissino had questioned, the purpose of writing itself in the face of such a broken political
system. The unbearable lightness of the *Mandragola* is lost on no one who
laughs and also recoils at the violence done to Lucrezia, the young woman
who is called both *accorta,* "astute," and *ingannata,* "tricked," whose virtue (chastity) is lost, and who, in the end, adapts to the new order.[41]

In a "metatheatrical reflection on the impossibility of both tragic action and political renewal,"[42] Machiavelli plays out the tension between
political expediency and literary ideality brilliantly through the alarming materiality of Lucrezia's "conversion" and through the surprising
conventionality of his *Mandragola,* whose simple plot contrasts with its
anarchic undertones.

In Machiavelli's writing, the nature of things and the appearance of
things enter into an ever-more-complicated relationship. In Trissino's
tragedy the ironic and self-divided *poetica imitazione* comes forth as a
friction between literary form and content. The lament of that breach,
before any later critic would voice it, became in Trissino's hands the substance of a new, modern tragedy.

Whether or not Trissino was under Machiavelli's influence, tragedy's
firstcomer dwelled on whether the utopia of literature could induce political change. Trissino, like Machiavelli, knew the power of art, the power
of the here-and-now of theater, as much as he knew the value of historical models. Two central, related questions shape *Sofonisba.* The first
is whether literature's marginality in relation to politics might be overcome by a rational and measured approach, and the second is whether
in the face of a devastating political landscape the utopia of literature

could induce change.[43] In Trissino's tragedy, the author's pessimism on both counts lies underneath a steady idealism expressed through art. We might take Trissino's piece as more than a theoretical exercise. We might take it as an artistic expression of those combined "sensibilities" that led the author to seek to assimilate the highest human ideals of the spirit into a politics of contingency. Giangiorgio Trissino had survived the invasions of 1494. Could grace and diplomacy, the characteristics imbued in his tragic Sofonisba, overcome the ravages of war?

In Trissino's heroine we find a dialectical mix of momentary optimism and profound pessimism. It might be useful to put aside originality and to view the alienation that accompanies a harmonization of eclectic sources—visual, literary, philosophical—across a broad spectrum: that is, a broad historical and critical spectrum that places at one end the uncomfortable intertextuality that is born of anachronism and, on the other end, the uncomfortable political reality that a workable theory built on past models could not assuage.

The vulnerability of Trissino's text as an experiment in Renaissance imitation links itself intimately to its layered, and in many ways incomplete, protagonist. This vulnerability, this misprision, constitutes Trissino's originality.[44] By choosing a historical plot, Trissino faced the discomfort of stepping outside the framework of divine providence and of abandoning a principle of apotheosis. How material reality failed to square with Platonic ideals and political unity constitutes both the success and failure of tragedy's firstcomer. Trissino responds to this challenge in part by folding together *locus* and *logos*—iconic presence and subjective discourse in the Sofonisba character, as I hope to have shown; but as political unity proved increasingly elusive, Trissino was forced to "reflect on the ruptures of history."[45] As Trissino moved from the ideality of literature to the materiality of history in hopes of cultivating their productive intercourse, Machiavelli staged his anachronistic performance as polemic.[46] In the end, Machiavelli would prove the better naturalizer. But their projects share more than tragic icons; they share an idea of dramatic literature as a brand of practical contemplation that sees the *human* as that space of ambiguity between the world in theory and the world of making. The discord that results from Trissino's inability to harmonize eclectic sources should lead us to investigate the author's need to confront the alienation that attends any effort to place the consequences of human action within a vision of unity. If we acknowledge that need, then we are on the right track.

Notes

I thank William West and Albert Ascoli for their attentive reading of this essay and for their many helpful suggestions for improvement. I also thank David Loewenstein for initially inviting me to give a talk on this topic at the Center for Early Modern Studies at the University of Wisconsin-Madison.

1. The scholarship devoted to the question of Renaissance imitation and originality is extensive, to say the least. One might start with Renaissance authors themselves, especially Ariosto, who, in defending his own "poetica imitazione" in his prologue to *Suppositi* (1508), provided the impetus for subsequent theoretical writing on imitation and, more importantly, on intertextual practice in drama itself. We need only examine the many comic and tragic prologues to glean specific attitudes about the use of ancient texts; nonetheless a number of treatises on dramatic literature (Robertellus, Castelvetro, Dolce, not to mention Trissino's own *Quinta divisione della poetica* of 1524) appeared as part of the editorial cycle. The complexity of this problem comes to the surface in Poliziano, whose philology problematizes its own alignment with poetry as art. Valla's epistemology, too, is crucial to the deepening concerns of literature during its simultaneous vulgarization. In this essay I have turned to a few modern critics who have focused on this question: Thomas M. Greene, *The Light in Troy: Imitation and Discovery in Renaissance Poetry* (New Haven: Yale University Press, 1982); Vittore Branca, *Poliziano e l'umanesimo della parola* (Torino: Einaudi, 1983); David Quint, *Origin and Originality in Renaissance Literature* (New Haven and London: Yale University Press, 1983); Leonard Barkan, *Unearthing the Past: Archaeology and Aesthetics in the Making of Renaissance Culture* (New Haven: Yale University Press, 1999); Giuseppe Mazzotta, *Cosmopoiesis: The Renaissance Experiment* (Toronto: University of Toronto Press, 2001); Frank Kermode, *The Classic: Literary Images of Permanence and Change* (New York: Viking Press, 1975); and Harold Bloom, *The Anxiety of Influence: A Theory of Poetry* (New York: Oxford University Press, 1973). Greene still offers a persuasive account of the sensibilities surrounding literary anachronism; the cogency of that account is paired with its overriding elegiac tone. Mazzotta argues for a political interpretation of anachronistic dissonance as Poliziano's foreboding prophecy about Medicean rule. In my discussion below of artistic reception, or beholding, I rely on the foundations of Gombrich, Baxandall, Belting, and Shearman in the social history of art, but more specifically, on the idea of figural anachronism forwarded by Christopher S. Wood and Alexander Nagel and discussed among art historians Michael Cole, Charles Dempsey, and Claire Farago. See note 11.

2. Few studies address Italian texts, but Rosemary Colie, *The Resources of Kind: Genre Theory in the Renaissance* (Berkeley, Los Angeles, and London: University of California Press, 1973), Frederic Jameson, *The Political Unconscious* (Ithaca, N.Y.: Cornell University Press, 1981), and of course Northrop Frye, *The Anatomy of Criticism* (New York: Atheneum, 1966 [1957]) should be mentioned.

3. Benedetto Varchi, *Lezioni* (Florence: Giunti, 1590), and Torquato Tasso, *La Sofonisba di Gian Giorgio Trissino con note del Tasso*, ed. F. Paglierani (Bologna: G. Romagnoli, 1884).

4. Marco Ariani, in *Tra classicismo e manierismo: Il teatro tragico del Cinquecento* (Florence: Olschki, 1972), blames De Sanctis in particular for setting the tone by calling Trissino "a pedant who was neither a poet nor a patriot" (*Storia della letteratura italiana* [Turin: Einaudi, 1958], 1:461).

5. Lienhard Bergel, "The Rise of *Cinquecento* Tragedy," *Renaissance Drama* 8 (1965): 198.

6. David Quint, *Origin and Originality in Renaissance Literature* (New Haven and London: Yale University Press, 1983), 7. Quint writes in the introductory chapter: "As a concept of value, originality is the byproduct of a historicist criticism which considers the work of art within its historical context without necessarily assigning value to the context itself. The comparison of the work to other similarly evaluated works measure what is distinctive and inimitable in it alone. Originality thus becomes virtually identical to the intrinsic strengths of the work of art" (5). Quint then places the problem in the period itself: "The new Renaissance appreciation of individual creativity and human differences could [thus] have its unsettling consequences."

7. *Renaissance Drama as Cultural History: Essays from* Renaissance Drama *1977–1987*, ed. Mary Beth Rose (Evanston, Ill.: Northwestern University Press, 1990). The volume contains one essay on an Italian work: Ronald L. Martinez, "The Pharmacy of Machiavelli: Roman Lucretia in *Mandragola*" (1983), 1–43.

8. For this article I have turned to more recent studies including Ariani, *Tra classicismo e manierismo*, and *Il teatro italiano: La tragedia del Cinquecento* (Turin: Einaudi, 1977); Giulio Ferroni, "Classicismo e riduzione di conflitto," in *Il testo e la scena: Saggi sul teatro del Cinquecento* (Rome: Bulzoni, 1980); Paola Cosentino, *Cercando Melpomene: Esperimenti tragici nella Firenze del primo Cinquecento* (Rome: Vecchiarelli, 2003); Renato Barilli, "Modernità del Trissino," *Studi italiani* 9 (1997): 27–46; Jonas Barish, "The Problem of Closet Drama in the Italian Renaissance," *Italica* 71, no. 1 (1994): 4–30; Beatrice Corrigan, ed., *Two Renaissance Plays* (Manchester: Manchester University Press, 1975), and "Two Renaissance Views of Carthage," in *Drama in the Renaissance*, ed. Clifford Davidson, C. J. Gianakaris, and John H. Stroupe, 116–29 (New York: AMS Press, 1986); Paola Mastrocola, *Nimica Fortuna: Edipo e Antigone nella tragedia italiana del Cinquecento* (Torino: Tirrenia Stampatori, 1996); Carla Bella, *Eros e censura nella tragedia dal '500 al '700* (Florence: Nuovedizioni E. Vallecchi, 1981); Federico Doglio, *Il teatro tragico italiano* (Parma: Guanda, 1972); Valentina Gallo, *Da Trissino a Giraldi: Miti e topica tragica* (Rome: Vecchiarelli, 2005); Marvin T. Herrick, *Italian Tragedy in the Renaissance* (Urbana: University of Illinois Press, 1965); Marzia Pieri, *La nascita del teatro moderno in Italia tra XV e XVI secolo* (Turin: Bollati Boringhieri, 1989); Louise George Clubb, *Italian Drama in Shakespeare's Time* (New Haven: Yale University Press, 1989); *Convegno di studi su Giangiorgio Trissino*, ed. Neri Pozza (Vicenza: Accademia Olimpica, 1980); and Salvatore di Maria, *The Italian Tragedy in the Renaissance: Cultural Realities and Theatrical Innovations* (Lewisburg, Pa.: Bucknell University Press, 2002). Most of these nod to Bernardo Morsolin's definitive biography of Trissino, *Giangiorgio Trissino: Monografia d'un letterato del XVI* (Florence: Le Monnier, 1894). Trissino's own treatise, *La Quinta Divisione della Poetica*, available in *Trattati di poetica e retorica del Cinquecento*, ed. Bernard Weinberg, (Bari: Laterza, 1970), 2:7–44, continues to provide historical perspective. Finally, the most salient treatment of Trissino's tragic enterprise to be found among recent studies is Ronald L. Martinez's concise essay "Tragic Machiavelli," in *The Comedy and Tragedy of Niccolò Machiavelli: Essays on the Literary Works*, ed. Vickie B. Sullivan (New Haven: Yale University Press, 2000).

9. Marco Ariani, "Utopia e storia nella *Sofonisba* di Giangiorgio Trissino," in *Tra classicismo e manierismo*, 9–52.

10. Ronald L. Martinez, "Tragic Machiavelli," and "The Pharmacy of Machiavelli." A reconciliation between formalist and historicist approaches to drama is well underway; in addition to Martinez, scholars such as Deanna Shemek, Jane Tylus, Maria Galli Stampino, Laura Giannetti, and Guido Ruggiero have enriched this field significantly by exploring the intersections between politics and aesthetics in comedy, tragedy, and pastoral.

11. Talking about painting specifically, art historians Christopher Wood and Alexander Nagel have argued for an analytical model that describes the emergence of the modern institution of the artwork as a reframing and redirecting of figural anachronism. They use the term "substitution" to describe the act of citing (literally importing in time, or substituting) in the new work known visual figures as if they were words or verses of an ancient text. This model is capable of tracking the self-divided artwork (ironically divided between old and new) as it distances itself from competing myths of origins and reinvents itself as the projection of a hypothetical world in which the image produces the effect of a collapse of time. Alexander Nagel and Christopher S. Wood, "Toward a New Model of Renaissance Anachronism," in "Interventions," special issue, *Art Bulletin* 87, no. 3 (September 2005): 403-15. The responses, printed in the same issue, include Charles Dempsey, "*Historia* and Anachronism in Renaissance Art"; Michael Cole, "*Nibil sub Sole Novum*"; Claire Farago, "Time Out of Joint"; and, importantly, Wood and Nagel's "Authors Reply."

12. See *L'Africa di Francesco Petrarca*, ed. Agostino Barolo (Turin: Chiantore, 1933), book 5, and in translation, Francesco Petrarca, *Petrarch's Africa*, trans. Thomas G. Bergin and Alice S. Wilson (New Haven: Yale University Press, 1977).

13. Trissino, *La Quinta Divisione della Poetica*, 18.

14. With a new valorization of the arts arising and patrons competing for cultural capital, the tragedians who tacked between Florence and Rome from 1511 to 1515 seized the opportunity for patronage by Leo X. In Rome Trissino befriended Baldassar Castiglione, who was in the Eternal City on a diplomatic mission, and the Venetian scholar Pietro Bembo. Trissino attended a well-publicized performance of Bernardo Bibbiena's *La Calandria*; Castiglione had organized the performance in order to honor Giuliano and Lorenzo de' Medici's new Roman citizenship in Campidoglio. Isabella of Mantua also attended the performance. Trissino had begun writing the *Sofonisba* in Florence. Perhaps encouraged by his friend Isabella when he stopped in Ferrara on his way to Rome, Trissino completed the tragedy in Rome and dedicated it to Leo X.

15. Barilli, "Modernità del Trissino," 39-40.

16. Ibid., 38: "E il nostro li affronta, i tre generi canonici, secondo . . . una modernità che a sua volta si pone come attenta erede del meglio che può venire dalla tradizione classica, vista però sempre come una tappa di passaggio, e non già come una meta in se stessa."

17. Corrigan, ed., *Two Renaissance Plays*, 13.

18. Riccardo Bruscagli, "La corte in scena: genesi politica della tragedia ferrarese," in *Il rinascimento nelle corti padane* (Bari: de Donato, 1977), 569-95.

19. Felix Gilbert has shed light on the nature of the Orti Oricellari meetings, explaining that there were two generational phases: the first revolved around Bernardo Rucellai and produced a number of traditional histories; the second revolved around Machiavelli, Trissino, and the younger Rucellai, Giovanni, Bernardo's son. This second phase, between 1511 and 1514, during which time Trissino wrote his tragedy of Sofonisba, is characterized by a new kind of thinking about history and humanist methods. (Felix Gilbert, "Bernardo Rucellai and the Orti Oricellari: A Study on the Origin of Modern Political Thought," *Journal of the Warburg and Courtauld Institutes* 12 [1949]: 101-31.) See also Carlo Dionisotti, "L'Italia del Trissino," in *Teatro del Cinquecento*, ed. Maristella Lorch, 11-23 (Vicenza: Accademia Olimpica, 1980), and "Machiavellerie (II)," *Rivista storica italiana* 83 (1971): 227-63. On the Orti see also G. Piccioli, "Gli Orti Oricellari e le istituzioni drammaturgiche fiorentine," in *Contributi dell'Istituto di Filologia Moderna*, Serie Storia del Teatro I, 60-93 (Milan: Vita e Pensiero, 1968), and Giuliano Lucarelli, *Gli Orti Oricellari: Epilogo della politica fiorentina del Quattrocento e inizio del pensiero politico moderno* (Lucca: M. Pacini Fazzi, 1979). Ariani (1972), Martinez (2000), and Corrigan (1975) likewise situate

the tragedy's genesis in the Orti discussions. Notably, Ferroni (1980) minimizes the impact of the Orti discussions.

20. Here I am thinking of Christopher Celenza's description of a microhistory of intellectuals, which focuses on "a limited group of people who possess a shared set of interests informed by common material for reflection." See Christopher S. Celenza, *The Lost Italian Renaissance: Humanists, Historians, and Latin's Legacy* (Baltimore: Johns Hopkins University Press, 2004), 75.

21. Louise George Clubb, *Italian Drama in Shakespeare's Time*, 5-9.

22. Ludovico Ariosto, prologue to *Suppositi*, in *La Cassaria - I Suppositi*, ed. L. Stefani (Milan: Mursia, 1997), 154.

23. E. H. Gombrich, *Art and Illusion: A Study in the Psychology of Pictorial Representation* (Princeton: Princeton University Press, 1961). Early cinquecento tragedy was primarily a written form. Recitation honed rhetorical skills while opening up debate on the uses of vernacular language, on poetic imitation, and on the nature of representation, especially regarding the nonperformative bent of Aristotle's prescriptions for the highest art. Neither *Sofonisba* nor Rucellai's *Rosmunda* was intended for the stage. Trissino was conscious that his tragedy would be a literary model. He offered it up as a poem whose refined verse and exemplary characters operated together in creating a powerful and moving image. The author maintained that tragic poetry ought not to rely on stage spectacle but should be able to portray events effectively by activating verbal imagery. In Trissino's view, the poet possessed the power to represent. We uncover this affirmation in the lines devoted to tragedy in Trissino's *Quinta divisione della poetica*, which, after giving due credit (as did Aristotle) to how stage representation impresses spectators, turns lastly to the first order of composition, the fable and its arrangement in verse. See also Jonas Barish, "The Problem of Closet Drama in the Italian Renaissance." Regarding the idea of cultural permeability and exchange, I still think that Richard Trexler's short essay "The Florentine Religious Experience," which first appeared in *Studies in the Renaissance* 19 (1972), and in alternate form in *Public Life in Renaissance Florence* (New York: Academic Press, 1980), provides an indispensable understanding of the entangled social functions of religious and scholarly practices. Some aspects of discussions of the beholder find a loose analogue in contemporary performance theory, such as Herbert Blau's *The Audience* (Baltimore: Johns Hopkins University Press, 1990): "Entranced by image, we are emptied into theater" (2).

24. Martinez, "Tragic Machiavelli," 107.

25. For an anthology of Sofonisba images see Paola Guerrini, "Iconografia di Sofonisba: Storia e teatro," in *Nascita della tragedia di poesia nei paesi europei*, ed. M. Chiabò and F. Doglio, 80-93 (Viterbo: Teatro Olimpico, 1991).

26. Jack M. Greenstein, *Mantegna and Painting as Historical Narrative* (Chicago: University of Chicago Press, 1992), 64.

27. Petrarca, *Petrarch's Africa*, trans. Bergin and Wilson, 86.

28. Petrarch's broader impact, as we will see, comes forth as part of a steady aestheticization of grace in poetry and art to the point at which it becomes, for Ficino, Botticelli, Trissino, Bembo, and Castiglione, the highest emblem of Platonic beauty. Trissino's *Ritratti*, Marco Ariani has argued, were among the first writings of the sixteenth century to suggest that an aesthetic unity of grace and form could lead to a consciousness and a demand for a historicization of grace in reality. See Ariani, *Tra Classicismo e manierismo*, 12-14.

29. Dante Alighieri, *Inferno* 33:4-5; *Sofonisba*, 425. See Salvatore di Maria, *Italian Tragedy in the Renaissance*, 45, 150.

30. On Petrarch and Eros in painting see Elizabeth Cropper, "On Beautiful Women, Parmigianino, Petrarchismo and the Vernacular Style" in *Art Bulletin* 58 (1976); "The Beauty

of Woman: Problems in the Rhetoric of Renaissance Portraiture," in *Rewriting the Renaissance: The Discourses of Sexual Difference in Early Modern Europe*, ed. Margaret W. Ferguson, et al., 175–90 (Chicago and London: University of Chicago Press, 1986); and especially "The Place of Beauty in the High Renaissance and its Displacement in the History of Art," in *Place and Displacement in the Renaissance*, ed Alvin Vos, 159–205 (Binghamton: State University of New York, 1995). For questions related to beauty and Platonism see the collection of diverse and informative essays presented by Francis Ames-Lewis and Mary Rogers (with an introduction by Elizabeth Cropper), *Concepts of Beauty in Renaissance Art* (Aldershot, UK: Ashgate, 1998).

31. This and the translation of "Voi ch'ascoltate in rime sparse il suono" below are from Robert M. Durling, *Petrarch's Lyric Poems: The "Rime sparse" and Other Lyrics* (Cambridge, Mass.: Harvard University Press, 1976), 151 and 36.

32. Di Maria, *Italian Tragedy in the Renaissance*, 118.

33. Ariani, *Tra classicismo e manierismo*, 67.

34. Herrick, *Italian Tragedy in the Renaissance*, 47.

35. See Ferroni, *Il testo e la scena*, 195–96.

36. As Salvatore Di Maria does, for example, on the nature of Trissino's Petrarchism: "whereas [Petrarchism's] influence on poetry might have been meaningful, it could hardly have been effective on an action-based genre such as theater. At its best, its dwelling on the characters' emotions succeeded in stifling dramatic action; at worst, language took on an importance all of its own, ignoring the necessary correspondence between words and deeds. Predilection for verbal communication is most damaging to theater, for it encroaches upon the basic function of the stage to represent dramatic action" (*Italian Tragedy in the Renaissance*, 11, 45).

37. Ariani contends that such insertions reset the tragedy's discourse as one that proceeds as reasoning (*ragionamento*) as opposed to pathos (my word choice here) (*Tra classicismo e manierismo*, 67).

38. My translation.

39. Valentina Gallo characterizes the dual nature of the Sofonisba tragedy as a "bipolarismo" that has driven some of the criticism of the play in a number of different directions. See Gallo, *Da Trissino a Giraldi*, 29.

40. Niccolò Machiavelli, prologue to *Mandragola*, ed. G. Bonino (Turin: Einaudi, 1979), 6; the translation is by Mera J. Flaumenhaft, in *Mandragola* (Prospect Heights, Ill.: Waveland Press, 1981), 10.

41. See G. Ferroni, *Mutazione e riscontro nel teatro di Machiavelli e altri saggi sulla commedia del Cinquecento* (Rome: Bulzoni, 1972), 19–137, the titular chapter of which appears in English as " 'Transformation' and 'Adaptation' in Machiavelli's *Mandragola*," in A. Ascoli and V. Kahn, *Machiavelli and the Discourse of Literature* (Ithaca, N.Y.: Cornell University Press, 1993). The critical literature on Machiavelli's *Mandragola* is vast. Here I will mention studies that focus on either the author's juxtaposition of comedy and tragedy or on the figure of Lucrezia. Jane Tylus's "Theater and Its Social Uses: Machiavelli's *Mandragola* and the Spectacle of Infamy," *Renaissance Quarterly* 53, no. 3 (2000): 656–86, deserves special note. M. Martelli, "La Mandragola e il suo Prologo," in *Il teatro di Machiavelli*, ed. Gennaro Barbarisi and Anna Maria Cabrini, 221–55 (Milan: Monduzzi Editore, 2005); Ascoli and Kahn, introduction to *Machiavelli and the Discourse of Literature*, 1–16; R. Martinez, "Tragic Machiavelli" and "The Pharmacy of Machiavelli"; C. Dionisotti, "Machiavelli: Man of Letters," trans. Olivia Holmes, in *Machiavelli and the Discourse of Literature*, ed. Ascoli and Kahn, 17–51, and "Appunti sulla *Mandragola*," *Belfagor* 39, no. 6 (1984): 621–44; M. Fleischer, "Trust and Deceit in Machiavelli's Comedies," *Journal of the*

History of Ideas 27 (1966): 365-80; E. Raimondi, "Il veleno della Mandragola," in *Politica e commedia: Dal Beroaldo al Machiavelli* (Bologna: Il Mulino, 1972), 253-64; J. D'Amico, "Power and Perspective in *La Mandragola*," *Machiavelli Studies 1* (New Orleans, La.: International Machiavelli Society, 1987), 5-15; J. Barber, "The Irony of Lucrezia: Machiavelli's Donna di virtù," *Studies in Philology* 82, no. 4 (1985): 450-59; M. De Panizza Lorch, "Women in the Context of Machiavelli's Mandragola," in *Donna: Women in Italian Culture*, ed. Ada Testferri, 253-71 (Ottawa: Dovehouse, 1989); D. Beecher, "Machiavelli's Mandragola and the Emerging Animateur," *Quaderni d'Italianistica* 5, no. 2 (1984): 171-89; S. Jed, *Chaste Thinking: The Rape of Lucretia and the Birth of Humanism* (Bloomington: Indiana University Press, 1989); F. Fata, "Machiavellian Strategies in the *Mandragola*," *Machiavelli Studies 2* (New Orleans, La.: International Machiavelli Society, 1988): 89-101; J. Francese, "La meritocrazia di Machiavelli: Dagli scritti politici alla *Mandragola*" *Italica* 71, no. 2 (1994): 153-75.

42. Martinez, "Tragic Machiavelli," 107.

43. The massacre at Prato in 1512 may also have been fresh in the minds of our authors. As for thematic and aesthetic questions as they relate to the futility of literature, I find Ariani's insistence on Trissino's declared neo-Platonism as the driving force behind his quest for unity very suggestive, albeit inconclusive.

44. See Thomas Greene, *The Vulnerable Text: Essays on Renaissance Literature* (New York: Columbia University Press, 1986), xii and xv: "The text under study, if it is worth studying, will in its own turn remystify itself, positively, productively, after its dissection."

45. Giuseppe Mazzotta, *Cosmopoiesis*, 9. Mazzotta concludes: "*La fabula d'Orfeo* is the sober divination of the imminent crisis. By the drunkenness in the final scene, it narrates that foundations shake and that we are no longer in the firm hand of understanding. It recalls a myth that plunges us into a world of evanescent shadows. It tells of transgressions and violence that eerily resemble the violence of the historical world" (23).

46. Ascoli and Kahn put it succinctly: "literature represents all that Machiavelli opposes in his intellectual and political life" (*Machiavelli and the Discourse of Literature*, 9).

Etruria Triumphant in Rome:
Fables of Medici Rule and
Bibbiena's Calandra

RONALD L. MARTINEZ

BERNARDO DOVIZI DA BIBBIENA'S comedy *Calandra* was first played in the ducal palace of Urbino on the last Sunday of Carnival, February 6, 1513. The performance occurred during a period unusually full of incident: just a few months after the return of the Medici to Florence (September 1, 1512), a few weeks before the death of the reigning Pope Julius II (February 20), and scarcely a month before the election of Giovanni de' Medici to the papacy as Pope Leo X on March 11.[1] The plays and festivities variously reflected events of political consequence:[2] if the *Calandra* intermezzi on that occasion—allegories of the four elements, in which Love puts an end to discord—might have appeared at first sight apolitical in content, they were nonetheless given political interpretation by Baldesar Castiglione, who in his celebrated letter describing the first performance was led by them to reflect on the war-torn state of Italy.[3] By the second and third performances of *Calandra*, in December and January of the following years 1514 and 1515,[4] the high-ranking audience at the Vatican in Rome (probably the original venue conceived for the play) could situate Bibbiena's comedy against an even richer background both of dynastic events and festive occasions. Even measured against the Florentine celebrations that attended the restoration of the Medici and Leo X's Roman *possesso* in April, the 1513 Parilia (or Palilia), the birthday of Rome, when two Medici scions were endowed with Roman citizenship, would have stood out as exceptional.[5] In such a rich context, Castiglione's interpretive reflex at the first performance offers a guide to contemporary reception of the *festa* that readers today would do well to heed.[6]

Calandra was in all likelihood planned during the months previous to the Medici return to Florence; since it took four months to build the Urbino stage set, the play had to have been in hand prior to September or October 1512.[7] Bibbiena's brilliant, if brittle play stands on the cusp of an epochal shift in papal style from Julian's militant to Leo's pacific stance, from a golden age won by arms to one enjoyed through art and leisure. Julius's obsession with the threat of the French and the Turks yielded to a proclaimed (if illusory) era of peace after the French disaster at Ravenna and Leo's apparently providential escape from captivity after that battle.[8] Given Bibbiena's role as the chief agent of favorable political outcomes for his patrons—we know from his correspondence that the recapture of Florence had been a chief object of his service, and it was widely accepted by contemporaries that he engineered the election of Giovanni de' Medici as Leo X—it comes as no surprise that the play alludes to Medici successes.[9] This essay will attempt to place Bibbiena's play within the dynastic and festival context of 1512 to 1514 and to suggest how the play *Calandra* delivers a carefully nuanced account of the triumphant passage of the Tuscan—or, rather, "Etruscan" Medici—from defeat to victory on the stage of history.

The celebration in the play of a Tuscan hegemony goes beyond political encomium, however. The proclaimed choice of vernacular prose in *Calandra* affirms and embodies the rising fortune of literary Tuscan. Fusing Latin comedy plots and the language from Boccaccio's *Decameron*, the play forged a model for learned comedy that outstripped competitors and became standard for subsequent comic drama in Italy. At the same time the comedy offers a sophisticated send-up of the Medici-fostered cult of ancient philosophy, *prisca theologia*, while setting in its place a jocular, Democritean view of human affairs, consistent with the characterization of that philosopher invoked by Castiglione's version of Bibbiena in the *Cortegiano* (2.45).[10] And it is in the spirit of that philosopher that the play deploys a facetious view of the triumphalist Renaissance papacy, whether wielded by the della Rovere or by the Medici. The astute, mercurial Bibbiena affirms things Florentine and "Etruscan" while subtly chaffing their excesses. Remaining unambiguous in the play, however, is the triumph of the designs and devices of theater, which is itself given an authoritative Etruscan aetiology.[11]

The Tuscan patina detected by Giorgio Padoan in the rare first printed edition of the play (Siena, 1521) is the trace of an elaborate program within *Calandra* affirming Tuscan linguistic and literary supremacy in the first decades of the cinquecento.[12] In light of Ariosto's vernacular adaptations of Plautine and Terentian models in the *Cassaria* and *Suppositi* (performed in Ferrara in 1508 and 1509, respectively), it could be argued that the arrival on the stage of the Tuscans was belated. But Bibbiena's prologue, proposing a play that is "in prose, not in verse; vernacular, not Latin; modern, not ancient" voices a forceful claim to the vernacular dramatic avant-garde in the face of the challenge presented by Ariosto and the theater-promoting dukes of Ferrara. Mention in the Argument of the acquisition of Florentine speech and manners by the fugitive twins means that the idea of exalting Tuscan is virtually explicit.[13] Bibbiena also salts his text with citations of the Tuscan canon: most conspicuous is Petrarch, quoted by Lidio to his pedantic tutor Polinico in defense of erotic pursuits ("bel fin fa chi bene amando muore" [a good end he makes who dies loving well], *Canz.* 140.14), and again in the same scene when repelling Polinico's moral tutelage: "if you think to dissuade me from loving her, you seek to embrace the shade and catch the wind in a net," adapted from a sestina.[14] Guinizelli's association of love and the gentle heart in his "doctrinal" canzone, echoed by Dante in the *Vita nuova*, and quoted by Bibbiena's Fessenio marveling over Calandro's invasion by love, who normally only captures noble hearts,[15] had been formulaic within the so-called *stilnovo* style Dante proclaimed in the *Purgatorio*.[16] Bibbiena offers, in short, a miniature anthology of Tuscan and Tuscanizing poets that attests his adherence to the Medicean promotion of the Florentine language. As the most influential Italian play of the sixteenth century, the ultimate role of *Calandra* in advancing the Tuscan linguistic project was considerable.[17]

The principal Tuscan influence in the prose *Calandra* is Boccaccio's *Decameron*, the text Bembo would consecrate as the benchmark for Tuscan prose, but which had already been singled out by Lorenzo the Magnificent, who praised its invention and range of styles. Bibbiena was not the first playwright to exploit the *Decameron*, but his mining of Boccaccio transcends past (and future) competitors and equals Bembo himself in the thoroughness of his scrutiny.[18] Most important perhaps, Bibbiena capped his close attention with the masterstroke of choosing as the model for Calandro Boccaccio's Calandrino, the most emphatically

Florentine gull in the whole collection of tales. For Calandrino fits, with anthropological exactitude, into a stereotypical division of Florentine society into the clever and the credulous, into *furbi* and *fessi*. He is a recurring character in Boccaccio, appearing in four tales (members of his *brigata* or social set appear in several more) and part of a trend within the *Decameron* itself that in its second half emphasizes the setting of stories in Florence and Tuscany. This Tuscan bias was to make Calandrino a fixture in plays and prose tales (*novelle*) that depend on Florentine origins and settings.[19]

But if the *Decameron* furnished the "grossa pasta," the raw material of Calandro's antic character,[20] Bibbiena's answer to Ariosto's challenge also required a distinct stance with respect to plot, the formal template of drama. Ariosto's early plays "contaminate" Plautine and Terentian elements, but Bibbiena seized instead on the more irreverent Plautus as a single ancient model, and especially on the ever-popular *Menaechmi*, with its double set of twins, servants and masters.[21] Bibbiena also drew on two other Plautine plays involving doubles that had been vernacularized by the early cinquecento though published only in the late twenties and thirties: *Bacchides* and *Amphitruo*.[22] Given that Fessenio, the astute servant of *Calandra*, has widely been seen as Bibbiena's partial portrait,[23] Plautine models were especially congenial to Bibbiena's personal interest in servant-master relations, bred from long experience as a trusted and powerful but still subordinate Medici courtier.[24]

Bibbiena's rivalry with Ariosto and his self-conscious virtuosity in capturing influences from Boccaccio and Plautus may be assessed by comparing instances of a comic routine that serves as a kind of trademark for early cinquecento playwrights: the comic distortion of the names of the characters.[25] In *Calandra* the wordplay seizes on the crucial name of the hermaphrodite: the exotic term is mangled by the supposed magician, Ruffo, whose name is also a pun that hints at a *ruffiano*, a procurer, his function in the play as he putatively assists Fulvia in bringing Lidio to her bed. With reflex metathesis, *ermafrodito* becomes in Ruffo's mouth first *merdafiorito* (flowered shit) and subsequently *barbafiorito* ("flowery-beard," dandy), reflecting the cross-dressing Lidio uses to gain access to Fulvia.[26] As we will see, the wordplay helps drive Bibbiena's parody of Florentine high philosophical discourse; but it is also a moment of cultural and linguistic affirmation. Ruffo, who is identified as *grosso* (uncouth) has difficulty with the high-cultural pedigree of the word, which comes from

Dante's use of the term in *Purgatorio* 26.82 ("our sin was hermaphrodite" [*ermafrodito*]), to describe heterosexual couplings like those that preoccupy Bibbiena's characters.

Indeed, the prodigious hermaphrodite, both name and concept, generates much of the play's verbal wit and comic business. Both the extraction and the distortion of the word suggest to what extent the play arises from linguistic legerdemain that is at the same time a meditation on Florentine literary idiom both high and low. The sexual vocabulary is present from the first scenes,[27] but it is at the end of act 3 and in act 4, that the language emerges with force, with Ruffo's ridiculing the possibility of a hermaphrodite, as if one could "slice through a man's root, and make a slit, and so make a woman; and sew up the mouth below, and stick on a peg, and so make a man" (4.2).[28] In the most important confusion of the play Fulvia, discovering that her Lidio has lost his ability to perform sexually because the "spirit" misunderstood her request for him "in the form of a woman" (she meant, disguised as one), asks for him to be better furnished on his next visit.[29]

Once sexual parts are in order, acts themselves must be described, whether of *changing* sexes (2.3, "they think I make and unmake what I wish," says Ruffo) with four more variations on the idea within the act;[30] or of *joining* the two sexes, which emerges apropos of Fessenio's plan to "join a gelding [Calandro] with a sow [the strumpet]."[31] Not usually remarked is that Bibbiena also links this series of linguistic invention with the routine about disassembling *Calandro* so that he may be transported in the chest, a tour de force in which Bibbiena draws on *both* Dante and Boccaccio.[32] Both the word for disassembly and the action that opposes it, that is, the reassembly of limbs during which mistakes can be made ("one takes the other's limb and puts it where he likes it best") are instances of the sex-conjunction paradigm just outlined for the play.[33] Indeed Fessenio, by syllabifying *Am bra cu llac* in the attempt to teach Calandro the magic that will make his disassembly possible, literally dismembers a word, and in so doing casts a reflexive light on Bibbiena's bold juxtapositions of borrowings from canonical Tuscans. Slicing and grafting terms into new contexts, much as Ruffo imagines sexes can be fashioned through cutting and sewing, Bibbiena's lexical play works like Dante's *ermafrodito* itself, which consists in the joining of male and female tallies, one part Hermes, one part Aphrodite. Moreover, by addressing in the prologue the accusation that the author is "a great thief of Plautus" with the suggestion that if the Roman playwright were inspected he would be found to "lack nothing he usually has," with obscene implication, Bibbiena marks how his own dramaturgical inspiration depends on genital additions and subtractions.

For in a sense general to the whole play, the frantic if illusory surgery below the belt is closely related to the "delightful exchanges" (*begli scambiamenti*) of persons and genders that drive the plot and that were to characterize the play's influence over the sixteenth century.[34] To be caught in an apparent sex-change (or cross-dressing), or indeed any kind of disguise is, as Fessenio alerts Calandro, to be "caught in a fraud" (3.3: *eri colto in frodo*), just as the hermaphrodite is itself patently a fraud.[35] Indeed, the suffix to *ermafrodito* evokes *frode* (fraud), reflecting the function of the word in perpetrating a deception achieved through verbal folderol. From the same tangent the verbal effects might appear typical results of the "spirito favellario," the "talking spirit" Ruffo supposedly possesses that can effect changes of sex. Given that *favellario* (talkative or confabulating) is Fannio's malapropism for *familiare* (familiar), it may serve as a pun for both the frauds (*frodi*) of the comic fable (*favola*) and for its speech (*favella*), the vivid and inventive Tuscan dialogue that is one of Bibbiena's achievements.

Bibbiena's use of the onomastic business is not confined to the *ermafrodito*, however. It is also at work implicitly in his choice of Boccaccio's character Calandro as the chief gull of the play. At *Menaechmi* 294, the cook, named, as often in Latin comedy, Cylindrus, from his rolling pin, is teased with the alternate kitchen-inspired name of Coriendrus (coriander). But in the 1486 vernacular *Menechini*, the exchange concludes by transforming Coriendrus into the name of Bibbiena's comedy: "per Chilindro e Calandra non ti voglio" (2.111–16).[36] Bibbiena could trace his main character's Boccaccian name through the vernacular version of the Latin play that most directly informed the plot of *Calandra*: the fortuitous pairing of preferred sources must have appeared a sort of lucky charm, and the use in *Menechini* of a feminine name for a male cook might have begun the reflections on the kinds of sex-change and cross-dressing that fill the language and action of Bibbiena's play.

Much of the recent discussion of the play has concentrated on the philosophical resonances of the "hermaphrodite." As several critics have proposed, Ruffo's paraphrase of Aristophanes' tale in Plato's *Symposium*, in which erotic desire is explained as resulting from the aboriginal bisection of humans by the gods, might suggest that the various loves of the characters can be roughly aligned with the species of divided hermaphrodites. In this view, homosexual love would be represented by Polinico, satirized in the first scene; heterosexual love by Fulvia's affair with Lidio; and sibling love by the desire of Lidio to find Santilla, and vice versa.

Earnest attempts to view the play as the serious expression of a universal Platonic Eros fail to persuade, however,[37] since the supposed quest of Lidio for his other half, his sister Santilla, despite being mentioned in the prologue, is visibly functional in the play only in the final recognition scene. Such a mythological "quest" is upstaged during most of the play by Lidio's sexual and economic exploitation of the wealthy Fulvia, Bibbiena's adaptation of the "fleecing" topic of Plautine comedy: thus Fessenio says in the first scene that Lidio "seeking his sister, found Roman Fulvia." What Lidio and Santilla repair during their recognition scene are not divided selves or souls, but political and economic fortunes; they recognize "how two fortunes are worth more than one" (5.12).

More convincing is a reading of the references in the play to Platonic icons and the *prisca theologia* dear to Renaissance humanism as consistently parodic of the Medici-fostered Platonism and philhellenism of Cristoforo Landino, Poliziano, Giovanni Pico della Mirandola, and especially Marsilio Ficino, which the young Bibbiena, as he grew to maturity in the Medici household, had witnessed at close range.[38] In this light the satire on the pederastic tutor Polinico gains added bite as a possible reminiscence of Poliziano's preceptorship in the Medici household.[39] That a joyous sexual consummation is achieved in the comedy only at the lowest social level, between Lusco and Fulvia's maid Samia (3.10), itself mocks Platonic rituals.[40] The offstage conjunction of domestics behind a closed door, veiled with systematic double entendres, constitutes the most authentic "mystery" of the play, though Fessenio, for all his perspicacity, never penetrates the arcanum of servile domesticity, never realizes what is going on.[41]

But if a metaphysical Eros is scarcely a serious motive in the plot of *Calandra*—Bibbiena's parody of it is beyond doubt—this is not to say that the scheme of the hermaphrodite is dramatically inert.[42] Bibbiena finds good use for Aristophanes' fable by reinvesting it with some of the topical political significance it has in Plato and of which Ficino's account in the *Commentary on the Symposium* had largely stripped it. In Plato's account, as translated by Ficino, Zeus and the gods, after having endured attacks by men, propose to mutilate human creatures—hitherto four-legged—by slicing them in two, thus keeping them weak and inoffensive and multiplying offerings and sacrifices receivable from them. Zeus performs the surgery, cutting "each of them lengthwise, and of each of them he made two, as do those who cut hardboiled eggs lengthwise with a hair . . . each of us is half a man, sliced like those fish called flounders."[43] Subsequently

> he bade Apollo, once the division was made, turn round the face of each half-neck attached to it towards the part that was cut, so that considering its bisection it might become more modest, and ordered that they be healed. So he turned the faces round, and gathering together the skin on what is now called the belly, as in a purse drawstrings make a single mouth, he bound it tightly in the middle of the belly. Which knot men call the navel.[44]

When Ficino has Cristoforo Landino comment on this passage, he omits profit and self-interest as motives of the gods, as well as eliding Plato's vivid artisanal imagery about the bisection and mending of the divided creatures.[45] Bibbiena in his turn avoids Landino's theological exposition of the human being as divided between "higher" and "lower" functions, between sense and reason, and approaches the issue in a manner closer to that of his friend Bembo, who in the Asolani updates Plato's account in terms of Italian political categories, describing humans as "divided down the middle by Jove, whose lordship they wanted to seize."[46] As we saw earlier, Ruffo, whom we can scarcely accuse of reading the *Symposium*, speculates in 4.3 on the fashioning of the sexes in artisanal terms. In his exploitation of Fulvia's credulity, and his preference for motives of economic gain, but also in his use of language from sewing and carpentry, Ruffo expresses Plato's fable in social and political terms: as an aetiology of the production of victims and gulls, of *fessi*.

In other words, Bibbiena recognizes that the division of the hermaphrodite into men and women is socially expressed: it is a division of human social and gender roles, as Bembo says in the *Asolani* (2.11), of "men and women destined to fulfill two different needs." The play's characters are not only divided between Calandros and Fessenios, between *furbi* and *fessi*, but also between two kinds of *fessi*, the stupid and credulous like Calandro on the one hand, and those handicapped by gender and social position—women like Fulvia and Santilla, servants like Fannio and Fessenio—on the other.

For even Fessenio, though he be the most *furbo* of those on the stage and the author's chief surrogate, fits into the scheme of humanity divided and incomplete. More than anyone else in the play his name appears derived from Italian *fesso*.[47] His internal division arises from a complex partition of loyalties: as he proclaims in the first scene of the play, he achieves the impossible by serving not two, but three masters: by turns Calandro, Fulvia, and Lidio.[48] Students of the play have thus argued persuasively that Fessenio's situation mirrors Bibbiena's own mixed allegiances while serving the often contradictory ambitions of both Julius II and Giovanni de' Medici.[49] In this context, Bibbiena's signature on his letters to Isabella d'Este as "servo moccicone" (snot-nosed servant), a designation of him adopted by his broader acquaintance, appears a form of defensive self-irony useful for navigating the shoals of courtiership.[50] That the emblematic *moccicone* is applied in the play (by Fessenio) to Calandro, the master played for a fool, and in the prologue to Plautus (by Bibbiena), the canonical author unable to protect his property, might point to both the fool and the author as projections of Bibbiena that betray the playwright's characteristic awareness of his own reputation for foolery while also working as protective disguise.

The evident philosophical parody and sociopolitical satire in the play should not obscure, however, the extent to which Bibbiena takes his cue from Boccaccio and Plautus; that is, it follows his reliable if still novel formula for fashioning a play out of canonical Tuscan and Roman materials. In *Calandra*, the program of philosophical parody is announced through the language of Boccaccio, by sketching Calandro, who demolishes all wisdom before him,[51] in the terms of Guccio Imbratta (*Decameron* 6.10.16), the assistant to Friar Cipolla whose vices were such that a single one nullified all the wisdom of Solomon, Aristotle, or Seneca.[52] By the same token, but relying on a different author, Fessenio's instruction to Calandro on how to "drink" a woman, read by Bottoni as referring to the Platonic soul-kiss and other mystagogic rites,[53] has a more everyday genealogy as part of the vocabulary of plunder, descending from Plautus's *Menaechmi* and *Bacchides*, where courtesans "drink," "eat," and "absorb" their customers, who therefore end up missing a nose or an eye, as in *Calandra* 1.7, where Fessenio warns Calandro not to allow his eye or nose to be so imbibed.[54] Even Fessenio's self-division among three masters is plausibly Bibbiena's rendition of the three virtuosic fleecings of Nicobolus achieved by Chrysalus in *Bacchides*,[55] while Bibbiena's self-deprecation itself owes a debt to Boccaccio's self-mocking Dioneo, indeed to Boccaccio's mischievous narrator himself.[56]

Other passages emphasizing the magical also prove to have theatrical pedigrees. Bottoni associates with Ficinian mysteries the comparison of Calandro to Martino da Amelia, the buffoon who could imagine himself becoming "a woman, god, a fish and a tree, at will."[57] But Martino's transformations are more immediately the felicitous results of theatrical imagination: the phrase for "at will" (*a posta sua*) translates *ad libitum*, which comes to Bibbiena as a device of Plautine theatrical magic from the *Amphitruo*, a play of doubly twinned characters (two Amphitruos, two serving Getas) that features the transformations of Zeus and Mercury into comic characters.[58] As in the case of the Platonic hermaphrodite, both necromantic and Ficinian magic are outdone by the magic of theatrical fiction.

That philosophy is inadequate to account for Love's folly, or that wisdom is indeed cancelled by invincible stupidity, while Love's miracles are perpetrated by the illusions of theater itself, are gestures to be expected from Bibbiena, whose philosophical orientation is plausibly consistent with the role given to Castiglione's Bibbiena in the *Cortegiano*, of discoursing on the "risible animal that is man."[59] As in Castiglione's Ciceronian source, the Urbino version of Bibbiena leaves the definition of laughter itself to Democritus,[60] known as the "laughing philosopher" because he surveyed human afflictions with a smile. Horace and Juvenal imagine Democritus's mirth when contemplating the pomps and shows of Imperial Rome,[61] and Renaissance reception typically opposed his laughter to the somber pessimism of Heraclitus.[62] *Democritus ridens, Heraclitus flens* was a commonplace known to Petrarch and cited widely in Bibbiena's Florentine milieu, especially by Ficino, who recalls in a letter that he had images of the two philosophers in his study.[63] As we saw, practical jokes are one of the categories of humor recommended in Bibbiena's exposition in *Cortegiano*. In real life, Bibbiena's supreme practical joke was undoubtedly his success in securing Giovanni de' Medici's election to the papacy by circulating the rumor that the young cardinal's anal fistula would prove mortal. Giovio's biography of Leo X suggests the relevance of the ruse to the emphases of *Calandra*: the cardinal was borne in to the conclave on a litter "propter innatum ab ima sede abscessum" (because of an abcess that had begun in his fundament),[64] and it was the rupture of the fistula that convinced the assembled cardinals to throw the election to Giovanni.[65] In this respect the future pope, too was, if only theatrically, a *fesso*, and fortunate to have as his conclavist a *furbo* who could decide a papal election with a trick, a *beffa*.

Indeed a fascination with anatomical fissures appears to be Bibbiena's signature as a writer of drama. The prologue to *Calandra* concludes with the audience invited to open their ears to the Argument that follows: "But here is one who brings you the Argument. Prepare to grasp it well, each of you opening wide the hole of your ear."[66] Rather than repeating a conventional appeal for attention,[67] Bibbiena relies on the alternative meaning of *argumento*, "clyster-pipe," which infuses the prologue's invitation with obscene suggestion.[68] Bibbiena's remark was memorable enough that it serves to characterize his entire oeuvre in Giovio's account of him and was echoed by later Tuscan writers of comedy.[69] That near contemporaries—expert ones, to be sure—used the sexual-metaphorical possibilities of language entering the hole of the ear as a shorthand reference to the play suggests to what extent Bibbiena's audience might have grasped the play's thematic and linguistic emphases on the divided and vulnerable human being, more forked animal than radiant androgyne.

The Tuscanizing linguistic project and Medicean ideological legacy that emerge when we sift the play's language also contribute to Bibbiena's naming of his characters and the articulation of his plot. The two Lidios and their servants are recent immigrants to Rome, having escaped the sack of Modon, in the Peloponnese kingdom of Morea, by the Turks in 1500.[70] That Lidio and Santilla are immigrants from Greece appears to echo the movement of Greek-speaking refugees from the sack of Constantinople in 1453, especially as Santilla and her servant Fannio pass through that city on their voyage to Rome. The choice and variety of itineraries, and their merging in Rome, is scarcely casual: it suggests the flow of hegemony from East to West (*translatio imperii*).[71] In the context of the large ambitions of Julian and Leonine Rome, and of a play set not in Florence or Urbino but in the Eternal City, the migrations of the twins also point to Roman associations. Even at the first performance in Urbino in February 1513, the hall was decorated with objects and motifs reminiscent of Roman history, including tapestries of the story of Troy,[72] and a triumphal arch whose spandrels represented the victory of the Horatii, which helped establish the ascendancy of Rome over Alba Longa, thus over Latium. Although the event was, as Stefani recalls, implicitly a statement of alliance between the Medici and Urbino,[73] certain ball-like decorations were taken after the fact as prophetic of the Medici capture of the papacy as well, thus instituting a discord with the specifically Urbinate meanings of the festival, which exalted Francesco della Rovere's role as papal gonfalonier in expelling the French invaders of Italy.[74] In a mythic and literary sense the Lidios, arriving in Rome to plunder the virtue and wealth of Roman Fulvia, reiterate in comic and parodic key the journey of Aeneas, who comes to the shores of Lavinia seeking an advantageous marriage and political alliances for his exiled Trojans.[75]

Yet though technically Modonesi, thus Greeks, the two Lidios evoke through their name a richer gamut of eastern origins. In Roman and Italian contexts, the name Lydus or Lydius designates an Etruscan,[76] for since the days of Herodotus this people was thought to have originated in Lydia, in Asia Minor.[77] When Virgil refers to the inhabitants of Latium, he calls them, among other things, *Lydia gens*.[78] Thus in Biondo Flavio's *Italia illustrata*, published in printed form in 1472, the Lydian origin of the Etruscans is set out based on ancient sources, and on Leonardo Bruni's history: in Bruni's account, the Lydians parallel the migration of the Trojans.[79] The name of Lidio is thus a convenient designation for the Modonese carpetbaggers to be identified (out of allegory) as Tuscans, that is, Florentines. In this sense the arrival and insertion of the Lidios, one into a native Roman, the other into a native Florentine household established in Rome, reflects not only the advantageous situations of the Medici, but the historical importance of Tuscans in the papacies Bibbiena served.[80]

Indeed, enthusiasm and study of things Tuscan, Etruscan, and Lydian, had been a marked emphasis of the cultural politics of Julius's court, and this emphasis only grew once Giovanni de' Medici became pope. During the earlier years of Julius's reign, Annio da Viterbo had made fraudulent, but widely accepted claims for the great antiquity of Etruscan language and culture.[81] Egidio da Viterbo, the Augustinian friar and papal orator who was Annio's disciple and who gave intellectual substance to Julius's imperial ambitions, wrote sermons on the Julian Golden Age that exalted the Etruscans for having fostered a Golden Age in Latium.[82] Under both Julius and Leo, Fedra Inghiramsi, prefect and later director of the Vatican library, and a native of Volterra, itself rich in Etruscan lore, continued the Tuscanizing emphasis with his concepts for Medici spectacles in Rome.[83] Thus when Giovio and others praised the Etruscan wit (*"ethruscos* sales") of Bibbiena's play at the expense of Greek and Latin comedy, they were granting palms not only to the Tuscan vernacular but also to a civilization whose modern flowering had, so the story went, noble and cultivated roots that preceded the Roman conquest of Latium.[84]

The Medici reacquisition of Florence and Leo's acquisition of the papacy brought the role of the Lydian-Etruscan-Tuscans to the forefront of Roman culture and politics. Both in Florence and in Rome, the festivities that attended the consummation of the Medici hegemony underlined the historical alliance between Rome and Etruria. In the first year of his papacy, Leo X restored the Palilia, the birthday of the city,[85] and made it the occasion for granting citizenship to two Medici scions, the younger Giuliano, Giovanni's brother, and Lorenzo di Piero, the pope's nephew. Celebrated September 13–14, 1513 (superimposed on the feast of the Exaltation of the Cross), the event was conceived by the Tuscan Fedra Inghirami and the Roman Camillo Porzio and organized and managed by a committee including the Roman Marc' Antonio Altieri.[86] The events were programmed for the Campidoglio, in a theater built and decorated for the purpose under the direction of Pietro Rosselli.[87]

Several accounts of the newly restored holiday survive. Festivities began on the eve of the feast (September 13), with a procession to the Capitol, followed by a solemn Mass, orations in praise of Giuliano (Lorenzo stayed in Florence), the conferral of citizenship, and a sumptuous, rowdy banquet. This was followed by allegorical triumphs devised by Camillo Porzio, leader of the Roman Academy, including one of *Roma* herself; a pastoral eclogue by the humanist Blosio Palladio; and an allegory of the ancient Tarpeian Mount, rejuvenated, who welcomed the coming of new gods in the form of the Medici. Then came the goddess Cybele drawn by lions and after her a masque of Rome, also rejuvenated and praising Leo and the Medici. On the second day, beginning at Vespers, there were further *rappresentazioni*, designed by the papal ceremonialist Evangelista Maddalena Capodiferro, including the figure of Clarice Orsini, Lorenzo the Magnificent's long-dead Roman wife and mother of Giovanni and Giuliano de' Medici, and one of both the Arno and Father Tiber, announcing an era of eternal peace, a new Golden Age. Plautus's *Poenulus*, directed by Inghirami and played in Latin by boys from Pomponio Leto's Roman Academy, ended the celebration.[88]

Underscored throughout was the union of the Tuscan and Roman people through the conferral of Roman citizenship on the Medici princes.[89] The theater was accordingly built in imitation of ancient models,[90] and celebrated both in images and with inscriptions the long history of political and cultural cooperation between Tuscans, that is Etruscans and Lydians, and Romans. Remembered were the assistance of Etruria at Aeneas's foundation of Rome, the magnanimity of Lars Porsenna, and early alliances between Etruscans and Romans,[91] with a bias in favor of the greater antiquity and cultural richness of Etruria.[92]

The ancient Etruscans had also nourished the upstart Romans by transmitting cultural lore, from military institutions and religious rituals to haruspication and augury, symbols and insignia, and the "erudition" of the Latin alphabet by the Etruscan.[93] For my purposes, of greatest interest is the importation to Rome of Etruscan *ludi scenici*—that is, theater. Palliolo describes a panel on which "is portrayed a capacious theater, filled with a large public, along with those who are playing the comedy on the stage, so skillfully depicted that they appear with their gestures, acts, and words to delight and give pleasure to the people watching them. Here is noted: *Scenic games begun from the Etruscans.*"[94]

That Etruscans had brought theatrical representation to Rome was in any case traditional lore. It had the authority of Livy and Tacitus, duly taken up by Renaissance antiquarians and historians of the theater. Livy records how *ludi scenici* were first brought to Rome and instituted in order to combat plague.[95] In the quattrocento, Flavio Biondo's *Roma instaurata* freely quotes Tacitus to similar effect and in the *Spectacula* (written about 1500), the Ferrarese Pellegrino Prisciani follows Biondo in quoting the Roman historian.[96] Leon Battista Alberti's treatise on architecture reiterates the aetiology as an introduction to his account of the Vitruvian theater:[97] in addition to the authority of antiquity, the very term *ludus* had been derived by medieval etymology from the origins of the Etruscans in Lydia, an association which the punning on *Lydus* and *ludus* in Plautus's *Bacchides*, one of the Latin plays that influenced *Calandra*, further warranted.[98] The iconography of the Campidoglio theater—where the Florentines were also referred to as Lydians—thus affirmed the Etruscan priority in theatrical *ludi* that Bibbiena's play instanced with its own frenetic brilliance and its plot of a "Lydian" conquest of Rome.[99]

Bibbiena continued to promote his play, which in the winter of 1514–15, the year after the Medici Palilia, received two performances, at least one for that avid consumer of drama, Isabella d'Este.[100] Though played first in Urbino eight months *before* the renewed Palilia, the plot of Bibbiena's play, in which the twin Lidios marry prosperously in Rome (one acquiring a Florentine, one a Roman fortune), neatly stages the fusion of Etruscan and Roman destinies celebrated at the Palilia, where the two nations were repeatedly envisioned as a single people under a single law.[101] Given the emphasis in the play on the identity of the twins—to which Bibbiena gives, in his prologue, a Roman analogue in the form of the brothers Antonio and Valerio Porcari—it is suggestive that the Palilia texts emphasize the Medici scions being honored as notional twins, while Romans and Etruscans could be understood as twin peoples.[102] The egglike resemblance of the two Lidios (5.2: "né l'uovo a l'uovo . . ."), a variation on the identical appearance of Plautus's *Menaechmi,* evokes the tutelary Roman twins, Castor and Pollux, born from one of Leda's eggs, and frequently mentioned in Palilia texts: Tuscan and Roman pairs of twins are superimposed.[103] So suggestive are the harmonies of play and pageant that one might venture that the play was conceived simultaneously with the Palilia—planning for which must have begun as soon as Bibbiena had secured Giovanni de' Medici's election.[104] In any case the play, the conclave, and the festival on the Campidoglio were bound by the common theme of triumph.

The subject of triumphs is explicit in the Argument to *Calandra,* where it is observed that Rome, once great enough to receive and absorb the whole world in its triumphs, is now so small it fits into the city of Urbino. This is followed by the flippant assessment: "Così va il mondo" (so the world goes). References to triumph also appear in the play, when Samia imagines Fulvia's triumph of sexual success if assisted by the "spirit" (2.3: "trionfa Fulvia"), and at the end, when Fessenio, absorbing the news of the planned marriages and combined fortunes, affirms that things are better in proportion to how much better Rome is than Modon, just as Italy is worthier than Greece:[105] "and we shall all triumph."[106]

All of these uses are, significantly, sardonic or ironic: Samia's ambition for Fulvia's love affair are of a piece with Fessenio's mockery of Calandro's infatuation with the disguised Lidio (3.1: "Behold, o spectators, the spoils of love" [*le spoglie amorose*]), which invokes the language of spoils in the Triumph of Love, of Petrarchan pedigree.[107] "Così va il mondo" evokes in turn the admonition to newly crowned popes, lest they overrate the permanence of their station: *sic transit gloria mundi.*[108] The observation of Rome's reduction in the Argument is pregnant: in the context of the first performance, it flatters the cultural "receptivity" of little Urbino (with obvious pun, on *Urbs,* antonomastic for Rome, and the diminutive *Urbino*), but also satirizes the imperial ambitions of the currently imperial

Julian Rome while staking its confidence on the revolutions of fortune—
sic transit gloria mundi—that will bring about a new pontificate and yet
another "new age," that of Leonine Rome. Taken as a whole, then, in what
is Bibbiena's most audacious gesture as a long-serving Medici partisan,
the Argument affirms, but also just discernibly mocks, the triumphalist
mode so much in evidence in the first years of the freshly reacquired
Medicean hegemony.

If Rome's reduction from former greatness is suggested, the reference
to Rome's absorbing the whole world recognizes the city for what it had
long been and still was: a cultural entrepôt, a destination for pilgrims,
and a diplomatic nexus as the seat of the papacy.[109] Rome's receptiveness
is itself a topic of triumph, evoking the great triumphs of the literary tradition, like that of Augustus on the shield of Aeneas in the *Aeneid,* where
peoples and rivers from various regions of the world arrive in the city.[110]

Conquered peoples and features of landscape could enter Rome because represented by marchers bearing signs and images. Thus in another
sense the words of the Argument underscore a triumph of representational and specifically of scenographic art. Discussions of stage set design
reiterate how perspective illusion can compress a great city onto a narrow stage: Shakespeare was able to cram the "vasty fields of France" from
the Hundred Years' War into the "cockpit" of the Globe.[111] In this sense,
reenactments of the triumphs of Rome are also a triumph of theatrical
sleight of hand that can outdo the necromantic sort disavowed in Bibbiena's Argument to *Calandra.*[112]

In any case the triumph was a theme, and an event, of which papal
Rome and Renaissance Italy could not get enough. During Julius's triumph
during the 1507 Palm Sunday entry into Rome after the conquest of Bologna, or the Roman Carnival of 1513, which reevoked that triumph, the
cities of Bologna, Parma, and Piacenza, as well as the Apennine mountain
chain were represented allegorically, and Italy itself displayed as a map
surmounted by a palm tree, signifying its liberation from tyranny.[113]

In addition to its ritual and celebratory instances the *triumphus* was a
literary and artistic genre, generating innumerable textual and visual examples that very often both imitated and illustrated Petrarch's triumphs
of love, chastity, death, fame, time, and eternity. These, along with celebrated triumphs such as that of Scipio, were depicted on *cassoni* and
spalliere and on birth salvers, or *deschi da parto.*[114] The prominence of
the triumph in Renaissance spectacle, literature, art, and indeed statecraft

and political propaganda can hardly be overestimated, and it has been viewed by some critics as an epochal artistic form whose dominance was in part enabled by the advent of artificial perspective, permitting "mastery of the world through the power of the eye."[115]

For my purposes here it is the association of the triumphal arch with the theater and with the scenography of early cinquecento plays that is most suggestive of the imbrication in *Calandra* of the triumph with the artificial perspective of the stage set.[116] The triumphal arch became a fixture of the canonical *tragic* stage set in Serlio's 1545 publication,[117] where such an arch is illustrated framing the vanishing point of the perspective.[118] That a similar design was used to interpret Vitruvius's Roman theater stage, often contradictory to or inconsistent with Vitruvius's text, is apparent from Gian Battista di San Gallo's marginal illustration in his copy of Sulpizio da Veroli's edition of Vitruvius (drawn around 1530).[119] A triumphal arch, either at the vanishing point or to one side of the stage, is a fixture of stage set drawings depicting Rome in the early- to mid-cinquecento, including existing designs by Peruzzi that have been repeatedly, if never convincingly, associated with *Calandra*.[120] Vitruvius, echoed by Alberti, Prisciani, and his translators, had in any case called for a *porta regia* or royal portal at the center of the *scaenae frons* itself, a portal that would in some instances become a triumphal arch.[121]

But it is Alberti who most closely associates the triumphal arch with both the location of the theater in the city and the architectural fabric of the theater itself.[122] The eighth book of Alberti's treatise explicitly adopts the trope of an excursion and follows the royal or imperial road past watchtowers and over bridges into the city (8.6, 145r), where triumphal arches—former gates of the city and markers of the expansion of empire (8.6.147r)—collect the trophies of past victories and act as suitable entrances to the forum, the heart of the city's civic life. Immediately afterward (8.7, 148r) Alberti discusses theaters, and other spaces for shows, which are like an "enclosed forum" and whose supporting porticos he recommends be constructed like triumphal arches.[123] Alberti's itinerary makes the theater and show buildings the focus of the public spaces of the city, the goal of the royal road.[124]

Is it possible to determine precisely the import of the triumphal arch for *Calandra*? What precisely the stage set of the first performances of *Calandra* looked like remains inconclusively disputed. Certain features are, however, attested: Castiglione reports that at the first performance there was to one side of the stage a triumphal arch, adorned with images of the victory of the Horatii, surmounted by a victorious mounted figure.[125] As we saw, the triumphalist tenor of the first performance was intended to celebrate Francesco Maria's role in helping Julius expel the barbarian invaders of Italy; but given that classicizing cityscapes of Rome typically included a triumphal arch, one would likely have been retained for the Rome performances, especially as we know Bibbiena requested details of the Urbino début performance, at which he was not present, in order to prepare the Vatican performances personally.[126]

More specifically, and in the context of a triumphalist semantics of the theater and stage set itself, the victorious mood that concludes *Calandra*, in the setting of the Rome performances during the Carnival season of 1514-15, reflects at once the Medici hegemony over Rome and the wealth of the papacy and the celebration of that very success in the affirmation of theater and spectacle during the Palilia. Not only did the Palilia bring triumphant pageants to the Capitoline, the traditional end point of Roman triumphal processions, it commemorated the Etruscan gift of theater to Rome on an edifice with an open central arch contemporaries described as *trionfale*.[127] The triumphalist ideology that the Medici wished to appropriate, as they wedded themselves to Roman history and joined Romans and Etruscans at the hip, was in full view.[128]

Though not recalled in the Palilia iconography, Bibbiena probably also knew from Flavio Biondo that the same people who brought theatrical *ludi* to Rome had also introduced the Romans to the triumphal pomps first used by the Etruscans.[129] And it is an additional bonus for my argument that the introduction of the Etruscan *histriones*, actors and mummers, traditionally coincided with one of the most lavish triumphs of the Republican era, that of Lucius Mummius, so that Roman comic theater and the Roman triumph hatched from the one Etruscan egg, so to speak.[130] In this light, the Lydian origins of comic theater and of the triumph are mutually implicated in their influence over Roman festival institutions of the Medicean restoration and papacy.

Notes

    1. The coronation was on April 11. For this period, see Paolo Giovio, "Vita Leonis X," in *Opera*, vol. 6 (*Vitarum, pars prior*), ed. Michele Cataudella, 62-67 (Rome: Istituto poligrafico e zecca dello stato, 1987): G. L. Moncallero, *Il cardinale Bernardo Dovizi da Bibbiena umanista e diplomatico (1470-1520)* (Florence: Olschki, 1953): 513-619, etc. Moncallero

1953: 317-58; Carlo Dionisotti, "Ritratto del Bibbiena," in *Rinascimento* s. ii 9 (1969): 51-67; John Shearman, *Raphael's Cartoons in the Collection of her Majesty and the Tapestries of the Sistine Chapel* (London: Phaidon, 1972): 9-20; Charles Stinger, *The Renaissance in Rome* (Bloomington: Indiana University Press, 1985): 55-57; Luciano Bottoni, *La messinscenea del Rinascimento: I. Calandra, una commedia per il papato* (Bologna: Francoangeli, 2005): 65-67.

2. The intermezzi for Grasso's *Eutichia*, staged along with *Calandra*, depicted a personified Italy appealing to the reigning duke of Urbino and nephew to Julius II, Francesco Maria della Rovere, for relief from foreign oppression. Nicola Grasso, *Eutichia*, ed. Luigina Stefani (Messina-Firenze: d'Anna, 1984): 7-32, esp. 8-13; Franco Ruffini, *Teatri prima del teatro: visioni dell'edificio e della scena tra Umanesimo e Rinascimento* (Rome: Bulzoni, 1983): 138-41.

3. Castiglione in Bernardo Dovizi da Bibbiena, *La Calandra, commedia elegantissima per Messer Bernardo Dovizi da Bibbiena*, ed. Giorgio Padoan (Padua: Antenore, 1985): 203-7, esp. 207: "Questo fu più presto speranza e augurio; ma quello delle guerre fu pur troppo vero per nostra disgrazia" (this was readily hope and good omen; but the part about the wars was alas too true, to our sorrow). Unless noted, translations in text and notes are mine. *Calandra* is cited as Bibbiena followed by act and scene number; other texts in that volume are cited by page number.

4. On the Rome performances at Carnival 1514-15, one at least was for Isabella D'Este: Paolo Giovio, "Gli elogi degli uomini illustri" in *Elogium virorum illustrium, Paoli Iovii Opera* vol. 8, ed. Renzo Meregazzi (Rome: Istituto Poligrafico dello Stato, 1972): 94; G. L. Moncallero, "Precisazione sulle rappresentazioni della *Calandria* nel Cinquecento" in *Convivium*, n.s. 6 (1952): 819-51; Fabrizio Cruciani, *Teatro nel Rinascimento: Roma, 1450-1550* (Rome: Bulzoni, 1983): 440-48; Franco Ruffini, *La commedia e festa nel Rinascimento; La* Calandria *alla corte di Urbino* (Bologna: Il mulino, 1986): 339-46; Padoan in Bibbiena 1985: 1-3.

5. For the festival, restored by Pomponio Leto in 1483, restored by Leo X to honor his brother Giuliano and his nephew Lorenzo di Pietro, see Fabrizio Cruciani, *Il teatro del Campidoglio e le feste romane del 1513, con la ricostruzione architettonica di Arnaldo Bruschi* (Milan: Il polifilo, 1969): xxxiii-lv; Charles Stinger, *The Renaissance in Rome* (Bloomington: Indiana University Press, 1985): 72, 97-98; Ingrid Rowland, *The Culture of the High Renaissance* (Cambridge: Cambridge University Press, 1998): 213-14.

6. Ruffini,(1986: 211-47) idealizes the intermezzi; recent English-language criticism of *Calandra* (e.g., Andrews) has also understated political meaning in the play. For the prevalence of political content in early cinquecento Florentine drama (Jacopo Nardi, Lorenzo Strozzi), see Francesco Bausi, "Machiavelli e la commedia fiorentina del primo Cinquecento," in Gennaro Barbarisi and Anna Maria Cabrini, eds., *Il Teatro di Machiavelli* (Milan: Cisalpino, 2005): 1-20.

7. Castiglione in Bibbiena 1985: 204: "so well finished that considering all the works in the state of Urbino it would not be possible to believe that it had been made in four months." June 1512 is a plausible date for the composition of *Calandra*, giving Bibbiena several months to prepare the play in time for the planning of Carnival 1513 to begin when the Medici regained Florence in September.

8. For the passage from disaster to glory and its transformation in Leonine legend, see Moncallero 1953: 316-43; John Shearman, "The Florentine *Entrata* of Pope Leo X, 1515, *Journal of the Warburg and Courtauld Institutes*, 38 (1975): 138-56 and 1972: 80-90; Stinger 1985: 55-57, 79-94, 296-301; Fabrizio Cruciani, *Teatro nel Rinascimento: Roma, 1450-1550* (Rome: Bulzoni, 1983): 379-405.

9. For Bibbiena's role in the Medici return to power, see Giovio 1987: 64–65; Dionisotti 1969: 51–67, esp. 60–65; Gaeta 1969: 72–73, 84–90. On the papal conclave, see Giovio 1987: 64–65; Franco Gaeta, "Bibbiena diplomatico," *Rinascimento* s. ii 9 (1969): 86; Bottoni 2005: 67–69.

10. Rafaello Alonge, "La *Calandria*, o il mito di Androgine," in *Struttura e ideologia nel teatro italiano fra '500 e '900* (Turin: Stampatori, 1978) and Ruffini 1986 read the play in terms of high Renaissance idealism.

11. In the play, twins Lidio and Santilla, separated at the sack of Peloponnesian Modon by the Turks in 1500, arrive in Rome: Lidio, accompanied by his servant Fessenio, via Bologna; while Santilla, who took her brother's name and gender for reasons of security when captured by the Turks along with her servant Fannio, arrives via Alexandria, whence ransomed by the Florentine merchant Perillo. Lidio claims to be searching for his sister, but the plot consists of amorous intrigues and conundrums: Santilla has been affianced to the daughter of her protector, Perillo, who is unaware of her real sex; Lidio pursues an amorous affair with Fulvia, wife to the vain and credulous Calandro, but as Lidio's passion seems to cool, Fulvia directs her servant Samia, with help from Fessenio, to rekindle his ardor. Meanwhile Calandro, who has fallen for Lidio after seeing him in the woman's disguise he uses to rendezvous with Fulvia, likewise employs Fessenio to advance his suit. Fessenio undertakes to bring Calandro to the embrace of the Lidio supposed female, but in fact devises a mating with a strumpet that comes to grief when customs agents inspect the chest in which Calandro is being borne to his assignation; Fessenio's quick thinking averts disaster, but Calandro is subsequently discovered by his wife in a compromising situation nevertheless. Fulvia's desperation over Lidio is the basis for an opportunistic conspiracy consisting of the disguised Santilla, Fannio, and Ruffo, another Greek refugee; they propose to reawaken Lidio's desire with the assistance of a necromancer, counterfeited by Ruffo. When Santilla, brought to Fulvia as Lidio, is discovered to be a woman, the error is treated as a miscommunciation with the magician's "spirit," and the conspirators claim that Lidio-Santilla is a hermaphrodite: the device will permit Ruffo and the "spirit" to remedy the problem before a return bout. In the frantic finale, thanks to Fessenio's belated realization of the presence of both twins, Santilla is substituted for Lidio in Fulvia's bedroom, preventing her disgrace. Santilla is destined for Fulvia's son Flaminio, while Lidio will supplant his sister in espousing Perillo's daughter Virginia. The twins wed wealthily in Rome, and Fessenio proclaims the general triumph.

12. Padoan in Bibbiena 40, of the 1521 edition: "si raccomanda . . . per la patina linguistica toscana." This program would bear its most important result in Bembo's *Prose sulla volgar lingua* (published in 1529); Bembo was in contact with Bibbiena from the days at the court of Urbino (1505-6) to the time of Bibbiena's cardinalate (1513-19); but such a hegemony was an objective of Medici cultural politics as early as the *Raccolta aragonese* or *Libro di Ragona* (1476) and Lorenzo de' Medici's commentary on his sonnets. For the Letter to Frederick of Aragon attributed to Poliziano, dedicatee of the *Raccolta*, see *Prose Volgari del Quattrocento, ed. Claudio Varese (Milan-Naples: Ricciardi, 1955): 985-90*; for the *Comento* (written or revised 1483-89), see Lorenzo de' Medici, *Opere*, ed. Tiziano Zanato (Turin: Einaudi, 1992): 313-20.

13. Argument: "i costumi e' l parlar pigliano" (they grasp the speech and habits). For identification of the linguistic program in the play, see A. Fontes-Baratto, "Les fêtes à Urbin en 1513 et la *Calandria* de Bernardo Dovizi da Bibbiena" in *Les écrivains et le pouvoir en Italie a l'époque de la Renaissance*, ed. André Rochon (Paris: Université de la Sorbonne nouvelle, 1974): 64-67, 75-78; Giulio Ferroni, "I due gemelli a Roma" in his *Il testo e la scena. Saggi sul teatro del Cinquecento* (Rome: Bulzoni, 1980): 89-90; Padoan in Bibbiena 1985: 13-14.

14. Bibbiena 1.2: "se tu pensi levarmi dello amore di costei, tu cerchi abbracciar l'ombra e pigliare il vento con le reti." See Petrarch *Canzoniere* 237.37, "in rete accolgo l'aura" (I gather the breeze in nets).

15. Bibbiena 1.7: "Amore che suole inviscare solo i cori gentili. . . ."

16. See Dante, *Purgatorio* 24.53-55. Guinizelli's canzone is cited in Lorenzo's *Comento* to his sonnets; see Lorenzo de' Medici 573.

17. *Calandra* enjoyed twenty-one printed editions in the cinquecento. Bibbiena's imitators include Machiavelli in both *Mandragola* and *Clizia* (see Padoan 1996: 35-39 and R. L. Martinez, "Comedian and Tragedian: Machiavelli and Traditions of Renaissance Theater," forthcoming in *The Cambridge Companion to Machiavelli,* ed. John Najemy), Ariosto in his *Negromante* (Padoan 1996: 46-48), and many others: Padoan lists passim some twenty plays between Aretino's *La cortigiana* (1525) and Giambattista della Porta's *Fantesca* (1592) that betray the imprint of Bibbiena's comedy, by authors from Ruzante to Agnolo Firenzuola. See also Bottoni 2005: 102-9.

18. Inventories of borrowings from the *Decameron,* all short of complete, are found in Fontes-Baratto 1974: 69-74, Padoan in Bibbiena 1985: 20-35.

19. Bibbiena's character informs Machiavelli's Nicia, the cuckolded husband of *Mandragola.* Franco Sacchetti's *Trecentonovelle* (ed. Antonio Lanza [Florence: Sansoni, 1993]) deploys Calandrino in several tales (67.4, 80.6, 84.28). See also Firenzuola's *Trinuzia* 4.6 in Agnolo Firenzuola, *Opere,* ed. Adriano Seroni (Florence: Sansoni, 1991): 683.

20. "Grossa pasta" is at Bibbiena 2.9; it is Boccaccio's phrase for Calandrino at *Decameron* 8.3.31.

21. Played in Ferrara 1486 and Florence 1488, and recently in Rome, 1511, on the Campidoglio (see Moncallero 1953: 544-60; Padoan in Bibbiena 13-14); significantly for Bibbiena's linguistic project, *Menaechmi* had been translated more than once into vernacular; see Giorgio Padoan, *L'avventura della commedia rinascimentale* (Padua: Francesco Vallardi, 1996): 9-10, 11, 12, 28n16, etc.

22. See Padoan 1996 on the translation of *Bacchides* (lost): 10n32, 56 (for peformances see 19n54). For *Amphitruo* translations by Pandolfo Collenuccio and Boiardo (both lost), see Padoan 1996: 10n31, 11-12, and 56 n34; for Plautus in *Calandra,* see Richard Wendriner, "Die Quellen von Bernardo Dovizi *Calandra,* " in *Abhandlungen Herrn Prof. Dr. Adolf Tobler* [. . .] *in Ehrerbietung dargebracht* (Halle a.S.: Niemeyer, 1895): 173 and Moncallero 1953: 551; *pace* P. D. Stewart, "A Play on Doubles: The *Calandria,* " in *Modern Language Studies* 14 (1984): 31.

23. For Bibbiena as Fessenio, see Moncallero 1953: 527; Fontes-Baratto 1974: 60-61, 75; Padoan in Bibbiena 1985: 33.

24. When Fessenio commends adaptability to the times (Bibbiena 1.2: "laudabile è accomodarsi al tempo"), he digests the servant Chrysalus's remark in *Bacchides:* "a man . . . must be good with the good and bad with the bad: whatever the deal is, that's what he must be" (*Bacchides* 658-60: ". . . bonus sit bonis, malus sit malis,/utcumque res sit, ita animum habeat").

25. Stefani's account is in Ludovico Ariosto, *Commedie: La Cassaria e I Suppositi,* ed. Luigina Stefani (Milan: Mursia, 1997), 180.

26. Padoan corrects the *barba fiorita* of the 1521 edition; see Bibbiena 41 (*barba* is also a vernacular term for an uncle).

27. Fessenio refers to the truffle, which causes erections in young men, farting in older men (1.2: "fa rizzar la ventura a' giovani, ai vecchi tirar corregge"); later he mistakes Calandro's reference to preparing the beast as referring to an erection (2.9: "la bestia è parata"); Samia's tryst with Lusco at 3.10 places "la chiave nella toppa" (the key in the keyhole) so that "il buco è pieno" (the hole is filled).

28. *Calandra* 3.17: "il sesso di donna e la radice d'uomo" (the sex of a woman and the man's root); 4.2: "tagliare la radice dell'uomo, e fare un fesso, e così fare una donna; e ricucire la bocca da basso, e appiccare un bischero, e così fare un maschio. . . ."

29. She asks that he come with "il coltel della guaina mia" (the knife for my scabbard; 4.2); this was again reiterated with the Boccaccio-inspired reference to the mortar and its pestle (4.3; compare *Decameron* 8.2.45); thereafter the desired male member is a branch or tail (*ramo, coda;* 4.6).

30. 2.3: "s'avvisano ch'io faccia e disfaccia cio che voglio"; 4.2: "fare una persona femina e maschio a posta sua" (make someone female and male at will), also 4.2, 4.3, and 4.4; and see 4.6, Fessenio speaking: "debbo credere però che per forza di incanti sia converso in femina . . . intendo vedere questo miraculo prima che maschio ridiventi" (must I then believe that by the force of enchantment he has been changed into a woman. . . . I intend to see this miracle before he becomes a man again).

31. Bibbiena 3.1: "andrò a congiungere il castron con la troia"; it has earlier been announced in the abstract (2.9: "la castroneria si congiungerà oggi con la lordezza"). Bibbiena transforms *Bacchides* 81, "lepidus cum lepida accubet" (let the handsome couch with the beautiful), referring to bedding a courtesan.

32. Drawn from Dante's *bolgia* of the sowers of schism, who "by putting apart [*scommettendo*] increase their load" (*Inferno* 27.136), the verb *scommettere* describes the removal of Calandro's limbs; for the stacking of the limbs, Bibbiena draws on Boccaccio's comparison of the plague dead to a ship's cargo: "stivati come si mettono le mercatantie nelle navi a suolo a suolo" (stowed tier upon tier like ships' cargo, each layer of corpses being covered over with a thin layer of soil; Giovanni Boccaccio, *Decameron,* trans. G.H. Mc-William (Penguin, 1972): introduction, p. 12); compare Bibbiena 2.6: "cosi stivate, come l'altre mercanzie, a suolo a suolo" (thus stacked, like other merchandise, layer upon layer). The *Decameron* parallel is noted in Moncallero 1953: 579.

33. Bibbiena 2.6: "l' uno *piglia* el membro dell'altro e sel *mette* ove più gli piace," terms echoed at the dénouement, where "*piglia* questo, *metti* su," (5.4) are Fessenio's orders for the hasty cross-dressing designed to save Fulvia's reputation.

34. *Calandra* 5.12: "begli scambiamenti"; see also 3.17: "sei colto in iscambio" (you are mistaken); and 5.10.

35. Other references to fraud in the play are at 4.2: "in queste cose assai fraude intendo si fanno" (I hear that in such business many frauds are done); 3.3: "eri colto in frodo, eri preso" (you had been found in a fraud, you were caught); 4.1, "O fraudolenti spiriti" (O fraudulent spirits).

36. Published 1528; see Padoan 1996: 28, 56; this version published by Tissoni Benvenuti and Maria Pia Mussini Sacchi (Turin: Unione Tipografico-Editrice Torinese, 1983).

37. For arguments using Platonic categories see Alonge 1978: 11; critiques are offered by Stewart 1984: 23–24, Ferroni 1980: 90–92, and Bottoni 2005: 72–74. Ruffini's "socratic" Bibbiena (1986: 303–4), reconciling all contradictions of earnest and game, strains belief; see Michael Wyatt, "Bibbiena's Closet: Interpretation and the Sexual Culture of a Renaissance Papal Court" in *Queer Italia: Same-Sex Desire in Italian Literature and Film,* ed. Gary P. Cestaro (New York: Palgrave Macmillan, 2004).

38. See Bottoni 2005: 25–34; 83–100.

39. Bottoni 2005: 25–34; 74; 83; the principal Platonic "teacher" envisioned is Ficino.

40. Where Samia's name evokes Samos, Pythagoras's homeland, Lusco's name is plausibly modelled on that of Lusca, the intrepid lady's maid who assists her mistress Lidia in the cuckolding of Nicostrato in *Decameron* 7.9; for discussion of this tale, see Albert R. Ascoli, "Pyrrhus' Rules: Playing with Power from Boccaccio to Machiavelli," *MLN* 114 (1999): 14–57.

41. That one of Fulvia's servants has the name Tiresias, famous for experiencing sex as both a man and a woman (see Ovid, *Metamorphoses* 3.322–38) is a sly addition to the same pattern.

42. Stewart (1984: 26) points out that the twins appear onstage together four times in various guises, exhausting gender/identity combinations. For the "system" of twins in plays derived from Plautus, see Ferroni 1980: 85–98 and 1981: 353–64; for the cross-dressing in the play, see Maggie Günsberg, *Gender and the Italian Stage from the Renaissance to the Present Day* (Cambridge: Cambridge University Press, 1997): 83–84, and Valeria Finucci, "Androgynous Doubling and Hermaphroditic Anxieties: Bibbiena's *La calandria*" in *The Manly Masquerade: Masculinity, Paternity and Castration in the Italian Renaissance* (Durham and London: Duke University Press, 2003): 189–224.

43. Ficino, *De amore,* cited in Bottoni 2005: 96.

44. Text from *Omnium divini Platonis opera* (cited at Bottoni 2005: 97): "Mandavitque Apollini, ut partitione statim facta, cuiusque vultum cervicisque dimidium in eam partem qua sectus est, verteret, ut scissionem suam considerans modestior fieret, reliquis autem mederi iussit. Ille continuo vultum vertit, et contrahens undique cutem in eum qui nunc venter vocatur, tamque contracta marsupia et os unum faciens, medio in ventre ligavit. Quem quidem nexum umbilicum vocant. . . ."

45. See Marsilio Ficino, *Commentaire sur le Banquet de Platon,* ed. Raymond Marcel (Paris: Les belles lettres, 1956), especially 4.1-2, pp. 168–71.

46. Pietro Bembo, *Prose della volgar lingua Gli asolani Rime,* ed. Carlo Dionisotti (Turin: UTET, 1966): 401 (*Gli asolani* 2.11): "partiti per lo mezzo da Giove, a cui voleano torre la signoria." On the text of *Asolani* 2.11, and references to the hermaphrodite in Ficino's vernacular *De Amore,* Castiglione's *Cortegiano,* and other works, see Bottoni 2005: 33, 97.

47. *Fesso* means, literally, "split." For Hannah F. Pitkin, *Fortune Is a Woman: Gender and Politics in the Thought of Niccolò Machiavelli* (Berkeley: University of California Press, 1984): 33–51, dyads of *furbi* and *fessi* structure Machiavelli's representation of the Florentine polity; see also Fontes-Baratto 1974: 69; Padoan 1996: 28. Richard Andrews, in *Scripts and Scenarios: The Performance of Comedy in Renaissance Italy* (Cambridge: Cambridge University Press, 1993): 59, remarks this opposition as operative in Bibbiena's play.

48. Bibbiena 1.1: "Io solo fo l'impossibilità. Nessuno potette mai servire a due e io servo a tre: al marito, alla moglie e al proprio mio padrone. . . ." (I alone do the impossible. No one could ever serve two, and I serve three: the husband, the wife, and my own master.)

49. Fontes-Baratto 1974: 61; see Moncallero 1953: 527, who quotes from Bibbiena's letters and dispatches. Fessenio's proclamation of divided duties also invokes the biblical "no man can serve two masters" (Matthew 6.24: "Nemo potest duobus dominis servire . . . homo servire non potest et deus et mammona").

50. For letters to Isabella d'Este signed this way, see G. L. Moncallero, *Epistolario di Bernardo Dovizi da Bibbiena,* 2 vols. (Florence: Olschki, 1955): I, 242 (and note), 249, 251; 2.13; Bottoni 2005: 68. Isabella's dialect form of the address (*mozicon*) is remarked in Bottoni 2005: 88–89. Gaeta 1969: 70-71 remarks Bibbiena's *astuzia* and *doppiezza;* Dionisotti 1969: 56, 60 his self-deprecation; see also Fontes-Baratto 1974: 55–56 and Bottoni 2005: 57–58, 67–68 for Bibbiena's ironic self-fashioning.

51. Bibbiena 1.3; related is Love's superiority to philosophy in stimulating ingenuity; see 3.13: "O Love, how great is your power! . . . Every kind of wisdom, anyone else's doctrine is slow compared to yours."

52. The parallel with Guccio Imbratta is noted in Fontes-Baratto 1974: 71. That Friar Cipolla of Certaldo is one of Boccaccio's surrogates in the *Decameron* is in the background here as well.

53. Bottoni 2005: 88; he also cites a Carnival song by Lorenzo de' Medici, 47.

54. To Bibbiena 1.7 ("se una ti bevesse il naso, una gota o un occhio"), compare *Tito Macchio Plauto [Plautus] Anfitrione [Amphitruo] Bacchidi [Bacchides] Menecmi [Menaechmi]*, ed. Margherita Rubino, trans. Vico Faggi (Milan: Garzanti, 1993): 194-95, said of a courtesan, "iam oportebat nassum abreptum mordicus" (you'd already have bitten off his nose); also *Bacchides* 372: "sorores, quae hominum sorbent sanguinem" (sisters, who drink men's blood); and 471: "apsorbet ubi quemque attigit" (she swallows whomever she touches). Boccaccio furnishes language from *Decameron* 9.5.37 (a Calandrino story) for Calandro's desire to kiss Lidio-Santilla: "E mi par mille anni *succiar* quelle labbra ver-migliuzze. . . ." (2.6; I can't wait to suck on those ruby lips); passages noted in Wendriner 1895: 175; Padoan in Bibbiena 1985: 21.

55. Chrysalus models his triple play on the *tria fata*, the three signs to be fulfilled for the fall of Troy (*Bacchides* 953-56); for the three deceptions as besting Menander's origi-nal play, see William M. Owens, "The Third Deception in Bacchides, 'Fides' and Plautus' Originality," *AJP* 15 (1994): 381-407.

56. Dioneo calls himself a nitwit at *Decameron* 9.10.4 ("sento anzi dello scemo che no"); and for the narrator, see conclusion 22-23.

57. *Calandra*, prologue (Bibbiena 61): "diventare donna, dio, pesce ed arbore a posta sua." Bottoni's reading of the play as a parody of Ficinian mysteries underlines Ruffo's nec-romantic observation to Samia that magic requires the conjunction of disparate elements according to the doctrine of signatures (3.15: "bisogna accozzare stelle, parole, acque").

58. Bibbiena repeats the idiom in the play at 2.9: "saprò morire e rivivere a mie' posta" (I'll know how to die and live again at will), repeated at 3.1; 4.2; 5.4; 5.12. See *Amphitruo* 120-24: "vorsipellem se facit *quando lubet* "(he can change his skin when he wills); and 860-64: "fio Iuppiter *quando lubet* " (I become Jupiter when I please). See Martinez, forthcoming.

59. The exposition of Castiglione's version of Bibbiena in the *Cortegiano* (2.45) associ-ates his comic flair with the theater, for it begins with a discussion of entertainments and theaters in classical antiquity.

60. See Castiglione 2.87 (compare. Cicero, *De Oratore* 2.235). Moncallero (1953: 205) characterizes the historical Bibbiena as Democritean.

61. See Horace, *Epistle* 2.1, 187-200, esp. 93-94: "captive ivory, captive Corinth, are borne along. Democritus, were he on earth, would laugh. . . ." (*Works of Horace*, trans. C. Smart and T. A. Buckley, New York: Harper, 1855); see also D. Iunii Iuvenalis [Juvenal] *Saturae* XIV, ed. J. D. Duff (Cambridge: Cambridge University Press, 1962): 10.33-35. See August Buck, "Democritus ridens et Heraclitus flens," in *Wort und Text: Festchrift für Fritz Schalk*, ed. Harri Meier and Hans Sckommodau (Frankfurt am Main: Klostermann, 1963): 167-86.

62. Bibbiena also likely knew Democritus to be an authority on scenography, recalled in Vitruvius Pollio, *Ten Books on Architecture*, trans. Ingrid Rowland, 2 vols. (New York: Cambridge University Press, 1999): 87.

63. See Petrarch, *De remediis utriusque fortunae* 2.89 and *Familiares* 11.9; also Ficino 1975, letters 35, 57, 58, 59 (to Landino), 61. Letter 58 begins: "You have seen painted in my academy a sphere of the world; on one side Democritus laughing, and on the other Hera-clitus weeping."

64. *Abscessum*, etymologically, suggests a slice or a cut (*ab-scissum*, "cut away"); the 1557 vernacular translation of Giovio's biography of Leo (cited in Bottoni 2005: 69) renders the term with *taglio*, "cut" or "slice."

65. Giovio 1987: 65: "because on the previous day from that ruptured abcess [*disrupto eo abscessu*] that he had in his seat, such a foul stink from the flowing pus had filled the

room, that like one infected by a mortal plague, he was not believed likely, in the opinion of doctors, to survive much longer."

66. *Calandra*, prologue (Bibbiena 63): "Ma ecco qua chi vi porta lo Argumento: preparatevi a pigliarlo bene, aprendo ben ciascuno il buco dell'orecchio."

67. As in the prologue to the vernacular *Menechini*, referring to the device of distinguishing the twins: "Appra adunque ciascun le orecchie soi/senza tropo variar la fantasia:/e stati ben attenti e riguardati/accio che l'un per l'altro non togliati" (Each then open his ears,/without too much shifting his imagination/and be attentive and look closely/so that you not take one for the other) (Tito Maccio Plauto, *Menechini*, in *Teatro del Quattrocento: Le corti padane*, ed. Antonia Tissoni Benvenuti (Turin: UTET, 1983): 90.

68. Compare Ludovico Ariosto, *Il negromante*, in *Opere*, ed. Giuliano Innamorati (Bologna: Zanichelli, 1967): prologue, 61-65: "non aspettate argomento né prologo,/che farlo sempre dinanzi fastidia./Il variare, e qualche volta metterlo/di dietro, giovar suol; ne la comedia/dico. . . ." (don't expect an argument or prologue, because it's boring to always do it in front; variation, and putting it sometimes in the rear, tends to bring benefits: I mean, in the play). Ruffini (1986: 324-25) derives Bibbiena's expression from Latin comedy, as in the appeal to "benignis . . . auribus" at *Menaechmi* 4; but Plautus's appeal lacks any sexual double meaning.

69. See Giovĩo 1972: 91: "Abdicant in ea numeros primus, ut vernaculos sales dulcius atque liquidius foeminarum auribus infunderet; quo multi risus hilarior voluptas ecitaretur"; and Firenzuola 1991: 633: "Voi sapete che gli argomenti son molto atti ad allargare il buco dell'orecchio dello intelletto, sì che più facilmente tutta la materia della favola penetri, anzi, come dire, vi sdruccioli dentro. . . ." (you know that arguments are suited to expand the hole of the ear of the intellect, so that the matter of the fable more easily penetrates, rather, as it were, slides into you).

70. The 1480 Turkish sack of Otranto affords the preamble to Ariosto's plot in *Suppositi* (5.4). Bibbiena's historical reference had contemporary resonance: the despot of Morea was present at the 1513 Palilia in Rome; Egidio da Viterbo records the loss of Modon and the Peloponnese as an occasion of sorrow for Alexander VI, though one relieved by Julius's Golden Age; see John W. O'Malley, "Fulfillment of the Christian Golden Age Under Pope Julius II: Text of a Discourse of Giles of Viterbo, 1507," *Traditio* 25 (1969): 311.

71. Inclusion of Bologna and Florence reveal Bibbiena's interests, as he had accompanied Julius II in Romagna during the pope's campaigns; his center of dutiful interest was the Medici return to Florence, though his personal ambitions pointed toward Rome; see Dionisotti 1969: 60; Fontes-Baratto 1974: 55.

72. Ruffini 1983: 138-41. The tapestries were removed when Cesare Borgia conquered Urbino; their restoration emphasized the return of della Rovere rule; see also Ruffini 1986: 185-88.

73. See Stefani in Grasso 1984: 21-27.

74. The accounts of the Urbino performance are Castiglione in Bibbiena 1985: 203-7 and Vat. urb. lat. 490 in Bibbiena 208-12; see also Fontes-Baratto 45-51; Stefani in Grasso 18-28; Ruffini 1986: 177-220.

75. By contrast, the names of Fulvia, of her son Flaminio, and of Virginia, Lidio's ultimate wife, have Roman associations: Fulvia recalls the wife of Marc Antony; Virginia was a name hallowed in Roman annals; Flaminio's name evokes the ancient circus Flaminius, the Porta Flaminia, and the Via Flaminia.

76. Padoan corrects *Lydio* to *Lidio* at 3.v in his edition of the 1521 Sienese imprint; see Bibbiena 1985: 41.

77. DNA evidence has now shown this long disparaged aetiology to be plausible.

78. See Vergil, *Aeneid* 8.479: "urbis Agyllinae sedes, ubi Lydia quondam/gens, bello prae-clara, iugis insedit Etruscis" (the site of the city Agylla, where a Lydian people, renowned in war, has long since held the Tuscan heights); see also *Aeneid* 2.781 and 9.10–11. Latin text from P. Vergili Maronis *Opera*, ed. R. A. B. Mynors (Oxford: Clarendon, 1969): 297.

79. Biondo Flavio, *Italy Illuminated*, vol. I (books I–IV), ed. and trans. Jeffrey A. White (Cambridge and London: Harvard University Press, 2005): 45, citing Livy and Justin: "Tuscorum gens . . . ex Lydia Asiae provinciae veniens pulsis umbris incoluit hanc Italiae partem . . . Leonardus autem Arretinus primo Historiarum dicit Etruscos venisse ex Moeonia, unde Lydi, gens maxima, navibus in Italiam adveni sunt" (The Etruscan people . . . actually came from the Asian province of Lydia . . . Leonardo Bruni tells us in the first book of his *Histories* that the Etruscans came from Maeonia, from where the Lydians sailed in great numbers to Italy).

80. Stinger (1985: 28) notes the flourishing Florentine banking community in Rome serving the papacy (25 to 35 banking houses); they were recognized by Leo X as a nation in 1515.

81. See at least Giovanni Cipriani, *Il mito etrusco nel Rinascimento fiorentino* (Florence: Olschki, 1980): 33–36; Walter Stephens, *Giants in Those Days: Folklore, Ancient History, and Nationalism* (Lincoln: University of Nebraska Press, 1989): 98–138; Rowland 1998: 53–59.

82. On Egidio da Viterbo in Julian Rome see Heinrich Pfeiffer, *Zur Ikonographie von Raphaels Disputa. Egidio da Viterbo und die christlich-platonische Konzeption der Stanza della Segnatura* (Rome 1975): 171–209, 241–54 (excerpts from the *Sententiae ad mentem platonis*); John W. O'Malley, *Giles of Viterbo on Church and Reform* (Leiden: E. J. Brill, 1968): 30–31, 123–24, and 1969; Rowland 1998: 143–50, 214–15.

83. For Inghirami at the courts of Julius and Leo, see Cruciani 1980; Christiane L. Joost-Gaugier, *Raphael's Stanza della Segnatura: Meaning and Invention* (Cambridge: Cambridge University Press, 2002): 18–42, 69–94, 151–63, 180–91; Rowland 1998: 147–57, 212–15.

84. In the anonymous remark in ms. Vat. lat. 3351 (193v): "Caedat Aristophanes tuscoque Terentius ori/Ethrusci superant graeca, latina sales" (Let Aristophanes and Terence yield to Tuscan speech/Etruscan wit overcomes that of Greek and Latin); also Giovio 1987: 94: "Poetices enim et ethruscae linguae studiosus, comoedias multo sale multisque facetiis refertas componebat. . . ." (zealous for poetic art and the Tuscan language, he composed comedies stuffed with plentiful wit and many jests).

85. For this festival, restored by Pomponio Leto in 1483, then restored again by the Medici, see Cruciani 1969: xxxiii–lv; Fabrizio Cruciani, "Il teatro dei ciceroniani," *Forum Italicum* 14 (1980): 279–85; Stinger 1985: 72, 97–98; and Rowland 1998: 213–14.

86. Castiglione's Bibbiena is represented as familiar with both Fedra (*Cortegiano* 2.62, a joke at the expense of cardinals) and Camillo Porzio (Porcaro, in the vernacular spelling, *Cortegiano* 2.65).

87. The involvement of Peruzzi and Antonio da San Gallo is likely; see Bruschi in Cruciani 1969: 141–67; and Götz Pochat, *Theater und Bildende Kunst im Mittelalter und in der Renaissance in Italien* (Graz: Akademische Druck-u.Verlagsanstalt, 1990): 251–55.

88. Accounts are found in Stinger in Rosenberg 1990: 142–52 and notably Cruciani 1969, with the accounts of Marcantonio Altieri, Paolo Palliolo, and Aurelio Sereno, among others.

89. See Palliolo in Cruciani 1969: 56; Clarice speaks: "Rome wishes to have you gathered into her blessed lap and to have made you hers: by nature you are Tuscans, but let the privilege make you Roman; in any case the one people and the other are joined by blood [*l'una e l'altra gente è congiunta di sangue*] such that now the Tiber is said to be Tuscan. . . ." See also Palliolo in Cruciani 1969: 89, when Rome speaks: "Let there between you be one same love and one same mind and one same will; long may you live in concord

[*concordesque diu vivant*] and let Florence by the Medici and Rome by Leo be ruled with paired auspices. Therefore establish eternal fealty between yourselves."

90. Discussion of the theater, and reproduction of the Codex Coner drawing of it, in Bruschi in Cruciani 1969: 141-67; see also Pochat 1990: 251-55.

91. See Palliolo in Cruciani 1969: 29. Cipriani (31-36) details how Medicean constructions of Etruscan history, in accord with their own preference for centralized power, privileged Lars Porsenna, featured on the Campidoglio theater scenes, rather than the *lucumones,* the leaders of the confederated cities.

92. See Stinger (1985: 97) on this festival as designed to coopt what had been a Roman popular festivity; also (Stinger 1985: 72) on the first Palilia restoration by Pomponio Leto; see also Cruciani 1980: 279-85.

93. Palliolo in Cruciani 1969: 31-32.

94. Palliolo in Cruciani 1969: 32: "Nel III è ritratto uno amplissimo theatro, pieno di gran populo, con quelli che recitano le comedie in la scena, chiamati histrioni, mimi, et pantomimi, tanto artifitiosamente dissegnati, che parieno con suoi atti, gesti et parole dilettare et dar piacere al populo che li guarda. qui è notato: *Ludi scenici ab Hetruscis adcoepti.*" Another witness describes the same panel as the *mise-en-abîme* of the festive event itself; see Cruciani (1969: li) reporting the account by Benricevuti da Prato.

95. Livy's discussion of the origins of Roman theater mentions Fescennine verses (an alternate etymon for Bibbiena's Fessenio, in addition to his relation to Plautus's Messenio in *Menaechmi*), Atellan farce, and the introduction of extra actors by Livius Andronicus (*Ab urbe condita* 7.2): "quia iste Tusco verbo *ludio* vocabantur, nomen histrionibus inditum." (because the Tuscan word for an actor is *istrio,* so the native performers were called *histriones*).

96. Biondo, *Roma instaurata* 2.110 (cited in Cruciani 1983: 98): "Tacitus does not deny that the model for theatre was taken from the Greeks; he however attributes to the Etruscans the labor and the art of these games when he says that the ancient Romans did not abhor the pleasure of these spectacles given the prosperity their republic enjoyed, and having brought actors from Etruria and equestrian contests from the Tyrians performed much better the games they had possessed from the Greeks and Asians." Biondo cites freely from Cornelius Tacitus, *Annales* 16.21; see also Pellegrino Prisciani, *Spectacula,* ed. Danilo Aguzzi Barbagli (Ferrara: Franco Cosimo Panini, 1992): 37 (f.18v).

97. Leone Battista Alberti, *L'Architettura (de re aedificatoria),* 2 vols. (Milano: Il Polifilo, 1966): 8.7, 148v.

98. Isidore, *Etymologiarum libri* (book 20, 2.2; in *Patrologia latina* 82.651), has the Lydians settle in Etruria and establish their spectacles; these are borrowed by the Romans, therefore, "ludi a Lydis vocati sunt" (games are named after the Lydians).

99. Palliolo in Cruciani 1969: 57: "Born among the laurels of Apollo and the lilies, here where the flourishing youth of Lydia [*flos Lyda pubes*] ornaments with walls, temples and manners the city that is the flower of the Italian people."

100. Giovio records the performance for Isabella in his life of Leo X and in his *Elogium;* see Giovio 1987: 94 and Giovio 1972: 91. On the Vatican performances, see Moncallero 1952: 819-51 and Cruciani 1983: 440-45.

101. Palliolo in Cruciani 1969: 54, Cybele speaking: "Let us make of the two cities one sole people. O Roman and Tuscan, under the same laws, let yours be a single love, a single mind, and a single will [*sotto le medesime leggi sia el vostro un medesmo amore, una mente et una voluntate*]. Live long in concord. Let the Medici rule Florence, and Leo rule Rome, with equal auspices, and establish between you an eternal confederation." See Palliolo in Cruciani 1969: 89 for the Latin version.

102. Given that Giuliano was not present, the twins could also appear to be Lorenzo and Leo. See Palliolo (in Cruciani 1969: 86) for Rome's reference to the Medici as "twin" Roman citizens: "et nomine cives/Romanos geminos vocat." See also Aurelio Sereno in Cruciani 1969: 104.

103. Plautus *Menaechmi:* 1,088: "neither water and water nor milk and milk were ever more similar, believe me." See Sereno in Cruciani 1969: 104: "Thus, spectators, we point out the truth to you, that you be attentive to the great announcement of the brothers: now a certain Pollux and Castor reign in the city [*Pollux cum Castore regnat in urbe*]."

104. For the Capitoline theater to be built as specified, its design would have been required by March or April of 1513 (see notes in Bruschi in Cruciani 1983, esp. 142-43).

105. Such proportional comparisons, using *quanto magis* (so much the more) are recalled by Stinger 1985: 204 and 374n137 (speech of Piero da Monte for Nicholas V on Petrine primacy); 244 (Biondo in *Roma Triumphans* on the greater glory of Christian Rome); also 384n39 (Marcello's *Oratio ad Leonem X Pont. Max.,* ms. Vat. 3646, fol. 17v.).

106. Bibbiena 5.12: "e tutti trionferemo." Fessenio's crowing echoes Chrysalus's in *Bacchides* 1,070-74.

107. For Renaissance adaptations of Petrarch's *Triumphi,* see Pochat 1990: 185-200; Konrad Eisenblicher and Amilcare A. Iannucci, *Petrarch's Triumphs: Allegory and Spectacle* (Toronto: Dovehouse, 1990).

108. The phrase is echoed at 2.7, "come va il mondo," with which Samia taxes Lidio's fickleness concerning Fulvia. The reference to the papal *possesso* seems unmistakable; see Cruciani 1983: 390-405, esp. 391 (on Leo's *possesso*); Shearman 1972: 13-20; Stinger 1985: 53-57.

109. For Rome's receptivity, see Stinger 1985: 39 (pilgrims), 74 (citizens), 244 (Rome extends universal citizenship), 156 (the public emporium of whole globe). The receptivity of Rome was a topos for describing the city; see Cipriani 1980: 47, who cites Francisco Albertini's *Opusculum de mirabilibus novae et veteris urbis Roma* (Rome, 1510): "Rome, unequalled and second to none, where nearly the whole vanquished world is in triumph received [advectos triumphos recepit]." Rome is also linguistically receptive in Bembo 108 (*Prose,* 1.13): "those languages that in Rome, because of the variety of peoples that like the rivers flow to the sea and gather from every place, are surely infinite. . . ."

110. *Aeneid* 8.722-28: " . . . vanquished nations march in long procession/as varied in their language as in their armor and their dress;/Here Mulciber had fashioned Nomads and ungirt Africans,/here the Leleges, the Carians, and the Geloni, bearing arrows;/and there went the Euphrates, its waves now tamed,/there the Morini, most remote of men, the Rhine with twin horns,/the Dahae unsubdued, and the Araxes, resentful of its bridge." At the Capitoline festivities of the Palilia in 1513 a shield granted to Giuliano alluded to the scene in the *Aeneid* of the shield of Aeneas; see Palliolo in Cruciani 1969: 85-86. Biondo's account is based on the triumph of Titus and Vespasian as reported by Josephus (*Jewish War* 7.5; summarized in Payne 1962: 169-71), of which a visual record was preserved in the Arch of Titus.

111. Bembo 1966: 183 (*Prose* 3.1) recalls how Rome affects artists: "the arches and the baths and the theaters and other various buildings, which still remain erect in some places, they zealously search out, and preserve the forms of them in the small space of their paper [*picciolo spazio delle loro carte*]." Vasari (1555), cited in Bibbiena 213, and echoing Serlio's 1545 account of perspective scenes, gushed of the Peruzzi set for the 1514 Rome *Calandra* that "Nor can it be imagined how he in such a narrow place [*in tanta strettezza di sito*] could fit in so many many streets, palaces, and fanciful temples." [Sebastiano Serlio] *Sebastiano Serlio on Architecture,* vol. I (*Books I-V of Tutte l'Opere d'Architettura et Prospetiva, by Sebastiano Serlio*), translated with introduction and commentary by Vaughan Hart and Peter Hicks (New Haven and London: Yale University Press, 1996-2001).

112. Bibbiena 66 (prologue): "don't believe that they've come here from Rome so quickly because of necromancy, however." The Argument conserves the adaptation of the play to the Urbino performance.

113. For these entries, see Cruciani 1983: 320-26; Stinger 1985: 235-42, Stinger in Rosenberg, 1990: 193. Albertini's *Opusculum* (Cruciani 1983: 321) suggests a parallel to the triple triumph of Augustus (a third Julian triumph, over infidels, was yet to come); Biondo's account of the Roman triumph in *Roma triumphans* X, drawing parallels with the triumph of contemporary princes of the Church, is quoted in Cruciani 1983: 102-12 and cited in Stinger 1985: 383n23.

114. Examples illustrated in Pochat 1990: 167-200; Bonner Mitchell, *The Majesty of State: Triumphal Progresses of Foreign Sovereigns in Renaissance Italy* (1494-1600), (Florence: Olschki, 1986): 411. Other examples in editions of the *Triumphi* (e.g., Venice, 1488) and in more eccentric form in the illustrations to the *Hypnerotomachia poliphili*, published in 1499 by Aldus Manutius. The much admired Mantegna "Triumphs of Caesar" provided a visual account of the triumph that met exacting standards of antiquarianism and furnished the set for a play at the Mantuan court; see Andrew Martindale, *The "Triumphs of Caesar" by Andrea Mantegna in the Collection of Her Majesty the Queen at Hampton Court* (London: Harvey Miller, 1979).

115. Randolph Starn, "Renaissance Triumphalism in Art," in *The Renaissance World,* ed. John Jeffries Martin (New York: Routledge, 2007): 343; see also Roy C. Strong, *Art and Power: Renaissance Festivals 1450-1650* (Berkeley: University of California Press, 1984): 32-35.

116. Castiglione's Bibbiena (*Cortegiano* 2.45), as he begins his exposition on the risible, notes that ancient rulers constructed theaters and public buildings for the purpose of providing shows.

117. Existing scenographies may indicate a period when a single scene adaptable to tragedy or comedy was the rule; see Ruffini 1980: 171. For Alberti's distinctions, see his texts cited in n. 123.

118. Pochat 1990: 306-18; also Serlio 1996-2001: 83-93.

119. Illustrated in Pochat 1990: 314. Robert Klein and Henri Zerner, "Vitruve et le théâtre de la Rénaissance italienne," in Jacquot 1964: (51-55) demonstrate how strict Vitruvian reconstructions and the perspective *scena picta* of Renaisssance plays diverged,although contemporaries often did not distinguish them; see also George R. Kernodle, *From Art to Theater: Form and Convention in the Renaissance* (Chicago and London, 1944): 176-79.

120. For interpretation of Vasari's description of the 1514 *apparato* associated with Peruzzi, see Ruffini 1983: 125-96; Cruciani 1983: 467; Fabrizio Cruciani and Daniele Seragnoli, *Teatro italiano del Rinascimento* (Bologna: Il Mulino, 1987): 220-24; Pochat 1990: 286-91. Vasari's account of the Rome stage sets of Peruzzi is in Bibbiena 213; see also Thomas A. Pallen, *Vasari on Theatre* (Carbondale: Southern Illinois University Press, 1999): 61.

121. Vitruvius 5.6.8; see Prisciani 45 (22r): "with exits, doors, and with one in the middle like a royal one [*si come regale*] for the adornment of temples"; Alberti 1988: "One passageway . . . should be more generous than the rest; this I call the royal entrance [*apertionem regiam*], because it leads to the royal road" (8.7, 150r). Magagnato pointed out that the *scaenae frons* of the Teatro Olimpico in Vicenza (1585), based on designs by Palladio developed from his collaboration on Daniele Barbaro's edition of Vitruvius, constitutes a triumphal arch.

122. Non-Vitruvian images of dramatic "scenes," such as the Lucretia panel at the Isabella Stewart Gardner Museum in Boston attributed to Botticelli's workshop (see Baskins 1998: 128-59, esp. illus. 148-49) or the cityscape in the Uffizi attributed to Bramante dated

1500 (reproduced in Pochat 1990: 279), also have centralized triumphal arches and could represent stage sets; so also the notorious Baltimore, Urbino, and Dresden panels; for which see at least Richard Krautheimer, "The Tragic and Comic Scene of the Renaissance: The Baltimore and Urbino Panels," *Gazette des Beaux-Arts* 44 (1948): 327–47; Klein and Zerner 1964; Hubert Damisch, *The Origin of Perspective*, trans. John Goodman (Cambridge, Mass.: MIT Press, 1995).

123. Alberti 1988: "the most suitable place to build an arch is at the point where a road meets a square or a forum, especially if it is a royal road" (8.6, 147r); "a show ground [*spectaculum*] is nothing but a forum surrounded with steps" (8.6, 145v); "The portico behind the cavea is to be constructed solidly with robust walling, their lineaments taken from the triumphal arch [*ex arcu triumphorum*]" (8.7, 151r).

124. Cruciani (1980: 26–31) and Ruffini (1983: 125–92 and 1986: 249–92) assert, as a methodological premise, systematic homologies of city, court, and theater.

125. Castiglione in Bibbiena 204: "Da l'un de' capi era un arco trionfale. . . ." (at one extreme there was a triumphal arch). Vasari reports that Girolamo Genga, a disciple of Bramante transferred to the court of Urbino, and usually taken to have designed the apparatus of the first performance (Sabine Eiche, "Girolamo Genga the Architect, an Inquiry into his Background," in *Mitteilungen des Kunsthistorischen Institutes in Florenz* 35 (1991): 317–24 casts doubt on the attribution, however), devised triumphal arches and comedy apparatus; see Pallen 1999: 74.

126. On the evidence of the report of manuscript Vat. urbinate lat. 490, now attributed to Urbano Urbani; see Cruciani 1983: 440–48, esp. 441; Bibbiena 208. See Cruciani (1983: 441–48, esp. 444–47) for doubtful attributions of Peruzzi drawings as stage sets for *Calandra;* for a different hypothesis, see Ruffini (1986: 339–46).

127. See Cruciani 1983: lxiii; Bruschi in Cruciani 1983: 154–55; and Sereno in Cruciani 1983: 97: "more triumphalis dehinc ianua ponitur arcus" (a door is placed in the fashion of a triumphal arch). A triumphal entry of Henry II of France was the occasion of the Lyons performance of *Calandra* in 1548 (an account is in Bibbiena 214–36); Ruffini (1986: 328) notes how, in its use of a triumphal arch and in its reference to Lorenzo de' Medici, made a citizen of Rome in 1513, the Lyons apparatus "cited" the Campidoglio theater in architectural and iconographical terms.

128. Palliolo in Cruciani 1969: 21: "the new triumph [*il novo triompho*] celebrated at the promotion of the Magnificent Giuliano and Lorenzo de Medici to the Roman patriciate"; Palliolo 49, Monte Tarpeio speaks: "for whom are the lofty edifices and the show of a splendid triumph [*splendido triompho*]?"; see also Palliolo 77, 84–86. Notturno Napolitano's account of the Palilia, versifying Palliolo's, is titled *Triomphi de gli mirandi spettaculi . . .* and is formally divided into sections labeled *triomphi;* Cruciani 1983: 421–34.

129. Biondo, *Roma illustrata*, 1.4: "It is clear from Livy's report that the Etruscans were a most impressive people, since the Romans took over from them the purple-bordered toga, robes of state, the decorative insignia of their horses, equestrian finger-rings, decorated togas and togas embroidered with palm-leaf patterns, triumphal cars [*currus triumphales*], ceremonial rods, lictors, trumpets, and the curule chair." For detailed analysis, see Robert Payne, *The Roman Triumph* (London: Robert Hale, 1962): 19–23; H. S. Versnel, *Triumphus: An Inquiry into the Origin, Development, and Meaning of the Roman Triumph* (Leiden: E. J. Brill, 1970): 196–98 and 394–97.

130. As recalled by Alberti 8.7, 148v, for example, quoted above in the text. These are the "Etruscan" pomps satirized by Horace and Juvenal; see note 61.

"Ma che potrà succedermi se io donna amo una Donna": Female-Female Desire in Italian Renaissance Comedy

LAURA GIANNETTI

I N NICOLÒ SECCHI'S comedy *Gl'inganni* (first performed in 1547), the protagonist Ginevra, much like Lelia in the better known *Ingannati*, pretends
to be a man called Ruberto in order to live as a servant in the house of her
beloved, Gostanzo.[1] There, disguised in masculine attire, she causes Portia,
Gostanzo's sister, to fall in love with her, and not knowing how to "sadisfar a
le voglie di Portia" (satisfy her desires; Argomento, c. 5r), she has her brother,
Fortunato, substitute for her in bed with Portia before the play begins. When
Ginevra's nonmasculine identity is discovered, Portia, pregnant and about to
give birth, continues to insist to her father, Massimo, that Ginevra is her lover
and thus father of her child. In the face of that unlikely claim he decides to
send his friend Tullio to find out what has actually happened. But it is not so
easy to figure out how a young woman might have fathered a child, and Tullio can only reiterate what Portia's father already knows about Ginevra's sex.
Clearly this hardly satisfies the outraged father who rails

Che di Ruberto, ah sfacciata crede di vendermi vesciche? Cavar gl'occhi alla
verità? *Pascermi dell'impossibile?* Non hai tu messo a fronte l'un dell'altro. Che
disse quando seppe, che Ruberto è donna come lei, come si salva? (5.3.c. 85;
emphasis mine)

What is this about Ruberto? Ah, she [Portia] is a shamed woman who tries to sell
me this crap? Is truth blind? *Should I make a meal of the impossible?* Didn't you

confront the one with the other? What did she say when she saw that Ruberto
was a woman like her?

Tullio assures his friend that Portia continues to insist on her version of
the facts in the face of the incontrovertible evidence to the contrary:

> Cosa che v'empierà di *meraviglia, e stupore.* Crederete voi, che Portia vince
> d'argomenti, di ragioni, di luoghi, di tempi . . . Crederete che quest'altro non
> negando quel che Portia dice, tace, piange, e si può dir, che confessa, *ma come ve-*
> *dete l'impossibile lo difende* . . . Facciam, che sia vero tutto quello che Portia dice,
> *non può una fanciulla baciare, e toccar l'altra, che mal è questo?* Non si baciano
> ogni di in presentia nostra tra loro le donne? (5.3. c. 85–86; emphasis mine)

> It is a thing that will fill you *with wonder and incredulity.* You would think that
> Portia would be won over by arguments, reason, the times and places. . . . You
> would think that this other young person is guilty for he does not deny what Por-
> tia said [about going to bed together] and is silent, cries and one might say, con-
> fesses. *But as you can see the impossibility of the deed defends him* [as a woman
> he cannot have impregnated Portia]. . . . Let's admit that everything Portia says is
> true. *Can't a young girl kiss and touch another young girl? What harm is there*
> *in that? What evil?* Don't women kiss each other in front of us everyday?

Tullio, then, believes that the *impossibility of the deed* exonerates
Ruberto—since he is really Ginevra and thus could not have been responsible for the pregnancy—and sees nothing wrong with the physical
expression of affection between the two women.

The humorous confusion of Tullio and Massimo is indicative of what may
be seen as the two most widespread cultural assumptions at the time about
love between women: on the one hand, that it was *impossible*—a cultural
prejudice typical of a phallocratic society that assumed that women could
not have sexual relations with other women—and, on the other hand, that
physical intimacy between women was *innocuous,* as it did not threaten
the family or society. Even if such relationships remained anathema for
the church and the occasional target of moralists and prescriptive literature, this vision helped to render such desires and deeds less troublesome
in everyday culture onstage and off. Neither of the two assertions, however, are particularly relevant to modern critical questions of deviance or
normativity, heterosexuality or homosexuality; the first case made love a
wonder or a marvel—a category much more typical of the period—and the
second case made it irrelevant.[2] Yet the insistence on *impossibility*—the
idea that such a sexual relationship was "impossible" is repeated two times

in two relatively brief speeches—actually calls attention to the fact that in this comedy the idea of love and sex between women is imagined as *possible* at the same time as it is proclaimed not to exist.

This trope of the *impossible* has become also, in a certain sense, a trope of the modern critical discourse, which neglected until recently to analyze any portrayals of love between women in the premodern era and assumed them to be invisible because they were impossible to conceive at the time. Valerie Traub, author of one of the most influential studies on the topic, *The Renaissance of Lesbianism in Early Modern England,* begins her analysis with the paradigmatic example of an English comedy, John Lily's *Gallathea,* which portrays the love between Gallathea and Phyllida, two young women, both cross-dressed.[3] For Traub this comedy is a text that repeats the trope of *impossibility* but that also makes it *possible* to open a window on a less narrow vision of love between women.[4] Her suggestion that we study more carefully "the puzzle of an impossibility that *can* be practiced" is one that can be applied profitably to the study of portrayals of love between women in the culture of Renaissance Italy, a period when these representations became increasingly explicit and frequent, especially in dramatic literature, preparing the way for what would later happen on the English stage.[5]

Even if the comedies rarely describe directly the practice of women loving women, they are rich with information on contemporary ways of understanding it. One finds reflected in the scripting of such love, or in the telling silences about it, a complex balance of and/or tension between diverse factors, including most notably: social custom and practice, the rules of canon and civil law, misogynist prejudices, proto-feminist influences of the *querelle des femmes,* erotic influences from translations of Latin literature, and the impact of philosophical debates on love and everyday attitudes toward women.[6] In addition, newer Renaissance socioeconomic factors must also be considered: the creation of a more popular printing press, which granted women public access to and greater participation in written culture, and the activity of a few academic societies that contributed to the success of genres such as comedy and epic poetry in which innovative images of women circulated more freely. The cinquecento was thus a particularly privileged period for the exploration of this topic because the cultural and literary milieu saw a growth in references to and testimonies of female desire and love in a wide range of cultural productions such as short stories, epic poetry, and above all, theatrical comedy. It was not by chance, then, that a number of the studies on the representation of love between women in English Renaissance literature recognized the importance of an Italian influence on that literature, from Ariosto's *Furioso* through Italian adaptations of Ovid and on to the tradition of the *commedia erudita;* by turning to Italy, English literature was drawing on a rich and diverse literary and cultural discourse.[7]

The encounter between the woman warrior Bradamante and Fiordispina in canto 25 of *Orlando furioso* set the stage for a number of subsequent representations of eroticism and desire between women in Italian, as well as European, literature. The celebrated episode portrays Fiordispina's desire for Bradamante as unnatural and asserts that it falls short of the superiority of the "better sex" (*miglior sesso*), that is, the male.[8] After realizing that Bradamante is not a man, Fiordispina begins her famous "lament" in which she claims that neither humans nor animals have ever found that a "female loves a female." Because of this she begs all the gods to change her beloved Bradamante into the "better sex."[9] As is well known, Fiordispina's *impossible* love for Bradamante would find a "natural" solution in Bradamante's brother Ricciardetto, who is substituted for her and has what "Nature" has not given his sister (i.e., a penis).[10] The same trope of impossibility is resolved in the popular Ovidian story of Iphis and Ianthe in a way more typical of classical Latin literature: Iphis is magically transformed into a man so that she can marry her beloved, Ianthe.[11] It is possible that Ariosto's tale was inspired by this classical Ovidian story, even if the idea of substituting twins of the opposite sex for the magical transformation is a major break from the classical tale.[12]

It may be, however, that Ariosto was more influenced by the cross-dressed twins in Bernardo Dovizi da Bibbiena's *Calandra* (1513), one of the most popular comedies of the early sixteenth century both in terms of productions and printings and well known before Ariosto published his epic poem. In *Calandra,* the twin Santilla, dressed as a man, faces sexual performance risks having to demonstrate her sexual maleness in several situations in the comedy—most notably perhaps in the planned meeting with her male twin's mistress Fulvia, a meeting where she is supposed to pass as him and somehow calm Fulvia's pressing sexual desire for the young man. Santilla repeats the trope of impossibility to her servant Fannio who had suggested the plan:

Mo non sai tu, sciocco, che, s'io fo prova di me paleso quel ch' io sono . . . Come vuoi che si faccia? (4.4.158, 55)

Don't you realize, you fool, that if I try to satisfy her [Fulvia], I won't have the right stuff. . . . How do you plan for me to carry this one off?[13]

Santilla's trope of impossibility had already been confirmed in her earlier encounter with Fulvia, when the latter, convinced that she was with the real Lidio, hungrily touched Santilla's body and did not find what she was seeking. Suggestively, however, Santilla is not unmoved by that earlier encounter and admits late in the comedy that "Fulvia mi è ben ne l'animo e nella memoria" (Fulvia is indeed in my soul and memory; 5. 2. 173, 63), hinting perhaps at an attraction for the woman based on that encounter.

The Renaissance popularity of the translations and adaptations of *Metamorphoses, Orlando furioso,* and of Bibbiena's comedy suggests that the notion of women loving and desiring other women and the possibility of female-female erotic encounters were not unimaginable. These literary works revealed the significance of cultural presuppositions about such practices; most notably they underlined the assumed superiority of the male sex in satisfying women and the supposed female incapacity to do the same. This, however, was not the last word on the subject, for at much the same time a different vision began to be expressed in other literary sources—a vision that considered instances of love, erotic desire, and pleasure between women independent both of men and of the rhetorical trope of impossibility. A number of texts, including most notably two works by Agnolo Firenzuola, *Ragionamenti* (a novella collection from around 1525) and *Celso. Dialogo delle bellezze delle donne* (published in 1548), contributed greatly to this changing perception.[14] In the second story of the first day of the *Ragionamenti,* the unhappily married Lavinia wants to make love to her maid Lucia, who is actually the cross-dressed Fulvio. Lavinia, however, believes Lucia to be a woman and is not at all worried about any impossibility in fulfilling her own desire with her. Moreover, when Lavinia discovers Lucia is a man, her unhappiness contradicts what might have been expected given the phallic predilection of many literary tales and the master narrative of male sexual superiority. Firenzuola's tale is important because it admits the possibility of desire between women, which becomes a theme that continues in several comedies of the sixteenth century and in his own later philosophical work *Dialogo delle bellezze delle donne.*

What was referred to until a few years ago as an "insignificant handful of references,"[15] takes on a very different perspective when one looks more closely at the signs and indications furnished by *novelle,* by dialogues on love, and, above all, by the corpus of Italian Renaissance comedies. Though continuing to imitate models like *Calandra* and *Orlando furioso,* a number of later comedies played in intriguing ways with the idea of erotic attraction, love and sex between women, giving increasingly less weight to the trope of impossibility, and not merely from a rhetorical point of view. Stage comedies, possibly because they were considered part of the middle-to-low comic genre, had perhaps the most freedom to explore and chart such changes in the scripting of women desiring and making love to other women. Playwrights most often approached the subject via the common "theatergram" of heroines cross-dressing as men.[16] This allowed their female heroines the necessary freedom of movement and the possibility for revealing misunderstandings of sex and gender. Louise George Clubb was the first to underscore, and rightly so, the importance of the character who cross-dresses for love and who "unintentionally" attracts the love of another woman; but in such attractions things can be much more complex than the notion of mere accidental attraction might seem to imply. Clubb referred specifically to the model of Lelia in *Gl' ingannati,* who, dressed as a man, arouses the erotic desire of Isabella. This scenario was widely followed by later comedies.[17] Isabella, however, is completely unaware that her beloved Fabio is a woman, Lelia, and the latter, although amused by the idea of kissing Isabella, is not particularly interested in Isabella as a woman. Thus *Gl'ingannati* does not develop intentionally the scenario of women loving women but does start the play of misunderstandings and gender confusion that will animate many later cinquecento comedies.

A number of the heroines cross-dressed as male, however, who seemed to have been derived from Lelia's example, did fall in love with characters that they believed to be women like themselves—a very different situation indeed. In this context the theme of love between women was intentionally developed in *Alessandro* (1544) by Alessandro Piccolomini, *La Cesarea Gonzaga* by Luca Contile (printed in 1550), *Gli inganni* by Curtio Gonzaga (printed in 1592), and it was at least referred to explicitly in *Anconitana* by Ruzante (written around 1520) and other plays written in the second half of the sixteenth century. In these works the heroines who have been cross-dressing for a long time for varying motives not only attract the love of other women, but fall in love with them in turn. It matters little for our argument that the female beloved does not realize that the person who woos her is a woman, because the heroine in love realizes full well that her love is for a person of the same sex.[18]

One of the earlier comedies of the sixteenth century, Ruzante's *Anconitana,* is particularly interesting, not as an analysis of the representation of female homoerotic desire in itself—as it is only mentioned—so much as for what it says about Renaissance society's changing perception of such desire.[19] The servant Ruzante is the only character in the play who knows from the beginning that two other characters, Caco and his servant-boy, are in truth Ginevra and her servant-girl Ghitta. Ginevra is from Ancona and has put on male clothing to follow the man she loves, Gismondo, to Padua, not realizing that he is also a woman cross-dressed. When Ginevra and her servant meet Ruzante, they admit to him their true identities and ask for his help in winning Gismondo. Ruzante agrees for two reasons: first, for the money Ginevra promises him in exchange for that help, and, second, because the game makes "la pí bela fiaba al mondo" (the most beautiful tale in the world; 3. 2. 831).

To Ruzante it is the "most beautiful tale" because it represents the marvelous and heroic power of love: Ruzante marvels that, in the name of love, a woman (Ginevra) disguised as a man crossed the sea and faced an infinite number of dangers to win the love of another woman. Ginevra does not know that Gismondo was a woman in disguise, and naturally this ultimately disqualifies her love as a representation of female homoeroticism. But the reaction of Ruzante, who knows that, under their clothes, both lovers are women, opens a different perspective on the perception of love between women. The character Ruzante repeats the traditional trope that their love is impossible and even adds that it has never been heard of in the past, something that the author Ruzante should have been aware was not true, given the classical examples well known at the time. Yet all the same, he neither stigmatizes it nor judges it negatively; on the contrary, he adds a new positive evaluation. Their love, the coupling of "a woman with a woman," has a power that he judges has never been seen before, a power that leads a woman to do heroic things like cross the sea and place herself in great danger. Women lovers had become, for a moment at least, heroic, even as they remained an impossibility, and in doing so they took on characteristics such as courage and heroism that were typically gendered male. *Anconitana* was written just before 1520, and it was staged around 1525; with its performance we can affirm that the scripting of *woman with woman* began to acquire a concrete and positive *visibility* in Renaissance comedy.

The only comedy where no cross-dressing is required to present sexual play between women is the anonymous comedy *La Veniexiana*.[20] In this play, a young, rich, and beautiful widow, Angela, has spotted Julio, a fascinating foreigner visiting Venice, from her window and fallen madly in love with him. In the scene in which Angela appears for the first time, she is going to the room of her servant Nena to try to quell her passions and the erotic desire she feels for Julio.[21] Like Lavinia in Firenzuola's short story, Angela, too, sees no *impossibility* in her search for pleasure with a woman, even if ultimately the pleasure she really longs for is with a young man. Once in her servant-girl's room, Angela approaches Nena, who is lying on her bed, embraces her, and asks her to make love to her. While Nena tries at first to push her away, Angela nevertheless presses ahead and Nena accepts her mistress's amorous advances.[22]

In this scene Nena even expresses a certain playful competitiveness with Angela's desire for the young man. Consider the following passage, in which she asks her mistress what she would do if she actually had Julio in bed:

ANGELA: Butarghe cusì le braze al collo, zicar quelle lavrine, e tegnirlo streto, streto.
NENA: E po,' no altro?
ANGELA: La lenguina in boca.
NENA: *Meio lo saverae far mi, che esso.* (1.3.41. *290–91;* emphasis mine)
ANGELA: I want to take him in my arms like this (*lying down with Nena and taking her in her arms*) and taste his lips and hold him tight, very tight.
NENA: And then? That's it?
ANGELA: Then the tongue in the mouth.
NENA: *I could do it better than he could.*

Nena's "better" is as a woman with another woman. And while it is true that Angela asked Nena to impersonate Julio, saying to her "Biastema el corpo de Cristo, menzona le parolle sporche: co' fa i omeni" (swear on the body of Christ, say dirty words like men do; 1.3.43, *292*), it is also evident that Angela, before "playing" with Julio's body—as the prologue suggested—had decided to play with Nena's first.[23] The comedy leaves no doubt of that:

NENA: Sté indrio, ché me sofoghé!
ANGELA: Caro, dolçe pì che no xè el zùcaro!
NENA: Vu no v'arecordé che sun donna.
ANGELA: Sun morta, mi. Sudo in aqua, tuta.
NENA: Gran merçé! perché vu fe matiere. (1.3.41, *291*)

NENA: Enough, you're suffocating me!
ANGELA: Dear boy, sweet, sweeter than sugar!
NENA: You're forgetting that I am a woman.
ANGELA: I'm about to faint away. I'm all hot and bothered!
NENA: What do you expect, with all the crazy things you're doing?

In sum, Angela reverses the figure of impossibility by showing that sex between women is possible, that it is a source of pleasure, and that there is no need for the topical lament of the heroine in love with another woman with no hope of satisfaction. Angela openly displays clear signs of desire for another woman, and this is not merely suggested but rather clearly identified by "performative" remarks such as "gèttame cussì le to braze" (take me in your arms like this; 1.3. 41, *291*), made by Angela to Nena, and others such as "Voleu cussì?" (like this?) in response to Angela's desire to be taken into the arms of her own servant.[24]

In this scene sexual practice between women is not only openly portrayed, it is also dissociated from the traditional vision of women as sexually passive. Angela is the initiator of sexual play—without a man—in the name of erotic pleasure. But that play is perhaps dangerous, and together with the other scenes of active feminine desire in the comedy it may have been dangerous enough to be kept secret. The anonymous author added a claim at the end of the comedy that is revealing: "This is not a fable or a comedy but a true story" followed by a warning in Latin to the reader—"read, learn and keep silent" (*V, Finis*, 123, *321*). What should the reader have learned and kept secret? Perhaps that the practice of adultery, which is extensively developed with the other woman lover in the play, Valeria, and the erotic practices between women that are openly displayed, were a "true story" in the sense that they involved people who actually lived and whose names thus had to remain hidden.[25] It is suggestive to think that this warning was followed, for the comedy remained silent, lost until the manuscript was discovered in 1928.[26] One wonders if there were other works that were as transgressive that still remain silent, lost, destroyed, or unread because they fell outside of what could be presented. Certainly they were unlikely to become a part of any canon of comedies selected by male critics who preferred passive women and happy marital endings.

Outside of Venice, the other important center for the elaboration of themes in comedy with a strong interest for women was the city of Siena.[27] The later comedy *Alessandro* (1544) written by the Sienese intellectual Alessandro Piccolomini (1508–79), one of the members of the Accademia degli Intronati, is another "foundational" text for the emergence of the "woman with woman" theme.[28] This comedy once again deals with the trope of impossible love and resolves it with the more typical solution of the final revelation of the true sex of characters who turn out in the end to be of the opposite sex. Perhaps following Firenzuola's novella discussed earlier, however, this comedy went a step beyond the Ovidian tradition of magical transformation or the switching of twins of the opposite sex that Ariosto used, offering a happy ending that provides pleasure and closure.

Alessandro is a comedy in which the cross-dressed male and female characters play a key role. Lucrezia, a young woman, has lived disguised as a young man, Fortunio, who has been working as a servant for various people since her kidnapping by pirates as a child, a kidnapping that had separated her from her betrothed, Aloisio. In the first scene where Lucrezia/Fortunio appears, following the trope of impossibility, she immediately complains to the audience about how badly fate has treated her; for as if all the hardships she has suffered were not enough, she now has fallen in love with another woman, Lampridia:

Oh, che vita infelice è la mia! Io son pur lo scherzo e 'l giuoco di te, Fortuna; gli altri, se ardon per amore, almen godan di quella fiamma sperando che, vinta la crudeltà de l'amante loro, ogni cosa ritorni in gioia; ma io amo con tutto 'l cuore e, se ben io vincesse con la mia servitù la durezza di Lampridia, ch'avrei fatto? Io son donna com'è lei, e rimarrebbe ingannata del caso mio. (2.1.2-10)[29]

Oh, my life is so unhappy! I am both your joke and your plaything, Fortune. The others who burn with love at least can enjoy in that fire the hope that once they have overcome the cruelty of their lovers, all their travails will be repaid with joy. But I love with all my heart and even if I overcome with my servitude the hardness of Lampridia, what will I have won? I am a woman as is she, and she will be unhappily tricked by me.

What Lucrezia/Fortunio does not know is that perhaps thanks to Fortuna, her fiancé Aloisio is actually hiding beneath the female attire of

Lampridia. Fleeing with his father who has been banished from their city, Aloisio disguises himself as a woman to escape the negative consequences of being the son of a banished father. Not knowing this, Lucrezia is forced to face the "joke" which Fortuna has played on her (in making her fall in love with another woman), as well as the fear that even if she wins her love, she will not be able to satisfy her.

Desperate to succeed in love, Lucrezia as Fortunio asks for the help of the servant Niccoletta who, unaware of her real identity and assuming her to be a male, advises him to try to go beyond the letters and messengers he has sent, which have not produced results, and get on with it by "using his hands." Niccoletta promises to get him into Lampridia's room at an opportune moment. The ensuing monologue by Lucrezia/Fortunio is very revealing:

Or che farai, misera Lucrezia? . . . S'io l'accetto, e ch'io vada da Lampridia, *e che le persuada a far quanto ch'io voglio,* e ch'ella conosca puoi ch'io son femina, non sarà uno scorgimento? Oltra che, scopertami poi per femina e saputosi per Pisa, mi sarà cagion di maggior pericolo. *Da l'altra parte, io arei pur un gran contento di trovarmi seco e baciar il volto e 'l petto di sì bella donna. Io già non son la prima donna ch'amasse donna;* ella m'arà per iscusata e, per mio bene, s'io ne la prego, terrà segreta la cosa, *in modo che da'l far questo non me ne può venir se non piacere.* Andarò, dunque, e l'assalirò mentre che dormirà, e me scoprirò. . . . Me n'andarò a casa e, dopo desinare, mi metterò arditissima a questa impresa. (2.1. 171–86; emphasis mine)

Now what will you do poor Lucrezia? . . . If I accept it and I go to Lampridria *and persuade her to do what I want,* and then she finds out that I am also a woman, won't it be disconcerting? And then after I have revealed myself to be a woman and it is known all over Pisa, it will be the cause of greater danger. *Still I would have a great pleasure to find myself with her and to kiss the face and the breast of such a beautiful woman. I am not the first woman ever who has loved a woman.* She will forgive me, for my sake, if I beg her to keep it secret *in that way doing it can't give me anything but pleasure.* I'll go then and coming upon her when she is asleep reveal myself. . . . I'll go home and after dinner I'll take on with the greatest zeal this challenge.

Although Lucrezia/Fortunio is aware of the danger she would court if ever her true identity is discovered, she quickly overcomes her doubts and decides to take the initiative in declaring her amorous passion for Lampridia in order to have the pleasure promised by the encounter with the "beautiful woman." It is not clear whether the risk she fears is simply being discovered as a woman who has passed as a man for so long or of being accused of sodomy with another woman.[30] In contrast with Firenzuola's novella, here it is a cross-dressed woman who loves another woman and takes the initiative; thus, she faces an additional danger as the perpetrator of the deed. As in that tale, however, what really matters to her is the *pleasure* promised by the erotic encounter with another woman whom she loves. Lucrezia even emphasizes the carnality of her attraction, noting that she wants to kiss her beloved's face and breast. Clearly she sees this as a physical and sexual attraction, not as simple friendship.

In a soliloquy, Lucrezia takes comfort in the thought that she is not the first woman to love another one. Where did this conviction come from? Did it originate in other literary examples, like *Orlando furioso,* where Fiordispina continues to love Bradamante despite her discovery that she is a woman?[31] Or did it reflect daily life and the sexual play between young women that *La Veniexiana* seems to evoke? Or did it come from the reading of tales like those written by Firenzuola, whom Piccolomini knew well as a friend and collaborator? If, in the *Anconitana,* Ruzante finds it extraordinary that a woman would cross the sea in pursuit of another woman, in *Alessandro,* as in *La Veniexiana,* things progress one step further: erotic attraction between women is considered possible, practical, and relatively unproblematic as long as it is kept secret.[32]

The comedy *Alessandro* is an important example because it dwells long enough on the idea of "woman with woman" in a way that suggests that readers or spectators would have found the scripting of such love attractive, credible, and relatively unproblematic. The topos of impossibility does reappear briefly in the second act, but it seems almost like a "required" rhetorical device (or as an *escamotage* to complicate the plot and provoke pity for the heroine). There, Lucrezia presents herself again as the desperate heroine who wonders how she can satisfy her lover and retain her honor if she is discovered to be a woman:

. . . E s'ella, fatta pietosa de miei dolori, *si lasciarà al fin vincer come molte fanno, che farò io per far cosa che le sodisfaccia?* O ella conoscerà ch'io son femina o no; se lo conoscerà, si pigliarà per iscorno tutto l'amore e tutte le dimostrazioni che io ho fatte verso di lei, e si accenderà di voglia di vendicarsi; s'ella non lo conoscerà, oh che risa, oh che beffe si farà di me, *che a guisa d'un cuculo tenghi l'ale basse poco manco ch'un uom di pasta!* Può esser maggior scorno a un giovine innamorato che condursi solo con la donna sua e mancargli su 'l buono? Oh, che strania fortuna è la mia! *non veggio modo da riuscir da questa impresa con onore.* Ma faccia Iddio. Io pur l'abbracciarò e baciarò mille volte e, chi sa, forse che Amore non abandona chi 'l serve con fede? (3. 2. 58-72; emphasis mine)

. . . And if she took pity on my pain *and let herself be conquered as many do, what would I do to satisfy her?* Either she would know that I am a woman or she would not; if she did she would take for scorn all the love and all the expressions [of it] that I have made to her and what vengeance she would take; if she did not realize it, oh what laughs and cruel jokes she would make at my expense *because like a cuckoo bird I kept my wings furled* [with her] *little better than a man of putty!* . . . Oh how cruel is my fortune! *I don't see any way to escape from this trial with honor.* Whatever happens happens. But still I will embrace her and kiss her a thousand times and who knows maybe Love will not abandon someone who serves him so faithfully?

Upon close reading, Lucrezia's concern looks more and more like the literary trope of impossibility revisited, at the same time as it is a tribute to Ludovico Ariosto. The central part of her monologue is, in fact, very similar to the considerations that the narrator of *Orlando furioso* attributes to Bradamante to justify the decision to reveal to Fiordispina that "he," too, is a woman.[33] The most important new element in Lucrezia's monologue with respect to the scripting of "woman with woman," however, is that she considers for a moment the idea that sexual satisfaction might be possible for them both, hoping that Love might take pity on her and miraculously make her a man for an hour. But tellingly this is a wish in which she places little hope. Her main hope is that her love, her desire, and her kisses will win over her love when they are together and bring them both the pleasure that she desires.

Alessandro is one of the comedies of the period that gives the greatest voice to female desire; in a cultural atmosphere that was anxious to ignore the topic, this text seems to desire to believe in representing the possibility and the appeal of eroticism between women. Even if one must not forget that the audience knew in advance that Lampridia is actually a man[34]—and this awareness certainly softened the audacity and transgressive nature of Lucrezia/Fortunio's monologue—the discussion nevertheless emphasizes a female sexuality dissociated from a reproductive discourse and from a connection to the institution of matrimony or the theme of honor in a traditional sense; it substitutes a discourse of desire and pleasure between women. Moreover it is interesting to note that Lucrezia wishes to succeed in giving her love pleasure with "honor," thus giving this crucial term a completely different meaning. Rather than referring to the chastity and modesty of a woman, in this text "honor" refers to her sexual prowess and ability to give pleasure to the woman she loves; performance, not passivity, is the key.

In the course of the plot, the miraculous sex transformation that Lucrezia/Fortunio wishes for herself ("make me for an hour a man") becomes Aloisio/Lampridia's fate instead, and not just for an hour. In the servant Niccoletta's account, Fortunio (i.e., Lucrezia) returns from the encounter with Lampridia with the marvelous news of the discovery of the male anatomy under her beloved's skirts:

Or, di lì a poco il giovinetto [Fortunio/Lucrezia] tornò a me e mi disse come, mentre che la [Lampidria/Aloisio] dormiva, l'aveva pian piano tramenata e baciata mille volte senza destarla, e, volendole metter le mane giù a la . . . tu m'intendi, *vi trovò una cosa la più grossa che tu vedesse mai; ond'egli, stupito, non ritrovandola femina come si pensava, senza destarla tornò a me, lamentandosi ch'io l'avevo ingannato; e, raccontandomi il caso, mi fe' maravigliare.* . . . (4.5, 394-402; emphasis mine)

Then a little while later the youth [Fortunio/Lucrezia] returned to me and said that while she [Lampridia/Aloisio] slept, he had very quietly touched her and kissed her a thousand times and wishing to put his hand down there . . . you understand where, *he found a thing larger than you could imagine and thus was stunned not finding her a woman as he imagined. And immediately he returned to me complaining that I had tricked him. As when he told me this, it seemed a marvel.* . . .

Much as had been the case for the protagonist of Firenzuola's short story, for the disguised Lucrezia the discovery of her beloved's male sex does not immediately make her happy, solve her problems, or even reconstitute the traditional sexual order. Instead Lucrezia as Fortunio complains to her servant about *having been deceived* and wants an explanation. She had anticipated a sexual encounter with another woman whom she loves and desires and returned to Niccoletta protesting when that turns out not to be the case.

As Niccoletta later explains to a servant friend, she responded to Fortunio (i.e., Lucrezia) with an obvious question: "però che, che voleva far d'un maschio?" (4.5. 405-7; "what did he want to do with a man?"). The response of Fortunio/Lucrezia was even more problematic in Niccoletta's eyes; she reports that he suddenly became "più focoso e più inamorato che prima" (407-8; more ardent and in love than before) and decided to return to Lampridia's room, apparently contradicting his earlier complaints about having been deceived. Lucrezia desires Lampridia as a woman, and when she realizes that her beloved is actually a man and overcomes the shock of the revelation, she decides that she can love the supposed Lampridia (i.e., the cross-dressed Aloisio) as a man as well. The meeting seems largely driven by the need to have closure and to reestablish a normalizing sex/ gender system, with women and men physically and culturally correctly identified, clearing the way for the recognition scene between the two long-separated lovers and the happy closure of the comedy.

But it also turned on the contemporary assumption, found in a number of other comedies, that love and desire did not necessarily have one fixed object in members of the opposite sex; Lucrezia's desire is never solely for a woman or for women. There might be technical difficulties in women loving women, given the phallocentric vision of the time, but the desire itself is wholly "natural" even if it occurs often silently and out of sight. The opportune transformation of Lampridia into a man, then, begins to restore the "correct" order that the erotic attraction between the two supposed women had threatened to overturn. Marriage, family interests, and reproduction safely return to the prominence they commanded in the Renaissance social order, and youthful love, pleasure, and play fall back to their required secondary positions, even though we might wonder if spectators and readers of the comedy would have so easily forgotten Lucrezia's heroic desire and search for pleasure with another woman.

Historically, a woman's decision to love another woman (in *La Veniexiana,* for example) was not necessarily more transgressive than the decision to love a man who had not been selected by her family for marriage. Comedies like *Alessandro, La Veniexiana,* and others suggest that erotic practices between women were guided more by the search for pleasure, in that they seemed to support a counter-discourse that privileged love, desire, and pleasure.[35] Moreover, in sixteenth-century texts where the scripting of such pleasures occurred, there is no mention of the dangerously evil and lustful woman who is close to the devil because of her unrestrained passion and desire (a common figure, for instance, in the medieval tradition). In fact, women who love women are not even portrayed as foolish for such desires. They are seen invariably in a positive light and often as heroic in their desire.

Focusing on *Alessandro,* there is too much space dedicated to the theme of "woman with woman" in the comedy to believe that the author considered it unimportant, impossible, or unattractive to an audience.

The prologue of the comedy, in fact, directly addresses the "women of Siena," as is often the case with Piccolomini's works and the works of the Intronati.[36] But there are more concrete reasons to suggest that Piccolomini was sympathetic to the theme of "woman with woman," particularly his publicly stated interest in collaborating with the women of Siena and with Laudomia Forteguerri (1515–53?) in particular. In 1540, a few years before *Alessandro* was written, Piccolomini held a lesson at the Accademia degli Infiammati in Padua, which focused on the analysis of a sonnet Laudomia addressed to Margaret of Austria (Duchess of Parma and Piacenza, 1522–86).[37] The names of these two illustrious women had already appeared as a sublime example—thus apparently well known at least in humanist and upper-class society—of female love in Firenzuola's *Dialogo delle bellezze delle donne*. In the preface to the printed version of his lesson, Piccolomini explains how the two women met two times when the daughter of the emperor Charles V passed through Siena on her way to Florence to marry Duke Alessandro dei Medici.[38] As Konrad Eisenbichler has pointed out in his important study of this relationship, the phraseology that Piccolomini uses to describe the love between the two women might seem to be mere empty imitations of typical Petrarchan *topoi* of love, "but they are not so when applied to the affections felt by two flesh-and-blood contemporary women for each other."[39] In the preface to his lesson, Piccolomini typifies the love shared by the two women as a lofty and noble sentiment in the context of well-known Renaissance/neo-Platonic theories.[40] In his lesson as well as in *Alessandro*, Piccolomini presents the love between two women as possible and positive, as erotic in his comedy and as sublime in his lecture, attributing it to invented characters, on the one hand, and to real and well-known people, on the other.

The scripting of "woman loving woman" found in *Alessandro* would be taken up again a few years later in a comedy of great interest, Curtio Gonzaga's *Gli inganni*, which was published in Venice in 1592, but apparently written around midcentury. The title of the comedy clearly places it in the "family" of plays influenced heavily by *Gl'ingannati* by the Intronati, while its plot and themes show strong similarities with *Alessandro*. *Gli inganni* seems to be the only comedy written by Gonzaga and was staged in 1554 in Mantua for the wedding of Isabella Gonzaga and Don Ferrante Davalo, Marchese of Pescara.[41]

Gonzaga's comedy uses many of the *topoi* of sixteenth-century *commedia erudita*. Long before the opening action of the comedy, two soon-to-be fathers, Giulio and his friend Lorenzo, make a bet: if one of their wives gives birth to a girl and the other to a boy, the father of the boy would have to pay 2,000 florins to the father of the girl as a dowry.[42] Lorenzo's wife has a son, and Giulio's wife has twins, a boy and a girl. Giulio, perhaps figuring that he had only half lost the bet anyway, disguises the male child as a girl and gives the female child away to a relative to be raised, thus winning the 2,000 florins.[43] When the comedy's action begins, Giulio's male son Scipione had grown up with everyone believing that he was a girl named Lucretia.[44] His father in the meantime had gone off on a trip and not returned, which meant that as Lucretia, Scipione lived on alone with his mother, Cencia.

At this point a youth, Cesare, begins to visit their house, having been sent there originally by Cencia's brother on an errand. To keep things complicated this Cesare is actually a woman named Ginevra, who had been disguised by her father as a male when he was exiled from Siena years earlier. Cencia begins to worry about the intentions behind the frequent visits of the youth who spends so much time with Lucretia and thus decides to tell her brother the truth about Lucretia. Her brother in turn reveals that Cesare is actually a "well-mannered" woman. None of the other characters, however, know the truth about the cross-dressed pair, including the youths themselves. Thus the maid, Filippa, aggressively urges Cesare to do something with Lucretia, who she believes to be in love with him. Cesare attempts to stall by telling her that he has to be careful and mindful of a noblewoman's honor, as he is a foreigner and does not want to risk being kicked out of the city and thus never able to see Lucretia again.

This conversation between Filippa and Cesare is very revealing of Renaissance understandings of the perceived differences, both physical and cultural, between men and women. Filippa laments to Cesare that he is like one of those "giovanetti, a' quali sa ancora la pelle di piscio!" (1.4. c.18v; whose skin still smells of piss!), a not very elegant way of saying that he is still green and inexperienced. And she continues to claim that while he wants to seem like a man, he is so young that he is, in truth, much closer to being a girl. Of course she is not claiming that he is a girl, just that he is at that age when male youths are still passive, delicate, and virtually interchangeable with girls.[45] That is confirmed, she notes, by Cesare's behavior, which is not what it would have been if he were an older, more mature male—that is, active and aggressive. She even suggests that, given his age, he is not really in love with Lucretia at all and is probably looking for "something else harder," in other words, a male lover of his own (1.4. c. 19r). Despite all of these factors, she does believe him to be male, just too young to actually function as an adult male would; she thus characterizes him as a youth with "arms that do not penetrate." In the face of this, Cesare, who is trying his best to keep his female identity hidden, responds that he really is in love with Lucretia and agrees to a rendezvous with her.

It may seem that Cesare accepts Filippa's proposal to go to Lucretia in order to hide his/her true sex, but the ensuing monologue by "the female Cesare," as the character is labeled in the text, reveals that there are other reasons behind this decision. Cesare, like Santilla in *Calandra* and Lucrezia in *Alessandro,* appears alone onstage and inveighs once again against the cruelty of Fortune:

O infelice Ginevra, doveva pur contentarsi la Fortuna d'averti cacciata di casa tua, con la perdita della madre, dei parenti, et di tanti beni, et con la grave, et aspra ruina di tuo padre, il quale per troppa gelosia, che tu non fossi ammazzata, ti fece vestir da huomo, *senza indurti anco ad amare ardentemente una femina com'è questa Lucretia,* . . . Che farò io adunque? farò buon animo, et vi andrò, *sperando che la bontà della mia Lucretia risguarderà più tosto al grand'amore, ch'io le porto, che all'impossibilità mia,* et mi averà compassione. *Non son io la prima che amasse femina: ne sono piene le istorie antiche, et moderne, la ricordanza delle quali è stata ésca a questo focile, che mi consuma.* Ben è vero che niun Padre doverebbe imparar lettere alle figliuole, alle quali dee bastar di sapere adoprar l'ago, e 'l fuso *senza cercar quello che pare la natura con ogni poter suo ci vieti;* ma la colpa è della nostra usanza di Siena, la quale ha poco men donne, che huomini, studiose, et di mirabile ingegno. (1. 5. c. 21r-v; emphasis mine)

O, unhappy Ginevra, Fortune should have been content with having thrown you out of your house, with the loss of your mother, relatives, and so much wealth, and with the cruel ruining of your father who so very fearful that you might be killed made you dress as a man, and now Fortune *even forces you to ardently love a woman like this Lucretia.* . . . What can I do now? Be of good spirit and go to her hoping that *the kindness of my Lucretia will focus her attention more on the great love that I have for her, than on my impossibility* [to satisfy her] and that she will have pity on me. *I am not the first person who loved a woman. Histories, ancient and modern, are full of accounts which have reinforced this fire that consumes me.* Certainly it is true that no father should have his daughters study literature. For them it is enough to learn the needle and the spindle *rather than to search for what it seems Nature with all her power has tried to deny them.* But the problem is with our customs here in Siena where there are hardly fewer women than men who study and show great learning.

The first part of this monologue seems to recycle all the tropes of the impossibility of love between women. Moreover, Cesare/Ginevra blames her masculine dress and a cruel fortune for her love of Lucretia. Her unhappiness in the face of these facts is compounded by her fear that her beloved will feel that she has been tricked when she discovers that Cesare is not a man. Nonetheless, like Fortunio/Lucrezia in *Alessandro,* she decides to meet with her love hoping for compassion from her. Once again Cesare/Ginevra points out that she is not the first woman to love another. But in a striking departure from earlier comedies, she adds an explanation and a justification for her love. She has read "histories, ancient and modern" that speak of love between women, and the memory of those accounts has inflamed her love for Lucretia. This venting of emotions by Cesare/Ginevra, typical of many suffering Renaissance heroines, continues with the claim that it would be better if fathers did not teach their daughters to read because then they would not be tempted to go in search of things that were forbidden by Nature. This misogynist claim that women should not study, however, is immediately balanced by Cesare/Ginevra's recognition that in Siena it is "our custom" to have educated daughters of "great learning."

The reference to Siena and the education of daughters there would not have been surprising to the audience of the comedy. The city was noted for this, and it was also a well-publicized program of the Intronati and intellectual leaders such as Alessandro Piccolomini. Moreover, through its echoes in title, dialogue, and plot, this comedy reveals its debts to *Gl'ingannati* by the Intronati and Piccolomini's comedy *Alessandro.* With these connections to Siena in mind, and the Intronati's program of making literature available to women, it is difficult to take literally Cesare/Ginevra's appeal to Sienese fathers to stop this local "custom," thereby limiting their daughters to the stereotypic "needle and spindle." Rather, in this context, her lament seems to be an ironic reference to a practice in Siena that made Sienese women—and Cesare/Ginevra herself—women of "great learning" and better than other women.

When Cesare/Ginevra explains that her memories of "histories, ancient and modern" have inflamed her love for Lucretia, she is probably referring to Ovid and Sappho for ancient literature. The reference to modern history, on the other hand, is less clear and leads to some interesting speculations that reinforce the interpretation that Cesare/Ginevra's apparent attack on learned Sienese women is an ironic one that actually allows the author to compliment Sienese women on their learning. It may well be an homage by the author Curtio Gonzaga to his friend the poet Maddalena Campiglia (1553–95), perhaps added to the comedy when it was printed. Campiglia, significantly, was noted for her poems that explored the theme of women loving women. The comedy was published for the first time in 1592, and, tellingly, it was accompanied by a letter of dedication written by Maddalena Campiglia to her patron, "The Most Excellent Noble Lady Marfisa da Este e Cibo." In that letter the poet speaks about the comedy and notes that its author, Gonzaga, "gave it to me explicitly and publicly as a gift."[46] The letter also suggests that Maddalena Campiglia and Curtio Gonzaga had a strong connection: the poet had been given the text and had it in her possession in the nineties. Thus she was the person who finally had it printed, and she dedicated it to one of her aristocratic woman patrons.

Maddalena Campiglia was one of the few female poetic voices that explored the theme of "women loving women" in the cinquecento. Both her *Flori* and *Calisa* portray chaste love between women. In the pastoral drama *Flori,* the nymph Flori loves Amaranta, while in the eclogue *Calisa,* Maddalena Campiglia again portrays herself as the nymph Flori "to express her devotion to Pallavicino Lupi" (i.e., Isabella Pallavicino Lupi, 1550–1623, another of her aristocratic woman patrons).[47] It seems highly likely that both *Flori* and *Calisa* (published in 1588 and 1589) were read and admired by Gonzaga, as they were dedicated to him. While *Flori* and *Calisa*—texts of pastoral poetry—explore the discourse of chaste love between women, Gonzaga's comedy published by Campiglia went a step beyond: it portrays love between women that included erotic attraction. This close relationship, in many ways, leaves little room for doubt about the irony of Cesare/Ginevra's lament about the dangers of women reading.

Looking more closely at Cesare/Ginevra's use of ancient and modern books to justify her attraction to another woman, it is noteworthy that she places this explanation in a broader context of the opposition between nature and culture, and we might add, from a modern perspective, between sex and gender. If, as Cesare/Ginevra suggests in his/her monologue, nature prohibits love between women, culture (or at least the various readings to which Ginevra refers) not only suggests that it is *possible,* but actually inspires it. Even if it is dangerous to attribute any modern significance to these words, it is tempting to see how Cesare/Ginevra transfers the idea of sexual attraction from the domain of nature to that of culture. Thus even if Nature tried, in every way possible, to make love between women impossible, such love could still be *learned* in books or by examples from ancient and modern history. Could the cross-dressed Ginevra be an early heroine that shows us, with much anticipation, the emergence of a constructed "lesbian" identity? This is an unlikely, but attractive, idea that might again suggest Ginevra's (and the playwright's) positive vision of the accomplishments of the women of Siena.

The opposition between nature and culture, which seems so obvious from a modern critical perspective, cannot be so easily applied to the premodern period.[48] The nature to which Cesare/Ginevra refers did not have the more limited sense that we give it today or that even Galileo Galilei gave it in the next century, as historians of science such as Katharine Park and Lorraine Daston have cogently pointed out.[49] In the usage of the cinquecento, "nature" was a polyvalent term that referred to all that was inherent in the order of things and thus included customs, traditions, and moralistic structures, as well as (significantly) those social strictures that constrained women to specific roles and behaviors that were "naturally" theirs.[50] So that what "nature" forbade did not necessarily refer to a fundamental inner identity in a modern sense, but to those things that Renaissance society saw as part of the much broader natural order of things. And even though that broader "natural" order of society and things prohibited love and sex between women, literature nonetheless reveals it as a concrete *possibility*. Given the many ways in which cinquecento culture and society tried to limit every discourse on love and pleasure between women, the evidence furnished by this comedy and by the plays analyzed earlier is of great importance for demonstrating that things were never so simple or neat.

That these comedies were published in the second half of the sixteenth century is yet another indication that the idea of love between women was emerging from the shadows that Firenzuola, Piccolomini, and others had already begun to disperse in the first half of the century. Across the century this "loss of invisibility" of the theme of "woman with woman" was progressively realized, a fact reinforced by a growing attention to it in artistic representations as well.[51] This article has shown that with the help of comedies modern scholars, much like the character Cesare/ Ginevra in *Gli inganni,* can *learn* about the existence of love and erotic desire between women in the Renaissance, even if it means reading beyond a canon that largely ignored works that discussed such themes.

The comedies examined here offer a fresh and rich perspective on the sixteenth-century perception of female sexuality and homoeroticism. In general, they provide revealing depictions of love and sexual desire between women independent from men and patriarchal imperatives. Given that many intellectuals of the period—moralists, philosophers, and doctors in general—did not refer to women as human beings endowed with sexual desires distinct from those of men, the first "novelty" that these comedies reveal is that women could be seen as more than mere sexual objects of men whose sexual identities were based on conformity to male concepts of honor and chastity. A second point, which is closely linked to the former, is that these comedies and the other texts analyzed here reveal a clear concept of an active female sexuality directed toward the search for pleasure; this contrasts with the traditional view of the time that saw women as passive recipients of male sexual advances and desire and thus made female desires for other females virtually invisible and impossible. And, in turn, this vision of active women seeking their pleasure and expressing their desires for other women challenged the phallocentric logic that maintained that women lacked what was necessary to function sexually, as well as that they adhered to the basic passive/active dichotomy of sex and gender division of the day.

The literary topos of the impossibility of female with female sexuality is one that comedies cited regularly and that their female protagonists just as regularly take on and overcome. Love between women was presented as possible and, significantly, not as transgressive as either adultery or a woman's attempt to marry a man that her family had not chosen for her. Rather, it was regularly presented as a positive, even heroic motive for noble deeds. Moreover, the fact that a number of these comedies accepted without hesitation that sexual pleasure was possible with a man or a woman suggests that sexual relationships were perceived as a continuum that swung from passive and female-like reception (but not limited to women) to active and masculine-like action (but not limited to men),[52] rather than a simple binary division of sexual practices between heterosexuals on the one hand and lesbians and homosexuals on the other. Women in comedies could be active and aggressive in their desire and lovemaking, and men could be passive and receptive. While such behavior, if it was too pronounced or not correctly motivated by love, could be looked upon negatively, comedies that feature young women loving or desiring other women usually treat it positively and even at times with a sense of the heroic adventure that one finds in the chivalric literature of the day. The comedies discussed here reveal that well. They show a not unsurprising awareness of the standard discourse on love and sex that featured marriage, family, reproduction, and chaste and passive women, but they also positively portray a very different vision of love between women aimed at pleasure and not marriage, where women were active, not chaste, and attractive heroines nonetheless.[53] As a result, what begins to emerge from the Renaissance trope of invisibility and impossibility is a rich and complex world of love, pleasure, and heroines seeking to find happiness and fulfillment, at least for a moment, as women in love with other women.

Notes

The quotation in the title is from *Comedia del Contile chiamata la Cesarea Gonzaga* (Milan: Francesco Marchesino, 1550), 3.4 c. 25r. For an analysis of *Cesarea Gonzaga* see chapter two of my *Lelia's Kiss: Imagining Gender, Sex, and Marriage in Italian Renaissance Comedy* (Toronto: University of Toronto Press, 2009). All translations in this article are mine unless otherwise noted. For quotation from the comedies the act, scene, and page number (for *Alessandro,* line numbers are given in lieu of page numbers) of the edition cited appear in the text itself in parentheses following the quote; e.g., (1.4. 23). For *Calandra, Veniexiana,* and *Ingannati* translations are drawn from the volume I co-translated with Guido Ruggiero, *Five Comedies from the Italian Renaissance* (Baltimore: Johns Hopkins University Press, 2003). After the act, scene, and page reference to the Italian edition, I have added the page number of the English translation, cited in italics; e.g., (3. 2. 55, *178*). This essay is a shortened version of the second chapter of *Lelia's Kiss.* Finally, I would like to thank Albert Ascoli and William West for their generous help with the revisions of this article.

1. *Gl'inganni. Commedia del Signor Nicolò Secchi. Recitata in Milano l'anno 1547 dinanzi alla Maestà del Re Filippo* (Florence: I Giunti, 1568). *Gl'inganni* by Secchi is a comedy partially derived from *Gl'ingannati* by the Accademia degli Intronati (performed in January 1532). See Louise George Clubb and Robert Black, *Romance and Aretine Humanism in Sienese Comedy, 1516: Pollastra's Parthenio at the Studio di Siena* (Siena: La Nuova Italia, 1993), 170, and Robert C. Melzi, "From Lelia to Viola," *Renaissance Drama,* o.s., 9 (1966): 67–81.

2. On female figures of wonder in sixteenth-century comedy see the chapter "Woman as Wonder," in Louise George Clubb, *Italian Drama in Shakespeare's Time* (New Haven and London: Yale University Press, 1989), 65–89. On ideas of the marvelous see Lorraine Daston and Katharine Park, *Wonders and the Orders of Nature: 1150–1750* (New York: Zone Books, 1998); *Wonders, Marvels, and Monsters in Early Modern Culture,* ed. Peter G. Platt (Newark: University of Delaware Press, 1999); Douglas Biow, *Mirabile Dictu: Representations of the Marvelous in Medieval and Renaissance Epic* (Ann Arbor: University of Michigan Press, 1996).

3. See also the earlier work by Terry Castle, *The Apparitional Lesbian: Female Homosexuality and Modern Culture* (New York: Columbia University Press, 1993).

4. Valerie Traub, *The Renaissance of Lesbianism in Early Modern England* (Cambridge: Cambridge University Press, 2002), 5.

5. Ibid., 6.

6. See introduction to *Same-Sex Love and Desire Among Women in the Middle Ages,* ed. Francesca Canadé Sautman and Pamela Sheingorn (New York: Palgrave, 2000), 1-47; Jacqueline Murray, "Agnolo Firenzuola on Female Sexuality and Women's Equality," *The Sixteenth Century Journal* 22, no. 2 (1991): 199-213.

7. For the Italian influence on English literature see Ian Frederick Moulton, *Before Pornography: Erotic Writing in Early Modern England* (New York: Oxford University Press, 2000); Traub, *The Renaissance of Lesbianism;* and more recently, the essay by Rachel Poulsen, "Women Performing Homoerotic Desire in English and Italian Comedy: *La Calandria, Gli Ingannati* and *Twelfth Night,*" in *Women Players in England 1500-1660: Beyond the All-Male Stage,* ed. Pamela Allen Brown and Peter Parolin (Aldershot, UK: Ashgate, 2005), 171-91.

8. On Bradamante-Fiordispina see the chapter "Transvestite Love: Gender Troubles in the Fiordispina Story," in Valeria Finucci, *The Lady Vanishes: Subjectivity and Representation in Castiglione and Ariosto* (Stanford: Stanford University Press, 1992), 201-25; Mary-Michelle DeCoste, "Knots of Desire: Female Homoeroticism in *Orlando furioso,*" in *Queer Italia: Same-Sex Desire in Italian Literature and Film,* ed. Gary Cestaro, 55-69 (New York: Palgrave, 2004).

9. Ludovico Ariosto, *Orlando furioso,* ed. Lanfranco Caretti (Turin: Einaudi, 1992), 2: xxv, 37, 742-43.

10. Here it should be noted that even the "natural" is to a great extent a cultural construction in the Renaissance, as will be discussed later in this essay. In this, even the apparently clear distinction between sex as physical (i.e., "natural") difference between males and females and gender as the cultural constructs that surround those distinctions and give them meaning is actually less clear than claimed. For even physical distinctions (including medical and scientific distinctions) tend to have significant underlying cultural dimensions, often unrecognized but nonetheless significant. As a result, in this essay "sexual difference" refers to distinctions that are seen as physical and often turn on genital configurations, especially the penis, while "gender distinctions" refer to nonphysical characteristics more usually associated with behavior, but always with the realization that the two concepts are tightly interrelated because of their cultural dimension. See Londa Schiebinger, *Nature's Body: Gender and the Making of Modern Science* (Boston: Beacon Press, 1993), and Thomas Laqueur, *Making Sex: Body and Gender from the Greeks to Freud* (Cambridge, Mass.: Harvard University Press, 1990), as well as the debate the topic has generated.

11. Ovidius Naso, *Metamorphoses,* trans. Frank Justus Miller (London: Heinemann; New York: Putnam, 1916), 2: 50-61.

12. On twins in comedy see Giulio Ferroni, "Tecniche del raddoppiamento nella commedia del Cinquecento," in *Il testo e la scena: Saggi sul teatro del Cinquecento* (Rome: Bulzoni, 1980), 43-64; Angela Guidotti, *Specchiati sembianti: Il tema dei gemelli nella letteratura* (Milan: Franco Angeli, 1992); Bianca Concolino Mancini, "Travestimenti, inganni e scambi nella commedia del Cinquecento," in *Atti dell'Istituto Veneto di Scienze, Lettere ed Arti* 147 (1988-89): 199-228.

13. The referenced edition is *La Calandra commedia elegantissima per Messer Bernardo Dovizi da Bibbiena,* ed. Giorgio Padoan (Padua: Antenore, 1985).

14. See "I ragionamenti" in Agnolo Firenzuola, *Le novelle,* ed. Eugenio Ragni (Rome: Salerno Editrice, 1971), 1-199, and Agnolo Firenzuola, *Celso. Dialogo delle bellezze delle*

donne, in *Opere,* ed. Delmo Maestri (Turin: UTET, 1977), 713–89. The theme of love between women—as a means by which women might protect their chastity—is suggested in *I ragionamenti* by Fioretta, one of the characters of the group. The queen's response is negative, and she reveals an intensely bitter moralism. It is important to note nonetheless that the queen's discourse confirms an awareness of the existence of desire between women. The second story of the first day (*Le novelle,* 106–19) is very important as far as the discussion of love between women is concerned, for it displays dramatic elements that would be typical of many later Renaissance comedies; see Eugenio Ragni's Introduzione, especially xxviii–xxx. Firenzuola, who wrote the main body of the work in the 1520s, died without finishing it. Lodovico Dolce completed and published it in 1543.

15. Murray, "Agnolo Firenzuola on Female Sexuality," 209. Other "references" are found in Pietro Aretino, *Ragionamento Dialogo,* ed. Giorgio Bàrberi Squarotti (Milan: Rizzoli, 1988); Pietro Aretino, *Il piacevol ragionamento dell'Aretino: Dialogo di Maddalena e Giulia,* ed. Claudio Galderisi (Rome: Salerno, 1987); and in Pierre Brantôme [Pierre De Bourdeille], *Les Dames Galantes* (Paris: Garniere Frères, 1960; rpt. of 1566 ed.).

16. Clubb, "Theatergrams," in *Italian Drama in Shakespeare's Time,* 1–26.

17. Clubb and Black, *Romance and Aretine Humanism in Sienese Comedy,* 169–75 (173).

18. Writing in *The Renaissance of Lesbianism,* Traub expresses the belief that it is an error to consider cross-dressing comedies to be the principal source for studying erotic attraction between women, affirming among other things that "Despite the confusions wrought by a change of clothes, the status of a normalizing gender, mapped on to a normalizing eroticism, remains" (170). Denise Walen, on the other hand, bases her analysis in *Constructions of Female Homoeroticism in Early Modern Drama* (New York: Palgrave, 2005) primarily on English cross-dressing comedies.

19. Ruzante (Angelo Beolco), *Anconitana,* in *Ruzante Teatro,* ed. and trans. Ludovico Zorzi (Turin: Einaudi, 1967), 773–881.

20. All quotations are from the critical edition by Giorgio Padoan, *La Veniexiana* (Venice: Marsilio, 1994). The date of the comedy is much debated (1536 according to Padoan), and it was apparently never staged.

21. Angela: "Ti xé in letto, e mi nel fogo che me consuma." Nena: "Che diseu, de fuogo? Le mie carne brùsciano. Moro de doia" (Angela: "You're in the bed, and I'm in the fire, and it's burning me up!" Nena: "What? What fire?" Angela: "My flesh is burning up. The pain is killing me"). *La Veniexiana* (1.3 39, *290*).

22. *La Veniexiana* (1.3. 41, *291*).

23. ". . . And you will hear of her boldness and her determination to have him, and then the happy play and pleasure that she enjoyed with him." *La Veniexiana,* Prologus (25, *286*).

24. See 291n9 in *Five Comedies,* ed. Giannetti and Ruggiero.

25. Padoan suggested that Angela and Valeria were recognizable as women "belonging to the most important patrician families of Venice: Angela Valier was widow of the important politician Marco Barbarigo and Valieria Valier the wife of Giacomo Semitecolo, Avogador di Comun." *La Veniexiana,* Introduzione, 13.

26. The *Veniexiana* was found in the manuscript (dated around the first half of the sixteenth century) It. IX 288 (=6072) in the Marciana Library in Venice. The text was transcribed and published by Emilio Lovarini in 1928 (Bologna: Zanichelli, 1928).

27. On the Sienese contribution to Italian Renaissance drama, see Daniele Seragnoli, *Il teatro a Siena nel Cinquecento: "Progetto" e "modello" drammaturgico nell'Accademia degli Intronati* (Rome: Bulzoni, 1980); and Clubb and Black, *Romance and Aretine Humanism in Sienese Comedy.*

28. The comedy was composed around 1544. It was performed for the first time by the Intronati during Carnival of the same year and was a great success, as its numerous editions and various stagings attest. See Florindo Cerreta, *Alessandro Piccolomini: Letterato e filosofo senese del Cinquecento* (Siena: Accademia Senese degli Intronati, 1960), 52–56.

29. All quotations are from *L'Alessandro di Alessandro Piccolomini,* ed. Florindo Cerreta (Siena: Accademia Senese degli Intronati, 1966), 109–238.

30. In Renaissance Italy sexual activity between individuals of the same sex fell into the general catchall category of sodomy or unnatural sex—in other words sexual activity not aimed at reproduction or not conducted in a "natural" way.

31. After Fiordispina discovers Bradamante's identity, she does not change her mind about being attracted to the latter; see *Orlando furioso,* 2: xxv, 32,741.

32. Heterosexual adultery, with its risk of illegitimate children, could be seen as more problematic.

33. "And she was correct; it would have been absolutely base, the conduct of a man of straw, if he had continued to speak with a woman that he was with [who was] so beautiful and as sweet as nectar and yet still kept his wings folded like a cuckoo" (*Orlando furioso,* 2: xxv, 31, 740–41).

34. In the first half of the cinquecento in Italy it was customary that male actors played women's roles, and this fact was not contested by moralists and theater critics of the time. Male actors cross-dressing as women encountered a different reaction in the later English theater, however; they have been the object of numerous well-known studies on English Renaissance drama.

35. The enjoyment of pleasure may have included that of a male audience, which could have been attracted by representations of female–female sex (see for instance Pietro Aretino, *Ragionamento Dialogo*).

36. The comedy was quite popular at the time. The dedication of a sixteenth-century edition consulted states that it was performed during Carnival in Bologna "before all the nobility of the city to great applause." See the Dedica in *Comedia intitulata Alessandro del Signor Alessandro Piccolomini, Conominato il Stordito* (Venice: Bindoni, 1550), c. 2r-v.

37. Laudomia wrote five poems for Margaret, probably during the period 1535–40; Konrad Eisenbichler, "Laudomia Forteguerri Loves Margaret of Austria," in *Same Sex Love and Desire Among Women,* 277–304. See also Marie-Françoise Piéjus, "Les poétesses Siennoises entre le jeu et l'écriture," in *Les Femmes écrivains en Italie au Moyen Âge et à la Renaissance"* (Aix-en Provence: Publications de l'Université de Provence, 1994), 315–32, especially 319–22.

38. Quotations are from Eisenbichler's study, which reconstructs the encounter between the two women as well as the cultural context that made it possible: "Laudomia Forteguerri Loves Margaret of Austria," 282–83.

39. Ibid., 283.

40. Ibid., 284.

41. *Gli inganni. Comedia dell' Illustrissimo Signor Curtio Gonzaga* (Venice: Rampazetto, 1592). Curtio Gonzaga (1530–99), author of *Il Fidamante* (published 1582) and *Rime* (published 1585), belonged to a minor branch of the Gonzaga family. The comedy *Gli inganni* was probably written around midcentury. On Curtio Gonzaga see Oler Grandi, "Di Curzio Gonzaga e delle sue opere," in *Per Cesare Bozzetti: Studi di letteratura e filologia italiana,* ed. Simone Albonico, Andrea Comboni, Giorgio Panizza, and Claudio Vela, 535–46 (Milan: Mondadori, 1996). This *Gli inganni* is not to be confused with the comedy *Gl'inganni* by Nicolò Secchi (first performed in 1547). On *Gl'inganni* by Sechi see n. 1.

42. The cost of female dowries was often seen at the time as one of the most negative aspects of having a daughter. For this and a review of the extensive literature on the subject see Joanne Ferraro, *Marriage Wars in Late Renaissance Venice* (Oxford: Oxford University Press, 2001), especially chapter 6.

43. It might seem strange today that Giulio gives away his daughter to cross-dress his son to win a bet requiring a daughter, but this underlines the importance placed in the Renaissance on sons over daughters. Better to keep a son, even if he has to pretend to be a daughter, than to keep a real daughter.

44. On male characters disguised as women and on the construction of male gender identity see chapter 3, "Men in Women's Clothing: Male Cross-Dressing Plays and the Construction of Masculine Identity," in my forthcoming book *Lelia's Kiss.*

45. On this see again chapter 3 of *Lelia's Kiss;* the introduction to *Five Comedies* by Giannetti and Ruggiero; and Guido Ruggiero, *Machiavelli in Love: Sex, Self, and Society in the Italian Renaissance* (Baltimore: Johns Hopkins University Press, 2007).

46. Maddalena Campiglia, "All'Illustrissima et Eccellentissima Signora Donna Marfisa da Este e Cibo," in *Gli inganni. Comedia dell'Illustrissimo Signor Curtio Gonzaga,* c. 5v.

47. Maddalena Campiglia, *Flori a Pastoral Drama,* ed. Virginia Cox and Lisa Sampson, trans. Virginia Cox (Chicago: University of Chicago Press, 2004), 27.

48. *As You Like It,* however, makes a clear distinction from the outset between nature and culture. The complex relationship between nature and art (or nature and culture) was a central topic for early modern authors; see for instance in *Orlando furioso* the case of Alcina's garden, which is a clever culturally constructed example of "nature."

49. Lorraine Daston and Katharine Park, "The Hermaphrodite and the Orders of Nature: Sexual Ambiguity in Early Modern France," in *Premodern Sexualities,* ed. Louise Fradenburg and Carla Freccero (New York: Routledge, 1996), 117–36 (136).

50. As a result "nature" had a strong cultural dimension; thus, although it was presented as a given, much like the modern concept "gender," it was essentially a cultural construct.

51. Patricia Simons, "Lesbian (In)Visibility in Italian Renaissance Culture: Diana and Other Cases of *donna con donna,*" in "Gay and Lesbian Studies in Art History," special issue, *Journal of Homosexuality* 27 (1994): 81–122.

52. See note 10.

53. As Murray cogently expressed it, "Women were bound by the strictures of their society. Thus the recognition of female sexuality by an articulate masculine voice may suggest that by extension, there was a similar recognition by the inarticulate female" ("Agnolo Firenzuola on Female Sexuality," 211).

Performance as Profanation: Holy Tongue and Comic Stage in Tsahut bedihuta deqiddushin

YAIR LIPSHITZ

W ISDOM, AS SHE opens the prologue of the first Hebrew play known to us, declares

בראותי כי חכמי הגוים ללשונותם בארצותם, מדי יון כתים ודודנים, התפארו על אשר מצאו דרך ישר
לפניהם בתענוגות בני האדם לחבר מילין אשר יסופרו לפני שרים ונכבדי ארץ ושם יחדו יהיו תמים התענוג
והתועלת. . . והמה חשבו לחסרון ופחיתות אל ילדי העברים כי עד הנה נפקד מאתם התענוג והתועלת הזה
בסיפוריהם ובחיבוריהם—הנה בחרתי היום הזה להראות לכל עמי הארץ, כי לא נופל הלשון העברי לכל
מלאכת מחשבת מכל לשונות הגוים, אך אמנם גדלה למעלה למעלה תפארת גדולתו ולו יתר שאת ויתר עז
על כל אשר יתפארו בו גויי הארצות. ואם לא ראו עד עתה חבור וספור במילי דבדיחותא כאלה משמחי לב,
לא יחשב לו לפחיתות, יען כי הלשון הקדוש הזה בחר לו בראשיתו דברים עתיקים ונוראים במאד מאד ויבז
בעיניו לדרוש ולחקור בתענוגות בני אדם שדה ושדות. ומה שעשוי יתר הלשונות עטרת לראשם עשה הלשון
הקדוש הזה עקב לסוליתו. ובא האות והמופת מאשר תראו עתה, ואם חדש הוא בלשון הזה, כי על כלם
יתגדל ויתהדר גם בדברי משלים וחידות המשמחים לבב אנוש.

I realize that the wise of many lands [whether of Greece, Cyprus or Turkey], have taken pride in the way that they employ language to delight mankind. Their works have been performed before men of distinction and high degree, and in their words pleasure and utility are perfectly conjoined. . . . Now they have looked down upon the Jews because these seem to lack this literary facility. It is for this reason that I have this day resolved to show all the nations of the earth that the Hebrew language is not inferior in its artistic power to any of the gentile tongues. On the contrary, the splendor of its greatness is much loftier, and it holds outstanding dignity and power, more than anything the gentiles of the lands can take pride in. Hence, people should not deem it a defect in that language because they have not seen it cast, ere now, into a pleasing comedy. Rather, it is because the words that constitute this Holy Tongue are of

127

most ancient and wondrous origin, and it has seemed unworthy for such sacred words to be used solely for human pleasure. Indeed, what is a crowning glory for other languages is used as nothing but a shoe-sole by this Holy Tongue. But now I will prove that, even if it is a novelty in this language, the Holy Tongue can do better than all other languages also in the field of tales and riddles which give pleasure to the heart of Man.[1]

Thus, the prologue of *Tsahut bedihuta deqiddushin* (usually translated as *A Comedy of Betrothal*), attributed to Mantuan Jewish playwright and esteemed cinquecento man-of-theater, Leone de' Sommi (or Yehudah Sommo, as was his Hebrew name), clearly frames the play as an endeavor focusing on language. To be more precise, the words of Wisdom invite her audience to decipher the theatrical event they are about to witness as an exploration of the possibilities of recasting the Holy Tongue into comic performance. The playwright is completely aware of the novelty of his project: as Hebrew-speaking drama was practically a nonexistent phenomenon before de' Sommi's times (and still an extremely rare one for a long while afterward)—his play constitutes a daring attempt in re-locating Hebrew from the field of Jewish textual culture to the one of Renaissance Italian theater.[2] Indeed, while other Italian Jews in de' Sommi's times have been involved in writing Hebrew texts in various humanist literary genres which were new to Jewish culture—such as historiography and biography[3]—de' Sommi does something more in writing *Tsahut bedihuta deqiddushin:* he uses Hebrew not just as a language for written literature, but, probably for the first time in Jewish history, as a language designated for embodied theatrical praxis.

The play itself is an intriguing piece of cultural interaction: written in the genre of Italian *commedia erudita*—with its love intrigues, urban setting, and stock characters—*Tsahut bedihuta deqiddushin* nonetheless remolds this genre into a Jewish and Hebrew cultural context. Located in the Mediterranean city of Sidon, the play's plot features mainly Jewish characters—all of whom speak Hebrew (and a little Aramaic)—who are involved in an intricate web of intrigue, love, and money. The series of tricks and counter-tricks that sets the comic plot in motion, as it does in the well-established tradition of New Comedy, is constituted mainly of manipulations of halakhah (Jewish law), including some which are motivated by greed and lust, while others attempt to foil these maneuvers (ending, as can be expected, with the young lovers' reunion). Thus,

Tsahut bedihuta deqiddushin's setting, characters, language—indeed, its very comic mechanism—all derive from Jewish cultural tradition, as well as from the Western tradition of New Comedy and its specific articulation in Renaissance Italy. As such, the play offers an occasion for these cultural traditions to intersect and illuminate each other on the new, "other" space of the Italian comic stage.

Yet, the very otherness of Italian culture vis-à-vis Jewish culture must be delineated with care. Italian Jews of the Renaissance hardly closed themselves off from their surrounding culture. Rather, many of them participated in their contemporaries' humanist project. At the same time, however, they were conscious of maintaining well-defined (if not always rigid) cultural and social borderlines. While the intercultural encounter was surely not without its tensions and anxieties, neither the concept of "assimilation" nor that of "separatism" would suffice to describe these dynamics. David Biale gives a lucid formulation of these dynamics when he writes

Indeed, the Jews should not be seen as outsiders who borrowed from Italian culture but rather as full participants in the shaping of that culture, albeit with their own concerns and mores. The Jews were not so much "influenced" by the Italians as they were one organ in a larger cultural organism, a subculture that established its identity in a complex process of adaptation and resistance. Jewish "difference" was an integral part of the larger mosaic of Renaissance Italy.[4]

More specifically to the field of theater, one should recall that while the Italian comic stage was definitely a new space for Hebrew writing, it was hardly foreign for Italian Jews. Jewish culture up until the Renaissance had not usually been theatrically active, but the Jews of early modern Italy—and especially the Jews of Mantua—were involved with the theatrical praxis around them: during the sixteenth century, and well into the seventeenth, the Jews of Mantua had performed theatrical pieces for the Gonzaga court in Carnival, at festivals, and on special occasions.[5] As Dunbar H. Ogden reminds us, this participation was not only a moment of Jewish creative participation in Italian culture, but also "a kind of tax, a sort of blackmail"[6] through which the performances in front of the rulers of Mantua served as a "vivid manifestation of their political, economic, and cultural power that very much included the Jewish community of Mantua held in a kind of servitude, even bondage."[7] And yet, complex as

the power structures embedded in the Jewish performances at the Mantuan court might have been, they still allowed for a theatrical activity exceptional in Jewish cultural history prior to the late nineteenth century.

Leone de' Sommi himself is a remarkable figure in this field. Not only
a prolific playwright, de' Sommi was an artist of the theater as an art of
performance. His now celebrated treatise on play production, *Quattro
dialoghi in materia di rappresentazioni sceniche,* puts unique emphasis
on theatrical performance rather than on dramatic writing—an emphasis for which the treatise is considered by Kristine Hecker to be the first
"true poetics of staging"[8] and which earned de' Sommi the title of being
a forefather of the modern concept of directing as art form.[9] While most
of de' Sommi's Italian plays were destroyed during the fire at the National
Library of Turin in 1904, the surviving manuscripts—which are described
by Cristina Dal Molin as "original and irreproducible draft-scripts, defaced
with corrections and erasures"—attest according to Dal Molin to de' Sommi's refusal of "publication and disseminations of his own scripts, for he
was convinced that the dramatic text, lacking in any intrinsical value, was
primarily intended for its final destination: the theatrical performance."[10]
De' Sommi's only fully surviving comedy in Italian, *Le tre sorelle,* is indeed
considered by Massimo Ciavolella to be a rare example of a *commedia
erudita* "in which text and performance are strict functions of each other,
to the extent that only with their fusion is 'meaning' actually acquired."[11]
In the case of his Hebrew play, I would argue, de' Sommi specifically explores the dynamics between text and performance, between the Hebrew
tongue with its many layers and the Italian comic theater.

These intersections between Jewish culture and Italian comedy, which
constitute much of *Tsahut bedihuta deqiddushin*'s hybrid quality, have
been assessed by Shimon Levy as superficial. Levy claims that in essence,
the play "is an Italian Renaissance morality play, with *commedia erudita*
and *commedia dell'arte* influences, dressed up in Jewish clothes and
speaking Hebrew." Therefore, he considers it to be "a Jewish *adaptation*
and not an 'organic' Jewish play in the strict sense of the word . . . a Hebrew version of an Italian play, an adopted dramatic child."[12] As Arthur
M. Lesley writes with regard to Jewish-Italian culture in the Renaissance,
however, to "assume that a minority culture that has long survived, such
as that of the Jews, automatically imitates whatever it encounters in the
surrounding society both ignores the internal dynamics of Jewish life and
reduces intercultural relations to simplistic alternatives of borrowing or

complete originality."[13] Bearing these words in mind, it would seem more productive to regard *Tsahut bedihuta deqiddushin* not as a "Jewish" text borrowing "Italian" elements from its surroundings, nor vice versa (indeed, what should be questioned is precisely the "strict sense" of such "organic" cultural identities evoked by Levy)—but as a text that is double-voiced to its core, which maintains intricate intertextual relations with both Jewish and Italian cultural traditions, and which fully participates in (rather than being "influenced by") both. It is through such a participation, I would maintain, that *Tsahut bedihuta deqiddushin* explores a unique, performative route through which Italian comedy can offer new horizons of knowledge of Jewish textual culture and of the Hebrew language itself.[14]

The Meaning of Hebrew

Textual activity may well be considered one of the most central endeavors of Jewish communities throughout the ages. From the inceptive moments of midrash, both halakhic and haggadic, Jews were involved in interpreting and reinterpreting their textual canon, thus establishing themselves as paradigmatic examples of what Moshe Halbertal calls "text-centered communities."[15] This phenomenon is reflected in the high incidence of explicitly intertextual writing in Jewish literature. Every word, every phrase, echoes other, earlier phrases and interprets them in the process.

Specifically in Jewish Mantua, one of the main textual practices was the development of Hebrew, its grammar, style, and vocabulary.[16] Indeed, even though Hebrew did not serve as a Jewish vernacular in early modern Italy, Hayyim Schirmann argues that it is highly probable for de' Sommi to have had an audience who would be fluent enough in Hebrew to watch and enjoy a theatrical performance of *Tsahut bedihuta deqiddushin.*[17] Mantua was also a center for Christian Hebraism, and the non-Jewish residents of Mantua are mentioned in several sixteenth-century texts as specifically fluent in the Holy Tongue.[18]

What could it mean then to write a comedy in Hebrew in Renaissance Mantua? As seen above, de' Sommi himself declares in the prologue that he wishes to prove that Hebrew is not inferior to Italian and that a distinguished literary humanist genre such as comedy can be written in it. Such a claim is a common one among Italian-Jewish authors of Hebrew works written in humanist genres that were foreign to Jewish culture up until that time—such as rhetoric and historiography. Not once was it declared that Hebrew could serve the goals of humanism just as well as any other language.[19]

On the other hand, we might wish to consider the prologue of *Tsahut bedihuta deqiddushin,* with its preoccupation with issues of language, comedy, and cultural identity, as a revealing mirror-image of another, more famous prologue, that of Bibienna's *La calandria:*

Oltre che, la lingua che Dio e Natura ci ha data non deve, appresso di noi, essere di manco estimazione né di minor grazia che la latina, la greca e la ebraica: alle quali la nostra non saria forse punto inferiore se la esaltassimo, la osservassimo, la polissimo con quella diligente cura che li greci e altri ferno la loro. Bene è di sé inimico chi l'altrui lingua stima piú che la sua propria. So io bene che la mia mi è sí cara che non la darei per quante lingue oggi si trovano. E cosí credo intervenga a voi.

Moreover, given that Italian is the language that God and Nature have given us, it shouldn't be less appreciated or enjoyed than Latin, Greek or Hebrew. Our language wouldn't be inferior if we praised, practiced and polished it with the same diligence that the Greeks and the others did theirs. For those who appreciate other languages over their own are their own enemies. I know that as far as I'm concerned I hold my own language more dear than any other, and I believe the same is true for you.[20]

Several decades after Bibienna[21] felt the need to empower Italian vis-à-vis the classical (and thus prestigious) tongues—with Hebrew among them— de' Sommi wishes to do the same for Hebrew, with Italian being now the "other" language in front of which Hebrew needs to reassert its qualities.

Hebrew, then, has a double role in this case: like Italian, it serves in comedy as a language forming a group's cultural identity.[22] And yet, like Latin, it is also a "classical" language—and, even more so, one which is derived from the sacred sphere. Indeed, what de' Sommi seems to tackle in his prologue is the possible opposition from people in the Italian-Jewish community to his mundane, perhaps even sacrilegious, use of the Holy Tongue in comedy:

ואל נא תשיתו לבבכם, חברים מקשיבים הנאהבים והנעימים, אשר באולי יביעו ידברו עתק הנעלמים לעגי מעוג, כי דבר ריק הוא להוציא לשון קודש בדברי הבאי; כי גם בזה תשובתם בצדם, יען כי אם ישכילו באגדה זו אשר שמתי לפניהם, יכירו וידעו כי יסודתה בהררי התבונה התועלית, לקוחה מאוצר אגדות החכמים הקודמים הקוראים בשמי, ולתהלה ולשם ולתפארת, להגדיל תורה ולהאדירה, ללמוד וללמד, לשמור ולעשות הטוב והישר בעיני אלקים ואדם. ואני החכמה בדעת ותבונה החזקתי בידם, ואני אהיה בעזרתכם לתת עליכם היום ברכה שמחה וששון . . .

Do not heed, dear and beloved audience, those who speak with arrogance, those mocking hypocrites, who contend that it is improper to use the Holy Tongue in a profane fashion. I have an answer for them: for if they would delve into the legend that I have placed in front of them, they will realize that its source is in the mountains of beneficial sapience; that it is taken from the treasury of legends told by the ancient sages, who spoke in my name, for glory and splendor, to expand the *Torah* and exalt it, to learn and to teach, to observe and to do all that is good and right in the sight of G-d and man. And I, Wisdom, have placed knowledge and understanding in their hands, and I shall be your aid to give you today blessings, happiness and joy . . . (30 [68])

Thus, de' Sommi addresses not only the issue which preoccupied Bibbiena in his prologue—that is, professing that the language (Italian or Hebrew) is worthy enough for the writing of Comedy—but also the opposite concern as well: reassuring that Comedy is worthy enough a genre to be written in Hebrew. This double valence stems from the multiple qualities of Hebrew for de' Sommi: a sacred tongue,[23] as well as one that participates in the "secular" (if such a sharp dichotomy is at all applicable for early modern culture) project of establishing an ethnic-national cultural identity.

And yet it is precisely those elements of Hebrew which are derived from the sacred sphere that stand at the core of de' Sommi's playwriting in *Tsahut bedihuta deqiddushin*. In terms of the play's use of language, its most evident feature is the fact that the dramatic dialogue consists almost entirely of quotations and allusions to texts canonized by Jewish culture, such as the Hebrew Bible and the Talmud. The play's allusiveness is perhaps the most prominent tool used by de' Sommi as he explores Hebrew as a language intended for the stage. Indeed, one may assume that for a text-centered community such as that of early modern Jewish Mantua, the onstage performance of allusions to canonical texts, in Hebrew, would have particular resonance. This resonance should be located specifically within its theatrical context—that of Italian Renaissance comedy—for it is through comic performance that a dialogic tension is established in *Tsahut bedihuta deqiddushin* between textual tradition and theatrical moment. Through performance, the theatrical genre of Renaissance comedy determines possible routes of rereading Jewish canon and reusing the Holy Tongue.

The Performance of Allusions:
Scripture Through Body and Space

The phrase "performance of allusions" can be fruitfully understood in two ways regarding *Tsahut bedihuta deqiddushin:* first, it could relate to the theatrical moment in which such allusions were to be performed onstage; and secondly, it could help pose the question of how these allusions themselves, as an "event in the text,"[24] perform a rereading of their source-text while being performed. In other words, it seems that the play traces the possibilities that open up for Jewish textual culture when one relocates quotations and allusions into a medium that has as one of its most characteristic traits its quality as a junction between text and other (visual, performative) sets of discourse. In de' Sommi's theater, the stage indeed becomes a medium for exploring the textual canon anew.

Perhaps it would be simpler to begin the discussion by showing how the use of allusions in the play offers new horizons of textual meaning through their mere presence in the dramatic dialogue. In its most basic function, of course, the allusion charges the dialogue with meaning and offers new options for the interpretation of the dramatic scene. A good example of such a process can be found in the dialogue between Amon and Dvorah, the parents of the young Beruriah, after they discover the fate of Yedidiah, who is engaged to their daughter (act 1, scene 1). Yedidiah's father passed away and did not bequeath anything, so it seems, to his son. Yedidiah is now penniless, and Dvorah refuses to allow him to wed her daughter.[25] Amon tries to defend Yedidiah, and the following dialogue is exchanged between the two:

דבורה: ככה עלה לפניי במחשבה מוחלטת ואין עליה להוסיף, כי אחרי דבריי לא אשנה.

אמון: אם כן הוא, למה זה אנכי? האהיה כלא אהיה?

DVORAH: This is what I've thought of—and nothing more is to be said, for I shall not change my word.

AMON: Therefore, why am I to exist? Shall I be as one that is naught? (34 [72])

This dramatic moment is rich with textual allusions. Dvorah's words "This is what I've thought of—and nothing more is to be said," echo the words of God in a legendary story appearing in the Babylonian Talmud, Tractate *Menahot* 29b. According to this tale, Moses asks God to show him the distinguished sage, Rabbi Aqiva. After he gets acquainted with the marvelous scholarly abilities of the latter, Moses returns to God and wonders, "You have such a person—and you give the Torah to me?" God's answer is definite: "Be silent. This is what I've thought of"(שתוק, כך עלה במחשבה לפניי). Afterward, Moses asks God to see what became of Rabbi Aqiva and then watches him being tormented by the Romans. Moses protests against such injustice ("This is *Torah* and this is its reward?")—and God answers once more in the same definite, arbitrary manner: "Be silent. This is what I've thought of."

When Dvorah answers Amon's argument regarding the injustice of her behavior with the words "This is what I've thought of—and nothing more is to be said," she is actually playing God against Amon-Moses. Amon's reply continues this line: The first part of his words—"Therefore, why am I to exist" (אם כן הוא, למה זה אנוכי?)—is an allusion to the words of the pregnant Rebecca, going to seek answers from God (Genesis 25:22). Amon addresses Dvorah in the manner of a human being addressing God. Like Dvorah's earlier words, the allusion Amon uses also charges the dramatic relationship between the two with echoes of the relationships between Man and God.

The Man-God relationship is hardly a neutral association in this scene, as the dramatic conflict between the couple concerns the issue of authority. The two argue about who will have the last word in the household. Dvorah's paraphrase of God's "Be silent. This is what I've thought of" is not just a speech-act aimed at shutting Amon up. Dvorah is fashioning herself as the "God" in the power struggle of husband and wife: she is the one with the final authority who can, like God, act in an arbitrary manner, with no need for self-justification. Likewise, Amon, although trying to re-establish his patriarchal authority, only reinforces (for the audience) Dvorah's true position as the masculine "God" of the two, as he uses a quotation of a mortal woman, seeking God in order to explain her misery, thus inadvertently continuing the reversal of gender hierarchies in the household. Likewise, it is hardly coincidence that Amon's subsequent words of protest about his lost authority—"Shall I be as one that is naught?" (כלא אהיה האהיה?)—are in fact an act of self-negating God's name, as it appears in Exodus 2:14: "I shall be Whoever I shall" (אהיה אשר אהיה).

Thus, the dramatic situation of a bourgeois couple bickering with each other is charged—through de' Sommi's use of allusions—with other "dramatic scenes" from the Hebrew Bible and the Talmud, allowing the audience new levels of interpretative insight into the performed scene. Just as the relationship between God and Man charges the one between Amon and Dvorah with meaning, however, so can the bourgeois marital life of the couple be interpreted as a comical image of the relationship between God and Moses (or Man in general): a petty, quarrelsome set of never-ending power struggles, where God plays the shrewish, dominating wife, following the long tradition of comic *ma-tronae*. In other words, the world of Renaissance comedy—with all its plots and stock characters—becomes an interpretive paradigm for Jewish canon and myth.

Yet de' Sommi's dialogue with the canon does not occur on the textual level alone. In fact, it is the onstage performance, in Hebrew, of allusions to canonical tradition that makes *Tsahut bedihuta deqiddushin* a sophisticated, multilayered drama. The most fascinating aspect in de' Sommi's dramaturgy is perhaps the fact that even nonverbal elements—such as space, movement, and mise-en-scène—maintain a reciprocal dialogue with the presence, traces, and echoes of biblical and Talmudic texts in the play. In a sense, it seems that de' Sommi already reads his canonic tradition "as theatre,"[26] extracting space, body and movement from texts—only to remold them into onstage performative moments.

As an example, let us review another scene: in act 1, scene 4, the young lover Yedidiah—accompanied by his slave, Pash'hur—knocks on the door of his beloved Beruriah. Beruriah's maid, Yeqarah, answers

יקרה: מי הוא הדופק על הדלת?

ידידיה: פתחי לי, אחותי היקרה!

YEQARAH: Who is it that knocks on the door?
YEDIDIAH: Open up, my dear sister! (37 [76])

The scene is to be performed using all the spatial conventions of Italian Renaissance comedy: the male lover standing outside (at the city square or at a street corner), wishing to enter the interior space of the house, where his female beloved resides.[27] But a quick inspection of this short piece of dialogue reveals that its textual allusions direct the audience to a famous biblical scene as well—Song of Songs 5:2, in which another male lover is trying to enter *his* beloved's house: "I am sleeping, but my heart is awake. The sound of my beloved knocking: 'Open up, my sister, my bride, my dove, my perfect one—for my hair is wet with dew, my locks with the drops of the night.'" (אני ישנה ולבי ער, קול דודי דופק: פתחי-לי אחותי, רעיתי, יונתי, תמתי, רסיסי לילה). De' Sommi, so it seems, extracts here the biblical scene's implicit mise-en-scène (the lover knocking on his beloved's door) and applies it, through the dramatic dialogue, to the performed mise-en-scène—which is conducted completely by the conventions of the Renaissance comic stage. Thus, an exploration of biblical (textual) space is achieved through its Renaissance theatrical manifestation—so that, at this moment, the dramatic space is "double voiced": charged with meanings from both Jewish and Italian cultural traditions.

For, once again, the dialogue between the Hebrew text (the biblical allusion) and its performance within the conventions of Renaissance comedy's dramatic space can also open up new options of meaning with regard to the biblical text itself: spatial aspects that are usually only implicit in the Song of Songs—a text meant mainly for the purpose of reading or reciting—are moved to the foreground at the moment the allusion is performed within a specific space. The cultural contexts of such theatrical space, evolved in a different cultural heritage, enable de' Sommi also to reexplore the possibilities of the Song of Songs, often interpreted allegorically in Jewish tradition, as a human text relocated in its urban setting.

This urban setting, of course, is also an eroticized one. It has already been noted by many that the dramatic space of Renaissance comedy is highly gendered: the interior space of the house is many times also a feminine space, while the male lovers' various attempts throughout Renaissance drama to enter these houses from the outside may well be read as a metaphor for sexual penetration, thus playing upon the linkage between the interior space of the house and that of the female body prevalent in Western imagination since antiquity.[28]

The alluded-to scene from the Song of Songs, of course, sustains the same gendered space—as well as its erotic connotations of sexual penetration. (Consider, for example, the erotic use of space made in verses 4 and 5 of the same chapter of the Song of Songs—where words such as "hand," "hole," and "lock" might serve as metaphors for the sexual organs: "My beloved put in his hand by the hole of the door, and my heart was moved for him. I rose up to open to my beloved and my hands dripped with myrrh, and my fingers with sweet smelling myrrh upon the handles of the lock.") As the scene continues, de' Sommi highlights the sexual spatial symbolism of the Song of Songs through the bluntly erotic use of the alluded-to space made by Pash'hur. The slave asks Yeqarah to allow him also into the house—but while she claims that the door is already wide open, Pash'hur clarifies that where he really wants to enter is her "Garden of Eden." Yeqarah then answers with yet another allusion to Song of Songs, 4:12, replying that "the garden is locked, and the fountainhead is sealed" (הגן נעול והמעין חתום). Thus, the space of the Song of Songs reveals its bold, erotic aspects as the romantic idyll is being reread as a flirtatious scene in which the two servants negotiate just how far each of them is willing to carry their dalliance. In this sense, the scene from *Tsahut bedihuta deqiddushin* is reminiscent of the sexual use of the space of the doorway in the following scene—again from *La calandria*. In act 3, scene 10 (which might maintain by itself an intertextual relationship with the spatial erotic metaphors of the Song of Songs), the male servant Fessenio comes knocking at the door, while the female servant Samia, who locked herself in the house with her lover, answers from inside:

FESSENIO: Tic, toc; tic, toc. Sete sordi? Oh! oh! Tic, toc. Aprite. Oh! oh! Tic, toc. Non udite?

SAMIA: Chi picchia?

FESSENIO: Fessenio tuo. Samia, apri.

SAMIA: Ora.

FESSENIO: Perché non apri?

SAMIA: Io mi alzo per metter la chiave nella toppa.

FESSENIO: Presto, se vuoi.

SAMIA: Non truovo il buco.

FESSENIO: Or escine.

SAMIA: Eh! eh! eimè! non si può ancora.

FESSENIO: Perché?

SAMIA: Il buco è pieno.

FESSENIO: Soffia nella chiave.

SAMIA: Fo meglio.

FESSENIO: Che?

SAMIA: Scuoto quant'io posso.

FESSENIO: Che indugi?

SAMIA: Oh! oh! oh! Laudato sia il manico della vanga, Fessenio, ché ho fatto el bisogno ed ho tutta unta la chiave perché meglio apri.

FESSENIO: Or apri.

FESSENIO: (*Knocking.*) Are you deaf in there? Hey! Hey! (*Knocking again.*) Open up. Hey! Hey! (*Knocking harder.*) Don't you hear me?

SAMIA: (*After a moment.*) Who's knocking?

FESSENIO: Your Fessenio. Open up, Samia.

SAMIA: Right away.

FESSENIO: Why don't you open up?

SAMIA: I'm getting up to put the key in the lock.

FESSENIO: Hurry up, please.

SAMIA: The key can't seem to find the hole.

FESSENIO: Come, now, come on.

SAMIA: Oh! Ohhh! Mmmm. I can't yet.

FESSENIO: Why not?

SAMIA: The hole's all plugged up.

FESSENIO: Blow on the keyhole.

SAMIA: Ohhhh! I can do better than that.

FESSENIO: What?

SAMIA: I'm going as fast as I can.

FESSENIO: What's gotten into you?

SAMIA: Oh! Ohhh! Ohhhhhh! Blessed be the shovel handle! Fessenio, I've taken care of the problem, and I've lubricated the key so well that it should open the door just fine now.

FESSENIO: So open it.[29]

As the scene between Yeqarah and Pash'hur goes on, the maidservant continues to reject Pash'hur's obscene attempts—and Pash'hur starts to get more physical. Yeqarah, cursing Pash'hur strenuously, demands that he leave her alone, and he replies: "I shall not leave you—unless you bless me, to replace your curses!" (לא אעזבך, כי אם ברכתיני חלף קללתך קללתך זאת). Yeqarah retorts: "You shall be blessed. . . . Now leave me!"

Pash'hur's words are highly evocative in the context of the performed scene. They are an allusion to Genesis 32:27, where similar words are being spoken by Jacob as he wrestles with the Angel. Jacob refuses to release the Angel unless the latter will bless him (לא אשלחך כי אם ברכתני). Subsequently, the Angel complies and changes Jacob's name to Israel. Now, when we consider the implicit mise-en-scène of the biblical scene between Jacob and the Angel, we can discover striking similarities between it and that of the scene in *Tsahut bedihuta deqiddushin*—performed according to the Renaissance theatrical tradition of *zanni* scenes. Both scenes involve a struggle—between Pash'hur and Yeqarah, or between Jacob and the Angel. Furthermore, the struggle in both scenes is focused around the groin: the Angel catches Jacob at the hollow of the thigh (at *Gid Ha'Nasheh,* which the Israelites are not allowed to eat since that mythic battle)—while Yeqarah demands Pash'hur, later during their dialogue, to move his hand away from her bosom (and Pash'hur merrily invites her to touch all of his "goods"—using another biblical allusion, to a dialogue between Jacob and Laban in Genesis 31:37).

And so the biblical wrestling turns from a mythic moment of the formation of "Israel" into a sexual, vulgar *zanni* scene. As before, the performance of these specific words within this specific "double-voiced" mise-en-scène—referring as it does both to Jewish textual tradition and to Italian performative conventions—offers to read this myth anew. It reveals the myth's erotic potential—perhaps even its homoerotic potential, if we are to recall that the struggle in the biblical myth was conducted between two male characters. As the scene in *Tsahut bedihuta deqiddushin,* like those of many other plays during the first half of the sixteenth century, was also (as Hayyim Schirmann suggests) probably intended to be performed by two male actors, it might be the case that the male bodies of the biblical text are still to be theatrically present during the scene between Yeqarah and Pash'hur.[30]

As the dialogue continues, so does the blatant eroticization of Scripture: Yeqarah inquires what Pash'hur wishes to receive for him to leave her alone at last, and Pash'hur replies: "the arm and the cheeks" (הזרוע והלחיים) (38 [76]). Pash'hur is quoting Deuteronomy 18:3, where "the shoulder [literally: "the arm"] and the two cheeks" of a sacrificed animal is mentioned as part of the gifts that priests are entitled to receive from each Israelite bringing a sacrifice to the Temple. The image of "cheeks" is used by Pash'hur on yet another occasion in the play to insinuate the female genitalia, as he tries to persuade Yedidiah to sleep with Beruriah and (alluding to Song of Songs 6:2) "pluck the lily of her cheeks" (תלקט שושנת לחייה) (60 [100]). Combining this phrase with the phallic "arm," then, Pash'hur substitutes priestly gifts with sexual favors. The biblical priest is thus replaced by a lustful servant, while carnal imagery is transferred from Temple sacrifices to sexual intercourse.

The unique trait of the theater as a medium that maintains a dialogue between text and space, movement or the performing body, becomes therefore an opportunity for de' Sommi to explore new possibilities of meaning (comic, erotic, physical) in Jewish textual tradition that can be fully realized *only* through the performance of the text. The prospective audience of de' Sommi—the Jews of sixteenth-century Mantua—might return from the theater (if the play was indeed performed at the time) to the textually centered spaces of the synagogue or the *Beit Midrash* (hall of learning) with broader reading horizons. They might reread the canonical texts with new associative contexts made possible by what they have just seen. Indeed, the Italian Renaissance stage allowed de' Sommi—and his audience—to reimagine Scripture in ways hitherto unimagined.

Destabilizing Hebrew: *Tsahut bedihuta deqiddushin* and the Tradition of Purimic Parodies

The play's use of Hebrew stems partially from an earlier Jewish literary, nondramatic tradition echoed in the play: that of the parodies written for the carnivalesque festival of Purim, mainly *Tractate Purim,* composed

by Kalonymos ben Kalonymos, and *Megillat Setarim,* attributed to Ger-
sonides—both written at the beginning of the fourteenth century and
first printed, in Pesaro, around 1513. These texts parody Talmudic trac-
tates, applying "upside-down" midrashic techniques originally used in
rabbinic literature to extract laws and morals from Scripture's verses promoting carnivalesque subversiveness.[31] Thus, as a parody on the Talmud,
they expose the instability of the Jewish hermeneutic act—as well as
displaying the ability to manipulate it in favor of "anticultural" values.

Tsahut bedihuta deqiddushin, intended for performance in Purim, is
full of allusions to *Tractate Purim* and *Megillat Setarim.* The two students of Rav Hamdan (Rabbi Greedy), Yair and Yoqtan, recite Purimic
Midrashim in the *Tractate* style—as carnivalesque acts of biblical exegesis
that justify their desire for food and idleness (67 [107–8]). Furthermore,
the two also mention some of the grotesque rabbis populating the Purimic parodies—such as Rabbi Bibi, whose name is derived from the Latin
bibere, and can thus be translated as "Rabbi Drunkard." In fact, even the
name of Rav Hamdan himself—the greedy charlatan rabbi of the play—
appears as one of the reversed rabbis that teach carnivalesque halakhah in
these parodies.[32] While Rav Hamdan is only one of the characters whose
opinions are being "cited" in the topsy-turvy Talmudic discussion, de'
Sommi turns him into a dramatic character who speaks on his own behalf
and becomes a dramatic force that destabilizes the play's society. Thus, de'
Sommi finds in the Jewish textual tradition of Purimic parodies material
for participating in the emerging comic portrayal of corrupt representatives of religious establishments in early modern drama, from Fra' Timoteo
in Machiavelli's *La mandragola* to Molière's Tartuffe.[33] It would seem that
this is yet another exemplary instance of a "double-voiced" element in de'
Sommi's drama—a character maintaining simultaneous intertextual relations to both Italian and Jewish cultural traditions.

While Yair and Yoqtan apply exegetic techniques on biblical verses in
order to subvert their meaning and celebrate carnivalesque values, Rav
Hamdan is active in offering halakhic ways for leading morally corrupt
lives while remaining legally kosher. This aspect of Rav Hamdan's character is expressed most fully in his dialogue with Yedidiah, as he offers
the young man a solution for his plight: as Beruriah's parents refuse to
wed her to her betrothed and have engaged their daughter to another
man, Rav Hamdan proposes that Yedidiah stage a fake rape, sleep with
Beruriah in the field, and thus leave her parents no alternative but to allow

the young couple to wed (act 3, scene 5).[34] The scheme is punishment-proof, argues the rabbi, as Beruriah can claim she had sex with Yedidiah against her will—while Yedidiah should insist that he did not know while sleeping with Beruriah that their betrothal had been annulled.[35] While sexual intercourse with one's betrothed is hardly encouraged, halakhah does not prescribe as serious a punishment for such an act as it does when a person sleeps with another person's betrothed. The scandal in Rav Hamdan's proposal lies, therefore, in that while being correct in the legal details of Jewish halakhah—its overall aim is to pave the way for a young man to satisfy his sexual desires, as well as forcefully compel his beloved's parents into changing their minds:

רב חמדן: אם כן הוא, שבתי וראיתי, כי שלושה המה החומרות העיקריות הסובבות את מרכז תשוקתך בדרוש הזה לבוא אל תכליתו: הראשונה דבקה בנפש ובדחלתא דשמיא; השנית—על רכות לבב הנערה ופחדה; והשלישית—בסכנת עצמך, פן יוונה אליך רעה—חס ושלום—בגופך. אמנם אם מצד הסיבה הראשונה—דע נאמנה, כי נקי תהיה מגזרת עירני שמיא, יען כי על הדין ועל האמת לא נתפסה הנערה הזאת בקידושין אשר קיבלה בערמה מבלי הסכמתה, ובוחן כליות יראה ללבב ולא למראה עיני ההמון. ואנוכי מגן לך לעלמא דאתי מדינה של גיהנם.

פשחור: אם תיתן ערבון עד בואך שמה!

ידידיה: זה כלל גדול בגופא דעובדא.

רב חמדן: אם מצד תשועת ברוריה להצילה מדין קשה—הלא גלוי וידוע לכל בי רב דחד יומא, כי אף תהיה מאורשת לאיש, אין לנערה משפט מוות, אם בשדה מצאה החושק, ובזאת תוכל ברוריה להינצל, אם תתראה כאנוסה . . .

RAV HAMDAN: If these are the facts of the case under review, then you have three major concerns which serve as obstacles to your fulfilling your desire: the first is the fear to violate G-d's law, and therefore to put your soul in jeopardy; the second has to do with the faintheartedness and fearfulness of the maiden; the third is your own fear that, G-d forbid, you would be physically punished for having sexual relations with Beruriah. Now, with regard to the first concern, I guarantee that your soul will be forever clean from the decree of Heaven's Angels—since, according to truth and to the law, the maiden is not bound by the second betrothal ceremony, since the arrangement was entered into deceitfully and without her consent. And He, who searches one's interiors, will see one's heart rather than the exterior appearance, as it is perceived by the crowd. And I shall be your defender in the World to Come from the verdict of Gehenna.

PASH'HUR: If only you could put down a deposit to guarantee your defense, until you reach that place yourself!

YEDIDIAH: This is a great legal principle, at the very core of the case.

RAV HAMDAN: If what concerns you is Beruriah's rescue and your desire to save her from the extreme penalty for adultery—well, then, the rankest law student knows that even if she is betrothed to another man, a maiden will not be condemned to death—if the man who desired her found her in the field.[36] And in this manner, Beruriah can be saved, if it would seem that she was raped. (63 [103–4])

The scene constitutes a parody of rabbinic scholarly discourse, not just by the seemingly logical structure of Rav Hamdan's arguments (the threefold division, the unpacking of each concern one at a time, and so on), but also through the language itself: the dialogue of this scene displays the highest density of Aramaic phrases in the play. Almost all of these are being spoken by Rav Hamdan: "Fear to violate G-d's law" (דחלתא דשמיא); "Heaven's Angels" (עירין דשמיא); "in the World to Come" (לעלמא דאתי); "the rankest law student" (בר בי רב דחד יומא)—yet even Yedidiah is momentarily swept into Aramaic, perhaps wishing to impress his interlocutors with his own scholarly knowledge: "at the very core of the case" (בגופא דעובדא). This is hardly coincidental, for as Aramaic (and not Hebrew) is the prominent language of the Talmud—the scene deliberately mocks rabbinic discourse, with its Aramaisms and legalistic articulations. As Yonatan Dubossarsky comments, Aramaic serves de' Sommi here as a Jewish equivalent to the Latin characterizing the stock characters of the *dottore* and the *pedante* prevalent in Renaissance comedy.[37]

Like his two students, Rav Hamdan is also active in hermeneutic manipulations of Scripture—manipulations designed to promote lasciviousness and greed. (The rabbi, unaware that Yedidiah is supposedly impecunious at the moment, plans to be well paid for this piece of halakhic advice, besides utilizing the scheme for the advancement of his own personal vendetta against the family of Beruriah's second betrothed.) Yair and Yoqtan are indeed good disciples of their master as they follow his steps in exploring the playful aspects of the Jewish hermeneutic system and by using these aspects for their own pleasures. Thus, all three function as a parody of rabbinic interpretive discourse—unveiling its fluidity, its elasticity and inherent openness for manipulation. Yet, unlike his students', Rav Hamdan's manipulation of Jewish law is not pleasantly amusing. As Rav Hamdan juggles his knowledge of halakhah to convince Yedidiah to sleep with Beruriah and feign a rape, his function as a parody of rabbinic discourse exposes the manners by which this discourse itself can be manipulated toward sin. As parody, it is quite poignant: it delineates the dark, uneasy side of the Jewish community's main site of authority.

Rav Hamdan, as a character derived from the carnivalesque world of the Purimic textual parodies, and his two students, interpreting biblical verses in the parodies' style, form therefore a whole school for themselves. This school, emerging from these textual parodies of Talmud and midrash, is a topsy-turvy Purimic one, promoting anarchic and hedonistic values, from the rabbi's corruption to his students' idleness. Through them, we are acquainted with the fluidity and perhaps even fickleness of the Jewish hermeneutic system and of language itself—whether in its comic, light-hearted manifestation (Yair and Yoqtan) or in its dark, destabilizing one (their rabbi). Indeed, Rav Hamdan—now a dramatic force rather than the literary pun he was in the earlier Purimic parodies—is a true threat to the play's society. The carnival of *Tractate Purim* and *Megillat Setarim,* being remolded into the drama of *commedia erudita,* reveals its anarchic, threatening depths.

Yet de' Sommi does something more by relocating these Purimic texts from the halls of learning (or wherever these parodic texts were actually to be read) to the theater. As has been discussed earlier, the performance of allusions in *Tsahut bedihuta deqiddushin* does not only charge the theatrical moment with connotations from the Jewish canon, it also offers new horizons for the reading of canon itself. The marital arguments of Dvorah and Amon suggest a new, comic perception of the relationship between God and Man; the flirtations of Pash'hur and Yeqarah eroticize the biblical scene of Jacob and the Angel and relocate the spatial metaphors of the Song of Songs in the urban space of Renaissance comedy, with its own sexual connotations. These new horizons of textual meaning, as has been noted before, are possible only through theatrical performance—through the conjunction of text to performing body, dramatic moment, and theatrical space. Thus, if *Tractate Purim* and *Megillat Setarim* are parodies of Jewish hermeneutics, in which interpretation transforms the law into its inverted, carnivalesque mirror image, then *Tsahut bedihuta deqiddushin,* intended to serve as a Purimic event, is indeed some sort of *Tractate Purim,* an occasion for comic and erotic interpretations of the canon. Yet, in de' Sommi's play, these interpretations do not occur on the textual level alone (as in *Tractate Purim* and *Megillat Setarim*), but through theatrical performance. *Tsahut bedihuta deqiddushin,* therefore, does not only participate in theatrical interpretation of the canon, it actually builds itself up as a performative version of the Purimic parodies' exegetic carnival. This version explores, like the parodies, the subversive possibilities of the Jewish hermeneutic system. By relocating interpretation to these new, performative sites of body and space, however, *Tsahut bedihuta deqiddushin* charges the hermeneutic act with a corporeal, physical, and erotic thrust that *Tractate Purim* and *Megillat Setarim,* as written texts, must somewhat lack. Thus, de' Sommi examines the manners by which theater—and Renaissance Italian comedy in particular—is able to participate in one of Jewish culture's most fundamental projects, that of textual interpretation. Indeed, the Italian comic stage allows de' Sommi to do something that very probably was not done by any other Jewish writer before him: to initiate an embodied, playful exploration of Jewish canon and the Holy Tongue.

The Two Rabbis: Dramatic Conflict and Linguistic Tensions

As the pinnacle of carnivalesque hermeneutics, Rav Hamdan's fickle use of language is put in dramatic conflict in the play with that of the virtuous Rabbi Amitai (Rabbi Truthful). This is the rabbi who finally gives the good advice in the play, solves the plot, and saves Yedidiah from his perils. The conflict between these two rabbis has its manifestations also in language. Each rabbi is characterized with a different register of Hebrew: while Rav Hamdan's Hebrew is more Talmudic in orientation and is adorned with many Aramaic phrases, as noted above, Rabbi Amitai's Hebrew is more biblical and is constructed mainly from the language of the prophets (compare 80–81 [123]). It is striking to note that Rabbi Amitai actually uses no Aramaic at all.[38] Rabbi Amitai's prophetic, biblical rhetoric is thus contrasted with Rav Hamdan's scholarly, Talmudic style, in favor, perhaps surprisingly, of the former. Thus, the Jewish traditional distinction between Sage and Prophet as two alternative models of religious-spiritual leadership serves to inform the dramatic conflict between the two rabbis and its linguistic manifestation.[39]

Indeed, the highly intertextual quality of Jewish literature enables de' Sommi to reconsider dramatic conflict not only as conflict between characters, but also as a conflict between texts. This possibility, in fact, is further enhanced in comedy. As Francesco Loriggio comments regarding the function of language in comedy:

There is a mixedness to comedy, additional to and quite aside from the quality inherent to it as theatre and according to which it will appear to us now as a fixed, written text, now as an audiovisual text changing with each adaptation or performance. This quality, typical of the genre whether it is read or listened to or watched, is perhaps most immediately brought home to us by the language:

comedy has always been polyphonic, has always allowed contrasting stylistic registers, contrasting vernaculars to cohabit.[40]

Such a polyphonic cohabitation of contrasting textual traditions is present in de' Sommi's comedy, as can be seen above, in the form of dramatic conflict. De' Sommi uses the trait of comedy, formulated by Loriggio, to expose potential conflicts within the language of textual canon itself. In *Tsahut bedihuta deqiddushin,* the different strata of the Hebrew tongue, as well as the different texts from which it is compiled, become a source and a model for dramatic conflict.

Yet the linguistic conflict between the two rabbis relates, in fact, to a cultural tension within the Jewish communities of Renaissance Italy regarding language and the Jewish canon. On one side stood the Biblical Hebrew, which was considered as more "honest" and sublime. On the other side there was the Talmudic principle of *Pilpul,* which, its cultural prestige notwithstanding, was regarded as linguistically suspect. This tension was already, to some extent, dramatized in the literature of Italian Jewry in the fifteenth century in a poem describing a debate between the *Passuk*—the biblical verse—and the Talmud. In this poem, the *Passuk* indeed accuses the Talmud of being potentially useful for deceit and corruption, while praising itself as the foundation for the study of Hebrew grammar.[41]

This dichotomy had its social manifestations as well: while the *Italiani* (the native Jews of Italy) were considered to have superb Biblical Hebrew and to be experts in Hebrew grammar, the Ashkenazi Jews who immigrated to Italy from across the Alps were perceived as superior Talmudists but also as having crude Hebrew, which the *Italiani* considered barbaric.[42] In fact, there seem to be several clues in the play suggesting that Rav Hamdan himself—the villainous master of *Pilpul*—is indeed an Ashkenazi Jew: he, like many of the Ashkenazi Jews, is an immigrant within the play's society (68 [109]).[43] Furthermore, he refers to other people as *Italiani,* thus revealing that he himself is not one of them (compare 39; 48 [77; 87]). One might suggest, of course, that Rav Hamdan is a Sephardic Jew—like many others who also immigrated to Italy after 1492—but the Sephardim, at least in Mantua, were not an influential cultural force and usually joined either the *Italiani* or the Ashkenazi communities.[44] If de' Sommi is making some social reference here—as it indeed seems likely—he is probably referring to the more dominant Ashkenazi Talmudist culture.

The play therefore posits two strata within the canonical Hebrew language itself, setting one against the other. The dramatic conflict is also an intertextual conflict between biblical and Talmudic texts, a conflict that participates in the cultural and social tensions of Renaissance Italian Jewry. In other words, the conflict between texts becomes a model not only for the dramatic conflict between Rav Hamdan and Rabbi Amitai, but also for the broader cultural and social conflicts manifested in the drama.[45]

Thus, the fundamental element of drama, that of conflict, as well as the polyphonic quality of comedy's language, allow de' Sommi to address his Jewish textual tradition in a new light. Reading this tradition as drama, as Renaissance comedy, enables the Jewish-Italian playwright to reveal its seams, its fissures and fractures, its sites for potential dramatic conflict. The canon itself is therefore reconsidered not as monolithic Tradition but as dramatic polyphony. And even as *Tsahut bedihuta deqiddushin* ends with the apparent victory of Rabbi Amitai's linguistic integrity and the downfall of Rav Hamdan's fickle hermeneutics, one cannot help but wonder whether the play, given its carnivalesque renditions of Scripture, does not in fact amount to a theatrical celebration of the latter.

Conclusion: Performance as Profanation— Playful Knowledge and the Question of Use

In the concluding remarks of his essay, "Towards a 'Philosophy' of Renaissance Theatre," Riccardo Scrivano writes

Sufficient for now is an invitation to recognize how much the theatre of the Renaissance offers to the means of human knowledge. It is much more than an occasion for escapism. With the audacity of its fictions, its hypotheses, its capacity to cancel the usual modes of conduct, it reveals to us different ways of organizing knowledge, and thus different ways of knowing.[46]

Following Scrivano's remark, it is possible to see how the comedy of *Tsahut bedihuta deqiddushin* offers its Jewish audience new ways of knowing their shared textual canon. The play's intertextualities reveal a multilayered drama of voices and texts encountering one another: Jewish textual tradition is conjoined with Italian theatrical culture into "double-voiced" performative moments; the Purimic parodies are put in conflict with Jewish canon; and even the Aramaic of the Talmud is put in dramatic opposition to the Hebrew of the Bible. As suggested above, these intertextual encounters enable the Jewish community to broaden its reading horizons vis-à-vis the textual canon. Since such potentialities manifest themselves fully only through performance within the theatrical conventions of *commedia erudita,* it would seem that de' Sommi indeed suggests Italian-Hebrew theater as a new path for Jewish knowledge. Bearing in mind Laura Giannetti's assertion of the centrality of the concept of *gioco* (both "play" and "game") to Italian Renaissance comedy,[47] the final paragraphs of this essay will try to characterize more fully the kind of playful knowledge proposed by *Tsahut bedihuta deqiddushin* and to articulate its possible cultural work.

De' Sommi's playful use of language might maintain dialogue not only with the Purimic parodies discussed above, but also with Boccaccio's *Decameron,* arguably one of the texts that exerted the greatest influence on Renaissance Italian comedy. In his exploration of the concept of play in the *Decameron,* Giuseppe Mazzotta notes the "radical instability of figurative language" exposed in some of Boccaccio's *novelle.*[48] Mazzotta points out the process in which Boccaccio employs figurative language and images taken from allegorical-religious discourse in order to subvert and reread them in the realm of physical eroticism. Thus, claims Mazzotta, with regard to the final story of the *Decameron's* third day, what is fundamental to the story's humor is "the strident and close union of the spiritual and physical activities . . . the ease with which the two registers are 'exchanged.'"[49] The startlingly easy exchange between the spiritual and the physical takes place, according to Mazzotta, specifically in figurative language. By using the "technique of indirection—the strategy of *not* naming sexuality directly"[50] and by claiming in his *Conclusione dell'autore* that the figurative words used in the *Decameron* in order to speak of sex "are not obscene in themselves and that the tales are not more harmful than the Scripture have been to some readers,"[51] Boccaccio reveals that "all writings, sacred and profane alike, are morally neutral allegories," thus implying that "Scripture and the *Decameron* have in common a dangerous ambiguity."[52] Lying at the core of this ambiguity is the notion that the erotic imagery of religious figurative language renders medieval allegorizations susceptible to becoming a kind of pornography, "because the erotic story they tell is contrabanded as a moral myth."[53]

As can be seen from de' Sommi's rereading of the biblical scene of Jacob and the Angel, as well as in many other instances in the comedy, the playful use of language in *Tsahut bedihuta deqiddushin* is in many ways close to Boccaccio's, since in de' Sommi's theatrical moments one may also witness a collapsing of the spiritual and the physical one into the other, thus radically destabilizing Scripture. By writing in Hebrew, however (and possibly because allegory is, all in all, less prominent a strategy in the Jewish hermeneutic system than it is in the Christian one),[54] de' Sommi does not expose the instability of figurative language and allegorical image alone. His use of Hebrew destabilizes the Holy Tongue as such, its textual heritage and hermeneutic practices as a whole. How should one further formulate, then, the cultural work of de' Sommi's playful, bodily use of language?

In order to delineate a possible answer, I would like to turn to Giorgio Agamben's recent formulation of play as a form of profanation, which I find highly fruitful for a discussion of *Tsahut bedihuta deqiddushin*. In his essay, "In Praise of Profanation," Agamben defines religion as "that which removes things, places, animals or people from common use and transfers them to a separate sphere." Agamben adds that "not only is there no religion without separation, but every separation also contains and preserves within itself a genuinely religious core."[55] Therefore, drawing on Carl Schmitt's notions of political theology and Walter Benjamin's concept of capitalism as religion, Agamben wishes to distinguish between two processes—secularization and profanation:

Secularization is a form of repression. It leaves intact the forces it deals with by simply moving them from one place to another. Thus the political secularization of theological concepts (the transcendence of God as a paradigm of sovereign power) does nothing but displace the heavenly monarchy onto an earthly monarchy, leaving its power intact.

Profanation, however, neutralizes what it profanes. Once profaned, that which was unavailable and separate loses its aura and is returned to use. Both are political operations: the first guarantees the exercise of power by carrying it back to a sacred model; the second deactivates the apparatuses of power and returns to common use the spaces that power has seized.[56]

Play, claims Agamben, could be seen as a preferred model for profanation:

The passage from the sacred to the profane can, in fact, also come about by means of an entirely inappropriate use (or, rather, reuse) of the sacred: namely, play. . . . In analyzing the relationship between games and rites, Emile Benveniste shows that play not only derives from the sphere of the sacred but also in some ways represents its overturning. The power of the sacred act, he writes, lies in the conjunction of the myth that tells the story and the rite that reproduces and stages it. Play breaks up this unity: as *ludus,* or physical play, it drops the myth and preserves the rite; as *iocus,* or wordplay, it effaces the rite and allows the myth to survive. . . . This means that play frees and distracts humanity from the sphere of the sacred, without simply abolishing it. The use to which the sacred is returned is a special one that does not coincide with utilitarian consumption.[57]

By suggesting play as a kind of relation to the sacred, a relation which profanes the sacred without "simply abolishing it," Agamben might offer a productive paradigm for understanding de' Sommi's playful theatrical use of Hebrew and the Jewish textual canon. Profanation is fully in force on the stage of *Tsahut bedihuta deqiddushin* with regard to Jewish canon, as the process of enabling, through play, a new use of the sacred. Indeed, as we may recall, it is exactly the question of using the Holy Tongue that troubles de' Sommi in the prologue—and usage is the issue he feels the need to confront as a response to his prospective opponents.

On de' Sommi's stage, of course, one may find both *iocus* and *ludus,* both wordplay and physical play. Therefore, when dealing with *Tsahut bedihuta deqiddushin,* we might wish to slightly adjust Agamben's claim, following Benveniste, that play dismantles the sacred compound of myth and ritual. Neither the physical nor the textual is dropped or effaced in de' Sommi's play. Instead, what is playfully redefined in *Tsahut bedihuta deqiddushin* is the relationship between the textual and the physical, vis-à-vis the sacred canon. By imagining, for example, the wrestling of Jacob with the Angel as a *zanni* scene—while both quoting biblical verses and alluding to the implied corporeal dimensions of the biblical text—de' Sommi is in fact conjuring a new, profane theatrical compound of text and body, one in which myth and performance relate to each other anew.

As a matter of fact, since in Jewish ritual in de' Sommi's times myth was rarely performed at all but rather recited in the synagogue (and thus embodied in a rather limited manner), the playful, profaning use of the Holy Tongue and Jewish texts in de' Sommi's comedy stems precisely from the combination of Hebrew allusions with the theatrical physicality of the comic stage. Since much of the *ludus* in the play derives directly from the humanist tradition of the Italian stage, it seems that it is comic performance that allows de' Sommi to imagine his textual, mythical tradition in terms of physical play and to reinscribe a new kind of playful dynamics among Scripture, body, and space. Thus, the "new use" enabled through de' Sommi's profanation of the Holy Tongue, to be sure, has a very tangible meaning as theatrical praxis. Onstage, sacred text and Holy Tongue become materials to be embodied, enunciated, and performed by actors—indeed, to be bodily used. And—through the performers' usage of Hebrew and of the Jewish canon—the Jewish audience of Mantua is also offered a new kind of playful use, and knowledge, of their traditions.

The play's politics, to be sure, are more complex than the ones assigned by Agamben to the process of profanation. As much as the play opens up sacred texts and language for playful use, its self-declared political aim is to reaffirm a stable cultural identity for the Jews of Italy. Indeed, while Agamben sees play as a form of "freed behavior" that empties cultural forms "of any obligatory relationship to an end," thus turning into "pure means,"[58] the play's prologue insists precisely that it does have an end: it seeks to prove the virtues of Hebrew and strengthen Jewish-Italian cultural identity. In a sense, then, while fully participating in the Italian humanist project, the play at the same time makes a move of separation, delineating and maintaining some kind of borderline between the Jewish way of life, already set apart to some degree (legally, ritually, and culturally), and the nation around it. In this sense, not only does the prologue refuse to empty comedy "of any obligatory relationship to an end"—but the specific end announced in the prologue is one that reaffirms separations, hierarchies, and even the sacred status of Hebrew ("what is a crowning glory for other languages is used as nothing but a shoe-sole by this Holy Tongue").

And yet, one may discern some kind of tension between the claims of the prologue and the dynamics of the play itself. While the prologue offers Hebrew as a stable marker of cultural identity, the qualities of which can be shown through comedy without hindrance, the comedy's destabilizing theatrical play with Scripture seems to imply otherwise. The play juggles with the Holy Tongue and displays its fickleness—with Rav Hamdan serving only as the peak of carnivalesque playfulness taking place throughout *Tsahut bedihuta deqiddushin*. In the same manner that the explicit victory of Rabbi Amitai is undermined by the play's implicit celebration of Rav Hamdan's Talmudic playfulness—so are the self-declared claims of the allegorical prologue about the stability of language as a marker of cultural identity put into tension with the destabilizing forces of the comedy itself. While the social, sexual and halakhic order might well be resumed by the end of the play,[59] the linguistic order does not necessarily follow suit. De' Sommi's prospective opponents, the "mocking hypocrites" from the prologue, can hardly rest assured: through play, the Holy Tongue has been put to new use, and there are no signs of it fully returning to its supposed origin in the sacred sphere.

And as a marker of cultural identity, when employed by the genre of Italian comedy, the Hebrew of *Tsahut bedihuta deqiddushin* necessarily occupies a liminal or hybrid place, mediating as it does Jewish and Italian humanist cultural practices. Renaissance Jewish-Italian cultural identity emerges in the play as anything but univocal or self-enclosed, in a move which parallels (and is entwined with) the playful exploration of Jewish textual tradition as polyphonic, conflictual, and unstable: indeed, as the stuff of Renaissance humanist comedy.

Thus, some gap unfolds between the play's "end" (the assertion of Hebrew's qualities and of a distinct Jewish-Italian cultural identity) and its "means" (the playfulness of the comedy itself). This gap is inherent in the double nature of Hebrew in the play, noted above: both a sacred tongue and one that participates in the formation of a group cultural identity in Renaissance Italy. Serving as the latter, Hebrew must prove its qualities in the emerging genre of comedy, as Italian does—but being also the former, it cannot do so without risking, in a sense, its own qualities as Holy Tongue.

Risking, yet not "simply abolishing"—for the profanation of the Holy Tongue achieved by de' Sommi in his comedy in fact employs the function of Hebrew in the sacred sphere, its connotations, layers, and resonance, and opens it into "new use."[60] Within the framework of Italian Renaissance comedy, de' Sommi thus offers Jewish-Italian theater as a new space for the playful reuse of the Holy Tongue and of Scripture and articulates the possible meaning of Hebrew drama, hardly even beginning to emerge in his times—thus tracing what such a drama could be, what it can do.

Notes

Some of the material in this paper has appeared in different form as: "The Stage as a Space for *Midrash:* Theatre and the Jewish Hermeneutic Project," in *Jewish Theatre: Tradition in Transition and Intercultural Vistas (Assaph: Studies in the Theatre 22–23),* ed. Ahuva Belkin (Tel Aviv: Tel Aviv University Press, 2008), 11–23. The author would like to thank Mira Balberg, Carey Seal, Lilla P. Toal, Moulie Vidas, and the anonymous readers of *Renaissance Drama* for reading earlier versions of this essay, which benefited greatly from their useful suggestions and criticism. William N. West and Albert R. Ascoli were of immense help with their patience, dedication, and comments. Special thanks are also in order to Dror Yinon, for one casual—yet crucial—comment, which changed the course of this essay.

1. Yehudah Sommo, *Tsahut bedihuta deqiddushin*, ed. Hayyim Schirmann (Jerusalem and Tel Aviv: Tarshish/Dvir, 1965), 29–30. See also Leone de' Sommi, *A Comedy of Betrothal*, trans. Alfred S. Golding (Ottawa: Dovehouse, 1988), 68. As Golding's translation of the play does not always make full use of the allusions of the original Hebrew, most translations here will be my own (consulting Golding's), to emphasize the allusive quality of the text. References will therefore be made to Hayyim Schirmann's Hebrew edition, which will be followed, for the sake of convenience, by a parenthetic reference to the equivalent in the English translation.

2. The only extant play written by a Jewish playwright before *Tsahut bedihuta deqiddushin* is Ezekiel's *Exagoge*, a Jewish-Hellenistic tragedy written in Alexandria during the second century B.C.E. Only fragments of this play have survived. The *Exagoge*, however, was written in Greek, not Hebrew.

3. On this cultural process, see Arthur M. Lesley, "Jewish Adaptation of Humanist Concepts in Fifteenth- and Sixteenth-Century Italy," in *Essential Papers on Jewish Culture in Renaissance and Baroque Italy*, ed. David B Ruderman, 45–62 (New York and London: New York University Press, 1992).

4. David Biale, "Preface: Toward a Cultural History of the Jews," in *Cultures of the Jews: A New History*, ed. David Biale (New York: Schocken, 2002), xix. See also Robert Bonfil, *Jewish Life in Renaissance Italy*, trans. Anthony Oldcorn (Berkeley: University of California Press, 1994), 146.

5. See Shlomo Simonsohn, *History of the Jews in the Duchy of Mantua* (Jerusalem: Kiryat Sefer, 1962), 479–87 (in Hebrew).

6. Dunbar H. Ogden, "De' Sommi in '88: Dynamics of Theatrical Space," in *Leone de' Sommi and the Performing Arts*, ed. Ahuva Belkin (Tel Aviv: Tel Aviv University Press, 1997), 241. As the Jewish community was to cover the costly performances from its own pocket, these performances would have been a considerable financial burden for the community. See Simonsohn, *History of the Jews in the Duchy of Mantua*, 287–88.

7. Ogden, "De' Sommi in '88," 236.

8. Kristine Hecker, "The Concept of Theatre Production in Leone de' Sommi's *Quattro dialoghi* in the Context of his Time," in *Leone de' Sommi and the Performing Arts*, 189. Hecker mentions Giraldi Cinthio's *Discorso intorno al comporre delle comedie e delle tragedie* as the only earlier example in Renaissance Italy of a treatise dealing with issues of theatrical performance, albeit on a much more limited scale than de' Sommi's (190). According to Hecker, de' Sommi was certainly acquainted with the *Discorso*, and might have met Cinthio while in Ferrara.

9. See, among others, Toby Cole and Helen Krich Chinoy, *Directors on Directing: A Source Book of the Modern Theatre* (Indianapolis: Bobbs-Merill Co., 1963), 16–17; Georges Banu, "De' Sommi, or 'Stage Cement,'" in *Leone de' Sommi and the Performing Arts*, 211–19; J. Guinsburg, "Leone de' Sommi: A Precursor of Modern Theatricality," in *Leone de' Sommi and the Performing Arts*, 221–29; Anna Migliarisi, *Renaissance and Baroque Directors: Theory and Practice of Play Production in Italy* (New York: Legas, 2003), 13–60.

10. Cristina Dal Molin, "Recovery of Some Unedited Manuscripts by Leone de' Sommi at the National Library of Turin," in *Leone de' Sommi and the Performing Arts*, 114.

11. Massimo Ciavolella, "Text as (Pre)Text: Leone de' Sommi's *Three Sisters*," in *Leone de' Sommi and the Performing Arts*, 151.

12. Shimon Levy, "A Comparison of Theory and Practice in de' Sommi's *Dialogues* and *A Comedy of Betrothal*," in *Leone de' Sommi and the Performing Arts*, 186 (emphasis is Levy's).

13. Lesley, "Jewish Adaptation of Humanist Concepts in Fifteenth- and Sixteenth-Century Italy," 45.

14. While there is still no direct evidence that *Tsahut bedihuta deqiddushin* was indeed performed in de' Sommi's time, it is quite clear from the text of the play that it was written for performance and not merely to be read. See Schirmann's preface to his edition of *Tsahut bedihuta deqiddushin,* 22-23.

15. Moshe Halbertal, *People of the Book: Canon, Meaning and Authority* (Cambridge, Mass.: Harvard University Press, 1997), 1-3; 6-10. That said, I am hardly interested in promoting here a notion of Jewish culture as a purely textual one (as if such a culture can exist) that neglects, denies, or represses the visual. On the political dangers and scholarly problems inherent in such a totalizing notion, see Kalman P. Bland, *The Artless Jew: Medieval and Modern Affirmations and Denials of the Visual* (Princeton: Princeton University Press, 2000).

16. Simonsohn, *History of the Jews in the Duchy of Mantua,* 436-38. For more on the textual practices of early modern Italian Jews see Robert Bonfil, *Jewish Life in Renaissance Italy,* 149-51.

17. Hayyim Schirmann, "Theater and Music in the Jewish Neighborhoods of Italy," *Zion* 29 (1964): 70 (in Hebrew).

18. Simonsohn, *History of the Jews in the Duchy of Mantua,* 436.

19. Ibid., 438.

20. Bernardo Dovizi da Bibbiena, *La calandria* (Turin: Giulio Einaudi, 1978), 15; Bibbiena, "*La calandra (The Comedy of Calandro*)," in *Five Comedies from the Italian Renaissance,* ed. and trans. Laura Giannetti and Guido Ruggiero (Baltimore and London: Johns Hopkins University Press, 2003), 2.

21. It is in fact debated whether to attribute this prologue to Bibbiena himself or to Castiglione. See Bibbiena, "*La calandra (The Comedy of Calandro*)," 2n2.

22. On this process, see also Richard Andrews, *Scripts and Scenarios: The Performance of Comedy in Renaissance Italy* (Cambridge: Cambridge University Press, 1993), 6-8.

23. The issue of Hebrew's sacred status should also be considered vis-à-vis the Christian culture of the period. As a recent study by Daniel Stein Kokin shows, Christian Hebraists in Renaissance Italy were in fact forming new concepts of Hebrew as Holy Tongue—so that one may speak of a process of "a striking (re-)sacralization of Hebrew" taking place in the sixteenth century. See Daniel Stein Kokin, "The Hebrew Question in the Italian Renaissance: Linguistic, Cultural and Mystical Perspectives" (Ph.D. diss., Harvard University, 2006), 18. Kokin posits this narrative contra the one established by Marie-Luce Demonet-Launay, which claims that one may locate the opposite process in the Renaissance, in which Hebrew gradually lost its sacred status. See Marie-Luce Demonet-Launay, "La désacralisation de l'hébreu au XVIe siècle," in *L'hébreu au temps de la Renaissance,* ed. Ilana Zinguer, 154-71 (Leiden: E.J. Brill, 1992); Kokin, "The Hebrew Question in the Italian Renaissance,"197-98, 234. Since Christian Hebraism was prominent in Renaissance Mantua, as noted above, it is quite probable that de' Sommi was acquainted with this discourse as well. I am deeply grateful to Daniel Stein Kokin for allowing me to consult his work for the writing of this essay.

24. Michael Worton and Judith Still, introduction to *Intertextuality: Theories and Practices,* ed. Michael Worton and Judith Still (Manchester and New York: Manchester University Press, 1990), 12.

25. For a discussion of the play and its dynamics within the context of Jewish-Italian procedures of betrothal and marriage in the Renaissance, see Roni Weinstein, *Marriage Rituals Italian Style: A Historical Anthropological Perspective on Early Modern Italian Jews* (Leiden and Boston: Brill, 2004), 44, 345-49, 466.

26. The phrase is borrowed from Shimon Levy's theatrical readings of the Bible. See Shimon Levy, *The Bible as Theatre* (Brighton: Sussex Academic Press, 2002).

27. Hanna Scolnicov has explored the possible staging of *Tsahut bedihuta deqiddushin* within Serlian scenographic conventions. See Hanna Scolnicov, "Staging *A Comedy of Betrothal* on the Serlian Stage," in *Leone de' Sommi and the Performing Arts,* 1997), 119-32. Alfred S. Golding, however, argues that such stage design might be too expensive for the Jewish community—and suggests other scenographic possibilities from the practice of sixteenth-century Italian theater. See Alfred S. Golding, "*A Comedy of Betrothal:* Some Suggestions for a Reconstruction of its Premiere Performance," in *Leone de' Sommi and the Performing Arts,* 134-38. Either way, the play's conventions of dramatic space are those of most Italian Renaissance comedies: several houses surrounding an exterior public space.

28. Hanna Scolnicov, *Woman's Theatrical Space* (Cambridge: Cambridge University Press, 1994), 41-68; Maggie Günsberg, *Gender and the Italian Stage* (Cambridge: Cambridge University Press, 1997), 6-28. This linkage between women and the interior sphere of the house had, of course, its equivalents in rabbinic cultural tradition as well. See Charlotte E. Fonrobert, *Menstrual Purity: Rabbinic and Christian Reconstructions of Biblical Gender* (Stanford: Stanford University Press, 2000), 40-67.

29. Bibbiena, *La calandria,* 62; Bibbiena, "*La calandra (The Comedy of Calandro),*" 40-41.

30. Schirmann, Preface to *Tsahut bedihuta deqiddushin,* 23. For further discussion of the practice of casting male actors in female roles in sixteenth-century Italy, see also Günsberg, *Gender and the Italian Stage,* 58-59. In his *Quattro dialoghi in materia di rappresentazioni sceniche,* de' Sommi himself refers to this practice, as well as to the existence of female actresses in this transitional period. See Leone de' Sommi, *Quattro dialoghi in materia di rappresentazioni sceniche* (Milano: Il Polifilo, 1968), 39-43.

31. Israel Davidson, *Parody in Jewish Literature* (New York: Columbia University Press, 1907), 19-29.

32. Ibid., 26n58.

33. See Yonatan Dubossarsky, "The First Hebrew Drama Reconsidered," in *Studies in Literature—Presented to Simon Halkin,* ed. Ezra Fleischer (Jerusalem: Magnes, 1973), 2-3 (in Hebrew).

34. Resemblances between this plotline and Ariosto's *La lena* have already been noticed by Schirmann (Schirmann, Preface to *Tsahut bedihuta deqiddushin,* 20).

35. The extent to which Beruriah herself is part of the plan from the beginning is left disturbingly unclear in the comedy. Before being separated from Yedidiah (earlier in the play), Beruriah tells him that if he arrives to meet her at the field, she will grant him "all the tokens and proofs of her love," but not at the price of her honor (59 [99]). On the other hand, Yedidiah, after sleeping with Beruriah, reports how much both of them enjoyed the sex and that Beruriah has agreed never to be with any other man but him (73 [114-15]). But, much like the case of Callimaco's report on Lucrezia's response to having sex with him in *La mandragola,* given Beruriah's earlier words we might wish to consider a possible gap between Yedidiah's experience and that of Beruriah. A very different report of the event is given by Yeqarah, who is unaware of the scheme and, witnessing the sexual act from afar, indeed believes it to be rape. She speaks of Beruriah's "burning eyes" and "flushed cheeks" as signs of rage (while the audience might interpret them as signs of pleasure)—but even she admits, when interrogated by Amon, that Beruriah started screaming for help only *after* she noticed Yeqarah's presence. Before that, her lips only moved voicelessly, as Yedidiah was "biting her lips and tongue like a mute dog" (75

[116]). Beruriah herself does not appear onstage after these events, so the audience does not receive her point of view in an unmediated manner.

36. Rav Hamdan is referring here to the laws of seduction and rape, as they are formulated in Deuteronomy 22:23-27: "If there is a betrothed virgin, and a man meets her in the city and lies with her, then you shall bring them both out to the gate of that city, and you shall stone them to death with stones, the young woman because she did not cry for help though she was in the city, and the man because he violated his neighbor's wife. So you shall purge the evil from your midst. But if in the open country [literally: "in the field"] a man meets a young woman who is betrothed, and the man seizes her and lies with her, then only the man who lay with her shall die. But you shall do nothing to the young woman; she has committed no offense punishable by death. For this case is like that of a man attacking and murdering his neighbor, because he met her in the open country, and though the betrothed young woman cried for help there was no one to rescue her." Thus, it would seem that de' Sommi is turning away from the conventional space in Italian comedy for sexual encounters—i.e., the interior of the house—in order to charge dramatic space (an offstage space, in this case) with connotations derived from biblical law.

37. Dubossarsky, "The First Hebrew Drama Reconsidered," 2.

38. Ibid.

39. The classical study on this typology in rabbinic culture is still Ephraim Elimelech Urbach, "Prophet and Sage in the Jewish Heritage," in *Collected Writings in Jewish Studies,* ed. Robert Brody and Moshe D. Herr, 393–403 (Jerusalem: Magnes Press, 1999).

40. Francesco Loriggio, "Prefacing Renaissance Comedy: The Double, Laughter and Comic Structure," in *Comparative Critical Approaches to Renaissance Comedy,* ed. Donald Beecher and Massimo Ciavolella (Ottawa: Dovehouse, 1986), 103.

41. Menahem Silver, "A Debate Poem from the Fifteenth Century: The War between 'the Verse' and the Talmud," *Italia* 7, nos. 1 and 2 (1988): 7-28 (in Hebrew).

42. Simonsohn, *History of the Jews in the Duchy of Mantua,* 422, 437; Bonfil, *Jewish Life in Renaissance Italy,* 153.

43. The English translation here ". . . for I have lived in the land of Israel . . . I lived in the Galilee for two whole years...." seems to be incorrect. The Hebrew states כי גר אנכי בארץ . . . זה שנתים ימים שבאתי להתגורר בגליל הזה. Rav Hamdan uses the word גֵר (ger, which can be translated as "newcomer," "immigrant," or "noncitizen") and not גָר (gar, "living in"). His words here, rather, should be "for I am a newcomer in the land." These words are, in fact, an allusion to Psalms 119:19: "I am a sojourner [ger] on the earth. . . ." Furthermore, the reference to the galil (גליל) in the text does not indicate the Galilee, but refers to the more generic use of the word, that is, a land district. Rav Hamdan does not say that he lived in the Galilee for two years but, instead, that he has been living in "this district," that is, the city of Sidon, for *only* two years. All of this is used by Rav Hamdan in order to explain to Shoval why he does not recognize him and not, as the translation would have it, to reassure Shoval that he *does* recognize him.

44. Simonsohn, *History of the Jews in the Duchy of Mantua,* 363-64.

45. C. L. Barber's famous formulation of Shakespeare's use of ritual in his comedies might illuminate this process. Barber notes how Shakespeare "gives the ritual pattern aesthetic actuality by discovering expressions of it in the fragmentary and incomplete gestures of daily life. . . . In making drama out of rituals of state, Shakespeare makes clear their meaning as social and psychological conflict, as history." See C. L. Barber, *Shakespeare's Festive Comedy: A Study of Dramatic Form and Its Relation to Social Custom* (Princeton: Princeton University Press, 1959), 15. In de' Sommi's case, of course, "rituals of state" are less central (even though the Purimic rituals of the community certainly are crucial

here), as he finds social conflict and cultural tensions in the Jewish community's textual (both mythic and hermeneutic) traditions and practices.

46. Riccardo Scrivano, "Towards a 'Philosophy' of Renaissance Theatre," in *Comparative Critical Approaches to Renaissance Comedy*, 12.

47. Laura Giannetti, "On the Deceptions of the Deceived: Lelia and the Pleasures of Play," *MLN* 116, no. 1 (2001): 54–59.

48. Giuseppe Mazzotta, *The World at Play in Boccaccio's Decameron* (Princeton: Princeton University Press, 1986), 130.

49. Ibid., 118.

50. Ibid., 119 (emphasis is Mazzotta's).

51. Ibid.

52. Ibid.

53. Ibid. Mazzotta continues exploring how in fact allegory and pornography are structurally similar: "pornography is an allegory, for like allegory it needs a cover. In allegory, the ambiguities are provided by the husk that envelopes the moral kernel; in the present figuration of pornography, morality is the chaff hiding the erotic fruit" (ibid.). By the cinquecento, however, pornographers such as Aretino have in fact moved away from this mode of indirection and, as Paula Findlen puts it, "often presented their work as the end of metaphor. . . . They loudly proclaimed that their works laid bare the truth, stripped of all the metaphorical witticisms and allegories that characterized the contemporary culture of learning. . . . Pornography purported to unveil 'the thing' itself." See Paula Findeln, "Humanism, Politics and Pornography in Renaissance Italy," in *The Invention of Pornography: Obscenity and the Origins of Modernity, 1500–1800*, ed. Lynn Hunt (New York: Zone Books, 1993), 77.

54. The Jewish tradition of interpreting the Song of Songs allegorically notwithstanding. As a matter of fact, as can be seen above, de' Sommi indeed employs the Song of Songs in a manner similar to that which Mazzotta finds in Boccaccio's treatment of the Song (see Mazzotta, *The World at Play in Boccaccio's Decameron*, 111–12).

55. Giorgio Agamben, *Profanations*, trans. Jeff Fort (New York: Zone Books, 2007), 74.

56. Ibid., 77.

57. Ibid., 75–76. Agamben is referring here to Émile Benveniste, "Le jeu comme structure," *Deucalion* 2 (1947): 161–67.

58. Agamben, *Profanations*, 86.

59. See also Giannetti, "On the Deceptions of the Deceived: Lelia and the Pleasures of Play," 59.

60. We might thus posit the playful profanation of Hebrew taking place in de' Sommi's comedy vis-à-vis Gershom Scholem's famous fear of the modern secularization of Hebrew that he dreads will plague Zionism. In a letter from 1926, Scholem writes to German-Jewish philosopher Franz Rosenzweig that "another threat confronts us that is a *necessary* consequence of the Zionist undertaking: What about the 'actualization' of Hebrew? . . . The secularization of language is only a *façon de parler*, a ready-made phrase. It is absolutely impossible to empty out words filled to bursting, unless one does so at the expense of language itself." See Gershom Scholem, "Confession on the Subject of Our Language," in Jacques Derrida, *Acts of Religion*, ed. Gil Anidjar (New York and London: Routledge, 2002), 226. While such secularization, according to Scholem, is actually a repression of language's religious charge, the profaning use of the Holy Tongue in *Tsahut bedihuta deqiddushin* might be seen as one that, instead of "emptying out words filled to bursting," simply (or maybe not so simply) plays with them.

Sincerity, Fraud, and Audience Reception in the Performance of Early Modern Poverty

ROBERT HENKE

As Erving Goffman argues in *The Presentation of Self in Everyday Life,* the degree to which the everyday performer believes in his or her own public presentation may vary widely:

> When an individual plays a part he implicitly requests his observers to take seriously the impression that is fostered before them. . . . At one extreme, one finds that the performer can be fully taken in by his own act; he can be sincerely convinced that the impression of reality which he stages is the real reality. When his audience is also convinced in this way about the show he puts on—and this seems to be the typical case—then for the moment at least, only the sociologist or the socially disgruntled will have any doubts about the "realness" of what is presented. At the other extreme, we find that the performer may not be taken in at all by his own routine. . . . When the individual has no belief in his own act and no ultimate concern with the beliefs of his audience, we may call him cynical, reserving the term "sincere" for individuals who believe in the impression fostered by their own performance. It should be observed that the cynic, with all his professional disinvolvement, may obtain unprofessional pleasures from his masquerade, experiencing a kind of gleeful spiritual aggression from the fact that he can toy at will with something his audience must take seriously.[1]

Early modern begging, as it was practiced in the roads, streets, and piazzas of a sixteenth-century Europe overwhelmed by poverty and demographic disruption, was a ubiquitous "poor theater" characterized by widely differing degrees of belief in the performance, both on the part of the beggar and on the part of the potential almsgiver. Contemporary literature on the beggar written in Germany, Italy, Spain, France, and England usually simplified this complex exchange, claiming that many beggars had no belief in their own performance and delighted in manipulating their audiences, like Goffman's cynical performer. According to the unmasking and debunking "beggar's book," whose immense transnational success rather reflects collective anxiety about the new multitudes than it describes their actual conditions, the performer merely aimed to defraud his audience, and the vigilant author—standing in for the municipal representative charged with the problem of crowd control and poor relief—had to convert the audience's naïve, absolute belief to thoroughgoing disbelief.

But Goffman goes on to argue that the "sincere" and the "cynical" performers plot two extremes in a spectrum and that most everyday performers fall somewhere between the two poles.[2] In fact, the early modern individual presenting himself as a beggar in a highly mobile and flexible street theater could run the gamut between full belief in his own destitution and the cynical manipulation of his audience. For the latter's part, they might totally believe the beggar, altogether disbelieve, or experience a mixture of credence and skepticism, even at different points of the performance. It is not difficult to configure the various permutations: an audience totally believing a cynical manipulator, an audience totally disbelieving a sincere and deserving indigent, and various degrees of performer sincerity measured across one axis that could be plotted with points drawn from a similarly varying axis of audience belief.

Considering the practice of begging in the present day may clarify this phenomenon of complex audience response. It might fairly be generalized that European begging, in cities such as Rome, tends to employ long-established, formulaic, and exaggerated gestures (such as prostration) and vocal inflections, as well as the strategic use of physical spaces like the church threshold and the echoing, acoustically resonant piazza. It is possible for the potential almsgiver both to note the stylization and exaggeration of the European beggar and to feel enough belief and charity to still give money. American beggars, less availing of established gestural-vocal forms and symbolically and acoustically advantageous public places, both sacred and profane, tend to favor narrative in their attempt to arrest the moving target of charity: the causally concatenated story of catastrophe meant to elicit both pity and charity from the passerby.

In the American paradigm, it is particularly clear that the audience may both partially believe and partially disbelieve the narrative; furthermore, the performer might even be rewarded for the sheer power of his or her story, irrespective of its truth claims. In the recent film *Ray,* about Ray Charles, when the blind African-American musician pleads with an unsympathetic, racist busdriver to give him a ride and is finally driven to invent the story that he has been blinded while serving in the Normandy invasion, we as the film audience may well believe that his "lie" qualifies as something like truth.

Singing for his supper, performing for his life in a high-stakes itinerant street theater, the early modern beggar deployed the performative arts of voice, costume, makeup, gesture, and facial expression to present a story that would convince the bystander of his or her need. Beyond the fact that mere begging amounted to a kind of performance, there was a thin line in the period between begging and obviously performative forms of itinerant poverty, such as musical performance, mountebank activity, fortune-telling, and, indeed, acting.[3] The "scene" of the variously incarnated beggar and bystander could be one of skeptical debunking, charitable belief, or a complex and performatively interesting combination of both. The beggar-bystander relationship therefore had much in common with the theatrical encounter between actor and audience member in the early modern period, which while certainly capable of proto-Brechtian distancing effects also often involved illusionistic complicity between spectator and actor, as contracted by the Chorus in the prologue to Shakespeare's *Henry V.* Furthermore, the actor, always already itinerant from the dawn of the internationally influential *commedia dell'arte,* was often conflated by the authorities with beggars and itinerants.[4] It is, therefore, no surprise that, beginning with Italian early modern theater, the beggar-bystander relationship was frequently fictionalized in improvised and scripted drama. Italian, Spanish, or English theatrical renditions of this encounter, codified in either script or scenario, could be extremely compelling onstage, especially when they staged the very drama of audience belief.

For an opening example of complex "sincerity" on the part of the beggar-performer, which also illustrates the ways in which begging tended to assume stylized and exaggerated forms, we might consider a moment from the third chapter of the Spanish picaresque novel *Lazarillo de Tormes,* published in 1554. In this episode, Lazarillo's new master is a delusional example of the so-called shame-faced poor: those from the upper classes who had fallen on hard times but were often protected by special in-stitutional dispensations from having to present themselves publicly as beggars. Not benefiting from any institutional support, Lazarillo's master, who calls himself a squire, cannot publicly admit that he is poor, and at a certain point the famished and desperate Lazarillo is finally driven to the streets to perform the forms of poverty:

Desque vi ser las dos y no venía y la hambre me aquejaba, cierro mi puerta y pongo la llave do mandó y tórnome a mi menester. Con baja y enferma voz y inclinadas mis manos en los senos, puesto Dios ante mis ojos y la lengua en su nombre, comienzo a pedir pan por las puertas y casas más grandes que me pa-recía. Mas como yo este oficio le hobiese mamado en la leche (quiero decir que con el gran maestro el ciego lo aprendí), tan suficiente discípulo salí, que aunque en este pueblo no había caridad ni el año fuese muy abundante, tan buena maña me di, que antes que el reloj diese las cuatro ya yo tenía otras tantas libras de pan ensiladas en el cuerpo, y más de otras dos en las mangas y senos.

When I saw that it was two o'clock and he still hadn't come back, and I was going through the tortures of hunger, I shut the door and put the key where he'd told me to and went back to plying my old trade. In a low, sickly voice, with my hands drooping over my breast with God in front of my eyes and His Name on my tongue, I set about begging bread at the doorways of whichever big houses looked most promising. It was a calling which I'd sucked in with my mother's milk; what I mean is, I'd learned it in my youth from a great master, the blind man, and I'd turned out to be such a good pupil that though there was scant charity in that town and it had not been a very prosperous year, I was able to work the art to very good effect, so that before the clock struck four I had as many pounds of bread stowed away inside me and another two tucked into my sleeves and the front of my shirt.[5]

Lazarillo's begging is palpably theatrical, and in twenty-first century terms it resembles performance art more than it does traditional mimetic theater. Although nothing prevents a skeptical bystander from interpret-ing Lazarillo's performance as a sham persona aesthetically disparate from the supposed real person—who would then be revealed as a shifty and lazy charlatan—much like the performance artist, Lazarillo creates a heightened awareness of his own exaggerated and italicized body, which becomes autobiography: the speaking text of poverty.[6] The concentrated, distilled, exaggerated, and skilled use of voice, gesture, gait, grimace, and narrative, and the manner in which Lazarillo conjures an invisible spiri-tual third party—God in front of his eyes—provides a performance that stages his own belief and entreats that of the audience. That Lazarillo's begging is the accomplished product of many years of training does not necessarily compromise its "sincerity," since the "calling," or "trade" (*menester*) has been acquired under conditions of real poverty. In a way that would have been particularly compelling in a Catholic culture that had long sanctioned the itinerant mendicant orders, Lazarillo aims to sanctify the formal "corpograms"[7] of degradation, asking his audience to lend him an aura of belief as they would the traveling friar. A lifetime of hunger has pressed desire-based forms into existence that are exaggerated and grotesque, like the bulge of the *commedia dell'arte* mask or the ironically distended stomach of the *zanni*.[8] In the Latin sense of "performance," by which *per* can means "through to its completion," Lazarillo performs his very real destitution by extending physical and vocal forms to an exaggerated and "completed" degree—as developed by a lifetime of practicing his *menester*.

Lazarillo's performance, if closest to Goffman's pole of sincerity for the readers of the novel, nicely represents the complex early modern mode of performativity that, I would argue, characterized both actual begging and begging as it was represented in both literary and visual texts. This early modern mode can be illuminated by contrasting it with the two extremes of Goffman's spectrum as they manifested themselves in medieval and early modern culture: the medieval paradigm and, as already mentioned, the debunking beggar's book.

The medieval practice of charity, at least in the ideal model, can be seen to exemplify the pole of externally codified "sincerity" on behalf of both performer and audience. Historians of poverty such as Bronislaw Geremek have corrected the tendency to romanticize the medieval perception of poverty, demonstrating that the suspicion that the poor combine idleness and deceit certainly pervaded medieval discourse on the poor.[9] English ordinances against "idlers and vagabonds," which aim to distinguish between the "legitimate" and "illegitimate" poor, may be found at least as far back as 1284.[10] Still, churches, monasteries, and confraternities provided an institutional frame that ritually legitimated the performance of poverty. Collective acts of charity publicly performed by religious institutions, such as the calendrically regulated mass distributions of food performed at monasteries such as the Abbey of Cluny, involved large and theatrical demonstrations that certainly did not threaten the social order.[11] When Saint Louis, as a nearly contemporary observer recorded, distributed alms to churches, hospices, leper hospitals, and even to those at his own table, it was a theatrical performance, by which socially codified forms guaranteed the efficacy of the exchange.[12] The very felicity of the performance rendered it less theatrical than the early modern cases we are investigating here, since persuasion, belief, and choice—central to the theatrical experience—were not dynamically in play.

What underpinned these public acts of charity was the fact that medieval habits of mind tended to judge in favor of the poor, according to the formula *in dubio pro paupere* (in doubt [believe] the poor person). When the itinerant mendicant, priest, preacher, relic-seller, or pilgrim was conflated with the vagabond, it tended to be the latter who was sanctified, rather than the priest who was tainted. What was clear—and marks a difference of degree between medieval and early modern periods—was that palpable advantages were accorded to the rich for giving to the poor, even if the latter were lying, since the rich were rewarded for their charitable intent. The beggar-almsgiver exchange was really a contract, and as a performance was more stable in both theatrical and socioeconomic terms than what is here proposed as the early modern paradigm: the rich gave to beggars so that the latter would pray for their souls.[13] And so the beggar's petition—at least in the model medieval paradigm—was a felicitous speech-act, judged to be sincere, or sincere enough, by the dispenser of charity. The hierarchical, socially conservative structure of charity did not depend on compassion or any specific emotional response on the part of the almsgiver, nor even on the truth claims of the petitioner.

In the fifteenth century, the new poverty structurally required by the new wealth of early modern capitalism taxed the medieval system of charity beyond its limits, and the effects were evident throughout Europe. The medieval arrangement by and large had succeeded because monasteries and churches were able to address, more or less, rural poverty and thus avoid massive migration to the cities. But demographic growth in the fifteenth century tested the limits of agrarian technology, especially for peasants who could not compete with the capital, resources, and economies of scale enjoyed by the larger landholders, and country dwellers flocked to cities such as London, Venice, Paris, and Madrid.[14] The gains from new trading routes established in the age of discovery generated a pan-European price inflation that sharply lowered the real wages of small landholders. In the transition from a feudal to a capitalist society, and from agrarian to industrial structures, poverty for the first time became, in the words of Bronislaw Geremek, a "mass phenomenon."[15] The sheer volume of the new arrivals severely taxed urban resources, which had to develop new technologies of control and charity, with a particular concern about the spreading of the bubonic plague, typhus, and other infectious diseases by "foreign," itinerant beggars newly arrived in the city. Reflecting (and possibly influenced by) reforms taking place throughout western Europe in the 1520s, the Venetian state began to enact systematic social legislation, including a poor tax that rationalized and controlled the distribution of charity. As Brian Pullan has demonstrated in his magisterial account of poverty in early modern Venice, the vagrant poor were identified, counted, contained, disciplined, and, when necessary, evicted by new state apparatuses.[16] It was now essential to distinguish between presumed "illegitimate" and "legitimate" beggars.

Increased municipal scrutiny of the poor was coupled with an early Reformation critique of the mendicant orders and those beggars who drew upon their aura, and it is in the antimendicant discourse of Martin Luther and the beggar's books that the performative mode of sham theatricality is most fully articulated. In an introduction that Luther wrote to the 1528 edition of the anonymous German *Liber vagatorum* (*Book of the Vagabonds*), he declares that he too has been hoodwinked by charlatan indigents and promotes the book because it will help the reader identify the canny arts of the false beggars, which include elaborate verbal and visual codes.[17] For Luther, the *Liber vagatorum* usefully instructs princes, lords, and counselors, as well as innocent bystanders, on the semiotics of the street, providing cant glossaries that can help decode the charlatans' mysterious language (drawn from the Jews, claims Luther), and an extremely detailed visual semiotic guide that can help one distinguish between the truly deserving beggar and those who are just acting. Such rational scrutiny, for Luther, will help counteract the performative charisma of the fraudulent beggars, among whom the mendicant friars are the most pernicious because of their capacity to "place God in front of [their] eyes," as Lazarillo puts it. Heightened rational scrutiny of theatrical and fraudulent beggars, who for Luther are usually "foreigners," will help generate a more rational, state-controlled apportionment of charity, now redirected toward the deserving—local—poor. Having himself been a victim of the beggars' performative verve, Luther vigorously supports the *Liber*'s project of exposing them as imposters.

The classic beggar's book, of which the most familiar example to English speakers is Thomas Harman's 1565 *A Caveat for Common Cursetors*,[18] actually has origins in German municipal registers dating back to the 1340s, apparently written by clerks with a lively literary imagination, but still presumably with documentary intent. The German registers categorize beggars into various subspecialties, and in these archival registers from towns like Augsberg and Strasbourg, many of the categories are those of religious imposters. The registers' concern to eradicate the deceptive performance of religion thus anticipates Luther's introduction to the *Liber vagatorum*. The city records of Augsberg in 1342, already employing the technical vocabulary of cant, list those who pretend to be converted Jews (*Hürlentzer*); those simulating pilgrims and frequenting churches (*Clannier*); those pretending to be sick (*Grentzier*); beggars impersonating monks (*Münser*); and false penitents (*Serpner*).[19] In 1343, also in Augsberg, five categories are added, and the *Basler Betrügnisse der Gyler,* containing municipal depositions in Basle between 1411 and 1463, increases the categories to some twenty-four. Copied several times, and significantly modified by Mathias von Kemnat in 1475, the *Basler Betrügnisse* might well have influenced the *Liber vagatorum* and thus provided a conduit from the municipal records, which have a surprisingly literary color, to the early modern beggar's books.

In their fullest flower, between 1480 and 1520 on the continent, and a bit later in England, these books enumerate a dazzling panoply of performers: those feigning to be blind, deaf-mutes, lame, mad, deserting soldiers, peddlers, hermits, relic sellers, priests, escaped captives of the Turks, Jews repeatedly converting to Christianity, pilgrims, penitents, lepers, miracle mongers, those afflicted with gangrene, paralytics, tremblers, epileptics, teeth-shakers, and professors (these last further subdivided according to institutions, such as Cambridge or Oxford!). There appears to be almost no role that these prodigious masters of deceit cannot play. According to this literature of exposure, the canny impersonators dexterously employ the full range of theatrical technique: the arts of makeup (simulating wounds, for example); costuming (used by both false priests and professors); props (relic sellers, peddlers); the full range of voice; the exaggerated gesture; and the face distorted like a mask— a distilled "form" of poverty. A late fifteenth-century Latin text, *Speculum cerratanorum (Mirror of Charlatans)*, which was plagiarized into Italian a century later by Rafaele Frianoro,[20] nicely captures the peculiar blend of strangeness and distortion used in these spectacles, which were aimed at eliciting the poor man's version of pity and fear. Frianoro's Italian version notes one group "mandando fuori inarticolate voci, con bocca storta e occhi biechi" (sending forth inarticulate sounds, with twisted mouths and sullen eyes).[21] Also noteworthy is the skilled conjunction of grotesque, exaggerated gesture with a compelling narrative frame, usually of a religious nature, that aims to elicit belief from the audience. Consider, for example, the so-called Affarfanti of Frianoro:

> Percuotono il corpo con alcune leggere catenelle di ferro, ovvero fingono di percuotere e lacerar il petto con un gran sasso che tengono nelle mani, dando ad intendere che devono andare per tutto il mondo facendo questa penitenza.

> They strike their bodies with a few short iron chains, or they pretend to strike and lacerate their chests with a large stone that they hold in their hands, making everyone think that they must travel throughout the whole world doing that penance.[22]

The beggar's books, in fact, explicitly compare these spectacles to theater; according to Frianoro, people flock to see the false priests perform in the piazza "con non minor piacere che se andassero a veder spettacoli e a sentire commedie" (with no less delight than if they were going to see spectacles and to hear plays).[23]

These books, I would argue, are distortions of distortions. Like dreams, they extend, distort, and exaggerate in order to debunk and demystify that which were exaggerations to begin with, although in my view exaggerations with at least some measure of existential validity and socioeconomic justification. The beggar's books respond to the age's pronounced fear of a multitude grown beyond the control of the medieval institutions: a disordering, threatening, even frightening mass of wretches who were desperate for food and would perform for their lives to get it. The emotionally terrifying and socially threatening multitude could be defused by the relative calm of category, by subdividing the beggars' outrageous gestures and grimaces into discreet categories of specialization. The strange foreign sounds uttered by the beggars, especially in international crossroads such as Venice, could be disciplined by the cant glossaries and visual identifications. Bizarre, frightening gestures that might threaten to reach across the merely visual to the disturbingly tactile plane could be rationalized by a science of gesture. Ultimately, the aim of Pini, the anonymous author of the *Liber vagatorum,* and Harman was much like that of Samuel Harsnett in *A Declaration of Egregious Popish Im-postures* in his attack on the public exorcisms performed, for the most part, by Roman Catholics in Shakespeare's England: to expose a charismatic spectacle that manipulated the fears and anxieties of audiences as "merely" a theatrical fraud.[24] But whereas in the case of exorcism, except for those who might believe in the supernatural reality of devils inhabiting human bodies, one can confidently expose the exorcist's work as sham theatricality and naked fraud, the line between "genuine" and fraudulent performance in deinstitutionalized, postmedieval begging is difficult to draw.

Especially in actor-based theaters and works of playwrights who appeared to have some actual sympathy for the poor, intermediate modes of mendicant sincerity and audience belief are subtly explored in Renaissance theater (although the stage in this period could certainly also dramatize the sham theatricality of the beggar and the comic epiphany of his exposure). The theater of the semiprofessional Ruzante (Angelo Beolco) and the fully professional *commedia dell'arte* provided, in the terms of Louise George Clubb, theatergrams as well as corpograms of poverty—including the beggar-bystander "scene" and its complexities of persuasion and belief—that were later appropriated into continental and English theater. Both Ruzante and the *commedia dell'arte* place poverty, in the form of the destitute "Ruzante" (the principal character in many of Beolco/Ruzante's plays) and the famished *arte zanni,* at the heart of their character structures. The disadvantaged figure is usually matched with a master (for example, Pantalone) who counters the servant's scarcity with mercantile, capitalist plenty. Shakespeare's early comedies explicitly borrow from the *commedia dell'arte*—for example, one of the first English references to "Pantaloon" comes in *The Taming of the Shrew* to describe Gremio, a ridiculous suitor to Bianca—and it is possible to glimpse in *Shrew* (Grumio-Peteruchio) and *The Merchant of Venice* (Launcelot Gobbo–Shylock) something like the *arte*'s master-servant dyad, which in itself could articulate the performance of poverty.[25] Shakespeare, as Richard Andrews has pointed out, all but abandoned obvious *commedia dell'arte* character structures in his mature comedies, but these character-based theatergrams can be seen to reconfigure themselves in his tragedies: the braggart soldier and subversive servant in *Othello,* the pedantic counselor in *Hamlet,* and the foolish old man in *King Lear.*[26] If Shakespeare, in the *Lear* character Edgar, borrows from Harsnett's debunking tract against exorcism, he also manifestly—and perhaps even more explicitly—recirculates Harman's "Abraham Man" in Edgar's "Poor Tom" disguise. The horrible but also bizarre and "zany" performance of destitution implicit in the sect described by Harman and appropriated by Shakespeare in *King Lear,* I will argue, also needs to be seen both in the full context of the beggar's books and in the Italian theatrical arena of the hungry, performing *zanni*/Arlecchino.

No Renaissance theater maps and memorializes demographic migration as clearly as the *commedia dell'arte,* for the Bergamask *zanni* working for his master Pantalone in the big city reflects multitudes of Bergamask peasants who, displaced from their land by agricultural crisis and foreign wars, came to Venice to work as porters and servants. The countryman transplanted to the city thus reflects the very economic and demographic conditions of sixteenth-century European poverty. *Zanni* and Pantalone respectively represent the poles of scarcity and plenty, and the fundamental engine of their dyad is run by the *zanni*'s hunger and the verbal and physical persuasions that he performs to get his meal from his stingy master. But when the proverbially famished *zanni* implores his master for food, the medieval pair of beggar and almsgiver is translated from a sociotheological contract to a scene of earnest, multifaceted, and ingenious performance (on the *zanni*'s part) and, on Pantalone's part, skeptical assessment. The hospices, confraternities, monasteries, and churches have gone and Pantalone, the urban gatekeeper, stands in their place, wryly considering the material condition, the emotional appeals, and the truth claims of the beggar-*zanni*. The *zanni*'s hunger, probably believable enough from the audience's point of view, is for Pantalone one of the many possible ruses of his fecund mind. For Pantalone, the *zanni* is a glutton, already gastronomically surfeited, but since that view is refracted through the prism of plenty it is also possible to view the *zanni*'s proverbial gluttony as the photographic negative of starvation. The *zanni*'s gluttonous, hallucinatory fantasies, engendering a copious lexicon of alimentary plenty, negatively formalizes his scarcity and want, Pantalone's protestations to the contrary. The verbal and corporal theatergrams of gluttony performed by the destitute *zanni* provide another example of the distilled and exaggerated forms of poverty.

The *zanni*-Pantalone exchange becomes even more dramatically interesting when we consider the latter's epithet "dei Bisognosi" (of the Needy), and recognize that this "merchant of Venice" (a colleague of

Shylock?) obsessively clutches his purse because of the vulnerability of anyone engaged in early modern venture capitalism, such as Shakespeare's Antonio in *The Merchant of Venice*. Not only Pantalone, but many other early modern almsgivers might have seen in the beggar a disturbing reflection of what, in an economic crisis, they might become.

The *zanni* and his Gallo-Italian cousin Harlequin/Arlecchino perform poverty in various modes of sincerity, but usually with a theatrical brio that amounts to a genuine cultural production in its own right, and perhaps remunerable on that basis alone. Regularly included in the props lists from Flaminio Scala's monumental scenario collection[27] are items that characters would use to impersonate beggars: bread (to be given to real or pretended beggars), distressed traveler's clothing, and eye patches for actors impersonating blind indigents. In the Flaminio Scala scenario "La travagliata Isabella" (Day 15), the exiled Pantalone (who has fled to Rome because he believes that he has killed someone) disguises himself as a beggar, beseeching alms from door to door. This might be neatly categorized, with the charlatans from the beggar's books, as sham destitution, except that Pantalone's actual condition of destitute fugitive significantly overlaps with his disguise, and his famished servant Pedrolino, who accompanies him in his begging, very much begs in earnest. Tristano Martinelli, the first Harlequin/Arlecchino (the nationally hybrid role was conceived by the Italian Martinelli on tour in France), frequently projected the persona of a destitute beggar to the kings and dukes whose courts he entertained. Even after he had become prosperous enough to buy land in Mantua, the beggar persona that he continued to perform could be seen to distill years of hardship in a difficult métier, both as a street performer in Mantua and as an itinerant actor who probably shared some of the same roads used by vagabonds.[28]

Even years after Martinelli's career (roughly the same as Shakespeare's), when the *commedia dell'arte* was securely installed in Paris, the famous Harlequin Domenico Biancolelli virtuosically performed poverty when, in the scenario "La fille desobeissante" (1667), he assumed the disguise of a destitute and famished discharged soldier. Approaching the prosperous *innamorato* Cinthio, Biancolelli/Harlequin first declares, after giving a ceremonious verbal greeting, that he is mute. When Cinthio laughs and asks him how it is possible that he can speak, Harlequin first replies that he has been brought up to always respond to gentlemen, only to recognize his obvious absurdity and declare that he is actually deaf, eliciting an even louder guffaw from Cinthio. Confessing again to his mistake (he claims that hunger keeps him from thinking clearly), he announces that he is blind, to which the now extremely skeptical (but well-entertained) Cinthio aggressively thrusts his fingers toward Harlequin's eyes. After he instinctively recoils, to Cinthio's insistence that blind men do not react that way, Harlequin claims that he is only able to see in cases when people try to harm him, only then to confess again his stupidity and assume yet another guise that, effectively, could be taken straight from the pages of the beggar's books: he is lame. But when Cinthio lures him into a dash by showing him money and quickly drawing it away, then decrying him to be a *fourbe* (rogue), Harlequin pulls out the last stop: "Ouy Mr c'est ce que je voulois dire je ne pouvois pas trouver le mot je suis un fourbe" (Oh, yes, sir, that's what I really wanted to say but I couldn't find the word: I'm a rogue!). Claiming, to the last, to be a discharged soldier from "Porto Longone," Harlequin has adroitly performed with a virtuosic brilliance that may compensate for his insincerity, especially given the fact that he seems to operate out of conditions of actual destitution.[29]

Whereas Biancolelli's Harlequin lies close to the pole of insincerity, Ruzante is especially interested in the phenomenon of the indigent vagabond who, in Goffman's terms, convinces himself of the "truth" of a delusion. Ruzante certainly could understand the complexities of poverty: he was the illegitimate son of a upper-middle-class Paduan father and a peasant mother, and as the delegate of the patrician Alvise Cornaro had daily dealings with peasants in the Paduan countryside. In *Il parlamento de Ruzante che iera vegnu de campo,* which was first performed in 1530, the emaciated and degraded character Ruzante slouches into Venice as a deserting soldier and beggar.[30] After a long performance of his own destitution to the external theater audience in an opening monologue, he encounters his old comrade Menato, regaling him with various and sundry war stories that blend the obdurate truth of material reality with the fictive, exuberant license of the stand-up performer. With the entrance of his wife Gnua, who in his absence has taken up the trade of prostitution in order to survive, the encounter of Ruzante, Menato, and Gnua resembles the form of the *zanni* petitioning his skeptical master. (Ruzante precedes the advent of the *commedia dell'arte,* but his theater anticipates it in many respects.) Menato and Gnua mistrust his narratives, faulting him for not bearing the proper marks of the deserting soldier (a typical beggar disguise, as we have seen in Biancolelli), as if they had just studied the corresponding chapter in the *Liber vagatorum*. Whereas Ruzante's fictional invention had served him well during the wars—he had carried a two-sided shield with the insignia of both armies, which he could cleverly reverse as needed—his performance back home meets with absolute skepticism, and Gnua's pimp beats him into a pulp. The play, however, ends with Ruzante's virtuosic performance of the fiction that he has been beaten up not by one, but by a hundred men: a gag and a formal theatergram of destitution that Beolco repeatedly used and that Shakespeare deploys in the highwayman Falstaff's multiplying buckram men in *Henry IV, Part 1*.[31]

As an actor-writer, Beolco's genius lies in the forms and fictions of what might be called the hallucinatory mode, which in Goffman's terms could be considered a strange example of the performer completely believing his own deluded fiction. These forms, hyperdistorted and distended by hunger, are brilliant, perhaps compelling to the theater audience, but also solipsistic and of little practical avail within the fictions of the play. In several of his hunger plays can be located the scripted vestigia of a corpogram that surely was born from the body of the actor seeking new forms: the chilling gag of eating oneself, or autocannibalism, a version of which is still performed by Dario Fo.[32] In *Dialogo facetissimo,* the emaciated peasants Duozo and Menego propose various fantastic solutions to the problem of famine, such as suppressing defecation so that they can hoard what little food they have in their own bodies. For the early modern poor, deprived of some of the institutional support that they might have received in earlier years, the acute desire caused by material deprivation could spur desperate invention. The thousands of poems performed in Italian piazzas (and sold to a readership of an increasing social range) celebrating the fantastic pleasures of the Land of Cuccagna bespeak this structural relationship between desire and invention, and thus should not be dismissed as mere escapism. The Cuccagna poem in the hands of such writers as the blacksmith-poet Giulio Cesare Croce (who actually did experience severe poverty in his life) celebrates the hallucinatory joys of a land where one gets paid for sleeping and imprisoned for working, where the streets are lined with tortellini, where all manner of pleasure, including sexual, provides imaginative compensation for the poor.

Christopher Sly, described as a "beggar" in the Folio speech-prefixes of Shakespeare's *The Taming of the Shrew,* has Cuccagna thrust upon him by a lord who has been repulsed by the sight of him drunk and sleeping outside an alehouse door, where a dispute about some glasses that he has broken has led the tavern hostess to call for a constable. A self-described peddler, cardmaker, bearward, and tinker—and we recall that the line between outright beggars and the "working-poor" was very thin in the period—Sly evokes Shakespeare's native Warwickshire as much as any other character in his plays: he comes from Burton-heath, some sixteen miles south of Stratford and mentions a certain "Marian Hacket" from Wincot, four miles south of Shakespeare's birthplace.

Just as the exaggerated antipathy and the categorizing mania of the beggar's books respond to the public fear of gesticulating and gibbering indigent masses, the lord is extremely disquieted by the spectacle of poverty and bestiality evoked by Sly, which presents a disturbing emblem: "O monstrous beast, how like a swine he lies!/Grim death, how foul and loathsome is thine image" (Induction 1.1.32–33).[33] Just as the hallucinatory fictions of the Cuccagna poems can be seen to emanate from real social conditions, so the fantasy imposed by the lord on Sly is triggered, as a kind of nervous replacement for real charity, out of the real anxiety that wealthy people, especially those operating outside of institutional charity, must have felt when they saw the poor. Imposed, not with charitable good will but with a kind of aggressive aristocratic humor, this "flatt'ring dream or worthless fancy" of opulence resonates for Sly like the visions of Cuccagna, a poor man's version of Segismundo's dream in Calderón's *La vida es sueño:* the "fairest chamber" hung with "wanton pictures"; "warm distilled waters"; the "dulcet and heavenly sound" of music; a "silver basin/Full of rose-water and bestrew'd with flowers"; hunting regalia, costly apparel, and the sexual fantasies (if here given an Ovidian and mythological register) typical of the Italian popular poems: "a couch/Softer and sweeter than the lustful bed/On purpose trimm'ed up for Semiramis" (Induction 1.44, 45, 46, 49, 53–55; Induction 2.38–40). It could plausibly be argued that the lord merely realizes the aristocratic delusion conjured by Sly in his skirmish with the alehouse hostess: "Look in the Chronicles, we came in with Richard the Conqueror" (Induction 1.405). But the lord's careful theatrical direction of his page as Sly's "lady" more resembles a hostile *beffa* than a carnivalesque licensing of social mobility. Still, Shakespeare, who may possibly have poached the grounds of someone like this distinctly Warwickshire lord, treats his practical joke with cool distance and invites us to reassess the aristocratic treatment of the beggar Sly, which is so harsh that it redirects us toward a degree of sympathy for the drunken beggar.

A scene in *Henry VI, Part 2* dramatizes the beggar Simpcox's performance of poverty before two sharply contrasting audience members that effectively plot the extremes of credence and doubt. Drawn from the highly ideological work *Acts and Monuments* of the Protestant John Fox, the scene counterposes the naïveté of the holy, but ineffectual Henry VI with the sagacity and sophistication of the Lord Protector Duke Humphrey of Gloucester, praised by Fox for his capacity to distinguish between truth and impersonation.[34]

Just at the point when the enmity between state and church, the Duke of Gloucester and Cardinal Beaufort, reaches the breaking point, a blind man who has visited the shrine of St. Albans is reported to have regained his sight, although still suffering from lameness. (Comparisons with the Biancolelli scene are not inappropriate.) Shakespeare, following Fox, explicitly associates this "miracle" with Catholicism: the saint's shrine is a repository of relics and, like Joan de la Pucelle, the beggar Simpcox and his wife have heard voices that have drawn them to the shrine. Henry VI stands as the late medieval king who holds *in dubio pro paupere,* as Simpcox is triumphantly carried on a chair in a procession whose pictorial stasis visually monumentalizes the medieval valence of the poor: "Enter the Mayor of Saint Albans and his brethren, with music, bearing the man, Simpcox, between two in a chair; his wife and townsmen following" (2.1.68; stage direction). Henry's pietistic utterances ("Now, God be prais'd, that to believing souls/Gives light in darkness, comfort in despair" [2.1.66–67]) place him at the pole of absolute credence, and the questions that he directs at Simpcox (how long had he been blind; where was he born) merely elicit a preconfirmed narrative.

Gloucester, counterpointing the neomedieval holy king at the pole of radical state skepticism, then examines Simpcox with penetrating questions quickly establishing that the beggar could not have been blind before his "cure." Like Cinthio with Biancolelli's Harlequin, Gloucester proceeds to make short and cruel work of Simpcox's "lameness" by forcing him to jump over a stool, which he does quite featly. Finally ordering Simpcox to be whipped back to his native town of Berwick, Gloucester represents the early modern state policy (not unknown in the medieval period but enforced with new state discipline in the sixteenth century) of forcing vagabond beggars to return to their home districts.

The king and the queen clearly perceive that Gloucester has staged a theatrical spectacle, but their responses are quite different. Although the comic energy of the scene might favor the queen, Gloucester's cruelty renders Henry's response at least plausible.

KING: O God! Seest thou this, and bearest so long?
QUEEN: It made me laugh to see the villain run. (*2 Henry VI* 2.1.147–48)

In fact, by giving one of the last lines to Simpcox's wife, who declares "Alas! Sir, we did it for pure need," Shakespeare complicates the response to this performance of poverty, whose exaggerations and deceptions are reconfigured in the context of material need.

In the Poor Tom disguise of Edgar in *King Lear*, Shakespeare incorporates the Ruzantian genius for hallucinatory fictions also born out of "pure need" into a structure of social gestures that renders Edgar's fictions into truths that actually change the way people think. In discussing the intertextual resonance of Samuel Harnett's exorcism tract in Edgar's staged hallucinations, Stephen Greenblatt has illuminated the social and contextual pressures of Edgar's theatricality. But the theatrical role that Edgar explicitly adopts is not of someone about to be exorcised; it is rather that of a "Bedlam beggar" taken out of Harman's *Caveat,* employing the arts of makeup, costume (or anticostume), voice, and grotesque gesture in order to "enforce charity." So Edgar declares "My face I'll grime with filth,/Blanket my loins, elf all my hair in knots," and vows to emulate beggars who "strike in their numbed and mortified bare arms/pins, wooden pricks, nails, sprigs of rosemary" (2.2.180–81, 186–87).[35] As analyzed by Greenblatt, exorcism demonstrations were deadly serious performances that did not really admit of intermediate degrees of reception and had enormous consequence in this period of mortal religious rivalry. Most, or at least many, Catholics witnessing a public exorcism would have believed that the devil was really exiting the body; most Protestants would have scoffed at the spectacle as a pack of lies. But the role of Poor Tom as Bedlam beggar *overlaps* with the new actual state of Edgar in many ways: like Poor Tom, Edgar is displaced, humiliated, exiled, and bereft of material support. As the most consummate actor in the play, Edgar could certainly have chosen a different disguise, but this particular role clearly resonates with him, and the exaggerations and distortions to which he forces his body and his voice read like extensions of the truth, both to himself and to those who encounter him. Before Gloucester and King Lear, the sight of Edgar's body as autobiography clearly does move them to rethink the distribution of wealth and resources in radically new ways. So Lear:

> Poor naked wretches, wheresoe'er you are,
> That bide the pelting of this pitiless storm,
> How shall your houseless heads and unfed sides,
> Your looped and windowed raggedness, defend you
> From seasons such as these? O, I have ta'en
> Too little care of this. Take physic, pomp,
> Expose thyself to feel what wretches feel,
> That thou mayst shake the superflux to them
> And show the heavens more just.
>
> (3.4.28–36)[36]

That the tone of Edgar's grim performance is predominantly tragic need not preclude its filiation with Italian, French, and Spanish theatrical and literary performances of poverty cast in the comic vein. Placing Edgar in the performative context of early modern begging, whether viewed unsympathetically as in the beggar's books or more complexly as in the Spanish picaresque novel, the actor's theater of Ruzante, the *commedia dell'arte,* and the *comédie italienne* of Biancolelli, can demonstrate the complex and compelling overlap between the existential reality of the early modern poor and the exaggerated, distended forms that they used to "enforce," or perform, their charity before audiences who could respond anywhere between the poles of doubt and belief.

Notes

1. Erving Goffman, *The Presentation of Self in Everyday Life* (Garden City: Doubleday, 1959), 17–18.

2. Ibid., 19.

3. Patricia Fumerton, in *Unsettled: The Culture of Mobility and the Working Poor in Early Modern England* (Chicago: University of Chicago Press, 2006), has placed begging in the overall context of the "working poor" in early modern England, who practiced such trades as peddling, tinkering, preaching, relic-selling, musical performance, and other entrepreneurial "inventions of necessity."

4. See Robert Henke, "Representations of Poverty in the Commedia dell'Arte," *Theatre Survey* 48, no. 2 (2007): 233–34.

5. *La vida de Lazarillo de Tormes y de sus fortunas y adversidades,* ed. Alberto Blecua (Madrid: Castalia, 1972), 139, translated by W. S. Merwin, in *The Life of Lazarillo de Tormes: His Fortunes and Adversities* (New York: New York Review of Books Press, 2005), 68.

6. Marvin Carlson, *Performance: A Critical Introduction,* 2nd ed. (New York and London: Routledge, 2004), 5-6.

7. "Corpograms" extends to the realm of the body Louise George Clubb's extremely fruitful notion of "theatergrams"—flexible and transnationally moveable theatrical units such as dialogue structures, plot motifs, character dyads, and topics. See her *Italian Drama in Shakespeare's Time* (New Haven: Yale University Press, 1989), 1-26.

8. My observation that the exaggerated shapes of the *arte* mask amount to *forms,* is indebted to the performance and scholarship of Mace Perlman. See his "Reading Shakespeare, Reading the Masks of the Commedia dell'Arte: Fixed Forms and the Breath of Life," in *Transnational Exchange in Early Modern Theater,* ed. Robert Henke and Eric Nicholson, 225-37 (Aldershot, UK, and Burlington, Vt.: Ashgate, 2008).

9. Bronislaw Geremek, *Poverty: A History,* trans. Agnieszka Kolakowska (Oxford: Blackwell, 1994), 15-36.

10. Quoted by Paula Pugliatti, in *Beggary and Theatre in Early Modern England* (Aldershot, UK: Ashgate, 2003), 2, who cites C.J. Ribton-Turner, *A History of Vagrants and Vagrancy, and Beggars and Begging* (London: Chapman and Hall, 1887), 35.

11. Geremek, *Poverty: A History,* 37.

12. Jean, Sire de Joinville, *Histoire de Saint Louis,* ed. N. de Wailly (Paris: Renouart, 1868), 248. This roughly contemporary account, whose accuracy is generally validated by Jacques Le Goff, was written in 1309, thirty-nine years after the king's death. See Jacques Le Goff, *Saint Louis* (Paris: Gallimard, 1996), 473-78.

13. Geremek, *Poverty: A History,* 48.

14. In addition to Geremek, 73-177, a good pan-European account of poverty in the fifteenth and sixteenth centuries is that of Catharina Lis and Hugo Soly, *Poverty and Capitalism in Pre-Industrial Europe,* trans. James Coonan (Bristol: Humanities Press, 1979).

15. Geremek, *Poverty: A History,* 11.

16. Brian Pullan, *Rich and Poor in Renaissance Venice* (Cambridge: Cambridge University Press, 1971). The office of the Sanità was founded in 1485.

17. *Liber vagatorum* was first printed in 1510 (Nurnberg), and went through many different editions. For an English translation, see D. B. Thomas, ed., *The Book of Vagabonds and Beggars with a Vocabulary of Their Language,* trans. J. C. Hotten (London: Penguin, 1932). Luther's introduction is collected in Piero Camporesi, *Il libro dei vagabondi* (Torino: Einaudi, 1973), 289-90. Luther had first written about the problem in his 1520 appeal "To the Christian Nobility of the German Nation Concerning the Reformation of Christianity."

18. For a modern edition of Harman's text, see *Arthur F. Kinney, Rogues, Vagabonds, and Sturdy Beggars* (Barre, Mass.: Imprint Society, 1973), 103-53.

19. For a detailed discussion of the German municipal records, see Bronislaw Geremek, *Les fils de Caïn: L'image des pauvres et des vagabonds dans la literature européenne du XVe au XVIIe siècle,* trans. Joanna Arnold-Moricet, et al. (1980; Paris: Flammarion, 1991), 77-91.

20. The *Speculum cerratanorum* was written by Teseo Pini. The 1486 manuscript was recently discovered by Piero Camporesi, who published the full text in *Il libro dei vagabondi,* 5-77 (Torino: Einaudi, 1973). Camporesi also includes Frianoro's plagiarized version, the 1621 *Il vagabondo* (78-165).

21. Rafaele Frianoro, *Il vagabondo,* in Camporesi, *Il libro dei vagabondi,* 125. All translations from the Italian are my own.

22. Ibid., 117.

23. Ibid., 136.

24. Samuel Harsnett, *A Declaration of egregious Popish Impostures, to withdraw the harts of her Maiesties Subiects from their allegeance, and from the truth of Christian Religion professed in England, under the pretence of casting out devils* (London: Iames Roberts, 1603). For a penetrating analysis of exorcism, Harsnett, and Shakespeare's *King Lear,* see Stephen Greenblatt, "Shakespeare and the Exorcists," in *Shakespearean Negotiations: The Circulation of Social Energy in Renaissance England* (Berkeley and Los Angeles: University of California Press, 1988), 94-128.

25. See Andrew Grewar, "Shakespeare and the Actors of the Commedia dell'Arte," in *Studies in the Commedia dell'Arte,* ed. David J. George and Christopher J. Gossip, 13-47 (Cardiff: University of Wales Press, 1993).

26. Richard Andrews, "Shakespeare and Italian Comedy," in *Shakespeare and Renaissance Europe,* ed. Andrew Hadfield and Paul Hammon, 123-49 (London: Thomson Learning, 2005).

27. Flaminio Scala, *Il teatro delle favole rappresentative,* ed. Ferruccio Marotti, 2 vols. (Milan: Il Polifilo, 1976). In English, see Richard Andrews, *The Commedia dell'Arte of Flaminio Scala: A Translation and Analysis of 30 Scenarios* (Lanham, Md.: Scarecrow Press, 2008).

28. For a discussion of Martinelli's performance of poverty, see Henke, "Representations of Poverty in the Commedia dell'Arte," 236-40.

29. My considerable thanks to Virginia Scott for alerting me to this Biancolelli routine. The text of the scenario may be found in Stefania Spada, ed., *Domenico Biancolelli, ou l'art d'improviser* (Naples: Institut Universitaire Oriental, 1969), 18-23.

30. Also known as the *Primo dialogo.* For a definitive edition of the play, see Ludovico Zorzi, *Ruzante: Teatro* (Turin: Einaudi, 1967), 513-43.

31. For a more extended treatment of Ruzante, see my "Comparing Poverty: Fictions of a 'Poor Theater' in Ruzante and Shakespeare," *Comparative Drama* 41 (2007): 199-205.

32. Ruzante wrote a series of plays during or in the immediate aftermath of the terrible 1527-29 Venetian famine: *Dialogo facetissimo, Il Parlamento, Bilora, La seconda orazione,* and *La Moscheta.* For an excellent English discussion of Ruzante's work, including a precise dating of the plays, see Ronnie Ferguson, *The Theatre of Angelo Beolco (Ruzante): Text, Context, and Performance* (Ravenna: Longo, 2000).

33. Shakespeare, *The Taming of the Shrew,* ed. Brian Morris (London: Methuen, 1981).

34. See Appendix I, 179, in the Andrew S. Cairncross edition of *King Henry VI, Part 2.* (London: Methuen, 1957).

35. Shakespeare, *King Lear,* ed. R. A. Foakes (London: Thomson Learning, 1997).

36. In fact, Lear says this speech just before he sees Edgar for the first time, but it clearly anticipates his imminent arrival on the scene. Grigor Kozintsev's 1970 film version of *King Lear* has Lear delivering this speech in sight of Edgar, who is sheltering in a hovel with a throng of other beggars.

"Che indizio, che prova . . . ?" Ariosto's Legal Conjectures and the English Renaissance Stage

LORNA HUTSON

ARIOSTO, IT IS inevitably and rightly said, is the "father of modern comedy." The production of *La cassaria* during the 1508 Carnival at the court of Alfonso D'Este in Ferrara marked a watershed, a new beginning. Since at least 1486, the Este court at Ferrara had been entertained by festival performances of classical comedies translated into Italian—Plautus's *Menaechmi, Amphitryon, Asinara, Casina,* and others, Terence's *Andria, Eunuchus,* and *Phormio*—but never before had the courtiers followed a new plot composed in Italian especially for the occasion. What's more, as historians of theater also observe, the first performance of *La cassaria* was revolutionary in other ways, too. As a much-cited letter from Bernadino Prosperi to Isabella D'Este reported, the "best thing" about the festival that year was not Ariosto's play alone, but its performance in front of perspective scenery painted for it by Pellegrino da Udine:

Ma quello che è stato il meglio in tutte queste feste e representatione, è stato la scena dove se sono representate, quale ha facto uno M.ro Peregrino depinctore, che sta col S.re, che'è una contracta et prospectiva de una terra cum case, chiese, torre, campanili e zardini.

But the best thing in all these festivals and shows has been the scenery in which they have been performed, which was made by one master Peregrino [Pellegrino da Udine], employed by his Lordship, which was a contraction and view of land with houses, churches, towers, belfries and gardens.[1]

179

Prosperi's letter seems to signal something entirely new, "an illusion of three-dimensional space created around the realistic acting of the characters," as Elena Povoledo put it.[2] If what is new in the vernacular Italian play is its unity of time and place (by contrast with the otherworldly, postmortem locations and temporalities, the paradises and hell-mouths of contemporary sacred *rappresentazioni*) then it does indeed seem as though "the perspective set and the unities of time and place" are not only, in Peter Womack's words, "historical twins," but inseparable twins, joined at the hip.[3] Richard Andrews puts the historical meaning of the 1508 performance thus:

> The excitement of the Ferrarese audience seems to show that perspective had not, to their knowledge, actually been used on stage before. . . . There is, however, a twofold coincidence. On the one hand, the perspective set coincides neatly with the first full-length *commedia* in Italian. More importantly, *perspective illusion as such coincides with and even reinforces everything which was innovatory about the new dramaturgical mode*—its setting in a street outside houses, its unchanging fictional time and space, its whole status as "overheard" drama with a well-defined dramatic space of its own. [My italics.][4]

In effect, then, the critical consensus seems to be that perspective illusion is integral to the mimetic project of a dramaturgy that aims to reproduce the particularity of everyday life through the precise temporal and spatial indicators associated with the neo-Aristotelian unities.

Yet if all this is taken for granted in histories of European drama, it remains an odd consequence that for Anglophone critics this mimetic achievement merely exists to be transcended, and in such a way that renders it strictly unnecessary in the first place. The psychological realism of Shakespeare, it is said, is both superior to the dramaturgical realism fostered by the humanist imitation of Terentian and Plautine comedy and is not in any way *dependent* on the humanist conventions of fixed-location staging or temporal precision. Shakespeare's earliest and most overtly classicizing plays—*The Comedy of Errors* and *Titus Andronicus*—are routinely said to be a kind of working through of Latin influences (including the unities of time and place) to get them out of the dramatist's system, as it were.[5] And even though now, long after "Leo Salingar made it impossible to doubt that Shakespeare's use of Italian elements was . . . [the] application of Italian methods to new purposes," and after Louise Clubb, whose words these are, extended critical awareness of Shakespeare's

Italian indebtedness to the *commedia grave* of the Counter-Reformation, even now critics repeatedly argue that Shakespeare's dramaturgy is defined by its rejection of Continental neoclassicism.[6] Helen Cooper, for example, has recently written that Shakespeare's plays are part of an art of "enactment, not description." Their emphasis on enactment, she continues, distinguishes them "from humanist or classical drama" in which plays "locate their action offstage and so privilege the spoken word. . . . The staging of Latin comedy requires little more than a series of entrances and exits."[7] Temporal fluidity, transformability of the acting space, flexible attitudes to genre and decorum—all of these are said to be reasons why Shakespeare's theater owes more to native medieval traditions than to neoclassical influences, and why its own emotional realism is so superior.[8] Yet this and similar subscriptions to what Peter Womack has recently described as the "comfortable English myth" of a rejected Continental humanism damagingly preclude our understanding of the vitally creative contribution made by both classical and neoclassical comedy to the achievements of the Renaissance English stage. To write, "as if the medieval tradition consisted of nothing but spontaneous practices, and Renaissance humanism of nothing but codified regulations" is, Womack argues, to fail to see that "the makers of the unitary stage" were not "prohibiting something but . . . *producing* something."[9] What these makers—including Ariosto—produced was, moreover, vital to the mimetic achievements of both Shakespeare and Jonson as these authors each, in different ways, developed their own striking modifications of Continental neoclassicism for English audiences. To argue this, I will begin by focussing not on the much-discussed realism of the perspective scenery painted for Ariosto's two earliest comedies—*La cassaria* and *I suppositi*—but on the realistic effects produced by Ariosto's following of Plautus and Terence in their uses of forensic rhetoric. I will then go on to show first the significance of Jonson's adaptation of *La cassaria* in *Volpone,* and finally the ambiguous tribute paid by Shakespeare to the mimetic power of Ariosto's *I suppositi* in *The Taming of the Shrew.*

The Wealth of Conjecture: *La cassaria (The Coffer)*

As we've seen, the innovation of *La cassaria* as an Italian version of the Plautine and Terentian plot is inevitably associated with the innovation of the "prospectiva" or "perspective" scenery painted for it by Pellegrino da Udine. Yet if the invocation of perspective scenery works to prevent us asking what it was in Ariosto's text that conjured up this three-dimensionality, this vivid illusion of substance, presence, and extension in space and time, then it's worth temporarily bracketing off the question of the perspective scene's impact in order to consider more fully the textual effects it is supposed to have reinforced.

There is, indeed, more than one historian of Italian theater whose work would support such a move. Ludovico Zorzi wrote in 1977 of doubts as to whether the term "prospettiva" as used by Prosperi actually referred to a fully realized scene in one-point perspective, a flat depiction of the perspective set in relief described by Sebastiano Serlio forty years later.[10] Elena Povoledo's work on Italian scenography establishes as the antecedents of the scene painted by Pellegrino a conventional set, worked out over thirty years or so in Ercole D'Este's court, which she calls the "città ferrarese." This city-scene was a hybrid—it borrowed from the late medieval set with its multiple juxtaposed mansions—but as it was developed for vernacular performances of Plautus and Terence in the Cortile Nuovo and later in the Palazzo della Ragione, these houses were taken to represent not cosmic divisions but locations in a specific earthly city on a specific day. As Povoledo writes, extrapolating from the descriptions of the diarist Bernadino Zambotti and from the anonymous *Diario Ferrarese:*

The diaries all emphasize the limited number of "houses," the fact that they could be used, and that they sought to convey the impression of a city. This idea of a city, that is of a single and fixed location, is in fact the basis of the Ferrarese set, and involves the rejection of the coexistence of several simultaneous sets, which had been inevitable in the sacred *rappresentazioni.* But in this city of Ferrara, there were at most six houses, and the crenellated walls, which were intended to limit the view of the city, were painted on the plinth of the proscenium. . . . One cannot go so far as to talk of a perspective set which followed the humanist principles of the three unities, nether can one speak only of "mansions," for this would be to ignore a manifestly new element which freed the *citta ferrarese* from the traditions of religious drama. . . . Four or six houses did not constitute a perspective view; they were mansions which had been up-dated in accordance with a new concept of theatre. . . . It was therefore a conventional set . . . however it was still intended to represent a city "with superb houses and wide streets," in accordance with the ideas of the humanists who filled the palace.[11]

Although Povoledo goes on to read Prosperi's letter on the scene for *La cassaria* as representing a new development, it is clear from her analysis here that elements of what she calls the *città ferrarese* set—the neighboring "houses" with functional doors lining a shallow proscenium—were necessary for its performance, since it requires, above all, that actors move in and out of these doors. Pellegrino's scene was a painted backdrop, not Serlio's innovative series of successive flats "with very long straight roads crossing others."[12] In spite of comically detailed directions to specific houses in the city—Volpino, for example, tells Trappolo to remember where he's to take the girl: "Ricordati passato el portico che tu trovi su per questa contrada, è la terza casa a man ritta . . . È una porta picola, fatta di nuovo" (Remember after you pass the portico down the street, it's the third house on the right-hand side. . . . It's a small door, newly built)[13]— the only two entrances and exits actually required by the plot are that of Erofilo's father's house and its next-door neighbor, the house of the pimp, Lucrano. (Trappolo, waylaid by drunken servants, never arrives anywhere near the third house on the right after the portico.) So while these detailed directions might, accompanied by gestures in the direction of Pellegrino's scenery, pay a sort of homage to its visual illusionism, the play would seem to have been staged on a shallow proscenium in which two "mansions" or houses with working doors enabled the necessary to-ing and fro-ing in and out of Crisobolo's and Lucrano's houses.

Thus, as Peter Womack points out, the considerable differences between the "open" stage of Elizabethan popular theater and the fixed-locale staging of Italian *commedia erudita* do not preclude certain basic similarities in their reliance on the common theatrical syntax of "mansions" or "houses" or *case* as places to which the actor retires when leaving the acting space. And this, in turn, produces a common "insistent externality" in both Italian and English Renaissance acting spaces that is distinct from the modern assumption that the natural dramatic location is a room. As Womack observes, "the Renaissance stage . . . *is* outside. When you exit, you go in."[14]

This paradox of Renaissance theatrical space is dazzlingly exploited by *La cassaria,* a play whose vivid effects of circumstantial reality are rhetorically produced, generated by the audience's urge to make sense of the rapid action of the plot by conjecturing an "interior" world beyond the doors through which the actors constantly enter and exit. These reality effects, then, work independently of perspective illusion.[15] Moreover, though invented on the fixed-locale stage, these strategies—essentially, arguments of circumstantial probability—could and did translate to the temporally and spatially flexible acting space of Elizabethan drama. They derive ultimately from what Adele Scafuro has called the "forensic disposition" of Greek and Roman New Comedy; and though it is the peculiar artistic challenge and pressure of representing offstage events and interior spaces on the fixed-location stage that originally calls forth the ingenious *enargeia* or *evidentia* of this forensically oriented drama, its techniques are later brilliantly assimilated by dramatists who write for the open English Renaissance stage.[16]

As we have seen, one of the artistically generative limitations of fixed locale staging, whether that of the *città ferrarese* of the 1490s and early 1500s, or of the English academic theater (universities and Inns of Court) in the mid-sixteenth century, was the fact that "interiority"—in the sense of conversations and actions appropriate to private space, the interiors of houses—becomes impossible to stage or enact as such. On the academic stage it is, as Alan Nelson notes, "virtually impossible . . . to play an interior scene. . . . All conversations, including the most private, must occur outdoors."[17] An often-noted effect of this is that characters give the most absurd reasons for calling interlocutors out from their houses into the street, even when secrecy is of the essence. Ariosto has fun inventing such reasons toward the end of *La cassaria* when Fulcio, trying to recover what he can from the wreck of a plot gone hopelessly awry, calls at the door of the merchant Crisobolo's house, planning to tell him a fib about legal charges being brought against him by his neighbor, the procurer, Lucrano. Fulcio, having knocked at the door, tells Marso to inform his master, Crisobolo, that the "Bassa" (the "Pasha," or Turkish governor of Mytilene, on the isle of Lesbos, where the play is set) has a message for him. Marso naturally asks Fulcio why he doesn't come in, and Fulcio gives a brilliantly absurd answer to Crisobolo himself, when he appears at the door:

CRISOBOLO: Chi a quest'ora importuna mi dimanda?
FULCIO: Non te maravigliare, e perdonami s'io t'ho chiamato qui fòra, che aven-
doti a dire cose segretissime, non me fido costa dentro di non essere udito
da gente che poi lo rapporti. Io mi porto meglio qui vedere a torno, né averò
dubbio che me ascolti omo che io non veggia. (5.4.1–8)

CRISOBOLO: Who wants me at this ungodly hour?
FULCIO: Don't be surprised, and forgive me for having called you outside, but I
have something highly secret to tell you and I was afraid that being inside we
might be heard by those around who would then report what I say. Out here
I can easily look around and be sure I'm not overheard by someone whom I
cannot see. (5.4)

But Fulcio's crazily inverted opposition of spy-ridden private space to the controllably "secret" space of the public street—an opposition even more ludicrously and hilariously invoked at the opening of *I suppositi,* when the nurse brings Polinesta "outside" on to the stage, so "seremo certo almeno di non essere da alcuno altro udite" (we can be sure at least of not being overheard by anyone else), ; *I Suppositi,* 1.1.2–3)— should draw our attention to more than the mere structural limitations imposed by the neoclassical rule of unity of place and the architecture of fixed-locale staging. For Fulcio's formulation is remarkable for its joking insistence that the audience is not *witnessing* the play. There's the hint of an ethical question at work here on what it means to be an audience at all, but more immediately the playfulness of Fulcio's lines draws his audience into the centrality of the related legal concepts of the witness (*testimonio*) and proof (*la prova*) to the action of *La cassaria* as a whole. It is in the context of the discourse of proof in Roman Law, or more generally in the context of asking how it is that we come to know what we think we know—especially what we think we know concerning "interiority," the physical and mental spaces we can't actually see— that the theatrical innovation of Ariosto's earliest comedies, and its later significance for the mimesis of the English Renaissance stage, emerges most clearly.

The plot of *La cassaria,* as many critics have detailed, derives elements from several Plautine and Terentian comedies.[18] More specifically— though I have not read any discussion of this—Volpino's plot to get Erofilo and Cassidoro their girls in *La cassaria* is clearly a variant on Milpho's legal entrapment plot in Plautus's *Poenulus* (*The Little Carthaginian*). Characters in Plautus's *Poenulus* exhibit all the hallmarks of what Scafuro calls the "forensic disposition" typically displayed by the dramatis personae of Greek and Roman New Comedy. That is to say their behavior is marked by the "staginess" that comes from a readiness to anticipate the legal consequences of their actions and to imagine any scenario in terms of its retrospective power to convince in a courtroom. Characters constantly, for example, call on friends and even strangers as legal witnesses to whatever action happens to be taking place. Scafuro quotes a plaintiff in fourth century Athens:

For you all know that whenever we enter upon any course of action that we foresee might require the use of witnesses [*marturoi*], we customarily round up our closest friends and relatives as witnesses for such actions; but of unforeseen and sudden events, each of us uses any chance person.[19]

In *Poenulus,* hired witnesses play a crucial part in the plot to entrap the pimp, Lyscus, into an unwitting act of *furtum manifestum,* theft caught in the act. The plot works thus: Agorastocles, a wealthy enough young man is, like Erofilo in *La cassaria,* enamored of a courtesan being kept in the house of his next-door neighbor, Lyscus, who happens to be a pimp. Agorastocles' slave, Milphio, counsels him that the best way to make the girl his freedwoman without going to any expense is to send his bailiff, Collybiscus, to the procurer's house disguised as a foreigner, a Carthaginian, with a bit of money and in search of a girl. Agorastocles is then to inquire of the pimp whether his slave is at the pimp's house; the pimp, not knowing Collybiscus, will deny it, and Agorastocles will be able to bring a charge, before witnesses, of the pimp's being a thief and having stolen his man and money—when the case comes to court, the praetor, as Milphio says, "will adjudge his entire establishment to you."[20]

The similarity of Milphio's strategem to that which Volpino outlines at length to the bemused Erofilo in act 2, scene 1 of *La cassaria* is clear. Volpino, too, plans to ensure Erofilo's attainment of a girl in Lucrano's clutches by sending a servant disguised as a merchant to visit the procurer with the purpose of purchasing a courtesan. Moreover, just as Lyscus doesn't know Collybiscus, so, too, it's important for Volpino's plot that the servant he has chosen—Trappolo—has never been to Mytilene before, so no one knows him, least of all the procurer, Lucrano. Trappolo, of course, is not to hand over a purse with money, but the eponymous coffer, replete with precious textiles and filched from the house of Erofilo's father, Crisobolo. And this is where the crucial difference between the two entrapment plots comes in. It is essential for Milpho's plot that Agorastocles provide himself with hired witnesses—*avocati*—who will be there to *see,* and to testify later before the praetor that they have seen, Lyscus take hold of the money from Collybiscus and usher the latter into his house. The Twelve Tables of Roman law reserved severe penalties for *furtum manifestum,* notorious theft, and though opinions of jurists differed as to the definition of *manifestum* (whether the theft had to be detected as it was actually being committed or whether it was enough to see the thief at any time with the stolen object in his hands), it is clear from the comic asides between Agorastocles and seasoned court-hirelings he has recruited, that their general function is to bear witness to the "theft" in the moment that it takes place.[21] Comically lazy, however, they try to shift this role onto Agorastocles himself. "Specta a dextram," they tell Agorastocles in act 3, scene 4, "tuos servos aurum ipse leoni dabit" (look to the right—your slave himself will be giving the money to the pimp; 712-13). In the following scene, Lyscus leaves Collybiscus in his house while he emerges carrying the purse with money. Agorastocles seizes his opportunity and accuses the pimp: "Manifesto fur es mihi!" (you're a thief of my goods, caught in the act!; 785).

Ariosto obviously remembered Plautus's plot in detail and appreciated, in particular, its invocation of the Roman definition of *furtum manifestum,* since he has Crisobolo, whose coffer it is, enter Lucrano's house with witnesses and accuse Lucrano of being "ladron manifesto," a manifest or notorious thief (4.5.18).[22] But what Ariosto leaves out of the original plot of entrapment is, precisely, the element that made the *furtum* manifest in *Poenulus*—the element of witness. In outlining the plan to the bemused Erofilo, Volpino explains that it will be possible to accuse Lucrano of theft, and be believed, not because of any handy witnesses of the theft, but because no other explanation of how the coffer found its way into his house is going to seem *as likely,* as easy to *conjecture.* As soon as the coffer has been left in Lucrano's house, Volpino explains to Erofilo and Caridoro, they will go to the *Bassa,* Caridoro's father, and the governor of Mytilene, and, he continues, "tu farai querela che questa cassa ti sia stata di casa tolta, e che suspetti ch'un ruffiano, vicin tuo, te l'abbia tolta" (you will complain that this coffer has been taken from your house and you *suspect* that a procurer, a neighbor of yours, has stolen it; 2.1.163-64; my italics). Then, of course, the house will be searched, possibly by a *bargello* (a senior law enforcer specially appointed by the prince or governor), and the coffer will be found. Lucrano will tell the truth—that it was left ostensibly as security for the purchase of one of his women. But, concludes Volpino triumphantly, no one will believe him, for "chi vorrà credere che per cosa che val cinquanta a pena, si lassa la valuta di più di mille assai?" (who will believe that someone would leave goods worth more than a thousand ducats for something scarcely worth fifty?; 2.1.177-78). The procurer, "having been found guilty," will, he concludes with a deadpan relish of cruelty, be imprisoned and perhaps hanged, maybe even drawn and quartered, but what will they care? They will have got the girls.

Excising the witnesses, Ariosto makes the success of the entrapment turn on what legal rhetoricians called "artificial proof"—the use of arguments from the circumstantial topics of time, place, motive, opportunity, and character—to make people believe a narrative account of what no one could have seen, because it did not happen. The dramaturgical illusion is paralleled by the forensic one: just as the audience could never see beyond the door of Lucrano's house, but will imagine the "interior" where the coffer (with its equally evocative and illusory interior) snugly nestles, so the governor, lacking witnesses to give an account of how the coffer came to be there, will believe what the generative rhetorical topics of artificial proof lead him to think most probable: Lucrano is a pimp, probably a liar, and who would believe that something so valuable could have been left as security? By 1508, when he wrote *La cassaria,* Ariosto had already gained both practical experience in the performance and staging of Plautine and Terentian comedy (he was among the courtiers whom Ercole D'Este took to Milan in 1493 to act in comedies, including *Poenulus,* before Ludovico Il Moro) and academic experience in the study of Italian civil law, including its codified systems of artificial proof.[23] This conjunction of two different forms of practical experience in the dramaturgical and rhetorical operations at the heart of Roman New Comedy was decisive in shaping *La cassaria,* a play that revels in the recognition that classical drama was all about persuading people to believe in things and people that they would, in the course of the drama, never be able to *witness.*

Ariosto clearly relished the power of what Italian legal treatises on proof referred to as *indicia*—the signs drawn from topics of circumstance that might be adduced when a "full proof" (confession or two unimpeachable witnesses) was lacking.[24] He also saw that to work, the manipulation of *indicia* relied not only on the speaker's rhetorical skill in producing credible circumstantial narrative, but on the imaginative complicity of the auditor, on the play of fear and desire. Giraldi Cinthio praised *La cassaria* above all Ariosto's comedies because of the marvellous ingenuity of both its "knot" (*nodo*) of errors and its solution (*soluzione*), but in fact both the knot and the solution rely on one and the same tactic: the skillful use of *indicia,* or circumstantial proofs, to persuade an auditor to believe in the fantasy being painted in words before him.[25] Thus, when Volpino's clever plan goes horribly wrong—Trappolo loses the girl, and Crisobolo, Erofilo's father, returns home unexpectedly early—he tries to persuade Crisobolo that his coffer is missing because Lucrano has stolen it and that Crisobolo should accuse him before the governor. "Che indizio, che prova gli saprò dar io per farli constare che sia così?" (what evidence, what proof can I give him to convince him that this is so?; 4.2.148–49). Volpino, desperately confident, says that if they just go to the governor's house, he will present "tali indizii e conietture e prove, che non potrà, se ben volesse, negare di crederti" (so many indications and conjectures and proofs that even if he didn't want to he couldn't help but believe you; 4.2.159–61). Meanwhile, Volpino improvises a brilliantly, hilariously circumstantial narration of how the coffer came to be lost, appealing throughout to Crisobolo's knowledge of the rather curmudgeonly character of his chief servant, Nebbia, on whom Volpino plans to pin all the blame. But Crisobolo is not completely taken in: "Non m'hai, con tutte quest ciance, produtto alcuno indizio che'l ruffiano, più che altri, abbi avuta la mia cassa," he comments (with all your chattering you haven't come up with a single proof that it's the procurer rather than anyone else who has my coffer; 4.2.258–60). This circumstance is corroborated, however, by the discovery of the coffer at Lucrano's house, and for a moment Crisobolo seems inclined to believe Volpino's fabrications. But Crisobolo's return to his own house, and subsequent discovery of the hapless Trappolo dressed in his (Crisobolo's) clothes, casts the narrative of theft into doubt and forces Volpino into a hysterical last-ditch attempt to salvage the situation by attempting one more time to improvise corroborative circumstances that will fasten the blame on Nebbia. Inspired, he tells Crisobolo that Trappolo is a deaf-mute and proceeds, hilariously, to "interpret" the dumb man's gestures. Someone from this very house took his clothes, interprets Volpino, "Someone tall and thin, who has a large nose and white hair and who speaks hurriedly." Crisobolo jumps in on cue with a recognition: "I think he means Nebbia"—the circumstances are almost beginning to cohere with those of Volpino's earlier account. But—brilliantly skeptical—Crisobolo's credulity snags on a detail of witnessing: "But how does he *know* he speaks hurriedly? *Can he hear then?*" he asks (4.2.59; my italics). The game, for Volpino, is up.

As it happens, Fulcio repairs all Volpino's disasters with exactly the same techniques. He frightens Lucrano with a story that Crisobolo has gone to the governor and accused him of stealing, enhancing the effect of terror by seeming to hear the corroborative sounds of pursuit: "mi pare non so che sentire, e son certo ch'è il bargello" (I think I hear something, I'm certain it's the police; 4.11.59–60). Surely Jonson remembered and hyperbolized this in *Volpone* when Volpone, thinking his game is up (for he is, after all, guilty of attempted rape) vividly imagines not only that he hears the *saffi,* or Venetian constables, at the door to arrest him, but that he feels the hot branding iron "Hissing already, at my forehead."[26] In Ariosto's play, Fulcio succeeds where Volpino failed, but his techniques are identical. The coffer, a tantalizingly enclosed but imaginatively generative repository of wealth (the figure of Tantalus is explicitly invoked in relation to the riches inaccessibly hidden in Crisobolo's house [1.5.15]) is transformed into the issuing forth or exiting (*uscire*) of the fears and desires that motivate people to believe what they haven't any real reason to credit. Lucrano thinks he hears the *bargello,* because secretly, internally, he knows he's guilty of plotting to leave Mytilene with the coffer, just as, in Jonson's later play, Volpone's guilt calls forth the hallucinatory pain and shame of branded flesh. But in Ariosto's first play, this new potential for dramatic and psychological realism is played, finally, as a joke on the audience, who might be so taken in as to think they could join Fulcio and Volpino at the Moor's Tavern for a drink. "You in the audience may as well go home," Fulcio tells them, disappointing their implied hopes, "for the girl whom I'm going to take *doesn't want to be seen coming out* [*non vuole esser veduta uscire*]. And, as the procurer has to flee, *it would not be proper for there to be too many witnesses* [*tanti testimonii*]" (5.5.25–26).

I Suppositi: The Crisis of Conjecture

La cassaria experiments intricately with the wealth of conjecture that issues from the hidden, offstage interior and the unwitnessed story, but the sense that such a dramaturgy of conjecture might have profound affective potential is not really exploited by Ariosto until the following year, in *I suppositi.* This play brilliantly demonstrates that the emotional power of probable conjecture is enhanced, not subverted, by the scandal of adventitiousness and, indeed, of downright mendacity that haunts a dramatic denouement based on proofs of recognition. The whiff of fraud lingering about the play's concluding *soluzione* (solution) of its *nodo,* or knot of error, is all the more edgily disturbing for issuing from the mouth of a lawyer who, at the height of the play's perturbation, or the tightening of its knot of errors, had declared the law incompetent to prove precisely those questions of identity that he pronounces himself so certain about in the final recognition scene of the play. The impact of this extraordinarily subversive play on writing for the English stage was complex and considerable: George Gascoigne's English version, composed for performance in the legal setting of Gray's Inn in 1566, was as overtly skeptical as Ariosto's original, but was followed by Gascoigne's contribution to a new English genre of neoclassical "detective" drama, which upheld, rather than undermined, the power of the judge or magistrate to detect and prove identity frauds and other abuses of the civic order.[27] Shakespeare, in turn, reacted to the 1570s "detective" genre by redeeming, in *The Comedy of Errors* (also performed at Gray's Inn), the subversively skeptical uses of paralogism, or false conjecture, so brilliantly deployed in *I suppositi*. In *The Comedy of Errors* Shakespeare proved that it was possible for a dramatist to exploit, as Ariosto had done, the emotional and psychological effects of mistaken inference (what the mistake reveals to us about the one who makes it) without having endorsed a drama of deliberate deception. In Shakespeare's Ephesus, unlike Ariosto's Ferrara, no one sets out to deceive, though everyone feels betrayed and deceived. In *The Taming of the Shrew* Shakespeare reacted more negatively to *I suppositi*'s tolerance of a degree of sexual freedom in women, composing a play that worked to disassociate the emotional power of a conjectural drama from the stigma of an "Italian" sexual licentiousness.

I suppositi plays, as does *La cassaria,* on the affinity between artificial legal proofs—*indizi, conietture, manifesti segni*—and strategies of deception. In *I suppositi,* however, the vertiginous sense of infinite recess and of social subversion inherent in this affinity is much more explicit than it is in the earlier play. There are several reasons for this, but among these is that the fraud being perpetrated by the young lover and his servant involves multiple thefts and exchanges of status and identity not in some fictitious "Athens" of Roman Comedy, but in a simulacrum of the Ferrara that lay outside the Ducal Palace in which the audience was seated.[28]

Erostrato, a Sicilian studying in Ferrara, has changed identities with his servant, Dulipo, in order to infiltrate a bourgeois Ferrarese household and deflower the daughter of the house; between them, master and servant plot to counter the dowry negotiations of the daughter's other lover, the lawyer, Cleandro, by persuading a visiting Sienese merchant to pose as the false Erostrato's father and sign a false bond. The arrival of Erostrato's real father from Sicily is then met with disbelief by the Ferrarese citizens, who refute his claims with those of the fakes, Dulipo and the Sienese merchant, while Ferrara's magistrates and laws prove incapable of helping him prove his identity or find the son whom he begins to think must have been murdered by Dulipo. The very setting of the play

in Ferrara, and the transformation of the "returning father" motif of Roman New Comedy into the arrival of a disoriented foreigner, who has no
privileged access to the city's judicial authorities (as does Crisobolo in *La
cassaria,* through Caridoro's father) works to disturb the Roman comic
tradition and to skew *I suppositi*'s putative function, within the tradition
of festival performances of humanist comedy in 1490s, as an idealizing
celebration of Ferrara under Este rule.

As in *La cassaria,* in *I suppositi* the invisible interiors of houses are
furnished, and their occupants' identities established, by the power
of conjecture. In act 1, scene 3, the false Dulipo (that is, Erostrato disguised as his own servant), searching for the true Dulipo (known in
town as Erostrato) asks his boy, Caprino, whom he sees coming out into
the street, "O, Caprino, che è di Erostrato?" "Di Erostrato?" replies Caprino, "Di Erostrato sono libri, veste e denari e molte altre cose ch'egli ha
in casa." ("O, Caprino, what of Erostrato?" "Of Erostrato? Of Erostrato
there are books, clothes, money, and many other things that he has in
the house." [1.3.1-3]) This fraudulent Erostrato, metonymically identified
with the wealthy foreign student's accoutrements that have brought him
such credit in Ferrara, then explains to the real Erostrato how he has also
plotted to acquire the father necessary to secure Polinesta as a bride.
As all act 2, scene 1 of *La cassaria* consists of Volpino's elaborating the
scheme that will ensure the entrapment of Lucrano, so 2.1 in *I suppositi*
is entirely taken up with Dulipo's or the false Erostrato's narration of the
outrageous lies by which he convinced a Sienese merchant that Este hos-
tility to Siena was so great that if he wanted to stay in Ferrara he'd better
pose as Filogono, a Sicilian merchant, wealthy father to Erostrato. In 2.2
the Sienese merchant and his servant (the latter evidently acted by the
player of Trappolo in *La cassaria*) enter the door of the false Erostrato's
house. In act 4—the usual act in which such a crisis occurs—the real
Erostrato's real father, Filogono, and his servant Lico, wearied by their
long journey from Sicily, arrive at this very door. Their knocking, however, arouses the hostile response of Erostrato's cook, Dalio, who claims
that the lodgings are full, indeed that Filogono himself is already *inside.*
Then the Sienese imposter issues forth and rehearses, as his own life
story, the circumstances leading up to Filogono's arrival in Ferrara. The
real Filogono splutters in disbelief as Dalio shuts the door in his face.

At this moment, when Filogono, instead of meeting his longed-for son,
finds himself shut out of his son's house, the object of Dalio's obscenities,

the effect is more disturbing than anything comparable in Roman comedy. And the peculiar nature of the disturbance derives from the relationship between the increasingly demented, disorienting evidential contradictions and the invocation of Ferrara as a civic ideal. For it is also at this point, having witnessed Filogono's experience as a stranger—bullied, abused, and told outrageous lies by a man occupying his accommodation and claiming to be him—that the audience first meets the citizen (called simply "Ferrarese") who speaks patriotically of the city's good government and especially of its judicial system. After a dig at the proverbial falsehood of the Ferrarese (in a pun on the Italian *fe* or *fede* for "faith"), Lico accuses the bystanding Ferrarese citizen of belonging to a city without due respect for law, where officers allow such cheating to go on. "Che sanno li officiali di queste trame?" replies the Ferrarese (what do the officers know of these things?; 4.6.9–10), introducing a more material, less idealizing view of the problems of judicial administration in Ferrara. But it is when the Ferrarese citizen attempts to vindicate the honesty of his city by presenting the Sicilian stranger with his son Erostrato that the most marked—if still darkly comic—departure from the Roman tradition takes place. In this moment we experience not only an unsettling subversion of the Ferrarese's civic idealism, but, in our sympathy with Filogono, a brush with the everyday possibility of tragedy. The well-meaning Ferrarese introduces the disguised Dulipo to Filogono as the old man's son. Filogono, having longed to see Erostrato, suddenly realizes that the man whom all Ferrara takes to be his son is the very servant into whose care he had entrusted his son—with dawning horror, he conjectures or imagines the scenario most likely to explain such a bizarre situation: "Ahi lasso!" Filogono laments,

costui dunque, che al mio carissimo Erostrato diedi per famiglio e scorta, averà o venduto o assassinato el mio figliolo, o di lui fatto qualche pessimo contratto; et averassi, non solo e panni e libri e ciò che per il vivo suo di Sicilia conducea, ma el nome ancora di Erostrato usurpato, per potere le lettere di cambio et il credito che io davo al mio figliolo senza altro impedimento usare a beneficio suo. Ah misero et infelice Filogono! Ah infortunatissimo vecchio! Non è Giudice o Capitano o Podestà o altro rettore in questa terra, a cui mi possa ricorre?

Alas! This man whom I gave as a servant and escort to my dearest Erostrato has either sold or murdered my son or has made him agree to some hideous contract. And not only has he usurped the clothes, books and other possessions which Erostrato brought with him from Sicily, but his name as well, so that he could, without hindrance, use to his own benefit the bills of exchange and letters of credit that I gave to my son. Ah, wretched and unhappy Filogono! Ah, most unfortunate old man! Isn't there a Judge, a Captain, a *Podestà,* or some other official in this city to whom I can have recourse? (4.8.25-36)

No *senex* figure of Roman comedy sounds quite so distraught on discovering how he's been made a dupe in his absence. The difference from Roman comedy lies in Ariosto's brilliant exploitation of the horror of surmise: Filogono's imagined scenario of his son's murder is indeed more likely than the play's "real" explanation, and its pathos plumbs unexpected emotional depths in the comic convention of paralogism, or mistaken conjecture.

Another shadowy element of disturbance to the comedy, however, lies in what Filogono's plight exposes about the limitations of human proof, the possibility of fundamental error that haunts all questions of identity, legitimacy, and paternity once they become questions.[29] Though the Ferrarese gamely insists on the infallibility of Ferrara's legal system— "Ci abbiamo e iudici e podestà, e sopra tutti un Principe iustissimo. Non dubitare che ti sia mancato di ragione, quando tu l'abbia" (We have judges and a *podestà* and, above all, a most just prince. Don't doubt but that you will get justice, if your cause is just; 4.8.37-39)—Lico has already anticipated the technical problem with such idealism: "Si tutti li altri testimonii in questa terra sono così fatti, si debbe provare ciò che si vuole" (if all the other witnesses in this city are like this one, people here can prove what they like; 4.8.13-14). When Filogono cried out for a captain, or a *podestà,* he, too, was acknowledging the problem Lico perceived—both captain and *podestà* (chief law enforcer and senior judge respectively) were, in most northern Italian cities, nonnative appointments, who were explicitly forbidden to enter into kinship relations with local inhabitants.[30] But the prospect for Filogono only looks bleaker when, instead of going straight to one of these impartial, nonnative representatives of justice, he finds his case being handled by a lawyer who is none other than Cleandro, rival suitor to the man claiming to be Filogono's son. Cleandro, far from expressing confidence in his client's case, declares that it will be almost impossible to prove: "Ma come mostrarai tu che costui non sia Erostrato, essendoci la publica presunzione in contrario? E come, che tu sia Filogono di Catania, quando quest'altro col testimonio del simulato Erostrato lo nieghi, e che sia quello esso pertinacissimamente contenda?"

(But how will you prove that this fellow isn't Erostrato when the public presumption is against you? And how will you prove that you're Filogono of Catania, when that other man, supported by the *testimony* of the sham Erostrato, denies it and obstinately claims that he is? [5.5.1–6; my italics] Although Beame's and Sbrocchi's excellent English translation does not register the technical legal sense of "presumption" here, translating *la publica presunzione* simply as "everybody knows," the term resonates with equally technical words for proof used by Cleandro in the recognition scene about to unfold in the next few lines. "Presumption" is a Roman and Italian civil law term, enormously important in the contexts of evidence and proof, for the law's ability to assume the truth of a certain matter for the purposes of inquiry.[31]

What happens, of course (the real Erostrato, meanwhile, lying imprisoned in Polinesta's father's house), is that Cleandro's anticipation of the problematic, expensive, and ultimately ineffective nature of the mode of proof Filogono proposes becomes redundant as the conjectural work of the denouement's "recognition" takes over: Cleandro begins to piece together clues and fragments of proof that suggest that Dulipo is, in fact, the son he lost long ago at the battle of Otranto. The predictable romance denouement obviates the need for dwelling further on the legal impasse momentarily glimpsed in the discussion of how inadequate Filogono's testimony and proofs would be, but it no less clearly raises further questions of likelihood and probability. As Cleandro finds out from Filogono that Dulipo's former name, as a foundling, was "Carino," he immediately claims that "Carino" was the name of his own son, whom he lost at Otranto. From the perspective of the strangers to Ferrara, however, this simply looks like another trick, another set of circumstantial lies to prove a false identity and kinship. As soon as Cleandro asks Filogono for details of Dulipo's origins, Lico is on guard, "Non ti disse io, patrone, che siamo in terra di Bari, e credavamo essere in Ferrara? Costui, per privarti del servo tuo, se lo vorrà qui con ciance adottare per figlio." (Didn't I tell you, Master, that we're in Bari [punning on *barare*, "to cheat"], and we thought that we were in Ferrara? Just to deprive you of your servant this man would adopt him with stories about his being his son. [5.5.109–12]) When Cleandro comes to his "recognition" finale, Lico narrowly avoids an obscene response to his request to see the birthmark that would clinch the story that Dulipo and Carino are one and the same person. "Non ho bisogna di piu manifesti segni oramai," announces Cleandro, "questo senza alcuno dubbio è el mio figliolo, che, già diciotto anni, ho perso e mille volte ho pianto, et aver debbe un neo di buona grandezza ne l'umero sinistro." (I don't need proofs more manifest than this: this is without doubt my son whom I lost eighteen years ago and for whom I've cried a thousand times. He must have a rather large mole on his left shoulder. [5.5.136–40]) Lico replies acidly, displacing the audience's urge to laugh at the pat rehearsal of these proofs: "Che maraviglia, se te l'ha detto, che tu lo sappia? El neo vi ha purtroppo: così vi avessi egli." (No wonder you know it, if he told it to you. Of course there's a mole, I wish he had. . . . [5.5.141–42]) In Gascoigne's 1566 *Supposes*, Lico's obscenity, and the skeptical response to the recognition that it jarringly registers, is fully spelled out: "He hath a moulde there in deede: and an hole in an other place, too. I woulde your nose were in it."[32]

"If She and I Be Pleased, What's That to You?": Conjecturing Female Consent in English Law and on the English Stage

Ariosto's conjectural dramaturgy, though composed for a humanist, festival theater in which experiments with perspective scenery and fixed-locale staging were an essential part, was perfectly adaptable to the open stage of English Renaissance drama later in the century. I will conclude by showing, briefly, how both Jonson and Shakespeare responded specifically to Ariosto's legally inflected rhetorical games with the power of "indizii e conietture" (indications and conjectures).

Shakespeare and Jonson were both acutely aware of the shared rhetorical ground between skeptical modes of inquiry into "the fact, and the circumstances thereof" in a legal case and the modes of circumstantial inquiry that offer audiences a vivid sense, in the theater, of unstaged events and places contributing to the characters' lives, histories, and psychological realities.[33] In English common law, unlike in the Romano-canon tradition informing Italian law, witnesses did not constitute proof, but only "evidence" before a jury, though of course the Romano-canon system of proof was valid in English ecclesiastical law.[34] It is notable, however, that Gascoigne translates Cleandro's "Non ho bisogna di piu manifesti segni," as "What nedeth me more *evident tokens*?" (*Supposes*, 5.5.128). For Ariosto, working with the Romano-canon system of proofs, the "manifest" sign was already a circumvention of the requirement of full proof (two witnesses or a confession). In England, the circumvention was itself unnecessary, for witnesses were not proofs, but themselves merely those who, in Sir Thomas Smith's words, can "give any . . . tokens which we call in our language evidence" to prove the case.[35] In this sense, the English system was already more amenable to the deconstruction of the opposition between seeing and imagining, or that between "witness" and "conjecture," than that in which Ariosto had worked. An English sense of the affinity between legal and dramatic rhetoric was further encouraged by the fact that the English word "evidence" so clearly derived from the Latin *evidentia,* a rhetorical term meaning "vividness" or "clarity." For Quintilian, a favorite author of Jonson's, *evidentia,* translating the Greek term, *enargeia,* was the vividness that a clever lawyer could give to a narrative of the facts, whether true or false, by making all the circumstances seem coherent and plausible.[36] And the English word "evidence" could be used as a term of praise for dramatic action so vividly conveyed by circumstantial narration that it seemed to be presented onstage. Thus George Chapman went so far as to praise Jonson's tragedy, *Sejanus* for

> Performing such a lively Evidence
> in thy Narrations, that thy Hearers still
> Thou turnst to thy Spectators.[37]

Just as it would be a mistake to think that Shakespeare was not concerned with the dramatic *evidentia* of circumstantial narrations—recall Hamlet's unstaged sea voyage, narrated to Horatio, or Ophelia's narrative of Hamlet's bursting into her closet—so it would be wrong to assume that Jonson did not see in the dramaturgy of conjecture and circumstantial inquiry a technique of psychological revelation. In the quarto text of Jonson's *Every Man in his Humour*—the text of the version set in Italy, and in which Shakespeare was an actor—there's a brilliant scene in which a merchant, Thorello, who, having debated whether or not to absent himself from his wife and home for an appointment with another merchant, is met, while away from home, by his neighbor, Cob, of whom he receives what he thinks are alarming reports about how things are progressing back at his own warehouse. Everything Cob says actually refutes Thorello's suspicions of sexual freedoms being taken, but Thorello is unstoppably eager to supply the evidence Cob denies. The scene opens as Thorello asks Cob to say exactly how many young men he has seen entering his warehouse. Cob isn't sure exactly how many, prompting Thorello to imagine "a swarm." Thorello then says he is sure his sister and wife would welcome these gallant young men. "Like enough," Cob concedes, in a general way, "yet I heard not a word of welcome." Thorello supplies an inference as fantastic as it is swooningly erotic: "No, their lips were sealed with kisses." He then asks, desperately, "Cob, which of them was't, that first kissed my wife?/My sister, I should say. My wife, alas,/I fear not her. Ha? Who was it, sayst thou?"[38] Cob's professions of ignorance are in vain, and Thorello's next move is to dash back to his house to confront the orgy he has conjured so powerfully from such meager fragments of discourse. It is not hard to see, in the wake of Jonson's creation of Thorello, the possibility of a play like *Othello,* in which the passionate, irresistible complicity of the hearer in the production of lurid evidence of his wife's infidelity is presented as pitifully tragic.

Jonson's great comedies, however, exploit an intense awareness of the relations between evidence manipulation and theatrical illusion in ways that bespeak a continued engagement with Ariosto's *indizii e conietture.* In *Volpone* the games Mosca plays with plots of entrapment, witnessing, and conjectural proof recall Volpino's improvisings in *La cassaria.* In act 3, scene 3 of *Volpone,* Mosca tells the young heir, Bonario, that he will bring him where he will be "a witness of the deed" of his father's disinheriting him (3.3.60–64). What Bonario actually witnesses, however, is Volpone's attempt to rape Celia. Bonario and Celia, innocent victim and honest eyewitness, immediately go to the police, and when the judges or *avocatori* come into the courtroom in the trial scene in 4.4 they are ready to think Volpone guilty. Mosca, however, not only primes the advocate Voltore to plead the opposite case—accusing Celia of whoredom—he actually recruits a complete outsider as unwitting corroborative witness. Earlier, in 3.5, Mosca had rid Volpone of the annoying Lady Would-Be by exciting her suspicion that her husband was seeing a courtesan on the Rialto. In 4.6, in a brilliant tour de force, Lady Would-Be comes on to *identify* Celia in court as the prostitute with whom her husband apparently consorted in a gondola (4.6.1–4; see 3.5.19–20). The case is altered: the advocates believe not the true eyewitnesses, but the extraordinarily coherent illusion fabricated by Mosca's cunning circumstantial evidence and Lady Would-Be's snobbery and jealousy.

Filogono's horrified surmise of his son's death in *I suppositi* opened up, for Shakespeare, a sense of the possibilities, as well as the risks, of employing the drama of false conjecture as a means of accessing emotional and psychological depths onstage. Shakespeare's *Comedy of Errors*, played at Gray's Inn nearly twenty years after Gascoigne's English version of *I suppositi*, subtracts the element of deliberate deception from Ariosto's urban intrigue plot. Though treachery and fraud reputedly characterize Shakespeare's Ephesus, as they did Ariosto's Ferrara, the hurts inflicted in the play are the result of confusion, shaped by paranoid imaginings into something emotionally revelatory of the vulnerabilities, relationships, and characters of those involved.[39]

Something quite different, however, happens to Ariosto's drama of conjecture in *The Taming of the Shrew*. As Louise Clubb has written, Ariosto's Counter-Reformation successors, the authors of *commedie gravi*, endowed the theme of love and of woman's constancy with a greater moral seriousness than had Ariosto himself, producing a "more spiritually specialized version of the inamorata" from whom we can see a clear line of descent to Helena of *All's Well* or Isabella of *Measure for Measure*.[40] In *The Taming of the Shrew*, however, Shakespeare's transformations of the earlier form of heroine—Polinesta from *I suppositi*—render her a peculiarly charged locus of conjecture, and one which, arguably, has to do with England's peculiar legal status as subject neither to the laws of the reformed Church nor to those of the Counter-Reformation.

In Womack's suggestive discussion of the dynamic relations of the fixed-locale and open stages of the Renaissance, he proposes that the most obvious referent of the "outside/inside" binarism of the stage "is sexual. The young man is out in the street, and the object of his desires is inside one of the houses . . . because it is the house of a blocking father or husband."[41] It is easy to see how this scheme applies to *La cassaria*, where the women are supposedly inside Lucrano's house, or *I suppositi*, where Polinesta is supposed, except for her initial revelatory appearance, to be inside Damone's house. It is easy to see, too, how in more stylized ways this binarism catalyzes action and enables sexual conjecture in Shakespeare and Jonson. One example would be Antipholus of Ephesus barred from his own door and imagining what's going on behind it in *The Comedy of Errors*, 3.1. Another would be the example just given of Thorello's lurid conjectures of the goings-on behind the doors of his warehouse in *Every Man in his Humour*.

In *The Taming of the Shrew*, however, Shakespeare's juxtaposition of Ariosto's variant on Terence's *Eunuchus* (a plot in which a young stranger disguises himself to enter a house and deflower a citizen's daughter) with a wife-taming plot derived from folk culture put the binarism to work in new ways that effectively rewrote the history of marriage in Western culture, leading later readers and critics of Shakespeare to conjecture an affectionate intimacy as the explanation of the enigma that is Petruchio's and Katherina's final relationship.[42] Critics have long argued that a chief distinction between Ariosto's play and Shakespeare's imitation of it in *Taming* involves the enlargement of the woman's role and the apparent development of her "character." In Ariosto's play, a critic wrote over forty years ago, "supposed identity never serves to transform the characters . . . Polynesta's value is neutral throughout," whereas, by contrast, "in Bianca, Shakespeare greatly expands this restricted role of the woman in Roman comedy, and not only brings her into the shrew theme, but also initially puts us under suppositions of her character that prove in part false."[43] The same critic also proposed that the Ariostan drama of conjecture (or, in Gascoigne's and Shakespeare's preferred usage, "supposing") should be seen as "the guiding principle of Petruchio's strategy in winning and taming the shrew."[44] Shakespeare's celebrated "character-realism" has, in *The Taming of the Shrew,* then, something to do with the positioning of women in relation to conjecture or supposition, a point that feminist attempts to ironize or distance the taming plot fail to engage. For what needs to be understood is the way in which Shakespeare's juxtaposition of the two plots involves a chiasmus, or crossover, of the public/private or witness/suppose binarism as each plot traces a distinct move from one to the other, based on two distinct legal models of marriage.

In English common law, husband and wife were said, by the legal fiction of *coverture,* to be one person, and that person was the husband. He looked after her, and she was incapable of owning separate property or of making her own contracts.[45] Marriage and courtship, however, were under the jurisdiction of the ecclesiastical courts, which operated according to quite a different model of female personhood. The Church and canon law had, since the twelfth century, emphasized "the union of two hearts" and made the legal validity of the marriage depend on *voluntary* consent, as signified in courtship and spousal promises, whether witnessed or not.[46] Even after the Council of Trent's 1563 decree, which made parental permission a legal requirement for marriage in Counter-Reformation Europe, England persisted into the seventeenth century with an ecclesiastical law that validated a marriage made by two persons in private if there was evidence of voluntary consent. And in popular English practice, as social historians tell us, the private beginnings of matrimonial contracts were reconciled to the wider community by way of increasingly public witnessings of the couples' promises, until the marriage was gradually accepted and formalized by the parish at large.[47] According to English canon law, then, the woman's consent, whether witnessed or unwitnessed, was essential to the validity of any marriage; her consent had to be sought, *she had to be courted,* however privately. According to English common law, however, the unity-of-person doctrine rendered the concept of the married woman's consent unnecessary; the woman's thoughts—her consent, her dissent—were inaccessibly hidden as she herself was said to be *coverte,* covered by the person of her husband.

In the traditional fixed-locale-stage courtship plot, as Womack says, "the young man is out on the street and the object of his desire is inside one of the houses." The insides of houses are also, on the fixed-locale stage, imaginatively generative: generative of supposes and conjectures. In *The Taming of the Shrew,* Shakespeare interwove a plot of covert courtship, in which a young man uses false conjecture to deceive his elders (the bride's father and his own) to ascertain the affection of his love-object, with a plot of common law *coverture,* in which the husband's conjectures finally dictate the wife's reality. Thus, Lucentio's disguised courtship of a Bianca "closely mew'd . . . up" in her father's house, though deceitful, is motivated by the need to win her love and voluntary encouragement.[48] In this the Lucentio-Bianca plot corresponds with some precision to the traditional popular model, whereby relatively informal, clandestine promises would lead to increasing publicity, solemnization before witnesses, and acceptance by the community. Lucentio courts in private, sends his rivals packing, and, having found a "suppos'd" father to forge the assurance of Bianca's dower, takes his bride privately and *voluntarily* ("if she be so contented") "to th'church," with "the priest, clerk and some sufficient honest witnesses" before revealing their contract to both their fathers (4.5.88–90 and 5.1.105–6) who are then sufficiently reconciled to allow Bianca to preside at a wedding feast (5.2). By contrast, Petruchio's wooing of Katherina is marked by a refusal of the repetitive rhythms and leisure of courtship, the slow process by which one tests one's own and another's inclinations and feelings: "My business asketh haste,/And every day I cannot come to woo," he says (2.1.114–15). After one interview with her, which even the most traditional critics concede reveals her spirited resistance to his courtship, he concludes by producing a fiction of her consent that effectively renders her speech and signs opaque, uninterpretable to the others: "If she and I be pleased, what's that to you?" he challenges the others, "Tis bargain'd twixt us twain, *being alone,*/That she shall still be cursed in company" (2.1.296-98). Having destroyed the public legibility of any distinction between the voluntary or involuntary in his betrothed ("will you, nill you, I will marry you"; 2.1.264), Petruchio moves swiftly to secure the other elements of marital legitimacy according to canon law. Having mocked the ceremony in the church (as we hear from Gremio's narration; 3.2.155-80), he proceeds to defy the custom of the public witnessing and solemnity that signals the community's participation in the marriage of two young people: the bridale, or marriage feast. His "haste" and "business," he says, calls him away from the feast, to the obvious dismay of his kinsfolk and neighbors who "entreat" him to stay. And then, tellingly, he states his rights as they now stand in the *common law,* threatening a common law *action* on anyone who denies his right to deny his wife's desire to preside at her own wedding feast:

> I will be master of what is mine own.
> She is my goods, my chattels, she is my house,
> My household stuff, my field, my barn,
> My horse, my ox, my ass, my any thing.
> And here she stands. Touch her whoever dare!
> *I'll bring my action on the proudest he*
> That stops my way in Padua. (3.2.227-33)

Lucentio's covert courtship of Bianca, and her voluntary responsiveness to him, encourages an audience to read her as sexually forward and potentially deceitful. (Her "development," as critics say, amounts to a revelation that she is not as "submissive" as she first seemed, but "assumes many of the characteristics of her shrewish sister" once married.)[49] By contrast, Petruchio's common law coverture of Kate, his legally sanctioned removal of her, and the removal of the stage action from the public space of the wedding feast to the private space of his house, renders her thoughts and desires completely unreadable to the community and to us. It is this trajectory toward privacy that encourages our conjecture, producing, in effect, the desire of so many critics and audiences, traditional and feminist, to believe that Katherina's opacity constitutes proof of our exclusion from a profound intimacy with her husband, to which no other can have access: "they surrender to the fact of their affection" as one critic puts it.[50] That generations of readers of Shakespeare have been so ready to believe in Petruchio's and Kate's postmarital romance, is due in no small part to Shakespeare's figuration, through the Lucentio-Bianca plot, of the license of Ariosto's conjectural drama as the mobility and deceitfulness of the desiring woman herself.

Notes

1. No. 138, "Lettera di Bernardino Prosperi a Isabella D'Este," 1508 8 Marzo, in Michele Catalano, *Vita di Ludovico Ariosto Recostruita su Novi Documenti*, 2 vols. (Geneva: Leo S. Olschki, 1931), 2.83–84. The letter is cited in Douglas Radcliffe-Umstead, *The Birth of Modern Comedy in Renaissance Italy* (Chicago: University of Chicago Press, 1969), 65–66; *The Comedies of Ariosto*, trans. and ed. Edmond M. Beame and Leonard G. Sbrocchi (Chicago: University of Chicago Press, 1975), xix–xx; Richard Andrews, *Scripts and Scenarios: The Performance of Comedy in Early Modern Italy* (Cambridge: Cambridge University Press, 1993), 36–37.

2. Nino Pirrotta and Elena Povoledo, *Music and Theatre from Poliziano to Monteverdi,* trans. Karen Eales (Cambridge: Cambridge University Press, 1982), 311–34.

3. Peter Womack, "The Comical Scene: Perspective and Civility on the Renaissance Stage," *Representations* 101 (2008): 32–56 (35).

4. Andrews, *Scripts and Scenarios,* 38.

5. See, for example, Anne Barton in *The Riverside Shakespeare* (New York: Houghton Mifflin, 1997), 111: "Shakespeare may well have felt . . . that it would be a useful discipline to submit himself to the three unities even . . . if he saw no subsequent need to employ them."

6. Louise George Clubb, *Italian Drama in Shakespeare's Time* (New Haven: Yale University Press, 1989), 3, and 49–63; Leo Salingar, *Shakespeare and the Traditions of Comedy* (Cambridge: Cambridge University Press, 1974).

7. Helen Cooper, "Shakespeare and the Mystery Plays," in *Shakespeare and Elizabethan Popular Culture,* ed. Stuart Gillespie and Neil Rhodes (London: Arden, 2006), 18–41, 19–20.

8. Cooper, "Shakespeare and the Mystery Plays," 29.

9. Womack, "Comical Scene," 37–38.

10. "Dubito tuttavia che il termine 'prospettiva' usato dal Prosperi si riferisca a un impianto realizzato effettivamente secondo i canoni della regola prospettiva; o non intenda piuttosto indicare la 'scena di teatro,' secondo il lessico divulgato dai traduttori di Vitruvio." Ludovico Zorzi, *Il teatro e la città* (Torino: Enaudi, 1977), 27–28.

11. Pirrotta and Povoledo, *Music and Theatre from Poliziano to Monteverdi,* 306–7.

12. Ibid., 317. Povoledo includes at plate 21, and discusses at p. 319, a tracing of a sixteenth-century sketch in the *Biblioteca Ariostea,* possibly for *La cassaria* or for *I suppositi,* which shows "the city alive in the background" of a play that requires only two houses with functional doors. See also Sergio Costola, "Ludovico Ariosto's Theatrical Machine: Tactics of Subversion in the 1509 Performance of *I suppositi*" (Ph.D. diss., UCLA, 2002), 86–88.

13. Ariosto, *La Cassaria,* 3.1.2-12, in *Tutte le opere di Ludovico Ariosto,* ed. Cesare Segre, 5 vols., (Milano: Arnoldo Mondadori Editore, 1964-84) 4: 22; Ariosto, *The Coffer,* in

Comedies of Ariosto, trans. and ed. Beame and Sbrocchi, 43. Further references to both of these editions will appear in the text.

14. Womack, "Comical Scene," 43.

15. Some critics, of course, have argued for the significance of the analogy between visual perspective and narrative realism; see Alistair Fowler, *Renaissance Narrative Images in Literature and Art* (Oxford: Oxford University Press, 2003).

16. Adele C. Scafuro, *The Forensic Stage: Settling Disputes in Graeco-Roman New Comedy* (Cambridge: Cambridge University Press, 1997), 25.

17. Alan H. Nelson, "The Universities: Early Staging in Cambridge," in *A New History of English Drama,* ed. John D. Cox and David Scott Kastan (New York: Columbia University Press, 1997), 64.

18. Radcliffe-Umstead mentions *Mostellaria, Pseudolis, Andria,* and *Heautontimorumenos* (*Birth of Modern Comedy,* 66–67).

19. Scafuro, *Forensic Stage,* 42.

20. Plautus, *Poenulus* (*The Little Carthaginian*), 185–86, in *Plautus,* trans. Paul Nixon, 5 vols. (Cambridge, Mass.: Harvard University Press, 1932), 4.18–19.

21. On *furtum manifestum* and *Poenulus* see Alan Watson, *The Law of Obligations in the Later Roman Republic* (Oxford: Clarendon Press, 1965), 230–32. Scafuro, *Forensic Stage,* 458–59, discusses the problems of assuming the play accurately represents the law.

22. For Ariosto, "manifest," meaning something like "notorious," would be understood within the Romano-canon system of proof as a category of fractional proof introduced by Italian jurists in the thirteenth century to enable conviction in the absence of the full proof of two unimpeachable witnesses or a confession. See Barbara J. Shapiro, *Beyond Reasonable Doubt and Probable Cause: Historical Perspectives on the Anglo-American Law of Evidence* (Berkeley: University of California Press, 1991), 120–21.

23. Catalano, *Vita di Ludovico Ariosto,* 1.123; 1.93. In his *Satires,* Ariosto says he spent five years uselessly studying law.

24. Shapiro, *Beyond Reasonable Doubt,* 120–21; John Gilissen, "La Preuve en Europe (XVIᵉ-XIXᵉ S.)," *Recueils De La Société Jean Bodin Pour L'Histoire Comparative Des Institutions,* XVII, *La Preuve: Moyen Age et Temps Modernes* (Bruxelles: Editions de la Librairie encyclopedique, 1965), 755–833, 759–69. For German criminal procedure and *indicia,* see John F. Langbein, *Prosecuting Crime in the Renaissance: England, Germany, France* (Cambridge, Mass.: Harvard University Press, 1974), 272–79.

25. Giovambattista Giraldi Cintio, *De' romanzi, delle comedie e delle tragedie ragionamenti,* ed. Eugenio Camerini, 2 vols. (Milan: G.Daelii, 1864; facsimile reprint A. Forni, 1975), 2.21.

26. Ben Jonson, *Volpone,* ed. Philip Brockbank (London: A&C Black, 1968), 3.7.19. Further references to this edition will appear in the text.

27. See Lorna Hutson, *The Invention of Suspicion: Law and Mimesis in Shakespeare and Renaissance Drama* (Oxford: Oxford University Press, 2007), 207–16.

28. Costola, "Ariosto's Theatrical Machine," 88.

29. See Terence Cave, *Recogntions: A Study in Poetics* (Oxford: Clarendon Press, 1988), 252.

30. See David S. Chambers and Trevor Dean, *Clean Hands and Rough Justice: An Investigating Magistrate in Renaissance Italy* (Michigan: Ann Arbor, 1997), a study of the office of *podestà* in Ferrara and Mantua in this period, 49–50. Interestingly, Ariosto's own grandfather, Niccolò Ariosti, broke the kinship rule when he was captain of the *cittadella* of Reggio in the 1480s; Catalano, *Vita di Ludovico Ariosto,* 1:26, 39–40.

31. See James Bradley Thayer, *A Preliminary Treatise on Evidence at the Common Law* (Boston: Little, Brown & Co., 1898), 314-15, discussing Andrea Alciati's definition.

32. George Gascoigne, *Supposes*, 5.5.131-32, in *A Hundreth Sundrie Flowres*, ed. G. W. Pigman III (Oxford: Clarendon Press, 2000), 53. Further references by act, scene, and line will appear in the text.

33. See Hutson, *Invention of Suspicion*. The quotation is from Michael Dalton, *The Countrey Justice* (London: assignes of John More, 1635), 295.

34. Hutson, *Invention of Suspicion*, 75-77.

35. Sir Thomas Smith, *De Republica Anglorum*, ed. Mary Dewar (London: Cambridge University Press, 1982), 114.

36. Quintilian, *The Orator's Education*, ed. and trans. Donald A. Russell, 5 vols. (Cambridge, Mass.: Harvard University Press, 2001), 2.250-51, book 4.2.64-65.

37. George Chapman, "In Seianum Ben Ionsoni," in Ben Jonson, *Sejanus his Fall* (London: 1605), sig. ¶ 4v.

38. Ben Jonson, *Every Man in his Humour* (1601 Quarto), ed. Robert S. Miola (Manchester: Manchester University Press, 2000), 3.3.30-32.

39. Hutson, *Invention of Suspicion*, 147-57, 202-9.

40. Clubb, *Italian Drama*, 67-69.

41. Womack, "Comical Scene," 43.

42. On the taming plot's folktale origins, see Jan Harold Brunvand, "The Folktale Origin of *The Taming of the Shrew*," *Shakespeare Quarterly* 17, no. 4 (1966): 345-59. For a typical conjecture of affection—as prescribed in humanist texts of companionate marriage—as the explanation for Kate's obedience to Petruchio, see John C. Bean, "Comic Structure and the Humanizing of Kate in *The Taming of the Shrew*," in *The Woman's Part: Feminist Criticism of Shakespeare*, ed. Carolyn Ruth Swift Lenz, et al., 65-78 (Urbana: University of Illinois Press, 1983).

43. Cecil C. Seronsy, "'Supposes' as the Unifying Theme in *The Taming of the Shrew*," *Shakespeare Quarterly* 14, no. 1 (1963): 15-30, 18.

44. Ibid., 16.

45. J. H. Baker, *An Introduction to English Legal History*, 2nd ed. (London: Butterworths, 1979), 395.

46. See Georges Duby, *Medieval Marriage: Two Models from Twelfth-Century France*, trans. Elborg Forster (Baltimore: Johns Hopkins University Press, 1978), 15-17.

47. See Diana O'Hara, " 'Ruled by My Friends': Aspects of Marriage in the Diocese of Canterbury, ca.1540-1570," *Continuity and Change* 6, no. 1 (1991): 9-41 (20); Subha Mukherji, *Law and Representation in Early Modern Drama* (Cambridge: Cambridge University Press, 2006), 21-26.

48. *The Taming of the Shrew*, ed. Brian Morris (New York: Methuen, 1981), 3.1.43. Further references to act, scene, and line of this edition will appear in the text.

49. See Brian Morris, introduction to *Taming of the Shrew*, 112.

50. Seronsy, " 'Supposes' as the Unifying Theme," 16.

"Bawdy Doubles": Pietro Aretino's Comedie (1588) and the Appearance of English Drama

BIANCA FINZI-CONTINI CALABRESI

Si trovaria più tosto casta e sobria Roma che un' opra corretta.
You would sooner find a chaste and sober Rome than a book without misprints.
—Pietro Aretino to Jacopo Barbo (December 10, 1537)

"S'IO NON ERRO" (if I don't err) begins the printer's address to the reader in the first single-author collection of vernacular plays to be produced in England—Pietro Aretino's *Quattro comedie*—published in London by John Wolfe in 1588. Having earlier promised (pseudonymously) to publish Aretino's letters in accessible editions, Wolfe would have been aware of Aretino's equally improbable visions of a reformed Rome and a correct text. Indeed, instances of error and errancy, trespass and transgression, appear throughout Wolfe's collection, the first English anthology solely devoted to drama.[1] In good humanist fashion, Wolfe provides an extensive list of printer's omissions, mistakes, and typographical errors at the end of his book. His work errs in a broader sense, however: it represents itself as a "wandering" international text, both subject to emerging standards of accuracy and, at the same time, committed to *errare* "roving, gadding, erring up and down" within and across boundaries, national, textual, commercial, and sexual.[2] Wolfe's edition thus links *errore,* "error, . . . ouersight . . . trespasse," and *erronìa,* "mocking or scoffing, a figure in speaking meaning contrary to the word," to create a text doubly *erronico,* that is, a text that functions "in another sense" from what it seems and is patently "erroneous, false, erring, mistaking" (Florio 120).[3] Such self-referential doubleness complicates the still-current assumption that Wolfe's edition falsely represents itself as having been produced, indeed printed, in Italy and suggests rather that the edition

207

plays with what it means to desire Italianate books and bodies as well as with what national drama "should" look like in the period.

The *Quattro comedie* were one of a number of Italian-language works published by Wolfe in the 1580s, most notably texts by Machiavelli, Aretino, Castiglione, and the like, authors who had been placed on the Indices of Prohibited Works by the Vatican in 1559 and 1564 or were otherwise suspected of heretical or unflattering statements about the Catholic Church.[4] Although issued from his shop in London, and often registered with the Stationer's Company under his name, many of these editions include fictitious places of origin and false publishers' identities on their title pages and in their prefaces. Claiming to have been printed in Palermo, Naples, Rome, and Bengodi—this last a particularly significant reference, as I will discuss—Wolfe's books have been taken as intentional "forgeries" or "fakes" meant to be passed off for sale at the Frankfurt Book Fair and elsewhere as "Italian imprints," thanks to their seeming Italian provenance.[5] But there are serious limitations to this view of Wolfe's publishing as a marketing scam, not the least for the Aretine corpus that he issues in this period. In brief, the investment of the *Quattro comedie* in Italianate practices is at once extravagant and incomplete; the edition's lapses in authenticity undermine claims to have been "made in Italy," even as the fiction of Italian identity it creates itself emerges as a kind of authenticating mark of its Italian origins in a deeper sense.

In some ways it is not surprising that the first anthology of drama printed in England appeared in Italian: Italian publishers had been producing single-author collections of drama since at least midcentury (for example, editions of *comedie* by Giovanni Maria Cecchi, Ludovico Ariosto, and Anton Francesco Grazzini were published in 1550, 1562, and 1582, respectively). Wolfe's edition introduces English readers to the possibility of a marketable collection solely made up of vernacular drama. At the same time it offers itself to an international market that already has responded to Aretino's innovative printing of plays in the 1530s and the subsequent recognition by Italian publishers that single-author collections of drama could participate profitably in the emerging interest in vernacular octavos.

Sold in Britain as well as abroad, the *Quattro comedie* appear in the first catalogues of the Bodleian Library, as well as in the collections of Sir William Cecil and William Drummond, to name just a few influential bibliophiles.[6] That Wolfe intended these books to pass as Italian to English readers, if not to a European audience at large, has become something of a truism among critics. Robert Miola, for example, wrote in 1998 (and reiterated in 2000), "John Wolfe faked Italian imprints to boost the sale of his books," citing Wolfe's reasoning variously as an attempt at "forgery . . . wherein an anterior text pretends to be an original" and as a result of "the market for Italian books [being] so good in London."[7] More recently, Alan Farmer likewise repeats the presumption that "the reputation of English printed books even led some printers, most famously John Wolfe, to print surreptitiously books in foreign vernacular languages (with false imprints listing fictitious Continental origins) as a way to avoid the stigma of an English imprint."[8] Other commentators are more equivocal, stating merely that Wolfe's "Italian" publications suggest "intimate acquaintance with the shadier side of international printing."[9] Although not fakes in the sense meant by these critics, Wolfe's editions do create a fiction of originating elsewhere in space if not in time.[10] They thus raise questions about how readers in the Renaissance might distinguish between a text authentically *home-made* and one authentically *alien,* as well as why such categories might matter to early modern readers.[11]

One group of readers who appear to have been taken in by the prima facie "Italian" origins of Wolfe's *Quattro comedie* were the first administrators of the Bodleian Library. The opinions of its initial keeper, Sir Thomas Bodley, on the worth of printed vernacular drama are by now well known. Repudiating the many "idle bookes, & riffe raffes" to be found among "our London bookes," he famously writes in 1612 against admitting what he terms "baggage bookes" into the library:

I can see no good reason to alter my opinion, for excluding suche bookes, as almanackes, plaies, & an infinit number, that are daily printed, of very vnworthy maters & handling, suche as, me thinkes, both the keeper & vnderkeeper should disdaine to seeke out, to deliuer vnto any man. Happely some plaies may be worthy the keeping: but hardly one in fortie.[12]

Critics, however, have less frequently noted his praise of foreign plays in direct contrast to English printed drama:

For it is not alike in Englishe plaies, & others of other nations: because they are most esteemed, for learning the languages & many of them compiled, by men of great fame, for wisedome & learning, which is seeldom or neuer seene among vs. (Bodley 221)

Bodley approves the acquisition of foreign drama because of the high opinion in which it is held by others—specifically for its use in "learning the languages"—and because of the status of their compilers, "men of great fame." (In Bodley's ambiguous formulation, it is unclear whether the compilers are famous for "wisedome & learning" or whether the plays are printed to increase the "wisedome & learning" of their readers.) In any case, such conditions are "seldom or never seen" in English circles, according to Bodley. Wolfe himself would hardly have qualified as a personage of the sort Bodley intends, despite his notoriety in England by the end of the century. How well Aretino's works, themselves, might serve the ends of "learning the languages" and "wisedome & learning" might also be questioned, as I discuss below.

Wolfe seems to have had firsthand experience with the work of Italian editors and publishers; two mid-1570s imprints bearing an Italian version of his name have been taken to suggest that he spent several years training in Florence, perhaps under the Giunta family.[13] His later adoption of their device as his printer's mark—the Florentine Giglio (or iris)—may be an attempt to call attention to that apprenticeship or simply may be a more general advertisement of his Tuscan credentials, concomitant with his creation of an Italian persona for both his works and their producer. That persona offers the Italian—indeed Tuscan—*burla* or *beffa* (a mocking jest or practical joke) as a model of performative identity by which the translated textual and sexual desires of publisher and reader might be gratified.[14] As a quintessential distinguishing mark of the newcomer from the *conoscitore,* the *beffa* epitomizes a particular form of Italianate culture to which Wolfe's editions aspire, one that permits those texts to differentiate between the initiated and the overly literal reader—to do the social and cultural work of discriminating between sophisticate and gull—whether abroad or at home.

While much has been written of the Elizabethan concern over Englishmen acquiring Italian dress and mores in their travels, the deceptive work of textual Italianness has been less thoroughly examined. In his notorious attack on *l'Englese Italianato,* Roger Ascham links the two—body and book—as shape-shifting and monstrous in form as well as unduly subject to erotic female power: "These be the inchantementes of Circe, brought out of Italie, to marre mens maners in England," he writes in the 1571 *Scholemaster.*[15] In Ascham's (limited) transnational experience, errant, border-crossing texts perform like their human counterparts. He famously decries those "precepts of fonde books, of late translated out of Italian into English, sold in euery shop in London, commended by honest titles the soner to corrupt honest maners: dedicated ouer boldlie to virtuous and honorable personages, the easielier to begile simple and innocent wittes."[16] Thanks to his indefinite phrasing, Ascham's "fonde books" may be read simultaneously as books *about* desire, books desired *by* readers, and, as personified versions of the *Englese Italianato,* entities governed by a desire for the same libertine excesses in London that Italy purportedly offers abroad.[17]

For Ascham, transnational books, like transnational Englishmen, embody Italianness in themselves and in their influence on others, most notably in their ability to beguile tender English wits and lend ammunition to already corrupt English women: "these books, made in Italie, and translated in England . . . open, not fond and common ways to vice, but such sutle, cunnyng, new, and diuerse shiftes, to cary yong willes to vanitie, and yong wittes to mischief, to teach old bawdes new schole poyntes, as the simple head of an English man is not hable to invent. . . ."[18] In Ascham's formulation, books abet female panderers—specifically aiding bawds by introducing them to deceptive and seductive practices of which the innocent English man cannot conceive. As I'll discuss below, Wolfe's editions cast printers rather as masculine panders, who produce and market books which cater to female as well as male desires.

In 1582, Christopher Barker enjoined "Wolfe, leave your Machevillian devices, and conceit of your forreine wit, which you have gained by gadding from countrey to countrey."[19] In his accusation of "conceit of . . . forreine wit" and excessive "gadding," Barker, a senior official of the Stationer's Company, seems already to recognize Wolfe's production of an errant "Italianate" persona, based on a notion of alien or unfamiliar humor, that Wolfe's edition of Aretino's *Comedie* further extends and expands upon. But if Wolfe appeared to many as a quintessential "Italianate Englishman," would his "Italianate English" books have appeared as equally itinerant and foreign to early modern readers such as Bodley's administrators? To answer this question, we need to consider what kind of a text a prospective sixteenth-century buyer picking up the *Quattro comedie* from a stall in Frankfurt or St. Paul's churchyard would encounter, asking how his or her expectations of the Italian or English nature of the edition, and printed drama in general, might be confirmed or conditioned by the material object held in his or her hand.

Initially, Wolfe's *Quattro comedie* suggest nothing suspicious about their place of origin: given the title, the reader might reasonably assume that she or he was about to purchase a work "made in Italy." Classical in design, with roman majuscules and miniscules for type, a portrait medal at its center, and text entirely in Italian and Latin, Wolfe's edition might seem anomalous only in the absence of place name or publisher's name at the bottom of the page, logistical information commonly included to direct the reader to where the book could be bought, but increasingly also used as a means to advertise the publisher's own involvement in the creation of the work. The lack of publication data is sufficiently unusual in such an edition, and yet integral to this particular one, that the Corrector to Wolfe's edition points out its omission disparagingly in his end remarks appended to his errata list. He laments among other mistakes that this ottavo text appears "senza nome dello stampatore, ne meno del luogo" (without the name of the printer nor even the place name) where it was produced.[20]

In other ways, the title page of this small edition accords quite closely with emerging standards for collections of printed drama by well-known Italian authors and with the appearance of printed works by Aretino in the midcentury in particular. Although lacking a conventional printed border, the title of the work heads off the frontispiece, set in a well-spaced, centered roman capital that includes the author's name and a laudatory epithet. Below, Wolfe lists the individual plays contained within the collection: "*Cioè*/Il Marescalco/La Cortegiana/La Talanta/L'Hipocrito" (*Quattro comedie,* title page). This too is in keeping with developing conventions in Italian printing: the *Comedie* of Ariosto, published by the Gioliti in Venice in 1562, include a list of the works contained within the volume: "*CIOE,/I Suppositi, La Cassaria, La Lena,/Il Negromante, & la Scolastica.*"[21] As is common in the period, both works advertise that their contents are being reprinted; here the claims diverge, however. Whereas the Ariosto edition emphasizes that the plays have been submitted to a new level of scholarly rigor, the Aretino invokes a different reason for the reissue: the requests of readers who recognize the worth of these temporarily dimmed works, "nouellamente ritornate, per mezzo della stampa, a luce, a richiesta de conoscitori del lor valore" (newly returned, by means of the press, to the light, by request of connoisseurs of its value; *Quattro comedie,* title page).[22]

This short description of collaboration between press and readers—*stampa* and *conoscitori*—hints at Aretino's questionable, transgressive status in Italy and England in this period, a status somewhat differently defined in each locale. In the 1580s on the Continent Aretino was known equally for his religious writings (his works on Genesis and on the life of the Virgin, for example), for his unprecedented published correspondence with the great and the learned, and for his critiques of court and clergy that had earned him the title "il flagello / dei principle, il Divin Pietro Aretino" in Ariosto's 1532 *Orlando furioso* (46.14). In England, rather, while these other works were becoming known thanks to publications like John Florio's bilingual dictionary, Aretino was primarily associated with the "Aretine . . . printes" invoked in Jonson's *Volpone* and, increasingly, for the "curtisan politiques" of the *Raggionamenti* (published in England by Wolfe in 1584) in which Nanna and Pippa discuss the sexual status of the three roles for women ostensibly available in cinquecento Italy: nun, wife, or whore.[23] Even as Wolfe's *Quattro comedie* purportedly seek to emphasize his status as "D. Pietrus Aretinus. Flagellum Principum," it was these latter printed works that had earned Aretino the epithet in England of "Italian ribald" and associated him with the polymorphous erotic identity, as a "courtier or rather courtisan" responsible for the appearance of the "infamous Capricio, or apologie of Pedarastice" and other "vilest impostumes of lewde corruption" that Wolfe's editions evoke.[24] The "valore" or value of Aretino's *comedie,* which spurred *conoscitori* to ask for them again, is thus a matter of considerable current, and international, dispute. The peruser of the *Quattro comedie* is invited nonetheless to join the circle of knowing readers ("conoscitore = an acknowledger, one that knoweth") familiar with Aretino's works, both in the sense of having read them and in understanding how to value them.[25]

As I discuss below, the extradiagetical matter contained within the *Quattro comedie,* for example the letter from "Lo Stampatore a coloro, che stimano le opera di questo grande Scrittore," further emphasizes this picture of collaboration between printer and reader in rescuing Aretino's work and reputation from such attributions. On the title page of the Aretino, however, despite the valorizing mention of the press's role in this act of rehabilitation, the figure of the publisher is less present than in similar works produced in Italy. In the collected Ariosto, for example, the printer's mark of the Gioliti emphasizes and reiterates the role of that publishing empire in bringing the plays to the press: in the Wolfe edition, a medallion portrait of Aretino takes the customary place of the printer's device.[26] In another sense, this portrait would have served as a significant confirmation of the edition's authority and authenticity. Wolfe manages to reproduce with considerable accuracy the image used on many of the frontispieces of Aretino's individual works from circa 1539 on (including the editions published in Venice by Agostino Bindoni in 1550).[27] Like the medal on which it was based, the title-page portrait emphasizes Aretino's self-appointed role as castigator of contemporary Rome (called for example the "coda mundi" rather than *caput mundi* in *Cortegiana,* the second of the plays published in Wolfe's edition), by figuring him as an exemplar of an earlier, more correct Rome.[28] In both medal and print, Aretino is dressed *all'antica,* framed by Ariosto's epithet, now translated into Latin and presented in roman capitals and classical punctuation. The portrait appeared as well on editions of Aretino's celebrated *Lettere* printed by Marcolini (and others) throughout the 1530s and on single editions of *Il Marescalco* and *Cortegiana* printed by Antonio Bindoni in 1550. Thus it quickly left the hands of any single publishing house and became, rather, a recognizable sign of Aretino's work and his growing print presence.[29]

At once a mark of authorial identity and of textual dissemination beyond the reach of any one printing house's particular control, the portrait medal marks the *Quattro comedie* as belonging to Aretino regardless of the other producers involved, a considerably different claim from the title pages of other collected drama in Italy up to this point, whether single-author compilation or anthology.[30] At the same time, Aretino's portrait also identifies the work as something mass-produced and open to wandering, valued yet ubiquitous. On the proliferation of his image, Aretino himself wrote to Juneo Petreo in 1545:

in this matter of my being famous, you don't know the half of it. . . . Besides the medallions stamped or cast in gold, bronze, copper, lead, and plaster, I have had a lifelike copy made of my portrait which is on the façade of palaces and had it stamped upon comb boxes, on the frames of mirrors and on majolica platters just like Caesar, Alexander and Scipio. (Waddington, 60)

To Marcolini himself he writes, in that same year, of "the great pleasure I have in seeing a medallion of myself set between Caesar and Alexander on the comb boxes which they vend" (Waddington, 201–2), again coupling elevated status with market presence. The desire for Aretino's image, if not the image itself, traveled at least as far as the Americas. A letter from his former secretary, who accompanied Cabeza de Vaca into what is now Paraguay, asks that "Quattro effigie sue di Gioaniacobo, & sua Medagli" (four effigies . . . and . . . medals [Waddington, 200]), be sent along with the next shipment of trade goods. At the furthest extreme from Bodley's standards of acquisition, Aretino's image becomes literally "baggage" as it joins other objects of exchange in an expanding world market.

In a move particularly appropriate to Aretino's own self-production, then, the title page of the *Quattro comedie* all but erases the presence of any particular publisher and print shop, at the same time further permitting the work's apparent ability to wander without penalty or limitation across international borders. If this view of works seems at odds with Bodley's valuation of estimable cultural property, other aspects of the edition's appearance accord more closely with the library founder's notion of an appropriate text in general and Italian printed drama in particular. The end matter to the edition, for example, emphasizes a collaborative origin and scholarly function for vernacular literature that is more in keeping with Italian printing practices of the sixteenth century and Bodley's own collecting practices of the early seventeenth century.

Facing the concluding letter from Aretino regarding his two later plays, the extensive errata list provided at the work's end again solicits participation from those committed to Aretino's works, advising them, "Ammenderansi gli errori scorsi nella stampa, nella seguente maniera" (amend the errors escaped from the press in the following manner; *Quattro comedie,* Oo6ʳ). It then provides a brief set of instructions on how to interpolate the subsequent corrections into the reader's own volume, "sapendo come il primo numero significa la carta, e'l second la riga, l'A la prima facciata della carta, & la B. la seconda facciata" (knowing that the first number indicates the page and the second the line, "A" the first [recto] side of the page and "B" the second face; *Quattro comedie,* Oo6ʳ). The list of *Errori* not only corrects misprints to the plays but includes errors "Nella lettera dello stampatore" (*Quattro comedie,* Oo6ʳ), found within "the letter of the printer" itself, suggesting that its object is a corrected edition overall, not simply a correct set of Aretine texts. Some of these misprints seem to have been caused by errors in casting-off (distributing) earlier forms of type (for example, the missetting of a long *s* for an *f* as in "fin sine" for "fin fine"). Others seem to be corrections made to bring the text closer to linguistic conventions considered more correct or elegant—amending "chi Amor" to "che Amor," for example, or "areccare" to "arecare, & cosi sempre" (i.e., with instructions to do so at every following instance, *Quattro comedie,* Oo6ᵛ).

This extensive advisory on *Errori* is followed by another letter purporting to come directly from the "Corretore al benigno Lettore" explaining further the presence of the errata list. The Corrector, "auenuto, nella
fine della stampa di queste belle Comedie" (having come on the job near
the end of the printing of these *belle Comedie*) found the texts unacceptably damaged and altered, having been reprinted "da testi molto corrotti"
(from very corrupt texts; *Quattro comedie,* Oo8ᵛ). Comparing an edition
of *L'Hipocrito* printed by Marcolini in ottavo "nel XLII," he has found "in
diuersi luoghi . . . le line intiere di piu, . . . come ognuno potre vedere,
che si prendra piacere di confrontare I detti testi insieme" (in diverse
places . . . entire lines added . . . as anyone can see who cares to compare the two texts; *Quattro comedie,* Oo8ᵛ). The corrector sees nothing
untoward in readers conducting similar techniques of textual authenti-
cation as he himself has used—for example, comparing two editions in
order to determine the proper condition of the text. Less acceptable to
some, he suggests, is the advertising of such errors publically, a move
that has been thought to hamper sales, which he dismisses as "vana opin-
ione, che alcuni hanno, che lo stampare gli errori, impedisca la vendita
de libri" (the false opinions of some that to print the errors would get
in the way of selling books; *Quattro comedie,* Oo8ᵛ). For one thing, he
imagines his readers as potential publishers themselves: he provides this
information "accioche se ad altri venisse voglia di far ristampare queste
Comedie, lo possa perfettamente fare" (so that if others find they want
to reprint these Comedies they can do so perfectly; *Quattro comedie,*
Oo8ᵛ). Primarily, however, he sees this errata list as allowing the owner
to emend the text before reading, so as not to be "da predetti errori stur-
bato" (disturbed by its aforesaid errors)—down to "certi piccioli errori"
(certain small errors), which he leaves to the reader's judgment, "come
vna E per vna C, vna V rouerscia, vna Virgola, o un Punto posto piu in vn
luogo, che in vn'altro" (like an E for a C, a reversed V, a comma or a period
put in one place rather than another; *Quattro comedie,* Oo8ᵛ). By involving the reader in applying a shared system of substantive and accidental
errors, the Corrector too creates a hierarchy of knowing and unknowing
readers—elevating the current user to one who needs the list of *Errori*
only to make reading the text more regular, less disruptive, rather than
as one who might otherwise unwittingly replicate such textual errors
himself. Likewise the reader is cast as a potential producer and buyer of
multiple and international texts, acquired more for scholarly purposes of
comparison and valuation than for pleasure.

In *Print Culture in Renaissance Italy,* Brian Richardson extensively charts the developments and changes in Italian editorial practice for sixteenth-century Italian vernacular texts. A mark of the canonization of particular Italian authors, as well as of the preeminence of the Tuscan tongue, the inclusion of the apparatus of scholarly commentary and editorial correction in literary works becomes a sign of a well-printed, commercially respectable Italian book.[31] Whether "corretto" meant "corrected (according to current ideals)" or "correct, authentic"—and in the case of the *Quattro comedie* it seems to mean both—editorial intervention in a text was a sign of its production in and legitimation by major Italian printing centers like Venice, Florence, and Rome.

Bodley's acquisitiveness for foreign, particularly Italian, texts is well documented: in several letters he describes "the multitude of bookes, which I haue heere sent out of Italy and other places" (Bodley 85). Indeed he is quite adamant that he wants only works produced in significant printing centers on the Continent, writing to Thomas James in August of 1602,

And if yow please to send me a note of the principal bookes in fol. printed in Italy, Paris, or Lions, of those which yow haue lately collected to be wanting in the Libr. I will presently conuey it, to Io. Bille, who is nowe in Paris. I would onely haue suche as are printed in those places, or els where therabout, and not all in fol. that yow haue gathered, but some of the principal, for the more expedition, of your copieng of them out. (Bodley 53)

At the same time, the list of Italian print centers and peripheries from which he hopes to acquire texts is extensive and unusual in its breadth; in addition to Venice, he is pleased to announce that his deputy, the aforementioned Bille,

hath bin already, at . . . Ferrara, Padua, Verona, Brescia, Mantua, Pauia, Milan, Florence, Pisa, Rome &c. and hath bought as many bookes, as he knewe I had not, amounting to the summe, of at the lest, 400li. besides those that he may haue bought, sins his last vnto me, which was in December. (Bodley 76)

Thus Wolfe's edition might have seemed to gratify Bodley's interest both in Italian publications and in scholarly extradiagetical matter for printed drama, although these latter were features particularly of *classical* dramatic texts printed in England and on the Continent (and, increasingly, also of nondramatic vernacular works by canonical authors, like Dante, Petrarch, and Boccaccio). For example, Bodley writes in 1604 from London asking whether, "Yow haue Aristophanes in Greeke with an old Greeke Scholia vpon it. I pray yow send me worde, in half a line, howe the scholia doth beginne, vpon the I. Comoedie Πλουτος: and where your booke was printed" (Bodley 96). While sixteenth-century editions of Terence similarly contained extensive prefatory commentaries and line-by-line explanations in the margins of *Andria* and the like, collections like that of Ariosto's *Comedie* discussed above remain without such extradiagetical matter and, moreover, lack the scene divisions and plot summaries that characterize Greek and Roman plays printed in translation in this period.[32]

In short, first (as well as last) impressions prove deceptive in the case of the *Quattro comedie.* In fact, vernacular printed *dramatic* texts issued in Italy, whether singly or in collections, almost never included errata lists, let alone one of such an extensive nature. Moreover, the play text of Wolfe's *Comedie* itself demonstrates several markedly "non-Italian" features. The play's dialogues, as well as its speech prefixes, all appear in roman lettering rather than the almost ubiquitous italic lettering used for editions of *comedie,* from the earliest editions of *Il Marescalco* and *Cortegiana* in the 1530s and the *Due Comedie* of Lorenzo Comparini in 1554, through the collected Ariosto of 1570.[33] Printed almost entirely in roman letters, the *Quattro comedie,* would thus look somewhat "strange"—or rather oddly familiar—to anyone conversant with Italian printed drama from the period, resembling as it does the emerging conventions for English printed plays of the 1580s more closely than the standard body text used for Italian drama throughout the century.[34] Wolfe was hardly indifferent to such typographical distinctions in his publications. His trilingual edition of Castiglione's *Il cortegiano* of the same year (1588) prints the Italian text in italics, the French in roman (as prescribed increasingly by Francois I for vernacular texts in the sixteenth century), and the English translation in black (gothic) letter or the "English letter," as it was then commonly known.[35] Indeed, his joint edition of Guarini's *Il pastor fido* and Tasso's *Aminta,* printed in 1591, conforms much more closely to Italian convention, printing the text entirely in italics (even as it continues to provide a more extensive errata list than those found in contemporaneous Italian printings of the play). Wolfe's *Quattro comedie* thus appears visually anomalous, albeit in keeping with his stated claim that the plays are "worthy of being compared to any of the ancients or the moderns as well" (Aretino, *Quattro comedie,* A3ʳ). Yet neither does the roman font of the *Quattro comedie* gesture to classical or canonical texts published in the period, which themselves were printed in italic.[36] Wolfe's statement that the edition is *degne d'essere paragonate* openly invites comparison of the edition with its contemporaries, just as the Corrector does at its end. Such a comparison reveals, however, that questions of textual identity are more complicated and claims to national origin less useful than they first appear. Wolfe's edition turns out to be authentically and simultaneously both and neither Italian and English, disavowing through its appearance, provenance, and travels the distinction made by Ascham, Bodley, and others between supposedly native and foreign works.

But what of Bodley's assertion that foreign plays allow "learning of the languages" and his own instructions to acquire texts from a variety of Italian regional markets? John Florio recommends Aretino as well as other authors (and markets his own Italian-English dictionary), for just such late-sixteenth-century English readers in search of the breadth of Italian tongues. In his dedication of *A Worlde of Wordes* to "Roger *Earle of Rutland,* Henrie *Earle of Southampton,* Lucie *Countesse of Bedford"* (Florio a3^r), Florio writes of the difficulty of certain vernacular texts even for such experienced readers of Italian as they:

I haue seene the best, yea naturall Italians, not onely stagger, but euen sticke fast in the myre, and at last giue it ouer, or giue their verdict with An *Ignoramus. Boccace* is prettie hard, yet vnderstood: *Petrarche* harder, but explaned: *Dante* hardest, but commented. . . . How then ayme we at *Peter Aretine,* that is so wittie, hath such varietie, and frames so manie new words? . . . How shall we vnderstande so manie and so strange books, of so seuerall, and so fantasticall suiects as be written in the Italian toong. How shall we, naie how may we ayme at the Venetian, at the Romane, at the Lombard, at the neapolitane, at so manie, and so much differing Dialects, and Idiomes, as be vsed and spoken in Italie, besides the Florentine? (Florio a4^r)

Florio's exposition serves to advertise the dictionary's value as a source of foreign vocabulary, much as does the list he provides of texts consulted in its compilation, which includes extensive works by Aretino, including the *Quattro comedie.* Wolfe's Aretino edition likewise offers itself as a repository of unusual words: the Corrector finds it necessary to "alert" the reader that Aretino not only creates convincing characters by having them *speak* in Lombard voices and other strange accents but that he *writes* their lines in Lombard and in the "manner" of strangers: "those, being written in Lombard and the manner of strangers, should not be attributed, either to me or to others, as Error" (*che non pure ha vsato le voci lombarde, & le straniere, ma quelle ha etiandio scritte alla lombarda; & alla strauiera maniera, che ne a me, ne ad altri douerai attribure per errore* [*Quattro comedie*, Oo8ᵛ]).

An annotated 1539 octavo edition of *Il Marescalco* suggests that Aretino's comedies did indeed introduce vocabulary even to native Italian speakers. The "new words" for which Aretino becomes a resource, however, are terms like *fecciosa* and *moccichini*—hardly the stuff of an elevated or well-edited Tuscan tongue. A marginal note in an elegant early italic hand explains *fecciosa* as *brutta* (ugly) but a rougher contemporary italic hand substitutes *sporca* (dirty) instead. (Florio defines *feccioso* as "dreggie, slimie, filthie, drossie" [Florio 128] in turn.) *Moccichini* elicits a longer addendum in the bottom margin: "Mocci sono quelle sporchezze che vengano fuora / del Naso, onde Mocciebino; per il fazzoletto, et moccicone; quasi se habbia mocci, sula faccia, chioè sotto"—(Snots are those dirts that come out of the Nose, thus "Snot-rag" for handkerchief, and "snot-face" almost as if one had snot on the face, that is, "dolt"). (Again Florio's definitions mainly concur: *mocci* are "the snots or snuffing of ones nose" and hence a *Moccicone* is "a snottie, slouenlie, lubberly fellow, a gull, a ninnie" [Florio 228].) But the writer of this marginalia may be missing another, regional use of the term—Moccinigo—which is, according to Florio, "a kinde of coyne vsed in Venice"—and which better suits the context of the word in the play, in which one character promises to give another "quatro moccichini di rensa" (four bits of linen/flax; Bviiʳ).

If a reader looked beyond the first and last pages to the brief address purportedly from the Printer or "Stampatore," then, she or he might well have recognized the improbability that this work was either simply a scholarly edition of drama attempting to rehabilitate a writer whose condemnation by Catholic authorities might well endear him to English readers or an Italian import seeking to introduce its readers to new and profitable vocabulary from abroad—in other words what its title-page and end matter purport it to be. In short, she or he might be alerted to the danger of appearing a *moccicone* rather than a *conoscitore* vis-à-vis the text she or he was about to purchase.

Like the title page, the prefatory epistle initially suggests nothing untoward about the edition. In keeping with the work's final matter, the letter addressed from "Lo Stampatore a Coloro, che stimano le opera di questo grande Scrittore" (The Printer to Those, who esteem the works of this great Writer; *Quattro comedie*, A2ʳ) returns the nonauthorial producers of the text to a central role, printer and reader alike, and invokes again their collaboration. This epistle from the printer "to those who esteem the works of this great Writer" reminds those "spiriti nobili" (noble spirits) that, if the current publisher "does not err," there were "vi fu, pochi anni sono, presentate dal grande Stampatore, e libero huomo maestro Barbagrigia romano, le sei giornate di M. Pietro Aretino" (a few years back, presented from the great Printer and liberal man master Barbagrigia, Roman, the "sei giornate" of M. Pietro Aretino), and that Barbagrigia, in his own, earlier letter to his readers, had promised to give them many other examples of Aretino's work. The current printer then claims uncertainty as to why this was never accomplished, whether "egli, occupato in altri suoi affari, o pure da la graue sua etade, o piu tosto da l'importuna morte impedito" (was prevented by other business, advanced age or rather by his importunate death from making good on his offer; *Quattro comedie,* A2ʳ). Regardless, this printer writes, he now will bring "a luce" (to the light) again, "quattro delle sue diletteuoli comedie, per mezzo de la mia stampa, la quale perauentura non vi parra inferior a la sua, se ben non intend di gareggiar con vn cotanto stampatore" (four of his delectable comedies, by means of my press, which peradventure will not seem inferior to his, although of course I don't intend to compete with such a printer; *Quattro comedie,* A2ᵛ), although—of course— that is exactly the rivalry his allusion invites. The *Quattro Comedie del Divino Pietro Aretino, cioè Il Marescalco, La Cortegiana, La Talanta, L'Hipocrito, Nouellamente ritornate, per mezzo della stampa, a luce, a rechiesta di conoscitori del lor valore,* does indeed bring together four of Aretino's six published plays, most of which had appeared in numerous single editions in Italy from the 1530s through 1550. In the preface the publisher apologizes for the absence of a fifth comedy, *Il Philosopho,* and Aretino's tragedy, *L'Hortensia;* an unusual afterword following each play requests information about specific works by Aretino such as these that the publisher hopes to issue in the future. This desire for completeness accords with Wolfe's other printing endeavors in the 1580s and follows the complicated mentions of rival and hereditary printing rights, past and present, in Wolfe's other Italian prefaces.[37] But it also, by its mention of Barbagrigia, implicates the reader in a hierarchy of error and judgment similar to the one described by the Corrector in the final pages, one as equally interested in sexual transgression, however, as in the textual errors the Corrector addressed.

Barbagrigia first appears as an entity in these editions in Wolfe's 1584 publication of the *Prima Parte* where he is purported to be the printer of the work, addressing the "amatori del sapere" (lovers of wisdom) who are his "Gentilissimi Lettori."[38] Barbagrigia characterizes himself as moved by the same "greatest desire" shared by the readers—a desire whose nature he conceals momentarily until locating it in the wish to see Aretino's works republished—"di vedere ristamparesi l'opere del valente M. Pietro Aretino" (*Prima parte,* A2ʳ). Barbagrigia purports to be inspired as well by the sad history of Boccaccio's *Decameron,* which has been badly mishandled, indeed lacerated, according to the requirements of post-Tridentine Italian publications ("Le quali anchora vn giorno spero di darui a leggere cosi compiute, come egli le compose, & non lacerate, come hoggi I vostri fiorentini ve le danno a leggere, con mille ciancie loro" [which I hope one day to give you to read complete as they were written and not . . . as your Florentines today give them to you . . . , with a thousand of their own babblings/fables; *Prima parte* A2ʳ]): the *Decameron* was one of the texts most *riformato* by editors in the seventies and eighties according to Richardson.[39] It is telling, in this context, and given the new standards of post-Tridentine editing, that *corretto* could also mean "punished, chastised, controuled" (Florio 88). Aretino himself links sexual and textual errancy in the mock lament about his volume of letters resembling the state of Rome in its lack of chastity (see my epigraph) which, like Wolfe's editions, toys with the longstanding humanist connection between the castigation of texts and the castigation of female bodies.[40]

Purportedly heralding from "Bengodi ne la già felice Italia a xxi. D'Ottobre M.D.LXXIIII" (*Prima parte,* A3ᵛ), Wolfe's *Prima parte* reveals its ironic relationship to its aetiology even as it reinforces its humanist literary credentials. After the explicit reference to the misprinting of Boccaccio's *Decameron* on its first page, the implications of a provenance in "Bengodi" would be unlikely to escape any early modern reader of Italian.[41] The traditional Land of Milk and Honey in Italian legend, "a fained name of a countrie where they say dogs run away with whole shoulders of mutton" (Florio 42), Bengodi in the *Decameron* is, of course, the purported Land of Cockaigne to which the Florentine painters Buffalmacco, Bruno, and Maso del Saggio lead Calandrino, the perennial dupe of the final chapters. According to the Florentines, Bengodi contains "una montagna tutta di formaggio parmigiano grattugiato, sopra la quale stavan genti che niuna altra cosa facevano che far maccheroni e raviuoli e cuocergli in brodo di capponi . . . ."[42] Bengodi represents the locale where every desire is satisfied, where the carnivalesque—as evoked by the province in which it can be found, Berlinzone—has free reign.[43] That Calandrino's desires run primarily to "a mountain entirely of grated parmesan cheese on which there are people with nothing other to do than make gnocchi and ravioli and cook them in capon broth" only further emphasizes his simplicity, gullibility, and eventual humiliation (the capon being that still customary feast-day delicacy in Italy—castrated rooster). In the case of Wolfe's Aretino, the use of the place-name Bengodi necessarily casts doubt on the sincerity of the preface and, by extension, on the reliability of the edition itself. Savvy readers can then enjoy the presumed spectacle of those less-knowing newcomers to the text, who, like Calandrino, are pulled along by the force of their own unrealistic, presumptuous desires into a land that does not exist outside of the imagination but from which they will emerge authentically humiliated, the "già felice Italia"—the "once" or "already happy Italy"—in which Bengodi may be found.

Barbagrigia's Bengodi exists only in the text—however wished for or however well meant (the invocation "Bengodi" also means "enjoy yourself" or "well fare your heart"). The suggestion follows that the "già felice Italia" of these prefaces might well be equally fantastical if equally sought after by readers and publishers, an already or once happy Italy in which religious and erotic texts exist side by side, produced by the same pen and press. Like Buffalmacco, the Stampatore is happy to oblige such a desire on the part of his audience with his projected publications and, indeed, to further the illusion by the pseudonym Barbagrigia itself, representing as it does a historical personage known precisely for such a confluence of activities and texts.

The historical Barbagrigia, or Antonio Blado di Asola, while particularly celebrated as a publisher to the courts and Vatican circles of Rome, was also well connected to the Florentine patron Monsignor Giovanni Gaddi, Clerk of the Apostolic Chamber, and through him to Annibal Caro, Benvenuto Cellini, Pietro Bembo, and Sebastiano del Piombo. (To Gaddi he dedicated editions of Machiavelli's *Discorsi* and *Historie* in 1531 and 1532.) Wolfe and his readers would have been familiar with his works for and participation in the "semi-serious Academy of Virtue" with Caro, particularly his publication of Caro's *La Ficaia* or "Cunt-ry Matters" (a *ficaia* is, in Florio's words, "A discourse made of figs, or rather of women's quaints" [cunts]).[44] They might equally have recognized Blado's status as job-printer to the pope, issuing papal bulls and encyclicals at a consider-able rate.[45]

The twin scandalous products of the Italian press thus come together in the figure of Barbagrigia as memorialized in Wolfe's prefaces and by Caro in *Gli Straccioni.* The latter play begins, like Aretino's printed *Cortegiana,* in a new Rome—restructured after its sack in 1524 by Charles V's troops and the building projects of the Farnese family and pope—a city particularly disorienting to newcomers and those returning to it after that intervening decade.[46] For Pilucca and Demetrio (servants to the Scruffy Scoundrels of the title), the only remaining landmark is the printing house of the notorious publisher: in the opening scene, after wandering blindly through an unrecognizable city, Pilucca exclaims with relief, "Oh! Ecco qui la bottega del Barbagrigia stampatore" (Hey! Hey it's the printer's shop . . . what's his name . . . Barbagrigia).[47] While business seems to be booming, the audience never sees Barbagrigia at work printing or selling books.[48] Rather, he is characterized more as an advocate of women, and in particular as a "good neighbor and friend" to the rich widow who lives on his street (the aptly named Signora Argentina), than as a producer and pur-veyor of texts. Thus the most significant narrative function for Barbagrigia in the play is as go-between in the liaison of the "young handsome new-comer," Gisippo, and the well-off, amorous, and willfull Roman widow.

BARBAGRIGIA: O benedetta sia questa mia comare! Almanco la dice come la 'ntende, e intendela benissimo, second me. Poiché Pilucca afferma che 'l marito è morto, dice di volerne un altro e, senza consiglio de' parenti, giovine, fore-stiero e povero. E, alle ragioni che assegna, mi pare una savia donna.

O blessed be this dear friend of mine! At least she says what she thinks, and she thinks straight as far as I can see. Now that Pilucca has assured her that her hus-band is dead, she says she wants another one—young, a foreigner, one without means of his own, and that she'll have him without consulting her parents. The reasoning behind all this reveals a wise woman.[49]

In this alliance, the print shop plays a crucial role, being the place not only where Argentina first met her prospective non-Roman suitor but also where the arrangements for the liaison and the marriage are subse-quently made:

Ed un gran pazzo mi parrebbe questo Gisippo, ch'ella dice d'aver giá tentare, se non la pigliasse. Mi si fa mille anni che passi qui da bottega, come suole ogni giorno, per fare questa sensaría alla comare. . . . Non ha cattivo gusto la comare, no; un copertoro appunto da vedova.

This Gisippo, whom she's already approached would be a pure fool to turn her down. It seems like a millennium since he started passing my shop—and that's when he began to meet with her every day. . . . Her taste isn't bad, I must admit; he's just the right sort of bed-warmer for a widow.[50]

Like his Aretine counterparts in Wolfe's edition—and their author— Barbagrigia is both genuine advocate of Argentina's desires and complicit participant in a larger cultural misogyny regarding female eroticism.[51] On the one hand he states of Argentina, "Oimè Dio, bellezza, onestá, ric-chezza ed amore insieme, e in una patria come Roma!" (My God! Here's beauty, honesty, wealth, and love rolled into one and all in a country like Rome), and protests indignantly when Gisippo hesitates in marrying her: "che si trovano forse ad ogni uscio delle sue pari?" (do you think there are women like her on every street corner?).[52] On the other hand, when Demetrio orders him to "Fate che la vedova sia a ordine, ché li farò fare ogni cosa" (make sure the widow is ready and I'll look after the rest), Barbagrigia asserts that "Le donne sono a ordine sempre" (women are always ready). As spokesman for the needs and desires of the body, he insists that "altro ch'anello bisogna metterle" ([the alliance] has got to be sealed with more than a ring); "Voglio che gli facciamo incarnar questa sera medesima" (it's got to be flesh into flesh this very evening).[53]

Whether his readers would have caught the over-determined refer-ences to this Italian (potential) counterpart in printing, Wolfe certainly knew that the historical Barbagrigia himself had published the Italian edi-tion of *La Ficaia,* more commonly known under the name Wolfe uses— *Il Commento di Ser Agresto*—when he appends it to the *Prima Parte* of Aretino's *Raggionamenti.* The evocation of printer and printshop as meeting point or locus of untoward desire carries over to the prefaces Wolfe creates for his other reprints of Barbagrigia's former publications and through them to subsequent quarto and ottavo collections of ver-nacular drama printed in England.[54]

Like Wolfe's other works, the preface to *La Ficaia* is also signed as if written "di Bengodi" but now the date reads "a 12. Gennaio MDLXXXIV."[55] For the reader of the two books together (and according to Woodfield they were produced as a pair and consistently bound together in the sixteenth century), the use of the Gregorian calendar at the end of this second preface, providing a date at odds with that of the first preface, hints at an openly English provenance despite the Italian genealogy. At the same time, the continued use of the names Bengodi and Barbagrigia suggest a wish to associate Aretino's text with a distinctly Italian mode of border-crossing foolery. Nino Borsellino noted some time ago the link between the *beffe* practiced by Boccaccio's Florentine artists on Calandrino the artist in the *Decameron* and those performed by Aretino's Romans on Maco, the would-be courtier, in the *Cortegiana*.[56]

Castiglione's *Il cortegiano,* published in a trilingual edition by Wolfe in the same year as the *Quattro comedie* (1588), mentions Boccaccio's eighth-day stories, and the accounts of Calandrino in particular, as exemplary "Boordes or Merry prankes" asking "Who laugheth not when *Iohn Boccaccio* in the eight journey of his hundredth tales declareth how the Priest of Varlungo strained himself to sing a *Kyrie* and a *Sanctus,* when he perceived *Belcolore* was in the Church" and stating "there be also pleasant declarations in his tales of *Calandrino,* and many others."[57] Aretino situates his own *burle* in the context of Castiglione's *Il cortegiano* by having Maco seek a copy of the text (or one similar) from a bookseller in the opening pages of the play.[58] The rhetorical question "who laugheth not" at the tales of Calandrino and others again calls attention to distinctions between types of readers—knowing and unknowing—distinctions that, as I've discussed, Wolfe's publications of Aretino further employ and elaborate on as well.

Wolfe's edition of the *Quattro comedie* makes one "error," however, that repositions the relation of these two particular texts that he published in 1588. Not noted in the list of *Errori* nor by critics by and large, the 1588 *Quattro comedie* adds the article "La" to the title of Aretino's play on the frontispiece. In so doing, it transforms the ambiguous title *Cortegiana,* interpreted variously as "Courtly Matters," or "The Play of the Court," to the seemingly straightforward "The Courtesan."[59] With the added article, *La Cortegiana* gains a certain symmetry with *The Courtier/Il cortegiano* as well as with the other titles of the *Comedie, Il Marescalco, La Talanta,* and *L'Hipocrito.* It also more clearly parallels a work widely attributed to Aretino in England, *La puttana errante* (coyly known in Florio's book list as "La P. Errante del' Aretino"), in which errancy and desire are more explicitly linked and the boundaries of Europe are more clearly crossed or dissolved. Most obviously, it peddles a more overtly female text than the ambiguously gendered title *Cortegiana* allows.[60] While the infinitive of *cortegiana* (*cortegianare*) means, variously, "courtings, courtiers-hollie-water trickes, courtesans prankes or deuises," *La Cortegiana* means simply "a curtezan, a harlot, a strumpet, a whore" (Florio 88). Wolfe's altered title to Aretino's play reinforces the representation of publishers as panders of desirable texts, rather than as reformers or correctors, even as it masks its own performing of such "hollie-water trickes . . . prankes or deuises" in the creation of the edition.

"To coosen the expectation, one notable point in a Comedie," wrote Gabriel Harvey in the margins of his edition containing Gascoigne's *Supposes,* "and one of the singularities of . . . Aretino in his courting Italian Comedes." Like his other Italianate publications, Wolfe's edition of the *Quattro comedie* appropriates and rewrites such traditions of Continental cousinage, inserting his textual production into a genealogy that passes from Boccaccio to Aretino (via Castiglione) to himself, as Stampatore rather than Scrittore. But if Gascoigne's translation continues a genre now recognizably Italian, whereby characters are "supposed" to be unrecognizable to one another, Wolfe makes the readers' suppositions about the text itself the subject of his *beffa.* A graphically hybrid work, Wolfe's innovative edition of the *Quattro comedie* eschews stable determinations of its geographical sources, and of error itself, placing itself everywhere and nowhere, and thus privileging the illusion of movement as a way of transgressing—as well as capitalizing on—emerging notions of national literature.

Notes

The epigraph text was cited in Raymond B. Waddington, *Aretino's Satyr: Sexuality, Satire, and Self-Projection in Sixteenth-Century Literature and Art* (Toronto, Buffalo, London: University of Toronto Press, 2004), 35 and 180n12.

1. See David Scott Kastan's insightful summary of collected plays printed in English prior to 1623 in *Shakespeare and the Book* (Cambridge: Cambridge University Press, 2001), 62-64. In 1573, and again in 1575, Richard Smith issued collections of George Gascoigne's "Poesie" or "Posies," which included Gascoigne's liberal translations of a "Comedie called Supposes" and "Tragedie of Jocasta" (reissued as well in Gascoigne's *Whole woorkes* in 1587). Their significantly different format provides a telling contrast to Wolfe's edition. For example, both plays are printed in black (or English) letter, rather than in Wolfe's roman type. Moreover, as with the publications of plays by John Day earlier in the decade, the inclusion of drama within a larger written corpus bore a different status than a group of plays without the buttress of the author's work in other genres (as, for example, with Day's issue of *All such treatises as haue been lately published by Thomas Norton . . .* , [London, 1570]). See Douglas A. Brooks, *From Playhouse to Printing House:*

Drama and Authorship in Early Modern England (Cambridge: Cambridge University Press, 2000), 36-42.

2. John Florio, *A Worlde of Words or a most copious, and exact Dictionarie in Italian and English . . . .* (London, 1598), entries for *Errare, Errore,* and *Errónico,* 119-20. Hereafter cited in the text. For a brilliant exploration of errancy in Renaissance Italian literature, see Deanna Shemek, *Ladies Errant: Wayward Women and Social Order in Early Modern Italy* (Durham, NC: Duke University Press, 1998).

3. Lexicons like Florio's promote such explicit punning of *errore* with the Greek figure of Eironia or "irony," making these distinct words seem more phonetically and graphically connected through variant spellings (e.g., *erronia*).

4. In 1584, Wolfe issued *La prima [seconda] parte de ragionamenti di M. Pietro Aretino.* The same year he published *I Discorsi di Nicolo Machiaveli sopra la prima deca di Tito Livio* and *Il Prencipe di Nicolo Machiauelli,* followed three years later by Machiavelli's *Libro dell'arte della guerra* and *Historie.* Finally, in 1588, several months before the *Quattro comedie,* he published *Lasino doro di Nicolo Macchiauelli* and Baldassare Castiglione's *Il Cortegiano,* and, in 1589, *La terza, et vltima parte de Ragionamenti del diuino Pietro Aretino.* The *Quattro comedie* thus appear toward the end of Wolfe's Italian publishing ventures and take on some significance from this context. See Clifford Chalmers Huffman, *Elizabethan Impressions: John Wolfe and His Press* (New York: AMS, 1988); Harry R. Hoppe, "John Wolfe, Printer and Publisher, 1579-1601," *The Library,* 4th ser., 14 (1933): 241-88; Fabio Massimo Bertolo, "John Wolfe, un editore Inglese tra Aretino e Machiavelli," *Il Rinascimento Italiano di fronte alla Riforma: Letteratura e Arte,* ed. Chrysa Damianaki, Paolo Procaccioli, Angelo Romano, 199-208 (Roma: Vecchiarelli Editore, 2005); Jason Lawrence, *"Who the devil taught thee so much Italian?": Italian Language Learning and Literary Imitation in Early Modern England* (Manchester: Manchester University Press, 2005), especially 187-201. On attitudes toward Castiglione, see Brian Richardson's account of the censoring of *Il cortegiano* in *Print Culture in Renaissance Italy: The Editor and the Vernacular Text 1470-1600* (Cambridge: Cambridge University Press, 1994), 142-43.

5. See, respectively, Joseph Loewenstein, *The Author's Due: Printing and the Prehistory of Copyright* (Chicago: University of Chicago Press, 2002), 133, and Robert S. Miola, "The Italian *Every Man in His Humor,*" in *The Italian World of English Renaissance Drama: Cultural Exchange and Intertextuality,* ed. Michele Marrapodi, 208-24 (212) (Newark: University of Delaware Press; London: Associated University Presses, 1998).

6. For collections in which the *Quattro comedie* appear, see John L. Lievsay, *The Englishman's Italian Books: 1550-1700* (Philadelphia: University of Pennsylvania Press, 1969), 36, 38, 40, 50. Lievsay describes an additional edition of Aretino's collected plays as listed in the first Bodleian catalogue; for the moment, I have found no record of its existence outside of that 1605 catalogue entry which reads, "Com. di P. *Aretino.* 1535. In 8°. A. 21. It. L'Horatia.*Ven.*1549. It. le lettere del Medesimo.1538.in 8°.A.24" (Thomas James, *Catalogus Librorum Bibliothecae Publicae Quam Vir Ornatissimus Thomas Bodleivs. . . .* [Oxford: 1605], 285). One might compare the listing for Ariosto *Comedie diverse* on page 283. Rather than a collected edition, these catalogue entries may indicate one or more of the individual comedies that were produced in 1534-35 in a format that allowed them to be sewn together into one volume. For precedents for this type of group binding, see for example the listing of "Diuers Playes by Shakespeare—1602" in the Countess of Bridgewater's London library, of which Heidi Brayman Hackel writes "Perhaps a volume in which diverse separate quartos were bound together, the first of which was printed in 1602" (Heidi Brayman Hackel, *Reading Material in Early Modern England: Print, Gender, and Literacy* [Cambridge: Cambridge University Press, 2005], 266).

7. Robert Miola, "Seven Types of Intertextuality," in *Shakespeare, Italy, and Intertextuality,* ed. Michele Marrapodi (Manchester: Manchester University Press, 2000), 38. Citing Giordano Bruno on his printer's belief that fictitious foreign imprints improved sales of his works, Denis B. Woodfield claims that the English market would have been impressed by the seeming Italian origin of these works: "The explanation probably lies in the bad reputation which English printing had by then acquired in this field." Denis B. Woodfield, *Surreptitious Printing in England: 1550-1640* (New York: Bibliographical Society of America, 1973), 9.

8. Alan B. Farmer, "Cosmopolitanism and Foreign Books in Early Modern England," in "English Cosmopolitan and the Early Modern Moment," ed. Jean E. Howard, special issue, *Shakespeare Studies* 35 (January 2007): 58-65.

9. Loewenstein, *The Author's Due,* 31.

10. Even as she reiterates the belief that "Italian books were more easily marketed both on the Continent and at home if they were of Italian origin," and hence that "the false imprints . . . function as a sign of the text's authenticity," Alexandra Halasz in *The Marketplace of Print* calls attention to another potential effect of this aetiology, pointing out that Wolfe's "false imprints tacitly call attention to the papal proscription, mocking it by manifesting its relative impotence" in limiting the circulation of works by Machiavelli and Aretino; Alexandra Halasz, *The Marketplace of Print: Pamphlets and the Public Sphere in Early Modern England* (Cambridge: Cambridge University Press, 1997), 32. (See also Bertolo, "John Wolfe, un editore Inglese," 203.) Likewise, Michael Wyatt, in *The Italian Encounter with Tudor England: A Cultural Politics of Translation* (Cambridge: Cambridge University Press, 2005), skillfully begins to unpack the "game of cultural one-upmanship" of these prefaces and their allusions. While he claims that Wolfe's "inconsistent chronology, provenances, and fictional presses all aim with varying means to deflect attention from London as their point of origin" (189), at the same time, he points out that such feigned aetiologies would have had little success in convincing European readers. Wyatt argues that Wolfe's extradiagetical pranks would have been recognized by experienced readers: he astutely suggests that "what exactly Wolfe had in mind in creating a false provenance for these, and for his other editions of Machiavelli and Aretino, will never perhaps be entirely settled but clearly has something to do both with the intended audience for such books and the cultural milieu from which they issued" (189).

11. Lievsay seems to have been among the first to recognize the "transparently fictitious places of publication (Bengodi, Valcerca)" and "ready-made pseudonym" that Wolfe adopts (Lievsay, *The Englishman's Italian Books,* 18). For a discussion of forgery that focuses on its ability to bridge past and present (but less centrally on geographic difference), see Anthony Grafton, *Forgers and Critics: Creativity and Duplicity in Western Scholarship* (Princeton, NJ: Princeton University Press, 1990), particularly p. 5, where Grafton notes the type of fake that would seem best to describes Wolfe's productions: "At one extremity, . . . [forgery] borders on mystification, the production of literary works meant to deceive for a short time only, as practical jokes."

12. Sir Thomas Bodley, *Letters of Sir Thomas Bodley to Thomas James,* ed. G.W. Wheeler (Oxford: Clarendon Press, 1926), Letter 220, January 1, 1612, and Letter 221, January 15, 1612, 219-21. Hereafter cited in the text.

13. Woodfield, *Surreptitious Printing in England,* 6; Bertolo, "John Wolfe, un editore Inglese," 200-201.

14. See Florio, *A Worlde of Words,* 41 and 51.

15. Roger Ascham, *The English Scholemaster* (London, 1571), Iii^v.

16. Ibid.

17. Ascham is adamant about the link between such licentiousness and heresy, whether protestant or papist: "They mocke the Pope: They raile on Luther: They allow neyther side: They like none, but onelie themselues: The marke they shote at, the ende they looke for, the heauen they desire, is onelie, their owne present pleasure, and priuate profit"(Iiiiᵛ). The irreligion of these corrupted Englishmen manifests itself in their modes of reading: both the readers and their books "haue in more reuerence, the triumphes of Petrarch: than the Genesis of Moses: They make more accounte of Tullies offices, than S. Paules epistles: of a tale in Bocace, than a storie of the Bible"(Iiiiⁱ).

18. Ibid., Iiiᵛ.

19. Cited in Loewenstein, *The Author's Due*, 31. Along with purported travels to Italy and the German Provinces, Wolfe was and remains better known for his errancies in the London publishing world, domestic transgressions which in turn have influenced the reading of his "Italian" publications of the 1580s. As Loewenstein points out, Christopher Barker's statement predates Wolfe's first publication of Machiavelli by more than two years and seems to refer most explicitly to his illicit printing of English books whose patents were owned by others.

20. Pietro Aretino, *Quattro comedie del Divino Pietro Aretino Cioè Il Marescalco, La Cortegiana, La Talanta, L'Hipocrito* (London: 1588), Oo8ᵛ. Hereafter cited in the text. Most critics concur that the Corrector was Petruccio Ubaldini, an Italian émigré who assisted Wolfe on a number of his Italian printing projects. Woodfield argues that Ubaldini also was responsible for the prefaces from "Il Stampatore" in Wolfe's editions of Machiavelli and Aretino: "The prefaces . . . contain a number of stylistic peculiarities such as the frequent use of parentheses and the habit of assuming an air of modesty by continually inserting 's'io non erro' or 's'io nom m'inganno' which are also found in the texts of the books written by . . . Ubaldini" (Woodfield, *Surreptitious Printing in England*, 12). Woodfield's claims are compelling. In this context, however, I am more interested in the publishers' creation of a textual persona, and the fictional positions they take vis-à-vis error and desire, than in the historical identities behind the pose.

21. Ludovico Ariosto, *Comedie di M-Lodovico Ariosto, Cioè, I Suppositi, La Cassaria, la Lena, Il Negromante, & la Scolastica Di Nvovo Ristampate; & con somma diligenza ricorrette, Per Thomaso Porcacchi* (Venice: Gabriel Giolito de Ferrari, 1562).

22. On the possibility that this edition is a reprint of an earlier collection see note 7.

23. Ben Jonson *Workes* (London, 1616), 487. By the 1590s, thanks in part to Wolfe's own publications and Florio's description, Aretino's seemingly paradoxical publishing history was also becoming part of his English persona. Compare Gabriel Harvey's description of his works in *A New Letter of Notable Contents* (London, 1593): "[Aretino] Paraphrased the inextimable works of Moses, and discoursed the Capricious Dialogues of the rankest Bawdry. [He] penned one Apology of the divinity of Christ, and another of Pederastice, a kinde of harlatry, not to be recited: [he] published the Life of the Blessed Virgin, and the Legende of the Errant Putana: [he] recorded the history of S. Thomas of Aquin, and forged the most detestable Blacke-booke, *de tribus imposteribus mundi*" (sig. D; 1289–90), cited in Ian Frederick Moulton, *Before Pornography: Erotic Writing in Early Modern England* (Oxford and New York: Oxford University Press, 2000). Moulton perceptively argues that "to understand the place of Aretino in Elizabethan culture one must take into account the many works that were commonly, if falsely, ascribed to him. . . . These works . . . contributed greatly to the establishment of Aretino as an emblematic figure of erotic and authorial transgression in early modern England" (147).

24. Gabriel Harvey, *A Theological Discourse on the Lamb* (London, 1590), cited in Moulton, *Before Pornography*, 163.

25. Florio, *A Worlde of Words,* 82.

26. On Aretino's participation in visual "self-fashioning" more broadly, see, among others, Waddington, *Aretino's Satyr,* 41–44; Fabio M. Bertolo, *Aretino e la stampa: Strategie di autopromozione a Venezia nel Cinquecento* (Roma: Salerno, 2003), 25; Johanna Woods-Marsden, "Aretino e la costruzione visuale dell'intellettuale," in *Pietro Aretino nel Cinquecentenario della nascita* (Rome: Salerno Editrice, 1995), 2:1,099–1,125; and Susan L. Gaylard, "Shifty Men Writing Monuments: Creating a Permanent Self in Early Modern Italian Literature" (Ph.D. diss., University of California, Berkeley, 2004), chapter 4, especially 121–26.

27. This print in turn had been adapted from a 1537 portrait medal struck by Leone Leoni that became widely known as a model for other representations of Aretino in a variety of media. It appeared on the title page of *Il Genesi di M. Pietro Aretino* published by Marcolini in (Venice, 1541) and prior to that on Marcolini's edition of *La vita di Maria Vergine* of circa 1539. Wolfe's version is not identical to the Italian image: the eye and nose in profile differ slightly from those in Marcolini's print. The medal itself is described by Waddington as "atypical of the surviving Aretino medals in being struck, rather than cast, possibly calculated from the outset for wide distribution" (Waddington, *Aretino's Satyr,* 75). See also *Il Marescalco Comedia di Messer Pietro Aretino Nuovamente Ristampato* (Venegia: Agostino Bindoni, 1550) and *Cortigiana Comedia di Messer Pietro Aretino Nuovamente corretta & ristampata* (Vinegia: Bindoni, 1550).

28. The description of Rome changed between the 1525 manuscript and 1534 print versions, from *caput* to *coda.* For a discussion of this and other differences between the two, see Paul Larivaille, "Teatro e realtà a Roma nel 1525: La prima redazione della *Cortigiana,*" in *Varia Aretiniana (1972-2004)* (Roma: Vecchiarelli Editore, 2005), 269–88; and Raymond Waddington's introduction to Pietro Aretino, *Cortigiana,* trans. J. Douglas Campbell and Leonard G. Sbrocchi, Carleton Renaissance Plays in Translation (Ottawa: Dovehouse Editions, 2003), 11. On Aretino as censor see Paul Larivaille, "Pietro Aretino tra infrazione e censura," and Raffaella Castagnola, "Aretino 'censor del mondo' e 'de la verità nuncio e propheta,'" in *Pietro Aretino nel Cinquecentenario della nascita,* 1:3–21 and 1:349–404, respectively.

29. In discussions of his professional misdeeds, Wolfe has often been cast as the antithesis of an emerging authorial claim to property. Loewenstein surveys what he sees as Wolfe's long history of printing questionably legitimate works, arguing that "Wolfe ushered in a tradition, if not an age, of sometimes piratical claiming" and concluding that as a result what we conveniently call "Jonsonian authorship is in some ways a by-product of John Wolfe's reformation" (Loewenstein, *The Author's Due,* 40–41). In her close reading of the prefaces to the Machiavelli editions, Halasz comes nearest to unlocking the stimulus to desire and to acquire these editions, to which the prefatory and editorial matter contribute. Identifying the locus of textual value in an "alliance between publishers and book buyers constructed in the prefaces," Halasz recognizes that the production of fictitious editions stems at least as much from the wish to create a "collective narrative" whose goal "is not that of establishing an authorial text, but rather that of establishing the texts as property" (*The Marketplace of Print,* 32). Yet here, Halasz, like Loewenstein in his reading of Wolfe's Italian productions, displaces an English dichotomy of author and publisher onto an Italianate form. In Wolfe's Aretine works, at least, as in Aretino himself, publisher, consumer, and author come together in a nexus of desire that excludes none except the unsophisticated, provincial, or overly moralistic reader. The particular demonstration of intimacy and interdependence between author and publisher that emerges from Aretine and Italian circles in this period is part of what Wolfe imports provocatively to England with his pseudo-imported editions.

30. It differs as well from the view of sixteenth-century printed drama as collaborative in the ways that Brian Richardson and Julie Peters have outlined. See Richardson, *Print Culture in Renaissance Italy*, 79, 121, and Julie Stone Peters, *Theatre of the Book 1480-1880: Print, Text, and Performance in Europe* (Oxford: Oxford University Press, 2000), 131-35.

31. Richardson, *Print Culture in Renaissance Italy*, 3 and passim.

32. For example *Comedie di Terentio nuovamente di latino in volgare tradotte* (Venice, 1538). In contrast, see the Marcolini and Bindoni editions, as well as editions of the *Cortegiana* of 1537 and *Il Marescalco* of 1539. *Due Comedie di Lorenzo Comparini Fiorentino . . .* (Vinegia: Giolito de Ferrari et Fratelli, 1553), however, contains scene divisions: see Peters, *Theatre of the Book,* 323-24n33 for a discussion of the inconsistent usage of such divisions in the period.

33. Mark Bland describes Wolfe's Italian editions as following "continental practices, with the editions of Machiavelli's and Aretino's plays set in long primer roman, and their prose works in italic" (Mark Bland, "The Appearance of the Text in Early Modern England," *TEXT* 2 [1998]: 91-154 [103]). Likewise, in *Theatre of the Book,* Peters writes that "the norm in Italy was roman for both Latin and vernacular works. Once in a while, italic was used for an entire text, particularly if the editor wished to emphasize its poetic qualities (the 1538 Italian vernacular Terence *Comedie* is an example) but heavy roman tends to dominate" (322). I have not found this to be the case, at least in the extensive collection of cinquecento Italian printed drama in the Biblioteca Nazionale Firenze.

34. Both Gascoigne's *Supposes* and *Iocasta* are set in black letter like most of the rest of the 1573, 1575, and 1587 collections. By contrast, John Lyly's *Campase* (London, 1584) contains act and scene divisions set off by large uncials, with the body text set in roman type.

35. See Bianca F.-C. Calabresi, "Gross Characters: The Unseemly Typographies of Early Modern Drama" (Ph.D. diss., Columbia University, 2003), especially chapter 1. According to Stephen Orgel, the publication of Sidney's *Arcadia* marks the regular appearance of italic as a body text in England (Stephen Orgel in conversation, June 2008). Wolfe prints several quarto texts entirely in italics as early as 1584 (Bland, "The Appearance of the Text," 103).

36. On other visual markers of classicism in printed English drama see Zachary Lesser, *Renaissance Drama and the Politics of Publication: Readings in the English Book Trade* (Cambridge: Cambridge University Press, 2004), 63-71. Lesser excludes "plays in collection" from his excellent survey, however (66n24).

37. See ibid., 2; Halasz, *The Marketplace of Print;* and Wyatt, *Italian Encounter with Tudor England.*

38. *La Prima Parte de Ragionamenti di M. Pietro Aretino* (London: John Wolfe, 1584), A2^r. Hereafter cited in the text.

39. Richardson, *Print Culture in Renaissance Italy,* 143, 161, 164.

40. For quattrocentro Italian associations of *corretto* with chastised female bodies and corrected texts, see Stephanie H. Jed, *Chaste Thinking: The Rape of Lucretia and the Birth of Humanism* (Bloomington and Indianapolis: Indiana University Press, 1989), passim, especially chapters one and two. Beginning with the printing of *Gorboduc (Ferrex and Porrex)* by Wolfe's master John Day in 1570, the printed play-text as a wandering or errant (fallen) woman ready to be reformed by the current publisher emerges as a powerful trope in England (having already appeared considerably earlier in Italy (see Peters, *Theatre of the Book,* 140, and Brooks, *From Playhouse to Printing House,* 31-32, 48). Aretino's dedicatory letter to "La magnanima Argentina Rangona" at the start of the first of the *Quattro comedie, Il Marescalco,* distinguishes at length between the Honorata Signora to which the play is dedicated and the anthropomorphized female text, "che sendo femina, non è punto differente de la natura de le Donne" (who, being female, is no

different from women's nature in general). He entrusts his wayward, desirous text to this famously chaste patron, "che hauete fatto de la casa vostra il tempio di pudicitia" (who have made your house into the temple of modesty), explicitly using the language of error and castigation. By contrast, the presentation of the Stampatore as follower and emulator of Barbagrigia reformulates the metaphor of elevated patron and prostituted work, instead emphasizing the printer/publisher's role as pander, catering to his public's polymorphous desires.

41. Nonetheless the reference seems to have escaped most critics writing on Wolfe. Michael Wyatt was practically the first to identify Barbagrigia correctly; he points out that "Wolfe's engagement with Italian print culture bears a distinctly theatrical imprint" that includes the use of the name Barbagrigia: "taken from Annibale Caro's 1543 *Straccioni*, where he represents a kind of Boccaccian/Falstaffian excess . . . a figure patterned after a friend of Caro's, the Roman printer Antonio Blado d'Asola" (Wyatt, *The Italian Encounter with Tudor England*, 197).

42. *Tutte le Opere di Giovanni Boccaccio,* ed. Vittore Branca (Milano: Mondadori, 1976), 4:682. On Berlinzone and Bengodi in Boccaccio see Branca's note 8, p. 1,412, in *Tutte le Opere di Giovanni Boccaccio* 4: "Comincia la fantasmagorica girandole di nomi favolosi con cui Maso, . . . stordisce e incanta Calandrino. Berlinzone (anche nella VIII 9, 23) . . . è nome probabilmente coniato su 'berlingare' *ciarlare,* 'berlingaio' *giottone,* 'berlingaccio' *giovedì grasso.* . . . Trasparente, nella sua formazione, il senso favoloso di Bengodi, il mitico paese di Cuccagna del favolello *Dit de Coquagne:* gioconda creazione della fantasia medievale."

43. On Calandrino as a surrogate for the reader, and more generally on the linguistic and discursive complexity of the *beffa,* see Giuseppe Mazzotta, *The World at Play in Boccaccio's Decameron* (Princeton: Princeton University Press, 1986), 198 and passim.

44. The letter to the reader in Wolfe's edition of *La Ficaia* continues the theme of "Amorevole Lettore" (Loving readers) and their complicity with the "heirs of Barbagrigia" in gratifying or being unwitting subjects to their textual desires. Indeed, the readers of *La Ficaia,* as the Proem of the Commentator suggests, will accept that "cunts" can be both masculine and feminine—(Il soggetto sono i Fichi, o le Fiche; chè nell'un modo e nell'altro sono chiamati dall'Autore)—and that the text encompasses multiple forms of desire: "it is enough for now to know that the Poet . . . baptizes them [*fichi/fiche*] Hermaphrodites and that throughout the work you'll find that they have confusingly two essences and two senses, and of these one is according to the letter and the other according to the figure." (Bastivi per ora di sapere che il Poetra, non senza misterio, li battezza Ermafroditi, e che per tutta l'opera troverete, che hanno confusamente due essi, e due sensi; e di questi uno è secondo la lettera, l'atro secondo il misterio.) For a recent discussion of Caro and the *beffa,* see Patricia Simons and Monique Kornell, "Annibal Caro's After-Dinner Speech (1536) and the Question of Titian as Vesalius's Illustrator," *Renaissance Quarterly* 61 (2008): 1,069–97.

45. See A. F. Johnson, *Periods of Typography: The Italian XVI Century* (London: Ernest Benn, 1926), 9–10, for the range of Antonio Blado's printed work: Blado "appears to have printed some 430 books, . . . more than half of those were offical publications, bulls, encyclicals, etc., . . . Erasmus in writing to Francesco Asolano in 1523, said of him 'insanit in libros sacros.' He also printed a considerable number of popular broadsheets dealing with contemporary events, . . . In 1539 Blado was chosen by Paul III and Cardinal Cervini to print the Greek MSS. of the Vatican library. . . . Other Greek books in octavo are the *Electra* of Euripides printed in 1545." On Blado's connections, see also the introduction to Annibal Caro, *The Scruffy Scoundrels (Gli Straccioni),* trans. with intro and notes by Massimo Ciavolella and Donald Beecher (Waterloo, Ontario: Wilfrid Laurier University Press, 1980),

v, and *Opere di Annibal Caro,* ed. Stefano Jacomuzzi (Torino: Unione Tipografico-Editrice Torinese, 1974).

46. Caro, *Scruffy Scoundrels,* vi–xiv.

47. Annibal Caro, *Opere,* ed. Vittorio Turri (Bari: Laterza, 1912), 1:192; Caro, *Scruffy Scoundrels,* 8.

48. When Pilucca asks, "How are things with you?" Barbagrigia replies, "Bulgin' at the seams, as you can see" (Caro, *Scruffy Scoundrels,* 8).

49. Caro, *Opere* (1912), 208; Caro, *Scruffy Scoundrels,* 27.

50. Caro, *Opere* (1912), 208; Caro, *Scruffy Scoundrels,* 27.

51. Ian Moulton writes of the *Ragionamenti,* for example, that "though they are profoundly ambivalent about women's moral status, they offer, nonetheless, a scathing indictment of the social options facing women in early modern Italy. And while they were often read as an attack on female corruption, they also sympathized with the cunning, cleverness, and energy of their female protagonists to a greater degree than almost any other text in the period" (Moulton, *Before Pornography,* 131).

52. Caro, *Opere* (1912), 209–10; Caro, *Scruffy Scoundrels,* 28.

53. Caro, *Opere* (1912), 213; Caro, *Scruffy Scoundrels,* 33.

54. The next two single-author nonfolio collections of printed plays issued in England, several decades later, likewise present the publisher as equally or more central to satisfying the reader's desires than the author. Moreover, both the publishers of Lyly's octavo *Six Court Comedies* (1632) and of Marston's quarto *Workes . . . Being Tragedies and Comedies Collected into one Volume* (1633) in their own way affirm that they are catering to female as much as male appetites in producing these collections. Lyly, his publisher Edward Blount writes, was particularly beloved by women in Elizabethan times, not the least by the queen, who recognized him as "a Rare and Excellent Poet." Likewise the Muses held him "such a sonne, as they called their Darling"(A5ʳ). But it is court ladies who particularly interest Blount as readers both in Elizabeth's and now in James's time: "All our Ladies were then his Scolers; And that Beautie in Court, which could not Parley, *Euphueisme,* was as little regard; as shee which now there, speakes not French" (A5ʳ). And so, he argues, situating more clearly the "Reader" to whom this epistle is addressed, current women will equally enjoy the author's diverting presence in their private rooms: "Thou canst not repent the Reading of them [the plays] ouer: when Old *Iohn Lilly,* is merry with thee in thy Chamber" (A6ʳ). Moreover, they will recognize the publisher's singular role in brokering such interactions: "Thou shalt say, Few (or None) of our Poets now are such witty Companions: And thanke mee, that brings him to thy Acquaintance. / Thine. Ed. Blount"(A6ʳ). Whereas Blount claims to have brought "Old John Lilly" anew to his female readers' chambers, William Sheares offers himself, "ready prest and bound" to his patron, Elizabeth Cary, like one of Marston's erotically charged Italianate servants (named variously *Balurdo, Dildo,* and *Catzo*—Idiot, Dildo, and Prick). With this further association of body and book, the publisher now panders *himself* as well as his errant text to his reader, like Barbagrigia offering himself at liberty to satisfy whatever pleasures his bibliophiles desire. This is itself a distinctly Boccaccian move: see the *Decameron* as "cognominato Prencipe Galeotto" as well as the claims of the *Proemio* and *Conclusione dell'Autore* to be particularly responsive to female desires (Giovanni Boccaccio, *Decameron,* ed. Vittorio Branca [Milano: Mondadori, 1985], 3, 6–7, 913–14).

55. *Commento di Ser Agresto da Ficarvolo Sopra La Prima Ficata del Padre Siceo* (London: John Wolfe, 1584), Dd2ᵛ. According to Woodfield, this seemingly earlier date "does not mean that the second volume was printed before the first, as has been often stated; rather, the second date is old style and should be understood as 1584–85"

(Woodfield, *Surreptitious Printing in England,* 10). Compare the claims of the colophon to *La Seconda Parte* that it was "Stampata, con buona licenza (toltami) nella nobil citta di Bengodi, ne l'Italia alter volte piu felice, il viggesimo primo d'Octobre MDLXXXIV" (Cc6ʳ).

56. Nino Borsellino, *Rozzi e intronati: Esperienze e forme di teatro dal' Decameron'al "Candelaio"* (Roma: Bulzoni, 1976), 211-28. Both Calandrino and Maco are "new" men come to the city to make their fortune (both are Tuscan). According to the Boccaccian text, the Calandrino tales in particular are located in Florence and told to insiders distinguished from the dupe of the story at the outset (see Boccaccio, *Tutte le Opere,* 4:681: "Nella nostra città, la qual sempre di varie maniere e di nuove genti è stata abondevole . . .").

57. In Wolfe's trilingual edition, the English uses *declarations,* the Italian *narrative,* and the French *contes* for this generic component: *The Courtier of Count Baldasar Castilio . . . done into English by Thomas Hoby* (London, 1588), 129.

58. For a discussion of this connection, see among others, Giulio Ferroni, *Le voci dell'istrione: Pietro Aretino e la dissoluzione del teatro* (Napoli: Liguori, 1977), 36-40; J. Guidi, *Visages de la vie de cour selon Castiglione et l'Arétin: Du "Cortigiano" à la "Cortigiana,"* in *Culture et société en Italie: Du Moyen-Age à la Renaissance, Hommage à André Rochon* (Paris: Université de la Sorbonne Nouvelle, 1985); Christopher Cairns, *Pietro Aretino and the Republic of Venice: Researches on Aretino and His Circle in Venice, 1527-1556* (Florence: Olschki, 1985), 31-47; and Jodi Cranston, *The Poetics of Portraiture in the Italian Renaissance* (Cambridge: Cambridge University Press, 2000), 150-51.

59. The simpler title only *appears* to be less complicated: the courtesan at the center of the play, while named and known as an historical personage, is in fact conspicuously absent. For the multiple meanings of the original title see Waddington, introduction to *Cortigiana,* 13-15.

60. On the commensurability of the world of the courtier and the courtesan as a fundamental Aretine point see Nuccio Ordine, "Le 'Sei Giornate,'" in *Pietro Aretino nel Cinquecentenario della nascita,* 673-716, esp. 715.

Imitating Othello:
The Handkerchief, alla Italiana

JANE TYLUS

WITHIN THE INCREASINGLY cramped frame of a play that ends with a horde of soldiers crowded into a bedroom, Shakespeare entertains, for the briefest of moments, a fantasy. Cassio has been ordered to take Othello's place as general in Cyprus, and the deposed Othello in turn is set to go "into Mauritania, and take away with him the fair Desdemona" (4.2.224–25).[1] So we might be tempted to catch our breath and imagine that in the midst of what has seemed to be a tragedy hurtling toward the inevitable conclusion, some other ending is possible. And yet the phrase "fair Desdemona" and the idea for the Mauritanian trip are simply another lie of Iago's, as he tries to convince Roderigo to murder Cassio that very evening—thereby preventing Othello's departure not to Africa, but back to Venice. Thus the flight to Africa offers only cold comfort even as it conveys a momentary escape from the overwhelming claustrophobia of the play to a place where Desdemona could be "fair" again and Othello no longer jealous. Lie though it is, Iago's fantasy embodies what Leslie Fiedler has called "what Desdemona dreams, or rather Shakespeare dreams through her," "a symbolic marriage of all that Europe and Africa might mythically mean: civilization and barbarism, courtesy and strength, belonging and freedom. . . So long as the marriage holds, it signifies a miracle, a *discordia concors* in the flesh."[2] Yet such *discordia concors,* by the time of Iago's remark, seems gone forever—and with it a world that flickers occasionally across the stage in *Othello* to tease its characters and audience alike.

This is the world of Italian romance, as defined largely by a text that dominated the European literary scene for much of the sixteenth century, Ariosto's *Orlando furioso*. The *Furioso* has received considerable attention in recent years from Shakespeare scholars who have suggested that Orlando's jealous rage after his beautiful Angelica runs off with a young Moorish page may well be behind not only *Othello* but *Much Ado About Nothing*.[3] Yet as this essay will argue, Shakespeare's real interest in the *Furioso* was the hero who in many ways has more in common with Othello, given his African roots: the converted Muslim Ruggiero, about whom we first hear in the second canto of the *Furioso* as "un cavalliero / che d'Africa passò col re Agramante" (2.32),[4] whose mentor Atlante is from the Mauritania that Iago briefly evokes, and whose wanderings for forty-five cantos make him akin to the "errant barbarian" of Shakespeare's play.[5] Like that "barbarian," Ruggiero marries his Christian Desdemona, the woman warrior Bradamante. But it is in Shakespeare's revisions of a passage from the final canto describing Ruggiero's and Bradamante's marital festivities that we can discover the real subtleties of Shakespeare's reading of the *Furioso*— a reading that not only shaped his play but reflects an acute grasp of the tradition of Italian romance as defined by Ariosto. And this grasp was in turn conditioned by the fact that as the nature of those revisions strongly suggests, he read about Ruggiero not in John Harington's magnificent if problematic translation of 1591, but in Ariosto's original Italian.

When the long-awaited festivities are over, we learn in canto 46 of the *Furioso,* the African hero and his European bride will consummate their marriage on a "genial letto fecondo"—a fertile, happy bed placed within a sumptuous pavilion or "prezioso velo" (46.84) on which is embroidered the life of one of the couple's descendants, Ariosto's patron, Ippolito d'Este. Before describing that life, Ariosto attends to the genesis of the pavilion itself:

> Eran degli anni appresso che duo milia
> che fu quel ricco padiglion trapunto.
> Una donzella de la terra d'Ilia,
> ch'avea il furor profetico congiunto,
> con studio di gran tempo e con vigilia
> lo fece di sua man di tutto punto.
> Cassandra fu nomata, et al fratello
> inclito Ettòr fece un bel don di quello. (46.80)

The gorgeous pavilion was embroidered almost two thousand years earlier. A Trojan damsel, in prophetic furor, had devoted long vigils to making it all with her own hand. Her name was Cassandra, and she made a nice gift of the thing to her famous brother, Hector.

In the 1920s, Cassandra's "furor profetico" caught the attention of John Semple Smart, who noted its relevance for a suspenseful moment from act 3 of *Othello*.[6] Desdemona has just failed to produce the handkerchief that is possibly theater's most famous prop, and an enraged Othello expounds on the object's provenance, investing it with a history and a potency thus far unbeknownst to all:

> There's magic in the web of it;
> A sibyl, that had number'd in the world
> The sun to make two hundred compasses,
> In her prophetic fury sew'd the work;
> The worms were hallow'd that did breed the silk,
> And it was dyed in mummy. (3.4.67-72)

As long as the "work" first given to Othello's mother by an Egyptian "charmer" was in a woman's hands, it would "subdue" her husband ignorant of its powers "entirely to her love"—much as the pavilion wafted in for Ruggiero's wedding is said to be understood not by Ruggiero but only by his bride ("Ruggiero, ancor ch'a par di Bradamante/non ne sia dotto"; 46.91). Lost, however, the handkerchief would give the husband license to be unfaithful to his wife and thus enable him to wield power over her instead: "his spirits should haunt/After new fancies" (3.4.60-61).

Othello's account of his gift to Desdemona is not a literal translation of Ariosto's lines, of course. But as she embroiders the handkerchief with "magic," the sibyl engages in a "prophetic fury" that exactly translates the "furor profetico" of Cassandra—a phrase that Harington had omitted from his own translation.[7] Yet the generativity of the fecund bed tucked within the pavilion starkly contrasts with the tragic fate of the couple entangled within the web of the magic handkerchief. Arguably the explicit textual reference Shakespeare makes to this poem with a happy ending only heightens the poignancy of Desdemona's and Othello's own interfaith marriage—a marriage that, like Ruggiero's and Bradamante's, can only thrive if the groom's problematic past is definitively silenced.

To this extent, the two works can be said to end in strikingly similar ways. In the *Furioso,* immediately after the pavilion is introduced, the

African Rodomonte arrives to disturb the ceremonies and accuse Ruggiero of having betrayed his Muslim past. Proving his baptism and his allegiance to the Christian and French cause, Ruggiero slaughters Rodomonte after a protracted battle, stabbing the "impious pagan" in the face to end his life as well as the *Orlando furioso* itself, as Rodomonte's angry spirit flees to Acheron. Or as John Harington would suggest in his "Allegorical Reading" of the final canto, "the unbridled heat and courage of youth" must be "killed and quite vanquished by marriage" since "after that holy state of matrimonie is entered into, all youthfull wildness of all kinds must be cast away."[8] Wildness, to be sure, is "cast away" in this moment, but so is Ruggiero's African past, his years of allegiance to King Agramante, his teacher Atlante, and comrades such as Rodomonte beside whom he once fought the Christians. Similarly, in the closing moments of Shakespeare's play, Othello reenacts a moment when he defended a Christian against a "malignant and turban'd Turk" who has "traduc'd the state": "I took by the throat the circumcised dog,/And smote him thus" (5.2.352-57)—upon which he stabs himself, dying not merely "upon a kiss," but upon the bed made up in his "wedding sheets" (4.2.107). In this final scene, the Turk who "traduc'd the state" can be seen as Rodomonte, while in avenging Desdemona's own "traduction"—her defamation or slander—the hand by which Othello commits suicide is that of the convert Ruggiero. Falling alongside Desdemona's body in a perverse act of lovemaking, Othello attests to his conversion and his willingness to embrace the handkerchief as a guarantor of the "fertile marriage bed." But, of course, he does so only belatedly, and the Este dynasty to which Bradamante and Ruggiero give rise is a far cry from the sterile outcome of *Othello*.

Shakespeare's allusion to Ariosto's fabric and subsequently to Ruggiero's vanquishing of his past may thus let us know just how far *Othello* is from achieving a *discordia concors* of the kind that we witness at the close of the *Furioso*—and how near it might have been. It might have offered Othello and his own fair bride a history very much like that of the African convert Ruggiero and Bradamante. Does not Desdemona devour Othello's tales and Othello refer to her as his "fair warrior" (2.1.180), while she calls herself later in the play his "unhandsome warrior" (3.4.150)? And might they not have produced a progeny as distinguished as that of Ruggiero and Bradamante—one that could have prevented the historical Cyprus from going over, as it would after Othello's death, to the hands of the Turk? To that extent, the relationship between the play and the romance poem can be seen as one of belatedness and nostalgia, a belatedness only accentuated by Othello's suicide and his embrace of his beloved on the "fecund bed" after she is dead.[9]

This is at least one plausible reading. Yet to look more closely at the world of Ariosto's romance is to ask if it really *is* that distant from *Othello*. Shakespeare himself may provide us with a clue to a less benign vision of Ariosto's poem—or at least of its maker—in the passage about the pavilion just cited. As readers will have noted, Ariosto has the Trojan prophetess Cassandra embroider the wedding pavilion, but Shakespeare's Othello ascribes the handkerchief's creation to a sibyl. It is possible that he simply invented her, but it is equally possible that he encountered her in a passage about another pavilion from another Italian poem, Matteo Maria Boiardo's unfinished *Orlando innamorato,* the fifteenth-century predecessor to Ariosto's *Furioso:*[10] "Una Sibilla (come hagio sentito)/Già stete a Cuma, al mar napolitano,/E questa aveva il pavaglion ordito/E tuto lavorato di sua mano" (A Sibyl [as I have heard] lived at Cuma, on the sea of Naples, and she's the one who had warped the pavilion and embroidered it with her own hand; 2.27.51). Possessed of what the narrator calls divine gifts ("Io credo ben, signor, che voi sapiati/Che le Sibile fòr tute divine"; 52), the Sibyl, like her "sisters," is in the position to design "gran fatti, e degne historie e peregrine,/E presenti, e futuri, e de' passati": to tell of "great deeds, worthy and foreign histories, and things of today, as well as the future and the past." Insofar as this passage immediately follows another conversion and another wedding and describes a textile that represents other descendants of the Este line, it is clear that Ariosto's own pavilion, introduced at a climactic moment in the *Furioso,* derives, like so much of his poem, from Boiardo's fabric. And as with so much else in the *Furioso,* this overtly self-conscious passage willfully ignores its origins in Boiardo's *Orlando innamorato.*

In juxtaposing these two moments in Italian romance with *Othello,* I would like to speculate on Shakespeare's fidelity to Italy and to an Italian language with which he seems to have had more than a passing acquaintance, as a number of works from the early twentieth century and more recent scholarship have suggested—much of the latter prompted by the pioneering studies of Louise George Clubb.[11] Shakespeare speculated in turn about the fidelity of Italian texts to one another, hence producing a profound meditation on the role of *fede* in the romance tradition that the end of *Othello* would seem to nostalgically invoke. Eduardo Saccone powerfully demonstrated how crucial the question of *fede* or faith is to Ariosto's poem, and it is a faith that would seem to be brought to triumphant culmination in Ruggiero's and Bradamante's long-delayed wedding.[12] And yet it may be that the textile within which the couple will consummate their marriage is less benign than may appear at first glance, and with it the tradition from which *Othello* both does and does not depart. How does the fabric itself, arguably a model for Othello's exotic handkerchief, taint the *discordia concors* that seems to be celebrated at the close of the poem? And how does Shakespeare use it to identify a moment not of faith but of betrayal within the literary tradition in which he and Ariosto worked?

Albert Ascoli has been one of the few critics to address the ironies inherent in a pavilion embroidered by the prophetess Cassandra, the woman who spoke the truth but was cursed never to be believed, and the fact that she is the producer of the fabric suggests that we can hardly take the pavilion's celebration of Ippolito's life at face value. And ultimately, as Ascoli points out, the coupling of Bradamante and Ruggiero within this problematic tent will lead not to the happy conjoining of Africa and Europe, but to betrayal—the end point beyond Ariosto's poem that is, as Ascoli argues, "the meaning of Ruggiero's conversion and marriage, his access to political power, his triumph over demonic forces." "And the meaning of that death," Ascoli continues, "is more violence, more betrayals, more deaths."[13] For as we know from an earlier passage in the *Furioso*, marriage with Bradamante will lead all too soon to Ruggiero's death. It is a future about which Melissa informs Bradamante in no uncertain terms early in the *Furioso*, long before she transports the pavilion from Constantinople to the wedding. In an eerie calling up of spirits from the future, she demonstrates to Bradamante in elliptical fashion that Ruggiero will die at the hands of traitors from the Maganza clan and will in turn be avenged by his son Ruggierino, showing her the "sangue vermiglia" or vermilion blood of a member of the Maganza family slain by Ruggierino. "Vendicato il tradimento e il torto / contra quei che gli avranno il padre morto": "So was such treachery and wrong avenged on those who will have [Ruggierino's] father killed" (3.24). That Bradamante learns of Ruggiero's violent death so early on in the *Furioso* is significant, but she and Melissa are not the only ones with such knowledge. The Mauritanian Atlante, Ruggiero's mentor and possessed, like Melissa, of prophetic powers, seeks for the better half of the poem to prevent

Ruggiero from what would seem to be his inevitable destiny, a destiny of which he was already aware in the *Innamorato* where he tried—and failed—to prevent Ruggiero from going into battle against the Christians: "a tradimento fia occiso con pene" (a painful death will come to him through an act of treachery; 2.16.53), he cries out in tears after Ruggiero asks for armor and a horse, and a prophecy which Ruggiero hears neither in the *Innamorato* nor in the *Furioso*. Atlante's death and disappearance from the *Furioso* opens the way for Ruggiero's marriage, as well, we must assume, as his premature death. Ruggiero is thus left without a protector, vulnerable to a future he does not fully understand—much as he is said not to fully comprehend the images on the pavilion Melissa transports to Paris in canto 46, even if he has heard of Ippolito d'Este on occasion from Atlante ("pur gli torna a mente/che fra i nipoti suoi gli solea Atlante/commendar questo Ippolito sovente"; 46.99).

The pavilion itself is in fact implicated in a long history of betrayals, as can be seen both from the images depicted on its surface and its problematic transmission. Originally woven by Cassandra, it passes from her brother Hector to the Greeks when Hector is killed—like the future Ruggiero—"a tradimento" and the Trojans are destroyed by "Sinon falso," the false, treacherous Sinon to whom they opened their gates (46.82). Over the centuries, it falls into the hands of the Egyptians when Menelaus travels to Egypt to reclaim Helen, and then to the Romans when Cleopatra is defeated by Octavius. Three hundred years later, the emperor Constantine "gives cause to Italy to grieve" when he departs for Constantinople, taking the pavilion with him, a break with Rome and the center of the western empire that Ariosto considered here and elsewhere a betrayal.[14] The pavilion has remained in Constantinople ever since, up to the time of Bradamante's and Ruggiero's wedding in Paris. And yet breaches in *fede* are limited neither to antiquity nor to the period of Charlemagne; rather, they will continue into Ariosto's own day as revealed by the representations woven on the tent itself, as though the curse of "tradimento" follows Hector's descendants to the town that they supposedly settled, Ariosto's and the Este's Ferrara. For one of the events of Ippolito's life stitched on the pavilion is his timely discovery of the conspiracy plotted by two of his brothers against a third, Alfonso: "trova, e fa veder per cosa chiara/al giustissimo frate il tradimento/che gli usa la famiglia sua più cara" (so he discovers the betrayal, and makes it known to his most just of brothers how his dearest family acts against him; 46.95). In fact, in 1506, Giulio and Ferrante d'Este had plotted against Alfonso—largely to get back at Ippolito, who had violently blinded Giulio for suspected adultery with his mistress (a detail Ariosto wisely glosses over)—and Ippolito's uncovering of the plot led to the lifelong imprisonment of the two brothers. The allusion to the conspiracy is included among many other details of Ippolito's life extending over thirteen stanzas: his great learning, his feats in battle, his ascent to the position of cardinal. But the future act of brotherly treachery will be quickly echoed by the accusation of betrayal already noted, and one that leads to the end of the poem. No sooner has the pavilion been unfurled and described than the African Rodomonte challenges Ruggiero to a duel on the grounds that he has been "infido" to his slain King Agramante and his Muslim roots: "Ben che tua fellonia si vegga aperta, / perché essendo cristian non pò negarla; / pur per farla apparere anco più certa, / in questo campo vengoti a provarla" (So that your treachery can be seen more openly, since you can hardly deny that you're a Christian; yet to make it appear even more of a certain thing, I come to prove it right here on this battlefield; 46.106).

Finally, and perhaps most suggestively for *Othello,* the figure who reveals to Bradamante her painful future in canto 3 and explains more fully to her the pavilion of canto 46 is herself a character deeply implicated in wily deceits, Melissa. What has long puzzled readers of the *Furioso* is her implication in a secondary plot that would seem to have little to do with the future of Ferrara and far more to do with her own selfish passions: the tale of a husband's jealousy found just a few cantos before the closing one. It is a story relayed not to Ruggiero and Bradamante but to the Christian soldier Rinaldo as he leisurely makes his way down the Po so he can set sail for the island of Lipadusa, where a fatal, final battle is to take place between Muslims and Christians. The novella-like story concerns the overwrought efforts of Rinaldo's Mantuan host to discern if his wife is faithful. He had been married for five years when a noblewoman from his town ("una femina nobil del paese") who has magical powers falls in love with him: she can "brighten the night, darken the day, stop the sun, and make the earth move" (sapea d'incanti e di malie / quel che saper ne possa alcuna maga: / rendea la notte chiara, oscuro il die, / fermava il sol, facea la terra vaga; 43.21). After he steadfastly refuses to return her affections, she convinces him to question the fidelity of his wife—a beautiful woman deft at "needlework and embroidery" ("bei trapunti e di riccami . . . / sapea"; 43.18), divine at playing and singing music ("il suono e 'l canto"), and possessed of a loving, gentle disposition (all features that describe Desdemona, particularly when Othello, confronted with the handkerchief in Bianca's hands, says, "Hang her, I do but say what she is: so delicate with her needle, an admirable musician, O she will sing the savageness out of a bear . . . and then of so gentle a condition!" [4.1.183–84]). And it is only at this point, well into his tale, as the host describes how he was devoured by "lo spron di gelosia malvagio"—the spur of evil jealousy—that he mentions the name of this *maga:* Melissa. So wrought does Melissa make the besieged husband about his wife's fidelity that he finally agrees to let her magically transform him into a rich suitor to see if he can seduce his unknowing wife with jewels "as rich as ever came out of the Indies or Ethiopia."[15] When the wife is poised to surrender, Melissa chooses that very instant to change the wealthy and exotic stranger back into the enraged husband, causing the marriage to end bitterly as the wife leaves her manipulative spouse for another man. Even if she has not fulfilled her own desires, Melissa has exacted revenge, although the Mantuan's hatred for her ultimately drives her away, "e in modo abbandonò questo paese,/che dopo mai per me non se n'intese" (and she left town in such fashion that afterward I never heard of her again; 43.46).[16]

But Melissa reappears, as it were, in the unfolding events of the *Furioso* proper—or more precisely, she has already appeared to readers of the poem in canto 3 when she reveals to Bradamante her future progeny. And Rinaldo will presumably encounter her shortly after he hears the tale of her troublesome romantic past, since he is one of the guests to attend the wedding festivities of canto 46. Thus the figure responsible for provoking Rinaldo's host to jealousy and ultimately to despair emerges as the protectress of the Franks' most valiant woman warrior and the guarantor of her marriage with Ruggiero.[17] On the face of it, the pavilion might seem far removed from the narrative about infidelity in which Melissa's would-be lover too easily believes and the witchcraft which enabled the *maga* to enact revenge on the host. Yet the same dark powers underlie both webs. Melissa's pavilion is carried to Paris with the help of "infernali stigi," and when in canto 3 she summons spirits up from the deep to show Bradamante her descendants—and prophesy Ruggiero's betrayal—Ariosto's commentator wryly observes, "Avea de spirti un gran numero eletto,/non so se da l'inferno o da qual sede": "She had a great number of spirits at her behest, and I don't know if they came from hell or some other place" (3.20). The "furor profetico," that is, is hardly a furor that promises happiness untarnished by tragedy, and prophets are not immune from the kinds of human weakness exhibited elsewhere in the poem. The prize won in each case, moreover, is inevitably compromised. The host gains knowledge along with eternal unhappiness, while Ruggiero's submission to Christianity, to Bradamante, and to the *maga* Melissa who transported Cassandra's pavilion to France ensures his glory and sets him up for future betrayal.

That Shakespeare may have imagined Iago as a male Melissa adept at weaving webs in which he ensnares Desdemona and Othello seems eminently plausible. Indeed, Iago emerges as the genuine embroiderer of the play. He promises to make of Desdemona's goodness "the net/That shall enmesh 'em all" (2.3.352–53); Othello demands to know in the final scene "why he hath thus ensnar'd my soul and body?" (5.2.302); and in the closing lines of the play Lodovico instructs him to look at the "tragic lodging" of the bed: "this is thy work" (5.2.364–65). Yet the passage with the sibyl suggests that Shakespeare may have been prompted to reflect on more self-consciously literary forms of betrayal. As already noted, the pavilion Melissa transports to France in the *Furioso* is modeled on an earlier one found toward the end of book 2 of the *Innamorato*.[18] In canto 27, the warrior Brandimarte, a recent convert to Christianity, arrives in a verdant field in "Barbaria," outside of Carthage, where he and his bridal entourage have been blown thanks to a tempest, like an Aeneas of long ago (2.27.44–45). He uses the occasion to challenge the African king Agramante to a duel, but before he goes off to battle, Boiardo spends some six stanzas describing the pavilion that will house him and his new wife Fiordelisa, whose father Dolistone gave them the pavilion as a wedding gift. After calling attention to the tent's beauty, Boiardo describes the pictures embroidered on its surface. They depict the origins of the Este family that will one day rule Ferrara, symbolized by twelve Alfonsi whose virtues will culminate in the Alfonso I of Boiardo's day. The first nine leaders he dispatches quickly; the tenth, the Aragonese Alfonso il Magnanimo, king of Naples from 1442 to 1458, is described in two stanzas that linger over his defeat of the Tunisian pirates who threatened Sicily, and Africa is seen "kneeling before him, with its wicked people" (stava davante/Ingienochiata col suo popul rio; 2.27.54). Yet just as Africa is "vinta a lui," so is he "vinto" by Italy, where he chooses to live rather than in his native Spain, just as Hercules was once defeated by his love for a Lydian woman. The latest Alfonso, born in 1476 and hence just several years before Boiardo would have written the canto, is lauded as a young child who had such beauty and splendor that everyone could say about him, "Questo è 'l Dio d'amore!" (This is the god of love!; 2.27.58).

As he begins his description of the tent, Boiardo notes that "era sì legiadro e sì polito/Che un altro non fo mai tanto soprano" (2.27.51): it was so beautifully and carefully done that its like had never been made. And as he completes the description, he suggests that the work is so intricate that no one understands it, not even Brandimarte himself, who sleeps within its folds: "molt'altre cose a quel gentil lavoro/vi for ritrate, e non eran intese" (2.27.60).[19] These are all suggestions Ariosto will take up when displaying the tent in canto 46. None of the viewers admiring the pavilion understands its story, with the exception of Bradamante, to whom Melissa has explained all. The very fact, moreover, that Melissa is, as Pio Rajna notes, "a character invented by Ariosto,"[20] suggests that this femme fatale and prophetess is herself ignorant of Ariosto's precursor— surely an intentional gesture on Ariosto's part. Ariosto moreover will condense the twelve "Alfonsi" to focus on a single Este. And he will take Boiardo's "un altro non fo mai tanto soprano" and extend it into the future so as to claim a uniqueness for *his* pavilion that will never be effaced by time: it was "in all the world, the richest, the most ornate, the loveliest that was ever fashioned—either in times of war or peace, or before then, or since" (il più ricco, il più ornato, il più giocondo/che già mai fosse o per guerra o per pace,/o prima o dopo, teso in tutto 'l mondo; 46.77). At the same time, Ariosto introduces into Boiardo's pavilion an imperial history that takes not only the pavilion but the epic genre itself through key moments until it arrives in his own day, as he describes the tent's travels from Greece to Alexandria, to Rome, to Constantinople, and finally to Paris for the wedding. In moving directly from Charlemagne's era to his own, and in insisting that nothing like this "padiglione" adorned with the life of a member of the Este family ever existed before, or since, Ariosto omits the poem that was Boiardo's *Innamorato*—as well, of course, as Ippolito's ancestors—to stress both Ippolito's and the *Furioso*'s uniqueness.

This is where Shakespeare's own intervention may furnish a telling commentary on the discussion of magical fabrics and the people who make them, as he exchanges Cassandra for Boiardo's Sibyl, and as through his tragic figure of Othello, the voice through which the world of Italian romance effectively enters the play, he reminds us about another kind of *fede* and its betrayal: that of one literary figure to another.[21] This becomes all the more likely when we consider that the pavilion appears only two cantos after one of the most painful events of the *Furioso* as a whole: Brandimarte's unexpected death at a duel in Lipadusa after his comrades—Rinaldo among them—arrive too late to help him.[22] By killing Brandimarte off, Ariosto refuses to honor the fecundity associated with his wedding pavilion as described in Boiardo, displacing it onto Ruggiero's marital *padiglione* instead. The fact, moreover, that Melissa brings the pavilion from Constantinople and thus from the heart of the Byzantine empire, where she claims it has been ever since Constantine arrived there in the fourth century, suggests that it never *did* belong to Brandimarte and hence, to Boiardo. Far from copying the tent, Ariosto claims to invent it, even as he associates Brandimarte with a more modest textile shortly before his death. This is the black vestments he asks his wife Fiordiligi (Fiordelisa in Boiardo) to make for him for what turns out to be his final battle: clothing that in a foreboding dream she sees interwoven with "goccie rosse" or red drops that prefigure his blood that will soon stain the garment she "avea trapunta e di sua man contesta" (embroidered in her own hand; 43.155).

This prophetic female embroiderer thus replaces Boiardo's Sibyl, as the garment she sews becomes in her dreams an irrevocable text about her husband's death—and hence another link between the product of a woman's weaving and a man's submission to its narrative. The substitution obscures the fact that with Brandimarte—and Boiardo—now dead, there is no one to contest this apparent breach in literary *fede* when Ariosto does turn, three cantos later, to his much larger, more ambitious pavilion. Thus can Ariosto move to what can be called the grand finale of his ending, in which the fabric transported by Melissa becomes the material realization of the poem Ariosto has frequently referred to as a tapestry, using throughout the poem the verbs *lavorare, ordire* (to warp), and *tramare* (to weave; also, to plot).[23] Like the garment Helen weaves in book 3 of the *Iliad,* the pavilion of canto 46 can serve as a synecdoche for the poem itself: beautifully *lavorato* and prophetic, albeit misread and misunderstood.[24] With this final tour de force, Ariosto also seems to announce a definitive closure of the tradition that he had inherited from his predecessor Boiardo, whose adherence to the oral modalities of the *cantastorie* created a poem with a very different manner of presentation.[25]

Is Shakespeare's reference to a sibyl a fluke, a mistranslation of Ariosto, or, as Othello might call it, a "traduction"—a defamation of his source?

The allusion to Boiardo is an intriguing touch that Shakespeare might have gleaned from a Renaissance commentary on Ariosto and incorporated, unmindful of his source, into Othello's fabric. Alternately, he may have known Boiardo directly, since numerous copies of the *Orlando innamorato* were in circulation in England after Domenichini's revision of the text in 1545; Richard Tofte translated the first three cantos of the poem into English in 1598, dedicating them to Lady Margaret Morgan, wife of John Morgan, the knight and captain of her majesty's horsemen. (Tofte would go on in 1615—a decade after *Othello*—to write *A Blazon of Jealousy,* a loose translation of Benedetto Varchi's 1545 lecture on a poem by Della Casa about the monster of jealousy.)[26] If this evidence seems unconvincing, then perhaps since this essay began with Iago's fantasy about a boat bound for Mauritania that would have saved Othello from his fate, let it move toward its conclusion with a not altogether improbable fantasy about Shakespeare paying homage to Ariosto's precursor, Boiardo. This is a precursor whom David Quint argues Ariosto turned into the magician Atlante, who continues in the *Furioso* to try desperately, but unsuccessfully, to keep his charge Ruggiero from his destiny, and hence, literally speaking, in Mauritania.[27] Placing the pavilion at the end of the *Orlando furioso* is Ariosto's way of accentuating the poem's insistence on its textuality, torn definitively from the oral traditions of the *cantastorie* that everywhere mark Boiardo's poem. Thus might Shakespeare have been exposing the betrayals that writers perform on one another and for which there is no reliable test save that enacted by careful readers with an eye for catching what constitutes the "original," whether that be a passage in Ariosto's *Furioso* gone untranslated by Harington, or a textile in Boiardo gone missing in Ariosto.

Lest one presume too much about Shakespeare's sympathy for the unsung writer of an unfinished epic poem, however, one must add an extended note about Shakespeare's own infidelities to an Italian text—not Ariosto's or Boiardo's, but his principal source for *Othello,* Giraldi-Cinzio's novella about Disdemona and the Moor from the *Ecatommiti* of the mid-sixteenth century. As scholars have long known, this is a novella that provided Shakespeare with all the essentials of his tale. An unnamed African warrior (il Moro) turned Venetian officer wins the heart of a young Disdemona who goes with him to Cyprus, where he is swayed by the wickedness of his Ensign who has tried, and failed, to seduce the

Moor's faithful wife. With the Ensign's help, the Moor kills the innocent Disdemona, and the tale is related by the Ensign's widow, much as Emilia reveals Iago's guilt.[28] In this story, the handkerchief plays an essential role. Yet the magical origins of Othello's cloth distance it from the more prosaic handkerchief in Giraldi's tale. There is, moreover, an essential difference between play and novella regarding the status of the handkerchief as an imitable fabric and the role of women in the creation of such fabrics. Like Iago, Giraldi's Ensign plants a handkerchief that he has pilfered from an unsuspecting Disdemona in the chambers of the captain or "capo di squadra" who fulfills the role of Cassio, but despairs that nothing may ever come of his designs. Yet one day he has good luck. A woman in the captain's employ—a "donna in casa" whom Giraldi carefully distinguishes from the prostitutes with whom the captain consorts—finds the handkerchief in the house. As it so happens, she has marvelous skills in embroidery, and she recognizes the cloth as Disdemona's because it has an intriguing pattern subtly woven on it "alla moresca": in the Moorish style. Or, as Giraldi writes, in a passage worth quoting in full:

Aveva il capo di squadra una donna in casa, che maravigliosi trapunti faceva sulla tela di rensa; la quale veggendo quel pannicello, e intendendo ch'era della donna del Moro, e ch'era per esserle reso, prima ch'ella l'avesse, si mise a farne un simile; e mentre ella ciò faceva, s'avvide l'Alfiere ch'ella appresso una finestra si stava et da chi passava per la strada poteva essere veduta, onde fece egli ciò vedere al Moro. Il quale tenne certissimo che l'honestissima donna fosse in fatto adultera. Et conchiuse coll'Alfiero, di uccidere lei et il Capo di squadro.[29]

The captain had a housekeeper, who made marvelous stitches on a loom; and when she saw the handkerchief that belonged to the Moor's wife, she set about to make a copy of it before she gave it back to her. While she was copying it, the Ensign realized that she was sitting near a window that let anyone see her who was passing through the street, and he made sure that the Moor saw her too. At this point, the Moor decided there was no question that his most honest wife was an adulteress. And along with the Ensign, he decided then and there to kill her and the Captain.

This is the turning point in Giraldi's story, as two men watch a woman at the window pursue her craft, prompting the Moro to decide irrevocably that Disdemona must die. There is, simply, no equivalent in Shakespeare's play, even if *Othello* has its share of women skilled at embroidery. In fact, Shakespeare can be said to go out of his way to make sure that Othello's handkerchief is *not* copied. When Emilia first picks up the handkerchief that has fallen to the ground in the wake of Othello's anger, she immediately declares, "I'll ha' the work ta'en out" (3.3.300). Iago's appearance onstage a moment later, however, forces her to surrender the precious object, which he labels a "trifle light as air" that "to the jealous, [is] confirmation strong/As proofs of holy writ; this may do something" (327-29). In the scene from act 4 that most closely corresponds to that of Giraldi's embroidering woman, Othello is safely sequestered to watch a play within a play as Cassio himself is confronted with Shakespeare's version of the weaving woman, Bianca. A scene earlier, Cassio gave Bianca the handkerchief, asking her to copy it: "I like the work well; ere it be demanded,/As like enough it will, I'll have it copied;/Take it, and do't" (3.4.187-89). In act 4, however, she approaches him in the street where he is laughing about her with Iago and accosts him, saying, "What did you mean by that same handkerchief you gave me even now? I was a fine fool to take it; I must take out the whole work, a likely piece of work, that you should find it in your chamber, and not know who left it there! This is some minx's token, and I must take out the work; . . . wheresoever you had it, I'll take out no work on 't" (4.1.146-53)—presumably throwing the handkerchief back at the surprised Cassio and prompting in the meantime what seems to be Othello's own moment of recognition: "By heaven, that should be my handkerchief!" (4.1.155). And yet, this moment that throws into negative relief the peripeteia of Giraldi's tale does not serve to convince Othello of Desdemona's infidelity. When Bianca and Cassio have both departed, and Iago and Othello are left alone onstage, Iago asks, "And did you see the handkerchief?"; Othello confusedly responds, "Was that mine?" (4.1.169-70). Here the ocular proof that was so effective in Giraldi's suggestive link between the Ensign and the embroidering *donna* has been cast into doubt, as Othello's use of the conditional in "that should be my handkerchief!" suggests. Thus, if in the final scene Othello tells Desdemona he saw Cassio with the cloth—"I saw my handkerchief in his hand" (5.2.63)—he does so only because Iago tells him that is what he saw ("Yours, by this hand"; 4.1.171). No longer able to trust his own eyes, Othello must rely on Iago, traitor and circulator of textiles, for confirmation.[30]

In *Othello*, Emilia wants to copy the handkerchief but Iago grabs it from her hands; Cassio asks Bianca to copy it, but she refuses, thinking that he's had it from some "minx." That the unusual phrase "take the work out" is uttered in all of these contexts to denote copying suggests an almost primordial fear that imitation will deeply undermine the status of the original, depriving it of its potency. One definition from the *Oxford English Dictionary* connects "taking the work out" to the skill of limning: "A prettie devise to take out the true forme and proporcion of any letter, knott, flower, image, or other worke"; "taking out" thus means imitating a "letter" or "image" through excising or removing the wood so as to create the outline of a pattern with one's knife. Another example cited is from a 1530 grammar book of the French language, *L'esclarcissement de la langue française,* by the linguist and teacher John Palsgrave, who uses the language of carving to refer to copying a piece of writing, as though he were creating what seems to be a commonplace book or miscellany: "I take out a writyng, I coppy a mater of a booke, je copie"—apparently referring to the act of extracting a passage from one book and putting it in another, much as the term was used almost exclusively in the nineteenth century.[31] As Palgrave's thrice-repeated "I" emphasizes—once in French—copying is an act of appropriation and translation: it is not simply about "taking out" but taking over, taking away, denotatively if not connotatively.[32] Or as Richard Wilson has succinctly put it for *Othello,* the repeated use of the phrase makes it unclear to characters and audience alike "whether the embroidery is copied or removed" from the cloth.[33]

Thus, Shakespeare does not merely associate the fateful handkerchief with Ariosto's enchanted and paradoxically inimitable textile. In borrowing that textile for himself, he also aligns himself with an Ariosto who likewise places his pavilion—and by extension his poem—outside the realm of copying and the inevitable deformations and betrayals that accompany the act of imitation. At the same time, two final caveats are in order. Othello, of course, gives not one but two different accounts of the handkerchief's transmission. If his first words about the lost "napkin" draw on Boiardo and Ariosto as he dwells on its mysterious Egyptian origins and its transmission from one woman to another, the second reference, from the final scene, is the far more cursory "it was a handkerchief, an antique token / My father gave my mother" (5.2.216-17), suggesting that the purloined fabric derives not from the world of powerful and at times insidious women who dominate Ariosto's romance, but from Giraldi's more prosaic novella. Was the dense allusion fabricated from borrowings of Italy's great romance poems simply manufactured by Othello as a way of intimidating Desdemona into thinking that she no longer had the ability to "subdue" him and bring him into her sway?

And does its displacement by a second, contradictory narrative serve to emphasize that such a power, and the romance that embodied it, were no more than fictions? For what we have in Giraldi's tale of Disdemona and the Moro is a romance shorn of its magical components, in which the unnamed "donna di casa" takes the place of the prophetic sibyl or Cassandra. Or to put it in terms Giraldi used in his own treatise on the *Furioso*, "la fabbrica" or the fabric—a word Giraldi frequently used to refer to the romance poem, which necessarily proceeds in a "continuo filo" or continuous thread—without its prophetic embroidering.[34] Once a singular cloth linking a converted African to a Christian woman, in the novella the pavilion is reduced to a handkerchief that becomes the basis for "ocular proof," the vehicle through which Disdemona is unofficially tried and indicted, and the marriage dissolved. Othello's paradoxical doubling of stories about the handkerchief's origins serves in its own way to enact a form of inexact copying—or at least to acknowledge the twin sources from which Shakespeare drew his play.

The second caveat is that Shakespeare's deeply ironic alliance with Ariosto and his refusal to acknowledge the status of the "copy" may take on another dimension when one considers Italy's relationship to the Turkish threat as well as the fate of the Este dynasty that had patronized Ariosto, Boiardo, and Giraldi alike. Cyprus, still in Venice's hands when Giraldi was writing his *novelle,* was definitively lost to the Ottomans in 1570, and the Christian forces that gathered at Lepanto a year later failed to reclaim it despite their otherwise much vaunted victory against the Turks. Thus the tale of Othello is already a tale locked in a past of Venetian naval glory—a glory that the English would increasingly come to claim for themselves in the later sixteenth and early seventeenth centuries. And the Este family celebrated on Boiardo's pavilion with a seemingly endless series of Alfonsi would come to an end in 1597, some seven years before *Othello* was first performed, when Alfonso II died without heirs. The town of Ferrara founded by Hector's descendants and celebrated in the *Orlando innamorato* and the *Furioso* alike devolved to the papacy, along with the considerable lands that stretched from Liguria to the Adriatic. Hence the world that Shakespeare allusively gives us, one populated by scheming enchantresses, brave Italian women, and former Muslims ready to make the ultimate sacrifice for their bride and their new faith, is effectively no more, and the murder of Rodomonte—the ghost of Ruggiero's, and Othello's, past—comes too late to save either Othello or his bride.

Yet Ariosto could be argued to have intuited this dismal future through his very choice of the subject of Cassandra's tent: a single Ippolito, rather than a dozen Alfonsi. When Boiardo was writing book 2 of the *Orlando innamorato* in the early 1480s, the most recent Alfonso—Alfonso II— was a young child; he reigned as duke while Ariosto was writing the *Furioso,* and his son Ercole II would succeed him in 1534, not long after Ariosto's own death. Ippolito, however, Alfonso's brother and for whom the pavilion was woven by the mysterious Cassandra, died in 1520, several years after the first edition of the *Furioso* was published. Ariosto did not remove the pavilion from subsequent editions, nor did he alter the passage in the closing canto in which it is described.[35] Thus while Boiardo's—and Brandimarte's—wedding tent is testimony to an ongoing and seemingly eternal presence in Italy of "Alfonsi," the pavilion of Ruggiero and Bradamante looks only to a particular moment in time, one embodied by the inimitable Ippolito who left no heirs, and whose life can only be memorialized by Cassandra's weaving in the *Furioso*'s 1521 and 1532 editions. If the sibyl looked to a potentially endlessly unfolding sequence of dynastic rulers, Cassandra turned to a single individual who cannot escape time's constraints and who leaves no future generation behind him: what is unique necessarily dies, leaving no copy behind. For readers of the poem after 1520, the historical moment prophesied by the tent several millennia before is already over, the story of Cassandra is already a thing of the past.

Shakespeare may thus be true to Ariosto in the most genuine sense. Uncopied, its work never "taken out," Othello's handkerchief fails to achieve new life in an age in which Christian Cyprus and the Este dynasty no longer exist. At the same time, as the handkerchief presumably returns to Venice in Cassio's keeping—"How came you, Cassio, by a handkerchief,/That was my wife's?" (5.2.320–21) are Othello's last words on the matter—it may be that Shakespeare foresaw an as yet unwritten future for this textile and its forlorn prophecies after all.

Notes

My thanks to Troy Tower and the editors of this volume for their helpful comments on a penultimate draft, as well as to Louise Clubb and other colleagues at the Renaissance Society of America conference in 2005 and colleagues at the Theatre Without Borders workshop in Prague in 2007, when earlier versions of this essay were read.

1. All references to *Othello* are from the Arden Shakespeare edition, edited by M. R. Ridley (London: Methuen, 1965).

2. Leslie Fiedler, *The Stranger in Shakespeare* (New York: Stern and Day, 1973), 174.

3. In "The Story Is Extant and Writ in Very Choice Italian," in *Shakespeare, Italy and Intertextuality*, ed. Michele Marrapodi (Manchester: Manchester University Press, 2004), 91–106, Jason Lawrence sees the playwright Robert Greene as a mediating influence between the *Furioso* and Shakespeare; see the further development of Lawrence's argument in his recent *"Who the Devil Taught You So Much Italian?": Italian Language Learning and Literary Imitation in Early Modern England* (Manchester: Manchester University Press, 2005), 151–63. Lawrence argues that the presence in *Othello* of the *Orlando furioso* accounts "for the most significant addition to material derived from [Giraldi's] novella" (102), thereby generating the heroic dimensions of a largely domestic tale. See also Maristella de Panizza Lorch for an earlier consideration of the impact of Ariosto on *Othello:* "Honest Iago and the Lusty Moor: The Humanistic Drama of Honestas/Voluptas in a Shakespearean Context," in *Theatre of the English and Italian Renaissance,* ed. J. R. Mulryne and Margaret Shewring (New York: St. Martin's, 1991), 204–20. Lawrence Rhu talks about Orlando's bracelet as an irrevocable sign of love that affects Shakespeare's plot in *Much Ado About Nothing* in "Agons of Interpretation: Ariostan Source and Elizabethan Meaning in Spenser, Harington, and Shakespeare," *Renaissance Drama* 24 (1993): 176–79.

4. All citations from the *Orlando furioso* are of the two-volume edition of Lanfranco Caretti (Turin: Einaudi, 1966). Translations are my own.

5. See Peter Marinelli's suggestive discussion of Ruggiero's African origins in the *Orlando innamorato* of Boiardo: "Ruggiero's 'Saracen-ness' is an extreme representation of a condition common to all who have not yet been moved to conversion by grace. Obviously no Este ever believed he had a demi-Saracen among his ancestors. However, all of them knew about having to work the 'infidel' out of their natures; and that, in essence, is what the story of Ruggiero begins to record. The grand, complex elaboration of this story was the work of Ariosto in the third and last stage, but Boiardo provided the crucial incentives"; *Ariosto and Boiardo: The Origins of Orlando Furioso* (Columbia: University of Missouri Press, 1987), 53.

6. John Semple Smart, *Shakespeare: Truth and Tradition* (London: Kessinger, 1929), 183. Perhaps one of the best arguments supporting Shakespeare's reading of Ariosto in Italian is furnished by Roger Prior in "Shakespeare's Debt to Ariosto," *Notes and Queries* 48 (2001): 289–92. As he begins a painstaking reading of the comparable passages from *Othello* and the *Furioso,* Prior writes, "The two accounts thus share key narrative elements, and there can be no doubt that Shakespeare borrowed from Ariosto those which were not in Cinthio. In theory he could have got them from Sir John Harington's translation of *Orlando,* but in fact there is little evidence that he consulted it. He studied Ariosto, however, with considerable care" (290). Prior's reading focuses not only on the stanza with the Sibyl, but also on the several stanzas concerning the pavilion and its transmission, noting, for example, the resonances between "seta" and silk, the "vermo infernal" (infernal worm) and "hallowed worms," and "il mondo" and "in the world."

7. While Harington is at pains to tell us far more about Cassandra's sad fate than is Ariosto, he does not translate the phrase "furor profetico" when he writes of the pavilion's skilled embroiderer, giving us instead

> Two thousand years before, or not much lesse,
> This rich pavillion had in Troy bene wrought
> By faire *Cassandra,* that same Prophetesse

That had (but all in vaine) in youth bene taught
Of future things to give most certain guesse
For her true speech was ever set at naught.
She wrought this same with helpe of many other
And gave it *Hector* her beloved brother. (Stanza 64)
Orlando furioso, ed. Robert McNulty (Oxford: Clarendon, 1972), 549.

8. John Harington, *Orlando Furioso,* "Allegorie to Canto 46," 557.

9. Recently, Jean Howard has suggested that "in the play's kaleidoscope of possibilities, the handkerchief is at times a symbol of hope—the hope that a foreigner and a native can bridge the cultural and racial gap that makes their marriage seem an impossibility to members of the Venetian community such as Brabantio." And she continues: "But it also becomes a symbol of seemingly unbridgeable cultural difference—a love token freighted with a threat if its unfathomable [to Desdemona] codes of passage and preservation are violated" [brackets in original]; Jean Howard, "*Othello* as an Adventure Play," in *Approaches to Teaching Shakespeare's Othello,* ed. Peter Erickson and Maurice Hunt (New York: Modern Language Association of America, 2005), 98–99. Howard makes her point without reference to the *Furioso;* I am interested in extending it in a way that takes Ariosto's poem into account.

10. This was the discovery of Peter Alexander, in *Review of English Studies* 8 (1932): 99–101: "In Boiardo's *Orlando innamorato,* the work is done by a sibyl as in Shakespeare. It would be too much to conclude from this that Shakespeare drew on both passages, but it is certainly a possibility" (100). More recently, Andrew Cairncross mistakenly concluded in "Shakespeare and Ariosto: *Much Ado About Nothing, King Lear,* and *Othello,*" *Renaissance Quarterly* 29, no. 2 (1976), that the phrase "furor poetico" "might conceivably have come from another source, and the handkerchief is already in Cinthio" but then adds, "the sibyl and the magic come from Ariosto alone" (181).

11. Michele Marrapodi has edited several collections in the last decade aimed at identifying the diverse and often contradictory meanings of Italian literature and culture for the English Renaissance. In addition to the volume cited in note 3, they include *Shakespeare's Italy: Functions of Italian Locations in Renaissance Drama,* coedited with A. J. Hoenselaars, Marcello Cappuzzo, and L. Falzon Stantucci (Manchester: Manchester University Press, 1993); *Italian Studies in Shakespeare and His Contemporaries* (Newark: University of Delaware Press, 1999); and *Italian Culture in the Drama of Shakespeare and His Contemporaries* (Hampshire: Ashgate, 2007), in which Marrapodi argues that he and his colleagues are interested not in the "passive influence of Italian source material on Elizabethans" but the "ways in which the otherness of Italy and the politics of resistance that it implies worked on the ideological construction" of English drama ("Appropriating Italy: Towards a New Approach to Renaissance Drama," 4–5). Michael Wyatt's *The Italian Encounter with Tudor England: A Cultural Politics of Translation* (Cambridge: Cambridge University Press, 2005) is a thorough study of the presence of Italians in England, focusing in its second half on John Florio as an intermediary figure between the two cultures. Earlier work did often focus on source studies, but the occasionally pedantic nature of this scholarship and cavalier judgments about the relative merits of English vis-à-vis Italian works have prompted subsequent scholars to ignore this rich literature. See in particular the valuable studies of M. A. Scott, including her "Bibliography of Elizabethan Translations from the Italian," which appeared in a series of articles in *PMLA* from 1895 to 1898; Lewis Einstein, *The Italian Renaissance in England* (New York: Columbia University Press, 1902); and Richard Garnett, *Italian Literature* (London, 1898). It seems to me that as

bracingly theoretical as much recent work on the relationship of Shakespeare to Italy is, it could benefit from deeper familiarity with this earlier scholarship.

12. Eduardo Saccone, *Il soggetto del Furioso e altri saggi tra quattro e cinquecento* (Naples: Liguori, 1974). More recently, Marc Schachter, following Saccone's lead, has suggested that "fidelity is the *Furioso*'s problem, fidelity, or the impossibility of fidelity," in "'Egli s'innamorò del suo valore': Leone, Bradamante and Ruggiero in the 1532 *Orlando Furioso*," *Modern Language Notes* 115 (2000): 64. Clearly, it would seem that the poem vacillates between the two—a vacillation in which the fidelity of literary imitation should also be seen as playing a role, as I will go on to suggest.

13. Albert Ascoli, *Ariosto's Bitter Harmony: Crisis and Evasion in the Italian Renaissance* (Princeton: Princeton University Press, 1987). For the quotation on betrayal, see 387; for comments on Cassandra as weaver and "surrogate poet-figure" for Ariosto himself, see 389–92. Ascoli ultimately concludes that just as Cassandra is betrayed by an Apollo who curses her after she refuses to sleep with him, so is Ariosto betrayed by his patron and his public. "[Cassandra] embodies the poet's mute and resigned protest of his reader's inability to hear and believe him. She stands for his fate as victim of a betrayal—less by those readers than by poetry itself . . . which lends its own most serious utterances to trivialization and laughter" (391). Peter Marinelli suggests that such an emphasis on betrayal throughout the *Furioso* is already present in the *Orlando innamorato* and ultimately looks back to the world of the *Aeneid*: "In Boiardo's hands, popular romantic history becomes part of a cyclical movement, and the disasters that fall on all the children of Hector's line . . . recall the death by treachery of Aeneas, the widowhood of Lavinia, [and] the orphaning of Ascanius"—as well as shadowing "the lives of those descendants as far as Bradamante"; *Ariosto and Boiardo,* 63.

14. See the fragment cited by Pio Rajna in *Le fonti dell'Orlando furioso* (Florence: Sansoni, 1975), 382, from the *Opere minori* (1:125) in which Ariosto calls attention to the wars and devastations of Italy resulting from the transfer of the seat of the Roman empire to Constantinople. Interestingly, the piece is placed in the mouth of the Sibyl of Cuma to dissuade the emperor from leaving Rome.

15. Might not Desdemona's and Emilia's exchange in 4.3 be a comment on this story, as Desdemona asks, "Wouldst thou do such a thing for all the world?" and Emilia eventually suggests that "I think it is their husbands' faults/If women do fall"; 4.3.67; 86–87.

16. For a recent reading of the interpolated tale of the manipulative spouse and the dangerous *maga,* see Ronald Martinez, "Two Odysseys: Rinaldo's Po Journey and the Poet's Homecoming in *Orlando furioso,*" in *Renaissance Transactions: Ariosto and Tasso,* ed. Valeria Finucci (Durham: Duke University Press, 1999), 17–55.

17. These very different Melissas—one the beneficial enabler of Bradamante and Ruggiero's wedding, the other the vindictive *maga* who ruins a couple's love—have led some scholars to protest that there are, in fact, two Melissas in the poem. Yet the only defensible argument is a weak one: that in his haste Ariosto overlooked the fact that he gave the "nobil donna" of canto 43 the same name as his favorite sorceress; Donato Internoscia, "Are There Two Melissas, Both Enchantresses, in the *Furioso*?" *Italica* 25, no. 3 (1948): 217. I have not had a chance to see the recent paper by Gerarda Stimato, "Doppia Melissa," given at the December 2007 conference of the Istituto di studi rinascimentali di Ferrara.

18. Just as Boiardo's tent is modeled on previous pavilions from earlier chivalric poems; see Pio Rajna, *Le fonti,* 378–83. Rajna also cites Catullus's epithalamion for the parents of Achilles, with its fertile bed ("pulvinar . . . geniale") and nuptial cover, as a possible source for Ariosto (381).

19. Just two cantos earlier, Brandimarte becomes the privileged spectator of a series of representations depicting the future Este family; see 2.25.41-56. While here, as in 2.27, his own implication in the unfolding narrative is more casual than not, Boiardo seems to have privileged this convert to Christianity as a vehicle, albeit an unwitting one, for the *Innamorato*'s prophecies about the Este.

20. Rajna, *Le fonti,* 130.

21. Boiardo's place in the English literary canon has been largely ignored, even among Spenser critics; see Charles Ross's measured comments on the possible impact of the *Innamorato* on the *Faerie Queene* in *The Spenser Encyclopedia,* ed. A. C. Hamilton (Toronto: University of Toronto Press, 1990), 101. My thanks to Professor Ross for an email exchange on Boiardo's presence in Elizabethan England. As for Shakespeare, the only works that came to my attention focus on an unlikely relationship between *Timon* and *Timone Comoedia,* a Latin play by Boiardo: Richard Garnett, *Italian Literature* (London, 1898), and R. Warwick Bond, "Lucian and Boiardo in *Timon of Athens,*" *Modern Language Review* 26 (1931): 52-68. Bond closes his article by turning to Florio's *First Fruites,* as he argues that while it is impossible to "argue fully the larger question of Shakespeare's knowledge of Italian," it is unquestionable that Shakespeare was familiar with Florio's works—and perhaps with Florio himself. He closes with the rhetorical question, "Does an intelligent and busy Shakespeare study conversation-manuals at this rate, unless he is learning Italian?" (67).

22. Ronald Martinez makes the intriguing suggestion that "Rinaldo's tardiness, rather than merely undercutting the character, is the narrator's ploy for multiplying the goals of the paladin's journey, which remain suspended between the vision of future Ferrarese glories and the tragic death of Brandimarte"; "Two Odysseys," 46; see also David Quint, "Death of Brandimarte," *Annali* 12 (1994): 75-85. One might add that here again, Melissa is indirectly responsible for Brandimarte's death, as she is largely the genetrix of the tale that Rinaldo listens to as he sails down the Po.

23. See Eric MacPhail, "Ariosto and the Prophetic Moment," *Modern Language Notes* 116, no.1 (2001): 44: "For the poet who describes his own activity with the verbs 'ordire' and 'tramare' or 'lavorare,' history resembles a *tela Penelopes* constantly rewoven in new and unexpected patterns." The title of Peter Wiggins's book acknowledges directly the weaving metaphors at work in Ariosto's poem: Peter DeSa Wiggins, *Figures in Ariosto's Tapestry: Character and Design in the "Orlando Furioso"* (Baltimore: Johns Hopkins University Press, 1986).

24. As Ascoli elaborates; *Ariosto's Bitter Harmony,* 262-63.

25. The orality of the *Innamorato,* of course, is only a fiction, even as Boiardo often attempts to re-create the dynamics of the *cantastorie* or minstrels. See Dennis Looney on metaphors of weaving in both Ariosto's and Boiardo's poems and on the extent to which the narrator of the *Innamorato* occasionally "drops his pose as 'cantastorie' and refers to the act of reading the poem"; *Compromising the Classics: Romance Epic Narrative in the Italian Renaissance* (Detroit: Wayne State University Press, 1996), 56. On Ariosto's competitive relationship to Boiardo—he sought not to "sfruttare la scia del successo di Boiardo, ma superarlo col proprio," as distinct from the efforts of other poets more faithful to Boiardo—see Giuseppe Sangirardi, *Boiardismo Ariostesco: Presenza e trattamento dell'* Orlando Innamorato *nel* Furioso (Lucca: Maria Pacini Fazzi, 1993), 29. As Antonio Franceschetti notes in "The *Orlando Innamorato* and the Genesis of the *Furioso*" (in *Ariosto Today: Contemporary Perspectives,* ed. Donald Beecher, Massimo Ciavolella, and Roberto Fedi [Toronto: University of Toronto Press, 2003]), Ariosto's opening lines ("Cosa non detta in prosa mai né in rima") demonstrate that in the *Furioso* there is "no reference

to the previous poem or its author as is to be found in the first octave of the fourth book published by Niccolò degli Agostini" (33).

26. See *The three first Bookes of that famous Noble Gentleman and Learned Poet, Matteo Maria Boiardo, Earle of Scandiano in Lombardia. Done into English Heroicall Verse by R[obert].T[ofte]. Gentleman* (London, 1598)—the first three "books" are really the first three cantos—and *The Blazon of Jealousie. A subject not written of by any heretofore. First written in Italian by that learned gentleman Benedetto Varchi, sometimes Lord Chauncelor unto the Signorie of Venice, and translated into English, with speciall notes upon the same, by R[obert]. T[ofte]. Gentleman* (London, 1615).

27. See David Quint, "The Figure of Atlante: Ariosto and Boiardo's Poem," *Modern Language Notes* 94 (1979): 77-91, particularly 81: "The identification of Atlante as a surrogate figure for Boiardo . . . suggests that the enchanted palace may be a microcosm not so much of the *Furioso* as of the *Innamorato.*"

28. This analysis begs the question as to whether Giraldi had Ariosto in mind while writing his novella. He knew the *Furioso* well, defending it and the romance genre more generally against conservative Aristotelians in his treatise *Discorso intorno al comporre dei romanzi*. More pertinently, as we have seen, the novella was hardly an alien form to the *Furioso,* and at least several stories from the *Ecatommiti* share plots with interpolated tales from Ariosto's poem. Whether the tale of the Moro and Disdemona looks back to either the all-encompassing story of Ruggiero's and Bradamante's long courtship or to one of the many tales within the *Furioso*—such as that of a jealous husband and a manipulative *maga* frustrated in her own designs to consummate an adulterous passion—must remain speculative.

29. *Gli Ecatommiti* (Florence: Borghi, 1833), 935. Translations are my own. There is a partial translation by Raymond Shaw of the story about Disdemona and Othello in M. R. Ridley's edition of *Othello*, appendix 1, 239-45. For Giraldi's impact on Shakespeare, see Kenneth Muir, *The Sources of Shakespeare's Plays* (New Haven: Yale University Press, 1978), 182-86; Daniel Vitkus, *Turning Turk: English Theatre and the Multicultural Mediterranean: 1570-1630* (New York: Palgrave, 2003); and Barbara Majelli, "Riscrivendo 'L'alfiere': Cinthio, Greene e la figura di Iago in *Othello,*" in *Intertestualitá Shakespeariane,* ed. Michele Marrapodi (Rome: Bulzoni, 2003), 253-73. Louise George Clubb calls attention to a third Italian source on *Othello*, that of the *commedia dell'arte*, in her brief remarks in "Italian Stories on the Stage," *The Cambridge Companion to Shakespeare,* ed. Margreta de Grazia and Stanley Wells (Cambridge: Cambridge University Press, 2001), 45.

30. For a suggestive article on the way that *Othello* "disrupts women's historic relation to textiles"—"textiles mark and then signify the contested female body, which can be possessed entirely by men, and, thus reduced, may be disposed of violently"—see Susan Frye, "Staging Women's Relations to Textiles in Shakespeare's *Othello* and *Cymbeline,*" in *Early Modern Visual Culture: Representation, Race, and Empire in Renaissance England,* ed. Peter Erickson and Clark Hulse (Philadelphia: University of Pennsylvania Press, 2000), 215, 221.

31. Cited in the *Oxford English Dictionary.*

32. This is something that Palsgrave seems to have felt fairly strongly about, since he made special provisions for his proofs to be corrected by no one but himself or his "assigns." He likewise insisted that no one should buy a copy of his book without "his own special consent." Henry Morley, *English Writers: An Attempt Towards a History of English Literature* (Oxford: Oxford University Press, 1887), 14.

33. See Richard Wilson, *Secret Shakespeare: Studies in Theatre, Religion, and Resistance* (New York: Palgrave, 2004), 177. Only a few critics have noted the discrepancy

regarding the copying of the handkerchief. Lynda Boose, "Othello's Handkerchief: The Recognizance and Pledge of Love" [1975], reprinted in *Critical Essays on Shakespeare's Othello*, ed. Anthony Gerard Barthelemy (New York: G.K. Hall, 1994), notes that "whereas Cinthio's 'Bianca' is spied in the act of copying the patterned handkerchief, Shakespeare's Bianca comes onstage to emphasize her inability either to copy or 'take out' the work" (60). For Boose, the failure to copy symbolizes the uniqueness of this "symbolic token, the act between one husband and one wife"; it exists as "a unique absolute and is therefore not subject to duplication or eradication."

34. The citations are in Looney, *Compromising the Classics*, 98–99, taken from Giraldi's *Discorso intorno al comporre dei romanzi* of 1549.

35. Ariosto's alterations to what was canto 40 in the 1516 *Furioso*—canto 46 in the 1521 and 1532 editions—were relatively minor; the most significant one involves the omission of the final stanza of the description of the pavilion (40.71) in which Ippolito is mentioned as the protector of not only Ferrara but the entire "dominio" on occasions when Alfonso was absent; Ludovico Ariosto, *Orlando Furioso secondo la princeps del 1516*, ed. Marco Dorigatti (Florence: Olschki, 2006), 1005.

Misreading and Misogyny: Ariosto, Spenser, and Shakespeare

KASEY EVANS

I N ACT 2, scene 1 of *Much Ado About Nothing,* the city of Messina celebrates the victorious return of the Aragonese army with a masquerade,
rehearsing in a comic key the motifs of disguise and misrecognition that
will later modulate into tragic threats. Beatrice seizes the opportunity
to torment her rival Benedick, pretending not to know him under his
mask, railing about him in the third person. Her teasing hits home, and
Benedick fulminates to the Aragonese Prince Don Pedro:

> She speaks poniards, and every word stabs. . . . I would not marry her, though
> she were endowed with all that Adam had left him before he transgressed. She
> would have made Hercules have turned spit, yea, and have cleft his club to make
> the fire too. . . . I would to God some scholar would conjure her, for certainly,
> while she is here, a man may live as quiet in hell as in a sanctuary, and people sin
> upon purpose, because they would go thither. . . . (2.1.231–43)[1]

Repeatedly, Benedick imagines Beatrice assuming the masculine part.
Her verbal assaults take the form of phallic penetration. She seems simultaneously to play the prelapsarian Adam and his imaginary widow
("endowed" in the particular sense of "possessing a dowry")—roles that
both entail the exercise of masculine prerogatives.[2] To Benedick, Beatrice seems more emasculating even than Ovid's Omphale, who enslaved
Hercules, dressed him in women's clothes, and forced him to spin like a

261

maid; Beatrice would render him "turnspit": a dog running on a tread-wheel to turn a roasting spit over the fire (OED 1). Emphasizing the sexual nature of this humiliation, Benedick describes Hercules's phallic club "cleft" like the female genitalia and consumed as kindling in the roasting fire. Benedick's defense against these effeminizing threats is an explicitly theatrical one; he imagines a scholar performing a conjuration, exorcising Beatrice to hell like an evil spirit.[3] This speech thus establishes a constellation of concerns central to *Much Ado About Nothing* and to early modern English culture: disguise and identity; reading and misreading; gender and sexuality; performance and efficacy. Specifically, the speech identifies Benedick's virulent misogyny as a consequence of misreading and sexual anxiety. Supposing himself incognito, Benedick interprets Beatrice's "poniards" as public slander, texts that render him an object of common scorn. He experiences this textualization as emasculating and retaliates with this misogynistic rant. Finally, his fantasy of exorcism, the imagined performance that will expel Beatrice's scorn, calls attention to the masquerade, the actual performance that has engendered her mockery. Theatricality here is both cause and consolation for a threatened sense of masculinity.

I begin with this scene not just because it encapsulates prominent concerns in *Much Ado About Nothing;* the claim that a Shakespearean comedy demonstrates the subversive potential of gender performance hardly needs rehearsing. Instead, I want to locate these concerns at the end of a sixteenth-century textual genealogy that begins with Ludovico Ariosto's *Orlando furioso* (1516, 1521, 1532); enters the English canon with Spenser's *Faerie Queene* (1590, 1596); and makes its transition to the English stage with *Much Ado About Nothing* (1598–99).[4] The Ferrarese poet's tale of Ariodante and Ginevra becomes Spenser's parable of Phedon and Claribella, which yields in turn to Shakespeare's plot of Claudio and Hero. The problems of theatrically staged misreadings and their misogynistic consequences, I will show, inhere in the tale from its Italian beginning. While Shakespeare's play offers one compelling, carnivalesque answer, these questions of gender and interpretation are cultural preoccupations spanning multiple decades, genres, and linguistic traditions. In using Ariosto and Spenser to trace the literary history of Shakespeare's tale of Claudio and Hero, then, I aim to limn an early modern intellectual tradition and to establish the ubiquity of ideas perhaps too narrowly understood, in Renaissance studies, as Shakespearean preoccupations.

Rinaldo: Reading as Writing

The mechanics of the Ariodante-Ginevra plot of the *Orlando furioso,* which remain relatively unchanged throughout this textual genealogy, might encourage the misprision that the poem shares the familiar early modern obsession with female chastity and circulation. The knight Ariodante and the princess Ginevra are betrothed and in love. Ariodante's envious friend Polinesso, resenting their happiness, seduces Ginevra's handmaid, Dalinda, who receives Polinesso at night on the balcony of Ginevra's bedchamber. Stationed below, Ariodante witnesses this apparent proof of Ginevra's infidelity and leaves the court in despair, while his loyal brother demands Ginevra's death. Her father schedules a tournament to try her innocence. Ariodante, surmising the truth, returns in disguise to defend Ginevra's honor and defeats Polinesso, who confesses before dying on the field.

Despite the ostensible importance of chastity in this plot, the narrative takes pains to establish interactions among men as its primary interest. In fact, opportunistic fraternal alliances characterize allegedly chivalric conduct from the outset of the *Furioso*. In canto 1, Charlemagne's knight Rinaldo forgets his political fealty and suggests joining forces with the Saracen knight Ferraù to capture the fleeing maiden Angelica: "Come l'avremo in potestate, allora/di ch'esser de' si provi con la spada" (Once we have her in our power, then we will fight for possession of her with our swords).[5] Rinaldo suggests abandoning their literal swords for their phallic counterparts, turning their *spade* not against each other but against Angelica. Their common sexual agenda trumps their divisive militaristic one, and masculine confraternity precedes and enables both sexual and martial virility. Whether we read the planned gang rape as a heterosexual encounter or a mediated homosexual one, the opportunistic union of Rinaldo and Ferraù effaces the possibility—or, here, the actuality—of female resistance. Singularly unconcerned with preserving female chastity, the knights instead forge a fraternal alliance dedicated to the plucking of Angelica's legendary rose.

These are precisely the stakes of the Ariodante episode, where fraternity confers the authority and the authorship to ignore, or to erase, the reality of the virginal female body. In this tale, male homosocial alliances serve as the guarantors of an authorial prerogative: the privilege of having one's readings and misreadings poetically performed and protected.

In defiance of the uxorious mandates of chivalric courtly love and bolstered by fraternal support, Rinaldo appropriates the female body as a text, an opportunity to author his own worldly reputation. Egregious and slanderous misreadings are the occasion for, and the consequence of, the masculine authorial prerogative.

The episode begins when Rinaldo travels to Scotland to draft troops for Charlemagne's holy war. Again, he forgets his martial responsibility in favor of a self-serving mission; and again, the narrative is concerned less with the damsel in distress than with Rinaldo's homosocial alliances. He immediately encounters an abbey, whose monks (*frati*) institutionalize and literalize fraternal bonds. When Rinaldo inquires "dove si possa in qualche fatto eggregio/l'uom dimostrar, se merta biasmo o pregio" (where by some notable deed a man could show whether he deserved blame or praise; 4.55.7–8), the monks reveal Ginevra's plight, but they warn Rinaldo against accepting the charge:

> Risposongli ch'errando in quelli boschi,
> trovar potria strane aventure e molte:
> ma come i luoghi, i fatti ancor sono foschi;
> che non se n'ha notizia le più volte.
> –Cerca (diceano) andar dove conoschi
> che l'opre tue non restino sepolte,
> acciò dietro al periglio e alla fatica
> segua la fama, e il debito ne dica. (4.56)

They responded that by wandering in those woods, he could find many strange adventures, but that deeds accomplished there often remained as hidden as the place itself, and frequently escaped notice. "Try," they said, "to go where you can be certain that your actions will not remain buried, so that your risks and triumphs will be attended by fame, who will recount them in turn."

The monks assert an authorial prerogative: the power to predict whose fame will endure and whose will remain buried. This preoccupation with worldly renown, a set piece of anticlerical satire, has a specific, local function here: extending this fraternity to the poet-narrator of the *Furioso*, who, not four stanzas earlier, offered a different prediction about Rinaldo's fortunes.

> Sopra la Scozia ultimamente sorse,
> dove la selva Calidonia appare,
> che spesso fra gli antiqui ombrosi cerri
> s'ode sonar di bellicosi ferri.

> Vanno per quella i cavallieri erranti,
> incliti in arme, di tutta Bretagna,
> e de' prossimi luoghi e de' distanti,
>
> . . . .
>
> Chi non ha gran valor, non vada inanti;
> che dove cerca onor, morte guadagna.
> Gran cose in essa già fece Tristano,
> Lancillotto, Galasso, Artù e Galvano,
>
> ed altri cavallieri e de la nuova
> e de la vecchia Tavola famosi,
> restano ancor di più d'una lor pruova
> li monumenti e li trofei pomposi. (4.51.5–4.53.4)

Finally he landed in Scotland, when the Caledonian forest appeared, where so often amid the ancient shadowy oaks one could hear the clash of warlike swords. Through that would travel knights errant, legendary in battle, from all over Britain, and from other places, near and far. . . . The man who lacks great valor should not venture within, for where he seeks honor he will earn only death. Great deeds were done there by Tristan, Lancelot, Galahad, Arthur, and Gawain, and other famous knights of the new Round Table and of the old. Proud trophies and monuments to more than one of their great deeds still survive.

The monks' counsel poses subtle, but crucial, challenges to the narrator's predictions. While the narrator cautions that unworthy adventurers will find death, the monks extend this grim fate to all deeds performed in the forest, which will go as unremarked as if entombed (*sepolte*). And while the narrator testifies to extant monuments of chivalric triumphs, the monks object that deeds remain *foschi,* shadowy as the woods themselves.

The narrator settles these disagreements by erasing the monks from the narrative altogether. In a silent intervention, the poet-figure thus obscures the challenge of the *frati* to his authorial prerogative, and the narrative goes on to fulfill his predictions (the *selva oscura* reveals, rather than buries, the truth of Ginevra's story, and the text of the *Furioso* spreads Rinaldo's fame). Robert Durling has ascribed this kind of despotic judgment by the *Furioso*'s narrator to a "divine analogy" between the poet-figure and God.[6] Exercising an omnipotent prerogative, the narrator effaces dissent from the poem. The appearance of the fraternity in the poem has served, in the end, as merely a temporary demurral of the power to erase resistance and opposition to the mandates of the narrator-author.

Conversely, the narrator rewards Rinaldo, a hero *degradato*[7] who satirizes the ideals of chivalric romance.[8] Although Rinaldo undertakes

Ginevra's defense, his intentions defy the chivalric mandate of uxorious worship of the unattainable woman:

> Sia vero o falso che Ginevra tolto
> s'abbia il suo amante, io non riguardo a questo:
> . . . .
>
> Non vo' già dir ch'ella non l'abbia fatto;
> che nol sappiendo, il falso dir potrei;
> dirò ben che non de' per simil atto
> punizion cadere alcuna in lei;
> . . . .
>
> S'un medesimo ardor, s'un disir pare
> inchina e sforza l'uno e l'altro sesso
> a quel suave fin d'amor, che pare
> all'ignorante vulgo un grave eccesso;
> perché si de' punir donna o biasmare,
> che con uno o più d'uno abbia commesso
> quel che l'uom fa con quante n'ha appetito,
> e lodato ne va, non che impunito?
>
> Son fatti in questa legge disuguale
> veramente alle donne espressi torti;
> e spero in Dio mostrar che gli è gran male
> che tanto lungamente si comporti. (4.64.1–4.67.4)

Whether it's true or false that Ginevra received her lover [on her balcony] does not concern me. . . . I cannot say that she did not do it; not knowing the truth, I might speak falsely. What I will say is that no punishment should fall on her for such an act. . . . If the same ardor, the same urge drives one sex and the other to the gentle consummation of love, which to the ignorant throng seems a grave sin, why should a woman be punished or blamed when with one or several men she has done the very thing a man does with as many women as he has an appetite for, and earns for it praise rather than censure? It is clear that this unequal law does women outright wrong. I hope by God to show what a great wrong it is that this law has survived so long.

Rinaldo remembers his Arthurian romance; however unjustly, he assimilates *this* Ginevra to her literary antecedent, Guinevere, the courtly adulteress *par excellence*. But Rinaldo seems less interested in the Arthurian tradition than in his own reputation; he passes quickly over the possibility of Ginevra's innocence in order to project his own condition, narcissistically, onto her plight. In the tortuous logic of his speech, Rinaldo imprecates the cruel author of the sexist law three times; he twice reiterates that he neither knows nor cares about Ginevra's actual innocence and twice declares that he would excuse Ginevra even if she had consummated her passion. His reluctance to blame resounds with the terms of his own endeavor in Scotland: proving himself worthy of *biasmo o pregio.* Empathetically identified with Ginevra's susceptibility to judgment, Rinaldo suddenly finds himself blame-averse. When he announces his intention to defend any woman who has committed sexual acts *con uno o più d'uno*—a description irrelevant to Ginevra's plight as he has heard it described—Rinaldo seems to be less concerned with Ginevra than with the project of defense in general. If he could only obviate the category of blame altogether, Rinaldo would secure not only Ginevra's pardon but also his own noble legacy.

Although unconcerned with Ginevra *per se,* Rinaldo is singularly preoccupied by the men whose legal precedents he will overturn. He curses "chi tal legge pose" (the man who founded this law; 4.63.5) and then "chi la può patire" (he who can endure it; 4.63.6). Rinaldo returns compulsively in his speech to various incarnations of this imaginary man. He repeats, "fu ingiusto o . . . fu matto / chi fece prima li statuti rei" (whoever first made these royal statutes was unjust or mad; 4.65.5–6), and when he concludes with a final reiteration of this conviction, his fraternity chimes in to agree: "Rinaldo ebbe il consenso universale, / che fur gli antiqui ingiusti e mali accorti, / che consentiro a così iniqua legge, / e mal fa il re, che può, né la corregge" (all concurred with Rinaldo that the ancients were unjust and careless when they consented to such an iniquitous law, and that the king did wrong in failing to right it though he could; 4.67.5–8). Rinaldo and his peanut gallery concentrate not on Ginevra's *difesa* but on the figures whom Rinaldo will overcome, whose imagined unjustness, madness, imprudence, and irresponsibility set the bar low for Rinaldo's chivalric success. In the tale of Ginevra, Rinaldo can read only the image of his projected success.

The misreading of Ginevra enabled by Rinaldo's projection and the monks' approval leads to an ideological erasure, similar to that effected by Rinaldo and Ferraù over Angelica or by the narrator over the monks. More specifically, and more importantly for the Spenserian and Shakespearean adaptations, the episode explores the gendered implications of such misreading, implicating Rinaldo in a sexual politics of gynophobia, slander, and misogyny. In Rinaldo's imagination, Ginevra is utterly available, in multiple senses of that word. She is available as a sexual object whose indefatigable appetites excuse the sexual aggression of her suitors. She is available narratively as an opportunity, an *impresa,* which the *frati* suggest he should exploit to advance his reputation; the submerged pun on *impresa* as sexual exploit emphasizes the continuity between these first two forms of availability (4.57.2). Finally, Ginevra is available rhetorically, to the terms of interrogation Rinaldo uses for self-evaluation: *biasmo e pregio,* blame and praise.

By thus assuming Ginevra's availability, Rinaldo begs the question of her consent, the *sine qua non* of medieval courtly love, specifically invoked by the Arthurian context of this episode. *Amour courtois* is defined by the mutual and free decision of both parties to enter into its bonds, a willingness that distinguishes courtly love from nonaristocratic servile relations. And although the Renaissance adaptation of courtly love typically omits the woman's consent, in Joan Kelly's famous argument, the result of this withholding is nonconsummation, not capitulation.[9]

Despite his transgressions against *amour courtois,* the narrator grants Rinaldo unqualified success; the tragic death predicted by the monks converts neatly into comedy. Stumbling across the runaway handmaid, Dalinda, Rinaldo scares away two villains who threaten to murder her. But it is Dalinda, not Rinaldo, who confirms Ginevra's innocence, and when he arrives at the tournament, Ariodante himself triumphs over his traitorous brother.[10] Despite his slander of Ginevra, despite flaunting the mandates of *amour courtois,* Rinaldo evades both literal and literary death. With the silent assistance of the Ariostan narrator, Rinaldo transforms Ginevra into a narrative occasion, a cipher onto whom he can project his own ambitions. And Ginevra succumbs entirely to this conscription, quietly eliding the paradoxes of Rinaldo's chivalric ethos. She makes herself rhetorically available for his purposes, allowing Rinaldo to earn his *pregio.* She does not, however, make herself sexually available, as Rinaldo suggested she might. The hero is thus forced neither to fulfill his most radical promises to reform the harsh laws of Scotland and to eliminate the sexual double standard for men and women nor to recant his outlandish speculations. Capitulating to the role of the traditional courtly woman, pledged to one man alone, Ginevra becomes the text of Rinaldo's projected fantasy.

Thus circumscribed by the exigencies of Rinaldo's *pregio,* Ginevra, like the monks, bears witness to the way the *Furioso* allows fraternal relations to foreclose the possibility of resistance and dissent. As if to punctuate this authorial accomplishment, the narrative figures Ginevra's doppel-gänger in Dalinda, her handmaid. Guilty of the very crimes that Ginevra avoids, Dalinda suffers for resisting the imperatives of the *Furioso*'s frater-nity. Unlike Ginevra, whose chastity secures Rinaldo's reputation, Dalinda is a figure of continued circulation. Most obviously, she yields her body to Polinesso's sexual advances. Furthermore, she opens the inviolate space of Ginevra's bedchamber to Polinesso, and, unwittingly, to the voyeuristic gaze of Ariodante and his brother, making the private public. Finally, as a narrator, Dalinda repeats her story to Rinaldo, who narrates it for the Scottish court, whence it passes to the poet-figure of the *Furioso,* record-ing Polinesso's conspiratorial plot for posterity. For revealing the truth, however, Dalinda receives not the *pregio* of a heroine but the *biasmo* of one disgraced: "molto sazia . . . del mondo" (tired of the world; 6.16.3–4), she leaves Scotland for a Danish convent, where she will be permanently removed from sexual and discursive circulation. Why, exactly, should Dalinda suffer this fate? The answer might lie once again in the fraternal alliances that organize the poet-figure's allegiances in the poem. While the pun on "plot"—Polinesso's conspiracy and the narrator's literary com-position—works less neatly in Italian than in English, the connection is im-plicit. Polinesso has "ordito" (5.85.8) and "tramato" his plot ("l'inganno") (87.8); *tramare* means "to plot, to scheme, or to conspire," but the derived noun, *trama* can refer both to a conspiracy and to the weave of a textile. *Ordire* can mean either "to plot, to hatch a plot," or, in relation to textiles, "to warp," relevant here because the narrator's primary metaphor for his poem in the *Furioso* is that of a great web or tapestry. The poet-figure describes his strategy of romantic narrative *entrelacement* using the verb *ordire*—the same verb used to describe Polinesso's handling of the *in-ganno:* "varie fila a varie tele/uopo mi son, che tutte *ordire* intendo" (I require many threads and cloths to weave my entire tapestry; 2.30.5–6, emphasis added).[11] Like Penelope resisting her suitors, Dalinda has the au-dacity to unweave the threads of masculine aggression, importunity, and narrative, and she suffers poetic excision for this audacity.

Rinaldo thus ends the episode comfortably ensconced within the narrative fraternity, protected by the poet-figure who has *ordito* the poem and its many *inganni.* This hero *degradato* enjoys the preroga-tive of sanctioned misreading. Ginevra's silent capitulation is a privilege of authorship extended by the narrator to the poem's chivalric frater-nity. At whatever cost—the monks' erasure, Ginevra's silence, Dalinda's exile—Rinaldo's narcissistic misreading effectively writes Ginevra into the role he needs her to fulfill.[12]

Phedon: Misreading and Rereading

From its outset, when the Redcrosse Knight confronts his own error in the form of a monstrous maternal body, *The Faerie Queene* associates acts of misreading with misogyny. In keeping with this correspondence, Spenser makes explicit what Ariosto's poet-figure would suppress. If the latter effaces Rinaldo's misogyny via narratorial intervention, the former introduces his first extended Ariostan adaptation of *The Faerie Queene* with a patent example of misogynistic misreading.

Immediately before encountering Ariodante's English double, Guyon is accosted by a madman and "a wicked Hag":

> In ragged robes, and filthy disarray,
> Her other leg was lame, that she no'te walke,
> But on her staffe her feeble steps did stay;
> Her lockes, that loathly were and hoarie gray,
> Grew all afore, and loosely hong vnrold,
> But all behind was bald, and worne away,
> That none thereof could euer taken hold,
> And eke her face ill fauourd, full of wrinckles old. (2.4.4)[13]

As Guyon will learn in a stern rebuke from his Palmer, this old woman is Occasion, the mother to the madman Furor and "the root of all wrath and despight" (2.4.10.9). In the classical tradition, occasion (L. *occasio*) is the climactic time of the event, in contrast to the undifferentiated time of delay (*tempus*). Renaissance emblem books embody this contrast in Occasion's pate, bald except for a single forelock; the time for action must be seized at once, ungraspable once it has passed.[14] Occasion is thus strict but not malevolent. In Geffrey Whitney's *A Choice of Emblemes,* for instance, she solicitously "warne[s] all people not to staye,/But at thee firste, occasion to imbrace,/And when shee comes, to meete her by the waye."[15] Even Reformation theology, prioritizing patient sufferance, sanctions the seizure of occasion, as in Luther's gloss on Ecclesiastes: "The maker of a thing hath nothing but his time and season. Till this cometh, he can do nothing. *If the houre be hit so doth he likewise hit it.*"[16] Occasion is not a threat but a reward: the moment of action, realization, culmination.

Guyon and the Palmer, however, treat Occasion as a menacing figure. Citing her "reprochfull blame" as the cause of Furor's wrath, the Palmer counsels, "With her, who so will raging Furor tame,/Must first begin, and well her amenage" (2.4.11). This apparently temperate counsel belies a metaphoric stratum of misogynistic violence. The iconography of *manège* as horsemanship goes back to Plato's *Phaedrus*, which allegorizes the mind controlling the passions as a charioteer reining a steed. Early modern writers embrace this metaphor, commonly depicting the appetitive body as an unruly horse that must be reined in by reason.[17] Occasion, though, is not a horse, and the Palmer's application of the equestrian metaphor to a woman is misogynistically suggestive.[18] Given Occasion's similarity to the medieval *Fortuna*,[19] this metaphor creates a sinister register for the Palmer's advice, for Renaissance writers often depicted Fortune as the wayward woman in need of physical domination. Machiavelli is only the most famous progenitor of this image, in this notorious passage from *The Prince:*

It is better to be impetuous than cautious, because Fortune is a woman and it is necessary, in order to keep her under, to cuff and maul her. She more often lets herself be overcome by men using such methods than by those who proceed coldly; therefore always, like a woman, she is the friend of young men, because they are less cautious, more spirited, and with more boldness master her.[20]

Machiavelli advocates what Sidney reproves: the deployment of misogynistic violence to ensure masculine sovereignty.

Guyon enthusiastically embraces the mandate of the Machiavellian *vir virtutis:* "Therewith *Sir Guyon* left his first emprise,/And turning to that woman, fast her hent/By the hoare lockes, that hong before her eyes,/And to the ground her threw" (2.4.12.1-4). He then binds her hands to a stake and secures her tongue with an iron lock; rather than seizing Occasion's "hore lockes" of hair—that transient opportunity that must be seized actively before it passes—Guyon turns his attention to a different sort of lock, one designed for complete immobilization.[21] This exchange of the hoarie lock for the iron one represents a failure of Guyon's nominal virtue. Instead of seizing Occasion at the appropriate moment, Guyon arrests her entirely, in a violent attempt to subdue the march of *tempus* to his authority. Even the "varlet" Atin finds Guyon's conduct reprehensible: "Vile knight,/That knights and knighthood doest with shame vpbray,/And shewst th'ensample of thy childish might,/With silly weake old woman thus to fight" (2.4.45.2–5). Guyon's zealotry here reveals its Machiavellian excess. It is one thing to "imbrace" Occasion, "and when shee comes, to meete her by the waye," and quite another to beat up on little old ladies. Spenser thus opens the canto by associating misreading, like that of the Ariostan episode, with Machiavellian misogyny, conflating the narrative violence of the *Furioso* with the physical violence of the Machiavellian *vir virtutis*.

The sexual-political stakes of misreading are thus in full view when *The Faerie Queene* undertakes its first major Ariostan revision, the story of Phedon and Claribella. Spenser's adaptation is simultaneously less and more dramatic—in every sense of that word—than the original. Characteristically, the oscillations between hope and fear are psychologized; much of the action occurs in Phedon's mind.[22] As an allegorical poem, though, *The Faerie Queene* projects Phedon's psychological dynamics onto the poem's landscape, realizing even Phedon's private affective states in the material world and staging, in an explicitly theatrical way, the problems of misreading. In what he comes to describe as "my trage-die," Phedon struggles with the sexual implications of the spectacle he thinks he sees. He faces a double threat of feminization: first as an emas-culated cuckold, and subsequently as a text, a theatrical spectacle, whose cuckold's horns render him legible to all audiences. In his desperation to remain the subject rather than the object of the feminizing gaze, Phedon misreads Claribella as unfaithful, gaining temporary and illusory inter-pretive control. Unlike Rinaldo, he suffers brutal repercussions, realizing precisely the humiliation he feared and assuming the burden of guilt.

The failure of Phedon's desperate salvo is finally complete when Guyon and the Palmer allegorize the event. Phedon has become their spectacle, their object of interpretive control, the malleable, Ginevran text to their definitive interpretive desire. Spenser's adaptation thus demonstrates the failure of two interpretive schemes. Neither masculine desire nor allego-rization provides control over *The Faerie Queene*'s female characters; neither Phedon nor Guyon can solve the interpretive problem that Cla-ribella presents. Phedon kills her, Guyon transforms her into an abstrac-tion, and the poem and its readers register the aporia, and the misogyny, of gendered misreading.

Phedon begins his narrative by articulating two complementary anxiet-ies: a sense of isolation in his masculinity and a fear of his own feminiza-tion. He begins, "It was a faithlesse Squire, that was the sourse / Of all my sorrow, and of these sad teares,/With whom from tender dug of commune nourse,/Attonce I was vpbrought" (2.4.18.1–4). Phedon shares with Philemon, Spenser's Polinesso, a wet nurse: a shadowy feminine presence who functions as nothing more than a measure of the boys' intimacy and betrayal. Otherwise, Phedon is alone, lacking Rinaldo's fraternal alliances. His friends and parents barely haunt the edges of the narrative, registered grammatically as objects of prepositions in subordinate clauses: "Accord of friends, consent of parents sought,/Affiance made, my happinesse begonne" (2.4.21.3–4). Thus isolated, Phedon doubts his masculinity. Philemon's intimations about Claribella's infidelity produce a "gnawing anguish and sharpe gelosy," which become "infixed in [Phedon's] brest" (2.4.23.1, 2); later, he confesses that he still harbors grief and fury "Of which in me yet stickes the mortall sting" (2.4.33.5). Later, Phedon explicitly feminizes such coronary penetration, describing the handmaid Pryene's response to Philemon: "glad t'embosome his affection vile" (2.4.25.3).[23]

Phedon's sexual uncertainty becomes increasingly explicit when Philemon positions him for the staged deception: "Me . . . in a secret corner layd" (2.4.27.5). "Layd" underscores his emasculation and passivity, "cast down from an erect position" (OED s.v. "lay," v.[1] 1) while his location in the "secret corner"—echoing the "darksome inner bowre" where Claribella allegedly welcomes her illicit lover (2.4.24.5)—suggests the fear and shame Phedon associates with female sexuality. Even before witnessing the staged infidelity, Phedon suffers from a sense of his feminized position and of the shameful unknowability of female sexuality, a foreboding of its "darksome" ensnaring potential.

What Phedon witnesses in the spectacle is not a resolution but a symptom of these anxieties. Philemon, disguised as the "groome of base degree," arrives at the appointed place along with Pryene, who is dressed in Claribella's clothes. But from his secret vantage, Phedon can see nothing more:

> . . . Her proper face
> I not descerned in that darkesome shade,
> But weend it was my loue, with whom he playd.
> Ah God, what horrour and tormenting griefe
> My hart, my hands, mine eyes, and all assayd? (2.4.28.3–7)

With this tortuous logic, Phedon moves precipitously from unknowing to certainty. He cannot see the face of the woman in lines 3–4; he suspects it to be Claribella's in line 5; but in line 6, after the full stop, the tenuousness of "weening" in a "darkesome shade" disappears. Phedon begins to experience his emotional pain as a physical assault from outside: his hands, his eyes, and "all" other senses are "assayed." In an instant, Phedon substitutes objectivity for uncertainty, preferring to believe the worst rather than to endure continued doubt.

In construing Claribella as unfaithful, Phedon tries to assert the authorial prerogative of an Ariostan narrator and thereby to forestall his own feminization. The paradox of his predicament is clear when he describes himself, ambiguously, as "the sad spectatour of my Tragedie" (2.4.27.6). Phedon is sad, which could make him either the subject of a tragedy or its theatrical audience, which, in the fears of Renaissance antitheatricalists, becomes like what it views. If "spectatour" seems to settle the question, "my Tragedie" reopens it. In what sense is Phedon the spectator of his own tragedy: as audience or performer, spectacle or spectator?

The dramatic vocabulary is crucial here. Spenser's theatricalization of the scene of misreading prepares the episode for its transition to the stage in Shakespeare's *Much Ado*. At the same time, this crossing of genres situates this instance of gendered misreading in a larger Renaissance context: the institution of the popular theater that provoked myriad concerns about performance, interpretation, and reality—the power of the spectacle to exert influence beyond the bounds of the stage.[24] Phedon imagines his unfolding narrative as a tragic play because even in the age of the expansive Marlovian stage, the play works through synecdoche—a few soldiers for a whole army, three hours for the passage of years. As Katherine Eisaman Maus argues, the metonymic nature of the stage play makes the audience conceptually equivalent to the cuckold: neither can intervene in the spectacle, neither has the "full view" of what it longs to see, but both find the imagined synecdoche more believable than the reality of the absence of "ocular proof."[25] The cuckold never gets the forensic evidence he simultaneously dreads and desires. But for the price of this frustration, the cuckold, like the theatrical audience, earns a measure of interpretive control. Like Rinaldo enjoying the authorial prerogative, the cuckold makes himself into playwright rather than spectator. It is the simultaneous occupation of these roles that produces Phedon's epistemological vertigo ("not descerned . . . /But weend"). As Maus explains, such bids for control are futile: "Once the cuckold's plight becomes public he . . . becomes himself a feminized spectacle at which others point mocking, phallic fingers. *Any* act of sexual assertion or self-justification thus threatens to emasculate him. . . . A gain of power in one direction inevitably entails a loss of power in another."[26] His oscillations between disavowal and knowledge underscore the sexual politics of Phedon's misreading. He gains the masculine privilege of authorship, but gains too the shame of the feminized cuckold. Phedon trades the story of Phedon-as-spectacle ("my Tragedie" as objective genitive) for the story of spectacle-by-Phedon ("my Tragedie" as subjective genitive), but he cannot escape the theatricality, or the tragedy, of his predicament.

Guyon and the Palmer complete the sequence of feminization with a final act of misreading, treating Phedon as a text in need of allegorical exposition. The Palmer calls him a "wretched man / That to affections does the bridle lend" (2.4.38.1–2), and Guyon advises:

> Wrath, gealosie, griefe, loue do thus expell:
> Wrath is a fire, and gealosie a weede,
> Griefe is a flood, and loue a monster fell;
> The fire of sparkes, the weede of little seed,
> The flood of drops, the Monster filth did breede:
> But sparks, seed, drop, and filth do thus delay;
> The drops soon dry vp, and filth wipe cleane away:
> The sparks soone quench, the springing seed outweed,
> So shall wrath, gealosie, griefe, loue dye and decay. (2.4.35)

Guyon and the Palmer seem to have lent only the most cursory attention to Phedon's story; they moralize him with the same vocabulary applied to Furor and Occasion before Phedon arrived. The "flood" of grief recycles the Palmer's claim about Furor's passions ("the tempest of his passion wood; / The bankes are ouerflowen, when stopped is the flood"; 2.4.11.7–9). Similarly, the image of wrath as a fire recalls how Occasion "kindles [Furor's] courage," and "the franticke fit inflamd his spright" (11.5, 7.3). The Palmer invokes the "bridle," recalling the reins of temperance that subtended Guyon's *manège* of Occasion.

With these recycled readings, Guyon and the Palmer reveal themselves as failed readers, heedless of Phedon's parable about the dangers of attempting to assert a masculine authorial prerogative over a feminized spectacle. Moreover, they fail to appreciate the specificity of Phedon's theatrical vocabulary. Phedon's narrative explains how "my Tragedie" as objective genitive—a fictional, scurrilous story *about* him, directed by his treacherous friend—was transformed into "my Tragedie" as subjective genitive—a true story of how Phedon killed his fiancée and best friend. It is a story about the dangers of theatrical performance: a familiar Renaissance antitheatrical complaint about the impact of staged fictions affecting and infecting the real world. Theatrical audiences who lust after female characters in a play might find themselves erotically drawn to the boy players; Faustus's fictional conjuration of devils onstage during a production of Marlowe's play might conjure real devils from hell; lowly actors who dress as noblemen onstage might find themselves inclined to violate early modern sumptuary laws.[27] Guyon and the Palmer fail to appreciate Phedon's lessons about the dangers of gendered misreading and misinterpretation inherent to the theatrical spectacle. Shakespeare, on the other hand, proffered a more appreciative audience.

Much Ado About Nothing: Reading the Unreadable

In the Claudio-Hero plot, Shakespeare's contribution to this legacy of narration and revision, *Much Ado About Nothing* too turns on by now familiar scenes of gendered misreading. But unlike Phedon's sober "tragedie," *Much Ado* embraces epistemological ambiguity. Its characters remain happily entangled in the oscillations between knowledge and uncertainty, between the visibility and invisibility of both fidelity and betrayal. Is the female body whole or inviolate? Is the male head horned or smooth? In *Much Ado,* these questions are unanswerable. Bodies are phenomenologically unstable, it insists, readable only as fragmentary, "distempered," and violable. The title's pun on the no-thing of the female genitalia is also a pun on know-thing: the impossibility of reading the body as definitive proof of the sexually coherent, stable subject. To the Ariostan scene and Spenserian critique of misogynistic misreading, the play posits a carnivalesque alternative: a joyful relocation of corporeal misreading from Thanatos to Eros and a cheerful abandonment of the fiction that authorial control can guarantee sexual identity.

Much Ado About Nothing begins with the transition from the masculine violence of the battlefield to the feminine world of leisure and rejuvenation. The triumphant Aragonese army returns to its peacetime haunt in Messina, and masculinity itself softens; the ideal of the martial "lion" (1.1.14) gives way to the ideal of the old man openly weeping in a "kind overflow of kindness" (1.1.25). And yet Messina is not all sweetness and light. The indomitable Beatrice asks after her rival Benedick: "I pray you, how many hath he killed and eaten in these wars? But how many hath he killed? For indeed I promised to eat all of his killing" (1.1.38–41). This proverbial expression[28] inaugurates a metaphorics of corporeal violence that persists throughout the play. Almost obsessively, characters are catalogued in parts, as if *Much Ado* is a five-act blazon.[29] Take Beatrice's description of her masculine ideal:

BEATRICE: He were an excellent man that were made just in the mid-way between him [Don John] and Benedick: the one is too like an image and says nothing, and the other too like my lady's eldest son, evermore tattling.

LEONATO: Then half Signior Benedick's tongue in Count John's mouth, and half Count John's melancholy in Signior Benedick's face—

BEATRICE: With a good leg and a good foot, uncle, and money enough in his purse, such a man would win any woman in the world—if he could get her good will.

LEONATO: By my troth, niece, thou wilt never get thee a husband, if thou be so shrewd of thy tongue.

ANTONIO: In faith, she's too curst.

BEATRICE: Too curst is more than curst: I shall lessen God's sending that way, for it is said, "God sends a curst cow short horns," but to a cow too curst he sends none.

LEONATO: So, by being too curst, God will send you no horns.

BEATRICE: Just, if he send me no husband . . . (2.1.6–24)

The proverb Beatrice cites implies that God limits the capacity of a fierce beast to inflict harm.[30] But in a play obsessed with sexual fidelity, these horns simultaneously evoke the cuckold, as Beatrice's final riposte implies. She feels the want of neither the horns she might lock with her mate, nor the horns she might confer on him through infidelity. These proverbial prostheses, then, transfer across genders and signifying functions. Belying the integrity of a body of either gender, the sign of Beatrice's temperamental "curse" is here appropriated to signify both her mate's sexual inadequacy and their marital union. These horns are the passage's final contribution to its blazon of body parts, one that contravenes the fantasy of the coherent sexual subject. Leonato and Beatrice imaginatively construct a physiological composite: half of Benedick's active tongue to animate Don John's laconic mouth; half of Don John's black bile ("melancholy") to temper Benedick's choler; a shapely leg and foot borrowed from Beatrice's fantasy; and the horns conferred by the would-be *amoreuse* herself. The masculine body whose appearance would please Beatrice is not an integral subject but a composite of temperamentally distinct parts.

The concept of "temperament" adduced here is *Much Ado*'s answer
to temperance, the virtue in whose name Guyon critiques Phedon's acts
of misreading. Referring both to the humoral composition of the body
and the subject's resulting disposition, "temperament" marks the convergence of the body in parts *per se* and the phenomenology of that body,
of the physical *corpus* and its readability. Both senses of "temperament"
are operative, for example, when Don John declares himself "born under
Saturn" (1.3.11), the planet directly associated with melancholic humor,
so that his villainous conduct is literally the disposition that "fits [his]
blood."[31] Similarly, suspecting that Don Pedro woos Hero for himself,
Claudio appears jaundiced, "civil as an orange, and something of that
jealous complexion" (2.1.276-77). Claudius's jaundice is the phenomenological counterpart to his sanguinary body: his behavioral temperament
derives from his humoral one.

The play's climactic scene, Claudio's public decrial of Hero on their
wedding day, demonstrates the interpretive difficulty posed by the temperamental body. Claudio misreads Hero's humoral temperament—and
infers her lustful disposition—from the phenomenology of the blush:

> Behold how like a maid she blushes here!
> O, what authority and show of truth
> Can cunning sin cover itself withal!
> Comes not that blood as modest evidence
> To witness simple virtue? Would you not swear,
> All you that see her, that she were a maid,
> By these exterior shows? But she is none:
> She knows the heat of a luxurious bed:
> Her blush is guiltiness, not of modesty . . .
> Out on thee, seeming! I will write against it. (4.1.33-56)

Rather than an "exterior show" of modesty, Claudio insists, Hero's blush
signifies a humoral temperament that leads to wantonness. His diagno-
sis rests on sound sixteenth-century physiology, which identifies "redde
coulour" as a chief symptom of "the hot bodye" prone to lechery.[32] Hero's
undiluted blood, Claudio imagines, improperly balanced by phlegm, flows
through her veins and into her face. The vow to "write against" Hero's
apparent chastity echoes the authorial prerogative repeatedly asserted
by sexually threatened male figures in Ariosto and Spenser. Claudio also
"write[s] against" Hero's "seeming" with his performative interpretation.
His misreading of Hero's temperament becomes an article of faith even

for Hero's devoted father, who echoes Claudio's accusation in believing he can read Hero's infidelity "printed in her blood" (4.1.122).

Like Phedon, Claudio asserts this authorial prerogative to shore up a threatened sense of masculinity.

> O my lord,
> When you went onward on this ended action,
> I look'd upon her with a soldier's eye,
> That lik'd, but had a rougher task in hand
> Than to drive liking to the name of love:
> But now I am return'd, and that war-thoughts
> Have left their places vacant, in their rooms
> Come thronging soft and delicate desires,
> All prompting me how fair young Hero is,
> Saying I lik'd her ere I went to wars. (1.1.276-85)

By collapsing the past and the present, Claudio here imagines his martial, masculine self dissolving into the feminine leisure of Messina. He refers proleptically to the "ended action" even as he describes Don Pedro setting out at the campaign's onset; at the conclusion of the passage, his newfound desires for Hero claim rights of prior occupation, asserting their importance not just to Claudio-the-lover, but to Claudio-the-soldier. For one whose youth makes his martial prowess surprising—Claudio surprised the Aragonese army by "doing, in the figure of a lamb, the feats of a lion" (1.1.13-14)—this temporal collapse undermines his hard-fought masculinity, ascribing Claudio's prowess to the lucky breaks of a lamb in lion's clothing.

Don Pedro exacerbates the problem by offering, impatiently, to broker Claudio's engagement: "Thou wilt be like a lover presently, / And tire the hearer with a book of words, / . . . / . . . thou shalt have her. Was't not to this end / That thou began'st to twist so fine a story?" (1.1.286-91). If Don Pedro grants Claudio a certain authorial prerogative with "book of words," he emphatically genders this version of authorship feminine. The threads of Claudio's confession, spun into a tale, identify him simultaneously with the loquacious woman gossiping while she spins[33] and with the writer of romance, genre of the disenfranchised, the emasculated, the feminized.[34] Don Pedro thus derides Claudio's manliness while aggrandizing his own epic-appropriate impatience, laying fertile ground for the fantasy of Hero's infidelity:

> I will assume thy part in some disguise,
> And tell fair Hero I am Claudio,
> And in her bosom I'll unclasp my heart,
> And take her hearing prisoner with the force
> And strong encounter of my amorous tale:
> Then after to her father will I break,
> And the conclusion is, she shall be thine. (1.1.301-7)

Don Pedro underscores the martial aggression of his wooing: his "force" and "strong encounter" will claim first Hero's ear and subsequently her affections as his "prisoner." In the only line suggestive of erotic intimacy—"in her bosom I'll unclasp my heart"—it is Don Pedro's heart, not Claudio's, unfolding within Hero's breast. The fragmented body reappears here to impugn Hero's chastity; she has, by the end of Don Pedro's speech, already been debauched, her body penetrated imaginatively by a man other than her betrothed. With Don Pedro having asserted the masculine prerogative of authorship and feminized Claudio, Don John need only capitalize on these anxieties to execute his plot.

Claudio tries to reassert the corporeal integrity that could guarantee either Hero's chastity or his own masculinity—his rejection of that shameful prosthetic, the cuckold's horns. Believing Don Pedro to be courting Hero for himself, he resolves never again to trust a proxy: "all hearts in love use their own tongues;/Let every eye negotiate for itself,/and trust no agent" (2.1.165-67). If the rest of Messina playfully imagines composite lovers ("half Signior Benedick's tongue in Count John's mouth") or vengefully imagines the dismemberment of the unchaste female body (if Hero is guilty, Leonato vows, "these hands shall tear her"; 4.1.191), Claudio hopes to reassert the integrality of his body, which will see and speak on its own behalf. As with Phedon, the prerogatives of authorship and authority wrest control of the male body back from the cuckolding woman, and thus compensate in part for the alleged betrayal.

When Leonato adopts this metaphor of authorship, he unwittingly reveals Hero's impossible predicament, bringing to the fore the tragedies that ended, in Ariosto and Spenser, with the erasure of Ginevra and Claribella from the text. When Hero declines to rebut her accusers, Leonato laments: "Could she here deny/The story that is printed in her blood?/Do not live, Hero, do not ope thine eyes;/For did I think thou wouldst not quickly die,/Thought I thy spirits were stronger than thy shames,/Myself would on the rearward of reproaches/Strike at thy life" (4.1.121-27).

With "the story that is printed in her blood," Leonato grants Hero a dubious sort of authorship: she has printed, made public for all to see, the blood that accounts for her lustful temperament.[35] But Leonato recants almost immediately. At the friar's suggestion, he determines to "publish" yet a different story, allowing Hero's staged death—metonymic referent of her "blood"—to testify to her virtue (4.1.204). Hero is granted the right to control her bodily signification only in the negative; her "blood" can speak of her innocence only when it has been taken from her by someone else (within the fiction of her death, by her accusers; within the play, by the friar and Leonato who execute this plan). It is Hero's postmortem silence that exonerates her, as in her epitaph:

> CLAUDIO (*Reading from a scroll.*):
> "Done to death by slanderous tongues
> Was the Hero that here lies:
> Death, in guerdon of her wrongs,
> Gives her fame which never dies:
> So the life that died with shame
> Lives in death with glorious fame."
> (*Hangs up the scroll.*)
> Hang thou there upon the tomb,
> Praising her when I am dumb. (5.3.3–10)

The story of Hero's death—what Claudio, were he Phedon, would call "my Tragedie"—speaks loudly enough of Hero's chastity to silence the disembodied "slanderous tongues," rendering her accuser "dumb." For the moment, this seems to be a victory as hard-won as Claribella's: heroism at the cost of perpetual silence, a kind of trial-by-ordeal in which only death, too late, can prove innocence.

Elsewhere in the play, too, silence constitutes female virtue and grants men authorial control. Don John, for instance, feigns punctiliousness about Hero's alleged transgressions: "Fie, fie, they are not to be nam'd, my lord, / Not to be spoke of! / There is not chastity enough in language / Without offense to utter them" (4.1.95–98). Feigning verbal nicety, Don John declares himself loath to detail Hero's affair; the truncated meter of line 94 itself enacts the silence that purports to stand for virtue. With this demurral, Don John invites his audience—both on the stage and in the theater—to make the vertiginous shift into certainty, to author a "story that is printed in [Hero's] blood" (4.1.122). To speak aloud of Hero's transgressions would be to participate in her sins. Silence stands as the guarantor of the accuser's own intact honor and the space in which he and his auditors, like Phedon, can entrench their positions as subjects, not objects, of this tale of unchastity.

Ultimately, though, the play rejects this double bind in which women must choose between disgrace and silence. This transformation is perhaps clearest in the trajectory of Benedick, who begins the play as a fervent believer in the virtue of female reticence. He rails against Beatrice, "my Lady Tongue" (2.1.258), who "speaks poniards, and every word stabs" (2.1.231). Blaming Beatrice's prolixity, Benedick swears off marriage altogether and mocks Claudio's marital ambitions:

BENEDICK: He is in love. With who? Now that is your Grace's part. Mark how short his answer is: with Hero, Leonato's short daughter.
CLAUDIO: If this were so, so were it uttered.
BENEDICK: Like the old tale, my lord: "It is not so, nor 'twas not so: but indeed, God forbid it should be so!" (1.1.195–201)

The "old tale" here is a morbid folktale about a serial killer named Mr. Fox, one which speaks directly to the relationship between female silence and dismemberment. In an analogue to the tale of Bluebeard, Lady Mary visits the home of Mr. Fox, where four written signs hang over four different portals. Three bear the same message—"Be bold, be bold, be not too bold"—while a final sign over the door of a chamber revises, "Be bold, be bold, be not too bold, lest that your heart's blood should run cold." When she opens the door, she finds the dismembered remains of scores of young women, her predecessors who have fallen into Mr. Fox's trap. Seizing a severed hand as evidence, Lady Mary escapes unnoticed. Several days later, at a dinner party with Mr. Fox among the guests, she entertains the company with her story, turning to Mr. Fox three times to insist on its fictionality with this refrain: "It is not so, nor it was not so." When she begins to describe the final bloody chamber, Mr. Fox interjects, "It is not so, nor it was not so, and God forbid it should be so." Lady Mary retaliates, "But it is so, and it was so, and here the hand I have to show," at which point she produces the severed limb. The dinner guests turn on Mr. Fox with their swords and cut him into a thousand pieces.[36]

In mentioning this "old wives' tale," Benedick joins Don Pedro in teasing Claudio about his compromised masculinity. As critics have long attested, fairy tales in the English Renaissance were considered with some disdain as childish relics of a preliterate, feminine sphere. The soft, effeminate boy who would have lapped up these nursery rhymes in his "mother tongue" came into manhood only when humanist pedagogy toughened him into "a 'hard' disciplined youth" trained up in "Roman masculinity."[37] But at the same time, this folkloric citation betrays Benedick's anxiety about the threats of Eros. Like *Much Ado About Nothing* itself, the tale of Mr. Fox represents the dangers of illicit sexuality—implied by Lady Mary's "bold" venture into her neighbor's home—as vivisection. Benedick quotes not the triumphant Lady Mary but the lying Mr. Fox, who tries unsuccessfully to silence a speaking woman, to disavow the inevitable truth, and to evade retaliation. For Benedick, maintaining his bodily integrity, avoiding Mr. Fox's Actaeon-like punishment, requires the continued silence—or, better, the nonexistence, says Benedick—of his imagined erotic partner. To admit a woman into a conversation, much less into his bed, is to risk effeminization, dismemberment, and death. Tellingly, Spenser quotes the same refrain from the Mr. Fox tale at the end of book 3 of *The Faerie Queene,* where the enchanter Busiraine writes "straunge characters of his art,/With liuing bloud . . . /Dreadfully dropping from [the] dying hart" of his chaste captive Amoret (3.12.31.2–4). The stakes are identical in the two texts: the violence of masculine authorship, and the costs it exacts in female silence and dismemberment.

The play ends, famously, with Benedick literally singing another tune (5.2.25–27). But crucially, these specific anxieties—about the fictions of bodily integrity on which authorship is premised—persist. After Borachio's confession, Dogberry makes a plea to Leonato, one based on a misprision about bodily integrity:

DOGBERRY: The watch heard [Borachio and Conrad] talk of one Deformed; they say he wears a key in his ear and a lock hanging by it, and borrows money in God's name, the which he hath used so long, and never paid, that now men grow hard-hearted and will lend nothing for God's sake: pray you examine him upon that point. (5.1.301–7)

Dogberry's report bastardizes the conversation between Borachio and Conrad in 3.3, when Borachio boasts about having deceived Claudio and Don Pedro: "Seest thou not, I say, what a deformed thief this fashion is, how giddily a turns about all the hot bloods between fourteen and five-and-thirty . . . ?" (3.3.127–29). The watchmen mistake Borachio's adjective for a proper noun: "I know that Deformed; a has been a vile thief this seven year; a goes up and down like a gentleman: I remember his name. . . . I know him, a wears a lock" (3.3.122–64). The watchman describes "Deformed" as wearing a lock (or "lovelock"), an artificial tress of hair common among Elizabethan courtiers. Just as Borachio tries to reveal the truth, the watchmen "deform" the revelation yet again with their own blunder.

This series of "deformations" continues with Dogberry's final speech. Just after Borachio confesses, a new image of Deformed appears, bearing an additional layer of misconstrual. Deformed's lock of hair has been transformed into a padlock, whose key hangs "nearby" in his ear—a misreading that echoes Guyon's transformation of Occasion's forelock into a lock for her tongue. The additional detail of the key suggests that Dogberry may have added to this palimpsest another image, this one an allegorical icon of feminine virtue.

This midsixteenth-century German broadsheet exemplifies an iconographic tradition that silenced women in the name of virtue.[38] But the virtue it grants with one hand is taken away with the other: the lock itself suggests women's incurable garrulity, a frequent claim from medieval antifeminist literature; the "mirror of Christ" in her right hand implies vanity, another charge familiar from the *querelle des femmes;* the snakes girding her waist, purporting to protect her from "poisonous scandal," associate the woman with Eve's satanic tempter; and her horse's hooves, allegedly representing the ability to "stand firm in honor," simultaneously evoke the cloven-hooved Satan.[39] Whether or not Woensam's image was known to Shakespeare, Deformed and the Wise Woman participate in a broad cultural imaginary of women's silence as the tenuous dividing line between the chaste female body and its lecherous double, between the blushing bride and the shamed adulteress. The interpretive ambiguity of Woensam's image echoes the phenomenological instability of Hero's blush; the temperamental body is too unstable to guarantee the integrity of the female corpus or of the male identity premised on its chastity.

Dogberry's specific misprisions about "Deformed" underscore *Much Ado*'s critique of the fantasy of corporeal integrity. When deformed becomes Deformed, an adjective assumes a body, a local habitation, and a name. Subsequently, when Deformed flirts with transsexuality, Dogberry's varlet converges with the cultural imaginary of the Wise Woman: the female figure whose silence testifies to her virtue. Attributing these transformations to the bumbling Dogberry and identifying them as "deformations," *Much Ado* derogates these fantasies. The assumption of any

Anton Woensam, *Allegory of Virtue*, 1558. *The Illustrated Bartsch*, vol. 13, entry no. 1 (473), reprinted courtesy of Abaris Books, Connecticut

single, integral body—much less that of the silent, chaste female—is a fiction in this play: the result of a laughable series of misinterpretations by an undeservedly cocky constable.

In its comic conclusion, therefore, *Much Ado* offers a wholehearted embrace of misreading. Benedick joyfully recants his fulminations against love, such as this vow to Don Pedro:

DON PEDRO: I shall see thee, ere I die, look pale with love.
BENEDICK: With anger, with sickness, or with hunger, my lord, not with love: prove that ever I lose more blood with love than I will get against with drinking, pick out mine eyes with a ballad-maker's pen, and hang me up at the door of a brothel-house for the sign of blind Cupid.
. . . .
DON PEDRO: Well, as time shall try. "In time the savage bull doth bear the yoke."
BENEDICK: The savage bull may; but if ever the sensible Benedick bear it, pluck off the bull's horns and set them in my forehead, and let me be vilely painted, and in such great letters as they write, "Here is good horse to hire," let them signify under my sign, "Here you may see Benedick, the married man." (1.1.229–48)

Benedick clings, here, to the fiction of bodily integrity. Falling in love amounts to dismemberment—his eyes picked out, his cuckold's horns plucked—and textualization. He imagines his body as a literal sign: Cupid advertising a brothel, or a warning against marriage. Like Phedon, he fears the loss of bodily integrity and interpretive control. To be enamored, for Benedick, is to be readable and read, a feminized text, powerless over his own signification.

United with Beatrice, Benedick retains these beliefs about the effects of love on his body and its readability. What changes is his attitude toward these transformations:

BENEDICK: . . . Here's our own hands against our hearts. Come, I will have thee, but by this light I take thee for pity.
BEATRICE: I would not deny you, but by this good day I yield upon great persuasion, and partly to save your life for I was told you were in a consumption.
BENEDICK: Peace! I will stop your mouth.
DON PEDRO: How dost thou, "Benedick, the married man"?
BENEDICK: I'll tell thee what, Prince; a college of wit-crackers cannot flout me out of my humour. Dost thou think I care for a satire or an epigram? No: if a man will be beaten with brains, a shall wear nothing handsome about him. In brief, since I do purpose to marry, I will think nothing to any purpose that the world can say against it; and therefore never flout at me for what I have said against it; for man is a giddy thing, and this is my conclusion. . . . Let's have a dance

ere we are married, that we may lighten our own hearts and our 'wives' heels! (5.4.91-118)

Benedick does assert a kind of constancy here; nothing can unseat his elated "humour," in the sense of "mood." And yet his intractability is marked by fragmentation. Benedick describes himself and Beatrice in parts (hands, hearts, mouth, brains, heels) that vie for sovereignty, the hands betraying the truth of the heart that the mouth would deny. He calls himself a "giddy" thing: he is ecstatic ("elated to thoughtlessness, incapable of serious thought or steady attention," OED 3a), but also physiologically affected ("having a confused sensation of swimming or whirling in the head, with proneness to fall; affected with vertigo, dizzy," OED 2a). What is constant about Benedick, he claims, is his humoral inconstancy. Crucially, he accepts that he will be read, interpreted, feminized as a text: he anticipates "wit-crackers" mocking his love in "a satire or an epigram." But this interpretive impotence is a source of joy, as he reveals when he turns the tables on the matchmaker Don Pedro: "Prince, thou art sad; get thee a wife, get thee a wife! There is no staff more reverend than one tipped with horn" (5.4.120-22). Benedick punningly suggests that Don Pedro should trade in his staff "tipped with horn"—walking sticks of the aged were often horn-tipped[40]—for the horns of the cuckold. Don Pedro's textualization will render him less stately ("sad," OED 2, 4), Benedick admits, but also less sorrowful (OED 5).

The embrace of epistemological chaos at the end of *Much Ado About Nothing* constitutes not so much a solution to, as an appreciation of, the complex problem of gendered misreading. The broad textual genealogy outlined here—spanning most of a century, two linguistic traditions, three literary modes (mythological, allegorical, mimetic), and multiple genres (epic, romance, comedy, drama)—testifies to an early modern preoccupation with the interpretation of the gendered body. Shakespeare's play, in a way we have come to recognize as characteristic, offers an incisive commentary on theatricality, performance, and gender as central categories of self-understanding and social intercourse. At the same time, *Much Ado About Nothing* demands recognition of the performative readings, misreadings, and deformations that are the condition of possibility for the comic ending. Interpretive history is indispensable to the preservation of social and cultural justice, as the antihero Dogberry repeatedly reminds his superiors ("masters, do not forget to specify, when time and place shall serve, that I am an ass"; 5.1. 249–50). *Much Ado About Nothing* ges-tures not only toward futurity and Benedick's marital emasculation; like Claudio's anxious collapse of his military past to his lovelorn present, it gestures backward toward the literary history that informs its central plot.

In fact, the fragmented body might serve not only intratextually as a paradigm for the lovelorn condition, but metaliterarily as a figure for the play as an intertextual olio, a theatrical assemblage of literary fragments. *Much Ado About Nothing,* like many of Shakespeare's "Italian" plays, borrows from Ariosto, Spenser, and the folkloric tradition, not system-atically—for example, according to the moralizing agenda that so many scholars have ascribed to English Protestant allegorization—but through what Louise George Clubb describes as "a common process based on the principle of contamination of sources, genres, and accumulated stage-structures, or theatergrams."[41] Clubb's coinage refers to portable, appropriable units of influence—patterns and conventions, rather than texts considered positivistically as indivisible entities—which circu-late within and among generic and national literatures, like the unruly women-qua-texts whom Ariosto's poet-narrator, Spenser's Phedon, and (if only briefly) Shakespeare's Claudio attempt to control with interpre-tive rigidity. Ariosto's hero *degradato,* as we have seen, succeeds, at least temporarily, in rendering his misreading performative, an executive act of authorial power. But at the same time, he sets the precedent for subse-quent, successful, strong misreadings, which generate a kind of double theatergram, both providing the narrative raw materials for Spenser and Shakespeare and implying a methodology of intertextual adaptation.[42] As Clubb and this tripartite study both suggest, neither the female body nor the textual fragment can be padlocked into silent immobility. Whether at the level of the phenomenological body or of the theatergram, defor-mity and misreading are the foundation of textual continuity, of literary *biasmo e pregio,* of comic and interpretive possibility.

Notes

For invaluable assistance at various stages, I am grateful to Janet Adelman, Albert Ascoli, Michael Farry, Coleman Hutchison, and Lorna Hutson.

Throughout this article, I refer to the OED online, 2nd ed., 1989. Translations are my own.

1. A. R. Humphreys, ed., *Much Ado About Nothing,* The Arden Shakespeare (London and New York: Routledge, 1981). Subsequent citations appear parenthetically in the text.

2. For widowhood as a state of socially and sexually subversive autonomy, see, e.g., Christiane Klapisch-Zuber, "The 'Cruel Mother': Maternity, Widowhood, and Dowry in Florence in the Fourteenth and Fifteenth Centuries," in *Feminism and Renaissance Studies,* ed. Lorna Hutson, Oxford Readings in Feminism (Oxford: Oxford University Press, 1999); Merry E. Wiesner, "Spinsters and Seamstresses: Women in Cloth and Clothing Production," in *Rewriting the Renaissance: The Discourses of Sexual Difference in Early Modern Europe,* ed. Margaret W. Ferguson, Maureen Quilligan, and Nancy J. Vickers, Women in Culture and Society (Chicago: University of Chicago Press, 1986).

3. In Reformation England, Anglican critics attacked exorcism and conjuration as the false theatrics of Catholicism; see Stephen Greenblatt, *Shakespearean Negotiations: The Circulation of Social Energy in Renaissance England,* vol. 4 of *The New Historicism: Studies in Cultural Poetics* (Berkeley: University of California Press, 1988), 94-128. For a discussion of acceptable forms of theatricality in the Reformation context, see Jean E. Howard, *The Stage and Social Struggle in Early Modern England* (London and New York: Routledge, 1994).

4. This genealogy omits several English adaptations, including Peter Beverley's "Ariodanto and Jenevra" (ca. 1566); George Whetstone's 1576 *The Rock of Regard;* and an anonymous 1585 dramatic production called *Fedele and Fortunio.* See Anne Barton's headnote to G. Blakemore Evans and J. J. M. Tobin, eds., *The Riverside Shakespeare,* 2nd ed. (Boston and New York: Houghton Mifflin, 1997), 361; A.R. Humphreys, ed., *Much Ado About Nothing,* The Arden Shakespeare (London and New York: Routledge, 1981); Charles T. Prouty, *The Sources of "Much Ado About Nothing": A Critical Study, Together with the Text of Peter Beverley's Ariodanto and Ienevra* (New Haven: Yale University Press, 1950). For an account of the English fascination with this tale, see Katharine Eisaman Maus, "Horns of Dilemma: Jealousy, Gender, and Spectatorship in English Renaissance Drama," *English Literary History* 54, no. 3 (1987): 561-83.

5. Ludovico Ariosto, *Orlando furioso,* ed. Marcello Turchi and Eduardo Sanguineti, 2 vols., I grandi libri Garzanti (Milan: Garzanti, 1985), 1.20.5-6. Subsequent citations appear parenthetically in the text.

6. See Robert M. Durling, "The Divine Analogy in Ariosto," *Modern Language Notes* 78, no.1 (1963): 1n1; Robert M. Durling, *The Figure of the Poet in Renaissance Epic* (Cambridge, Mass.: Harvard University Press, 1965), 112-81.

7. Mario Santoro, cited in Peter De Sa Wiggins, *Figures in Ariosto's Tapestry: Character and Design in the "Orlando Furioso"* (Baltimore and London: Johns Hopkins University Press, 1986), 18. For Rinaldo as a hero less *degradato* than displaced, see Michael Sherberg, *Rinaldo: Character and Intertext in Ariosto and Tasso,* ed. Jean-Marie Apostolidès and Marc Bertrand, Stanford French and Italian Studies 75 (Saratoga, Calif.: ANMA Libri, 1993), 63-64.

8. "Devotion to women was a primary article: protection of the weak was the professional concern of knights errant, only the brave deserved the fair, and the love of a noble woman inspired the perfect practice of chivalry." W. R. J. Barron, *Sir Gawain and the Green Knight,* rev. ed. (Manchester: Manchester University Press, 1998), 2. See also Maurice Keen, *Chivalry* (New Haven and London: Yale University Press, 1984).

9. On the elusiveness of the idealized woman of courtly love, see Ruth Kelso, *Doctrine for the Lady of the Renaissance* (Urbana: University of Illinois Press, 1956), chapter 6 passim, 206. For the ways in which Renaissance women had less agency in courtly love than did their medieval counterparts, see Joan Kelly, "Did Women Have A Renaissance?" in *Women, History & Theory,* Women in Culture and Society (Chicago and London: University of Chicago Press, 1984), 19-50.

10. Ultimately, the best we can say of Rinaldo is that "he comes upon this adventure in Scotland by accident, gets involved in it for the wrong reasons, learns the truth through no mental effort of his own, and brings a resolution to Ginevra's dilemma that would be most unsatisfactory were it not for the extraordinary resolution provided by Ariodante." Wiggins, *Figures,* 22.

11. See Durling, *The Figure of the Poet in Renaissance Epic,* 117-18.

12. It is worth noting that the *Furioso* does not always enact its narrator's misogyny so uncritically. For a reading of the ways in which such narrative manipulations reveal the alleged monstrosity not only of the female body, but of the male imagination, see Albert Russell Ascoli, "Body Politics in Ariosto's *Orlando Furioso,*" in *Translating Desire in Medieval and Early Modern Literature,* ed. C. A. Berry and H. Hayton (Tempe: Arizona Center for Medieval and Renaissance Studies, 2005). In "Like a Virgin: Fantasies of the Male Body in *Orlando furioso*" in *The Body in Early Modern Europe,* ed. Julia Hairston and Walter Stephens (Baltimore: Johns Hopkins University Press, forthcoming 2010), Ascoli discusses the ways in which several male knights in the *Furioso* find themselves losing the battle to assert both physiological and interpretive control over the female body. While the specific Ariostan episode I am considering here—the "theatergram" inherited by Spenser and Shakespeare, to borrow Louise George Clubb's designation—allows Rinaldo to realize his ambitions without confronting his misogyny, the poem elsewhere underscores and critiques the misogynistic potential of the masculine privilege of authorship and narration. For more on the "theatergram," see Clubb's *Italian Drama in Shakespeare's Time* (New Haven: Yale University Press, 1989), 1-26.

13. Edmund Spenser, *The Faerie Queene,* ed. A.C. Hamilton, Longman Annotated English Poets (London and New York: Longman, 1997). Subsequent citations appear parenthetically in the text.

14. James G. McManaway, " 'Occasion,' *Faerie Queene* II.iv.4-5," *Modern Language Notes* 49, no. 6 (1934); David W. Burchmore, "The Medieval Sources of Spenser's Occasion Episode," *Spenser Studies: A Renaissance Poetry Annual* 2 (1981): 93-120.

15. George Whitney, *A choice of emblemes, and other deuises, for the moste parte gathered out of sundrie writers, Englished and moralized* (Leyden: In the house of Christopher Plantyn, by Francis Raphelengius, 1586), 181.

16. Martin Luther, *An Exposition of Salomons Booke, called Ecclesiastes or the Preacher* (London: John Daye, 1573), sig. G4r, cited in Lorna Hutson, "Chivalry for Merchants; or, Knights of Temperance in the Realms of Gold," *Journal of Medieval and Early Modern Studies* 26 (1996): 47.

17. For more on the "reins of temperance," see *The Spenser Encyclopedia, "The Faerie Queene,"* book 2, ed. A.C. Hamilton (Toronto: University of Toronto Press, 1990). For the same image in *Orlando furioso,* see A. Bartlett Giamatti, "Sfrenatura: Restraint and Release in the *Orlando Furioso,*" in *Ariosto 1974 in America: Atti del Congresso Ariostesco—Dicembre 1974, Casa Italiana Della Columbia University,* ed. Aldo Scaglione (Ravenna: Longo Editore, 1974), and the later "Headlong Horses, Headless Horsemen: An Essay on the Chivalric Epics of Pulci, Boiardo, and Ariosto," in *Italian Literature: Roots and Branches,* ed. Giose Rimanelli and Kenneth John Atchity (New Haven and London: Yale University Press, 1976). For the Platonic roots of this iconography, see Theresa M. Krier, *Gazing on Secret Sights: Spenser, Classical Imitation, and the Decorums of Vision* (Ithaca, N.Y.: Cornell University Press, 1990), 85.

18. This application of *manège* to sexual relations is not original to Spenser. In Sidney's *New Arcadia* (1577-86), horsemanship serves as an ideal model for marital partnership; Musidorus's "spurs and wand . . . seemed rather marks of sovereignty than instruments of

punishment . . . [so] as he borrowed the horse's body, so he lent the horse his mind." But Sidney cautions against excessive misogyny, inveighing against women being "forced" into "thralldom" or treated like "cattle." Sir Philip Sidney, *The Countess of Pembroke's Arcadia: The New Arcadia,* ed. Victor Skretkowicz (Oxford: Clarendon Press, 1987), 153.

19. D. W. Burchmore, "The Medieval Sources of Spenser's Occasion Episode," 95; Frederick Kiefer, "The Conflation of Fortuna and Occasio in Renaissance Thought and Iconography," *Journal of Medieval and Renaissance Studies* 9, no. 1 (1979): 1-27.

20. Translated in Hannah Pitkin, *Fortune Is a Woman: Gender and Politics in the Thought of Niccolò Machiavelli* (Berkeley and Los Angeles: University of California Press, 1984), 152. See also Juliana Schiesari, "Libidinal Economies: Machiavelli and Fortune's Rape," in *Desire in the Renaissance: Psychoanalysis and Literature,* ed. Valeria Finucci and Regina Schwartz (Princeton: Princeton University Press, 1994), 180. Other proponents of physical mastery over Fortune, in more or less violent forms, include Leon Battista Alberti and Pico della Mirandola; see Kiefer, "The Conflation of Fortuna and Occasio," 7-9.

21. Compare this reference in a 1660 sermon by Samuel Rutherford: "indeed GOD has not put an Iron-Lock upon the Well of Life; But Christ by His Word and Sacraments opens the Well in the midest of us, and for Seventy Years and more in this Kingdom the Well has been Open." Here, the iron lock stands for permanence, prohibition, even death; it is antithetical to the living water of spiritual progress. Samuel Rutherford, *Christs napkin: or, A sermon preached in Kirkcubright at the Communion, May 12. 1633* (Scotland [?]: Imprint from the British Library, 1660), 18.

22. For Paul Alpers, such psychologization is characteristic of Spenser's adaptations of Ariosto. Paul J. Alpers, *The Poetry of "The Faerie Queene"* (Columbia and London: University of Missouri Press, 1982), 54-69. For a challenge to Alpers's reading, see Peter De Sa Wiggins, "Spenser's Use of Ariosto: Imitation and Allusion in Book I of the *Faerie Queene,*" *Renaissance Quarterly* 44, no. 2 (1991): 257-79.

23. "Embosom" too suggests Phedon's sexual confusion. It can mean both "to take or press to one's bosom; to cherish in one's bosom; to embrace," a clearly maternal image, and "to implant, plunge (a sting, weapon, etc.) in (another's) bosom," an obviously masculine one (OED). When the word appears for a second and final time in *The Faerie Queene,* it conveys a similar ambiguity. Acrasia threatens to "embosome . . . her guilefull bayt . . . deeper in [Guyon's] mind" (2.12.29); the sorceress effeminizes her victims with a kind of penetration.

24. The most comprehensive study of such anxieties is still Jonas A. Barish, *The Antitheatrical Prejudice* (Berkeley: University of California Press, 1981).

25. Maus, "Horns of Dilemma," 567-68.

26. Humphreys, ed., *Much Ado About Nothing,* 578, 572-73.

27. For transvestite boy players engendering sexual desire, see Stephen Gosson's 1582 *Playes Confuted in Five Actions,* discussed in Jyotsna Singh, "Renaissance Antitheatricality, Antifeminism, and Shakespeare's *Antony and Cleopatra,*" *Renaissance Drama* (1989): 104-5. For the story of the real devil cavorting among the players in the production of *Doctor Faustus,* see William Prynne, *Histrio-mastix: The players scourge, or, actors tragaedie* (London: Printed by E[dward] A[llde, Augustine Mathewes, Thomas Cotes] and W[illiam] I[ones] for Michael Sparke, and are to be sold at the Blue Bible, in Greene Arbour, in little Old Bayly, 1633), 556. For anxieties about theatrical flouting of sumptuary laws, see Phillips Stubbes's 1583 *Anatomy of Abuses,* discussed in Barish, *The Antitheatrical Prejudice,* 166-67.

28. Ibid., 91, n. to 1.1.40-41.

29. "Blazon" itself appears at 2.1.278, where it denotes Beatrice's evaluation of Claudio's "jealous complexion."

30. Humphreys, ed., *Much Ado About Nothing,* 110, n. to 2.1.20–21.

31. See, e.g., Nicholas Batman, *Batman Vppon Bartholome His Booke De Proprietatibus Rerum* (London: Imprinted by Thomas East, dwelling by Paules wharfe, 1582), Liber Octavus, 29–30.

32. Ibid., Liber Quartus, 25.

33. This association between spinning women and "old wives' tales" is perpetuated, e.g., in the 1510 *Gospelles of Dystaves,* Henry Watson's English translation of the anonymous antifeminist French text *Les evangiles de quenouilles.* See Susan E. Phillips, *Transforming Talk: The Problem with Gossip in Late Medieval England* (University Park: Pennsylvania State University Press, 2007), 176–202.

34. David Quint, *Epic and Empire: Politics and Generic Form from Virgil to Milton* (Princeton: Princeton University Press, 1993), 9 and passim.

35. Compare the reading of Shakespeare's *Rape of Lucrece* as a meditation on publication and sexual shame in Wendy Wall, *The Imprint of Gender: Authorship and Publication in the English Renaissance* (Ithaca, N.Y.: Cornell University Press, 1993), 214–20.

36. While this tale is already "old" by the late sixteenth century, it seems not to have been written down until 1821, when a Mr. Blakeway contributed to the Boswell-Malone Variorum Edition of Shakespeare a tale told to him by a great-aunt in 1715, who, he believed, had heard it from a narrator born during the reign of Charles II. See Appendix V of the Arden edition of *Much Ado* (232–33), and Mary Ellen Lamb, *The Popular Culture of Shakespeare, Spenser, and Jonson* (London: Routledge, 2006), 233n1.

37. Lamb, *Popular Culture,* 53, 45–62 passim.

38. Max Geisberg, *The German Single-Leaf Woodcut, 1500–1550,* ed. Walter L. Strauss (New York: Hacker Art Books, 1974), 4:1,511.

39. See the introduction to Heinrich Institoris, Jakob Sprenger, and Montague Summers, *Malleus maleficarum* (London: J. Rodker, 1928).

40. Humphreys, ed., *Much Ado About Nothing,* 217–18, n. to 122.

41. Clubb, *Italian Drama in Shakespeare's Time,* 5.

42. Clubb's theatergrams refer, of course, to conventions of cinquecento Italian *drama* that contaminate English Renaissance literature, and so I have indulged a certain definitional sloppiness by using the term for an episode in the *Furioso.* But as I have suggested, the theatricality of the Ariodante-Ginevra episode and of its English adaptations invites such semantic latitude.

Wrestling with Orlando: Chivalric Pastoral in Shakespeare's Arden

ALBERT RUSSELL ASCOLI

THE PRESENT ESSAY might be subtitled "a tale of two genres," which in turn roughly speaking relate to two of the traditional periods assigned to European cultural and social history: the Middle Ages and the Renaissance. The two genres, or perhaps "modes" is a better word in this case,[1] are, first, chivalric romance, the prose and verse tales of knights in shining armor—those from the court of an imaginary King Arthur and those from the court of an historical (but by then equally imaginary) Emperor Charlemagne—in which are played out the aspirations and the anxieties of a feudal nobility;[2] and, second, pastoral, that world of courtiers masquerading as love-sick shepherds, derived from the classical template of Virgil (who had it from Theocritus), the revival of which began, as the humanist Renaissance was first getting under way, in the fourteenth century, at the hands of (who else?) Dante, Petrarch, and Boccaccio.[3]

The pastoral mode—whose privileged status was definitively confirmed two centuries later in the *Arcadia* of Jacopo Sannazaro (1504) and the *Diana* of Jorge De Montemayor (1559)—would become a courtly mode par excellence, as the semi-independent barons of medieval times gave way to the increasingly refined, and increasingly subordinate, courtiers of the despotic *signoria,* the imperial papacy, and the nascent nation-state.[4] The medieval chivalric romance did not wither immediately, however. Far from it. The French *romans* and the Italian *cantari,* in fact, might be

293

said to have come into their own with the works of Matteo Maria Boiardo and his illustrious continuer, Ludovico Ariosto, in the *Orlando innamorato* (or *Innamoramento di Orlando;* 1494) and the *Orlando furioso* (1532), respectively. However, on the one hand, they were increasingly forced into a marriage of convenience with the classical epics of Virgil and his brethren[5] (whose genealogical emphasis perfectly suited the poet-courtier's encomiastic duties toward his princely patron, as well as fulfilling the humanist dream of classical revival) and, at the same time, with increasing explicitness, revealed themselves as the anachronistic fantasies they had decidedly become.

Neither of these two phenomena—the slow decline of the *romanzo cavalleresco,* and its eventual metamorphosis into the modern novel, also called *romanzo* in Italian,[6] and the rapid rise of pastoral (so mysterious to modern readers, who usually find it both incomprehensible and unutterably dull)—has escaped widespread scholarly attention; in fact, they are commonplaces of the literary-social history of early modernity. What I propose to do here, then, is to explore a specific aspect of this history that has perhaps received less attention than it might deserve, namely a series of significant contaminations and encounters between the two modes, which take place in European literatures over the sixteenth and early seventeenth centuries.

My attention will come to rest on what I take to be a particularly complex and illuminating encounter of this kind, namely Shakespeare's comic drama, *As You Like It.* Before doing so, however, let me briefly offer up some other symptomatic examples that will, I think, illustrate both how common the troubled marriage of pastoral and chivalric romance became in this period and why this was so.

As former baseball commissioner Bartlett Giamatti showed long before he plucked baseball's most notorious Rose, *Orlando furioso* is punctuated by a series of natural *loci amoeni*—natural "garden spots"—where the poem's ladies and knights, "donne e cavalieri," are put to the test.[7] In particular, and famously, the traditional hero of Carolingian romance, French Roland, Italianized as Orlando, experiences a "pastoral" moment that interrogates the values and the viability of the chivalric world that Ariosto inherited. The scene comes at the *Furioso*'s exact structural center, when Orlando, resting in a beautiful natural setting at what he has recently declared will be the end of his long, fruitless quest for the lovely pagan princess, Angelica,[8] gradually discovers that this same Angelica has married the low-born soldier Medoro, surrendering her long-defended virginity to him rather than to Orlando or any of a vast crowd of pagan and Christian knights who have pursued her throughout Boiardo's poem and then into Ariosto's. Once he has run out of excuses for disbelieving the obvious truth of the matter, Orlando goes stark-raving mad (*Orlando furioso*, 23.100–136; 24.4–14).

For our purposes, the following elements of the episode are key: that Orlando receives his knowledge about Angelica from a series of love poems carved by Medoro into the barks of trees, in a version of a *topos* deriving from the pastoral tradition (from Theocritus to Virgil to Sannazaro);[9] that Orlando experiences "the final blow" to his self-delusion about Angelica's devotion to him while spending the night in the humble abode of a shepherd (whose lowly status echoes that of Medoro); that upon descending into madness he sheds all external signs of his chivalric identity (most notably his famous sword and armor); and, finally, that in the first great expression of his madness he goes to war on the local population of shepherds, killing them and their herds randomly while at the same time turning the pastoral landscape into a desert by uprooting trees and plants, filling streams with rocks, and so on.[10] The encounter between chivalry and pastoral, then, represents the radical breakdown of a hierarchical world of class on which the former is predicated: Angelica, the princess, abandons her "knight in shining armor" for a lower-class person; Orlando surrenders his chivalric identity in the ignoble destruction of defenseless shepherds and domesticated animals.

A little less than a century later, a far more famous example of the encounter, indeed pathological symbiosis, between chivalry and pastoral punctuates the "first novel," Cervantes' *Don Quixote*. As Don Quixote, né Alonso Quijana, goes about the anachronistic and/or utopian pursuit of chivalric knighthood, which he has come to believe in through the reading of chivalric romances, like *Amadis de Gaul* and this same *Orlando furioso*, his adventures are regularly interrupted by encounters with the world of pastoral, or, better, with the world of upper-class people playing at being shepherd-lovers, following the literary model of the pastoral genre (for example, the tale of Chrysostom and Marcela in part 1 [bk. 2, chs.3–6], and the generically related episodes of Basilio and Quiteria [ch. 19] and of the two young "shepherdesses" [ch. 58] in part 2). In one of the many famous episodes of part 1, the Don, after his encounter with the love-mad Cardenio in the Sierra-Morena wilderness, considers imitating

the "pastoral" love madness of Ariosto's Orlando, only to opt instead for
that of Amadis, including the engraving of love poetry on tree bark (bk.
2, chs. 9–12). Perhaps even more to our point, near the end of part 2, having been tricked into binding himself by oath to forswear chivalry for a
full year, Quixote turns to an alternative fantasy, the creation of a pastoral
community of shepherd-poet-lovers, to include himself, Sancho, Sanson
Carrasco, and his two old friends, the barber and the curate (pt. 2, chs.
67 and 73). When, instead, he sickens unto death soon thereafter, poor
Sancho tries to revive him by re-presenting the pastoral fantasy, but to no
avail (pt. 2, ch. 74).[11]

Pastoral, then, is inextricably tied by both Ariosto and Cervantes to
the madness of chivalry—its increasing disjunction from the realities of
social and sentimental life—and, by Cervantes, to the death of the chivalric dream personified. Pastoral, in the *Quixote,* is where chivalry goes
to die. Curiously enough, we can find something very similar, though
in significantly abridged form, occurring in the case of Shakespeare's
most famous knight, Falstaff. In *Henry IV, Part 1,* the world of chivalry,
and its foremost value, honor, is schizophrenically torn between the ide-
alist ravings of the rebellious Hotspur, on the one hand, and, on the
other, the degraded picture of the historic knightly class drawn in the
figure of Falstaff ("What is honor? A word . . . air. . . . Honor is a mere
scutcheon. . . ." [5.1.132–33, 137]),[12] between the two of whom emerges
Hal, the princely politician, embodiment of a new, state-centered heroism for which honor, the myth of chivalry, is just one tool among many
others for the future ruler of a nation.[13]

Where, you might ask, does pastoral come in? Only at the end, and
then allusively. Two plays later, as Hal, now crowned Henry V, prepares
to go to war with France, where the chivalry of Charlemagne's court has
degenerated into the foppishness of the Dauphin (the crown prince, that
is), we hear, in the report of the Hostess (once Mistress Quickly), the dying words of the rejected Falstaff: "He's not in hell. He's in Arthur's bosom
if ever man went to Arthur's bosom. A made a finer end, and went away
an it had been any christom child . . . for after I saw him fumble with the
sheets, and play with flowers, and smile upon his finger's end, I knew that
there was but one way; for his nose was as sharp as a pen, and a babbled
of green fields . . ." (2.3.8–14).[14] As he dies, preparing to go to the heavenly court of the English chivalric king par excellence, Arthur, Falstaff

plays with flowers and "babbles of green fields" (linked by the image of the pen to a world of literature, or of art, if the Folio reading "tables" is taken instead):[15] he too takes the pastoral turn, as the degraded world of chivalry breathes its last.

Orlando, Don Quixote, Falstaff: three very different versions of chivalry, bound together, in madness and in death, by decisive detours into the pastoral—as natural landscape, and as literary mode. If each of these three texts, in its own way, uses pastoral as part of the process for representing the decline and fall of the chivalric ideal and the noble class that lived with and through it, there are other Renaissance texts that make a bid to rescue the genre of chivalric romance precisely by fusing it with pastoral:[16] I think, for example, of Sidney's *Arcadia* (1590, 1593) and of Honoré d'Urfé's *L'Astrée* (1607-27).[17] I think as well, and not by chance, of another English pastoral romance from the end of the sixteenth century—Thomas Lodge's *Rosalynde* (1590),[18] which Lodge may have composed with the help of his friend and sometime collaborator, Robert Greene,[19] himself the author of a dramatic, and radically unfaithful, version of *Orlando furioso.*

Lodge's story begins with the breakdown of a patriarchal ideal that is identified closely with the genealogical transmission of chivalric identity: Rosader, true heir to the chivalry of his father, John of Bordeaux, a member of the order of the Knights of Malta, is displaced by an older brother, Saladyn, whose name links him to the Saracen enemy of medieval chivalry; and, at the macrohistorical level, the twelve peers—the Paladins—of France, whose first appearance was in the court of Charlemagne, serve a usurper king, Torrismond.[20] The detour into the forest of the Ardennes—and into a world of pastoral marked by shepherd-lover-poets with traditional names like Montanus, Corydon, Silvius, and Phoebe—becomes the route (when the peers finally take action against the usurper) to restoring the true French king, Gerismond, and to giving Rosader back his birthright as true son and heir of John, finest chevalier of France. Chivalry's recovery from the corruption and delegitimation of Saladyn and Torrismond is sealed as Rosader not only enters the service of Gerismond in his father's place but also marries the king's daughter, Rosalynd, thus mitigating the potential gap between courtier and prince. On the margins of the tale lurks the potential for a dangerously topical allegory: the French locale and the thematics of usurpation point together toward the possibility of a Catholic restoration in the Protestant England of Elizabeth I, in keeping with Lodge's ill-concealed sympathies with the old religion and the social order it entailed.[21]

Enter, at last, Shakespeare and his Orlando. It has long been recognized, though (as far as I can tell) with little consequence for the interpretation of the play, that in taking up and adapting Lodge's narrative to his own dramatic purposes,[22] Shakespeare chose new names for Rosader and Saladyn that tied them directly to the literary tradition of chivalric romance: Oliver and Orlando, the most famous of Charlemagne's traditional paladins, and gave them a father, Rowland du Boys, whose name in French means "Roland of the woods,"[23] and that wood, again, is Arden, the anglicized Ardennes of Ariosto and the tradition to which his poem belongs.[24]

One might assume that Shakespeare was simply teasing out the implications of Lodge's patent effort to revive the institutions of medieval chivalry. Taken together, however, with the fact that Shakespeare at the same time suppresses the French element of Lodge's text (placing the action in an unnamed dukedom, removing references to the "twelve peers," and so on), I believe another possible interpretation emerges. Where Lodge sets out to effect a restoration of the *ancien régime,* chivalric, and perhaps religious, in an indefinite yet distinctly *present* tense and time (one thinks, for example, of the identification of John of Bordeaux as a Knight of Malta, an order that had existed under that name only since 1530),[25] Shakespeare turns back to a distinctly literary world at several removes from any present reality, whose nature might be emblematically figured by the descent from a semihistorical, French Roland, Rowland du Boys, to the Italianate "Orlando," who has left his historical origins far behind, dwelling, even by Ariosto's time, in a centuries-old world of literary fantasy.[26] In other words, Shakespeare restores the anachronistic element of chivalric romance before moving on to transform it into something very different indeed—into a pastoral comedy of happy marriage.

In the balance of this essay I will explore in greater detail how it is that Shakespeare invokes and transforms the categories of chivalric romance, primarily by submitting them to yet another version of pastoral.[27] As I do so, I will mark the connections of *As You Like It* to the trend in early modern literary and cultural history that I attempted to delimit at the outset by pointing to a series of homologies and analogies with Ariosto's poem,[28] though without claiming direct "influence" of the *Furioso* on Shakespeare's play.[29]

Let me begin with the curiously antichivalric exercise in "heroic" combat that Rosader/Orlando undertakes near the beginning of both *Rosalynde* and *As You Like It,* namely the wrestling match: with a gigantic "Norman" in Lodge and with one "Charles" in Shakespeare. In Lodge, the wrestling match is one event in a tournament staged by the king, which also includes more traditional chivalric activities like jousting. Where Shakespeare's Orlando seeks out the match himself to affirm his independence, Rosader is deliberately egged on to wrestle by Saladyn, who has arranged with the Norman to kill or maim him.[30] In both texts, wrestling—identified as a plebeian sport that brings a person of noble blood into agonistic contact with a member of the lower classes, dispensing with both of the trademarks of chivalry, armor and horse—is a marker of the degradation of chivalry.[31] In Lodge, however, it is a sign of the corruption introduced into the chivalric order by Saladyn (and Torrismond) that will eventually be set to rights, while in Shakespeare Orlando himself seeks out the challenge, and there is never any implication that he is destined for more traditionally chivalric heroism, as there is instead with Rosader. Such an interpretation might be reinforced if, as seems probable to me given the proximity to the names "Oliver," "Rowland," and "Orlando," Charles's name is meant to serve as a (degraded) reminder of the figure at the center of the tradition in play, namely the Holy Roman Emperor, Charles the Great.

Among other elements that Shakespeare introduces into the wrestling scene is one that strikes indirectly at the heart of the early modern iconography of heroism, notably as it is deployed in a chivalric text like Ariosto's. In *Rosalynde,* Lodge compares "the Norman" as he impatiently awaits any and all challengers to Hercules as he prepared to do battle against Achelous (a rival for the affections of Deineira),[32] an allusion generally in keeping with the classicizing Euphuism of the work as a whole (that is, its adherence to the mannered style identified with John Lyle's *Euphues* and fostered by Robert Greene in works such as the prose romance *Euphues his Censure* [1587]).[33] In *As You Like It,* Shakespeare makes much more limited and yet at the same time much more strategic use of classical allusion (for example, in Touchstone's comparison of his exile among the goats to Ovid's among the Goths, of which more later). In the case at hand, Shakespeare picks up the Hercules reference, but he transfers it to Orlando, in keeping with what we will soon see is a typical chivalric identification of the warrior-knight with the demigod who consistently impersonates the classical virtues, and particularly *for-titudo,* strength and endurance. As the match begins, Rosalind, already well on her way to love, cries out: "Now Hercules be thy speed young man!" (1.2.165). Moreover, Hercules in this case is implicitly linked to a much more predictable myth, namely the oft-allegorized wrestling match between Jove's son and the giant Antaeus since, shortly before Rosalind's comment, Charles has referred to Orlando as "this young gallant that is so desirous to lie with his mother earth" (1.2.157-58). The reference to Antaeus, who is the son of Earth, and derives his strength from her (so that Hercules can only achieve victory when he lifts his foe into the air and strangles him), is clear enough by itself, but it is then fully activated when Hercules is mentioned by name nine lines later.[34]

The myth of Hercules and Antaeus was widely known and used in the Renaissance, typically to figure the triumph of virtue over vice, and, since the literal story requires Hercules to go beyond his incomparable strength by the strategic use of his wits,[35] it also symbolizes the combination of *fortitudo* with *sapientia,* strength with wisdom, which is the time-honored possession of the true hero, and in particular of the chivalric hero.[36] There is no more appropriate text for illustrating the latter point than *Orlando furioso,* whose hero is linked, through the title and in other ways, with the Senecan tragedy, *Hercules furens,* and whose other hero, the genealogical protagonist Ruggiero, ostentatiously reenacts the famous choice of Hercules at the Crossroads, first choosing the right-hand path to virtue before being all to easily lured into the sinister arms of Circean vice, in the person of the seductress fairy, Alcina (*Orlando furioso* 6.55-56, 60).[37] Already in the Ariostan doubling of Hercules as madman and Hercules as personification of virtue we can see the by now familiar problematization of chivalric heroism at work. But it seems particularly significant in this context that both Ruggiero and Orlando are identified at crucial moments with both actors in the Hercules versus Antaeus drama.[38]

Let me cite one famous episode, that of Olimpia and Cimosco, in which this occurs, going very much to the heart of the "death of chivalry" story I am telling here. In the episode in question, Orlando, identified immediately by his "ercoleo aspetto" (Herculean appearance) betokening "virtù" (9.56.1-2), takes up the cause of Olimpia, whose fiancé, Bireno, is held hostage by the cruel king Cimosco. Cimosco is the possessor of a horrendous weapon, the *archibugio,* ancestor of the harquebus and cannon, in other the words the firearms introduced on a grand scale precisely in the early sixteenth century. Ariosto twice stops to rail against the antichivalric implications of this weapon, which evidently compromises irremediably the value of the individual valor of the single "cavaliere" (9.90-91 and, especially, 11.21-28). Ironically, as Herculean Orlando (whose body, like that of Achilles, is invulnerable to all assaults) overcomes the gun, which has been repeatedly compared to thunder and lightning (9.29, 66, 75, 88), he himself is assimilated to lightning (9.78.1-2), and specifically to its effects as it "penetrates into a place which encloses together carbon, sulfur, and saltpeter" ("[penetra] ove un richiuso loco/carbon con zolfo e con salnitro serra"; 9.78.3-4), that is, the ingredients of gunpowder. Orlando, paradigm of chivalry, is thus identified with the technological antithesis of chivalry.

At the same time, with equal irony, he metamorphoses from Hercules into Antaeus:

> Cade a terra il cavallo e il cavalliero . . .
> Quale il libico Anteo sempre più fiero
> surger solea da la percossa arena,
> tal surger parve, e che la forza, quando
> toccò il terren, si radoppiasse a Orlando. (9.77. 1, 5-8)

Horse and horseman fall to earth . . . Like Libyan Antaeus arose ever fiercer after striking the sands, so seems to arise Orlando, and so too did his force seem to redouble as he touched the earth.

Were we to take the reprise of this conflation of Hercules and Antaeus in Shakespearean Orlando as a specific echo of the *Furioso,* it would work simply to reinforce the degradation of chivalry already present in the reduction of horseman-knight to wrestler. In the immediate context of *As You Like It,* however, the allusive nexus has a rather different, if in the end related, valence. This Orlando, too, we soon learn to infer, is *both* Hercules and Antaeus in that even as he defeats Charles he is "overthrown" by "something weaker," namely Rosalind (1.2.212).

Orlando's "innamoramento" with Rosalind points to a second major area of analogy, if not influence, between the *Furioso* and *As You Like It:* namely, the insertion of Orlando-as-lover into a pastoral scene where love poems are to be found in the trees.[39] It may well be, in fact, that this combination of elements (pastoral love and arboreal verse), already present with Rosalynd and Rosader in Lodge's romance, helped to suggest the use

of the name "Orlando" to Shakespeare, whether via Greene's play, Har-
rington's translation, or some other means, indirect or direct.[40] For that
matter, Lodge may himself already have had the *Furioso* in the back of
his mind, especially given his ties to Greene. In any event, it is clear that
Shakespeare is following Lodge more closely than Ariosto, though there
are interesting modifications to be noted. Most obviously, where Ariosto's
Orlando goes mad after reading the arboreal verses reporting Medoro's
amorous conquest of Angelica, Lodge's Rosader and Shakespeare's Orlando (as, for that matter, Cervantes' Quixote) are themselves the authors
of love-poetry,[41] which eventually, after the "courtship of Ganymede,"
that is, Rosalind in disguise as a boy, leads to a happy marriage under
the allegorical auspices of the goddess Hymen, placing Shakespeare's Orlando structurally in the position of Ariosto's Medoro.[42]

In this regard, one touch added by Shakespeare that might well point
to Ariosto is Celia's apparent throw-away remark that she "found [Or-
lando] under a tree, like a dropped acorn" (3.3.196) and, here's the point,
"there lay he stretched along like a wounded knight" (3.3.201).[43] The remark is striking, first, because, unlike Lodge's Rosader, this is the one and
only time Orlando is referred to specifically as a knight, and even here
only in a simile. Secondly, and to my immediate purpose, it may well
recall the "innamoramento" of Ariosto's Angelica (disguised in "pastoral
e umile veste" [19.17.2]), who first encounters Medoro in the "alta selva"
"near death" from a wound inflicted on him by an unchivalrous man in
the company of the Scottish captain Zerbino, and, as she cures him with
magic herbs, receives the figurative wound of love herself (19.26–29 and
passim). If the echo is present, it completes the process of turning "Orlando," epitome of chivalric knighthood, into Ariosto's humble yet valiant
"Medoro," and of metamorphosing martial romance into a pastoral comedy of love. Whether or not an Ariostan intertext is present, however, it
is certainly the case that, apart from the reported battle with the lioness
threatening Oliver, in which Orlando is indeed wounded (4.3.93–151),
Shakespeare has omitted all of the other elements, of language and of action, from Lodge's forest scene that tended to keep Rosader's potential for
chivalric heroism in view, including the final battle between the usurper
king and the rightful monarch.[44]

In the same vein, it is worth noting that where for Lodge knighthood
and honor are the focus of repeated attention,[45] in Shakespeare, with the
exception just noted and two others I will come to shortly, chivalry is not

a central, explicit theme. What is repeatedly foregrounded, and what is correspondingly absent from Lodge, with a couple of perfunctory exceptions, are references to life at court and especially to the affectation and corruption of courtiership, beginning with the appearance of the frivolous courtier Le Beau in act 1, scene 2.[46] In other words, Lodge's anachronistic vision of chivalry and pastoral, reconciled in Arden, gives way in *As You Like It* to a tension between the court, where knights are domesticated as courtiers, and the country, where "winter and rough weather," the occasional lioness, and the smelly, realistic business of raising sheep (introduced in some detail by Corin in 3.3) have usurped the adventurous Ardennes of Ariostan romance knight-errantry.[47]

In addition to the strategic name changes insisted upon above, Shakespeare introduces a number of characters entirely absent from his primary model. Of these the most notable are, obviously, Jacques (with whom I am not concerned here) and Touchstone (with whom I am, as will appear). On the face of it, neither could be remotely compared to anything Ariostan, or, for that matter, anything inherent to the modes of either chivalric romance or of pastoral. To the long-time Ariosto scholar, such as myself, who sees the *Furioso* reflected not only in most books, but also in trees, stones, and running brooks, it is possible to discern a distant comparability between the function of metadramatic commentary exercised by those two, as occasionally by Rosalind (especially when "she/he" turns epilogue), and the intrusive narrating "I" deployed by Ariosto throughout his poem.[48] And this would be especially true of Touchstone, who, like that narrator,[49] both stands outside the action, commenting ironically upon it, and is also caught up in the world he comments upon (for example, in his courtship of and ill-augured marriage to the "foul slut" Audrey). The importance of this similarity, I think, lies not in any influence exerted (the device is central to Elizabethan-Jacobean theatricality and to Shakespeare's company and his oeuvre especially), but rather in how it may be related to the general literary cultural trends that I have associated with the juxtaposition of chivalric romance and pastoral.

It is, in fact, Touchstone, true to his name in this as in so many things,[50] through whom most of the play's reflections on its generic ancestry, and its poetic-dramatic nature, are articulated. Virtually all of the overt satire on courtliness, paired precisely with ironic commentary on the country life, is delivered by Touchstone. In addition, and to my final point, he is the primary vehicle, other than the allusive force of names, by which chivalry, bounded on one side by the new world of the centralized court and on the other by pastoral fantasies, is explicitly made a subject of discourse in *As You Like It*. I refer in particular to two speeches, one near the beginning, one near the end of the play, that surreptitiously place the action in a double context of literary and social history.

The initial passage is our introduction to the character of Touchstone, and it first seems, as Rosalind and Celia are inclined to understand it, as pointless foolery.[51] Here is the scene, whose potential significance perhaps will be more evident for its position in this essay:

CELIA: Were you made the messenger [by my father]?

TOUCHSTONE: No, *by mine honor*, but I was bid to come for you.

ROSALIND: Where learned you that *oath*, fool?

TOUCHSTONE: Of a certain *knight* that *swore by his honor* they were good pancakes, and *swore by his honor* the mustard was naught. Now I'll stand to it, the pancakes were naught, and the mustard was good, and yet was not *the knight forsworn*.

CELIA: How prove you that in the great heap of your knowledge?

ROSALIND: Aye, marry, now unmuzzle your wit.

TOUCHSTONE: Stand you both forth now. Stroke your chins, and *swear by your beards*, that I am a knave.

CELIA: By our beards, if we had them, thou art.

TOUCHSTONE: By my knavery, if I had it, then I were; but *if you swear by that that is not, you are not forsworn;* no more was this *knight, swearing by his honor*, for he never had any; or if he had, he had *sworn it away* before ever he saw those pancakes or that mustard. (1.2.47–63; emphasis added)

Knighthood, and the word most closely associated with it, "honor," and the "word of honor" by which a true knight defines a relationship both of referential truth and moral action to the world around him, is multiply degraded in this scene, which comes shortly before the antichivalric wrestling match. Touchstone's appropriation of "honor" to himself is in itself degrading, since he clearly belongs to a servant class that traditionally has no right to such a claim. In explaining that claim away (and, almost imperceptibly, admitting that he himself has no honor to swear by), he invokes a generic knight who wastes his word of honor on pancakes and mustard and who, in any case, has reduced "honor" to a mere word, to "air," as Falstaff puts it. Touchstone and his knight move chivalry in two directions simultaneously: toward an "ignoble" realism, a world of pancakes and mustard, on the one hand, and, on the other, toward pure literature, the "airy nothings" of imagination no longer able to assert a correspondence between its words and any reality that could truly be called "chivalric." It is, of course, the more overt clash between these extremes that Cervantes dramatizes throughout both parts of *Don Quixote.*

In my reading of *As You Like It,* this apparent throwaway scene fulfills its thematic and critical destiny in another, more famous rant of Touchstone, his lengthy discourse on the courtly duel that serves as a curious prelude to the quadruple wedding with which the play ends:

JACQUES: This is the motley-minded gentleman I have so often met in the forest; he [Touchstone] hath been a *courtier, he swears.*

TOUCHSTONE: If any man doubt that let him put me to my purgation. I have trod a measure; I have flattered a lady; I have been politic with my friend, smooth with mine enemy; I have undone three tailors; I have had four quarrels, and like to have fought one.

JACQUES: And how was that ta'en up?

TOUCHSTONE: Faith, we met, and found the quarrel was upon the seventh cause.

. . . .

JACQUES: . . . How did you find the quarrel on the seventh cause?

TOUCHSTONE: Upon a *lie, seven times removed* . . . as thus, sir. I did dislike the cut of a certain courtier's beard. He sent me word, *if* I said his beard was not cut well, he was in the mind it was: this is called "the retort courteous." *If* I sent him word again it was not well cut, he would send me word he cut it to please himself: this is called "the quip modest." *If* again, it was not well cut, he disabled my judgment: this is called "the reply churlish." *If* again it was not well cut, he would answer *I spake not true:* this is called "the reproof valiant." *If* again it was not well cut, he would say *I lied:* this is called "the countercheck quarrelsome." And so to "the *lie circumstantial"* and "the *lie direct."*

JACQUES: And how oft did you say his beard was not well cut?

TOUCHSTONE: I durst go no further than the *lie circumstantial,* nor he durst not give me the *lie direct;* and so we measured swords and parted.

JACQUES: Can you nominate in order now *the degrees of the lie?*

TOUCHSTONE: O sir, we quarrel *in print, by the book,* as you have *books for good manners.* I will name you the degrees: [*he repeats the list, ending with*] the sixth the *lie with circumstance;* the seventh, the *lie direct.* All these you may avoid but the *Lie Direct* and you may avoid that too, *with an "if."* I knew but when seven justices could not take up a quarrel, but when the parties were met themselves, one of them thought but of *an "if":* as *"if* you said so, then I said so"; and they shook hands and swore brothers. *Your "if"* is the only peacemaker. *Much virtue in "if."* (5.4.39–48, 60–88; emphasis added)

The richness of this passage, and its crucial thematic weight, has by no means gone unnoticed by critics of the play.[52] In terms of my topic, however, it has special resonance, and so I beg forgiveness for passing over what may seem to some readers very familiar turf. To begin, as pertaining to the "affair of honor," there is a distant yet substantive connection to the matter of the Knight of the Pancakes' hollow oath,[53] reinforced by the shared references to beards. More particularly, the passage elaborates a parody of the genealogical links that modern courtiers assert between themselves and the knights of yore. The duel is obviously the institutionalized heir of the chivalric single combat, which stands at the heart of the romance tradition—but it now follows elaborate protocols "by the book," specifically the dueling manuals,[54] which, as Touchstone himself points out, are comparable to the guides to courtiership, whose archetype is to be found in Baldassare Castiglione's *Libro del cortegiano* (1528) and in Thomas Hoby's Englishing thereof (1561).[55] Touchstone thus satirizes courtiership as a "literary" exercise in specific, degraded relationship to chivalric knighthood. And the play, in fact, has thus represented two degraded extremes of chivalric combat, wrestling and the mannerist duel,[56] without showing the thing itself.

The duel as Touchstone defines it is "by the book" and "in print," and its key categories are, precisely, the *"lie,"* given and received, and *"if"*: in other words, the untrue (though "untruth" related to the most trivial and "subjective" of matters—the cut of a beard and what one may or may not think of it) and, most crucially, the hypothetical-imaginary. More than one critic has pointed out that another aspect of the pervasive virtue of *if* is then made immediately present in the series of "ifs" that then allow the happy resolution of Shakespeare's comic drama (5.4.103–5):[57]

DUKE SENIOR: *If there be truth in sight,* you are my daughter.
ORLANDO: *If there be truth in sight,* you are my Rosalind.
PHOEBE: *If sight and shape be true,* why, then, my love adieu.

And then:

HYMEN: *If truth holds true contents.* (5.4.114)

That from a literal standpoint these "ifs," at least the first three, are quite untrue then appears pointedly in the epilogue when the boy-actor who has played the female Rosalind playing the boy Ganymede playing Rosalind concludes by saying "*If I were a woman,* I would kiss as many of you as have beards that pleased me, complexions that like me . . . " (Epilogue 13-15; emphasis added), and so on.

All of this, in turn, may be taken back to yet another famous speech of Touchstone, a little earlier in the play, during his first wooing of Audrey (3.4.5-6, 10-16; emphasis added):

TOUCHSTONE: I am here with thee [Audrey] and thy goats as the most capricious poet honest Ovid was among the Goths.

. . . .

TOUCHSTONE: . . . *Truly,* I would the gods had made thee [Audrey] *poetical.*

AUDREY: I do not know what *poetical* is. Is it honest *in word and deed? Is it a true thing?*

TOUCHSTONE: No, *truly,* for *the truest poetry is the most feigning,* and lovers are given to *poetry,* and what *they swear in poetry* may be said as lovers *they do feign.*

Poetic fiction then is, if not merely hypothetical, an outright lie, the antithesis of lovers' (and knights') oaths to be "true" in "word and deed." Chivalry gives way to pastoral, and both modes disappear into a world of fictional poetic imaginations and lies. This, then, is the last step in the process I have tried to describe in considering symptomatic aspects of the works of Ariosto, Lodge, Cervantes, and, of course, Shakespeare. The convergence of chivalric romance with pastoral, among other things, foregrounds the generic character of both spaces, their standing as subsets of an increasingly autonomous cultural domain, that of the "literary."

In a very different form, this same pattern is already on display in cantos 34 and 35 of Ariosto's *Orlando furioso,* written nearly a century before, and in another country. When the bizarre English prince and knight, Astolfo, sets off upon the Pegasean hippogriff of poetic imagination to heal the madness of Orlando *furioso,* his journey takes him, by now unsurprisingly, to the archetype of Christian pastoral, the garden of Eden, where he finds the guide who will lead him on the last stage of his journey—Saint John the Evangelist and author of Revelations, the personification of truthful biblical authorship. Together they ascend to the moon, where, in the midst of an extended allegorical landscape imaging the sum of earthly loss and lack, Astolfo recovers Orlando's wits, which are stored in a bottle. He then listens as Saint John unfolds the central

allegorical image of loss—Time despoiling human property and, in the
end, life itself—and the counterpoised remedy of poetic "fama," which
restores loss and brings the dead back to life, at least in words. This allegory, famously, takes an odd turn, as Saint John urges princely patrons
to treat their courtier-poets well and richly, since they are able to make
evil men seem good and good men (the example is Nero!) seem evil, depending on whether they are rewarded or not.[58] In Saint John's "authoritative" account, poetic language is, at best, inversely related to earthly
reality, and, at a nadir, entirely disconnected from it. Worse still, we then
learn, John and the biblical language he represents do not escape from
the economy of courtly fictions since, as he says in conclusion:

> Gli scrittori amo e fo il debito mio;
> ch'al vostro mondo fui scrittore anch'io.
> E sopra tutti gli altri io feci acquisto
> che non mi può levar né tempo né morte;
> e ben convenne al mio lodato Cristo
> rendermi guidardon di sì gran sorte. (35.28.7-29.4)

I love writers, and rightly so, since in your world I was a writer too. And above
all others was I repaid with that which neither time nor death can take away
[that is, eternal life in the earthly paradise]. And well it suited my much-praised
Christ to reward me for his great good fortune [that is, the fame I conferred on
him through writing].

What keeps Ariosto this side of overt blasphemy is that the whole episode has worked to unveil its own literariness in Touchstone's sense, its
ficticity—so that one immediately recognizes that this Saint John, like the
Carolingian chronicler and peer, Bishop Turpin, so often mockingly invoked as authoritative source in the *Furioso*, is a creature of the Ariostan
imagination, as much as the hippogriff.[59] Shakespeare, of course, does
not go so far, nor could he have, in the public theater and in Protestant
England, even *if* he had wanted to. And yet he also empties out any historical content of chivalric romance as he conflates it with the pastoral
mode, leaving behind an awareness of both as pleasure-giving literary
genres, whose delights are closely tied to their untrue and/or hypothetical nature. Beyond Touchstone's indications to this effect, "Rosalind"/
Ganymede as Epilogue says as much, and so, for that matter, does a title,
As You Like It, which describes the play's content solely in terms of audience expectation and enjoyment.

In other words, this exercise in literary history—my exploration of the motivated rewriting of chivalric romance through the distorting and ironizing filter of pastoral—has instead concluded with the recounting of an episode in the history of emergent "literariness" or "the literary" in a modern sense, one in which Ariosto and Shakespeare alike are "merely players."

In closing let me offer one final example of a text that represents the intertwining and transformation of pastoral and romance, though to apparently very different ends than those of *As You Like It,* much less *Orlando furioso.* When we talk about the pastoral of Milton's *Paradise Lost,* we usually refer to it in relation to yet another genre, *epic,* which it absorbs, Christianizes, psychologizes, and domesticates. And yet, this final episode leads out of epic, out of Eden, and down the road of romance, of errant wandering through the fallen world of human history:

> In either hand the hast'ning Angel caught
> Our ling'ring parents, and to th' eastern gate
> Led them direct, and down the cliff as fast
> To the subjected plain; then disappeared.
> They, looking back, all th' eastern side beheld
> Of Paradise, so late their happy seat,
> Waved over by that flaming brand; the gate
> With dreadful faces thronged and fiery arms:
> Some natural tears they dropped, but wiped them soon;
> The world was all before them, where to choose
> Their place of rest, and Providence their guide:
> They, hand in hand, with wand'ring steps and slow,
> Through Eden took their solitary way.[60]

Like Don Quixote and Falstaff, death awaits Eve and Adam on the far side of now-vacuous fantasies of epic warfare and of true pastoral bliss, but so does the long realistic *romanzo* (romance turned novel) that lingers on well beyond the "resolution" ostensibly provided by happy, comic marriages, even that of Rosalind and her Orlando.

Notes

My thanks to Janet Adelman, Louise George Clubb, Kasey Evans, and David Quint for suggestions that have helped me improve this essay, and to Jonathan Combs-Schilling for his indispensable bibliographic assistance in the latter stages of the project.

   1. On the genre/mode distinction, see Paul Alpers, *What is Pastoral?* (Chicago: University of Chicago Press, 1996), 44–78.

2. A good introduction to the romance tradition is Barbara Fuchs, *Romance,* in the series The New Critical Idiom (New York: Routledge, 2004). Although the "mode" of romance is usually traced back to the late classical Greek romances in prose of Heliodorus, Longus, and others, and even to the *Odyssey* or *Gilgamesh,* for the purposes of this essay the controlling model is the refashioning of the medieval chivalric romance, first in the popular Italian *cantare* and then in the works of Boiardo (*Innamoramento di Orlando*) and Ariosto (*Orlando furioso*), whose dominant influence in sixteenth-century Europe is visible, for instance, in Spenser's *Faerie Queene.* Not coincidentally, the latter part of the century saw a fierce debate over the legitimacy of romance as genre, provoked by the treatises of G. Giraldi-Cinzio and G. B. Pigna (respectively, *Discorso intorno al comporre dei romanzi* [1554] and *I romanzi* [also 1554]), and described by Bernard Weinberg in his monumental *A History of Literary Criticism in the Italian Renaissance,* 2 vols. (Chicago: University of Chicago Press, 1961), 2:432–52 and 2:954–1073 passim. Defining theoretical considerations of the question are in Northrop Frye, *The Secular Scripture: A Study of the Structure of Romance* (Cambridge, Mass.: Harvard University Press, 1976); Frederic Jameson, *The Political Unconscious: Narrative as a Socially Symbolic Act* (Ithaca, N.Y.: Cornell University Press, 1981), esp. 103–50; Margaret Doody, *The True Story of the Novel* (New Brunswick, N.J.: Rutgers University Press, 1996). On the Greek romances and their influence, see, to begin, James Tatum, ed., *The Search for the Ancient Novel* (Baltimore: Johns Hopkins University Press, 1994). On medieval romance, Kevin Brownlee and Marina Scordilis Brownlee, eds., *Romance: Generic Transformation from Chrétien de Troyes to Cervantes* (Hanover, NH: University Press of New England, 1985), and Roberta L. Krueger, ed., *The Cambridge Companion to Medieval Romance* (Cambridge: Cambridge University Press, 2000). On romance in the Renaissance, see Patricia Parker, *Inescapable Romance: Studies in the Poetics of a Mode* (Princeton: Princeton University Press, 1979); David Quint, "The Boat of Romance," in *Romance,* ed. Brownlee and Brownlee, 178–202; Sergio Zatti, *Il "Furioso" fra epos e romanzo* (Lucca: Pacini-Fazzi, 1990), partially translated by Sally Hill and Dennis Looney in Zatti, *The Quest for Epic: From Ariosto to Tasso,* ed. Dennis Looney, introd. Albert Russell Ascoli (Toronto: University of Toronto Press, 2006). See also notes 5 and 6 below.

3. On the history and significance of the pastoral mode see William Empson, *Some Versions of Pastoral* (London: Chatto & Windus, 1950); Thomas G. Rosenmeyer, *The Green Cabinet* (Berkeley: University of California Press, 1969); Harold Toliver, *Pastoral Form and Attitudes* (Berkeley: University of California Press, 1971); Laurence Lerner, *The Uses of Nostalgia: Studies in Pastoral Poetry* (London: Chatto & Windus, 1972); Renato Poggioli, *The Oaten Flute* (Cambridge, Mass.: Harvard University Press, 1975); Helen Cooper, *Pastoral: Medieval into Renaissance* (Totowa, N.J.: Rowman & Littlefield, 1977); Louise Adrian Montrose, "Of Gentlemen and Shepherds: The Politics of Elizabethan Pastoral Form," *English Literary History* 50 (1983): 415–59; Bryan Loughrey, ed., *The Pastoral Mode: A Casebook* (London: Macmillan, 1984); Annabel Patterson, *Pastoral and Ideology* (Berkeley: University of California Press, 1987); E. Kegel-Brinkgreve, *The Echoing Woods: Bucolic and Pastoral from Theocritus to Wordsworth* (Amsterdam: I.C. Gieben, 1990); Judith Haber, *Pastoral and the Poetics of Self-Contradiction: Theocritus to Marvell* (Cambridge: Cambridge University Press, 1994); Alpers, *What is Pastoral?;* Thomas K. Hubbard, *The Pipes of Pan* (Ann Arbor: University of Michigan Press, 1998). On pastoral drama more generally, see Louise George Clubb, *Italian Drama in Shakespeare's Time* (New Haven, Conn.: Yale University Press, 1989), 93–187; Robert Henke, *Pastoral Transformation. Italian Tragicomedy and Shakespeare's Late Plays* (London: Associated University Presses, 1997); Lisa Sampson, *Pastoral Drama in Early Modern Italy: The Making of a New Genre* (London: Legenda, 2006).

4. I loosely adopt the influential thesis of Norbert Elias, *The Civilizing Process: Socio-genetic and Psychogenetic Investigations,* rev. ed., trans. Edmund Jepbcott, ed. Eric Dunning, Johan Goudsblom, and Stephen Mennell (Oxford: Blackwell, 2000, first published in German, 1939). I am more directly influenced by David Quint's series of essays on early modern aristocracy: "Bragging Rights: Honor and Courtesy in Shakespeare and Spenser," in *Creative Imitation: New Essays on Renaissance Literature in Honor of Thomas M. Greene,* ed. David Quint, Margaret W. Ferguson, G. W. Pigman, and Wayne A. Rebhorn, 392–430 (Binghamton, N.Y.: MRTS, 1992); "Dueling and Civility in Sixteenth-Century Italy," *I Tatti Studies: Essays in the Renaissance* 7 (1997): 231–78; "The Tragedy of Nobility on the Seventeenth-Century Stage," *Modern Language Quarterly* 67 (2006): 7–29. See also Timothy Hampton, *Writing from History: The Rhetoric of Exemplarity in Renaissance Literature* (Ithaca, N.Y.: Cornell University Press, 1990), 205–36; David M. Posner, *The Performance of Nobility in Early Modern European Literature* (Cambridge: Cambridge University Press, 1999); Mario Domenichelli, *Cavaliere e gentiluomo: Saggio sulla cultura aristocratica in Europa (1513-1915)* (Rome: Bulzoni, 2002).

5. On the epic/romance question see again note 1, esp. the works of Parker, Quint, and Zatti, cited there, as well as Quint, *Epic and Empire: Politics and Generic Form from Virgil to Milton* (Princeton: Princeton University Press, 1993).

6. On "romance" (*romanzo*) as forerunner of the novel (*romanzo*), see, for instance, Jameson, *The Political Unconscious,* and Doody, *The True Story of the Novel;* and compare Ascoli, introduction to Zatti, *The Quest for Epic,* 1–12. For a relevant rereading of Cervantes' pivotal place in this process, see Quint, *Cervantes' Novel of Modern Times* (Princeton: Princeton University Press, 2003).

7. Giamatti, A. Bartlett, *The Earthly Paradise and the Renaissance Epic* (Princeton: Princeton University Press, 1966).

8. *Orlando furioso* 23.98.

9. For a brief but cogent history of the *topos* of writing on trees, see Rensselaer W. Lee, *Names on Trees: Ariosto into Art* (Princeton: Princeton University Press, 1977), esp. 9–11.

10. For a more detailed reading of the madness of Orlando in this key, see Ascoli, *Ariosto's Bitter Harmony: Crisis and Evasion in the Italian Renaissance* (Princeton: Princeton University Press, 1987), esp. 304–31.

11. Lee's focus is on the transformation of the *topos* in the *Furioso* and later visual representations thereof, but he notes its culminating appearance in *As You Like It* as well (5–7, 83).

12. William Shakespeare, *The First Part of King Henry IV,* ed. Herbert Weil and Judith Weil, The New Cambridge Shakespeare (Cambridge: Cambridge University Press, 1997).

13. See Quint, "Bragging Rights," 405–14. Andrew Barnaby, "The Political Conscious of Shakespeare's *As You Like It,*" *Studies in English Literature* 36 (1996): 373–95, points out (380) that *Henry V* and *As You Like It,* as well as *Julius Caesar,* all written in 1599, share a concern with "aristocratic identity." On *Julius Caesar* (not discussed here), see Hampton, *Writing from History,* 205–36.

14. William Shakespeare, *King Henry V,* rev. ed., ed. Andrew Gurr, The New Cambridge Shakespeare (Cambridge: Cambridge University Press, 2005). Joanne Altieri, "Romance in *Henry V*" (*Studies in English Literature* 21 [1981]: 223–40), makes the case for the presence of important elements of pastoral romance in the play; she does not refer to Falstaff's death scene or to the chivalric element in romance, however.

15. "Babbled of green fields," of course, is Theobald's eighteenth-century emendation, which has slight contextual, but no textual basis. Whichever reading is chosen, however, I believe that the references to "Arthur's bosom" (paradise) and to flowers impose a pastoral

motif, while the "pen" (which, according to the OED, could also refer to an instrument for engraving in this period) evokes representation, whether verbal or visual. For one among the various defenses of "table," see Ephim Fogel, " 'A Table of Green Fields': A Defense of the Folio Reading," *Shakespeare Quarterly* 9 (1958): 485-92.

16. The pastoral romance is, as is well known, a sixteenth-century innovation, beginning in earnest with Montemayor's Diana (1559)—compare Alpers, *What is Pastoral?*, 66-67.

17. For a reading of the latter text not unrelated to the concerns of this essay, Louise K. Horowitz, " 'Where have all the "Old Knights" Gone?': *L'Astrée*," in *Romance*, ed. Brownlee and Brownlee, 253-64.

18. Thomas Lodge, *Rosalind: Euphues' Golden Legacy Found After His Death in His Cell at Silexedra (1590)*, ed. and introd. D. Beecher, Publications of the Barnebe Riche Society 7 (Ottawa: Dovehouse Editions, 1997). All citations are to this edition (although the work is referred to throughout by its original title of *Rosalynde* rather than *Rosalind*, the modernized spelling adopted by Beecher).

19. For a succinct review of the state of the argument concerning the composition of *Rosalynde*, including Greene's possible contribution, see Beecher, introduction to Thomas Lodge, *Rosalind*,15-19. On Lodge, see also Katharine Wilson, *Fictions of Authorship in Late Elizabethan Narrative: Euphues in Arcadia* (Oxford: Clarendon, 2006), 144-53. See also notes 21-22, 25, 40, and 43 below.

20. I have not found a discussion of the French location of the play or its deliberate evocation of the court of Charlemagne.

21. For Lodge's Catholicism, see Beecher, introduction, 15. The name "Torrismond" and that of his deposed brother, "Gerismond" apparently derive from Torquato Tasso's tragedy, *Re Torrismondo* (1587), in which the female protagonist is "Rosamonda" (Beecher, 18-19). The reasons for the echo are not obvious to me, unless it be to create a general association with a Catholic poet most famous for his crusader-epic, *Gerusalemme liberata* (1581).

22. For a summary of criticism on the transformational process operated by Shakespeare on Lodge, see Beecher, introduction, 11-15. See also Albert H. Tolman, "Shakespeare's Manipulation of His Sources," *MLN* 37 (1922): 65-76; Helen Gardiner, "*As You Like It*," in *More Talking of Shakespeare,* ed. John Garrett, 17-32 (London: Longmans, Green, 1959); Edward J. Berry, "Rosalynde and Rosalind," *Shakespeare Quarterly* 31 (1980): 42-52; Nathan Strout, "*As You Like It, Rosalynde,* and Mutuality," *Studies in English Literature* 41, no. 2 (2001): 277-95. See also David Young, "Earthly Things Made Even: *As You Like It*," in *The Heart's Forest: A Study of Shakespeare's Pastoral Plays* (New Haven, Conn.: Yale University Press, 1972), 38-72, esp. 38-41; Maura Slattery Kuhn, "Much Virtue in 'If,'" *Shakespeare Quarterly* 28 (1977): 40-50 (46); Louis Adrian Montrose, " 'The Place of a Brother' in *As You Like It:* Social Process and Comic Form," *Shakespeare Quarterly* 32 (1981): 28-54, esp. 34-35, 43; Alpers, *What is Pastoral?*, 67, 69, 97-99.

23. References are to William Shakespeare, *As You Like It*, ed. Michael Hattaway, The New Cambridge Shakespeare (Cambridge: Cambridge University Press, 2000). That Shakespeare changed the names of his protagonists to link them to the chivalric tradition has often been noted, though its significance has not been fully explored. See, for example, Richard Knowles's notes on the cast of characters, in William Shakespeare, *As You Like It,* ed. Richard Knowles, A New Variorum Edition of Shakespeare (New York: Modern Language Association, 1977), 8; see also Miranda Johnson-Haddad, "Englishing Ariosto: *Orlando furioso* at the Court of Elizabeth I," *Comparative Literature Studies* 31 (1994): 324-50, esp. 339, 349n40. In perhaps the best and certainly the most influential of the social-political readings of the play, Montrose, " 'The Place of a Brother,'" convincingly asserts its central focus on the problematics of patriarchal lineage. My reading suggests that the father-son

duo of Rowland-Orlando makes it clear that this lineage is also literary-cultural, although I follow Montrose in arguing that this lineage betrays a crisis created by landmark shifts in class status and in relations between the aristocracy and the state.

24. For this reason, while accepting the possibility of secondary biographical references to the Arden of Warwickshire, not to mention Shakespeare's mother, I would insist that this "Arden" still should be referred primarily to the chivalric locus par excellence, as well as to the "ardent" passions of the lover-knights who wander, errantly, within it. Compare Stuart A. Daley, "Where Are the Woods in *As You Like It?*" *Shakespeare Quarterly* 34 (1983): 172-80; William Kerrigan, "Female Friends and Fraternal Enemies in *As You Like It*," in *Desire in the Renaissance*, ed. Valeria Finucci and Regina Schwartz (Princeton: Princeton University Press, 1994), 184-203, esp. 194-96; Swapan Chakravorty, "Translating Arden: Shakespeare's Rhetorical Place in *As You Like It*," in *Shakespeare and the Mediterranean*, ed. Tom Clayton, Susan Brock, and Vicente Forés (Newark: University of Delaware Press, 2004), 156-67, esp. 163-64.

25. *Rosalynde*, 97. Previously known as the Hospitaller Knights of Saint John, the order was based in Malta only from 1530 on. The knights were a distinctly Catholic order of Catholic *cavalieri* historically tied to the enterprise of the Crusades, thus bearing out the inference that Lodge's text may conceal a restorationist agenda.

26. Shakespeare's engagement here is in at least one way primarily "literary" rather than dramatic: the name "Oliver," key to identifying the drama not just with one famous character but with a whole chivalric tradition, appears only in the list of dramatis personae and in the paratextual markers of who is speaking, never in the words of the performed text.

27. There are, of course, numerous treatments of the complex and often critical relationship of *As You Like It* to the pastoral tradition. These include Harold Jenkins, "*As You Like It*," *Shakespeare Survey* 8 (1955): 40-51; R. P. Draper, "Shakespeare's Pastoral Comedy," *Études anglaises* 9 (1958): 1-17; C. L. Barber, "The Alliance of Seriousness and Levity in *As You Like It*," in *Shakespeare's Festive Comedy: A Study of Dramatic Form and Its Relationship to Social Custom* (Princeton: Princeton University Press, 1959), 222-39; Mary Lascelles, "Shakespeare's Pastoral Comedy," in *More Talking of Shakespeare*, ed. John Garrett 70-86 (London: Longmans, Green, 1959); Gardner, "*As You Like It*"; Albert Cirillo, "*As You Like It*: Pastoralism Gone Awry," *English Literary History* 38 (1971): 19-39; Young, "Earthly Things Made Even"; Rosalie Colie, "Perspectives on Pastoral: Romance, Comic and Tragic," in *Shakespeare's Living Art* (Princeton: Princeton University Press, 1974), 243-83, esp. 245-47, 253-61; Charles W. Hieatt, "The Quality of Pastoral in *As You Like It*," *Genre* 7 (1974): 164-82; Harry Morris, "*As You Like It: 'Et in Arcadia Ego,'*" *Shakespeare Quarterly* 26 (1975): 269-75; Judy Z. Kronenfeld, "Social Rank and the Pastoral Ideals of *As You Like It*," *Shakespeare Quarterly* 29 (1978): 333-48; Alpers, *What is Pastoral?*, 71-78, 123-24, 197-203; Barnaby, "The Political Consciousness of Shakespeare's *As You Like It*"; Linda Woodbridge, "Country Matters: *As You Like It* and the Pastoral-Bashing Impulse," in *Re-Visions of Shakespeare: Essays in Honor of Robert Ornstein*, ed. Evelyn Gajowski, 189-214 (Newark: University of Delaware Press, 2004).

28. The question of Shakespeare's direct knowledge of the *Furioso* remains open, though not his direct or indirect debts to it (in *Much Ado, Othello,* and, somewhat less plausibly, *Midsummer Night's Dream*), and to Ariosto's play, *I suppositi* (in *The Taming of the Shrew*). The most obvious possible intermediaries were John Harington's translation of the *Furioso* (1591) and Robert Greene's play, *The History of Orlando Furioso* (1594). For the general question of Shakespeare's literary culture, start with Leonard Barkan, "What Did Shakespeare Read?" in *The Cambridge Companion to Shakespeare*, ed. Margreta de Grazia and Stanley Wells, 31-48 (Cambridge: Cambridge University Press,

2001). For an overview of the influence of Italian culture on England in this period, see Michael Wyatt, *The Italian Encounter with Tudor England: A Cultural Politics of Translation* (Cambridge: Cambridge University Press, 2005). For the influence of Italian drama and literature on the English theater and Shakespeare in particular, see Clubb, *Italian Drama*, and "Italian Stories on the English Stage," in *The Cambridge Companion to Shakespearean Comedy*, ed. Alexander Leggatt, 32–46 (Cambridge: Cambridge University Press, 2002). See also the essays collected in Michele Marrapodi, et al., *Shakespeare's Italy* (Manchester: Manchester University Press, 1993); Holger Klein and Michele Marrapodi, eds., *Shakespeare and Italy*, in *The Shakespeare Yearbook*, vol. 10 (Lewisburg, Pa.: The Edward Mellen Press, 1999); and Michele Marrapodi, ed., *Shakespeare, Italy, and Intertextuality* (Manchester: Manchester University Press, 2004). On Ariosto's presence in the Elizabethan period and his influence on Shakespeare in particular, see also Anna Benedetti *L'"Orlando furioso" nella vita intellettuale del popolo inglese* (Florence: Bemporad, 1914); Mario Praz, "Ariosto in England," in *The Flaming Heart: Essay on Crashaw, Machiavelli, and Other Studies on the Relations between Italian and English Literature from Chaucer to T. S. Eliot* (Gloucester, Mass.: Peter Smith, 1966), 287–307; Alfonso Sammut, *La fortuna dell'Ariosto nell'Inghilterra Elisabettiano* (Milan: Vita e Pensiero, 1971); Andrew S. Cairncross, "Shakespeare and Ariosto: *Much Ado About Nothing, King Lear,* and *Othello*," *Renaissance Quarterly* 29 (1976): 178–82; Peter Brand, "Italian Romance and Elizabethan Comedy: Ariosto, Robert Greene, and Shakespeare," *Journal of Anglo-Italian Studies* 3 (1993): 40–51; Johnson-Haddad, "Englishing Ariosto"; Lawrence Rhu, "Shakespeare's Ariostan Skepticism," in *Shakespeare and Italy*, ed. Klein and Marrapodi, 359–73; Roger Prior, "Shakespeare's Debt to Ariosto," *Notes and Queries* 48, no. 3 (2001): 289–92; Jason Lawrence, " 'The Story is Extant and Writ in Very Choice Italian': Shakespeare's Dramatization of Cinthio," in *Shakespeare, Italy, and Intertextuality,* ed. Marrapodi, 91–106; Fernando Cioni, "Shakespeare's Italian Intertexts: *The Taming of a/the Shrew*," in *Shakespeare, Italy, and Intertextuality,* ed. Marrapodi, 118–28. See also the essays by Kasey Evans, Lorna Hutson, and Jane Tylus in the present volume.

29. In this my approach is closer to that of Clubb's seminal concept of the "theatergram" (*Italian Drama,* 1–26) than to the exploration of one-to-one engagements with privileged intertexts, although the notion has been loosened to allow for a relationship with themes and narrative patterns (especially those of chivalric romance), which fall outside the domain of the stage.

30. *Rosalynde,* 107–8.

31. Orlando's choice of wrestling to assert himself is closely associated with his lack of education and his consequent exclusion from a birthright of "gentility" (1.1.1–19, 53–59). As Cynthia Marshall describes in "Wrestling as Play and Game in *As You Like It*," *Studies in English Literature* 33, no. 2 (1983): 265–87, esp. 271–76, conduct and education manuals for gentlemen at once recommend wrestling as exercise and warn against its plebeian associations. Notably, while acknowledging the usefulness of wrestling as exercise (1.25, 3.3, 7) and its occasional necessity in warfare (1.21), in the *Cortegiano* Castiglione associates it with the lower classes and contrasts it negatively with the nobility of jousting and other tournament activities: "[Federico Fregoso:] 'Dico adunque che degli esercizi del corpo sono alcuni che quasi mai non si fanno se non in pubblico, come il giostrare, il torneare, il giocare a canne e gli altri tutti che dependono dall'arme. . . . Appresso dee considerar molto in presenzia di chi si mostra e quali siano i compagni; perché non saria conveniente che un gentilom andasse ad onorare con la persona sua una festa di contado, dove i spettatori e i compagni fossero gente ignobile.' / Disse allor il signor Gasparo Pallavicino: 'Nel paese nostro di Lombardia non s'hanno questi rispetti; anzi molti gentilomini

giovani trovansi, che le feste ballano tutto 'l dí nel sole coi villani e con essi giocano a lanciar la barra, lottare, correre e saltare; ed io non credo che sia male, perché ivi non si fa paragone della nobiltà, ma della forza e destrezza, nelle quai cose spesso gli omini di villa non vaglion meno che i nobili; e par che quella domestichezza abbia in sé una certa liberalità amabile.' 'Quel ballar nel sole,' rispose messer Federico, 'a me non piace per modo alcuno, né so che guadagno vi si trovi. Ma chi vol pur lottar, correr e saltar coi villani, dee, al parer mio, farlo in modo di provarsi e, come si suol dir, per gentilezza, non per contender con loro; e dee l'omo esser quasi sicuro di vincere, altramente non vi si metta; perché sta troppo male e troppo è brutta cosa e fuor della dignità vedere un gentilomo vinto da un villano, e massimamente alla lotta; però credo io che sia ben astenersene, almeno in presenzia di molti, perché il guadagno nel vincere è pochissimo e la perdita nell'esser vinto è grandissimo" (2.9-10; compare 2.12, 50). Cited from Baldassare Castiglione, *Il libro del Cortegiano,* ed. Ettore Bonora (Milan: Mursia, 1972). See also Ruth Kelso, *The Doctrine of the English Gentleman in the Sixteenth Century, with a Bibliographical List of Treatises on the Gentleman and Related Subjects Published in Europe to 1625* (Urbana: University of Illinois Press, 1929), 149. David Quint (private communication), points out that the final duel of *Orlando furioso,* between Ruggiero and the arch-pagan Rodomonte, degenerates into a wrestling match based on that between Tydeus and Agyellus in Statius's *Thebaid* (6.826-910). Throughout the *Furioso,* in fact, hand-to-hand combat signals the degeneration of chivalric combat into mad violence.

32. *Rosalynde,* 110.

33. In fact, the similarities with Greene's euphuistic style are the basis for the claim that he revised *Rosalynde* for publication (Beecher, introduction, 18-19, and bibliography referred to there).

34. The first to notice this allusion, perhaps exaggerating its importance for an interpretation of the play as a whole, was Richard Knowles, "Myth and Type in *As You Like It,*" *ELH* 33 (1966): 1-22, esp. 3-5.

35. On Hercules in the Renaissance see Erwin Panofsky, *Hercules am Scheidewege* (Leipzig: Teubner, 1930); G. K. Galinsky, *The Herakles Theme* (Totowa, NJ: Rowan and Littlefield, 1972); Marc-René Jung, *Hercule dans la Littérature Française du XVIieme Siècle* (Genève: Droz, 1966); Eugene Waith, *The Herculean Hero in Marlowe, Chapman, Shakespeare and Dryden* (New York: Columbia University Press, 1962); Ascoli, *Ariosto's Bitter Harmony,* 46-70 and passim; Christopher Braider, *Baroque Self-Invention and Historical Truth: Hercules at the Crossroads* (Burlington, Vt.: Ashgate, 2004).

36. For the topos of *sapientia et fortitudo* from the classics through the Renaissance, begin with E. R. Curtius, *European Literature in the Latin Middle Ages,* trans. Willard R. Trask, Bollingen Series 36 (New York: Pantheon, 1953; first published in German, 1948), 173-78.

37. Citations are to Ludovico Ariosto, *Orlando furioso,* 2 vols., ed. Emilio Bigi (Milan: Rusconi, 1982). Translations are my own.

38. For this identification, see Eduardo Saccone, *Il soggetto del "Furioso" e altri saggi tra Quattro e Cinquecento* (Naples: Liguori, 1974), 216-22; Ascoli, *Ariosto's Bitter Harmony,* 52-63 and passim.

39. Compare Johnson-Haddad, "Englishing Ariosto," 336-37.

40. Of course, Lodge's iterated references to the French court and the Paladins, of whom Roland was *primus inter pares,* would suffice as explanation.

41. On the motif of arboreal verse, see again note 9. Rosader engraves one of his poems in a myrtle (*Rosalynde,* 148-49) and recites several others. Orlando's verse, instead, is written on paper and hung on tree branches (*As You Like It,* 3.2.1-10; 3.3.65-72, 100-129).

Lawrence ("'The Story is Extant,'" 96-98), following Martha Hale Shackleford ("Shakespeare and Greene's *Orlando furioso*," *MLN* 39 [1924]: 54-56), develops the claim that Greene (*The History of Orlando Furioso*, 574-55) is Shakespeare's source for the hanging of verse on branches (as against engraving it on trees).

42. Greene's most prominent alteration of Ariosto's tale makes "Medoro's" poetic claims false and imposes a happy ending of marriage between Orlando and Angelica.

43. In Lodge, Aliena and Rosalynde come upon Rosader together and there is no comparable simile (149). For the genealogical implications of this and other arboreal imagery (beginning with Rowland du *Boys*), see Montrose, "The Place of a Brother," 43-44n35.

44. *Rosalynde*, 226-27. Compare Montrose, "The Place of a Brother," 43.

45. *Rosalynde*, 97-98, 103-4, 107-11, 142-43, 145, 173-75, and passim.

46. *As You Like It*, 2.1.3-4; 2.7.36; 3.3.1-62; 5.4.39-88. Compare *Rosalynde*, 134, 196-97.

47. Much criticism of the play, and notably that dedicated to the pastoral, focuses on the court/country contrast. See again note 27.

48. On the Ariostan "I," see Robert Durling, *The Figure of the Poet in Renaissance Epic* (Cambridge, Mass.: Harvard University Press, 1965), 112-50; compare Ascoli, *Ariosto's Bitter Harmony*, 295-97 and passim; Zatti, *Il "Furioso" fra epos e romanzo*, 173-212.

49. On the double place of the Ariostan narrator, see Ascoli, *Ariosto's Bitter Harmony*, esp. chapter 4, "Cassandra's Veil and the Poet's Folly."

50. Shakespeare may have found a suggestion for the name in this passage from early in *Rosalynde:* "Try, and then trust; let time be the touchstone of friendship and then friends faithful lay them up for jewels" (99). In support of this conjecture: the passage anticipates some key motifs of *As You Like It* (time; trust; friendship), which are closely associated with the character Touchstone.

51. And so it has seemed to many critics: a typical reaction is that of G. B. Shaw ("Who would endure such humor from anyone but Shakespeare?"), quoted in Kuhn, "Much Virtue in 'If,'" 43.

52. See especially Young, "Earthly Things Made Even," 46-50, and Kuhn, "Much Virtue in 'If'"; also Valerie Traub, "The Homoerotics of Shakespearean Comedy (*As You Like It, Twelfth Night*)," in *Desire and Anxiety: Circulations of Sexuality in Shakespearean Drama* (London: Routledge, 1992), 117-44, esp. 128-29; Strout, "*As You Like It, Rosalynde*, and Mutuality," 282, 288-89; William O. Scott, "'A Woman's Thought Runs Before Her Actions': Vows as Speech Acts in *As You Like It*," *Philosophy and Literature* 30, no. 2 (2006): 528-39.

53. Kuhn briefly notes a connection between the two scenes in her excellent reading of the pervasive thematics of (poetic) hypothesis in the play ("Much Virtue in 'If,'" 43-44).

54. In Italian, prominent examples are Girolamo Muzio, *Il duello* (1550); Giovan Battista Possevino, *Dialogo dell'honore* (1553); Annibale Romei, *I Discorsi* (1585). In English, see William Segar, *The Book of Honor and Arms* (1590); Vicentio Saviolo, *Saviolo his Practice* (1594-95). Secondary treatments are in Kelso, *The Doctrine of the English Gentleman;* Henry Charles Lea, *The Duel and the Oath*, ed. Edward Peters, additional documents trans. Arthur C. Howland (Philadelphia: University of Pennsylvania Press, 1974; Lea's text first published 1868); Frederick Robert Bryson, *The Sixteenth Century Italian Duel: A Study in Renaissance Social History* (Chicago: University of Chicago Press, 1938); Francesco Erspamer, *La biblioteca di Don Ferrante: Duello e onore nella cultura del Cinquecento* (Rome: Bulzoni, 1982); V. G. Kiernan, *The Duel in European History: Honour and the Reign of the Aristocracy* (Oxford: Oxford University Press, 1988); Edward Muir, *Mad Blood Stirring: Vendetta and Factions in Friuli During the Renaissance* (Baltimore: Johns Hopkins University Press, 1993); Franco Cuomo, *Nel nome di Dio: Roghi, duelli, e*

altre ordalie nell'Occidente medievale cristiano (Rome: Newton Compton, 1994); Quint, "Dueling and Civility." Quint's assertion that "the modern duel was the product of the printing press" (233), linked by him to Touchstone's rant, is apposite here.

55. On the European diffusion and enormous influence of Castiglione's dialogue, see Peter Burke, *The Fortunes of the Courtier* (University Park: Pennsylvania State University Press, 1995).

56. Marshall, in "Wrestling as Play," links the two activities around the idea of spectacularized violence (278–79).

57. See again note 52.

58. There is some doubt as to whether Saint John is suggesting that Nero was really good or just that he would have seemed good if he had paid his writers better (or at least stopped forcing them to commit suicide!). Two things, however, suggest that we are actually to entertain the hypothesis that Nero was good: first that his evil qualities are referred to in a condition-contrary-to-fact clause ("nessun sapria [saprebbe] se Neron fosse ingiusto" [35.26.4]), and second that Saint John concludes with the preposterous assertion that to know the truth of history one has to turn all received knowledge to its contrary ("tutta al contrario l'istoria converti" [35.27.6]).

59. On this question, see Durling, *The Figure of the Poet*, 146–49; Parker, *Inescapable Romance*, 44–53; Quint, *Origin and Originality in Renaissance Literature: Versions of the Source* (New Haven: Yale University Press, 1983), 87–92; Ascoli, *Ariosto's Bitter Harmony*, 286–96; Zatti, *Il "Furioso" fra epos e romanzo*, 199–202.

60. John Milton, *Paradise Lost*, ed. Scott Elledge (New York: W. W. Norton, 1975).

Coincidence of Opposites: Bruno, Calderón, and a Drama of Ideas

CHRISTOPHER D. JOHNSON

I N HIS INFAMOUSLY knotty *Epistemo-Critical Prologue* to *The Origin of German Tragic Drama*, Walter Benjamin announces: "Vom Extremen geht der Begriff aus" (the concept originates in extremity).[1] Testing this methodological dictum throughout his study of the Baroque *Trauerspiel,* Benjamin shows how this "eccentric" drama—a drama hitherto marginal both in terms of scholarly interest and, geographically, in terms of the main currents of European imitation, and one, most importantly, that he feels never reached the aesthetic perfection of Calderón and Shakespeare's plays—mediates extremes of language, character, and dramatic form, first, to express subjective, historical phenomena and, second, to adumbrate objective meaning (*Bedeutung*), or what he obliquely defines as the "being of truth" that inheres in "ideas."[2] That wrestling with extremes has since Hegel been central to most efforts in phenomenology, to say nothing of a great deal of structuralist and poststructuralist criticism, is reason enough to ponder its hermeneutic value.[3] But there are also more self-interested or self-reflexive reasons why students of late Renaissance thought and, more specifically, readers of Louise George Clubb's work on genre in Italian Renaissance drama might attend to Benjamin's play of extremes.[4] For as Benjamin indicates in the *Prologue,* by making the *Trauerspiel* the proving ground for his "philosophy of art," a place for combinatory thought, he discovers how the extravagant language and violent actions native to this dramatic form, which ultimately

319

yield the melancholic pleasures of allegory, necessarily mirror the philosophical critic's digressive, if dialectical apprehension of ideas. And since
"the idea is something linguistic," literary critics have a stake in securing
its origins.[5] Thus Benjamin's theory of Baroque allegory is (literally) preceded by the belief that critical exegesis and philosophy do not produce
"knowledge" (*Erkenntnis*), but rather "representation" (*Darstellung*).
"Truth, bodied forth in the dance of represented ideas, resists being projected . . . into the realm of knowledge."[6] In other words, if reading the
"antinomies of allegorical interpretation" will eventually yield Benjamin
a way of salvaging meaning from the Baroque ruins of a "profane world,"
this is because he has already learned to contemplate "extremity" as an
end in itself.[7]

    I must, however, leave to others the task of explicating the often gno-
mic notions of allegory, origin, nature, and history that riddle Benjamin's
treatise.[8] My aim instead is to focus on a crucial aspect of its method,
and with this in mind then to cast two remarkable late Renaissance plays
as exemplars of what I read as the dramatization, the theatrical performance, of ideas. Benjamin hopes to redeem, whether neo-Platonically,
kabbalistically, or otherwise, the "impoverished" aesthetic objects produced by Gryphius, Lohenstein, and other German Baroque dramatists.[9]
In doing so, he attends more to how ideas are used and less to what they
might ultimately mean. Likewise, this essay examines two early modern
instances in which phenomenological "extremity" is staged: Giordano
Bruno's *Candelaio* (1582) and Pedro Calderón de la Barca's *El mágico
prodigioso* (1637). It asks, in the light of Benjamin and his idiosyncratic
version of the "natural history" of ideas, how these plays perform an
idea at the heart of Renaissance intellectual culture.[10] Specifically, beginning with Nicholas of Cusa's negative theology, but also riddling much
of Renaissance neo-Platonism and the Baroque philosophies of Pascal
and Leibniz, the idea of the *coincidentia oppositorum* is central to early
modern intellectual history and its aftermath. My gambit in this essay
is to explore how the "coincidence of opposites" is played (out) in different but analogous ways in Bruno's *comedia vera* and Calderón's *comedia religiosa*.[11] Both these dramas heuristically remake the illogic of
the *coincidentia oppositorum*, as the search for *scientia* (knowledge
and skill) is variously transformed via the mediation of the language and
the devices of the stage into *sapientia* (wisdom). How, then, might the
coincidentia oppositorum serve both as a dramaturgical principle and

as what Benjamin calls a mode of "representation" available to the "philosophy of art"?

The most palpable "idea" emerging from Benjamin's *Prologue* concerns his refusal of conventional notions of genre:

> In the sense in which it is treated in the philosophy of art the *Trauerspiel* is an idea. Such a treatment differs most significantly from a literary-historical treatment in its assumption of unity, whereas the latter is concerned to demonstrate variety. In literary-historical analysis differences and extremes are brought together in order that they might be relativized in evolutionary terms; in a conceptual treatment they acquire the status of complementary forces, and history is seen as no more than the coloured border to their crystalline simultaneity. From the point of view of the philosophy of art the extremes are necessary; the historical process is merely virtual. Conversely the idea is the extreme example of a form or genre [*Gattung*], and as such does not enter into the history of literature. *Trauerspiel*, as a concept, could, without the slightest problem, be added to the list of aesthetic classifications. But not as an idea, for it defines no class and does not contain that generality on which the respective conceptual levels in the system depend: the average.[12]

The apparent paradox here dissolves if we consider Benjamin's distinction between "concept" (*Begriff*) and "idea" (*Idee*): the former is mainly the province of phenomenology, the latter of theology (or whatever species of mystical philosophy one ascribes to Benjamin).[13] As provisional or, if you will, performative representations, concepts are what the critic contemplates who is determined to find historical "origins" and is keen to spurn the Kantian emphases on cognition and transcendental ends. Concepts are manifested empirically in plays and in culture; they assume extreme linguistic form—thus Benjamin's attention to "bombast" and his celebrated theory of Baroque allegory. The latter, which explains the historicization of nature and thereby also its death, creates the hermeneutic space to contemplate an *Idee* such as the "mourning play" and how such an art form escapes subjectivity and contingency to become an "objective interpretation" worthy of philosophy.[14]

Where Benjamin ends his treatise—contemplating allegorical dramatizations of divinity and Calderón's *ponderación misteriosa*—depends on his notion of the "origin" (*Ursprung*). As Beatrice Hanssen observes, "the philosophical significance of Benjamin's theory of origin lies in the fact that it articulates an attempt to overcome the dualism between historical contingency and the ahistorical transcendent Ideas."[15] But Benjamin begins his study proper by immediately shifting from the philosophical to the literary. In doing so he signals his method: "The necessary tendency towards the extreme which, in philosophical investigations, constitutes the norm in the formation of concepts, means two things as far as the representation of the origin of the German Baroque *Trauerspiel* is concerned."[16] Extremity, we then learn, assumes either the form of plays whose expression is excessive and "eccentric" rather than perfected, or it is the decisive rejection of Aristotelian precepts by Baroque poetics.[17] The drama's "extremity" in plot and style are read chiefly, in other words, for their *affectus* and allegorical reach. Keenly conscious of his own belatedness vis-à-vis Baroque drama, but also insisting on parallels between its aesthetics and that promoted by expressionism in his own time, Benjamin appropriates Baroque melancholy and thirst for transcendence to read his own historical moment. Indeed, as an intellectual historian, Benjamin may be said to imitate Schelling and Hegel for this concept of historical consciousness, which includes rather than excludes earlier philosophical voices. Thus, for instance, to expound his *Identitätsphilosophie,* whereby conceptual extremes, especially that between multiplicity and unity, produces the thinking self, Schelling looks back to the early modern period when he publishes in 1802 a dialogue, *Bruno,* in which the Italian cosmographer is cast as an avid spokesman for such production.[18]

Like Schelling, Benjamin has enormous ambitions for his brand of dialectical idealism:

Ideas are timeless constellations, and by virtue of the elements being seen as points in such constellations, phenomena are subdivided and at the same time redeemed; so that those elements which it is the function of the concept to elicit from phenomena are most clearly evident at the extremes. The idea is best explained as the representation of the context within which the unique and extreme stands alongside its counterpart [*das Einmalig-Extreme mit seinesgleichen steht*]. It is therefore erroneous to understand the most general references which language makes as concepts, instead of recognizing them as ideas. It is absurd to attempt to explain the general [*das Allgemeine*] as an average. The general is the idea. The empirical, on the other hand, can be all the more profoundly understood the more clearly it is seen as an extreme. The concept originates in extremity [*Vom Extremen geht der Begriff aus*]. Just as a mother is seen to begin to live in the fullness of her power only when the circle of her children, inspired by the feeling of her proximity, closes around her, so do ideas come to life only when extremes are assembled around them. Ideas—or to use Goethe's term, ideals—are the Faustian "Mothers." They remain obscure so long as phenomena do not declare their faith to them and gather round them. It is the function of concepts to group phenomena together, and the division which is brought about within them thanks to the distinguishing power of the intellect is all the more significant in that it brings about two things at a single stroke: the salvation of phenomena and the representation of ideas.[19]

Of course it is Benjamin himself, forging concepts out of phenomena represented in the "eccentric" and flawed "sorrow-plays" of the German Baroque, who will be their savior and who will (re)represent the "ideas" expressed by them. Theatrical "representation" (*Darstellung*) and the "allegorical way of seeing" assuage the emptiness of the "empirical" world and the impossibility of gaining immediate access to Ideas.[20] "The being of ideas simply cannot be conceived as the object of vision [*Anschauung*], even intellectual vision."[21] It must be mediated by drama—just as Cusanus will depend on mathematics and paradox to achieve an analogous mediation. Hence, in the second half of his book, Benjamin will also become an allegorist of historical ruin as he interprets the narrative, characterological, and linguistic "extremity" in the *Trauerspiele*. But such interpretation, he insists in the prologue, should reject the conventional strategy of inducing and deducing concepts by examining a variety of plays; rather criticism should "take shape immanently, in a development of the formal language of the work itself, which brings out its content at the expense of effect."[22] Treating the tragic and comic as essential ideas or "structures," Benjamin thus applauds Benedetto Croce's "nominalism" when it comes to aesthetic genres.[23] Yet Croce is also faulted for relying too much on "intuition" in his attempt to provide an alternative, "genetic and concrete classification" of the artwork.[24] In brief, Croce does not go far enough; he stops short of contemplating the "origin" of the artwork from the point of view of its "natural life" in the history of ideas.[25]

Philosophical criticism ought to be Faustian in its ambition to encompass the whole. It should risk trading appreciation of particular phenomena (plays and their literary filiations) for a glimpse of the *explicatio,* or unfolding, of an idea via the play of extreme, opposing concepts. But to do so it must have at once an eye on the "essential" and how that being originates in the "phenomena" of history. It is in this sense that ideas for Benjamin are linguistic rather than transcendent.[26] To glimpse the "origin" (*Ursprung*) of the *Trauerspiel* is a situated, historical event in which a kind of Platonic telescope is set up to see "constellations of ideas."[27] And while Benjamin is historicist enough to appreciate the temporal *Sprung* ("jump" but also "fissure") in time needed for such a glimpse, still, his approach to his material is largely synchronic: "Philosophical history, the science of origin, is the form which, in the remotest extremes and the apparent excesses of the process of development, reveals the configuration of the idea—the sum total of all possible meaningful juxtapositions of such opposites. The representation of an idea can under no circumstances be considered successful unless the whole range of possible extremes it contains has been virtually explored."[28] Small wonder that Benjamin invokes Leibniz: "The idea is a monad—that means briefly: every idea contains the image of the world."[29] In short, concepts mediate between phenomena and ideas, but ideas are like Leibnizian monads, each one of which may stage or contain all the world. The question remains, however, whether individual plays can be monadic, a vehicle for an "idea" and its supporting "concepts."

"Methode ist Umweg" (method is a detour), Benjamin declares at the outset of the *Epistemo-Critical Prologue.*[30] More intuitive than inductive, more fragmentary than synthetic, such digressiveness marks his "natural history" of ideas as well as his interpretation of Baroque drama. The origins of this method are multiple, even as it has a singular aim; for digression must eventually yield to dialectics: "The baroque apotheosis is a dialectical one. It is accomplished in the movement between extremes. . . ."[31] Now, whether such "movement" ought to be imitated by critics hoping to test the viability of Benjamin's ideas remains, I think, an open question. Still, I need to detour briefly to trace the origins of an idea that not only strongly informs the neo-Platonism riddling Benjamin's treatise but which Bruno variously embraces and which Calderón stages in his religious comedy. The result, I hope, will be to set another, much more modest dialectic in motion.

Nicholas of Cusa (1401–64) makes *coincidentia oppositorum* the fulcrum of his epistemological stance of *docta ignorantia* (learned ignorance), which in turn fuels his negative theology.[32] And while there has been a tendency either to interpret the *coincidentia oppositorum* as a mystical abandonment of rational thought or to view it as a kind of proto-Hegelian *Aufhebung* lacking the third and final moment of synthesis, Cusanus himself insists that it is more a process of dialectical intuition than an idea possessing any fixed content of its own. Traditionally traced back to Parmenides' dialectic of the one and many, in Cusanus's hands the paradoxical aspects of the coincidence of opposites are sharpened to demonstrate the limits of reason and the necessity of a higher form of intellect or intuition. At its root is the notion of metaphysical and episte-mological unity guaranteeing not only that being and thought are one, but being and nonbeing as well.[33] In his discussion of the centrality of the *Koinzidenzlehre* in Cusanus's thought, Kurt Flasch gives the example of the coincidence of *rest* and *motion,* noting that it would be impossible to conceive of one without the other. In this sense, we ourselves, as mortal beings able to contemplate the divine *logos,* are the ultimate coincidence of opposites.

Most famously, Cusanus thoroughly reworks the hermetic common-place: *God is an infinite sphere the center of which is everywhere and the circumference nowhere.*[34] In other words, when taken to the infi-nite, all geometric shapes and their elements lose their essence and ul-timately coincide with one another. Mining the paradoxical aspects of this, Cusanus thus regards arguments for coincidences of opposites as illustrations rather than proofs.[35] For the mathematics they depend upon appeal to the understanding (*ratio*) and not to the higher intuition of reason (*visio intellectus*). God, Cusanus declares, is "beyond" or "above" the "coincidence of contradictories."[36] Still, our figures and demonstra-tions have a metaphoric function that aims to bring the mind closer to eternal ideas—but not to represent the ideas themselves—especially when the idea concerns God's infinitude. As Augustine might put it, mathematics thus remains a form of *scientia* rather than granting real *sa-pientia.* When Cusanus figures God as the maximum and individuals and individual things as minima, it means that these can never meet in our phenomenal world, although their absolute, paradoxical coincidence, as Bruno will also insist, can be intuited. Still, the maximum must be real, that is, God's immanent potential (*potentia*) is a kind of *complicatio* or "infolding," whereas that potential expressed as the world is *explicatio* or "unfolding."[37] For Cusanus, number is only the *explicatio* of the One. As he writes in *De docta ignorantia* (1440):

Non potest autem unitas numerus esse, quoniam numerus excedens admittens nequaquam simpliciter minimum nec maximum esse potest; sed est principium omnis numeri, quia minimum; est finis omnis numeri, quia maximum. Est igi-tur unitas absoluta, cui nihil opponitur, ipsa absoluta maximatas, quae est Deus benedictus. . . .

But unity cannot be a number, since number can always be exceeded and in no way can be simply the minimum or maximum. Unity is rather the origin of every number, because it is the minimum; and it is the end of every number, because it is the maximum. Absolute unity, therefore, to which nothing can be opposed, is absolute magnitude, which is blessed God. . . .[38]

Flasch thus concludes: "The doctrine of coincidences is accordingly no 'doctrine,' but rather a 'pair of glasses,' through which reason is permitted to see what must remain closed to understanding."[39] Or as Deleuze might say, the doctrine of coincidences is a vehicle of expression.[40]

The question for us, however, is how early modern drama might also be such a vehicle. In what follows I shall argue that in their theatricalization of opposites and extremes, Bruno and Calderón each cultivates a drama of ideas that self-consciously reflects on dramaturgical form and the conceptual limits of that form. In this sense, their plays are "successful" monadic representations of the extremity that yields concepts and eventually ideas. And while the ideas explored in these texts have different histories and are obviously played out in divergent cultural and historical contexts, when viewed synthetically they point to the kind of "philosophical history" that Benjamin suggests it is the task of criticism to adumbrate.

Written in 1582 around the time Bruno left Italy and arrived in France, *Candelaio* (*Candlebearer*) is Bruno's only known drama.[41] With its frenetic pace, myriad characters, converging plots, and copious declamations, it is as if Bruno wanted to condense the entire tradition of cinquecento comedy into a single play. Fusing elements of *erudita* comedy and *commedia dell'arte,* he even packs considerable *complicatio* into the play's title: the candlebearer in question is the chief protagonist, who fancies himself an ardent lover but who is also a *candelaio,* Neapolitan slang for "sodomite."[42] With the exception, perhaps, of Gianbernardo, a painter and therefore someone who discerns the superfluity and deceptiveness of language and so profits from the various intrigues, all the characters are parodic "theatergrams," stock characters whose words and actions lead to predictable results—they are also conceived in a manner as to critique the conventions of comedy itself.[43] The foolish *innamorato* (Bonifacio), the credulous dabbler in alchemy (Bartolomeo), and the pompous pedant (Mamfurio)[44] are each in turn mocked and gulled by characters from the lower classes who exploit these types, and the debased forms of humanism they represent, to make some money and have a laugh at their expense. The play produces more than just a dramatic *affectus,* however; its satire has a heuristic aim that corresponds neatly with the philosophical treatises Bruno will write in subsequent years, treatises that rely on allegory, bombast, and immense learning to undermine conventional cosmography and moral philosophy.

The play's motto is *In Tristitia hilaris: in Hilaritate tristis*—a coincidence of opposites to be sure, but a rather commonplace one. Bruno's self-appointed task of complicating and explicating this motto is pursued immediately in the array of paratexts preceding the play proper. Outdoing forerunners like Aretino and Bibbiena in the number and intricacy of his paratexts, Bruno offers, with his typical penchant for conceptual and rhetorical excess a title page proclaiming his authorship; a bawdy sonnet whose putative author is the "book" itself; a dedicatory letter to a "Lady Morgana B."; an extensive *argumento ed ordine della commedia;* an abusive Antiprologue; an ironic, meandering, learned Proprologue; and finally a short, rancorous speech by a "janitor" filled with unseemly imagery. While the effect of all of this is to preempt any narrative suspense that might have escaped the rules of convention, these texts also furnish the play with a hermeneutic—if we are willing and able to mediate Bruno's ironic *copia* of words and ideas.

In the dedicatory letter, sounding at times like Mamfurio the pedant whom he is about to skewer, Bruno addresses an unknown lady in a now obscene, now prostrate manner.[45] Having apparently lost in love before he left Italy, he presents the play as a kind of proof or testimony:

Adesso che, tra voi che godete al seno d'Abraamo, e me che, senza aspettar quel tuo soccorso che solea rifrigerarmi la lingua, desperatamente ardo e sfavillo, intermezza un gran caos, pur troppo invidioso del mio bene, per farvi vedere che non può far quel medesmo caos, che il mio amore, con qualche proprio ostaggio e material presente, non passe al suo marcio despetto, eccovi la candela che vi vien porgiuta per questo *Candelaio* che da me si parte, la qual in questo paese, ove mi trovo, potrà chiarire alquanto certe *Ombre dell'idee,* le quali in vero spaventano le bestie e, come fussero diavoli danteschi, fan rimaner gli asini lungi a dietro. . . .

Now that a great chaos, all too envious of my well-being, has descended between you, who bask in the bosom of Abraham, and me, who desperately burns and blazes without any hope of that succour with which you were wont to cool my tongue, with true pledges and this present gift I mean to prove to you that this same chaos cannot, for all its spite, obstruct my love; and so here then is the candle which is proffered to you by this *Candlebearer* which I send to you from this foreign land in which I find myself and where it may serve to throw light on certain *Shadows of Ideas* which in truth seem to frighten the beasts and, like Dantean devils, leave the asses gasping far behind. . . .[46]

Bruno first shows his skill in lampooning the Petrarchist rhetoric of opposites—a skill he will soon further refine in the dedicatory epistles to *Spaccio de la bestia trionfante* (1584) and *De gl' heroici furori* (1585). But then he refers to his treatise published immediately before the play, *De umbris ideorum,* which is an account of his version of the medieval memory theater, thereby casting his comedy as a variation on the same technique, but one that is accessible, or at least not terrifying, to "beasts" and "asses." Following his master, Lucretius, Bruno would cover the wormwood of philosophy with the honey of literature. Yet "how could," Gino Moliterno pointedly asks, "a boisterous and ribald *cinquecento* comedy throw light on the workings of these shadows of ideas?"[47] Moliterno's solution to read the play as a staging of Bruno's *ars memoriae* is at once ingenious and persuasive. Bruno, though, also suggests another way of distilling meaning from the play's "gran caos." At the end of the same dedication, he momentarily abandons the satiric mode to signal his philosophy of opposites:

Ricordatevi, Signora . . . Il tempo tutto toglie e tutto dà; ogni cosa si muta, nulla s'annichila; è un solo che non può mutarsi, un solo è eterno, e può perseverare eternamente uno, simile e medesmo.—Con questa filosofia l'animo mi si aggrandisse, e me si magnifica l'intelletto. Però, qualunque sii il punto di questa sera ch'aspetto, si la mutazione è vera, io che sono ne la notte, aspetto il giorno, e quei che son nel giorno, aspettano la notte: tutto quel ch'è, o è cqua o llà, o vicino o lungi, o adesso o poi, o presto o tardi.

Remember, Lady . . .: Time takes all and gives all; everything changes, nothing is annulled; one only does not change, one only is eternal and endures eternally one, similar and the same. With this philosophy my spirit swells and my intellect is magnified. Thus, at whatever point I may be in this night of waiting, if change is real, I who am in the night await the day and those who are in the day await the night: everything that is, is either here or there, either near or far, either now or future, either early or late.[48]

Superficially commonplace, this sequence of contraries proves to be proleptic. They point to Bruno's complicated embrace of the Cusan *coincidentia oppositorum* that characterizes both the style and the substance of his moral and cosmographic works. As Hilary Gatti recounts in *Giordano Bruno and Renaissance Science,* Bruno's concept of the infinite universe adapts and modifies Cusanus's distinction between divine *complicatio* and human *explicatio.* Yet "if Bruno's defense of his infinite world were to rest only on this logical concept of the *coincidentia oppositorum* in the mind of God, it could justly be accused of resting on a purely metaphysical basis. Much more physical consistency derives to it from the atomistic argument put forward by Bruno."[49] In other words, by leaning on predecessors such as Lucretius, Cusanus, and Charles Bovelles's *Ars oppositorum* (1510), Bruno discovers both a material and a metaphysical ground for the *coincidentia* in his attempt to forge a philosophical Copernicanism in texts like *La cena de le Ceneri* (1584), *De l'infinito, universo e mondi* (1584), and *De immenso* (1591).

Exemplary of Bruno's thirst for synthesis and satire is his Prefatory Epistle to the first of the Italian cosmological works he wrote in England, *La cena de le Ceneri.* Here Bruno flaunts his humanist learning with a long *omissio* describing what the book is not (". . . this book is not a banquet of nectar for Jove the Thunderer, signifying majesty . . . not that of Bonifacio for comedy. . . ."). This then yields another rhetorical balancing act:

Ma un convito sì grande, sì picciolo; sì maestrale, sì disciplinale; sì sacrilego, sì religioso; sì allegro, sì colerico; sì aspro, sì giocondo; sì magro fiorentino, sì grasso bolognese; sì cinico, sì sardanapalesco; sì bagattelliero, sì serioso; sì grave, sì mattacinesco; sì tragico, sì comico: che certo credo che non vi sarà poco occasione da dovenir eroico, dismesso; maestro, descepolo; credente, mescredente; gaio, triste; saturnino, gioviale; leggiero, ponderoso; canino, liberale; simico, consulare; sofista con Aristotele, filosofo con Pitagora; ridente con Democrito, piangente con Eraclito.

But this is a banquet so great and small, so professorial and studentlike, so sacrilegious and religious, so joyous and choleric, so cruel and pleasant, so Florentine for its leanness and Bolognese for its fatness, so cynical and Sardanapalian, so trifling and serious, so grave and waggish, so tragic and comic that I surely believe there will be no few occasions for you to become heroic and humble; master and disciple; believer and unbeliever; cheerful and sad; saturnine and jovial; light and ponderous; miserly and liberal; simian and consular; sophist with Aristotle, philosopher with Pythagoras; laugher with Democritus and weeper with Heraclitus.[50]

Gosselin and Lerner gloss this passage as informed by Bruno's adoption of the doctrine of *coincidentia oppositorum.* What the book is not corresponds to "the Cusan Minimum," while its myriad positive attributes point to the "Cusan Maximum."[51] But it is only at infinity, Bruno reminds us in *De l'infinito, universo e mondi,* that minima and maxima coincide.[52] In short, the excessive rhetoric of the Epistle points to Bruno's most urgent philosophical, if also mystical, task in his career: to create unity out of multiplicity.

The *Candelaio,* then, is the theatrical laboratory where Bruno first toys with solutions to this ancient conundrum. Despite appearances to the contrary, or more aptly put, because of the play of appearances, Bruno's farce creates a theatrical space where ideas and their consequences can be played out; it creates what Benjamin calls in his later work a *Denkraum* (thought-space). Here the gullibility of fools and the savoir faire of con artists placed in the crucible of Italian, mannerist comedy produce heuristic effects closely related to the cognitive effects Bruno cultivates in his philosophical dialogues. Still, after rehearsing Bruno's debts to Cusanus for the doctrine of coincidences, Antonio Calcagno flatly concludes, "the *Candelaio* is a satirical comedy and contains little or no philosophical speculation. It is related to other works in that there is a common anti-dogmatic stance. However, content-wise its central themes are not coherently related to the other works of Bruno."[53] Yet like any capable dialectician, Bruno first pursues negation in order to achieve subsequent syntheses. Both Bonifacio and Bartolomeo thus suffer debased forms of love, while Mamfurio vitiates the promise of Renaissance humanism with his fruitless verbal gymnastics and, in an inversion of Cusanus's *docta ignorantia,* his "dotta coglioneria" (learned idiocy; 2.7), which leave him penniless, whipped, blackmailed, and pleading with the audience for understanding. Mamfurio's punning attempt to join opposites is exactly the kind of empty rhetoric Bruno despises: "She is a muliercula, quod est per ethimologiam 'mollis Hercules,' opposita iuxta se posita" (1.5). With such nonsense the rule rather than the exception, no wonder Bruno spends so much time teaching the audience how to interpret the play. In the Proprologue, he warns

Considerate chi va chi viene, che si fa che si dice, come s'intende come si può intendere: ché certo, contemplando quest'azioni e discorsi umani col senso d'Eraclito o di Democrito, arrete occasion di molto ridere o piangere.

Eccovi avanti gli occhii ociosi principii, debili orditure, vani pensieri, frivole speranze, scoppiamenti di petto, scoverture di corde, falsi presuppositi, alienazion di mente, poetici furori, offuscamento di sensi, turbazion di fantasia, smarrito peregrinaggio d'intelletto, fede sfrenate, cure insensate, studi incerti, somenze intempestive e gloriosi frutti di pazzia.

Consider well who comes and goes, what is done, what is said, how to understand what there is to understand, for certainly, in contemplating these human actions and speeches in the spirit of a Heraclitus or a Democritus, you are sure to have great occasion to either laugh or cry.

Here then before your eyes are futile beginnings, feeble plots, vain thoughts, frivolous hopes, bursting breasts, heartstrings laid bare, false assumptions, alienated wits, poetic furors, clouded senses, distortions of fantasy, lost intellectual pilgrimages, unbridled faiths, absurd anxieties, dubious studies, untimely sowings, and the glorious fruits of madness.[54]

As the deixis ("Eccovi. . .") confirms, the entire play is meant to perform what the motto on the title page implies: one must interpret in the "spirit" of both Heraclitus and Democritus. More than heralding a tragicomedy, the *Candelaio,* Bruno's analysis of the play's contents and motives confirms, is an expression of multiplicity, a staging of myriad opposites, which hopes for a spectator steeped in the "one."

Such multiplicity involves the play's language as well. In the course of skewering his own "shadow," that is, Mamfurio, Bruno makes a dramaturgical weapon out of the very faculty he mocks:

Quanto ben dimostrano che essi son quelli soli a'quai Saturno ha pisciato il giudizio in testa, le nove damigelle di Pallade un cornucopia di vocaboli gli han sarcato tra la pia e dura matre: e però è ben conveniente che sen vadino con quella sua prosopopeia, con quell'incesso gravigrado, busto ritto, testa salda ed occhii in atto di una modesta altiera circumspezione. Voi vedrete un di questi che mastica dottrina, olface opinioni, sputa sentenze, minge autoritadi, eructa arcani, exuda chiari e lunatici inchiostri, semina ambrosia e nectar di giudicii, da farne la credenza a Ganimede e poi un *brindes* al fulgorante Giove. Vedrete un *pubercola* sinonimico, epitetico, appositorio, suppositorio, bidello di Minerva, amostante di Pallade, tromba di Mercurio, patriarca di Muse e dolfino der regno apollinesco,— poco mancò ch'io non dicesse polledresco.

How easy it is to see upon whose head exclusively Saturn has pissed down his wisdom and the nine handmaids of Pallas have unloaded their verbal cornucopia, so it is most fitting that they should parade their prosopopeia with grave steps, erect body, unmoving head and eyes in an attitude of modest yet proud circumspection. You will see one who masticates dogmas, reeks opinions, spits out aphorisms, pisses authorities, belches arcane learning, sweats banal and bizarre lines, sows the ambrosia and nectar of judgements which need to be tasted by a Ganymede before being raised as a toast to a fulgurating Jove. You will see a synonymic, epithetic, appository and suppository *pubercola*, janitor to Minerva, majordomo to Pallas, trumpet of Mercury, patriarch of the Muses and heir to Apollo's throne; there I was about to say drone.[55]

The ability to produce "un cornucopia di vocaboli," which Erasmus makes the cornerstone of his Christian humanism, is given here the authority of classical myth only then to be cast as the author's motive for satirizing how pedantry can become pederasty. Bruno presents his own *copia*—here his many puns and various forms of *amplificatio*—as paving the way for a theatrical spectacle (*opsis*) through which the audience will learn "to see" just how enormous the gap is between words and things. Such false verbal *copia* is the opposite of the kind of intuitive wisdom that will triumph in the play and that presumably the audience is being taught by watching it. In 2.1, Mamfurio's empty eloquence ("nostra dicendi copia") violently clashes with the bestial content of his verses—a disjunction that completely escapes his notice, but that the play works to sharpen until, in the last scene, Mamfurio's words are made to acknowledge his actual, debased bodily condition. In this way, and with the help of asides by the character Gianbernardo, who sometimes seem to speak for Bruno, the audience experiences the farce not only as a lesson in the folly of carnal desires and empty *scientia,* but also in the enormous tensions between contingent events and the claims of reason, thus paving the way for the discovery by Bruno's readers of decidedly more noble worlds in the philosophic dialogues to follow.[56]

Tracing the complications, convergences, and reversals of the three intertwining plots is beyond this essay's scope.[57] Still, I would note a few ways in which Bruno makes *coincidentia oppositorum* coincident, at least in debased forms, with the language and logic of the theater. With Bonifacio, *furor amoris* constantly verges on buggery as he vainly pursues a courtesan, all the while being gulled by various characters. As he is punningly warned early on: "From a candlebearer you're becoming an aurificer" (Da candelaio volete doventar orifice; 1.9).[58] This transformation from active sodomite to passive catamite is metaphoric as well. In 2.5, the play's chief rogue, Sanguino, tells a bawdy parable about a lion and an ass crossing a river, the upshot being that Bonifacio is figured as both ass and sodomite. Meanwhile, in the course of the play, Bonifacio's swindling doppelgänger, Gianbernardo, becomes the ersatz "candle" for Bonifacio's wife. Likewise, as he is realizing his true condition, Bonifacio is twice renamed "Malefacio" (5.19, 5.22).

Such peripeteia is also the rule in the second plot tracking the consequences of Bartolomeo's blind passion for alchemy. As Nuccio Ordine observes, Bruno's "technique of reversal" has analogues in Rabelais and Erasmus, for it creates a unique theatrical space where "the rigid antinomy between laughter and tears" can dissolve.[59] Specifically, Bruno wittily weds this technique to a parody of alchemists and their techniques. Often described as the art of manipulating contrary or antithetical substances, alchemy stands here for everything that is false about human *scientia*. The alchemist, Cencio, peddles his *pulvis Christi* to Bartolomeo and then disappears with his booty, only to be replaced in the plot by other peddlers of pseudoknowledge: a magician and astrologer, Scaramuré, and a pharmacist, Consalvo. In this sense, the entire play is presented as a kind of laboratory in which ideas and techniques are tried and proven to be mendaciously effective but bereft of any philosophical value. Like Bonifacio, Bartolomeo is a false lover of wisdom; moreover, whenever the two meet in the play, their antipathy and differences are underscored:

BONIFACIO: . . . Voi fate per li nominativi ed io per li aggettivi, voi co la vostra alchimia ed io co la mia, voi al vostro fuoco ed io al mio.
BARTOLOMEO.: Io al fuoco di Vulcano e voi a quel di Cupido. (4.5)

BONIFACIO: . . . Your passion is for nouns and mine is for adjectives, you resort to your alchemy and I to mine; you to your fire and I to mine.
BARTOLOMEO: I to the fire of Vulcan and you to Cupid's flame.

This pedantic *inflatus* is thoroughly deflated in the last act when Bartolomeo realizes the extent of his folly and disgrace. Indeed, Bruno stages this realization in such a way that Bartolomeo is also transformed into an ass, for he is tied to Consalvo who recounts, "as I tried to pull, he fell like an overloaded donkey and he brought me down with him; and then, out of spite, he wouldn't get up" (5.13).

Bruno's sharpest mockery, though, is reserved for Mamfurio, the bombastic, blinkered pedant. Presented as "a sheep for shearing" in the *Argumentum* because of his empty grandiloquence, Mamfurio is predictably, methodically, dehumanized of his tired humanism in the careening course of the play's seventy-five scenes. Again, while I cannot recount here the mechanics of Bruno's patient, merciless hoisting of scholarly *vanitas,* it may be that his most damning, if always implicit charge is that Mamfurio is immune to all dialogism; he hears but cannot listen.[60] The solipsism of "nostra dicendi copia" (2.1) is absolute. It is oblivious, like Bonifacio, to its own content. His absurd Ciceronianism barely can be deciphered by other characters, who take it as a sign of ignorance (while Bruno uses it as a springboard for endless wordplay). Thus Mamfurio is easily swindled, stripped of his dignity, his freedom, even his clothes, and left only with his empty words: "O me miserum! verba nihil prosunt.

O diem infaustum atque noctem!" (O miserable me! Words are useless. O unlucky day and night!; 4.16).

For Bruno, though, certain words retain great efficacy or, if you will, create fruitful ambiguity. In a dialogue between Barra and Marca, two of the men helping to orchestrate one of the scams, the former blithely if wittily inverts Christian dogma ("Far burla ad osti è far sacrificio a Nostro Signore" [playing a joke on an innkeeper is the same as offering a sacrifice to Our Lord]), while the latter observes

Concorsero molti, de quali altri pigliandosi spasso altri attristandosi, altri piangendo altri ridendo, questi consigliando quelli sperando, altri facendo un viso altri un altro, altri questo linguaggio ed altri quello: era veder insieme comedia e tragedia, e chi sonava a gloria e chi a mortoro. Di sorte che, chi volesse vedere come sta fatto il mondo, derebbe desiderare di esservi stato presente. (3.8)

Quite a crowd gathered, some amused by it all and some offended, some crying and some laughing, this person offering advice, that one receiving hope, people with different faces, speaking in this or that tongue. It was like seeing a comedy and tragedy together, with some people celebrating and others in mourning. Anyone who has ever wanted to see the world in miniature should have been there then.

Here in a nutshell is Bruno's reception theory for late cinquecento drama.[61] As Giulio Ferroni argues, what I have been calling a coincidence of opposites belongs to Bruno's "theoretical use" of the theater to discover and come to grips with the multiplicity and mutability of the world: "The alternation between the tragic and comic is a matter of perspective, a figure of the more general structure of the world, which constitutes itself in the alternation between contraries." (Lo scambio tra tragico e comico è un fatto di prospettiva, cifra della più generale struttura del mondo, del suo costituirsi nello scambio tra contrari).[62] Ferroni sees Bruno as imitating the deceptive Sileni of Alcibiades in the *Symposium,* as "the *Candlebearer* constructs a setting of continual mutability, of an always reversible farce."[63] Like Christopher Marlowe, whose *Doctor Faustus* (1588) mixes farce and tragedy to dramatize the struggle between good and evil, to stage the impossibility of reconciling the thirst for *scientia* and for *sapientia,* Bruno refuses to resolve such inconstancy into a stable allegory.[64]

But again, at least some of the characters in Bruno's play learn from this perspectivism. Scaramuré late in the play comments: "La vostra comedia è bella, ma, in fatti di costoro, è una troppo fastidiosa tragedia" (your comedy is certainly funny, but for these fellows it must be a bitter tragedy; 5.15). More dramatically still, Bruno's shadow, Mamfurio, is forced to deliver the *plaudite* in the play's final scene. Literally tearing the veil, Ascanio (Bonifacio's servant) urges him: "apri gli occhi, e guarda dove sei, mira ove ti trovi" (open your eyes and look where you are, see where you've ended up; 5.26). To which Mamfurio, after plowing through some more scholastic mumbo-jumbo about the physics of vision, finally exclaims: "Oh, veggio di molti spectatori la corona" (oh, I see a circle made up of many spectators). The subsequent exchange makes a spectator out of Mamfurio as well:

ASCANIO: Non vi par esser entro una comedia?
MAMFURIO: *Ita sane.*
ASCANIO: Non credete d'esser in scena?
MAMFURIO: *Omni procul dubio.*
ASCANIO: A che termine vorreste che fusse la comedia?
MAMFURIO: *In calce,* in fine: *neque enim et ego risu ilia tendo.*
ASCANIO: Or dunque, fate e donate il *Plaudite.* (5.26)

ASCANIO: Don't you feel that you're in a play?
MAMFURIO: *Ita sane* [exactly so].
ASCANIO: Don't you feel like you're on a stage?
MAMFURIO: *Omni procul dubio* [I hardly doubt anything].
ASCANIO: At what point would you like the play to be?
MAMFURIO: *In calce,* at the end: *neque enim et ego risu ilia tendo* [nor can I even hold my laughter].
ASCANIO: Well, then, initiate the *plaudite.*

From crocodile tears to coerced laughter, Mamfurio's anagnorisis, such as it is, consists in realizing that he is not alone, that other voices matter. Yet I would not go so far as Ferdinand Fellmann, who, reading Bruno's philosophy, asserts that "it is the coincidence of contraries [*Gegensatz und Zustand*] which permits one to be conscious of one's subjectivity."[65] In Bruno's elaborate *orbis theatrum,* the extremes, multiplicity, and ambiguity of language and character resolve not into a single point but into a characteristic way of thinking that informs all his philosophical and cosmographical writings. In his chapter, "The Ambiguous Space of Asininity," Ordine, quoting from Bruno's *Spaccio de la bestia trionfante,* reminds us: "In Bruno's view of things, *varietas* and *coincidentia oppositorum* converge in a common space where 'the beginning, the middle, and the end, the birth, the growth, and the perfection of everything we see is accomplished from opposites, by means of opposites, within opposites, toward opposites. Where there is opposition, there is action and reaction, there is movement, diversity, multiplicity, order, degrees, succession, and vicissitude.'"[66] In formal terms, that is, the dramatic techniques practiced in the *Candelaio* reappear in Bruno's later philosophical dialogues.[67] And while it may be too much to claim that in the theatrical space of the *Candelaio* Bruno learns to hear other voices, to become a better dialectician, still, we glimpse there the shadowy origin of his method resolving the many into one that will soon fuel his contentious expression of a Copernican *theatrum mundi*. In the *Candelaio* Bruno performs multiplicity even as he annuls it, just as he will when contemplating an infinite number of possible worlds.[68] In this respect, the play's chiasmic motto, *In Tristitia hilaris: in Hilaritate tristis*, points beyond a dramaturgical commonplace toward Bruno's central epistemological and ontological idea.

The opening scene of Calderón's *El mágico prodigioso* involves a scholar puzzling over the meaning and value of received knowledge. Having dismissed his two servants, Cipriano, a character based on Saint Ciprian, who was martyred in third-century Antioch, muses:

> Ya estoy solo, ya podré,
> si tanto mi ingenio alcanza,
> estudiar esta cuestión
> que me trae suspensa el alma
> desde que en Plinio leí
> con misteriosas palabras
> la difinición de Dios.
> Porque mi ingenio no halla
> este Dios en quien convengan
> misterios ni señas tantas,
> esta verdad escondida
> he de apurar.[69] (77–88)

Now I am alone and will be able, if my wit can achieve as much, to study this question, which holds my soul in suspense since I read in Pliny the definition of God with those mysterious words. Because my mind has not found this God in whom so many signs and mysteries can fit, I must investigate this hidden truth.

Preferring study and solitude to a festival honoring Jupiter, Cipriano initially is cast as a pagan whose "ingenio" is frustrated by the ineffability of "God." Eager to pierce "this hidden truth," he proves an easy dupe for the disguised Demonio, who appears immediately after these lines and speaks to him of a place where access to "ciencias" (119, 142) is had without laborious study. The Devil also gains Cipriano's sympathy by guessing the "mysterious words" of Pliny, which are: "Dios es una bondad suma, / una esencia, una sustancia, / toda vista y todo manos" (God is a supreme good / one essence, one substance, / all seeing and all doing; 169-71).[70] In the subsequent rather scholastic dialogue we learn that though Cipriano initially finds "repugnancia" (dissonance; 172) in this maxim—since he knows only the pagan gods with their human vices, and since he sees "contraries" (257) in the good and evil "genios" (spirits; 245) motivating human action—when left to his own "ingenio" (wit) he is indeed capable of apprehending if not comprehending the meaning of Pliny's words. Seeing this, the Devil vows to make Cipriano forget his "study" by blinding him with the "beauty" of Justina, who is a secretly practicing Christian in pagan Antioch. This will allow him to take vengeance on two people with one act: "sacaré / de un efeto dos venganzas" (I will extract / from one effect two vengeances; 314-15). In short, Calderón makes the ancient theological paradox concerning unity and multiplicity both the conceptual basis and the narrative motor for his *comedia religiosa*. What Benjamin asserts for German Baroque drama holds perfectly for Calderón's martyr-drama: "For a critical understanding of the *Trauerspiel*, in its extreme, allegorical form, is possible only from the higher domain of theology; so long as the approach is an aesthetic one, paradox must have the last word."[71] Moreover, Calderón's portrait of the ingenious Devil, whose role here is to help incarnate the delights and allegorize the follies inherent in the pursuit of knowledge, begs to be read as a kind of inverted self-portrait of the playwright as a vicarious, but fallen *magus* whose manipulation of dramatic action and appearances produces a vision of a lasting mystery.[72]

Bruce Wardropper comments that the Faust legend, although known in late Renaissance Spain, was a source that Calderón "omitted from employing."[73] Despite obvious parallels in plot and character, *El mágico prodigioso* differs from the legend (and from *Doctor Faustus*), as it eventually provides redemption for both Cipriano and Justina, granting them the mystical knowledge of martyrs. In this sense, the Faust legend is the negated absence in the play. (In a manuscript version of the comedy Justina was called Faustina). Also, as I suggested above, Calderón makes central to his drama the conflict between Cipriano's profane love for Justina and Justina's sacred but hidden love for Christ. In so doing, he exploits venerable Petrarchan and neo-Platonic rhetoric and conceptual tensions to help produce his chief protagonist's epiphany. In his final soliloquy, Cipriano announces his conversion after recounting his thralldom to Venus and his fruitless study of the Devil's hermetic arts:

> De su virtud despedido,
> mantuve mis sentimientos
> hasta que, mi amor pasando
> de un extremo en otro extremo,
> a un huésped mío, que el mar
> le dio mis plantas por puerto,
> por Justina ofrecí el alma,
> porque me cautivó a un tiempo
> el amor con esperanzas,
> y con ciencias el ingenio.
> De éste discípulo he sido,
> estas montañas viviendo,
> a cuya docta fatiga
> tanta admiración le debo
> que puedo mudar los montes
> desde un asiento a otro asiento;
> y aunque puedo esto prodigios
> hoy ejecutar, no puedo
> atraer una hermosura
> a la voz de mi deseo.
> La causa de no poder
> rendir este monstruo bello
> es que hay un Dios que la guarda,
> en cuyo conocimiento
> he venido a confesarle
> por el más sumo y inmenso. (2,893–2,918)

Dismissed by her [Justina's] virtue, I persevered in my feelings, until—with my love moving from one extreme to another extreme—I offered my soul for Justina to my guest, whom the sea gave as port for my complaints; for he captured me for a time, love with hopes, and the mind with sciences. I have been his disciple, living in these mountains; I owe his tiresome learning enormous admiration, for I can move mountains from one place to another. And though now I can achieve these marvels, I cannot attract a beauty with my desire's voice. The reason why I cannot overcome this beautiful monster is that there is a God who protects her and whose knowledge, I have come to confess to her, is the highest and greatest.

Here we have not only the entire narrative *in nuce,* but also an authoritative hermeneutic. The internal motion "de un extremo en otro extremo" that Cipriano experiences in love is repeated in the external movement of "los montes/desde un asiento a otro asiento"—an allusion to a scene I will discuss below—and then finally in his acceptance of powerlessness before Justina's unique, paradoxical mixture of faith, beauty, and disdain ("este monstruo bello"), all of which helps him to recognize God's absolute knowledge. In brief, as Calderón stages it, only the play of extremes is able to yield a realization of the divine idea first emblemized in the play by Pliny's maxim. But again, as Benjamin insists in his reading of the *Trauerspiele,* the "idea" also concerns the form of the drama itself.[74] Dramatic peripeteia produces epistemological certainty for Cipriano and reminds the audience of more timeless, stable truths.

Like his many *auto sacramentales,* Calderón's *comedias religiosas* aim to mediate Christian theology through the language and techniques of Baroque drama. The *autos,* performed during the Corpus Christi *fiesta,* usually atop an enormous cart that could be transported from town to town, were a more popular form of theater; the *comedias religiosas* sought to convey religious doctrine (*lección*) to a more theologically sophisticated urban and courtly audience.[75] Thus in *El mágico prodigioso* Calderón methodically stages the motions away from a subjective, terrestrial "centro" to a fixed, theological idea that is able, literally and allegorically, to mediate between the opposites of the human and the divine. To arrive at this idea—synonymous with the *ponderación misteriosa* in which God's grace and human free will (*libre albedrío*) coincide, in which objectivity and subjectivity, *complicatio* and *explicatio* prove identical—the play cultivates semantic, theological, and dramaturgical extremes.[76] The idea, as Benjamin might say, is "represented," even if it can never be fully understood as an object of knowledge.

"Every reader of Calderón is struck by the meaning of the word *centro.*"[77] In part this is because of the word's enormous semantic range. In his 1611 *Tesoro,* Covarrubias provides this remarkable gloss for *centro:*

Es un punto en la esfera o en el círculo que consiste en el medio; de manera que todas las líneas que se tiraren dél a la circunferencia, serán iguales. . . . El centro del mundo es aquel punto en el medio de la tierra, que para do quiera que se echaran las líneas a la superficie, serán iguales; y este es el que más dista del cielo, y así está diputado para el demonio y sus secuaces. . . . Este punto y lugar tira para sí de todos los elementos, con tanta fuerza, que si Dios se aniquilase el globo de la tierra y el agua, acudiría allí por todas partes el aire. Y por esta razón lo grave se va a este centro y no pasa de allí; de donde decimos cuando uno está contento, que no se acuerda de nada ni desea más de aquello de que está gozando, *que está en su centro*.[78]

It is the point in a sphere or circle that occupies the middle, such that all lines drawn from it to the circumference will be equal. . . . The center of the world is that point in the middle of the earth, from which wherever you send lines to the surface, they will be equal; and this point is the furthest from heaven, and thus it is ruled over by the devil and his minions. . . . This point and place attracts to itself all the elements, with such force, that if God annihiliated the globe of earth and water, the air from everywhere would meet up there. And for this reason heavy things go to this center and do not move from there; from which we say that when someone is content, neither regretting anything not desiring more than what he is enjoying, *that he is in his center*.

In the course of *El mágico prodigioso,* Calderón explores each of these meanings. And like Covarrubias he amalgamates late Renaissance science, theology, and psychology in an attempt to reconcile worldly multiplicity and a theological idea.

The play begins with the sun, a "gran cadáver de oro" (great corpse of gold), about "sepultarse en las ondas" (to bury itself in the waves; 24–28).[79] Just as the sun ominously finds its center, Cipriano compares all the roads leading from the mountains to Antioch to lines, which, bisecting a circle, necessarily touch the center (109–18). But when the disguised Devil appears, he deceitfully declares that he does not know how to profit from "las ciencias." As if on cue, after the brief dialogue about the Pliny maxim, the play turns first to the amorous theme, in which Cipriano, spurred by a parodic subplot of servants (*criados*) emulating their masters, literally finds himself in the center. Before he has lain eyes on Justina he tries to mediate between two rival young men enamored of her: "¿Qué es aquesto?/Lelio, tente; Floro aparta;/que basta que esté yo en medio,/aunque esté en medio sin armas" (what is this?/Lelio, stop; Floro, stand apart;/for it's enough that I am in the middle,/though I am in the middle without weapons; 331–34).[80] Agreeing then to pander for them, he immediately falls for Justina, who emerges as the play's other figure of the center and thus is accompanied by a series of solar images (407, 416, 419, 514). An orphan, found at the moment when her martyred mother is dying—and who describes her daughter as "being born from my tomb [*sepulcro*]"—Justina, with her unwavering faith and refusal to be courted by pagan lovers, comes to represent a symbolic antipode, an astronomical antinomy, to the dark, mortal center of human existence. Her presence in the play confirms what Klaus Uppendahl, in his reading of Calderón's *Mística y real Babilonia*, calls "the ambivalence of *center*-symbolism."[81] In other words, "the magnificent edifice of the universe" (62) is never stable for Calderón, since it has as its *centro* Hell itself, the locus of sin. As Covarrubias phrases it: ". . . y este es el que más dista del cielo, y así esta diputado para el demonio y sus secuaces." Thus after appearing in disguise on Justina's balcony to besmirch her honor, "the black shape," the Devil, "hurls itself from the balcony to the ground." Nor does he stop there:

> No sólo he de conseguir
> hoy de Justina el desprecio,
> sino rencores y muertes.
> Ya llegan: ábrase el centro,
> dejando esta confusión
> a sus ojos. (923-28)

Not only do I have to obtain now disdain for Justina, but also dissensions and deaths. Now they arrive: open the earth's center, leaving this confusion to their eyes.

But these "eyes" belong to the audience as well. For as we attend to Calderón's diction and metaphorics we learn to see this "confusion" and demonization of the *centro* as the proper order of things. In short, Calderón's universe is less Ptolemaic than allegorical; it is constructed along theological rather than cosmographical lines.

Meanwhile, the Devil labors to corrupt Cipriano with "nuevas ciencias" (2,012), with which Cipriano, in turn, hopes to seduce Justina. Hopelessly enamored, Cipriano declares his willingness to trade his soul for the chance to enjoy her (1,196-99). Hearing this, the eager Devil suddenly appears and immediately orchestrates a show. Yet aside from the stage directions indicating thunder, this spectacle is entirely mediated through Cipriano's words. This lends the scene enormous subjective force as well:

> ¿Qué es ésto, cielos puros?
> ¡Claros a un tiempo, y en el mismo oscuros!
> Dando al día desmayos,
> los truenos, los relámpagos y rayos
> abortan de su centro
> los asombros que ya no caben dentro.
> . . . .

> Todo nuestro horizonte
> es ardiente pincel del Mongibelo,
> niebla el sol, humo el aire, fuego el cielo. (1,201-6; 1,210-12)

What is this, spotless heavens? Clear one moment and dark in the next! Making
the day faint, the thunder, lightning abort from their center the terrors that no
longer fit within. . . . Our entire horizon is [painted] by the burning paintbrush
of Mount Aetna; fog [ornaments] the sun, smoke the air, fire the sky.

Parodying the convulsions felt by nature after Christ's passion, this astonishing tableau of the world upside down depends on the verb *abortar,* which signals a violent, unnatural motion. The center cannot hold as
monstrous nature becomes an artist.[82] More to the point, the Devil proves
a skilled con artist, as he also proceeds to paint a magnificently Baroque
shipwreck (1,215-37) out of which he emerges as the sole survivor. Then,
in a complicated, Miltonic soliloquy (1,295-1,418), he recounts his fall
("Fue bárbaro atrevimiento . . ." [It was a barbaric audacity . . .]), while
pretending to be no more than a learned magus willing to aid Cipriano
to fulfill his desires. His art, as he later confesses in an aside, consists of
pure "engaños" (deceits; 1,981).

   The Devil's art cannot then be separated from Calderón's still more ambitious art of *desengaño.*[83] In perhaps the play's most spectacular scene,
the Devil finally succeeds in getting Cipriano to sign away his soul by
virtue of another "prodigio," this time a mountain that moves itself "from
one part of the *tableau* to the other." The audience is surely meant to
share Cipriano's *affectus,* when he exclaims

> Pájaro que al viento vuelas,
> siendo tus plumas tus ramos;
> bajel que en el viento sulcas;
> siendo jarcias tus peñascos:
> vuélvete a tu centro, y deja
> la admiración y el espanto. (1,932-37)

Bird that flies in the wind, your feathers as your oars; ship that plows the wind,
your rocks as rigging: return to your center, and spare admiration and fright.

But then this lost *centro* is transformed again, becoming the explicit object
of Cipriano's desire when the Devil fashions an image of the sleeping Justina
and places it momentarily in the "oscuro centro" (dark center) of the mountain (1,945). This illusion is enough to persuade the idolatrous Cipriano:

> Divino imposible mío,
> hoy serán centro tus brazos
> de mi amor, bebiendo al sol
> luz a luz y rayo a rayo. (1,950-53)

My unattainable divinity, now your arms will be the center of my love, drinking from your sun, beam after beam, ray after ray.

Thus deluded Cipriano spends a year in a cave learning the Devil's magical arts before he sees that other sun again and tries to win Justina. For her part, with her honor in ruins, Justina seems to retreat into the sphere of herself "para acrisolar verdades" (to crystallize truths; 1,773). Her fierce subjectivity, her "libre albedrío," becomes thereby the play's unmovable center, immune to all blandishments and all "ciencia peregrina" (peregrine science; 2,314).[84] Indeed, just as Harry Levin was right to read *Doctor Faustus* as a tragedy of the overreaching will, *El mágico prodigioso* begs to be interpreted as a comedy of the free will, though one anchored in an absolute faith in God.[85] In the famous temptation scene, the Devil fails to move Justina's will even though he succeeds in corrupting her imagination (2,297-98). As the stage directions make clear, she literally will not be moved. In this way, Calderón gives the *coincidentia oppositorum* of *scientia* and *sapientia* one of its most Baroque dramatic expressions. A peculiarly theatrical species of *docta ignorantia* is produced from this coincidence; for the martyr's motives remain a mystery to the Devil, though they become palpable to the comedy's spectators.

Again, Cipriano's *desengaño* is orchestrated not by the Devil but by Calderón, who with all the tricks of dramaturgy utterly negates his protagonist's profane love and replaces it with a startling *memento mori.*[86] Struggling to resist the Devil's spell, Justina pointedly asks for a "blanket" to cover herself: "porque, en tanto/que padezco estos extremos,/tengo de ir al templo santo/que tan secreto tenemos/los fieles. . . En él tengo de templar/este fuego que me abrasa" (because, in so far/as I suffer these extremes,/I have to go to the holy temple,/which we faithful/keep secret. . . . In it I have to temper/this fire that burns me; 2,394-98; 2,399-400). With the aid of the pun on "templo" and "templar," Calderón achieves the *templanza* or mediation of "estos extremos," while his seemingly innocuous insistence on the blanket is the key to setting up the subsequent scene in which the Figure of Justina wearing a similar blanket is about to surrender itself to Cipriano. But just as this is about to happen the Figure flees offstage, only to be brought back onstage a moment later—as detailed in the play's most elaborate stage directions—carried in Cipriano's arms and completely covered in the blanket. Triumphantly discounting his damnation in light of the putative prize in his arms, Cipriano unwraps the blanket and beholds a skeleton that announces to the horrified lover: "Así, Cipriano, son/todas las glorias del mundo" (thus, Cipriano, are/all the world's glories; 2,549–50).[87] What Benjamin asserts of *memento mori* in the *Trauerspiel* holds exactly for Calderón's martyr-drama: "the corpse becomes quite simply the pre-eminent emblematic property. The apotheoses are barely conceivable without it."[88] Cipriano's embrace of the skeleton is the last step in his conversion. Rejecting now the Devil, who cannot deny God's intervention on Justina's behalf, he publicly embraces the Christian God. In so doing, Cipriano becomes the mean or *medio* between the extremes of the Devil's "ciencia" and God's "gracia" (2,575–76).

By the end of the play Calderón sharpens his allegory such that the imprisoned Cipriano and Justina are reconciled, and the opposition between the forces of Heaven and Hell collapses in the light of the ineffable truth spoken by Justina:

> No tiene
> tantas estrellas el cielo,
> tantas arenas el mar,
> tantas centellas el fuego,
> tantos átomos el día,
> ni tantas plumas el viento,
> come Él perdona pecados. (3,019–25)

The sky does not have as many stars, the sea as many grains of sand, the fire as many sparks, the day as many atoms, nor the wind as many feathers, as He pardons sins.

Here another kind of conversion or peripeteia occurs: the prodigious magician of the play's title no longer is the Devil or Cipriano, but as these and the comedy's last lines clarify, it is God—at once Pliny's God and the Christian God—who miraculously works the transformation of the mortal, natural *centro* into an infinite idea, an idea that allows the audience to say that a character like Justina or Cipriano *está en su centro*. On a theological level extremes are mediated by God-Christ's forgiveness of sins; but dramaturgically, through verbal wit, the inversion of the

Faustian plot, and the illusions created by stagecraft, Calderón proves the primacy of the dialectic between appearance and reality, *engaño* and *desengaño*. Thus Cipriano, rejecting the Devil's arguments late in the play, cites part of Pliny's maxim as evidence of God's will to intervene to save him from perdition: "Todo es vista,/y verá el medio oportuno. . . . Todo es manos:/Él sabrá romper los nudos" (All is seen,/and He will see the opportune means. . . . Being all-powerful: He will know how to untie the knots; 2,751–52). That Calderón refuses to stage a deus ex machina for his protagonists, "to untie the knots" of his plot, but rather makes their words gesture at another kind of salvation further confirms the subtlety of his allegory.

Benjamin's running, always invidious comparison between the *Trauerspiele* and Calderón's dramas rests on the Spaniard's "suppleness of form" in constructing his allegories.[89] While this is not the place to assess the reception of Benjamin's theory of Baroque allegory, it is important to note that for all its emphasis on the ruin, the fragment, "fallen nature," and "decayed objects" as the material for the melancholic allegorist to ponder, there is a less remarked, but equally powerful current in his thinking that solicits the transcendent and "the eternal" in these artworks.[90] Calderón figures in Benjamin's study mainly as a master of the secular drama of fate, a mastery that depends heavily on his ability to fashion antitheses.[91] Yet Benjamin explicitly invokes Calderón when, at the end of his book, and with a decidedly mystical tone, he cultivates another kind of *coincidentia* by refusing real, ontological existence to evil. Evil "exists only in allegory," thus rendering it a purely "subjective phenomenon."[92]

That this claim is more than recycled Platonism or revivified Augustianism may be confirmed by recalling the long passage I quoted at the beginning of this essay in which Benjamin speaks of "the distinguishing power of the intellect" that "brings about two things at a single stroke: the salvation of phenomena and the representation of ideas." The allegorist—be it Calderón or Benjamin (whose self-appointed task is the critical "mortification" of Baroque texts)—immerses himself in theatrical *realia* to learn how to mediate "extremes" and thereby arrive at an "objective interpretation" of the ways language and form may allow glimpses of less fleeting truths. By his own account, Benjamin is able to achieve this in his study of the German "sorrow-plays," not because his own *Geist* yearns to leave the material world behind, but because his "subjective perspective is entirely absorbed in the economy of the whole."[93] Embracing one last "extremity,"

Benjamin turns longingly to Calderón's method of *mystical ponderation:* "Subjectivity, like an angel falling into the depths, is brought back by allegories, and is held fast in heaven, in God, by *ponderación misteriosa.*"[94] And though such ponderation may well require an act of divine intervention, it also retains the particularly Baroque connotation, explicated at length by Baltasar Gracián in his remarkable treatise on wit and the poetic conceit, *Agudeza y arte de ingenio* (1642). To ponder wittily an object, event, or idea is an "act of understanding" that establishes "a harmonious correlation between two or three knowable extremes."[95] While they may diverge on how to use and value allegory, Gracián, Calderón, Bruno, Cusanus, and Benjamin agree on one point: the more extreme the representation of phenomena becomes, the stronger is its ultimate claim to be an expression of ideas.

Notes

1. Walter Benjamin, *Ursprung des deutschen Trauerspiels* (Frankfurt am Main: Suhrkamp, 1963), 16; *The Origin of German Tragic Drama,* trans. John Osborne, intr. George Steiner (London: Verso, 1977), 35; translation modified. Steiner dubs the prologue a "proem" (23).

2. *Ursprung,* 17; *Origin,* 36.

3. See, for example, Hans-Georg Gadamer, "Philosophy and Poetry," in *The Relevance of the Beautiful and Other Essays* (Cambridge: Cambridge University Press, 1986), 131–39. Gadamer writes: "In the case where language is the medium, we must ask a question that particularly concerns the relation between philosophy and literature: how do these two preeminent and yet at the same time contrary forms of language—the poetic text which stands on its own account, and the language of the concept which suspends itself and leaves everyday reality behind it—relate to one another? Following a tried phenomenological principle, I should like to approach this question from an extreme case. For this reason, I shall take as my starting point the lyric poem and the dialectical concept" (134).

4. See Louise George Clubb, "The Arts of Genre: *Torrismondo* and *Hamlet," ELH* 47, no. 4 (1980): 657-69; "Shakespeare's Comedy and Late Cinquecento Mixed Genres," *New York Literary Forum* 5-6 (1980): 129-39; also much of *Italian Drama in Shakespeare's Time* (New Haven: Yale University Press, 1989) is devoted to questions of genre.

5. *Ursprung,* 18; *Origin,* 36.

6. *Ursprung,* 10; *Origin,* 29.

7. *Ursprung,* 193-97; *Origin,* 174-77.

8. Steiner's introduction is a good place to start. See also Beatrice Hanssen, "Philosophy at Its Origin: Walter Benjamin's prologue to the *Ursprung des deutschen Trauerspiels," MLN* 110 (1995): 809-33; Bainard Cowan, "Walter Benjamin's Theory of Allegory," *New German Critique* 22 (1981): 109-22.

9. *Ursprung,* 31, 46; *Origin,* 46, 58. My translation.

10. *Ursprung,* 31; *Origin,* 47. Glossing this phrase, Hanssen writes, "inasmuch as the historical lies encased in the essence or 'nature' of the Ideas, natural history simultaneously signifies the historical 'dynamization' of the intransient Ideas or essences" (827).

11. As such my approach is more formalist than most recent efforts at fusing literary criticism and intellectual history. See Donald Kelley, *The Descent of Ideas: The History of Intellectual History* (Burlington, Vt.: Ashgate, 2002); Anthony Grafton, "The History of Ideas: Precept and Practice, 1950-2000 and Beyond," *Journal of the History of Ideas* 67, no. 1 (2006): 1-32. What generic label to apply to Bruno's play continues to be debated. But the solution of Vicenzo Spampanato, the first modern editor of the play (Bari, 1909 and 1923), remains the best one, when he points to Scaramuré's realization in 5.22 that he seems to be in "una comedia vera." The question, then, turns on the meaning of "vera."

12. *Ursprung*, 20; *Origin*, 38. Benjamin goes on to cite Max Scheler's early work, *Vom Umsturz der Worte* (Leibzig, 1919) as informing his refusal to think "inductively" about literary history, genre, and ideas.

13. Tellingly, Benjamin refers to Plato's ideas as "deified words and verbal concepts" (*Origin*, 36).

14. *Origin*, 47-48. But see also page 41 where discussing the "ideas" of the "renaissance" and "baroque," Benjamin asserts, "As ideas. . . such names perform a service that they are not able to perform as concepts: they do not make the similar identical, but they effect a synthesis between extremes."

15. Hanssen, 811.

16. *Origin*, 57.

17. *Origin*, 57-59. Thus he reads the German dramatists as rejecting the dogma of the three unities as promoted by neo-Aristotelian, cinquecento theory (60-62) . See Bernard Weinberg, *A History of Literary Criticism in the Italian Renaissance*, 2 vols. (Chicago: University of Chicago Press, 1961).

18. See F. W. J. Schelling, *Bruno, or, On the Natural and the Divine Principle of Things*, trans. Michael G. Vater (Albany: SUNY Press, 1984).

19. *Ursprung*, 16-17; *Origin*, 34-35. Later Benjamin urges attention to the form, or "theatrical representation" of the *Trauerspiel* (*Origin*, 50-51). The reference to "Faustian 'Mothers'" is to *Faust, Part 2* (1.5).

20. *Ursprung*, 183; *Origin*, 162.

21. *Origin*, 35.

22. *Origin*, 44.

23. *Origin*, 43. He cites a passage from Croce's *Brevario di estetica*, translated as *The Essence of Aesthetic* (1921). For a recent analysis of Benjamin's use of Croce, see Gabriele Scaramuzza, "Croce nella *Vorrede* al 'Dramma barocco,'" in *Giochi per melanconici: Sull' "Origine del dramma barocco tedesco" di Walter Benjamin*, ed. Andrea Pinotti, 269-73 (Milan: Mimesis, 2003).

24. *Origin*, 45. The quote is from Croce.

25. *Origin*, 47. In a note, Benjamin cites his own essay "The Task of the Translator" to gloss the notion of the "natural life" or historical becoming of the work.

26. Hanssen describes the paradox of "origin" as "a dialectic between historical singularity and repetition" (811).

27. As opposed to the *Aristotelian Telescope* (1654) that Emanuele Tesauro trains on the world to create an alternate universe of subjective wit.

28. *Origin*, 47.

29. *Origin*, 47. Glossing Benjamin's "Idea," Steiner comments, "it is 'ideally-ideationally' that discrete, fully autonomous objects—like baroque plays or renaissance paintings—enter into mutual compaction, into significant fusion without thereby losing their identity. The relevant paradigm is that of Leibniz's monads—independent, perfectly separate units which nevertheless and, indeed, necessarily enter into combinatorial, harmonic groupings and interactions. Thus the singular 'finds salvation,' i.e., realizes its potential of full

meaning, in the monadic plurality or, more precisely, in the representative manifold—the symbol, the icon, the declarative emblem—of 'Ideas'" (23).

30. *Ursprung*, 8; *Origin*, 28; translation modified.

31. *Origin*, 160. For all its theoretical debts to German romanticism, Nietzsche's *The Birth of Tragedy*, Scheler's phenomenology, and the "cultural-historical" interpretation of the Renaissance as championed by Warburg, Panofsky, Saxl, and company, Benjamin's method is driven by a series of intuitions that, frankly, often verge on the mystical. Indeed, Gershom Scholem reports that Benjamin had asserted that only someone steeped in Kabbalah could truly understand his prologue (cited by Steiner, *Origin*, 13-14).

32. For analysis of this and other tenets of Cusanus's thought, his debts to neo-Platonism, and his influence on other thinkers, see F. Edward Cranz, *Nicholas of Cusa and the Renaissance* (Aldershot, UK: Ashgate, 2000), and Dermot Moran, "Nicholas of Cusa (1401-1464): Platonism at the Dawn of Modernity," in *Platonism at the Origins of Modernity: Studies on Platonism and Early Modern Philosophy*, ed. Douglas Hedley and Sarah Hutton, 9-29 (Dordrecht: Springer, 2008). But see also Ernst Cassirer's *Individuum und Cosmos in der Philosophie der Renaissance* (Hamburg: F. Mainer, 2002), which places Cusanus at the center of the intellectual history of the Renaissance, and which was published in 1927, one year before Benjamin's *Trauerspiel* book.

33. I am especially indebted in my discussion of Cusanus's doctrine of coincidences to Kurt Flasch, *Nikolaus von Kues: Geschichte einer Entwicklung. Vorlesungun zur Einführung in seine Philosophie* (Frankfurt am Main: Vittorio Klostermann, 1998); "Nikolaus von Kues: Die Idee der Koinzidenz," in *Philosophie des Altertums und des Mittelalters*, ed. Josef Speck, 214-54 (Göttingen: Vandenhoeck & Ruprecht, 2001).

34. In *De docta ignorantia*, Cusanus approvingly writes, "those who considered the most actual existence of God affirmed that He is an infinite sphere, as it were" (Deum quasi sphaeram affirmarunt). And later: "For the minimum must coincide with the maximum; therefore the center of the world coincides with the circumference" (. . . quia minimum cum maximo coincidere necesse est. Centrum igitur mundi coincidit cum circumferential). Nicolaus of Cusa, *On Learned Ignorance: A Translation and an Appraisal of "De Docta Ignorantia,"* trans. James Hopkins (Minneapolis: A. J. Banning Press, 1981), 63, 114. For an incisive review of this "metaphor," see Karsten Harries, "The Infinite Sphere: Comments on a History of a Metaphor," *Journal of the History of Philosophy* 13, no. 1 (1975): 5-15.

35. Flasch, "Nikolaus von Kues: Die Idee der Koinzidenz," 241-48.

36. Cited in Cranz, 7.

37. Flasch, "Nikolaus von Kues: Die Idee der Koinzidenz," 246.

38. Nicholas of Cusa, *De docta ignorantia*, 1.5, *Philosophisch-theologische Schriften*, ed. Leo Gabriel (Vienna: Herder, 1982), 1:208-10. My translation.

39. Flasch, "Nikolaus von Kues: Die Idee der Koinzidenz," 216. Rather than being (merely) a form of mysticism, "the doctrine of coincidences is . . . not the renunciation of rational argumentation; it is still the attempt *to ground* rationality" (253).

40. While not discussing Cusanus in *Expressionism in Philosophy: Spinoza*, trans. Martin Joughin (Cambridge: Zone Books, 1990), where he first develops his cardinal concept of "univocity," Deleuze summarizes the thought of Spinoza and Leibniz in terms strongly resembling Cusanus's dialectic of *complicatio* and *explicatio*: "Expressionism . . . bears within it a double movement: one either takes what is expressed as involved, implicit, wound up, in its expression, and so retains only the couple 'expresser-expression'; or one unfolds, explicates, unwinds expression so as to restore what is expressed (leaving the couple 'expresser-expressed'). Thus there is in Leibniz, first of all, a divine expression: God expresses himself in absolute forms or absolutely simple notions, as in some divine Alphabet; such forms express unlimited qualities related to God as constituting his essence. God then re-expresses

himself on the level of possible creation: here he expresses himself in individual or relatively simple notions, monads, corresponding to each of his 'viewpoints.' These expressions in turn express the whole world, that is, the totality of the chosen world, which is related to God as the manifestation of his 'glory' or his will" (333-34).

41. Giordano Bruno, *Candlebearer,* trans. Gino Moliterno (Ottawa: Dovehouse Editions, 2000); *Candelaio,* ed. Isa Guerrini Angrisani (Milan: Rizzoli, 1976). All English translations are Moliterno's. Subsequent citations appear parenthetically in the text unless otherwise noted.

42. The full title is *Candelaio: Comedia del Bruno Nolano Achademico di nulla Achademia; detto il fastidito (Candlebearer: A Comedy by Bruno of Nola Academician of No Academy; also known as The Annoyed).*

43. Moliterno uses this term in his introduction, but it is borrowed from Clubb's *Italian Drama in Shakespeare's Time,* 1-26. Clubb calls the *Candelaio* an "anti-commedia" (32).

44. Moliterno renders the name as "Manfurio"; but for the sake of consistency I have changed it throughout back to the original "Mamfurio."

45. See Moliterno's introduction (20-21) for conjectures about her identity.

46. *Candelaio,* 118-19; *Candlebearer,* 59. Translation slightly modified.

47. *Candlebearer,* 26. In his introduction, Moliterno reads cinquecento comedy as a form of *ars combinatoria,* which he notes, also informs Bruno's art of memory. "Furnished with even a very schematic knowledge of the procedures of the art of memory in the *Shadows* we might now be able to see this textual deferral as something very like a process of mnemonic 'pre-inscription' of the comedy, of formatting the stage space, so to speak, of 'pre-constructing' the play in the mind of the reader-spectator" (27). He then links the *Candelaio* with Giulio Camillo's memory theater.

48. *Candelaio,* 120-21; *Candlebearer,* 60.

49. Hilary Gatti, *Giordano Bruno and Renaissance Science* (Ithaca, N.Y.: Cornell University Press, 1999), 113.

50. Giordano Bruno, *The Ash Wednesday Supper,* trans. Edward Gosselin and Lawrence Lerner (Toronto: University of Toronto Press, 1995), 67-68; *La cena de le Ceneri,* in *Opere Italiane,* 2 vols., ed. Giovanni Aquilecchia (Torino: UTET, 2002), 1:432.

51. Gosselin and Lerner, introduction to *The Ash Wednesday Supper,* 36.

52. See Dorothea Singer, *Giordano Bruno: His Life and Thought with an Annotated Translation of his Work, On the Infinite Universe and Worlds* (New York: Henry Schuman, 1950), 287. Bruno's late work *De monade, numero et figura liber consequens quinque de minimo magno et mensura* (1591) also meditates at length on infinity.

53. Antonio Calcagno, *Giordano Bruno and the Logic of Coincidence: Unity and Multiplicity in the Philosophical Thought of Giordano Bruno* (New York: Peter Lang, 1998), 62. For Bruno and Cusanus, see 29-33.

54. *Candelaio,* 139-40; *Candlebearer,* 69.

55. *Candelaio,* 144; *Candlebearer,* 71.

56. Similarly, in his dedications to Sir Philip Sidney in the *The Heroic Furies* and *The Expulsion of the Triumphant Beast,* Bruno will seize upon Petrarchism, declare it frivolous and inane, and then proceed to embrace it as a vehicle for his own cosmographic and epideictic purposes. In effect, his dedicatory sonnets out-Petrarch Petrarch. In one of his last lectures, Giovanni Aquilecchia, in addition to identifying Gianbernardo with Bruno, celebrates how the *varietas* of the play challenges a hierarchical conception of "Unity" and "diversity." See "Giordano Bruno as Philosopher of the Renaissance," in *Giordano Bruno: Philosopher of the Renaissance,* ed. Hillary Gatti, 3-14 (London: Ashgate, 2002), 7.

57. For a savvy attempt at this, see Anna Laura Puliafito Bleuel, *Comica pazzia: Vicissitudine e destini umani nel "Candelaio" di Giordano Bruno* (Florence: Leo. S. Olschki

Editore, 2007), esp. 129–35. Bleuel also contends that Bruno's chaotic plot, with its constant "contrapposizione realtà-apparenza," accomplishes larger ontological and ethical goals. See also A. Buono Hodgart, *Giordano Bruno's "The Candle-bearer": An Enigmatic Renaissance Play* (Lewiston, N.Y.: Mellen, 1997).

58. The pun is on *orefice* (goldsmith) and *orifizio* (orifice).

59. Nuccio Ordine, *Giordano Bruno and the Philosophy of the Ass,* trans. Henryk Baranski, with Arielle Saiber (New Haven: Yale University Press, 1996), 115. Comparing Bruno with Rabelais, Ordine writes: "The technique of reversal, as proposed by the particular nature of the Sileni, also directly determines the concept of the comic in both Bruno and Rabelais. The boundary between opposites, to which Erasmus was already alluding in his *Eulogy of Madness,* by means of universalizing the two faces of the Sileni, necessarily becomes blurred. The space of laughter and of tears no longer refers to two separate spheres, but constitutes a point of convergence where opposing elements engender each other reciprocally. The motto of the *Candelaio* (*In tristitia hilaris, in hilaritate tristis*) breaks the rigid antinomy between laughter and tears, by presenting itself as a particular expression of the general law of *coincidentia oppositorum*" (114–15).

60. In an intriguing reading of the play, Arielle Saiber, in *Giordano Bruno and the Geometry of Language* (Burlington, Vt.: Ashgate, 2005), argues, "The *Candelaio,* through impressive rhetorical finesse, reveals Bruno's epistemology and philosophy of the infinite via a satire of those who stubbornly see the world from only one perspective" (72). Given the many analogies between geometric and rhetorical figures, Saiber shows, for instance, how "through his satirical use of lists in the *Candelaio,* Bruno pointedly criticized the accumulation and amplification of a 'single line of thought'" (81).

61. The rogue, Sanguino, expresses the same sentiment in 5.23.

62. Giulio Ferroni, *Frammenti di discorsi sul comico,* in a volume Ferroni also edits, *Ambiguità del comico* (Palermo: Sellerio, 1983), 45, 52. My translation.

63. Ibid., 53. Similarly, Moliterno concludes: "Seeing the *Candelaio* not only as a scurrilous comedy but also as an erotic talisman, energised by celestial influences and animated by a simulacrum of Bruno himself, is surely an attractive proposition, not least because it allows us to better configure the play's dark, vicious energy and its irruptive, erotic intensity" (21).

64. Staged as a Manichean struggle between a Good and a Bad Angel (1.1, 2.3), and later (5.1) between an Old Man and Mephistopheles, but expressed more poignantly still in Faustus's monologues and asides where Marlowe paints his interior struggles as one between irreconcilable opposites, the battle for Faustus's soul knows no final resolution—while the Epilogue further muddies the play's theology. Faustus's desire that "spirits" would "resolve me of all ambiguities" (1.1.82) thus neatly captures the conceptual task Marlowe sets himself and his readers. For Faustus is made to embrace the means, no matter how infernal, to improve his *scientia,* all the while ignoring the pursuit of that *sapientia* praised by medieval and Renaissance theologians. That *sapientia* and *scientia* prove antithetical in the play does not mean, however, that they have equal worth in its dramatic calculus. Faustus's pursuit of the latter leads directly to his spectacular "hellish fall" (Ep. 4) and provokes him to exclaim in his last line, "I'll burn my books (5.2.115)." But Marlowe swerves here from his medieval models and declines to paint this "fall" in obvious allegorical colors.

65. Calcagno, 58.

66. Ordine, 26–27.

67. For instance, in *Giordano Bruno and Renaissance Science,* Gatti recalls Bruno's own caution not to confuse the opinions of characters with the author's own (225).

68. Ferrroni writes: "Tutta la filosofia bruniana si dà (in modo più netto ed esplicito nella struttura del *Candelaio* e delle opere in volgare) in una oscillazione tra l'accettazione

totale del teatro del mondo, dei suoi paradossi e delle sue infinite maschere, e una furia annullatrice, una tensione verso una verità capace di riconoscere e lacerare quelle maschere e quel teatro per affermare la propria luce totale. La scienza è coperta di stracci, lo stesso saggio è chiuso dentro un Sileno che sposta continuamente la sua superficie, che scambia senza fine l'interno e l'esterno: ma l'affermazione di questo essere solcato in due è già scoperta di una verità che porta lontano della stessa scena, che la distanza, che la guarda come estranea a sé" (53). See also Laura Sanguinetti White, " 'In tristitia hilaris, in hilaritate tristis': Armonie nei contrasti," *Quaderni di italianistica* 5, no. 2 (1984): 190–203. White approvingly quotes Erminio Troilo on how the motto condenses the ethical humanism that pervades all Bruno's works (191).

69. Pedro Calderón de la Barca, *El mágico prodigioso,* ed. Bruce W. Wardropper (Madrid: Cátedra, 1985). All references are to this edition; all translations are mine. Subsequent citations appear parenthetically in the text.

70. See *Historia naturalis* (2.5), which reads a bit more skeptically: "quisquis est deus, si modo est aliquis, et quacumque in parte, totus est sensus, totus visus, totus auditus, totus animae, totus animi, totus sui."

71. *Origin,* 216.

72. The Devil appears in over fifty of Calderón's *autos* and *tragedias.* See Alexander Parker, "The Devil in the Drama of Calderón," in *Critical Essays on the Theatre of Calderón,* ed. Bruce W. Wardropper, 3–23 (New York: New York University Press, 1965); Ángel L. Cilveti, *El demonio en el teatro de Calderón* (Valencia: Albatros Ediciones, 1977); Antonio Regalado, *Calderón: Los orígenes de la modernidad en la España del Siglo de Oro,* 2 vols. (Barcelona: Ediciones Destino, 1995), 1:873–99. Regalado writes: "El demonio calderoniano es una criatura del Barroco y, específicamente, de su creador, manifestándose como director de escena, manipulador de las apariencias, alegorista, generador de argumentos y actor que asume numerosos papeles" (874).

73. Wardropper, Introducción, 18.

74. The opposites of profane and divine love are given their most brilliant syntactic form, respectively, in lines 1,800–1,839 and 2,873–2,944. The former, a kind of *blasón,* is also emblematic of Calderón's signature technique of *enunciación* and *recolección,* which allows him first to compass the world's multiplicity but then to gesture at the unity of perception by crowding numerous substantives into a few lines ("al fin, cuna, grana, nieve,/campo, sol, arroyo, o rosa,/ave que canta amorosa . . . son las partes que componen/a esta divina mujer"). See Dámaso Alonso, "La correlación en la estructura del teatro calderoniano," in *Seis calas en la expresión literaria española,* ed. Dámaso Alonso and Carlos Bousoño, 113–86 (Madrid: Editorial Gredos, 1951).

75. Although *El mágico prodigioso* was first performed in a village near Toledo for Corpus Christi, the version that we have was produced in Madrid for the public theater and the more sophisticated tastes of the court.

76. Compare this with *Doctor Faustus,* where the tensions between divine *complicatio* and human, hubristic *explicatio* are represented as irreconcilable, despite Faustus's evanescent recognition of the solution. As Faustus admits: "For vain pleasure of four-and-twenty years hath Faustus lost eternal joy and felicity" (5.2.35–36). *Explicatio* encompasses all the human sciences, but these have proven fruitless, not even allowing, as with Cusanus and Bruno, a metaphoric glimpse of the divine. Alternately, *complicatio,* the surrender of philosophical and terrestrial ambitions in the name of *sapientia,* is never realized on Marlowe's stage.

77. "Jedem Calderón-Leser fällt die Bedeutung des Wortes *centro* auf." Hans Flasche, "Über die Raumterminologie ('Centro') bei Calderón zur Differenz der Sprache von Auto und Comedia," in *Über Calderón: Studien aus den Jahren 1958-1980* (Weisbaden: Franz

Steiner Verlag, 1980), 372–90; 372. Flasche traces the diverse semantic values that the word *centro* assumes in the *autos* but then demonstrates how these values are complicated by the syntactical structures that envelop the word in the *comedias.*

78. Sebastián de Covarrubias, *Tesoro de la lengua Castellana o Española,* ed. Felipe C. R. Maldonado and Manuel Camarero (Madrid: Editorial Castalia, 1995), 300.

79. Flasche notes that in Calderón's dramas, "the conjunction *sepultar* and *centro* is met with quite frequently" (380).

80. See also lines 365, 408, 975 for similar uses of *medio.*

81. Pedro Calderón de la Barca, *Mística y real Babilonia,* ed. Klaus Uppendahl (Berlin: Walter de Gruyter, 1978), 582.

82. According to the *Diccionario de Autoridades* (1726), poets used *abortar* metaphorically "quando el mar, los montes, u otras cosas no capaces de concebir arrojan de si algo que contenían." Cipriano's magic is also described as an *aborto.*

83. Anthony Cascardi makes a similar argument in his chapter on the play in *The Limits of Illusion: A Critical Study of Calderón* (Cambridge: Cambridge University Press, 1984), 96–106.

84. See also lines 1,898, 2,121.

85. Harry Levin, *The Overreacher: A Study of Christopher Marlowe* (London: Faber & Faber, 1954).

86. While the Devil is forced to confess his defeat in the face of Cipriano and Justina's martyrdom (3,105–30), he has up until this point practiced, as Parker puts it, "willful ignorance" (18).

87. For a contemporary discussion of Baroque stage machinery, see Nicolo Sabbatini, *Practica di fabricar scene e machine ne' teatri* (Ravenna, 1638).

88. *Origin,* 218–19. In the same section, Benjamin observes, "the allegorization of the physis can only be carried through in all its vigour in respect of the corpse. And the characters of the *Trauerspiel* die, because it is only thus, as corpses, that they can enter into the homeland of allegory" (217).

89. "The German drama of the Counter-Reformation never achieved that suppleness of form which bends to every virtuoso touch, such as Calderón gave the Spanish drama" (*Origin,* 49).

90. *Origin,* 177–82.

91. Calderón's "artifice" is stressed in achieving "the playful miniaturization of reality and the introduction of a reflective infinity of thought into the finite space of a profane fate" (*Origin,* 83).

92. *Origin,* 233.

93. *Origin,* 234. Steiner writes in the introduction, "In its motion of spirit, in the way in which idiom and organization enact the formal case, Benjamin's treatise is Hegelian" (12). By *Geist* I am thinking of the phrase applied to Benjamin's efforts in the treatise: "Geist kann man nicht habilitieren" (cited by Steiner, 11).

94. *Origin,* 235.

95. Baltasar Gracián, *Agudeza y arte de ingenio,* 2 vols. (Madrid: Editorial Castalia, 2001), 1:55. One of Gracián's definitions of the conceit reads: "Consiste, pues, este artificio conceptuoso, en una primorosa concordancia, en una armónica correlacíon entre dos o tres cognoscibles extremos, expresada por un acto del entendimiento" (55). The second kind of conceit is "de ponderación juiciosa sutil, y a ésta se reducen crisis, paradojas, exageraciones, sentencias, desempeños, etc." (63). According to Covarrubias, *ponderación* means "atención, consideración, peso y cuidado con que se dice o hace una cosa"; but *ponderar* can also be synonymous with *pesar, exagerar, encarecer,* and *contrapesar.*

Publish (f)or Paris?
G. B. Andreini in France

JON R. SNYDER

THE CRUCIAL ROLE played by Italian actors, especially those of the *com-media dell'arte* troupes, in the development of the early modern French theater has been studied extensively, starting in the nineteenth century.[1] As the renowned French historian Fernand Braudel long ago observed, Italian art and culture were exported throughout Europe far more extensively in the Baroque era than in the Renaissance.[2] Among Italian playwrights of the seventeenth century, none had greater international stature than Giovan Battista Andreini (1576–1654). Although his work lay largely forgotten for centuries after his death, and still has not been translated into French, Andreini in his prime—between the second and third decades of the Seicento—was a prominent figure on the theatrical scene in Paris, where he introduced the court of Louis XIII and the paying public to his unique version of the early modern Italian comedy now known as *commedia dell'arte* (or, as it is often called in English, "Arte"). In this essay I will consider a group of five plays published by Andreini in Italian in Paris in the pivotal year 1622. These include at least two landmarks of the Italian Baroque stage that were printed only this one time and only in the French capital. Rather than look closely at the texts of the plays themselves, I will examine the circumstances in which they first appeared in print while their itinerant author was on the road, far from his home base in northern Italy. Why did Andreini, the consummate actor-author of his generation in Italy, choose Paris as the preferred venue for his performances onstage and, later, on the page?[3] What were his goals as a theatrical professional, and what strategies did he adopt to achieve them in the prime of his career? Finally, how does the concept of border-crossings—between states, genres, genders, or media—come to define his position at the forefront of developments in the new art and culture of the post-Renaissance?

Andreini, born in Florence in 1576, was the eldest child in a famous professional theatrical family. His father, Francesco Andreini, specialized in the *commedia dell'arte* role of Capitano Spavento and served for many years as *capocomico* of the troupe known as the Compagnia dei Gelosi (or Company of the Jealous).[4] Isabella Canali Andreini, Giovan Battista's mother, was the first diva of the European professional stage. The only woman member of the learned Accademia degli Intenti in Pavia, she was able, with her humanist training and knowledge of languages, to play not only Arte roles, but roles in several other theatrical genres as well, from pastoral to tragicomedy.[5] Her pastoral, *Mirtilla* (1588), was the first play to be published in Europe by a professional woman of the theater, and her collection of Petrarchan verse, entitled *Rime* (*Poems,* first edition 1601), confirmed her reputation as one of the leading women poets of her generation and a legend in her own time. After being educated in Bologna, Giovan Battista joined his parents' troupe in 1595.[6] As an apprentice player specializing in the role of the *primo innamorato* with the stage name Lelio, Andreini seems to have performed with other companies as well as with his parents'. It is possible that he traveled to France with the Gelosi in 1599 when the company appeared by royal invitation at the court of Henry IV and his Italian-born wife Maria de' Medici. The troupe's visit to Paris was, by all accounts, a triumph. Isabella's poetry and pastoral drama (the latter in French translation) were soon afterward published in the French capital, cementing her star status before her untimely death in 1604.[7] In the early years of the new century, G. B. Andreini founded his own troupe, La Compagnia dei Fedeli (or Company of the Faithful), of which he was to be the *capocomico* and leading man. Although reorganized numerous times, the Fedeli were to endure for about fifty years, playing for Europe's great and powerful as well as for the paying public, from Paris to Prague to Venice. Louise George Clubb rightly remarks that Andreini's "ability to manage a company and maintain the favor of patrons in the courts . . . , even more than his celebrated acting and writing of plays and treatises, made him a model *capocomico,* the theatrical administrator around whom the organization of professional troupes would depend long into the future."[8]

Andreini did not travel with the Gelosi in 1603–4 on what was to be their final appearance in Paris. Almost a decade later, in the 1613 edition of his sacred play *L'Adamo* (*Adam*), dedicated to Maria de' Medici, the playwright states in the preface (dated June 12, 1613) that he is soon to depart for France with his wife, the renowned actress-singer Virginia Ramponi, to serve the queen.[9] Indeed, we now know that he subsequently took the Fedeli to Paris in the late summer of 1613 at the invitation of Maria de' Medici, who was at the time regent of France (Henry IV was assassinated in 1610, and their son Louis XIII was not yet of age). The Medici had long been patrons of the Andreini family of actors: between the closing years of the sixteenth century and the first decade of the seventeenth century, Maria de' Medici, her uncle Ferdinando, and her sister Eleonora showed themselves to be generous supporters of Isabella and Francesco Andreini as well as of their children.[10] Ferdinando died in 1609 in Florence and Eleonora passed away in 1611, however, leaving Maria de' Medici as the sole surviving Medici patron of G. B. Andreini (a Florentine by birth), for whom her patronage was invaluable, even though she was located so far away from his company's usual northern Italian circuit. The playwright's return to Paris with the Fedeli in 1620, by royal invitation, was undoubtedly meant to celebrate the (temporary) reconciliation of the queen mother with the young King Louis XIII after several years of estrangement.[11] Andreini's careful attention to Maria de' Medici's literary tastes and political interests is reflected in the play that he chose to dedicate to her, the dazzling *La centaura* (*The Female Centaur*). If, on the one hand, it is an avant-garde or ultramodern work of the most extreme Baroque taste, with its tripartite and hybrid structure—the first act is a comedy, the second is a pastoral, and the third is a tragedy—possessed of its own convoluted narrative logic of constant transformation and metamorphosis, the play also serves to celebrate the dynasty of the House of Bourbon that the queen mother had done so much to sustain through the political turbulence and instability of the first two decades of the seventeenth century.[12] Andreini in fact exhorts his royal patrons to remain reconciled in a prefatory poem included in the 1622 edition: "Thus all are united here by the bonds between you, / And no longer will speak with ease of taking leave; / Weave between yourselves a triple fleur-de-lys, / And rise to heights of glory."[13] In the same year and in the same city, the painter Peter Paul

Rubens was at work on the twenty-four paintings of his Maria de' Medici cycle, newly commissioned by the dowager queen to exalt her key role in the past, present, and future of the dynasty. Although Rubens's cycle was to become one of the most widely discussed allegories of seventeenth-century European art, while *La centaura* was to be largely forgotten, the latter wrapped its homage to Medici and Bourbon power in a much more radical—and boundary-breaking—aesthetic form.[14]

As a professional actor and man of letters, Andreini had to negotiate the visible and invisible boundaries—territorial, economic, political, and linguistic, as well as cultural—that cut across the Italian peninsula. He spent most of his working life in the Po River valley, which was—politically speaking—a crazy quilt of dynastic regimes large and small, with the exception of the ancient Venetian Republic. Depending upon the road taken by Andreini's troupe, traveling the few hundred kilometers that separated Venice from Milan might require them to traverse the respective territories of as many as four states, each with its own distinct political, cultural, and linguistic coordinates. Venice was both the publishing and the entertainment capital of Italy, and there Andreini published some of his early works for the stage; but others appeared all across northern Italy, from the small citadel city of Casale Monferrato to Ferrara, Milan, and Mantua.[15] The members of the Gonzaga dynasty in Mantua, who had ruled their small but wealthy state since the fourteenth century, were Andreini's principal patrons in this period, and it is not surprising that in 1616 he purchased a home in the Mantuan countryside. If the Gonzaga rulers financed a good many of the company's undertakings in its early years, however, Andreini also had influential supporters in Spanish Milan. The Count Pedro Fuentes, governor of Milan, may perhaps have been the godfather of one of the Andreini's children, and the actor-author published several important devotional works in that city, which played a central role in the Spanish imperial domination of northern Italy.[16] In the first phase of his career, then, Andreini did not follow a single path to the attainment of professional success in the theater, whether onstage or on the page. He constantly crossed geopolitical borders, moving from one urban center to the next in pursuit of patrons and public, negotiating ably with the book trade, emerging market forces in the theater, and the intricate etiquette of the Old Regime courts.[17]

In autumn 1620, the Fedeli once more departed from Mantua for Paris. Overland journeys to France for troupes of traveling players were long, arduous, and sometimes dangerous. The company brought its stage equipment, props, books, and so on in covered wooden carts that served the players as shelter against the elements, as well as providing them with a place to sleep during the night. The road systems of France and northern Italy were still quite poor in the first half of the seventeenth century, and few contemporary maps even bothered to show roads. If the route to be taken was from Turin to Paris via Chambéry and Lyon, as was most often the case, the Alps had to be crossed from Italy to France before the first snows fell on the high passes in early fall, and the return trip could not even be attempted until spring, when the snows had melted and the threat of blizzards had diminished. This period roughly coincided with the principal theatrical season in Paris, which began in September and reached its climax at Carnival (although performances could be put on both in spring and summer as well), making Lent a good time for travel. Progress toward their final destination—whether in France or Italy—could sometimes be excruciatingly slow for the traveling players, as heavy autumn or spring rains could quickly turn the unpaved post roads into quagmires or wash out bridges. Security was scarce, marauding armies could be on the march along the same highways, and highway robbers were not unknown. Companies might even be waylaid en route by powerful local nobles and forced to perform for them before continuing onward. Although Italian players were quite accustomed to the rigors of an itinerant existence, the journey to the French capital was nevertheless a risky and difficult business that was not to be undertaken lightly.

For the supremely ambitious Andreini, however, the potential rewards were well worth the gamble. The considerable expenses of the trip were normally covered by the French monarchs who invited the Fedeli to court, and payment for the company's performances there could be lucrative indeed. When not at court, moreover, the troupe could contract to play for the general public in Paris. During the 1613–14 season, the Fedeli performed at the Théâtre de Bourgogne, the first permanent theater in the city. Italian companies had been coming to Paris since the late sixteenth century, and the Théâtre de Bourgogne was often the venue in which they performed for the paying public.[18] This preeminent theater was owned and run by the Confrérie de la Passion et Résurrection de notre Sauveur et Rédempteur Jésus-Christ (Confraternity of the Passion and Resurrection of our Savior and Redeemer Jesus Christ), a religious organization of artisans and tradesmen that had originally held a monopoly on the performance of plays in Paris and the surrounding suburbs, as well as the rights to the only public playhouse.[19] By the beginning of the seventeenth century, the members of the confraternity had long since ceased to perform mystery or passion plays, had yielded their monopoly privilege, and instead leased their theater to traveling professional troupes.[20] They continued, however, to exercise considerable control over the theatrical scene in the city. In 1613–14 Andreini was accompanied to Paris by the renowned Arte comedian Tristano Martinelli, who was among the first to make famous the role of Harlequin in Paris many years earlier and who frequently appeared with Andreini's company.[21] The regent herself had selected the Théâtre de Bourgogne as the site for the company's performances (and paid the rent to the Confrérie), with the intent of providing the Parisians with a theatrical season for the first time in some years, following the closure of theaters in the wake of the assassination of Henry IV in 1610.[22] Far better known in France than Andreini at that time, and an expert in the ways of the profession, Martinelli surely played a key role in relations with the management of the Théâtre de Bourgogne, where a contract was signed with Jacques de Fontenoy, who had translated Francesco Andreini's *Le bravure del Capitano Spavento* (*The Courageous Captain Fright*) into French in 1608 and was one day to write a series of prefatory texts for the first edition of *La centaura*.[23] Such was their success there that when Andreini *fils* returned to Paris at the end of 1620 with the Fedeli and Martinelli, he once again contracted with the Confrérie for the use of their theater.

Andreini's reputation was so well established in Paris by this time that the company remained ensconced in the French capital until the conclusion of the 1622 Carnival season, with King Louis XIII regularly attending their performances at court. During the Fedeli's long sojourn in Paris, Andreini worked—between performances at court or in town—at completing the scripts of a number of plays, some apparently new and some perhaps already in the troupe's repertory. Five of these were printed as separate volumes in Paris in early 1622, before the company returned to Italy.[24] The five 1622 plays are *La centaura* (*The Female Centaur*), *La Ferinda* (*Ferinda*), *Amor nello specchio* (*Love in the Mirror*), *La sultana* (*The Sultan's Daughter*), and *Li duo Leli simili* (*Lelio and Lelio, the Identical Twins*). The French printer of all of these works, Nicolas de La Vigne, had only recently completed his apprenticeship and hung out his sign in the Rue Clopin on the Left Bank, an area known in these years for its bookmen.[25] We do not know how many copies of the plays were printed or whether they were later exported to Italy in any significant quantity. It seems unlikely, in any event, that there was a substantial print run or that more than a limited number of copies eventually made the journey across the Alps in Andreini's lifetime. The texts of the plays appear to have been proofread in haste, or sometimes not at all, and display numerous glaring errors or inconsistencies: *Amor nello specchio,* for instance, contains two lists of dramatis personae that do not match, and the name of at least one major character changes between the beginning and the end of the play.[26] Indeed, not all of the works contain a list of errata or *errori scorsi,* suggesting that there was only limited contact between author and printer during the final phases of the production process. Moreover, of the Fedeli's performances in Paris in the 1621–22 season based on the texts of Andreini's plays (both these and, presumably, others in the troupe's repertory), we know next to nothing at all. Although the leading Andreini scholar Siro Ferrone asserts that "in this period Andreini conceived, staged and published" all five of these works in Paris, there is in fact scant archival evidence to support the first of these claims.[27] Given his high rate of production in these pivotal years, it is nonetheless plausible to assume that Andreini did at least the lion's share of the work on these plays during this Paris sojourn. It is equally plausible to assume that (as is suggested by Andreini himself in more than one place) these plays were all seen onstage in Paris, although not necessarily in a public venue like the Théâtre de Bourgogne, prior to their publication. The printed texts themselves, however, offer incontrovertible evidence concerning his theatrical activities in the French capital.

From today's vantage point, it is not difficult to see that these five 1622 works, written in Italian, together make a signal contribution to the emergence of the modern theater on the continent.[28] Of the five Paris plays, none can be considered an Arte performance that has merely been transcribed for publication. Andreini's company certainly knew how to—and did—stage Arte productions while in Paris, but the plays from 1622 tend to be experimental, built around a concept that pushes the traditional representational practices of the theater as close to the breaking point as possible. Andreini often makes recourse in these plays to devices or themes involving doubles or doubling, in order to destabilize the difference between the authentic and the inauthentic, or between reality and illusion, in the mind of the spectator. In *Li duo Leli simili* identically named identical twins appear and speak together onstage in the final act when they must decide which of them is the "real" Lelio.[29] In *Amor nello specchio,* the polymorphous sexual desires of the female protagonist are resolved through marriage to a hermaphrodite, whose indecipherable body combines the traits of male and female. *La centaura* contains many doublings, including the mythological hybrid beings—half-human and half-animal—known as centaurs. The musical comedy *La Ferinda* systematically mirrors and reverses the language and structure of the court opera, dissolving tragic grandeur into laughter. Only *La sultana,* based on a preexisting Arte script (or *canovaccio*), seems to verge on the conventional in its mix of comedy and melodrama, revenge and recognition, although here too Andreini plays extensively with identity and gender-role reversals. The 1622 Paris plays undermine the established Western notion of the relationship between art and life. With their wholehearted embrace of the "modern" and the fundamentally antimimetic aesthetic of the Baroque, they dare to suggest that reality itself is representation and that the theater is a metaphor, rather than a mirror, of the real.[30]

None of these five "Parisian" plays is entirely original in its conception, for each is based on one or more prior texts borrowed from the Italian theatrical tradition: if in literature in general every work appears to be a sequel to an earlier work, this is even more the case in the early modern theater. *Li duo Leli simili* reelaborates an Arte scenario first developed by Andreini's father, Francesco. *La Ferinda* revises, in highly self-conscious fashion, the libretti of the first early modern court operas. *La centaura* is by no means the first hybrid play involving multiple genres to be composed for the Italian stage: that honor belongs to Guarini's hugely influential tragicomedy *Il pastor fido* (*The Faithful Shepherd,* 1590). On the other hand, *La sultana* draws extensively on the theatrical genre of *commedia grave* (or serious comedy), of which an outstanding example is Girolamo Bargagli's *La pellegrina* (*The Female Pilgrim*), performed in Florence at the same 1589 Medici wedding in which Andreini's mother, Isabella, gave one of her most acclaimed Arte performances. *Amor nello specchio* reworks the commonplaces of the sixteenth-century transvestite comedy, twisting that venerable (sub)genre in a new and unexpected direction by concluding with a marriage that precludes the full restoration of normative (hetero)sexual identity. This is, of course, typical of the literary culture of the age, in which writers sought to create the "new" and the "marvelous" by revisiting, recycling, and endlessly revising the

vast collection of ancient and modern plots, topoi, and themes that constituted the raw material of the Baroque literary system.[31] In each of the
above comedies, in point of fact, Andreini's importance as the author is
clearly foregrounded: the elaborately literary speeches invariably made
by the overwrought lovers, for example, serve to display his virtuoso
rhetorical and poetical talents. If Andreini the playwright and *capocomico* was a theatrical experimenter of the first order, however, he did
not see his own presence onstage as essential to the success of these five
works. In four out of five plays, the stock character of Lelio—the lover,
or *primo innamorato,* invariably played by Andreini in the company's
performances, and with which he was identified throughout his career—
appears (he is absent only in *La Ferinda*), but has a leading role in only
two of them. Thus Andreini the author, rather than Andreini the actor, is
the true protagonist of the 1622 Paris plays.

In his still-fundamental study of the central years of Andreini's career,
*Attori mercanti corsari: la commedia dell'arte in Europa tra Cinque e
Seicento* (1993), Ferrone argues convincingly that, by scripting and publishing these comedies in and around 1622, Andreini carried out a highly
effective coup d'état against the traditional Italian comic actors (such as
Tristano Martinelli) who played zanies and clowns by improvising more
or less freely onstage.[32] The actor playing the character of Harlequin, for
instance, was traditionally his own author, inventing and reinventing in
performance the great buffoon's traits while subverting any predefined
role assigned to him. Martinelli's performances as Harlequin thus "consisted above all in [impromptu] actions, gestures and words created on
stage and never transferred to the written page."[33] In the 1622 plays, on
the other hand, Andreini wove together complex and skillfully unified
tales around pairs of lovers rather than clowns, thus elevating plot to
the organizing principle of the "new comedy," as he called it. What was
required, in order to stage Andreini's plays, was a disciplined ensemble
of players, rather than an assemblage of individual actors each specializing in the portrayal of a single stock character. Andreini was the first
playwright in Italy, and among the first in Europe, to include elaborate
stage directions with his published works, a practice that has remained
important in the Western theater ever since.[34] Stage directions and other
paratextual materials addressing performance, when incorporated into
the texts of the plays, meant that freestyle improvisation by the actors on
stage—the staple fare of the *commedia dell'arte* clowns and zanies—was

to be much reduced, or even eliminated. For instance, at the end of scene 3 in act 5 of *Amor nello specchio,* the author gives precise instructions to the players concerning a gag when they attempt to exit the stage en masse: "Here we see that the players can't get through the door, and then all at once they go through it together."[35] In an appendix to the same play, entitled "Performance instructions for staging *Amor nello specchio* with great ease," Andreini even specifies that the servant Coradella's standard should be "not too big."[36] Such remarks can be found, in any case, throughout the corpus of Andreini's published work for the theater. By including in the printed versions of his plays not only the lines to be spoken onstage by the players but also the directions for stunts and gags, as well as detailed descriptions of props and special effects, and by binding all of these tightly to the plot structure, Andreini transformed the Arte tradition, transferring control over the performance to the single figure of the author-director-*capocomico.*

This transformation from stage to page, from public performance to literary text, was effected by Andreini with remarkable self-awareness. In the foreword to *La Ferinda,* entitled "A[i] benigni lettori," he makes a series of critical remarks concerning his intentions in writing the play. He starts by recounting his experiences, as a spectator in Florence and Mantua, of the new art of the court opera "with recitative and music."[37] His wife, Virginia Ramponi, had been the star of the pathbreaking 1608 production of Monteverdi's *Arianna* in Mantua. Such multimedia spectacles of *opera regia,* recounting mythological stories of "Orpheus, Ariadne, Sibyl, Daphne, Ceres, and Psyche, things that are indeed most marvelous," inspired Andreini to try to "compose a little knot of comedy in that genre."[38] This exercise in generic border crossing, however, turned out to be far more difficult than it had at first seemed to him. Not only is the material of comedy not of the same exalted status as classical mythology, Andreini complains to the readers of *La Ferinda,* but the scenery cannot be changed with the same frequency, because comedy is about humans rather than gods, and the latter do not usually cause "violent and rapid changes" in the affairs of everyday life. The play looks "cold" (*fredda*), Andreini laments, if the gods cannot be seen in all their glory by the spectators, and "enfeebled" (*snervata*) because of the absence of stage machinery, that is, "those machines which—whether by air, land or sea— do so much to make us admire their appearance."[39] At long last and after much reflection, Andreini announces in the foreword, he nevertheless found the inspiration to compose a contemporary version of the grandeur of the ancient gods. Why not set the libretto of this little comic opera (*operetta* or *commedietta musicale*) in Venice, the Queen of the Adriatic? Is not that marvelous city in the sea the closest that mankind has come to replicating the wonders of the heavens?

Although the stage set must remain the same throughout the play, as the laws of comedy require, the eye of the spectator will be endlessly delighted—the playwright assures us—by the miraculous sight of magnificent Venetian buildings balanced between land and sea. Instead of stage machinery with clouds and sky-chariots, Andreini adds, he will use gondolas and other common lagoon boats like the one-oared *fisolera*. The colorful and varied costumes of the Venetians will substitute nicely for the "sumptuous clothes" worn by the noble or divine characters in court opera. The narrator of the play's prologue, the muse Talia (seated on a seashell), will explain to the audience that it is time to stop weeping over the mythical Ariadne's fate, and to "cheer up with new delights" thanks to the powers of comedy. If the musical tragedy of the *opera regia* is performed "in a single language" (*in una istessa lingua*) suitable to tragic characters, this new musical comedy will instead employ "different languages" (*varii linguaggi*), making use of the dialects of Italy, from Ferrarese to Neapolitan, to bring laughter into the theater. There will of course be music, the playwright adds. This will include serenades, in homage to the "Pindaric" songs of serious opera, although here they are to be sung by "ridiculous" (comic) characters rather than noble ones. To complete the show, there will also be dances, which are an "excellent condiment" for such lighthearted music.[40] Andreini's keen awareness of literary genre and of the conventions of the literary system, forged in the fiery critical debates of the age,[41] allows him to create *La Ferinda* out of a series of carefully planned negations of the rules of court opera: nearly every component of the latter is neatly reversed and set in a new (comic) register obeying its own narrative and aesthetic logic. Thus, in the foreword to the play, we are given a privileged glimpse of Andreini's thought process at work, as he sets about transforming the Arte tradition of stage-based performance, with its potential for unscripted spontaneity, into a novel kind of theatrical text. He understood that the system of genres inherited from antiquity and the Renaissance could no longer contain the Baroque theater, in which generic boundaries had broken down and hybrid multimedia works had taken hold.[42] In *La centaura*, for instance, one of the characters in the play sings in the prologue: "Out of an indelible and fatal desire/I've brought new things into the world;/Everything in [this] work is both concordant and discordant,/All is calm, and all is stormy;/And it's the first to appear artfully/On paper as comedy, pastoral and tragedy."[43]

Let us now return to the question raised at the beginning of this essay. Why did Andreini choose to print these plays, composed in Italian, in Paris? Of the five, only *La centaura* was to be reprinted in Italy, and none of them was ever to appear again in France.[44]

There are at least two possible answers to this question. First of all, although he was from the very first a writer as well as an actor, and in fact devoted much of his career to trying to weld the prestige of literature to the still largely disreputable trade of the thespian, Andreini was ultimately less interested in polishing the printed texts of his comic plays than in generating live performances *from* them onstage. If a theatrical work could be useful to him in published form, perhaps to flatter a patron or to consolidate his intellectual credentials in a given literary or cultural context, then he would see it into print. Ferrone speaks, in this sense, of the "capitalization" of Andreini's performances through their transformation into printed texts.[45] Andreini was not wholly devoid of concern for the process of publication of his works: in 1604 he destroyed the entire first run of his only tragedy, *Florinda,* because of the unacceptably poor quality of the copies produced by Volcmar Timan's press in Florence.[46] The playwright does not seem, however, to have always held the publication of his comedies to these same standards. The print versions of the five 1622 Paris plays—all of which are comedies, with the exception of the hybrid *La centaura* (of which only the first act is a comedy)—appear in fact to have been produced rather hastily for a number of reasons. One function of these printed texts was to distinguish Andreini and the Fedeli from their leading Italian and French competitors in the crowded Paris theatrical market: other Arte actors usually did not write down fully, much less publish, what they performed onstage, rarely claiming any particular cultural prestige for their work.[47] Another key function was to consolidate the playwright's reputation with leading local patrons of the comic theater in Paris, some of whom were also members of the pro-Medici faction. If Andreini made gifts of copies of these volumes to his (potential or actual) patrons, as he surely intended to do in 1622, this was in order to further his standing in Paris as an actor-author of the first rank, one with whom it was beneficial for the powerful to associate. If Italian comedy and Italian players were in demand there in the early 1620s, as was in fact the case, Andreini consciously and paradoxically sought, by publishing plays written in Italian, to integrate himself, like Marino before him, into the foreign culture of France *as* an Italian, for his "otherness" was one of the primary sources of his cultural capital there.[48] As he reminds the great nobleman Bassompierre at the end of the dedication to *Amor nello specchio,* Andreini is a stranger in a strange land, "celebrating tirelessly and perpetually those many graces that your most liberal hand has granted to me on the two occasions in which I (a wandering actor) came to France by royal invitation."[49]

Andreini's written French was rudimentary at best, as can be seen from his few clumsy attempts to transcribe a name or address into French when addressing current or prospective patrons in the dedications to these plays ("Basampiere" for "Bassompierre," "Alui" for "Halluin," "Cloopin" for "Clopin," and so on). It is unlikely that his spoken French was much better, and he never attempts to represent the language in the printed versions of the five 1622 Paris plays, even though at least one of these (*La centaura*) includes prefatory material in French. By this time many French actors were playing Arte roles in local companies in and around Paris, but Andreini does not seem to have had much interchange with them during his periods in residence there. The playwright wrote reasonably well in Spanish, on the other hand, a language with which he was intimately acquainted for its importance in acquiring patrons in Milan, as well as for its identification with the Arte figure of the braggart soldier or captain (Capitan Matamoros, Capitano Spavento, and so on).[50] Although the Paris performances may perhaps have included some improvised wordplay in simulated French, since itinerant companies often included some reference to the local culture and language in their shows, the actors in Andreini's plays spoke principally in Italian or in some dialect of the peninsula, from Bergamasque to Bolognese. Many of the members of the French court were likely to have known literary Italian, given the prestige of its humanist culture and the political power of Maria de' Medici. Italian had first become a vernacular lingua franca among the intelligentsia in sixteenth-century Europe thanks in part to the prestige of the peninsula's great poets (particularly Petrarch, Ariosto, and Tasso), and most well-educated individuals in the early seventeenth century—both inside and outside France—could be expected to possess at least some knowledge of the language.[51] The same could not be said, naturally enough, for the average Parisian spectator. Nonetheless, conventional Italian *commedia dell'arte* shows for the French public, as well as for the court, proved popular for many decades, thanks to their blend of music, dance, acrobatics, stock characters, slapstick, sight gags, and plotlines readily recognizable to an audience familiar with the fundamentals of the Arte tradition. If clowns and zanies could hope for the familiarity of at least some spectators with a smattering of stock words and phrases of basic conversational Italian, allowing them to grasp small fragments of the dialogues in the Arte performances, this could certainly not be expected of the elaborately rhetorical speeches on love included in Andreini's 1622 Paris plays, although much clowning and tomfoolery is incorporated into the works. We may conclude from this that these five plays were destined principally for an aristocratic audience already familiar with Italian, although Andreini's showmanship and mastery of special effects, together with the virtuosi acting skills of the company's members, may likely have made some of them appealing to a broader public as well.

Andreini's economic strategy as *capocomico* in Paris, then, aimed not only to differentiate the Fedeli from the competition but also to exploit the international prestige of Italian theatrical and literary culture to cultivate patrons from the ranks of the French nobility. If his sometime rival and sometime partner Tristano Martinelli could rightly claim that King Louis XIII himself had held the actor's child during its baptism, Andreini was not to be outdone.[52] Andreini understood well the workings of the Old Regime courts: by 1622 he had not only frequented the court of the dukes of Mantua for close to two decades, but he now often corresponded with the current duke, Ferdinando I. As his successful quest for patronage in both Mantua and Paris demonstrates, Andreini knew how to maneuver within the taut and intricate web of social, economic, and political alliances and interests that defined the courts. *La centaura* is dedicated to Maria de' Medici, and even if the queen mother in 1622 no longer wielded the same political power at court that she had once held as regent, she was nonetheless a formidable and influential figure in the cultural life of the capital. *La Ferinda* is instead dedicated to Charles de Schomberg, who was the Duke of Halluin and a peer of France, while *Amor nello specchio* is dedicated to the duke's friend, the "Maréchal de France" François de Bassompierre, a renowned soldier, courtier, and rake who also belonged to the highest spheres of the nobility at court. *La sultana* is dedicated to "Monsieur le Grand," the honorific title of the Grand Squire of France, Master of the King's Stables: in 1622 this would have been Roger de Saint-Lary, Duke of Bellegarde and a prince of the blood (i.e., a legitimate member of the House of Bourbon). Last but not least, *Li duo Leli simili* is dedicated to the Duke of Nemours, Henri de Savoie, yet another wealthy and high-ranking noble courtier. In early 1622, when he published his five plays there, Andreini was clearly planning to return to Paris soon and wanted to ensure that his patronage network was in place: in fact, the Fedeli were once again in Paris by December of this same year for another triumphant sojourn.

There was likely at least one further, and very important, reason for the choice of Paris as the publication venue for these plays. The pressing issue of censorship in Italy could never have been far from Andreini's thoughts. The Counter-Reformation authorities' intolerance of the theater unquestionably had an impact on both the composition and the production of comedies across the peninsula, although the degree of official scrutiny varied widely from place to place. In Milan, for instance, the religious authority Charles Borromeo (1538–84) censored comedy and even called for an end to Carnival itself. Borromeo is known to have scrutinized the scenarios of the Compagnia dei Gelosi in 1583 in search of suspect dialogues and situations to suppress before they could appear onstage. He argued that comedy made a dangerous public display of every kind of vice, from adultery to prostitution; actors were troublemaking vagabonds to be banished from the city.[53] Actors were barred from burial in consecrated ground, and, in the Papal States, actresses were banned from the public stage.[54] Andreini knew all too well the ecclesiastical critique of comedy in Italy and made extensive efforts to counter it in writing his plays.[55]

His claims for "new comedy," as he termed his works for the comic stage, carefully take the problem of censorship into account. The "new comedy" was to be, Andreini argued in his theoretical writings, free of the frank immorality and subversive social critique so often found in the so-called learned comedies of the Renaissance. There would be no scathing portrayals of the Church or celebrations of adultery (as in Machiavelli's *La mandragola*), no attacks on government corruption (as in Ariosto's *La Lena*) or on the principles of absolutism (as in Aretino's *Il marescalco*), and little of the ribald sexuality that may be found in dozens of sixteenth-century Italian comedies or in the majority of Arte scenarios. This approach alone, Andreini contended, would allow comedy to flourish in the

Counter-Reformation climate.[56] For, as he remarked in the prologue to *Le-lio bandito* (composed shortly before he went to Paris in 1621), "although in comedies we often see lascivious acts and profane actions, they are not put there in order to teach us [how to perform] them, but in order to show us the way in which we may avoid them."[57] In other words, if comedy was to be a mirror of human life or "speculum vitae humanae," as he calls it in the preface to *Amor nello specchio,* this image of our existence—blemishes, warts, and all—was supposed to have a didactic moral effect on the spectator, who would then choose to avoid these errors in his or her own life.[58] Although such defenses of comedy are hardly original to Andreini—indeed, they have a very long history in European criticism and theory[59]—his repeated recourse to them over the course of his career shows that, both as playwright and *capocomico,* he well understood the obstacles that censorship in Italy had placed, and would continue to place, in his path.

The desire for moral improvement was surely not the chief reason that the Parisian public flocked to the Fedeli's performances at the Théâtre de Bourgogne: the crowds were drawn by the visual and other pleasures to be had in witnessing a spectacle comprised of supremely skilled Italian comic players, music, dance, special effects, and so on. Although by the beginning of the 1620s Catholicism had the upper hand in France, the regulation of public speech there was quite different from that in Italy. In the wake of the traumatic French Wars of Religion, no central censorship authority yet existed: Cardinal Richelieu would institute the Code Michaud only at the end of the decade (1629), giving him the power as chancellor to appoint censors who were to certify all manuscripts before publication. This is not to say that in 1622, before Richelieu's rise to the cardinalate, there was anarchic freedom in the Parisian publishing world. There was, however, considerably greater latitude for writers and printers than could be found anywhere in Italy. Nevertheless, when the libertine court poet Théophile de Viau's flamboyantly homoerotic verses appeared in Paris in this same year, in a collection published under his name and entitled *Le Parnasse des poètes satyriques,* they provoked a reaction by the French secular and religious authorities. Viau's poems were far more daring—even obscene—than anything that Andreini ever wrote, and, persecuted by the Jesuits, he was condemned to death *in contumacia* by the Paris parliament, although the sentence was later commuted to permanent banishment.[60] It goes almost without saying that there were limits to speech that could not be crossed without risk in France in 1622, even (or especially) by visitors.[61] Surprisingly, however, the 1622 edition of *La cen-taura* includes a prefatory poem by none other than Viau himself (identi-fied in the text only as "Théophile"), praising the work for its "délices" and "enchantements" while declaring the author's "madness/Not only for Italy/But in every climate to be found in the Universe."[62] Of Andreini's five Paris plays published for the first time in that year, only *Amor nello specchio* can be considered truly libertine, with its overt representation of same-sex love between women.[63] His patron for this play, François de Bassompierre, was widely reputed to be a freethinker, "one of atheism's leading lights."[64] Nevertheless, Andreini could not have ignored the con-troversies swirling around the famed Neapolitan poet Giambattista Ma-rino (1569–1625), who was resident in Paris during these same years while drawing a fabulous pension from King Louis XIII, because of Marino's far-from-clandestine ties to the culture of libertinism.

Paris—the largest city in Europe at the time—offered both playwright and players freedoms that could not be had elsewhere.[65] Even in the City of Light, however, Andreini had to watch his step carefully to avoid alien-ating authorities, patrons, or the public. The transgressive (and occasion-ally libertine) nature of these works for the stage suggests, on the other hand, that Andreini did not actively seek an opportunity to republish most of them after his return to Italy. At home, the problems posed by the Italian censors were real enough, but if Andreini had been able to se-cure new sources of aristocratic patronage through the publication of the plays, he might have chosen to do so. From the 1620s onward, however, northern Italy's sharp economic decline made such patronage increas-ingly difficult to obtain, and drove the Fedeli further and further afield in search of paying audiences.[66] Only *La centaura,* with its mythological and regal subject matter as well as its paeans of praise to dynastic rule, seemed suitable for the tastes of the northern Italian courts and was in fact reprinted at least once in Andreini's lifetime. It would appear that the actor-author was—despite the inclusion of Viau's brief poem in *La centaura*—keenly aware of what could or could not be said, or printed, in France or in Italy at this time. The evidence provided by his publica-tions suggests that Andreini carefully negotiated the circumstances in which he found himself in order to extract an advantage for his art and thus to enhance its economic, social, and aesthetic legitimacy.

As was often the case in early modern Italy, of course, the gap be-tween theory and practice could be substantial, and antitheatricalism among the Italian authorities was no different. Saint Charles Borromeo's proscription was not in fact embraced by many of the clergy, and there was no shortage of church leaders and organizations (such as the Jesuits) who saw in the theater a propaganda tool of great efficacy for the faith. Andreini's sacred plays, such as his three versions of the Mary Magdalene story, confirm that the religious potential of his special brand of theater was recognized by at least some Italian ecclesiastics.[67] Although the Fedeli continued to mount successful Arte performances as part of the repertory for many years, the *commedia dell'arte* itself was nonetheless sometimes made the target of censorship not only by religious but also by secular authorities in cities across Italy. Comedy tends to be a conservative genre, but the brash irreverence, subversive dialogues, and risqué antics of the Arte players could be perceived by those in power as a threat to public order itself. Ironically, as recent scholarship has shown, one of the main reasons for both religious and secular authorities' concern about the theater was the prominence of actresses in the companies. Municipal officials and clergymen railed against them, accusing actresses of every conceivable public and private impropriety. Yet of course the repertory developed by Andreini for the Compagnia dei Fedeli—which extended and transformed the Arte tradition—prominently featured female roles, and the troupe had numerous actresses among its members: of the five Paris plays, three of them have a female character in the title role (*La Ferinda, La sultana, La centaura*), and *Amor nello specchio* was primarily a vehicle for the actresses Virginia Ramponi (Florinda) and Virginia Rotari (Lidia). Because he understood so well what patrons, audiences, and authorities expected of his company and his work, Andreini the author-actor was able to perform a risky tightrope act that could keep the public's interest while avoiding interference from church and state.

When in Italy, as we have seen, Andreini preferred to publish or republish his comedies in the autonomous republic of Venice, with its deep-rooted theatrical culture, relatively tolerant authorities, and important printing trade: at the height of his powers as a playwright, between 1619 and 1633, ten of the twelve known printings or reprintings in Italy of his comic plays were done in Venice. However, seven more printings (including the two of *La campanazza*) appeared in Paris between 1621 and 1622. Thus, significantly enough, in these crucial years around ninety percent of Andreini's comedies appeared either in Venice or in Paris, with the latter playing a far from minor role in the printing of his works. It is worth noting, furthermore, that for the two comedies published for the first time shortly before 1622—*La venetiana* and *La campanazza*—Andreini decided to use a pseudonym.[68] This allows us to grasp better the significance of Paris to Andreini's lifelong project for promoting and transforming Italian comic theater, in which he played such an important role, through his "new comedy." For it was there that, despite differences in language and culture, some of his most visionary works (including those that could not appear publicly even in Venice, such as *Amor nello specchio*) first found their way to the stage and, ultimately, to the printed page. Unlike his comedies published in Venice or elsewhere in Italy, however, these often transgressive texts were not only shrewdly commercial but also *artistic* ventures seeking to probe the very limits of the Baroque aesthetic. They served not only to please great patrons, and perhaps the paying public, but also to allow the author-actor a unique opportunity to innovate freely, without the restrictions that so often came with performing or publishing in early seventeenth-century Italy.[69] Such remarkable works—sometimes revolutionary in design—not only define the distance between Andreini and his *commedia dell'arte* contemporaries in the professional theater; they also confirm his vanguard status in the culture of the age. Although he could have followed a much more conventional (and readily available) path to success as a comedian and as a playwright, he clearly chose not to do so.

By publishing these five plays in Paris in 1622, then, Andreini did not just seek to package his works as prestigious commodities for consumption by the French court or to avoid the interference of the Italian authorities. Their appearance in print is, in the last analysis, indicative of his ambitious project to emancipate and modernize his profession, which, as we have seen, could at that moment best be realized in France (although conditions would soon change there as well). From the outset of his career, Andreini turned all of his efforts to elevating the social and cultural status of the comic actor. If his parents had succeeded in earning public acclaim and admiration in Italy and France, the professional theater was nevertheless considered disreputable. Andreini therefore consciously sought to create a novel and strikingly modern figure—the actor-intellectual—who would be able to serve as an interface between official Counter-Reformation culture and the far less legitimate world of the stage, especially the comic stage. Wherever he traveled with the Fedeli, Andreini campaigned tirelessly as actor, poet, playwright, *capocomico,* and critic to integrate comedy and comedians into the domain of the contemporary arts—indeed, to convince patrons and public alike that the comic theater and "high" culture were inseparable.[70] The culture of the Baroque privileged the shock of the new, and the experimentalism of his brand of modern comedy, Andreini contended, was essential—rather than marginal—to the new aesthetic.[71] Nearly four centuries later, from the perspective of our current understanding of the early seventeenth century, the five Paris plays published by Andreini for the first time in 1622 offer convincing proof that he was right: in the Baroque, borders— wherever they may be found—exist only in order to be crossed.[72]

Notes

1. Among the positivist studies of the late nineteenth century, see Armand Baschet, *Les comédiens italiens à la Cour de France sous Charles IX, Henri III, Henri IV et Louis XIII . . .* (Paris: Plon, 1882; rpt. Geneva: Slatkine, 1969); Émile Campardon, *Les Comédiens du roi de la troupe française pendant les deux derniers siècles,* 2 vols. (Paris: Berger-Levrault, 1880; rpt. Geneva: Slatkine, 1970); and Luigi Rasi, *I comici italiani: biografia, bibliografia, iconologia,* 2 vols. (Florence: Bocca e Lumachi, 1897-1905)

2. Fernand Braudel, *Il secondo Rinascimento: due secoli e tre Italie,* trans. Corrado Vivanti (Turin: Einaudi, 1986), 83-87.

3. Andreini writes in the preface to the 1622 edition of *La centaura,* "as in Italy I printed works for the stage, likewise in France I give birth to theatrical compositions" (com'in Italia stampai opere recitative, così in Francia dò alla luce drammatici componimenti); G. B. Andreini, *La centaura, suggetto diviso in comedia, pastorale e tragedia* (Paris: Nicolas de La Vigne, 1622), n.p. Maria Galli Stampino, "Rôles et espaces de la *commedia dell'arte* à Paris," *Studi di letteratura francese* 26 (2001): 91, states that "l'analyse complète du théâtre français à la fin du seizième siècle et au cours du dix-septième doit prendre en considération la présence des troupes professionelles italiennes à la cour et dans la ville de Paris. Il est évident que la comparaison entre la situation en France et celle en Italie apporte des résultats qui nous aident à en comprendre les aspects contrastés."

4. Although a stock role (*maschera*) with roots in medieval Liguria, Capitano Spavento was made famous by Francesco Andreini's performances. For English-speaking readers unfamiliar with Arte terminology, traditions, and performance practices, see Richard Andrews, *Scripts and Scenarios: The Performance of Comedy in Renaissance Italy* (Cambridge and New York: Cambridge University Press, 1993), 169-203, and Robert Henke, *Performance and Literature in the Commedia dell'Arte* (Cambridge and New York: Cambridge University Press, 2002), 1-49.

5. M. A. Katritzsky, "Reading the Actress in Commedia Imagery," in *Women Players in England, 1500-1660: Beyond the All-Male Stage,* ed. Pamela A. Brown and Peter Parolin (Burlington, Vt.: Ashgate, 2005), 126-27. Most professional theatrical troupes in early modern Italy were capable of staging works in a number of genres.

6. Anne MacNeil, *Music and Women of the Commedia dell'Arte in the Late Sixteenth Century* (Oxford and New York: Oxford University Press, 2003), 238. MacNeil draws this information from a notarized document dated January 31, 1620, now in the Archivio di Stato in Mantua.

7. Ibid., 254, 256, 258.

8. Louise George Clubb, "Italian Renaissance Theatre," in John Russell Brown, ed., *The Oxford Illustrated History of Theatre* (Oxford and New York: Oxford University Press, 1995), 133.

9. G. B. Andreini, "Alla Maestà Christianissima di Maria de' Medici Reina di Francia," in *L'Adamo,* ed. Alessandra Ruffino (Trent: La Finestra Editrice, 2007), 5-7. A letter from Andreini to Ferdinando Gonzaga dated March 20, 1610, now in the Archivio di Stato in Mantua (b. 2718, c. 631), suggests that Andreini and his wife had intended to travel to France prior to 1613, although they did not do so.

10. MacNeil, *Music and Women,* 163.

11. Siro Ferrone, *Attori mercanti corsari: la commedia dell'arte in Europa tra Cinque e Seicento* (Turin: Einaudi, 1993), 66, and *Arlecchino: vita e avventure di Tristano Martinelli attore* (Bari: Laterza, 2006), 217-18.

12. Ferrone, *Attori,* 239, and *Arlecchino,* 217 (where *La centaura* is termed a "lunghissimo dramma dedicato proprio a Maria . . . con un finale che celebra proprio esplicitamente il trionfo della monarca medicea"). On Maria de' Medici's patronage of the arts, see Sara Mamone and Francesco Venturi, *Firenze e Parigi: due capitali dello spettacolo per una regina, Maria de' Medici* (Cinisello Balsamo [Milan]: Silvana, 1988), and Marc Fumaroli, ed., *Le 'Siècle' de Marie de Médicis* (Alessandria: Edizioni dell'Orso, 2002).

13. Andreini, *La centaura* (1622), n.p.: "Tutti uniti qui dunque in bel legame / Senza più favellar lievi partite; / Tra voi tessete triplicato stame, / A le mete di gloria alte salite."

14. On Rubens's cycle, see Sarah R. Cohen, "Rubens's France: Gender and Personification in the Marie de Médicis Cycle," *The Art Bulletin* 85, no. 3 (Sept. 2003): 490-522.

15. The sole exception to this pattern is Florence, capital of the Medici dynasty, where Andreini published *La saggia egiziana* and *La divina visione* in 1604, as well as the second printing of his first version of *La Maddalena* in 1612: see Silvia Carandini and Luciano Mariti, *Don Giovanni o l'estrema avventura del teatro: 'Il nuovo risarcito Convitato di Pietra' di Giovan Battista Andreini* (Rome: Bulzoni, 2003), 50-51.

16. Fabrizio Fiaschini, *L' "incessabil agitazione": Giovan Battista Andreini tra professione teatrale, cultura letteraria e religione* (Pisa: Giardini, 2007), 67.

17. See Ferrone, *Arlecchino,* 2-4, for superb maps of the routes regularly used by the Arte companies on their travels.

18. See, for instance, the late sixteenth-century Recueil Fossard, whose illustrations are believed to represent an Italian troupe's visit to Paris in 1577: *Le Recueil Fossard* (Paris: Librairie théâtrale, rpt. 1981).

19. John S. Powell, *Music and Theatre in France, 1600-1680* (Oxford and New York: Oxford University Press, 2000), 3, 6-7; and Ferrone, *Attori,* 61-67.

20. See the still valuable S.W. Deierkauf-Holsboer, *Le Théâtre de l'Hôtel de Bourgogne,* 2 vols. (Paris: Nizet, 1968).

21. Ferrone, *Arlecchino,* 209-20.

22. Ferrone, *Attori,* 66-67.

23. *La centaura* (1622), unnumbered pages containing an anagram, a quatrain and a sonnet; see also Carandini and Mariti, *Don Giovanni,* 45.

24. For example, the dedication of *Amor nello specchio* is dated March 18, 1622, that of *Ferinda* is dated March 20, 1622, and that of *La sultana* is dated March 22, 1622, while *La centaura* is instead dated January 1622 (but makes ample allusion to the reconciliation of the queen mother with Louis XIII, which occurred on January 27). See Ferrone, *Attori,* 239; and *Arlecchino,* 217-18.

25. Nicolas de La Vigne (159?-1679) was active for many decades as a printer in Paris, but these works by Andreini appeared less than two years after de La Vigne had become a *maître* in April 1620.

26. In *Amor nello specchio,* the Wizard is at first called "Stefasat," but thereafter is referred to as "Arfasat" (although this is duly noted and corrected in the list of errata included in the volume). The play has been published in a critical edition: G. B. Andreini, *Amor nello specchio,* ed. Salvatore Maira and Anna Michela Borracci (Rome: Bulzoni, 1997). An English-language translation will appear as *Love in the Mirror,* trans. Jon R. Snyder, The Other Voice in Early Modern Europe 2, n.s. (Toronto: CRRS, 2010).

27. Siro Ferrone, "Nota biobibliografica," *Commedie dell'arte,* 2 vols. (Milan: Mursia, 1986), 2:14.

28. I will not discuss here either *La campanaccia* (*The Bell*), which first appeared in Paris, printed by de La Vigne, in 1621, or *Le due comedie in comedia* (*The Two Plays Within the Play*), which was first printed in Venice in 1623, but both certainly belong formally and thematically to the works of this period. The former may perhaps have been ready for the press by the time the troupe reached Paris at the end of 1620, and the latter—unlike all the others—is not dedicated to an important French patron. The 1623 first edition of *Le due comedie in comedia* is instead dedicated to the Marchese Nicolò Tassoni Estense, a Ferrarese nobleman. *La campanaccia* was the Andreini comedy most successful with the reading public in Italy: it was reprinted six times in the seventeenth century and was his only work for the comic stage to appear in print after his death. This 1674 edition of *La campanaccia* was in fact the last of Andreini's comedies to be reprinted prior to the late twentieth century.

29. In an erudite note to the 1750 Florence edition of the satirical poem by the painter Lorenzo Lippi, published under the pseudonym Perlone Zipoli, *Il malmantile racquistato,* ed. Puccio Lamoni, Antommaria Salvini, and Antommaria Biscioni (Florence: Francesco Moücke, 1750), 566, this play of Andreini's is mentioned together with Giambattista Della Porta's *Gli duoi fratelli rivali* and the Arte scenario entitled *I duo simili.* This note, attributed to Biscioni, is one of the very few mentions of Andreini's work to be found in the eighteenth century.

30. "Il gioco e i suoi 'generi': conversazione con Luca Ronconi," ed. Aldo Viganò, in *La centaura,* by G. B. Andreini (Genoa: Il Melangolo, 2004), 215. On antimimetic tendencies in Baroque art, see Jon R. Snyder, *L'estetica del Barocco* (Bologna: Il Mulino, 2005), 21-23.

31. One of the most useful explanations of this system is to be found in Andrea Battistini, *Il Barocco: cultura, miti, immagini* (Rome: Salerno Editrice, 2000), 8-35.

32. Ferrone, *Attori,* 213.

33. Ferrone, *Arlecchino,* ix: "la sua opera geniale consistette soprattutto di azioni, gesti e parole create sulla scena e mai trasferite nella pagina scritta."

34. Ibid., 223-25.

35. Andreini, *Amor nello specchio,* 130: "Qui faranno vista di non poter entrare, e poi tutti in un tempo entreranno."

36. Andreini, *Amor nello specchio,* 141: "Ordine per recitare *Amor nello specchio* con gran facilità"; and 144: "un tamburo per Granello insegna per Coradella, non troppo grande. . . ."

37. The first performances of operas for a paying public in theaters would take place in Venice only some fifteen years later; see Ellen Rosand, *Opera in Seventeenth-Century Venice: The Creation of a Genre* (Berkeley: University of California Press, 1991).

38. G. B. Andreini, "A' benigni lettori" [Preface], *La Ferinda* (Paris: de La Vigne, 1622), n.p.

39. Ibid. The original text reads: "quelle macchine, e per l'aria, e per terra, e per mare, quali tanto fanno ammirande [sic] così fatte apparenze."

40. Ibid.

41. See Andrews, *Scripts and Scenarios*, 204-26.

42. Giovanni Battista Guarini (1538-1612), who first developed the tragicomedy in the late sixteenth century, influencing greatly the European literature, theater, and music of the seicento, had ardently defended the notion of the hybrid genre in the Italian critical debates of his time. See Bernard Weinberg, *A History of Literary Criticism in the Italian Renaissance*, 2 vols. (Chicago: University of Chicago Press, 1961), 2:679-84.

43. Andreini, *La centaura* (1622), n.p.

44. *La centaura* was republished in Venice in 1633; see Fiaschini, *L' "incessabil agitazione,"* 174, who does not recognize the attribution of a (lost) 1625 Venetian edition of the play made by Giammaria Mazzuchelli, *Gli scrittori d'Italia; cioè, Notizie storiche, e critiche intorno alle vite, e agli scritti dei letterati italiani* (Brescia: Giambatista Bossini, 1753), I: 710. The 1633 Venice edition, rather than the 1622 Paris one, is the basis for the 2004 edition (see note 30).

45. Siro Ferrone, *Comici dell'arte: Corrispondenze*, 2 vols. (Florence: Casa Editrice Le Lettere, 1993), 1:63.

46. G. B. Andreini, *La Florinda, tragedia* (Florence: Volcmar Timan Germano, 1604 [destroyed by author]; rpt. Milan: Girolamo Bordoni, 1606). Timan was termed "Germano" or "Todesco" [sic] because, although active in Florence in the early seicento, he was of German origin.

47. Important collections of Arte scripts and sketches were published not only by Francesco Andreini; see the two-volume *Teatro delle favole rappresentative*, by Flaminio Scala (Venice: Ginammi, 1610), which was to prove a milestone in the early modern Italian theater.

48. Ferrone, *Attori*, notes along these same lines that "indipendentemente dal copione che recitano, gli spettatori sanno che i comici, ciascuno con la sua peculiarità linguistica e la sua fisionomia etnica, non appartengono alla loro comunità" (xx).

49. Andreini, *Amor nello specchio*, 57: "celebrator inestancabile e perpetuo di quelle molte grazie che dalla sua mano liberalissima mi sono state compartite in due volte che m'è occorso (scenico peregrino) venir alla Francia, per servigi Reali."

50. In an appendix to *La Ferinda*, Andreini includes plausible Spanish-language versions of the songs to be performed by Guerindo, the play's braggart soldier, noting, "if ever this little opera were to deserve to be set to music, it seemed to me [useful] also to compose the part of Captain Guerindo in Spanish, because, if set in the musical style of *recitativo*, it would be excellent to listen to" (p. 3 of appendix). In *La sultana*, on the other hand, the Sultana, when she masquerades as a (male) Turkish slave, speaks both excellent Turkish and a lingua franca version of Venetian echoing that used in some parts of the eastern Mediterranean in the late sixteenth and early seventeenth centuries. See Robert C. Davis, *Christian Slaves, Muslim Masters: White Slaves in the Mediterranean, the Barbary Coast, and Italy, 1500-1800* (New York: Palgrave Macmillan, 2003), 113-15.

51. On the relationship between Italian and French culture in early modernity, see *Storia della letteratura italiana: Vol. XII, la letteratura italiana fuori d'Italia*, ed. Enrico Malato (Roma: Salerno Editrice, 2002).

52. Ferrone, *Arlecchino*, 186-87.

53. For Borromeo's attitude toward comedy, see his "Lettera al Cardinale Gabriello Paleotti, Arcivescovo di Bologna (luglio 1578)," now in Ferdinando Taviani, *La commedia dell'arte e la società barocca: la fascinazione del teatro* (Rome: Bulzoni, 1991 [1969]), 23-24. Taviani, 315-526, has also republished the important critique of Italian Baroque theater by Jesuit Giovan Domenico Ottonelli (1584-1670).

54. Andrews, *Scripts and Scenarios*, 224.

55. See, for instance, G. B. Andreini, *Prologo in dialogo fra Momo e la Verità* (Ferrara: Vittorio Baldini, 1612), now in Ferruccio Marotti and Giovanna Romei, *La commedia dell'arte e la società barocca: vol. 2, la professione del teatro* (Rome: Bulzoni, 1991), 473–88. Momo, one of the two interlocutors in the dialogue, asks, "How will you defend modern comedies, which are full of obscene, filthy and scandalous words?" (480). Truth counters by formulating an impassioned defense of comedy as a medium for "extremely wise and moral men" (481), in spite of appearances to the contrary.

56. Andreini published his plays in Italy with a regular imprimatur from the Church authorities: see, for example, the title page of *La turca* (Venice: Paolo Guerigli, 1620).

57. G. B. Andreini, *Lelio bandito: tragicommedia boschereccia* (Venice: G.B. Combi, 1624), 12: ". . . e benche nelle comedie molte volte si veggano atti lascivi & azzioni profane, non son introdotte per insegnarle: ma per mostrar il modo con cui ce ne possiano guardare. . . ."

58. Andreini, *Amor nello specchio*, 56.

59. See the invaluable collection of early modern critical texts concerning the theater, and Italian antitheatrical polemics, in Taviani, et al., *La commedia dell'arte e la società barocca*, vols. 1–2, as well as Jonas Barish, *The Antitheatrical Prejudice* (Berkeley: University of California Press, 1981).

60. Joan DeJean, *The Reinvention of Obscenity: Sex, Lies, and Tabloids in Early Modern France* (Chicago: University of Chicago Press, 2002), 21. The classic work on Viau remains Antoine Adam, *Théophile de Viau et la libre pensée française en 1620* (Paris: Slatkine, 2008 [1935]). See also Guido Saba, *Théophile de Viau* (Paris: Memini, 2007) for an extensive bibliography.

61. Giulio Cesare Vanini, the Italian philosopher, had been arrested, imprisoned, tortured, and executed in Toulouse in 1619 for his heterodox and suspect teachings; see Jean-Pierre Cavaillé, *Dis/simulations: Jules-César Vanini, François La Mothe Le Vayer, Gabriel Naudé, Louis Machon et Torquato Accetto: religion, morale et politique au XVIIe siècle* (Paris: Champion, 2002), 39–140.

62. Théophile de Viau, "Sur la Centaure du Sieur Iean Baptiste Andreini, dit Lelie," *La centaura* (1622), n.p.: ". . . folie / Non seulement pour l'Italie / Mais dans touts [sic] les climats qui sont en l'Univers."

63. On the representation of female same-sex desire in this drama, see the contribution of Laura Giannetti in this volume. —*Editors' note.*

64. Jean Orieux, *Bussy-Rabutin: le libertin galant homme (1618-1693)* (Paris: Flammarion, 1958), 46: "une des lumières de l'athéisme."

65. See J. Bradford De Long and Andrei Shleifer, "Princes and Merchants: European City Growth Before the Industrial Revolution," *Journal of Law and Economics* 36 (1993): 678, for a useful examination of the size of Paris relative to other European cities in this same period.

66. On the positive and negative aspects of the post-1620 economy, see Giovanni Muto, "Dopo l' 'estate di San Martino' dell'economia italiana," in *Italia 1650: comparazioni e bilanci*, ed. Giuseppe Galasso and Aurelio Musi (Naples: CUEN, 2002), 71–86.

67. The three versions are *La Maddalena* (Venice: Somasco, 1610; rpt. Florence: Eredi Marescotti, 1612); *La Maddalena, sacra rappresentatione* (Mantua: Aurelio e Ludovico Osanna, 1617; rpt. Milan: Malatesta, 1620); and *La Maddalena lasciva e penitente* (Milan: Giovan Battista e Giulio Cesare Malatesta, 1652; rpt. Bari: Palomar, 2006).

68. *Lelio bandito* is instead a tragicomedy. *La venetiana* (Venice: Alessandro Polo, 1619) was originally attributed to "Sier Cocalin de i Cocalini da Torzelo, academico Vizilante, dito el Dormioto," while the author of *La campanaccia* (Paris: De La Vigne,

1621) was instead supposedly "Giovanni Rivani da Bologna, detto il Dottor Campanaccio da Budri."

69. A glance at Andreini's biobibliography reveals that in early seventeenth-century Europe no author-actor after Shakespeare wrote as much for the theater as he did. See also Ferrone, *Attori* and *Arlecchino.* It should be added that we still do not know who paid for the plays to be published in Paris.

70. Among many other studies of this aspect of Andreini's theatrical project, see Rossella Palmieri, "Giovan Battista Andreini, la Maddalena e il 'tempo barocco,'" in G. B. Andreini, *La Maddalena lasciva e penitente,* ed. Rossella Palmieri (Bari: Palomar, 2006), 21–44.

71. I am indebted here to Fiaschini, *L' "incessabil agitazione,"* 12–13. On the culture of the Baroque, I refer the reader to the classic works by José Antonio Maravall, *Culture of the Baroque: Analysis of a Historical Structure,* trans. Terry Cochran (Minneapolis: University of Minnesota Press, 1986 [1975]), and Jean Rousset, *La Littérature de l'âge baroque en France: Circé et le paon* (Paris: José Corti, 1995 [1954]).

72. On the definition of the Baroque aesthetic, see Snyder, *L'estetica del Barocco,* 11–27 and 173–80.

Italy Versus France; or, How Pierre Corneille Became an Anti-Machiavel

KATHERINE IBBETT

"**D**'UN CÔTÉ CORNEILLE, de l'autre Machiavel" (on one side Corneille, on the other Machiavelli) claims Michel Prigent, the author of one of the most important recent books on Corneille's political tragedies.[1] Prigent's assertion, lining up the French playwright against the Italian political strategist, is certainly abrupt in its binarism, but it is not an unusual claim. His assessment, published in the mideighties, was echoed a decade later by the eminent scholar Marc Fumaroli, who maintained that "Les poètes français du XVIIe siècle ont tous été, ouvertement ou couvertement, du côté de la résistance à Machiavel, à Hobbes, à la politique moderne"[2] (French writers of the seventeenth century were all, openly or not, on the side of the resistance to Machiavelli, Hobbes, and modern politics). These statements are also in keeping with work such as that by Pierre Ronzeaud, who, in an essay entitled "La stratégie anti-machiavélique de Pierre Corneille," paints a picture of the "univers clos" (closed world) of Machiavellianism in contrast to the world of generous grace he sees in much of Corneille's work.[3] For Ronzeaud, Corneille takes on what he terms "l'espace verbal du machiavélisme" (the verbal space of Machiavellianism)[4]—that is, he imbues himself with a language redolent with the rich post-Machiavellian tradition—only to "démonter les stratagèmes argumentaires et les ruses oratoires des machiavéliques" (dismantle the arguments and oratorical ruses of the Machiavellians).[5] This kindly apology for the playwright reads a little like the plea of a defense attorney

379

eager to explain what his client has been doing hanging out with the neighborhood toughs. Corneille, in these readings, is trying to break the Machiavellian system down, from within, and it is the task of the critic-defender to tell us the good works the playwright *really* set out to do, "ouvertement ou couvertement."

Such readings, which make Cornelian tragedy the privileged site for "la confrontation entre les valeurs de l'héroïsme et la raison d'Etat" (the confrontation for the values of heroism and of reason of state), as Prigent puts it, are not merely a late-twentieth-century outcropping of conservatism.[6] They have a long and complicated history, drawing on a set of distinctions between France and Italy, style and values, ornamentation and clarity, that are at least as old as Machiavelli and that point to some of the complications inherent in the delineation of any national literary tradition in a Europe characterized by intense bouts of imitation, importation, and exchange. They may surprise the lay—perhaps more specifically, the foreign—reader of Corneille, who, as Ronzeaud acknowledges, often presents his readers with a tragic universe soaked in the imagery and language of post-Machiavellian reasons of state. In this essay, I set out something of the early modern history behind these brusque binaries and in particular the relation to Italy that haunts the retrospective formation of the neoclassical canon.[7] How did Corneille become an anti-Machiavel, and what does it mean to claim him as that? In what follows, I show how early modern resistance to the Italianate gave rise to a particular reading of the period, according to which Machiavellianism is understood as an affront to French values. I trace that resistance in the historical presentation of the fabled enmity between, in the "French" corner, Pierre Corneille, and, for the "Italians" or, as Ronzeaud would put it, in "l'espace verbal du machiavélisme," Cardinal de Richelieu, claimed as a notorious Machiavel.

The same sense of transalpine distinction that animates Ronzeaud's argument is fully present in the political pamphlets of midseventeenth-century France, the *mazarinades* that constituted the verbal space of the civil rebellions known as the Fronde.[8] The *mazarinades* took the Italian-born chief minister, Giulio Mazzarino, known as Jules Mazarin, as the focus of their ire, and in their frenzied productions the caricatured figure of the minister became the crucible for a more generalized rage against the rapidly centralizing power of the state. Though the force of the unrest was dissipated by 1652, the language of the *mazarinades* forged a template for protonationalist rhetoric and, in particular, for an understanding of Frenchness as a particular relation between style and values.[9] The *mazarinades* set forth a series of principles that were to become central to the developing sense of a French literary history and established an operative norm of Frenchness that underwrites readings of the period such as those I traced above.

As more and more Italians came to Paris in the years of Mazarin's ministry, the usual urban suspicion of court behaviors became increasingly targeted against Italians: in midseventeenth-century France, a suspicion of flowery language was a specifically anti-Italian sentiment.[10] One *mazarinade* even featured an allegorical France imagining an Italian lover whispering words of seduction to her, though the pamphlet suggests that the anti-Italian sentiment focused on the figure of Mazarin slid easily into a more generalized Latinophobia, since the lover's imagined whisperings are not in Italian but in Spanish instead: "su tesoro, su alma, su vida. . . ." (his treasure, his soul, his life).[11] This slippage notwithstanding, the politics of linguistic difference was a central concern in the *mazarinades,* and it drew upon over a century of concern about the dangerous influence of the Italian language, from Du Bellay's 1549 *Deffense et illustration de la langue francoyse* onward. In the late sixteenth century, and especially in the wake of the Saint Bartholomew's Day massacre and the consequent fury against the Italian queen Catherine de Médicis, much of the anti-Italian discourse had been motivated by sectarian prejudice and dominated by Protestant writers like Henri Estienne, Innocent Gentillet, and François de la Noue. Estienne's *Deux dialogues du nouveau langage François, italianizé, & autrement desguizé* (1578), for example, railed against courtiers' adoption of Italianate style and "vocables Transalpins" (transalpine vowels).[12] In much of this writing, Italian words are merely another form of imported luxury goods, rotting the straightforwardness of French identity; thus Gentillet upholds the values of the "bons et naturels François" (good and natural French) and rejects the superfluity of importing Italian goods, such as silk sheets, which will lead to dissolute behavior: "Et de faict quelle marchandise nous vient-il en France d'Italie qui nous soit necessaire? Ne nous passerions-nous pas bien de leurs draps de soye, qui ne nous servent qu'à dissolution & superfluité?"[13] (And in fact what necessary goods come to us in France from Italy? Wouldn't we do better without their silk sheets, which lead us only to dissolution and superfluity?)

Much of the anti-Italian language of the *mazarinades* drew upon another sixteenth-century commonplace, based on a false etymology, understanding "Frenchness" to be connected to "frankness": one pamphlet author calls upon the country to show "Qu'on est franc de nom, & d'effet,/Francs, montrez donc vostre Franchise,/Pour que la France soit remise. . . ."[14] (That we are frank in name, and in effect/ *Francs,* show then your frankness,/So that France may be restored.) The pamphlet writers often insist that they speak "avec sincerité & sans feintise" (with sincerity and without pretense) participating in a larger midcentury French concern with the transparency of language seen in the works of Vaugelas and other theorists of language.[15] In the pamphlets, though, what Boileau will later call the *clarté* of the French is understood to be a political platform, and writers attack "le mauvais usage de la Politique dans la pratique des maximes Italiennes, contraires à la simplicité des François" (the misuse of politics in the practice of Italian maxims, contrary to the simplicity of the French) according to which Italian intrigue has corrupted "la candeur Françoise" (French candor).[16] The same pamphlet declares

Les fourbes introduites par ce mal heureux estranger ne sçauroient jamais compatir avec la candeur Françoise, qui ne peut estre separée de la bonté de nostre Genie qu'avec des convulsions entierement mortelles à la tranquillité de nostre repos: L'hypocrisie est trop contraire à la sincerité que nous avons de tout temps tesmoignée pour l'exercice de la Religion: & cet esprit intrigueur avec lequel ce broüillon a constamment traversé le repos de l'Estat ne sçauroit jamais simboliser avec le naturel heroïque des François, qui font gloire de marcher plus rondement par les voyes de l'honneur, & de ne fuir rien avec tant d'horreur que ces infames détours des lâches, ou la vertu ne paroist jamais que dans les pasmoisons ou dans les fuites.[17]

The trickery introduced by this unhappy foreigner would never be compatible with French candor, for only convulsions that would kill the tranquility of our peace could separate us from the goodness of our Genius: Hypocrisy is too much opposed to the sincerity that we have for all time shown in the exercise of religion; and this spirit of intrigue with which this troublemaker has constantly beset the peace of the State would never conform with the natural heroism of the French, who count it a glory to walk more straightforwardly along the ways of honor, and who flee nothing with so much horror as they do these infamous detours of cowards, where virtue only appears in fainting fits and escape attempts.

For this writer, candor is inseparable from French *Genie.* The values of Frenchness are the values of straight talking, straight walking: "le naturel heroïque des François, qui font gloire de marcher plus rondement par les voyes de l'honneur. . . ." We see in this passage how French *style* becomes associated with French *values;* from a focus on the clarity and forcefulness of the French language, we have come to an assessment of national character and the values by which it is upheld.

The scorning of Italian (or generally foreign) ornamentation, and its development into a larger political assumption, was not confined to the *mazarinades.* In Guez de Balzac's *Socrate chrétien* of 1652 the same tallying of linguistic and political style is also apparent. Balzac, who began his career as a protégé of Cardinal Richelieu, only to fall out with him and retreat to the country, tells a story about pretentious cardinals returning to France after a stint in Rome and wanting to import the overblown titles of their time there:

> Les Éminences ont été reçues en ce Royaume, mais les Éminentissimes, les Excellentissimes, etc., n'ont point encore passé les Monts. Lorsque Monsieur le Cardinal de Perron revint de Rome, après la Négociation de Venise, il en apporta *l'Illustrissime Cardinal,* et la *Seigneurie Illustrissime,* mais personne n'en voulut.[18]

> The Eminences have been received in this kingdom, but the *eminentissimi,* the *excellentissimi,* etc., have not yet crossed the mountains. When Cardinal Perron came back from Rome, after the Venice negotiation, he brought The Most Illustrious Cardinal, and The Most Illustrious Lordship, but no one would have any of it.

The superlative—hallmark of the suspiciously flowery Italian, Balzac explains—is heartily rebuffed as a foreign import. Nonetheless, one man manages to impose the model: Richelieu, of whom Balzac comments acerbically that since he had conquered all else grammar could but follow.

> Il fallait que notre langue subît le joug, aussi bien que nos esprits et nos courages. Sans se mettre en peine des autres superlatifs, qu'il n'a pas jugés dignes de lui, il a employé son autorité pour réussir le plus important de tous, celui de GENERALISSIME, l'indépendant et le tout-puissant GENERALISSIME. . . . Généralissime est donc notre unique Superlatif, et nous sommes obligés de l'honorer en la personne de Monsieur le Cardinal de Richelieu.[19]

> Our language had to follow the yoke, since our minds and courage had already. Without a thought for other superlatives, that he had not deemed worthy to describe him, he employed his authority to make the most important one of all succeed, that of GENERALISSIMO, the independent and all-powerful GENERALISSIMO. . . . Generalissimo is therefore our unique superlative, and we are obliged to honor it in the person of Cardinal Richelieu.

In this comic indictment of the Italian excess figured by Richelieu, linguistic issues are themselves a form of political position.

Against this imagined excess, the fantasy of a neutral and transparent discourse was, as many critics have shown, central to the French neoclassical aesthetic.[20] It represented not just an acknowledgment but also an improvement of antiquity, and it also marked France's unique place among nations. The French "natural" style was imagined to be forged out of a balance between styles that the sixteenth century had placed in competition: the "Attic" simple style associated with figures such as Plutarch and Tacitus and with modern Spain, and the "Asian" virtuosic style seen in Cicero's oratory and Seneca's drama and thought to be the special preserve of the Italians and, more broadly, the Jesuits.[21] The critiques of Spanish and Italians littered throughout Dominique Bouhours's *Entretiens d'Ariste et d'Eugène* (1671) also suggest something of the nationalist pull of the praise of clarity, mocking Spanish and Italian as the languages of *matamores* and "charlatans," and insisting that French maintains "un juste temperament entre ces deux langues" (a golden mean between two languages).[22] This "juste temperament" was to crop up elsewhere, too; Samuel Chappuzeau's *Le théâtre français* of 1674 claimed that French theatrical style was not culturally specific but instead figured a universal style. Commenting on the excesses of other nations' theater, Chappuzeau boasts, "Les François ont sceu tenir le milieu entre les uns et les autres et par un heureux tempérament se former un caractère universel . . ."[23] (the French were able to keep to the middle between one and the other side, and through a happy temperament form a universal character for themselves). This labored formation of a style at once French and universal was lent a seemingly inalienable legitimacy by Nicolas Boileau's influential *Art poétique* of 1674. Taking up the earlier discourse of clarity as a *political* virtue, Boileau crowned clarity as the chief principle of Frenchness, a work of retrospective rearrangement that succeeded in powerfully shaping subsequent generations' reading of the period.[24]

Although substantial critical attention has been paid to the mixed origins of French classicism,[25] Boileau's imposed narrative of an exclusive and exclusively French style nonetheless remained central to a particular and powerful vision of early modern France, filtered in the nineteenth century through Hippolyte Taine's racialized versions of literary history to become a pedagogical platitude: what we today term "classicism" was the invention of the nineteenth century. Nonetheless, the instrumentalist notion of national values that the schoolbooks of the Third Republic worked hard to present is already recognizable in earlier reflections on national identity such as the *mazarinades.*[26] Indeed, we can trace in these textbooks a discourse that is strikingly similar to the insistent exhortations of pamphlet literature. Faguet's magisterial textbook, for instance, declares of the seventeenth century that "c'est bien à ce moment que l'esprit français . . . a trouvé la forme la plus précise, la plus nette, la plus éclatante comme aussi la plus élevée, de lui-même"[27] (it was at this point that the French spirit . . . found the most precise, the most clear, the most dazzling and also the most elevated form of itself). This precision and elevation of "l'esprit français" comes about through a battle against external forces, namely, as in the *mazarinades,* the "esprit" of both Italy and Spain:

Il est une sorte de lutte entre l'esprit français proprement dit et l'esprit italien, un peu aussi l'esprit espagnol, d'où l'on voit presque tout à coup l'esprit français se dégager et prendre conscience et maîtrise de soi avec une incomparable vigueur.[28]

There is a sort of struggle between the French spirit, properly described, and the Italian spirit, and to some extent the Spanish spirit, from which, almost all of a sudden, one sees the French spirit detach itself, and come to consciousness and mastery of itself, with an incomparable vigor.

Even in 1979, Lagarde and Michard's infamously influential textbook celebrated the seventeenth century as a crucible for Frenchness, arguing that the neoclassical unity of action in the theater is "la manifestation même du tempérament français, épris de clarté et de composition rigoureuse"[29] (the very manifestation of the French temperament, seized with clarity and rigorous composition).

Just as the *mazarinades* sought an antihero in the Machiavellian figure of Mazarin, so the textbook tradition seized upon a way to personify the French temperament by claiming the steadying figure of Pierre Corneille as the point of origin for this flourishing of national spirit. And, as Frenchness emerges in the *mazarinades* in contest with Italian encroachment, so here Corneille's importance is honed by a tendentious account of relations between the playwright and Richelieu. In 1637, Richelieu's newly founded Académie had launched its mission by critiquing Corneille's popular success, *Le Cid.* The nineteenth-century nationalist narrators of Corneille's significance understood that disapproval to be an ad hominem attack by the minister. A study guide for the *bacca-lauréat* of 1884 claimed that Richelieu disliked *Le Cid* because of "[sa] faiblesse de vouloir être poète" (his weakness of wanting to be a poet) and his consequent jealousy of Corneille's success.[30] Materials for the *bre-vet supérieur* examination of the same period tell the same story: "Le ministre ne sut pas dissimuler le dépit que lui causait le triomphe de son ancien collaborateur. Il suscita contre Corneille les haines rivales. . . ."[31] (The minister was not able to dissimulate the spite that the triumph of his former collaborator aroused in him. He instigated rival hatreds against Corneille.) These schoolyard explanations seem to have originated with Pellisson's 1653 history of the Académie française and were given further credence by Fontenelle's 1702 *Vie de Monsieur Corneille*.[32] They became a stock talking point in eighteenth- and nineteenth-century accounts of the period and were heavily romanticized by figures such as Michelet and Dumas. In these sensationalist accounts, Corneille's admirable qualities set him apart from his scheming rival.

The schema that opposes Corneille to Richelieu draws upon the same array of nationalistic engagements that we have already seen at work in the *mazarinades*. Corneille's virtues are celebrated as particularly French: one nineteenth-century literary history, written by a professor at the École Normale, exclaims, "À Dieu ne plaise que le grand Corneille cesse d'être populaire sur notre théâtre! Ce jour-là, nous aurions cessé d'être une grande nation."[33] (May it please God that the great Corneille should never cease to be popular on our stage! If that should happen, we would have ceased to be a great nation). In contrast, Richelieu's political engagements are understood to ally him with foreign and particularly Ita-lian influences, even, as we have seen, at the level of style. The minister was firmly associated with the figure of Tacitus, often an early modern cover for Machiavellian interests, and critics of his policies took this as evidence of his tyranny.[34] A contemporary wrote in his *Mémoires* that "Richelieu, né pour commander aux autres hommes, ami généreux, cruel ennemi, avait sur la même table son bréviaire et Machiavel"[35] (Richelieu, born to command other men, generous friend, cruel enemy, had on the same table his breviary and Machiavelli). Hay du Chastelet, a pamphleteer of the Cardinal, remarks in the introduction to his *Recueil* that Riche-lieu's enemies accused him "de pratiquer les maximes de Machiavel, de s'être fait cardinal par des moyens horribles"[36] (of practicing the maxims of Machiavelli, of having made himself cardinal by horrible means).

Little of the story of the Corneille-Richelieu enmity appears to be true.[37] But its persistence indicates something worth taking seriously, for it allows us to trace the construction of a particular account of literary value. To oppose Corneille to Richelieu is to oppose French integrity to Italian duplicity, and this opposition has proved surprisingly resilient in late twentieth-century criticism. The keyword attached to the curricular Corneille is *générosité,* a term associated with an aristocratic ethic of self-sacrifice. In this standardized reading, the famous Cornelian *générosité* entails a virtuous gesture performed without thought of its end, without economic calculations of profit and loss. That aristocratic ethic marks him, for the critics we considered at the beginning of this essay, as an upholder of stable French values set against the distortions of imported, Italian, political strategies.

But of course, as both Machiavellian treatises and Corneille's tragedies so successfully illustrate, the distinction between stable values as an absolute good and their instrumentalization in matters of political strategy is rather difficult to decipher. Machiavelli's deployment of the term *virtù,* for example, is famously slippery; as critics have consistently noted, the concept suggests not a timeless ideal, as it might have in humanist tradition, but rather what Victoria Kahn describes as a contingent "faculty of deliberation about particulars."[38] Just such a deliberation is advocated by the Roman ambassador Flaminius, in Corneille's *Nicomède,* who suggests "Qu'une vertu parfaite à besoin de prudence, / Et doit considérer pour son propre intérêt / Et les temps où l'on vit, et les lieux où l'on est"[39] (that a perfect virtue needs prudence / And must consider, for its own interest / The time and place in which we live). Flaminius is rather an outlaw figure, but again and again Corneille will stage a political learning curve wherein the figures of government realize that even the high-minded must turn from absolute ideals and grapple with just such particulars.

Corneille's interest in questions of vengeance and political memory, in the relation between the foundation of a state and its continuation, in the proper management of empire, in the role of counselors, in the figure of the malcontent, in dissimulation, and in the relation between virtue and crime, all mark him as a writer firmly engaged with the great production of post-Machiavellian writing so widely available in seventeenth-century France.[40] His 1643 tragedy *Cinna, ou la clémence d'Auguste* addresses the importance of the virtues shown forth by the prince and, in particular, the relation between that show of virtue and its strategic instrumentalization.[41] "Debbe ancora uno principe mostrarsi amatore delle virtù"[42] (a prince should also show himself a lover of the virtues),[43] Machiavelli tells us, but what does it mean to *show oneself* to be something?[44] That relation between virtue and show will become of particular interest in the French neoclassical theater, with its carefully decorous staging, where the delicate balance between what can be shown and what must be hidden is of such importance to both the dramaturgical structure and the social standing of the stage. In reflecting on the fraught relation between a virtue's essence and its show, *Cinna* places itself squarely in post-Machiavellian tradition. In her opening speech, Émilie, girding herself for revenge, apostrophically urges her love to "montre-toi généreux"[45] (show yourself to be generous): that is, to be ready for sacrifice. What, the play will go on to ask, is the relation between the verb and the adjective in this exhortation? Is a show of virtue set apart from its original substance? Is there such a thing as a virtue—or a theater—without show?

In some sense, the neoclassical tragedy—following on from the ancients, and in this case drawing on Seneca's text *De clementia*—is itself caught in this question of the lag between original and show, exhorting itself, as Émilie does, to show itself to be something that can be compared to past glories. Machiavelli's interest in the relation between virtue and exemplarity, explored in a well-known passage of the *Prince,* had presented a structure in which those who follow historical exemplars are always subject to a troubling gap between the ideal and its willed actualization.

Non si maravigli alcuno se, nel parlare che io farò de' principati al tutto nuovi e di principe e di stato, io addurrò grandissimi esempli; perché, camminando gli uomini quasi sempre per le vie battute da altri, e procedendo nelle azioni loro con le imitazioni, né si potendo le vie di altri al tutto tenere, né alla virtù di quelli che tu imiti aggiugnere, debbe uno uomo prudente intrare sempre per vie battute da grandi e quelli che sono stati eccellentissimi imitare, acciò che, se la sua virtù non vi arriva, almeno ne renda qualche odore. . . . (103)

No one should marvel if, in speaking as I will do of principalities that are altogether new both in prince and in state, I bring up the greatest examples. For since men almost always walk on paths beaten by others and proceed in their actions by imitation, unable either to stay on the paths of others altogether or to attain the virtue of those whom you imitate, a prudent man should always enter upon the paths beaten by great men, and imitate those who have been most excellent, so that if his own virtue does not reach that far, it is at least in the odor of it. (21–22)

As Timothy Hampton asks, "What, exactly, is the odor of *virtù*? How does one distinguish between virtue and its odor?"[46] Corneille's tragedies take place in the space of that odor; rather than upholding the high virtues for which those who claim him as anti-Machiavel celebrate him, he moves instead in the murkier world of those who seek to be virtuous but are sometimes unclear as to what that might mean or how it can be attained. For Corneille, the indeterminate relation between exemplary virtue and those that follow in its wake is expressed with the image not of scent but of a mirror. In the seventeenth century, the term *miroir* referred not only to a looking glass but also to an example, and Corneille frequently uses the term to suggest the apparently easy but actually distorted relation between the original and its would-be reflection. Far from imagining the mirror or example to be an absolute reproduction of a given scene or figure, Corneille has the mirror cast a crooked light on the imagined original. In *Horace,* the determined Roman hero's absolute eagerness to die for his country—"D'une simple vertu c'est l'effet ordinaire"[47] (it is the ordinary effect of a simple virtue)—is countered by his Alban counterpart Curiace's distancing from that certainty: "Nous serons les miroirs d'une vertu bien rare:/Mais votre fermeté tient un peu du barbare" (455–56; We will be the mirrors of a rare virtue/But your firmness is a little barbaric). Curiace's introduction of the mirror suggests that *vertu* can no longer be fully inhabited; though Horace continues to claim "solide vertu" (485), Curiace's mirroring of virtue shows it to be, instead, "âpre" (bitter, 504). Horace and Curiace, Roman and Alban, *do* mirror each other, or are set up as exact counterparts, but their precise exchanges reveal important differences that make a mockery of that pairing. Corneille's mirror, like Machiavelli's odor, introduces the sense of something not fully consubstantial with its mark; the example lags behind, trying to repeat the original but falling behind in its quest for absolute presence. The example fails to follow through on the promise of the original, just as the mirror can deceive; in a nicely tautological formulation, *Cinna*'s Auguste reminds his followers that "l'exemple souvent n'est qu'un miroir trompeur" (388; often an example is only a deceiving reflection).

This realization, however, is not marked by loss. Corneille's tragedy of moral *décalage* makes a pragmatic and humane attempt to come to terms with this inability to fully inhabit a stable ideal. Thus in *Cinna,* one by one, the characters must learn that *vertu* can be inflected by doubts, by sympathies, by emotion, and that these inflections in fact make not for a

weakened front but for a diversified and paradoxically stronger government. The rebels Cinna and Maxime initially have an essentialist and absolute understanding of virtue. For Cinna, virtue is an unshakable agent:

> Ma vertu pour le moins ne me trahira pas.
> Vous la verrez brillante au bord des precipices
> Se couronner de gloire en bravant les supplices. (312–14)

> My virtue at least will never betray me.
> You'll see it shining on the edge of the abyss,
> Crowning itself with glory by braving torture.

His coconspirator Maxime shares this sense, understanding *vertu* to be
firmly set against the troubles of uncertainty; of Brutus at the time of
his assassination of Caesar, he suggests, "il eut trop de vertu pour tant
d'inquiétude" (833; he had too much virtue for such worries). It might
seem that Maxime's dogged and end-inflected logic makes him the perfect Machiavellian in action: in table-thumping mode, he insists that in
freeing oneself from tyranny "tout s'appelle vertu" (488; everything can
be called virtue). As the play goes on, however, and the plotters' putative
actions are undone by Auguste's granting of clemency, we see that *vertu*
can also be defined more largely: not in the sense that all acts of force
are recuperated by calling them *vertu,* as in Maxime's understanding,
but because Corneille, following Seneca, introduces different behaviors
which, while keeping to the model of rationalist thinking proffered by
Maxime, point toward more flexible understandings of the relation between *vertu* and violence. This distinction is crisply expounded in act
4, scene 3, in the exchange between Auguste and his wife Livie. Livie,
giving "les conseils d'une femme" (1,197; a woman's advice), suggests a
more tractable approach to the threatened rebellion: clemency. In this
iteration, clemency is understood to be not an absolute virtue, but rather
an instrumentalist and rationalist response to threat. Livie's suggestion is
structured functionally:

> Essayez sur Cinna ce que peut la clémence,
> Faites son châtiment de sa confusion,
> Cherchez le plus utile en cette occasion. (1,210–12)

> Try how clemency works on Cinna,
> Turn his confusion into his punishment,
> Look for the most useful strategy on this occasion.

In this formulation, clemency is not an abstract noun but a tool, a strategy that will bring about the resolution of crisis. Auguste worries that such strategizing is merely the sign of weakness: "Régner, et caresser une main si traîtresse,/Au lieu de sa vertu, c'est montrer sa foiblesse" (1,241-42) (To reign and caress such a treacherous hand/Is a show of weakness, not virtue). Livie's response suggests that clemency is, instead, *both* something likely to bring about the desired end (whereas severity, she notes, has produced "aucun fruit" [1,199; no fruit]) *and* "la vertu la plus digne des rois" (1,244; the virtue most worthy of kings): clemency's absolute virtue nonetheless admits of a means/end rationalization. It is both presence and sign: Livie argues "la clémence est la plus belle marque/Qui fasse à l'Univers connaître un vrai Monarque" (1,265-66; clemency is the most beautiful mark/That lets the universe know the true monarch). Corneille has Auguste draw on a habitual hemistich to suggest the zero-sum understanding of violence/weakness that has led Rome only to a cycle of vengeance—"Dont il faut qu'il la venge, ou cesse d'être Prince" (1,254; which he must avenge, or cease to be prince)—but Livie's version of clemency smoothes over the ferocious versification of her husband's speechifying.[48] In Livie's assertions, and in Auguste's subsequent claiming of them in the final scene, we see the triumph of a humanitarian force, whose eye to its own interests masks itself in generosity.

In *Cinna*, as elsewhere in his work, Corneille presents a political situation in which the figure of government acts in a way that is at once generous and self-interested: Auguste's actions can be claimed as a political machination or, as the late Gérard Defaux took pains to suggest, the happy product of divine grace.[49] Corneille's dedicatory words to Monsieur de Montoron suggest something of this indecipherability when he says of Auguste, "Ce monarque était tout généreux, et sa générosité n'a jamais paru avec tant d'éclat que dans les effets de sa clémence et de sa libéralité" (this monarch was completely generous, and his generosity was never so well displayed as in the effects of his clemency and his liberality).[50] In this formulation, in which the conjunction bears a great deal of weight, generosity is an attribute used adjectivally, but also something understood as strategic display that makes itself felt "dans les effets." Corneille goes on to comment on the relation between liberality and clemency, suggesting that "ce grand prince les a si bien attachées et comme unies l'une à l'autre, qu'elles ont été tout ensemble et la cause et l'effet l'une de l'autre . . ." (this great prince had so well joined the one to the other, that they were all together both the cause and effect of one another).[51] Here, cause and effect, attribute and strategy, swamp each other. The prince's job, like the playwright's, is to weave together origin and effect into a seamless whole and to present it so smoothly that the audience cannot begin to unpick what lies behind it.

The slipperiness of Corneille's treatment of *vertu* suggests something of his theatrical leanings toward a domain defined as Machiavellian. More than that, though, the ways in which Corneille presents a given virtue as both one thing and another suggest that the taking of sides evident in the work cited at the beginning of this essay is ultimately an unsatisfying procedure. The assertion that Corneille is an anti-Machiavel has been answered in part by French critics on the left, such as Hélène Merlin-Kajman.[52] But the French debate around such issues has tended to remain entrenched in a national narrative in which each "side" speaks back and forth across the body of Corneille's work.

In gleaning the historic antagonisms that have contributed to the presentation of Corneille's tragedies, I want to underline the critical importance of pursuing the traces of the other voices and other spaces that have been obfuscated by the rather more univocal French accounts of Corneille's work.[53] To pay attention to Corneille's Italian problem reminds us that early modern tragedy seized upon the difficult dialogue between national traditions. Corneille's tragedies, with their interest in the ways in which political entities are begun in certainty and continue in compromise, remind us that as cultures forge ahead they leave behind traces of those sacrifices. We would do well to remember the ways in which our own critical narratives too often do the same.

Notes

1. Michel Prigent, *Le héros et l'État dans la tragédie de Pierre Corneille,* Quadrige (Paris: Presses Universitaires de France, 1996), 284. Future references given parenthetically in the text. All translations in this essay, unless otherwise noted, are mine. This essay's discussion of Corneille's Machiavellianism and of anti-Italianism in early modern France in this essay draws in part on material from the introduction to my book, *The Style of the State in French Theater, 1630–1660* (Ashgate 2009).

2. Marc Fumaroli, *Le poète et le roi: Jean de La Fontaine en son siècle* (Paris: Editions de Fallois, 1997), 69.

3. Pierre Ronzeaud, "La stratégie anti-machiavélique de Pierre Corneille," in *Machiavelli attuale/Machiavel actuel,* ed. Georges Barthouil (Ravenna: Longo Editore, 1982), 171–79 (171).

4. Ibid., 174.

5. Ibid., 175.

6. Prigent, *Le héros,* viii.

7. For a larger history of French anti-Italianism and Italian cultural presences in early modern France, see Henry Heller, *Anti-Italianism in Sixteenth-Century France* (Toronto: University of Toronto Press, 2003); Jean-François Dubost, *La France italienne, XVIe-XVIIe siècles* (Paris: Aubier, 1997); *Rome n'est plus dans Rome: La polémique anti-italienne et autres essais sur la Renaissance* (Paris: Honoré Champion, 2002); Richard Cooper, *Litterae in tempore belli: Études sur les relations littéraires italo-françaises pendant les guerres d'Italie* (Geneva: Droz, 1997); Jean Balsamo, *Les rencontres des Muses: Italianisme et anti-italianisme dans les lettres françaises de la fin du XVIe siècle* (Geneva: Slatkine, 1992); Françoise Waquet, *Le modèle français et l'Italie savante: Conscience de soi et perception de l'autre dans la République des lettres 1650-1750* (Rome: École française de Rome, 1989); Franco Simone, "La reazione francese al primo umanistico italiano," in *Il rinascimento francese: Studi e ricerche* (Turin: SEI, 1961), 47-54.

8. On the *mazarinades,* see Hubert Carrier, *Le labyrinthe de l'État: Essai sur le débat politique en France au temps de la Fronde (1648-1653)* (Paris: Honoré Champion, 2004); Christian Jouhaud, *Mazarinades: La Fronde des Mots* (Paris: Aubier, 1985).

9. On the relation between the proclamations of the *mazarinades* and the *pasquinade* tradition of Rome, see Katherine Ibbett, "Who Makes the Statue Speak? Louis XIV and the *plainte des statues," Word & Image* 24, no. 4 (2008): 427-38.

10. On this link, see Lionello Sozzi, chapter 2, "Éloquence et vérité: un aspect de la polémique anti-italienne," in *Rome n'est plus dans Rome: La polémique anti-italienne et autres essais sur la Renaissance* (Paris: Honoré Champion, 2002). On the notion that the Italian court overplayed its compliments, see Marc Fumaroli, *L'âge de l'eloquence: Rhétorique et "res litteraria" de la Renaissance au seuil de l'époque classique* (Geneva: Droz, 1980), 691.

11. François Eudes de Mézeray, *La France en travail sans pouvoir accoucher faute de sage femme* (Paris, 1652), 8.

12. Henri Estienne, *Deux dialogues du nouveau langage François* (Geneva: Slatkine, 1980), iii.

13. François Anjou, *Briève remonstrance à la noblesse de France sur le faict de la Declaration de Monseigneur le Duc d'Alençon* (Paris, 1576), 11, 26. On Italy's luxury trade in France, see Dubost, *La France italienne,* 312.

14. *Le medecin politique, qui donne un souverain remede, pour guerir la France malade a l'extremité* (Paris: 1652), 26. On the establishment of French *franchise,* see Timothy Hampton, *Inventing the Nation: Literature and Nation in Sixteenth-Century France* (Ithaca, N.Y.: Cornell University Press, 2001), 2. On the double false etymologies of "franc," see Hélène Merlin-Kajman, *La langue est-elle fasciste? Langue, pouvoir, enseignement* (Paris: Seuil, 2003), 151.

15. *Le Fidèle Empirique ou le puissant hellebore d'un anti-Machiavel* (Paris, 1652), n.p.

16. *Le dereglement de l'Estat* (1651), 27.

17. Ibid., 21.

18. Cited by Hélène Merlin, "Langue et souveraineté en France au XVIIe siècle: La production autonome d'un *corps de langage." Annales HSS* 2 (March 1994): 369-94 (388).

19. Ibid.

20. For example, Alain Faudemay's work on the neoclassical language of clarity has shown the ideological weight behind the seemingly innocuous phrase "Il est clair que. . . ." Alain Faudemay, *Le clair et l'obscur à l'âge classique* (Geneva: Slatkine, 2001), 23.

21. On these distinctions see Marc Fumaroli, *L'âge de l'éloquence: Rhétorique et "res literaria" de la Renaissance au seuil de l'époque classique* (Paris: Albin Michel, 1994), 33.

22. Dominique Bouhours, *Entretiens d'Ariste et d'Eugène* (Paris: Bossard, 1920), 42.

23. Samuel Chappuzeau, *Le théâtre français*, 1674 (43).

24. Of course, as Alain Viala has argued, Boileau is so ferocious in his pronouncements because he is forming an aesthetic rather than merely recording it. Alain Viala, "Qu'est-ce qu'un classique?" *Littératures classiques* 19 (1993): 11-31 (22). For a reverential history of French *clarté* that demonstrates the centrality of Boileau's model, see Daniel Mornet, *Histoire de la clarté française: Ses origines, son évolution, sa valeur* (Paris: Payot, 1929).

25. Even René Bray asserted, in his stuffy *La formation de la doctrine classique* (Paris: Hachette, 1927), that "il me semble désormais difficile de contester que les sources du classicisme français sont en Italie" (47).

26. On that invention of classicism, see Hélène Merlin-Kajman, *La langue est-elle fasciste?*; Alain Viala, "Qu'est-ce qu'un classique?"; Peter Bayley, "Let's Dump Classicism," in *Racine et/ou le classicisme*, ed. Ronald Tobin (Tübingen: Gunter Narr, 2001), 261-64; and, in the same volume, John D. Lyons, "What Do We Mean When We Say 'Classique'?" 497-505; Domna Stanton, "Classicism (Re)constructed: Notes on the Mythology of Literary History," *Continuum* 1 (1989): 1-29. On education in the nineteenth century, see Mort Guiney, *Teaching the Cult of Literature in the French Third Republic* (New York: Palgrave Macmillan, 2004); Martine Jey, "Les classiques de l'ère Ferry: Les auteurs dans les programmes scolaires au tournant du siècle," *Littératures Classiques* 19 (1993): 237-47. See also Ralph Albanese, *La Fontaine à l'école républicaine: Du poète universel au classique scolaire* (Charlottesville, VA: Rookwood Press, 2003), and *Molière à l'école républicaine: De la critique universitaire aux manuels scolaires* (Saratoga, Calif.: ANMA Libri, 1992), both of which show in ample detail the ways in which these authors were codified and taught to schoolchildren.

27. *Histoire de la littérature française depuis le XVIIe siècle jusqu'à nos jours* (Paris: Plon, 1900), 178-79.

28. Ibid., 179.

29. A. Lagarde and L. Michard, *XVIIeme siècle* (Paris: Bordas, 1979), 89.

30. *Recueil de compositions françaises*, Tridon-Péronneau (Paris: Hachette, 1884), 226.

31. *Etudes Biographiques et Critiques sur les textes d'explication du brevet supérieur, prescrits pour les sessions de 1888, 1889, et 1890*, ed. Louis Tarsot and Maurice Charlot (Paris: Delalain frères, 1900), 1:3.

32. Paul Pellisson, *Histoire de l'Académie Française* (Paris: Didier, 1858), 86.

33. Désiré Nisard, *Histoire de la littérature française* (Paris: Firmin Didot, 1854), 2:143.

34. Etienne Thuau, *Raison d'état et pensée politique à l'époque de Richelieu* (1966; Paris: Armand Colin, 2000), 44. On Richelieu's "Tacitean moment," see also Jacob Soll, *Publishing the "Prince": History, Reading, and the Birth of Political Criticism* (Ann Arbor: University of Michigan Press, 2005), 47-48.

35. Abbé de Choisy, *Mémoires*, cited in Thuau, *Raison d'état*, 57.

36. Cited in Thuau, *Raison d'état*, 58.

37. The story was doggedly rejected by Louis Batiffol's 1936 study *Richelieu et Corneille: La légende de la persécution de l'auteur du "Cid"* (Paris: Calmann-Lévy, 1936). More recent materialist criticism has also explored the weak points of this story. Alain Viala has reminded us that Corneille was one of the most officially rewarded writers of the seventeenth century, and that even while the writer declared his independence from political power, he was in fact deeply indebted to the financial and cultural capital provided by the cardinal's support. Corneille received a pension from Richelieu and was briefly a member of Richelieu's Société des Cinq Auteurs; in 1637, the same year as the crisis over *Le Cid*, Corneille's father was ennobled. See *Naissance de l'écrivain: Sociologie de la littérature*

à l'âge classique (Paris: Editions de Minuit, 1985), which discusses Corneille and other authors of the time in the context of career strategies, intellectual property rights and pensions. On the dedication of *Horace* (1641) and Corneille's equivocal praise of Richelieu therein, see Hélène Merlin, "*Horace:* L'équivoque et la dédicace," *Dix-septième siècle* 182 (1994): 121–34, and, in response, Christian Jouhaud, "L'écrivain et le ministre: Corneille et Richelieu: Note sur l'épître dédicatoire d'*Horace* et tout particulièrement sur la place qu'y tient le visage du cardinal de Richelieu," *Dix-septième siècle* 182 (1994): 135–42, and a more fully explored version of the argument in his *Les pouvoirs de la littérature: Histoire d'un paradoxe* (Paris: Gallimard, 2000), 292–307.

38. Victoria Kahn, *Machiavellian Rhetoric from the Counter-Reformation to Milton* (Princeton: Princeton University Press, 1994), 31. On this question see also Timothy Hampton, *Writing from History: The Rhetoric of Exemplarity in Renaissance Literature* (Ithaca, N.Y.: Cornell University Press, 1990), 65.

39. *Oeuvres complètes,* ed. Georges Couton (Paris: Gallimard, 1984), 2:673, line 816.

40. On reason of state in Richelieu's France, see Etienne Thuau, *Raison d'état;* Jacob Soll, *Publishing the "Prince."*

41. On *Cinna,* see John D. Lyons, *The Tragedy of Origins: Pierre Corneille and Historical Perspective* (Palo Alto: Stanford University Press, 1996), 71–108; Mitchell Greenberg, *Canonical States, Canonical Stages: Oedipus, Othering, and Seventeenth-Century Drama* (Minneapolis: University of Minnesota Press, 1994), 119–27.

42. *Il principe* (Milan: Rizzoli, 1977), 180. All future page references are made parenthetically in the text and refer to this edition.

43. *The Prince,* trans. Harvey C. Mansfield (Chicago: University of Chicago Press, 1998), 91. All future page references are made parenthetically in the text and refer to this edition.

44. On Machiavelli and the question of spectacle, see Barbara Spackman, "Politics on the Warpath: Machiavelli's *Art of War,*" in *Machiavelli and the Discourse of Literature,* ed. Albert Ascoli and Victoria Kahn, 179–93 (Ithaca, N.Y.: Cornell University Press, 1993).

45. *Oeuvres complètes,* 1:914, line 50. All future line references to *Cinna* are made parenthetically in the text and refer to this edition.

46. *Writing from History,* 66.

47. *Oeuvres complètes,* 1:859, line 439. Future references in the text.

48. For a reading of *Cinna* and the logic of vengeance, see Éric Méchoulan, "Revenge and Poetic Justice in Classical France," *SubStance* 35: 1 (2006): 20–51 (41–43).

49. Gérard Defaux, "*Cinna,* tragédie chrétienne? Essai de mise au point," *MLN* 119 (2004): 718–65.

50. *Oeuvres complètes,* 1:905.

51. Ibid.

52. See, for example, her polemical piece "Corneille et la politique dans *Cinna, Rodogune* et *Nicomède,* " *Littératures classiques* 32 (1998): 41–61.

53. Among those other voices are those of American critics whose relation to Corneille's Machiavellianism has been more flexible: see, for example, Susan Read Baker, *Dissonant Harmonies: Drama and Ideology in Five Neglected Plays by Pierre Corneille* (Tübingen: Gunter Narr Verlag, 1990).

Notes on Contributors

Guest Editors

ALBERT RUSSELL ASCOLI is Terrill Distinguished Professor in the Department of Italian Studies at the University of California, Berkeley. He is the author of *Ariosto's Bitter Harmony: Crisis and Evasion in the Italian Renaissance* and *Dante and the Making of a Modern Author*. This is the first time he has published on Shakespeare.

WILLIAM N. WEST is an associate professor of English, classics, and comparative literary studies at Northwestern University. He is the author of *Theatres and Encyclopedias in Early Modern Europe*. He is currently at work on a book to be called "Understanding and Confusion in the Elizabethan Theaters" and on a project tracing the history of the idea of the Renaissance as a period.

Contributors

BIANCA FINZI-CONTINI CALABRESI specializes in book history and women's cultural production in Europe from 1500 to 1650. She received her Ph.D. from Columbia University with a dissertation on the typography of the early modern printed play. From 2004 to 2007 she was a Haarlow-Cotsen Postdoctoral Fellow at the Society of Fellows in the Liberal Arts at Princeton University. She is currently an assistant professor of literature at Fairleigh Dickinson University and a 2008–2009 fellow at the Italian Academy for Advanced Studies in America at Columbia University, where she is researching "The Female Narcissus," a book-length project on early modern women's writing technologies.

LOUISE GEORGE CLUBB is an emeritus professor at the University of California, Berkeley, where she is a member of the departments of Comparative Literature and Italian Studies. She is general editor of Biblioteca Italiana, the bilingual series published by the University of California Press and launched by her edition and translation of Della Porta's *Gli duoi fratelli rivali / The Two Rival Brothers*. A former president of the Renaissance Society of America, she has been director of the University of California's Centro Studi at Padua and the Harvard University Center for Renaissance Studies at Villa I Tatti, Florence, and a member of the Comitato dei Garanti at the University of Siena and of the Accademia Galileiana di Scienze, Lettere ed Arti in Padua. Her other books include *Giambattista Della Porta, Dramatist; Italian Plays (1500–1700) in the Folger Library; Italian Drama in Shakespeare's Time;* and, with Robert Black, *Romance and Aretine Humanism in Sienese Comedy.* She is the author of the chapter "Italian Renaissance Drama" in *The Oxford Illustrated History of Theatre* and numerous studies of Renaissance comparative literature.

KASEY EVANS is an assistant professor of English at Northwestern University. Her current book project investigates changing representations of the virtue of temperance in sixteenth- and seventeenth-century English texts.

FABIO FINOTTI is Mariano DiVito Professor of Italian Studies; graduate chair, Italian; and the director of the Center for Italian Studies at the University of Pennsylvania. His research explores the relationships among different national traditions, codes, media, genres, and social structures. He is the author of several books, including *Sistema letterario e diffusione del decadentismo; Critica letteraria e linguaggio religioso; Una ferita non chiusa: Misticismo, filosofia, letteratura in Prezzolini e nel primo Novecento;* and *Retorica della diffrazione: Bembo, Aretino, Giulio Romano e Tasso: Letteratura e scena cortigiana;* as well as many articles on literary theory and on Italian literature, from Dante to the twentieth century. He is currently working on the rhetorical metamorphosis and multiplications of the self in Italian literature, from the medieval age to contemporary writers.

LAURA GIANNETTI holds a Ph.D. from the University of Connecticut and is an associate professor of Italian at the University of Miami. Her main area of research has been Italian Renaissance comedy; her first book is *Lelia's Kiss: Imagining Gender, Sex, and Marriage in Italian Renaissance Comedy.* She has published articles in *MLN, Sixteenth Century Journal,* and *Quaderni d'Italianistica* on representations of gender and play as well as *Five Comedies from the Italian Renaissance,* newly translated and edited with Guido Ruggiero. During the academic year 2008–09 she held the Lila Wallace–Reader's Digest Fellowship at Villa I Tatti, The Harvard University Center for Italian Renaissance Studies in Florence, where she worked on a new book project tentatively titled "Food Culture and the Literary Imagination in Renaissance Italy."

ROBERT HENKE, a professor of drama and comparative literature at Washington University, is the author of *Pastoral Transformations: Italian Tragicomedy and Shakespeare's Late Plays* and *Performance and Literature in the Commedia dell'Arte.* With Eric Nicholson, he edited *Transnational Exchange in Early Modern Theater,* a collection of essays from the group Theater Without Borders, an international research collective that examines transnational approaches to Renaissance drama. He is the recipient of fellowships from Villa I Tatti, the Fulbright Program, and the National Endowment for the Humanities.

LORNA HUTSON is Berry Professor of English Literature at the University of St Andrews, Scotland. Her most recent book is *The Invention of Suspicion: Law and Mimesis in Shakespeare and English Renaissance Drama.*

KATHERINE IBBETT teaches French at University College, London. She has published on topics ranging from the genre of the speaking statue to the politics of landscape; her book *The Style of the State in French Theater, 1630–1660* was published in 2009. She is currently working on a book about compassion and toleration in early modern France.

CHRISTOPHER D. JOHNSON is an associate professor of comparative literature at Harvard University. He is the author of *Selected Poetry of Francisco de Quevedo: A Bilingual Edition* and the forthcoming *Hyperboles: The Rhetoric of Excess in Baroque Literature and Thought.*

YAIR LIPSHITZ is currently completing his Ph.D. in the Department for Theater Arts at Tel Aviv University, writing on the body as a hermeneutical site for Jewish textual culture in theater and drama. He is a junior fellow at the Shalom Hartman Institute in Jerusalem, as well as a lecturer in the

Department for Theater Arts at Tel Aviv University. He is the author of a forthcoming book in Hebrew, *The Holy Tongue, Comedy's Version: Intertextual Dramas on the Stage of a Comedy of Betrothal.* He has also published several papers dealing with early-twentieth-century Jewish theater and drama, as well as with issues of the body in rabbinic literature.

RONALD L. MARTINEZ is a professor of Italian Studies at Brown University. In collaboration with Robert M. Durling, he is currently finishing an edition with translation and commentary of Dante's *Paradiso.* In addition to the study in this issue of *Renaissance Drama,* essays by him on Italian Renaissance spectacle and on Machiavelli's career as a dramatist are forthcoming.

KRISTIN PHILLIPS-COURT is an assistant professor of Italian at the University of Wisconsin–Madison. She has published articles on writers including Bruno, Caro, Belcari, Castiglione, and Vasari. She is the author of *Perfecting Genre: Italian Renaissance Drama's Debt to Painting* (forthcoming), which has been designated the winner of the 2009 Aldo and Jeanne Scaglione Publication Award for a Manuscript in Italian Literary Studies. Upcoming projects include a study of grace in literature and visual art, a study of Giorgio Vasari's narrative strategies, and a translation of Giordano Bruno's *Spaccio della Bestia Trionfante.*

JON R. SNYDER is a professor of Italian Studies and comparative literature at the University of California, Santa Barbara. Snyder's bilingual edition of G. B. Andreini's *Love in the Mirror* and his *Dissimulation and the Culture of Secrecy in Early Modern Europe* are forthcoming. The author of numerous essays on Baroque culture and literature, Snyder has also published a book-length study, *L'estetica del Barocco.*

JANE TYLUS is a professor of Italian Studies and comparative literature and Vice Provost for Academic Affairs at NYU. She is the author of *Writing and Vulnerability in the Late Renaissance* and coeditor of the volume *The Early Modern Period* for the Longman Anthology of Literature. Her recent work includes *Reclaiming Catherine of Siena: Literature, Literacy, and the Signs of Others,* and her translation of the poetry of Gaspara Stampa is forthcoming.

green press

INITIATIVE

Northwestern University Press is committed to preserving ancient forests and natural resources. We elected to print this title on 30% post consumer recycled paper, processed chlorine free. As a result, for this printing, we have saved:

4 Trees (40' tall and 6-8" diameter)
2,010 Gallons of Wastewater
1 Million BTUs of Total Energy
122 Pounds of Solid Waste
417 Pounds of Greenhouse Gases

Northwestern University Press made this paper choice because our printer, Thomson-Shore, Inc., is a member of Green Press Initiative, a nonprofit program dedicated to supporting authors, publishers, and suppliers in their efforts to reduce their use of fiber obtained from endangered forests.

For more information, visit www.greenpressinitiative.org

Environmental impact estimates were made using the Environmental Defense Paper Calculator. For more information visit: www.papercalculator.org.